CW00545095

JAPAN'S FAVORITE MON-STAR

The Unauthorized Biography
of "The Big G"

JAPAN'S FAVORITE MON-STAR

The Unauthorized Biography of "The Big G"

STEVE RYFLE

ECW PRESS

Copyright © Steve Ryfle, 1998

All rights reserved. No part of this publication may be
reproduced, stored in a retrieval system, or transmitted
in any form by any process — electronic, mechanical,
photocopying, recording, or otherwise — without the prior
written permission of the copyright owners and ECW PRESS.

CANADIAN CATALOGUING IN PUBLICATION DATA
Ryfle, Steve
Japan's favorite mon-star: the unauthorized biography of "The Big G"
ISBN 1-55022-348-8
1. Godzilla (Fictitious character). 2. Godzilla
films – History and criticism. I. Title.
PN1995.9.G63R93 1998 791.43'651 C98-930251-2

Research associate and translator: Addie Kohzu.
Front-cover: Alex Wald
Back-cover photo: Koji Sasahara, AP/WIDE WORLD PHOTOS

Imaging by ECW Type & Art, Oakville, Ontario.
Printed by Webcom, Toronto, Ontario.

Distributed in Canada by General Distribution Services,
30 Lesmill Road, Don Mills, Ontario M3B 2T6.
Distributed in the United States by LPC Group,
1436 West Randolph Street, Chicago, Illinois, U.S.A. 60607
Toll-free: 1-800-243-0138.

Published by ECW PRESS,
2120 Queen Street East, Suite 200,
Toronto, Ontario, Canada M4E 1E2.

http://www.ecw.ca/press

PRINTED AND BOUND IN CANADA

Acknowledgments

This book would hardly be what it is without the support and assistance of several friends and family. Thanks to author and film scholar Stuart Galbraith IV, a mentor, durable traveling partner and trusted friend; *Japanese Giants* publisher Ed Godziszewski, whose knowledge and generosity are equally boundless; David G. Milner, a pioneer in the field of Godzilla journalism. Mark A. Schultz, an avid video collector who was generous with his time and tapes; Joal Ryan, who tolerated the eternal roars of warring monsters; and to my mother, Patricia, who started this obsession when she took me to see *Godzilla vs. The Smog Monster* in 1973.

I am also grateful to the translators who provided invaluable assistance in researching this book. My good friend Addie Kohzu, chief translator and research associate, worked many, many hours translating Japanese texts; Yukari Fujii helped arrange several interviews in Tokyo and also provided key translation assistance; Atsushi Sakahara, Osamu "Sammy" Kobayashi and Emiko Iijima acted as interpreters during interviews; and Sumiko Urquhart and Yasmin Sferella provided translation help. Thanks to all.

Quotations attributed to the following people without citing outside sources are derived from interviews conducted by the author between 1994 and 1997: Allyson Adams, Joseph Barbera, Bob Burns, Ricardo Delgado, Robert Dunham, Fred Dekker, Ted Elliott, Peter Fernandez, Saiko Genso, Kent Gilbert, Don Glut, Edmund Goldman, James Hong, Maestro Akira Ifukube, Richard Kay, Robert "R.J." Kizer, Ib Melchior, Steve Miner, Terry Morse Jr., Haruo Nakajima, Teruyoshi Nakano, Dana Olsen, Duane Poole, Tony Randel, William Ross, Terry Rossio, Steve Sandoz, Paul Schreibman, William Stout, Harry B. Swerdlow, Yoshio Tsuchiya, Peter Zinner. Many thanks to all the interviewees for their time and assistance.

Additional thanks to: Forrest J. Ackerman, Mark Altman, the American Film Institute, Andrew Asch, James Bailey, Dennis Bent, Herbert Byrd, Steve Biodrowski and Fred Clarke at *Cinefantastique*, John "*Ryuusei*" Cassidy, Brian Culver, Max Della Mora, Norman England, Robert Scott Field, Jim Figurski, Peter H. Gilmore, Ed Gross of *Retrovision*, R.M. Hayes, Brian Henderson, The Margaret Herrick Library, Japan Travel Bureau, Randy Joheson (for the cool custom-made shirt), David Kalat, Osamu Kishikawa, J.D. Lees, Sean Linkenback, Marmoset Man, Chad Neuping, Chon Noriega, John Rocco Roberto, Bruce A. Robertson, John T. Ryan, Judy Ryan, Ryan O. Ryan, Paul Sammon, Jeff Schnaufer, Ron Silverman at the *Chicago Tribune*, Aaron J. Smith, Alice Ryan Spark-Dogg, Alex Wald, The Warner Bros. Archives.

For photographs and illustrations, thanks to Acme Features Syndicate, Thomas Fitch, Bill Griffith, Dinosaur Interplanetary Gazette, Matt Groening, Holly Jones (AP/Wide World Photos), Jim Mallon (Best Brains), Lisette Nabut (*Miami Herald*), Mike Seeling (Arlington Heights *Daily Herald*), Sandy Spikes (*Chicago Tribune*), Universal Press Syndicate, Jim Walsh, Brad Warner (Tsuburaya Productions Co. Ltd.), Tim Wright (*People*).

Photos on pages 189–191 are copyright Tsuburaya Productions Co. Ltd., Japan. Used by permission.

Finally, thanks to Lori Perkins, my agent, for her tenacity, dedication and direction, to Jack David and everyone at ECW Press for fighting to keep this project alive, and to Stuart Ross and Scott Mitchell for a great job of editing the manuscript. Thanks, everybody, we made it.

DISCLAIMER: This book is a work of journalism that documents the history of the Godzilla movie series and its significance in film history. The name and image of Godzilla are trademark and copyright of Toho Co. Ltd. This book is not authorized or licensed by Toho, and ECW Press Ltd. is not affiliated with Toho.

Dedicated to the memory of
Tomoyuki Tanaka,
Ishiro Honda,
and Eiji Tsuburaya

Contents

INTRODUCTION: The Godzilla Era

PART 1: GROUND ZERO — The 1950s

1. Birth of a Legend
   Godzilla a.k.a. Godzilla: King of the Monsters! 19

2. You Can't Keep a Bad Monster Down
   Godzilla Raids Again
   a.k.a. *Gigantis: The Fire Monster* 61

PART 2: GOLDEN AGE — The 1960s

3. Clash of the Titans
   King Kong vs. Godzilla 79

4. Madame Butterfly
   Godzilla vs. The Thing 103

5. Enter the Dragon
   Ghidrah: The Three-Headed Monster 113

6. Voyage into Space
   Monster Zero 121

7. It Came from Beneath the Sea
   Godzilla versus The Sea Monster 133

8. All in the Family
   Son of Godzilla 139

9. War of the Worlds
   Destroy All Monsters 145

10. Unknown Island
    Godzilla's Revenge 155

PART 3: DARK DAYS — The 1970s

11. Toxic Avenger
    Godzilla vs. The Smog Monster 161

12. Twilight of the Cockroaches
    Godzilla on Monster Island 173

13. Lost Continent
    Godzilla vs. Megalon 181

14. Robot Monster
    Godzilla vs. The Cosmic Monster 195

15. Bride of the Monster
    Terror of MechaGodzilla
    a.k.a. *The Terror of Godzilla* 199

PART 4: RESURRECTION — The 1980s

16. The Legend is Reborn
    Godzilla (1984) a.k.a. Godzilla 1985 215

PART 5: SECOND COMING — The 1990s

17. The Name of the Rose
    Godzilla vs. Biollante 251
18. The Time Travelers
    Godzilla vs. King Ghidorah 265
19. Earth's Final Fury
    Godzilla vs. Mothra 279
20. Cyborg
    Godzilla vs. MechaGodzilla 287
21. Enemies: A Love Story
    Godzilla vs. Space Godzilla 295
22. Requiem for a Heavyweight
    Godzilla vs. Destroyer 305

PART 6: GODZILLA VS. HOLLYWOOD — The Future

23. Remade in America
    Godzilla (1998) 321

PART 7: APPENDICES

i.   Cast and Credits 351
ii. Godzilla on Video 367
iii. Cyberspace Godzilla 370
iv. Endnotes 371
v.   Bibliography 373

PERSONNEL FILES AND INTERVIEWS

The God(zilla) Fathers: Tanaka, Honda, Tsuburaya, and Ifukube 39
The Heavy: Raymond Burr 59
City-Smashing to the Beat: Masaru Sato 75
Monster Scribes: Shinchi Sekizawa, Takeshi Kimura 92
The King's Court: Actors and Actresses 94
The Controller Speaks: Yoshio Tsuchiya 127
The Rebel: Nick Adams 129
Successor to the Throne: Teruyoshi Nakano 167
Godzilla in the Flesh: Haruo Nakajima 178
White Guy in Monsterland: Robert Dunham 185
Modern-Day Monster: Kenpachiro Satsuma 261
Swan Song: Akira Ifukube 315
New Wave Godzilla: Terry Rossio and Ted Elliott 330

SIDEBARS AND SPECIAL SECTIONS

Godzilla's Birthplace: A brief history of Toho and the
Japanese movie industry 24
Godzilla Talk: English dubbing in Japanese monster movies 149
Godzilla, American Style: Hanna-Barbera's cartoon series 209
Pop Monster: Godzilla references in books, music, etc. 243
Godzilla Invades LA 317

THE G-ARCHIVES: UNMADE AND OBSCURE GODZILLA PROJECTS

Hot Lava: Synopsis of *The Volcano Monsters* 70
Moth Holes: The evolution of the *Godzilla vs. The Thing* screenplay,
by Jay Ghee 111
Godzilla Conquers the World: *Frankenstein vs. Godzilla*,
by Jay Ghee 119
Evil Brain from Outer Space: *Godzilla vs. The Space Monsters*,
by Jay Ghee 176
Monster for Hire: *Godzilla vs. Redmoon*, by Jay Ghee 177
Ultra-Goji: Godzilla and Japanese TV super-heroes 188
The Electric Kool-Aid *Kaiju* Test: Cozzi's colorized *Godzilla* 207
Godzilla versus . . . *Cleveland*? 224
Begin the Bagan: *The Return of Godzilla*, by Jay Ghee 226
Synopsis of *Godzilla: King of the Monsters in 3-D*, by Fred Dekker 227
The Giant Rat and the Killer Plant: the original story of *Godzilla vs.
Gigamoth*, by Jay Ghee 259
S.O.L. on the Satellite of Love: Godzilla vs. MST3K 276
Development Hell, Toho-Style: *Mothra vs. Bagan* and *Godzilla vs.
Biollante*, by Jay Ghee 284

THE GODZILLA ERA

His footsteps quake the Earth and echo like thunder.

His deafening battle-cry strikes fear in the hearts of his enemies, both man and beast.

His white-hot radioactive breath sets entire cities ablaze and obliterates the most sophisticated and powerful military weaponry.

According to the legends of Odo Island, he was a malevolent god living beneath the sea, whose wrath could only be appeased by human sacrifices and ritual.

Scientists believe he was a creature of the Jurassic Period that defied the laws of evolution, living peacefully through the ages on the ocean's floor until a Hydrogen Bomb baptized him in radiation, creating a grotesque mutation unlike any creature known before. A prehistoric giant resurrected by modern-day technology.

Enraged, he emerged from the depths seeking one thing: Revenge.

I am a Godzilla Fan. Hear me roar.

In this age of computer-generated realism, when a Tyrannosaurus Rex can leap off the screen with stunning believability, I prefer to watch a man in a rubber monster suit stomping through miniature cities with hell-bent fury. Forget the technical sophistication and cutting-edge special effects of the annual big-budget summer blockbusters. The hand-made craftsmanship that brings Godzilla to life has remained basically unchanged for nearly 45 years, and it still delivers an enthralling monster spectacle that stimulates my imagination in ways no digital dinosaur can.

And I am not alone. Godzilla's fans are legion, spanning across generations and geographic boundaries.

To the unconverted, the sight of Godzilla rampaging through Tokyo and battling other mutoid creatures is pure cheap camp, a symbol of low-tech, inferior moviemaking. They don't know what they're missing. Godzilla may not be the most true-to-life of monsters, but in his greatest film moments he is an awesome force, so terrifying and stunning that his very essence approaches something mythical. He embodies the power of Nature and the doomed destiny of mankind, fused within his uniquely Japanese, badass prehistoric personality. More than a modern dragon, Godzilla is the unknown made flesh, an archetype that reaches inside man's soul and stirs universal fears, like a bad dream.

Known in Japan by his real name, "Gojira," the monster was conceived in 1954 by movie producer Tomoyuki Tanaka as a celluloid allegory to the atomic bombs dropped on Hiroshima and Nagasaki nine years earlier. Two years after his self-titled film debut, he swam across the Pacific Ocean and invaded American cinemas with a vengeance in *Godzilla: King of the Monsters!*, the famously re-edited version featuring inserted footage of Raymond Burr posing as a wire-service reporter in Tokyo. Bigger than *King Kong*, meaner than the *Beast From 20,000 Fathoms*, and more incredible than all the other atomic-bomb mutations running wild during the heyday of science fiction movies, this "unstoppable titan of terror" grew into an international phenomenon. Even today, he reigns as the undisputed movie monster monarch.

On a gut level, Godzilla's appeal is obvious. It is the visceral thrill of seeing this sinister saurian carry out the ultimate tantrum as he flattens metropolises, swats and smashes planes and tanks like mere insects, deflects an array of futuristic missiles and lasers, and incinerates the pillars of society with his atomic breath, while mankind remains powerless to stop the onslaught and ignorant of its meaning. It is the excitement of Godzilla's titanic battles with a gallery of monster adversaries, ranging from the hideous, three-headed space demon King Ghidorah to the elegant and feminine Mothra, the awe-inspiring cyborg MechaGodzilla, and a Japanese rendition of the great King Kong.

For those who delve beneath the surface, Godzilla is no mere movie monster. He is a paradox of sorts — a horrible embodiment of the Bomb that created him, and yet a pitiable victim of it; a symbol of Japan's post-war regrets and nuclear fears and, alternately, the nation's rage and retaliation. His films have often carried political subtext, sometimes subtle, other times blatant. While the original *Godzilla* was an anti-nuclear treatise, *King Kong vs. Godzilla* and *Godzilla vs. The Thing* decried commercialism and greed, *Godzilla vs. The Smog Monster* warned against rampant pollution, *Godzilla 1985* touched on Japan's uncertain future during the Cold War, and *Godzilla vs. King Ghidorah* expressed Japan's trepidation about becoming a global economic superpower. In *Godzilla vs. Destoroyah*, Godzilla's attack on Hong Kong (on the eve of China's takeover) denoted Japanese fears of losing ground to an aggressive Asian economic rival. Admittedly, Godzilla's film career has its share of blemishes; no one would argue that *Godzilla vs. Megalon* is a classic, or that *Smog Monster*, with a flying Godzilla and monster battles set to weird psychedelic rock music, isn't a big hunk of cinematic cheese. But overall, perhaps in ways no Westerner can fully understand, Godzilla movies serve as a sort of Japanese cultural barometer. And, for anyone open-minded enough, they pro-

vide a doorway to other Japanese media like *anime* (Japanese animation), *sentai* (Japanese super-hero TV programs) and even the classic films of Akira Kurosawa.

Godzilla's name, his lumbering image and his screeching roar are part of our pop-culture lexicon and landscape. His image — an upright-walking, vaguely mammalian, dinosaur-like creature with a thick body, long tail, maple-leaf dorsal spikes running down his spine and a menacing stare emanating from big, expressive eyes — is recognized worldwide. The monster has been paid musical tribute by Blue Oyster Cult, played basketball with NBA star Charles Barkley on a Nike shoes commercial, and, most significantly, been the subject of a \$120-million Hollywood remake. Still, he remains something of an enigma. If Godzilla has so pervaded our consciousness, why don't we know much about him?

For one thing, Godzilla is not an easy subject to study. Outside his native land, relatively little has been written about him, and until recent years the availability of Godzilla-related information and merchandise was sporadic and spotty. Thus, even some longtime fans have remained in the dark, believing in untruths like the myth that there are two different endings to *King Kong vs. Godzilla*, and unaware that Godzilla has made a triumphant comeback in the 1990s with a new series of made-in-Japan movies that have been slow in coming to the U.S.

On the other hand, while stereotypes about cars and consumer goods that are "made in Japan" have faded, old prejudices still hound Japanese monster movies. Cultural snobbery is partly to blame, but the prevailing view that Godzilla movies are nothing more than mindless junk is, in large part, an unwitting reaction to the way the films were carelessly butchered by American distributors. Like many foreign imports during the 1950s and '60s, Japanese monster movies were dubbed into English (the target of perennial ridicule, and fuel for parodies on shows like *Mystery Science Theater 3000*) and needlessly re-edited, with incongruous "linking scenes" featuring Caucasian actors inserted and little thought given to continuity gaps caused by the removal and re-arranging of the original Japanese footage. For the past 20 or so years, these films — which were meant to be viewed on the big screen of a movie theater — have been relegated to the small-screen medium of television and home video, diminishing the illusion of gigantic creatures; worse yet, nearly all TV broadcasts and videotapes utilize old, scratched films, presented in the pan-and-scan format — their once-glorious widescreen vistas cropped away. Thankfully, letterboxed videos of several Godzilla movies have become available in recent years, allowing the King of the Monsters to be appreciated in all his glory.

The last Japanese Godzilla flick to be released in American cinemas was *Godzilla 1985*, which was hardly a box-office sensation. Even so, the "Big G" has remained one of the most well-known fictional characters in this country and around the world, recognized almost as widely as Mickey Mouse. Thus, in an era when pop-culture icons from *Batman* to *The Flintstones* have been subjected to big-budget make-overs, it was inevitable that Japan's juggernaut would get his turn and, in 1998, TriStar Pictures unleashed its much-anticipated, mega-budgeted, U.S.-made *Godzilla*. Despite a nationwide, high-profile marketing campaign and the fact that it was produced by the makers of the super-blockbuster *Independence Day*, the picture did only lukewarm business, but not because Godzilla had become an entertainment anachronism. On the contrary, audiences wanted to see the most spectacular Godzilla movie ever, a modern version of the Japanese prototype with the enhanced, in-your-face impact of computer-age SFX, but the American *Godzilla* missed the mark. Rather than a harrowing city-stomper, the new beast was a fleet-footed reptile that ran from danger, lived in underground tunnels and only wanted to be left alone to raise its young. The reaction from the critics, general audiences, and the hard-core fans to this digital impostor-monster was nearly unanimous: Bring back the rubber-suited, indestructible, analog Godzilla. Director Steven Spielberg, who has cited Godzilla as an inspiration for *Jurassic Park*, told *Entertainment Weekly*, "The only Godzilla I saw was the one with Raymond Burr. I purposely stayed away from seeing [TriStar's] *Godzilla* because I didn't want to get anything between me and my memory of my favorite Godzilla movie of all time."

In embarking on the odyssey that has resulted in this book, my goal was simply to learn as much as possible about my lifelong lizard-hero. My hope is that, in some small way, the book will help bring Godzilla the accolades he and his creators have long deserved, clear up some of the myths and misconceptions about him, and encourage more people to enjoy the incredible, wild-and-woolly world of Japanese monsters. Still, it is impossible to compile Godzilla's entire history into a single text (the plethora of Godzilla tomes published in Japan, covering everything from special effects to ancillary merchandising, is proof of this). Like Japan itself, the King of the Monsters is a complex and mysterious creature, and many volumes will eventually be published about him in English, as there are in his mother tongue.

Now is the ideal time to reevaluate Godzilla's place in the annals of filmdom. In many respects, the Cold War era was also the Godzilla Era, with the monster serving as a harbinger of the destruction awaiting should mankind continue to tempt fate by unleashing the mighty power of the atom. With the breakup of the Soviet Union and the fading of the global nuclear threat, that era ended. In 1995, perhaps sensing he'd outlived his symbolism, Godzilla took a suicidal overdose of nuclear radiation in *Godzilla vs. Destoroyah*, the 22nd and supposedly final entry in Toho's long-running series. But, in the late 1990s, there have been numerous reminders of the Bomb's looming threat to the planet's survival — nuclear tests by the French in the South Pacific, nuclear warheads unaccounted for in the former Soviet republics, an escalating arms race between India and Pakistan, and so on. Godzilla is just as relevant today as he was in 1954, when Tomoyuki Tanaka used him to portray the fears of nuclear holocaust resonating through Japan. Fittingly, in the final weeks of 1998, just before this book went to the printer, the Toho Company Ltd. announced that the King of the Monsters would return in December 1999, in an all-new, Japanese-made film titled *Godzilla Millennium*. This, combined with the prospect of one or more sequels to the American-made Godzilla, is ample proof of the monster's lasting legacy. As a new century begins, we are entering the Godzilla Era anew.

It's hard to believe that a monster spawned by the horror of nuclear destruction could bring so much enjoyment to so many people for so long. But then, Godzilla is no ordinary movie monster.

Hail to the King!

Steve Ryfle
December, 1998

Part 1

GROUND ZERO
The 1950s

"*Godzilla* . . . was the most masterful of all the dinosaur movies because it made you believe it was really happening."

— *Steven Spielberg, in* The Making of Jurassic Park *by Don Shay and Jody Duncan, 1993*

"Without the bomb, there could not have been a monster."

— *Kimi Honda, widow of director Ishiro Honda, in a BBC-TV documentary, 1998*

One

BIRTH OF A LEGEND

"George, here in Tokyo time has been turned back two million years. This is my report as it happens."

— Steve Martin, *United World News* reporter

GODZILLA: KING OF THE MONSTERS!

RATING (OUT OF FIVE STARS): ★ ★ ★ ★ ★

JAPANESE VERSION: GOJIRA (GODZILLA). Released on November 3, 1954, by the Toho Motion Picture Company. Academy ratio, black-and-white. Running Time: 98 minutes.

U.S. VERSION: Released on April 4, 1956, by Trans World Releasing Corp. and the Godzilla Releasing Company. Running Time: 80 minutes.

STORY: Hydrogen bomb testing in the Pacific Ocean reawakens a long-dormant prehistoric monster, which rises from Tokyo Bay, terrorizes the superstitious natives of Odo Island and finally burns Tokyo to the ground with its white-hot radiation breath. Dr. Daisuke Serizawa, a reclusive scientist researching the properties of oxygen, inadvertently invents a doomsday weapon, the Oxygen Destroyer; reluctantly, Serizawa deploys the device on the ocean floor and Godzilla is killed, but the scientist does not return to the surface — guilt-ridden, he cuts his air hose and dies with the monster, ensuring that his invention will never be used as a weapon of mass destruction.

ORIGINS

According to legend, Godzilla was born aboard an airplane.

It was spring 1954. As the story goes, **Tomoyuki Tanaka**, a producer with the Toho Motion Picture Co., was flying home to Tokyo from Jakarta, where plans for a Japanese-Indonesian coproduction titled *In the Shadow of Honor* had just fallen apart. The movie, the story of a Japanese soldier who fights alongside the Indonesians in their struggle for postwar independence, was to be one of Toho's major releases later that year, and now Tanaka was under pressure to come up with a replacement for it — fast. Nervous and sweating, he spent the entire flight brainstorming.

Suddenly, he had a stroke of genius.

Taking a cue from the successful American science fiction film *The Beast from 20,000 Fathoms* (1953), in which a dinosaur is resurrected by atomic tests in the Arctic and swims south to terrorize New York, Tanaka decided to make Japan's first giant celluloid monster, a creature that would not only be reanimated by nuclear weapons but serve as a metaphor for the Bomb itself, evoking the horror of the Hiroshima and Nagasaki holocausts still vivid in Japan's consciousness. "The theme of the film, from the beginning, was the terror of the Bomb," Tanaka recalled decades later. "Mankind had created the Bomb, and now nature was going to take revenge on mankind."[1]

Nine years earlier, at the end of World War II, Japan had suffered a defeat unlike any other nation in history. In August 1945, America's twin atomic bombs had killed nearly 300,000 civilians, and an estimated 100,000 more lives had been lost the previous March when B-29 planes firebombed Tokyo for three consecutive days. Cities across Japan were leveled, leaving millions dead, wounded, or homeless. Factories that had been converted to military production were now either destroyed or rendered useless, crippling Japanese industry and bankrupting the economy. The country's massive empire in the Pacific region was lost, and six million repatriated soldiers and civilians returned to a Japan whose mighty spirit was crushed. Then came the seven-year-long Occupation (1945–1952), in which a nation that had remained unconquered for thousands of years suffered the shame of being governed by foreign soldiers and forced to adopt a Western-style constitution that reduced the Emperor to a mere symbolic figure, abolished State Shintoism, and threatened other long-held traditions and beliefs. The late 1940s and early 1950s were a time of political, economic, and cultural uncertainty in Japan.

During the war, the Japanese film industry was booming, due in large part to the government's use of the movie studios to disseminate heavily regulated nationalist propaganda. Then, after the defeat of Japan's militarist regime, the Allied powers likewise censored the movies and other media in their efforts to democratize Japan, forbidding discussions of the war, the Bomb and America's role in the tragedy. After the Occupation a handful of Bomb-themed films began to appear, notably Kaneto Shindo's Children of the Atom Bomb (1952), a semidocumentary about a schoolteacher who returns to Hiroshima looking for former pupils who were victims at ground zero. Hideo Sekigawa's Hiroshima (also 1952) was an angrier film that portrayed the atomic bombings as a racist act in which the Japanese people were guinea pigs in a U.S. nuclear experiment. But in the 40-plus years since the American forces left and censorship was lifted, surprisingly few movies have directly addressed Japan's status as the only nation to be attacked with nuclear weapons. Film scholars cite prevailing feelings of shame, repression, and guilt but are unable to fully explain the Japanese cinema's ambivalence toward the Bomb, a subject that would seem to be important and compelling movie material.

During the 1950s and '60s, several Japanese movies made references to the atomic bombs and to radiation sickness, but only two major films tackled the Bomb as subject matter. The most critically lauded of the two was Akira Kurosawa's I Live in Fear (a.k.a. Record of a Living Being, 1955), wherein Toshiro Mifune plays a man nearly frightened to death by the specter of another nuclear attack on Japan; the most commercially successful was Tanaka's barely disguised allegory of the Bomb, manifested in a gigantic monster.[2]

By 1954, Japan was peaceful and relatively prosperous again, but fears of renewed annihilation were brimming below the surface, fueled by new nuclear threats. Cold War tensions were increasing and Japan was now caught — literally — between the two superpowers' nuclear-testing programs: the Soviet Union's on one side, and the Pacific Proving Ground established by the U.S. at the Marshall Islands on the other. The Korean War was escalating, raising fears that a hydrogen bomb might be dropped on neighboring North Korea or China and rain fallout over the region. It may have been a divine act or it may have been pure happenstance, but around the same time that Tanaka was forced to quickly invent a major new film, a historic, horrifying event was unfolding in the equatorial Pacific, an event that would forever change monster-movie history.

Early in the morning on March 1, the U.S. detonated a 15-megaton H-bomb — with 750 times more explosive power than the atomic bombs that destroyed Hiroshima and Nagasaki — near the Bikini Atoll, 2,500 miles southwest of Honolulu. The explosion, code-named Operation Bravo, was labeled a "routine atomic test" by the Atomic Energy Commission but it proved far more powerful than expected, vaporizing a large portion of Bikini and sending a plume of highly radioactive debris floating eastward over a 7,000-square-mile area of the Pacific Ocean. Into this nuclear nightmare zone errantly wandered a 140-ton wooden Japanese trawler, the Dai-go Fukuryu Maru (ss Lucky Dragon #5), which was on a tuna-fishing trip about 100 miles east of Bikini. The boat's 23 crewmen were showered with a sticky, white radioactive ash; within a few hours several men became sick with headaches, nausea, and eye irritation, and a few days later some of their faces turned strangely dark. The ship's captain, not understanding what was happening to his men, abandoned the fishing trip and returned to the boat's home port at Yaizu in Shizuoka Prefecture. Six months later, on September 23, Aikichi Kuboyama, the chief radio operator, died of leukemia in a Tokyo hospital. His last words, according to newspaper reports, were, "Please make sure that I am the last victim of the nuclear bomb." Five other crew members later died from cancers and other diseases that were believed to be bomb-related.

The incident was first reported on the morning of March 16 in the *Yomiuri Shimbun* newspaper. At first the U.S. government denied it was responsible for the "death ash" that had poisoned the ship; the Americans later admitted the ash was fallout from a hydrogen bomb but accused the *Lucky Dragon* of entering the restricted testing area on a spy mission. The U.S. government sent the dead fisherman's widow a check for 2.5 million yen as a "token of sympathy" in an attempt to put the matter to rest. Only years later would America admit that Operation Bravo was the most powerful nuclear bomb ever detonated and that it caused the single worst fallout incident in the H-bomb atmospheric-testing program.

Throughout 1954 and '55, the *Lucky Dragon* tragedy released Japan's pent-up anxieties about the Bomb — an unprecedented public outcry followed it, including a boycott of tuna and other radiation-contaminated fish, a national ban-the-bomb signature campaign (by August 1955, 32 million signatures were collected), the formation of the Council Against A- and H-bombs, and the rise of the Japanese peace movement of the 1950s.[3]

It also gave birth to the King of the Monsters.

THE MAKING
OF GODZILLA

Before there was a screenplay, a story line, or even a concrete idea of what his monster would look like, Toho producer Tomoyuki Tanaka decided on a working title: *The Giant Monster from 20,000 Miles Beneath the Sea*. His first task was to present his idea to **Iwao Mori**, a powerful executive producer who had overseen much of Toho's moviemaking operations since the studio's formation back in 1937, and whose approval was needed to get the project off the ground. Seizing upon the clamor

over the fallout-poisoned fishermen, Tanaka used newspaper clippings about the *Lucky Dragon* incident to show Mori that the time was right for a gigantic monster, stirred from an eons-long sleep by rampant atomic testing, to come ashore and trample Tokyo.

Tanaka's idea was outlandish — no Japanese movie studio had ever attempted anything like it. The moviegoing public was accustomed to war films, family melodramas, and *samurai* sagas. RKO's *King Kong* (1933), which was re-released internationally with great success in 1952, was the only comparable film that Japanese audiences had seen. But Mori was interested in this odd proposal. A decade earlier, he had orchestrated Toho's successful string of special-effects-laden war movies, and now he was looking for a new way to parlay the talents of Toho's chief special-effects man, **Eiji Tsuburaya**, into big box-office yen. Stopping short of green-lighting the project, Mori told Tanaka to meet with Tsuburaya and determine if it was technically feasible.

Tsuburaya was heavily influenced by *King Kong*, and he had long wanted to make his own monster movie utilizing the type of stop-motion animation trickery Willis O'Brien employed in that film. He was also a man who seldom refused a challenge to create something new, so he quickly latched onto Tanaka's wild idea. Tsuburaya and his craftsmen were well experienced in filming re-creations of military battles and other illusions rooted in reality, but now Tanaka was asking them to create a larger-than-life, fictional creature, something no Japanese filmmaker had ever done.

In mid-April 1954, with Tsuburaya on board, Iwao Mori approved both the production and Tanaka's choice for its director. Senkichi Taniguchi, who had been slated to make the aborted *In the Shadow of Honor*, had already been reassigned to film an adaptation of *The Sound of Waves*, a popular Yukio Mishima novel. In his place, Tanaka chose **Ishiro Honda**, who had worked twice with Eiji Tsuburaya on war dramas featuring heavy use of special effects, *Eagle of the Pacific* and *Farewell, Rabaul*. Mori also shortened *The Giant Monster from 20,000 Miles Beneath the Sea* to simply *Project G* (*G-Sakuhin*, the "G" an abbreviation for "Giant"), and ordered that the production be given classified status, with details kept top-secret among the participants. "It was even said that Mr. Mori highly recommended that if you even told your children about it, that they'd wring your neck," Tanaka recalled. Believing this could be a historic event for Toho and the entire

A Tall Tale?

Producer Tomoyuki Tanaka often said *Godzilla* was the product of his clutch creativity in a high-pressure moment. But was Godzilla really born while Tanaka was sweating nervously in a plane flying over the Pacific? While Tanaka's story is certainly rooted in fact, the events leading to the monster's creation actually transpired much less dramatically.

According to several Japanese-language books and articles, it went something like this:

FEBRUARY 16, 1954: Tanaka and director Senkichi Taniguchi leave for Jakarta to finalize a contract with the Indonesian government's film agency for production of *In the Shadow of Honor*. Things proceed well.

FEBRUARY 25: Tanaka and Taniguchi leave Indonesia, fly to Hong Kong for a meeting with actress Shigeko Yamaguchi, one of the film's stars, and then return to Tokyo on February 28. The movie is to begin shooting within a few weeks.

EARLY MARCH: The Indonesians contact Toho to report that filming will be delayed until April, due to rainy weather.

MARCH 20: Toho receives a letter from Indonesia saying that the script for *In the Shadow of Honor* is unacceptable and the project is canceled. The underlying problem, however, is the tenuous postwar relations between Japan and Indonesia. Tanaka suggests going to Jakarta to try and save the production, but executive producer Iwao Mori tells him instead to come up with an idea for another movie. A few weeks later, the cancellation of *In the Shadow of Honor* is officially announced.

Japanese movie business, Mori ordered Tanaka to minimize his work on the other films he was producing at that time and focus on *Project G*.

Just as the American science-fiction movies *It Came from Outer Space* and *The Beast from 20,000 Fathoms* were based on stories by acclaimed genre author Ray Bradbury, Tanaka sought to give *Project G* credibility and commercial appeal by hiring science-fiction and horror novelist **Shigeru Kayama** to write an original story. Although his works have faded into obscurity today, Kayama (1906–1975) was then riding a crest of popularity that began in 1947 when one of his early stories, "Orang-Pendek's Revenge" (based on a legendary, Bigfoot-like creature in the Sumatran rainforests), won a literary prize from *The Jewel* magazine; another work, "The Curious Stories from the House of Eel," won first prize from the Detective Story Writers Club of Japan in 1948. Kayama was one of the most prominent mystery writers in postwar Japan, and because his stories sometimes involved mutant reptiles and fish and other monsters, Tanaka felt he was the ideal choice. On May 12, 1954, Kayama accepted the assignment.

Around the same time, two key decisions were made. First, the monster was named "**Gojira**" (roughly pronounced *GO-jee-rah*, later Anglicized as "Godzilla" by Toho's foreign-sales department when the film was offered to the English-speaking world). Second, the monster was given a shape. Contrary to popular belief, it appears Tanaka did *not* decide from the outset that the monster would be of the prehistoric-reptile variety. In fact, it is possible that he originally imagined a gigantic gorilla-whale, as its name suggested (see sidebar, "Gorilla-whale vs. Godzilla"). In memoirs published in Japan, Shigeru Kayama recalled that when he was first hired, he was told Godzilla was a sea monster that was "a cross between a whale and gorilla." The first conceptual drawings of Godzilla by Kazuyoshi Abe (a cartoonist who had illustrated some of Shigeru Kayama's novels) show a monster definitely more gorilla-like than reptilian. Evidence suggests that, at least until the early stages of Kayama's story-writing, ideas about the monster's physical form were still being discussed. At one point, Eiji Tsuburaya suggested a story he had written years before, inspired by his love of *King Kong*, about a gigantic octopus running amok and attacking

Japanese fishing boats in the Indian Ocean. Screenwriter **Takeo Murata** has also recounted how he and Tsuburaya devised a scenario in which a gigantic, whale-like creature came ashore in Tokyo and caused havoc.[4] Ultimately, Tanaka followed the wildly successful example set by *The Beast from 20,000 Fathoms* and elected to make Godzilla a dinosaur-like creature capable of posing a major threat to Japan. Tanaka said he felt a giant reptile "was more suited to the time period."

Kayama worked fast (according to his diaries, he had written 50 pages after just 11 days' work) and turned in his completed story before the end of May. While he was writing, Kayama received input from several Toho officials, including Tanaka and representatives from Toho's literary department, a group of people charged with cultivating story ideas. But perhaps the most key contributions to the development of *Godzilla's* story came from the aforementioned Murata, who co-wrote the screenplay with director Ishiro Honda. Murata (b. 1910), had directed Japan's first 3-D movie, *The Sunday that Popped Out* (1953), and was one of Toho's senior assistant directors. Although Shigeru Kayama established the framework of the story including the four pivotal roles (Dr. Yamane, Emiko, Ogata, Dr. Serizawa), it was Murata who fleshed out the dramatic structure and refined the characters. Dr. Yamane, for example, was originally written as a wildly eccentric character reminiscent of the works of Edogawa Rampo (a Japanese horror novelist popular in the 1930s and '40s, whose name is a Japanization of "Edgar Allan Poe").

"He (Yamane) was wearing dark shades and a black cape, and he had a very strange feel in the original story," Murata recalled in an interview published in *Toho SF Special Effects Movie Series Vol. 3*. "He was the type of man who lived in an old, European-style house, and he only came out at night. No one knew what he did for a living. Godzilla himself was weird, so we didn't want to make the main character weird also. That would be overkill. So, I suggested that the doctor should be an ordinary person who had lost his wife, and he lived with his daughter. . . . They should be living a very ordinary life."

"Gorilla-Whale" vs. Godzilla

Godzilla owes his name to a bad joke aimed at a Toho employee whose co-workers found him very ugly. They combined *gorira* (gorilla) and *kujira* (whale) to form "Godzilla" in Japanese and slapped the impolite nickname on him."
— From an *Agence France Presse* story, July 29, 1994

According to Toho folklore, the monster Gojira was named after a big, burly stagehand who worked on the Toho Studios lot. This man had earned his nickname, a compound of "gorilla" and *kujira* (Japanese for "whale"), due to his huge physique.

Over the years, producer Tomoyuki Tanaka often recounted how he thought the man's moniker perfectly suited the monster. Even director Ishiro Honda, shortly before his death, reaffirmed the story. "There was a big — I mean *huge* — fellow working in Toho's publicity department and other employees would say, 'That guy's as big as a gorilla.' 'No, he's almost as big as a *kujira*.' Over time, the two mixed and he was nicknamed 'Gojira.'" Honda's version of events seems somewhat revised; it makes less sense that someone working in the publicity department would be known for his girth than would a laborer. Regardless, the real name of Gojira (the man) has never been revealed, nor his job in the company and when he worked there.

Just who was "Gorilla-Whale," and why hasn't the studio ever brought him forward? Perhaps it's because he never really existed. "I expect the [monster's] name was thought up after very careful discussions between Mr. Tanaka, Mr. Tsuburaya and my husband," Honda's widow, Kimi Honda, said in a 1998 BBC-TV documentary. "I am sure they would have given the matter considerable thought." As for the burly man called Gojira, she added, "the backstage boys at Toho loved to joke around with tall stories, but I don't believe that one."

Godzilla's Birthplace

A BRIEF HISTORY OF THE TOHO MOTION PICTURE COMPANY AND THE JAPANESE MOVIE INDUSTRY

Godzilla was born at the right time, and in the right place.

In 1954, fueled by a postwar economic boom, Japanese movie studios were entering a period of unprecedented productivity. The Toho Motion Picture Company, which had already established itself as an innovator in the film industry, was engaged in box-office battles with its rivals (Shochiku, Nikkatsu, Shin-Toho, Toei, and Daiei studios) as it attempted to solidify itself as Japan's biggest and most ambitious moviemaker. It was this competitive climate, in which movie studios would take chances in order to make a splash, that made *Godzilla* possible.[5]

Toho was founded in 1937 by the merger of four small production companies that had all embraced the production of sound films while older, more established movie studios were still clinging to the tradition of silent movies with live narrators (*benshi*). The merger was orchestrated by Ichizo Kobayashi, a railroad tycoon who had successfully revived the struggling Arima Electric Railway Co. in Osaka by combining transportation with show business. In the early 1930s, Kobayashi extended a new railroad line out to a sleepy Osaka suburb, and at the end of the tracks he built a theater staffed with an all-female opera troupe, the Takarazuka Company. Located off the beaten path and kept under monastic conditions, Kobayashi's girls developed a mystique and soon became all the rage — a burgeoning entertainment city sprang up around the theater, with a zoo, a circus, and restaurants, and Kobayashi made a fortune on his railroad. Then, in hopes of building an entertainment empire, Kobayashi began buying theaters in the Tokyo area, envisioning a nationwide chain of movie and opera houses. To produce "talkies" for his theaters, in 1935 Kobayashi acquired two movie studios, PCL (Photo Chemical Laboratory) and JO, and formed the Toho Motion Picture Distribution Company to distribute the two companies' movies, along with imported American films. Two years later, he bought out two more small companies and solidified the entire operation into the Toho Motion Picture Company. (The name "Toho" is actually an abbreviation for "Tokyo-Takarazuka"; the Chinese character "Takara" can also be pronounced "ho." Toho's birth date is usually listed not as 1937, but 1932, the year that its precursor PCL was established.)

Toho hit its stride in the late 1930s and early '40s by becoming the foremost producer of "national policy films," a nice name for war propaganda movies. ☞

Honda and Murata holed themselves up in a Japanese inn in Tokyo's Shibuya ward to write the screenplay, which took about three weeks. "Director Honda and I . . . racked our brains to make Mr. Kayama's original story into a full, working vision," Murata said. "Mr. Tsuburaya and Mr. Tanaka came by and pitched their ideas, too. Mr. Tanaka's stance as a producer was, 'Please don't spend too much money.' Mr. Tsuburaya's stance was, 'Do whatever it takes to make it work.' Mr. Tsuburaya gave us

such encouragement. Whenever I wondered, 'Can we do something like this?' he would say, 'I'll give it some thought.' Then he comes back the next day and says, 'This is how we can make it happen.' "

Murata and Honda also introduced the Ogata-Emiko-Serizawa love triangle (originally, Ogata and Emiko were lovers, while Serizawa was merely a colleague of Yamane's), which gave deeper meaning to the characters' actions and lent a profundity to Serizawa's suicide. They nixed Kayama's idea of

Godzilla's Birthplace *continued.*

Often involving the painstaking re-creation of aerial dogfights and naval battles with miniatures and pyrotechnics, these elaborate, expensive productions laid the foundation of Toho's special-effects department. Buoyed by the nationalist fervor that brought audiences flocking into movie houses to see its war movies, and by the company's own political ties (in 1940, Kobayashi was appointed to serve in a cabinet position in the Imperial government), Toho's fortunes flourished.

With the end of the war in 1945 came the U.S.-led Allied Occupation, however, and the Japanese movie industry entered a dark period during which Toho nearly folded. There were several reasons for the decline. The office of the Supreme Commander of the Allied Powers (SCAP) utilized the cinema as a tool in its plan to democratize and westernize Japan; the industry was heavily censored and many producers, directors, and actors who had made war movies or otherwise aligned themselves with the war effort were thrown out. The studios were dogged by high postwar inflation and other economic problems, and many of their theaters had been bombed out during the war. The new labor movement, a by-product of the Occupation reforms, also wreaked havoc. Between 1946 and 1948 there were three major strikes at Toho, the last of which left the company nearly bankrupt, but its fortunes began to improve in 1950 as the Korean War brought new prosperity to Japan with the production of American procurements. After the Occupation ended in 1952, executive producer Iwao Mori, forced by the SCAP to leave Toho for having overseen its production of war propaganda films, returned and rededicated himself to making the company a profitable producer of feature films.

Godzilla was released less than one year before the start of the Showa '30s (1955–1965), a decade regarded as the historical zenith of the Japanese film industry, during which more than one billion movie tickets were sold in Japan. At the apex of this period, in the late 1950s, Japan cranked out more than 500 films per year, compared to about 300 by the U.S. and 100 by Britain. Toho continued to grow and became Japan's largest studio, a position it has more or less retained until today, on the strength of a commercial movie crop that included *salaryman* comedies, melodramas, youth-oriented love stories, and musical comedies (such as the famous *Wakadaisho* ["Young Guy"] series starring heart-throb Yuzo Kayama, and the comedies of the Crazy Cats, a sort of Japanese-style Marx Brothers troupe). It was during this time that the *kaiju eiga* (monster movie) genre, spawned by *Godzilla*, blossomed and became one of Toho's trademarks.

Located in Seijo-Gakuen, a tree-lined, upper-middle-class residential suburb in Tokyo's Setagaya ward, Toho Studios was in its heyday a sprawling production facility comparable in size to most American studios, with numerous enclosed soundstages and outdoor filming areas (a small river divides the property between open and closed sets). In those days, thousands commuted to and from the studio daily. Today, although most of the studio remains intact (a few parcels of real estate having been sold away), it is a much quieter place, with only a few films made each year.

having Godzilla's entire physical appearance revealed during the hurricane on Odo Island, opting instead to create suspense and dread by gradually making the monster visible (Godzilla stealthily destroys the ships, its footsteps and roar are heard during its Odo Island rampage, a footprint is found on the beach, the monster pokes its head above the mountain, and, finally, its entire figure is shown). Murata and Honda created the characters of the reporter Hagiwara and Dr. Tanabe, and they reduced the role of Shinkichi, the orphaned island boy, who figured prominently in Kayama's original draft.

More than anything, it was Godzilla that underwent the greatest change between Kayama's initial story and the Murata-Honda script. Kayama had imagined Godzilla as more of a wild beast than a monster — a predator with quick reflexes that came on land primarily to feed on live animals, and that showed a gorilla-like interest in females. Kayama also placed far less emphasis on the destruction of

The offices of Toho Studios, located in the Setagaya section of Tokyo, circa 1979.
COURTESY OF WINTERGARDEN PRODUCTION

cities that would become the hallmark of this film and many of its sequels (interestingly, however, he had Godzilla attacking a lighthouse in a scene borrowed directly from *The Beast from 20,000 Fathoms*). But then, there was no way Kayama could have known what sort of epic-scale illusions Eiji Tsuburaya was developing on the Toho Studios lot.

MONSTER MAGIC: On July 5, 1954, Toho Studios officially announced that production had begun on *Godzilla*. Shooting of the film began about a month later, in early August, by three photography teams: special-effects photography (Godzilla scenes), headed by Eiji Tsuburaya, principal photography (dramatic scenes), headed by director Ishiro Honda, and composite pho-

tography. It was during that month between the announcement of production and the start of filming that Tsuburaya and his craftsmen created the world's first Japanese movie monster, or *kaiju*.

In the West, many film critics have for years wondered why Eiji Tsuburaya did not use stop-motion animation to create Godzilla, opting instead for a man clad in a rubber monster suit trampling miniature cities. A few writers are so biased against the man-in-suit method and Japanese sci-fi movies in general that they even suggest Tsuburaya was ignorant of the techniques Willis O'Brien utilized in *King Kong*, which is pure nonsense — as proof, one stop-motion effect was included in the film, an animated model of Godzilla's tail smashing the

Nichigeki Theater building. "Mr. Tsuburaya had originally thought of going with stop-motion for quite a while, but finally decided it wouldn't work," Fumio Nakadai, a longtime member of Tsuburaya's effects crew, said in the book *The Complete History of Toho Special Effects Movies*. "Using a costume was the last resort for him. He wasn't happy with the idea [but] he had been kind of forced into a situation where he had to use the costume method." Tsuburaya even sat in a small screening room on the Toho lot and watched *King Kong* to study O'Brien's work, but stop-motion was more expensive and time-consuming than *Godzilla*'s tight budget and production schedule would permit. Thus, Tsuburaya went in another direction — albeit reluctantly at first — that would eventually define his place in movie history. "Suitmation," as it is now called, is not nearly as technically sophisticated as O'Brien's animation or the Dynamation process pioneered by Ray Harryhausen in *The Beast from 20,000 Fathoms* and other pictures, but it proved a more effective method to portray the kind of destruction Godzilla would become famous for.

Godzilla's shape materialized when sculptor **Teizo Toshimitsu** and art director **Akira Watanabe** began design work under Tsuburaya's supervision. Both Watantabe and Toshimitsu had known and worked with Tsuburaya for years; a decade earlier, Watanabe was special-effects art director and Toshimitsu one of his assistants on *The War at Sea from Hawaii to Malaya*. The initial Godzilla designs by Kazuyoshi Abe were discarded because they looked vaguely humanoid. Instead, Toshimitsu and Watanabe referred to dinosaur books, plus an issue of *Life* magazine that featured an illustrated article on dinosaurs, and decided to base the creature on two upright-walking reptiles, the tyrannosaurus rex and the iguanodon. They also borrowed a distinctive feature of the quadrupedal stegosaurus: three rows of erect dorsal fins lining the spine, from neck to tail, with no function other than to give the creature a unique look (it was decided, after the fact, that the fins would glow when Godzilla emits his radioactive breath). In taking artistic license with evolutionary history, the designers were clearly more interested in creating something fantastic rather than realistic or logical, a spirit that marked the beginning of *kaiju* history.

Toshimitsu first sculpted a clay model upon which the Godzilla suit would be based, standing about 10 centimeters tall, with a large head, small hands and feet, and skin covered with scales. This design was rejected by Tsuburaya as still not dinosaur-like enough, so Toshimitsu next came up with a "warted Godzilla" whose body was covered with smooth, round bumps to give it an amphibious look. This was also rejected, but Tsuburaya, Honda, and Tanaka finally approved Toshimitsu's third design, which had a small head, stubby arms, and a body covered with rough-hewn pleats, similar to alligator skin, representing the monster's physical scarring by an H-bomb blast.

SUITING UP: Next, sculptor Toshimitsu and a team of costume builders went to work. Tsuburaya had decided Godzilla would stand 50 meters (about 165 feet) tall, just high enough to peek above the tallest buildings in Tokyo at that time. The costume itself was to be two meters (about 6-1/2 feet) tall, or 1/25 Godzilla's actual height. The chief costume builders were Kanji Yagi and his younger brother, Koei Yagi, both of whom had worked with Tsuburaya at his Special Effects Institute after the war, and Eizo Kaimai. Using thin bamboo sticks and wire, they built a frame for the interior of the costume; over that, they put metal mesh and some cushioning to bolster its structure, and finally they applied coats of latex. It was a crude operation: the men melted large chunks of raw latex and stirred it by hand, then covered the costume frame with it. Several coats of molten rubber were applied, then indentations were carved into the surface and strips of latex glued on to create Godzilla's scaly hide. But the stuff was heavy, and barely flexible when it dried, which made for big problems in the early going.

That first Godzilla suit weighed at least 100 kilograms (over 220 pounds), and some sources say it weighed as much as 150 kilos. The men chosen to don the cumbersome costume and portray Godzilla onscreen were **Haruo Nakajima**, an athletic young actor and stuntman, and **Katsumi Tezuka**, still in his teens. Both were adept at martial arts and other sports, and were chosen for their strength and endurance. In the coming years, Nakajima would be immortalized as Toho's principal Godzilla suitmation actor.

At the first costume fitting, held on Stage No. 2 on the Toho lot, Nakajima climbed inside the opening along the spine (where the dorsal fins were located) and took a test walk while Tsuburaya, Honda, and others observed. Immediately, Nakajima felt as if he were in a straitjacket. He could hardly breathe. His fingers could barely move. He could turn his head from side to side only a few

This bronze statue was erected in 1995 in Tokyo to commemorate Godzilla's death in *Godzilla vs. Destoroyah*, the 21st Godzilla sequel (see chapter 22). It resembles both the original Godzilla (*Shodai-Goji*) design by Teizo Toshimitsu — a bulky, muscular, upright-walking reptile based on an amalgam of several different dinosaurs and incorporating mammalian-like facial features — and the 1990s Godzilla designs, which are more cat-like, created by latter-day sFx director Koichi Kawakita.

PHOTO BY THE AUTHOR

inches. There was no slack in the joints, and the deadweight of dragging the immense tail was unbearable. After just a few steps, Godzilla fell down. The staff members rushed to Nakajima's aid, and he emerged from the suit drenched in sweat. "When I was inside the costume, I could hear someone saying, 'Yeah, this looks like it's going to work.' But, man, it was so rough walking in that thing. I knew then that the job wasn't going to be as easy as I had thought," Nakajima said. "I thought to myself, oh well, it's only the beginning, but there were a lot of problems with the costumes as the shoot proceeded."

Because of its immobility, the original suit was cut in half and fitted with rope suspenders so Nakajima could wear it, like a pair of overalls, for close-ups of Godzilla's legs and feet trampling the Ginza district; the upper half was used for scenes where Godzilla pokes his head above the waterline in Tokyo Bay. For full-body shots of Godzilla, the original costume was replaced by a second one, virtually identical but made of a lighter latex that was easier to maneuver, but Nakajima's working conditions were grueling nonetheless.

IT'S A SMALL WORLD: One reason for Eiji Tsuburaya's willingness to gamble on the new technique of suitmation must certainly have been his ample experience in the other half of *Godzilla*'s special-effects equation: the building, photographing, and destroying of miniatures.

Although it has gone mostly unappreciated outside of Japan, Tsuburaya's replication of the Tokyo cityscape rivals — and even surpasses — the scope and detail of the miniaturization of New York City and the Empire State Building in *King Kong*. Tsuburaya, special-effects art director Akira Watanabe (who supervised the miniature construction), and their crew made great efforts to ensure the accuracy and realism of the miniature cityscapes, knowing the movie's primary audience would be Tokyo residents. They scouted the locations Godzilla was going to trample, and viewed the city from the monster's vantage point by climbing atop the Akasaka TV towers and the rooftops of various buildings. A story has been retold hundreds of times over the decades about a humorous episode that happened when Tsuburaya, Watanabe, and others were scouting locations in the Ginza district. The men were standing on the roof of the Matsuzakaya Department Store (one of the buildings Godzilla trashes in the film), looking out over the city and charting the monster's path of destruction. An eavesdropping security guard heard them talking casually about setting fire to certain landmarks and ran to get a policeman. As the filmmakers were leaving the department store, the cop questioned them, letting them go only after they showed him their Toho business cards.

At the time *Godzilla* was made, Toho had no special-effects department to speak of. The team assembled by Tsuburaya to produce and film the effects sequences was the largest since his war movies of a decade earlier, and it was made up mostly of craftsmen he had known since his early days in the film business, people who had worked for him at his Tsuburaya Special Effects Institute after the war, and young rookies just entering the business. The special-effects team relied heavily on other studio departments for assistance, and to help with miniature-making they turned to the studio's large carpentry department, where movie sets were built. Using photographs of the city, art director Akira Watanabe and his men drew hundreds of blueprints for the miniature buildings, which were given to Kintaro Makino, the chief of miniature construction. Makino assigned about 30 to 40 workers from the carpentry department's staff of about 300 to build them. All told, it took more than a month to construct the scaled-down version of the Ginza.

The majority of the miniatures were built at 1:25 scale, the same as the Godzilla costume, although there were a few exceptions. The Diet Building had to be scaled down to 1:33 size to make it appear smaller than Godzilla, because in reality the building is slightly more than 65 meters high (15 meters taller than the monster). Buildings seen in close-up shots were built larger, while those on the horizon were made smaller to create a forced perspective. The framework for the buildings was made of thin wooden boards reinforced with a mixture of plaster and white chalk. Buildings set ablaze by Godzilla's radioactive breath had explosives installed inside them, and some were also sprayed with gasoline to make them burn easier. Those Godzilla was to destroy were made with small cracks so they would crumble easily. Still, it took considerable force to smash the buildings, and Godzilla actor Haruo Nakajima was under pressure to make them crumble correctly for the cameras on the first take, as there was neither time nor money to rebuild the miniatures.

There were a number of inevitable mishaps, beginning on the very first day of special-effects shooting. Everyone arrived around 9 AM at Stage No. 5 on the Toho Studios lot, eager to begin work on Godzilla's destruction of the Diet Building, the first effects sequence to be filmed. The miniature sets were built on wooden platforms that stood above the floor, allowing explosives or other devices to be installed underneath if needed and giving the cinematographer room to tilt the camera up to make the buildings seem larger. The Tokyo city streets were made by pouring plaster over a layer of sawdust so that Godzilla's foot would sink into the asphalt on camera and leave gigantic footprints. But the plaster streets created problems even before Godzilla stepped on them. A crew member who was putting last-minute touches on the set prior to filming broke through the surface of the street, damaging the Diet Building set as he fell. The crew rushed to repair the damage, which took several hours, and by the time everything was ready it was well past noon. Then, as Nakajima was led onto the set in the Godzilla suit, he stepped on the spot where the repair was made and crashed through the platform, again damaging the set. Luckily, Nakajima wasn't hurt, and nothing was seriously damaged, but it was dusk by the time filming got under way that first day.

In the end, there were more troubles with the crucial Diet-smashing scene. When Nakajima went to destroy the miniature, it didn't crumble quite right, and the film was unusable. If you look carefully at the scene, you'll notice that the shot of Godzilla looming over the parliament building is actually a composite shot of the real Diet Building and Godzilla — a slightly irregular matte line can be seen where the two film elements are joined. All that survived of the miniature Diet set on film is a wing of offices, seen briefly as Godzilla's legs trample through it.

Tsuburaya's monster suit and miniatures were the core of his special-effects trickery, but he also utilized other techniques that were crucial to Godzilla's success and which later became staples of Toho's giant-monster films. Two small puppets were used — a hand puppet equipped with a mist spraying nozzle in its mouth for close-ups of Godzilla spewing his atomic breath, and a mechanical puppet able to "bite" and move its arms, used when Godzilla chomps on the TV tower and peeks over the Odo Island mountain; a waist-deep outdoor pool was constructed for filming the ship disasters, the Odo Island typhoon, and scenes of Godzilla wading ashore and smashing the Kachidoki Bridge; there were extensive pyrotechnical effects, from kerosene-soaked rags set afire around the perimeter of the miniature Tokyo set to create the illusion of a city engulfed in flames, to the wire-rigged charges that simulate the impact of gunfire hitting

Godzilla's body and the explosions that occur when Godzilla's atomic breath hits its targets; wires were used to manipulate the fighter planes attacking Godzilla and the movements of the monster's tail; primitive optical animation techniques in which hundreds of cells had to be hand-drawn, one frame at a time, created the illusion of Godzilla's fins crackling with light and the eerily brilliant, long-shot views of the monster spitting his radioactive halitosis; and traditional matte paintings were skillfully used — some of the daytime shots of the electrical towers along the waterfront were actually painted on sheets of glass placed in front of the camera, and the faraway view of Odo Island was really a painting. By modern standards, and even in its day, virtually all Godzilla's special effects were low-tech, which makes the movie's lasting visual impact all the more amazing.

In all, the Godzilla special-effects crew spent 71 days shooting the picture: 32 days on indoor sets and sound stages at Toho, 25 days on open sets, two days on rented stages outside the studio, three days on location in the Tokyo area, and nine days of second-unit shooting on location outside Tokyo. Because of this incredibly tight schedule, the crew members basically ate and slept at the studio for two months straight. Movies were typically filmed between 9 AM and 5 PM, but because of the new methods used in this production and the inexperience of the crew members, Tsuburaya and his men often did not begin rolling the cameras until 5 PM or even later. They pulled many all-nighters, finally wrapping up the shoot at daybreak, and some crew members joked that Gojira's name rhymed with goji, which means "5 AM" in Japanese. Every morning after shooting was finished, brothers Kanji and Koei Yagi would put away the Godzilla costume in a storage shed on the far side of the studio. At first, they hauled the heavy load in a hand-drawn cart, but soon the studio took pity on them and rented them a truck. The Yagis dried out the sweat-soaked cotton lining inside the costume (Haruo Nakajima's perspiration was so intense they had to re-line the inside of the suit several times) and tried to repair whatever damages it had sustained.

ON LOCATION: Before Godzilla moved from pre-production into production, executive producer Iwao Mori borrowed a technique pioneered by animators at Walt Disney Studios in Hollywood to ensure continuity from scene to scene. Storyboards were virtually unheard of in Japanese moviemaking prior to Godzilla, but with several photography teams working independently, Mori wanted each shot to be carefully planned. At his request, SFX art director Akira Watanabe hired several part-time artists and spent about two weeks sketching out about 300 cuts. Then, meetings were held in the Toho commissary in which the storyboards were hung on a wall and screenwriter Takeo Murata explained each scene in detail to the crew. This extra planning step proved invaluable, as the intercutting between the principal and special-effects photography in *Godzilla* is often seamless. Storyboarding became a mainstay of Toho's special-effects films; today, the technique is called "continuity sketches," or *conte.*

Honda's principal photography team spent 51 days shooting the film and, like the SFX crew, most of its work was done on the Toho lot, where sets of the Maritime Safety Agency disaster center, the Yamane house, the interior of the Diet Building, Dr. Serizawa's laboratory, and other scenes were created. But much time was also spent on location on the Shima Peninsula in Mie Prefecture, an area familiar to director Ishiro Honda (several years before, he had shot his first feature film, *The Blue Pearl*, there), to create the fictional locale of Odo Island, which in the story is located off the Izu Peninsula. Honda's crew established their base at the small town of Toba and did much of their shooting at and around a nearby mountain, where Godzilla first reared his hideous head over the hillside. In this immortal scene, an alarm bell is sounded in village — a creature has been spotted atop the hill! — and a throng of Odo islanders run up the narrow pathway armed with sticks and guns to fight off the monster, but when they realize that Godzilla is larger than anything imaginable they immediately turn and retreat in terror. About 50 Toho extras were brought from Tokyo, and the crowd was augmented with several hundred local villagers. The camera was positioned high atop the hill in order to photograph the long line of villagers extending down the slope, but it was so high that the extras at the bottom had no way of knowing when "action" was called. There were no walkie-talkies, so an assistant director stood at the foot of the mountain and watched Honda and the camera crew with a pair of binoculars. At the top of the hill, assistant director Koji Kajita waved a white flag to signal that the camera was rolling, and the order was given to run.

Another important scene filmed in Mie is the *kagura* folk dance, which the Odo islanders perform to invoke benevolent spirits. The dance was performed by local villagers and filmed outside a Shinto shrine in Toba. Traditional *kagura* music using flutes, drums, and gongs was later written by Akira Ifukube and added to the scene. Honda also scripted and filmed several scenes on location in the Mie area that were ultimately cut from the final print. In one scene, shortly after arriving on Odo Island, Dr. Yamane, Ogata, and Emiko visit the graves of several victims killed by Godzilla during the typhoon. In another scene, Ogata and his crew conduct a series of tests, attempting to determine what caused the shipping disasters. Still another had Emiko and Ogata, strolling the beach, frightened at the sight of Godzilla's tail moving in the water. There was also an unused version of Godzilla's first appearance on the hilltop; originally, Godzilla had a bleeding cow dangling from his mouth (this was in keeping with Kayama's story, in which Godzilla came ashore to feed on livestock), but Eiji Tsuburaya felt the effect was unrealistic and ordered it reshot.[6]

Ishiro Honda and his crew spared no trouble to make *Godzilla* as authentic as possible. Toho negotiated with the Japan Self Defense Force (JSDF, which was officially established earlier in 1954) to film actual military drills, but the military agreed to cooperate only on a very limited basis. When Godzilla comes ashore at Shinagawa and the military opens fire with machine guns, there are shots of actual soldiers filmed at target practice on a military base outside Tokyo. The convoy of JSDF trucks and tanks deployed against Godzilla is an actual military platoon that was being transferred from a base at Utsonomiya to another in Chiba; Honda's crew filmed the caravan as it was departing the base, then jumped in their cars, rushed ahead, and filmed it again further along the route. Other location shots were less troublesome, but equally important to creating the picture's impressive scope. The huge girls' choir that sings the haunting *"Heiwa no Inori"* ("A Prayer for Peace," sometimes called "Oh Peace, Oh Light Return") at the film's pivotal moment was actually the entire student body of an all-girls high school in Tokyo. It has been rumored that a matte painting was used to make the choir seem larger than it was, but in truth more than 2,000 girls memorized the words to the song and mouthed them in their school auditorium.

A *KAIJU* CACOPHONY: The illusion of Godzilla's size and irrefutable power was reinforced by the thundering sounds of Akira Ifukube, who wrote

one of the most memorable musical scores in sci-fi movie history and who supervised the creation of Godzilla's distinctive, immortal roar. Despite his background in classical music and as a composer of serious dramatic films, Ifukube never shied away from Tanaka's oddball monster movie, not even when his contemporaries said it was beneath him and urged him not to do it. After just a few introductory meetings with Tanaka, Tsuburaya, and Honda to discuss the project, Ifukube enthusiastically accepted the assignment. "Something monstrous comes out and makes you jump out of your wits!" Ifukube said. "It is sheer fear, not an abstraction, and it is global. Moreover, my specialty was biology. I couldn't sit still when I heard that in this movie the main character was a reptile that would be rampaging through the city."

While *Godzilla* was in production, Tsuburaya was intensely secretive about his special-effects work, and only allowed members of his crew to watch rushes of the footage shot each day. He even refused to show the rushes to director Honda until much later, when all the composite work and optical effects were done. However, there are conflicting stories as to whether Ifukube was allowed to see what Godzilla looked like on-screen, in all his terrifying glory, before he wrote his monster music. In 1994, Ifukube told *Soundtrack*, "I only saw the model of Godzilla and I read the script. In Japan, in most cases a composer has only one week's time to compose film music after the film is finished. I didn't have enough time, so I composed my Godzilla music before I saw the film." But in other published interviews, Ifukube has indicated that he saw at least some of Tsuburaya's footage, even if Godzilla had not yet been matted into the frame. "Mr. Tsuburaya would not show the actual footage until the final cut of the movie was completed," Ifukube said. "He always left [the special-effects scenes] blank, and he would say, 'Right here, something like this will appear.' And I would ask, 'What does it look like?' And he'd say, 'Well, if you look at the expressions on the extras' faces you'll know how scary the thing is behind the mountain.' I was very confused, so I tried to make music that would remind you of something enormous." To do that, Ifukube wrote a score that uses low-pitch brass and string instruments to reinforce the monster's ponderous plundering.

Ishiro Honda came up with the idea that Godzilla should roar, regardless of the fact that reptiles do not have vocal chords, with this rationale: "Godzilla underwent some mutation. He is beyond our imagination." Sound recordist Hisashi Shimonaga and sound-effects man Ichiro Mitsunawa were put in charge of creating the monster's roar, but Ifukube immediately took an interest in devising sound effects for the film and became involved in the process. "From our first meeting together, I already sensed what an amazing musician he [Ifukube] was," Honda said. "He asked us what certain special sound effects we were going to use in certain parts of the movie, and about all kinds of details concerning the sound." Mitsunawa started out by recording the roars of lions, tigers, condors, and other birds and zoo animals, then playing them back at various speeds (the original *King Kong* roar was created the same way), but none of these proved satisfactory. Eventually, someone hit upon the idea of using a contrabass (double bass), one of the lowest-pitched string musical instruments in existence. Ifukube arranged to borrow a contrabass from the prestigious Japan Art University's music department, and the roar was created by loosening the instrument's strings and rubbing them with a leather glove. The sound was recorded and then played back at reduced speed, resulting in the melancholy, ear-splitting cry of the original Godzilla. This technique became Toho's standard method for creating monster roars for years to come (Godzilla's cry, however, would be sped up and changed into a high-pitched whine in the 1960s and '70s films); today, monster roars are recorded digitally.

Conflicting stories exist as to how the ominous sound of Godzilla's footsteps was created. Legend has it that a Japanese kettle drum was struck with a knotted rope, and the sound was recorded and processed through an echo box; Akira Ifukube, in an interview with *Cult Movies*, said the footsteps were created with a primitive amplifier that emitted a loud clap when struck, designed by a Toho sound engineer. But several Japanese texts reveal the footsteps were actually the "BOOM!" of a recorded explosion with the "OOM!" clipped off at the end and processed through an electronic reverb unit, producing a sound resembling a gigantic bass drum — or a monster's foot crashing down on the Tokyo pavement.

The audio technology utilized in *Godzilla* was less than primitive. The optical recording equipment had only four audio tracks, and of those, one was used for the principal dialogue, one for background chatter, ambient noise, and the sounds of tanks and planes and one for Godzilla's roar and footsteps (these effects were so loud they required an independent track to avoid bleeding over the music and other audio). That left only one track for the music and the crashing sounds of Godzilla's destruction. Unbelievable as it sounds today, the musical score and the foley (mechanical) sound effects of Godzilla's final, wanton rampage through Tokyo were recorded live, at the same time. At the recording session, Ifukube conducted the NHK Philharmonic orchestra while a foley artist watched Godzilla's attack projected on a movie screen, using pieces of tin, concrete debris, wood, and other materials to simulate the sounds of the monster walking through buildings. It was a precarious process — if the foley artist missed a cue even slightly, a new take would be needed for the entire scene — but somehow it resulted in a seamless work of discord.

HYPING THE MONSTER: While production was well under way, executive producer Iwao Mori was busy devising promotional strategies to generate public interest in *Godzilla* and ensure its box-office success. The most significant of these was a radio play called *Kaiju Gojira*, based on the *Godzilla* screenplay, 11 episodes of which were broadcast on consecutive Saturday nights from July 17 to September 25, 1954, on the NHK radio network. To build an air of mystery around the movie, Mori banned reporters from the set, and all information on the special-effects techniques and other behind-the-scenes details was barred from the media (including the fact that Godzilla was a man in a costume, which would officially remain a secret well into the 1960s). The image of the monster, however, was well publicized: pictures of Godzilla were printed on Toho's company stationery, cutout pictures and posters of the monster were displayed in theaters and stores, huge advertising balloons were flown over major Japanese cities, and a Godzilla doll was mounted on the back of a truck driven through Tokyo. Finally, Toho's theatrical trailer for *Godzilla* began running in cinemas October 20, 1954, proudly boasting that the film would surpass American special effects in quality.

On October 23, 1954, the day of reckoning finally arrived. A private screening of the finished film was held for producer Tanaka, director Honda, SFX director Tsuburaya, and the core members of the filmmaking crew. The men watched nervously as the film unspooled before them, and they were relieved to see that their mammoth efforts had

come to grand fruition. Then, on October 25, a Godzilla festival was held in front of a water fountain on the Toho studio lot. The Godzilla costume was stuffed and mounted on a makeshift Shinto shrine and prayers were given (the festival was quite an event — attendees included the great actor Toshiro Mifune!), and there was a screening for the entire cast and crew. When it was over, the audience congratulated one another and then filtered out of the screening room. Only story author Shigeru Kayama, who was visibly shaken by the movie, lingered behind, weeping for the tragic, misunderstood creature that paid twice for mankind's recklessness with the atom — once when it was disturbed from its peaceful sleep by a nuclear test and again when a new doomsday weapon claimed its life. Others in the audience were similarly touched, including the film's star, Akira Takarada. "When I first saw *Godzilla* at the studio screening, I couldn't help crying when I watched Godzilla become a skeleton," Takarada said. "I thought, 'Why did mankind have to punish Godzilla like that?' . . . Mankind seemed like a bigger villain than Godzilla, and I felt sorry for him. I think sympathy for him still exists today. If Godzilla were truly evil, people wouldn't have loved him so much. We were responsible for triggering Godzilla's violence."[7]

THE BOTTOM LINE: The official total estimated production budget for *Godzilla* was 62,893,455 Yen, the equivalent of about $900,000 in 1954 U.S. funds. More than one-third of the budget, nearly 27 million Yen, went to expenses related to special-effects filming, while location costs, the large number of extras employed for crowd scenes, and other factors shot the budget skyward. Advertising expenses and the cost of striking theatrical film prints further pushed the budget up to about 100 million yen (roughly $1.5 million U.S.) — according to some reports, this was as much as 30 times the cost of the average Japanese movie. *Godzilla* was the most expensive Japanese movie produced to date; the previous holder of that distinction was Akira Kurosawa's *The Seven Samurai*, which took more than one year to shoot and had higher-priced talent attached to it, yet still cost much less (about $500,000). Both pictures were considered risky megaproductions in their day, but Toho's gamble paid off in both cases. *The Seven Samurai* was the best-attended film of 1954 and has gone down in history as one of the greatest feature films ever made; on November 3, *Godzilla* broke the opening-day ticket-sales record in the city of Tokyo (previously held by *The Seven Samurai* and *Musashi Miyamoto*, both released earlier that year) and was the eighth-best-attended film of 1954 in Japan. In all, 9.6 million people went to see *Godzilla* during its theatrical run — a figure that seems staggering today — and its box-office earnings were about 152 million Yen ($2.25 million), netting Toho a nice return on its investment.

MONSTER METAPHOR

A Closer Look at Godzilla

Thud.

Deafening footfalls echo in the blackness. An ear-crushing wail splits the night. Then a title card rises, three *katakana* characters proclaiming the arrival of Japan's doomsday beast: GOJIRA.

Given Godzilla's prevailing repute as a campy icon and comic superhero, the original Japanese version of his first film is a revelation even today, when viewed at a distance of more than 40 years. And although hundreds of people contributed to the film's success, from low-echelon gofers to the special-effects crew to producers Tanaka and Mori, the sure guiding hand of director Honda is most evident throughout the picture, conducting something akin to an orchestra of drama and horror storytelling, stark visual style, and ominous sound and music, all of which meshes together and plays out like a grand nightmare.

The story is simple enough, with two common themes woven together. The first is a combination war drama and monster-movie scenario with Japan as the victim of a hostile and incomprehensible enemy that strikes without warning — like a ghost — and gradually reveals its physical form and the full fury of its destructive powers. The movie opens with a series of strange shipping disasters haunting Tokyo Bay, with freighters and fishing boats mysteriously wiped from the ocean's surface, evoking the real-life terror of the recent *Lucky Dragon* mishap. The authorities are powerless to respond, mystified as to whether the culprit is a military enemy or some strange phenomenon. At first, the only people who truly understand the magnitude of the approaching doom are a superstitious Odo Island elder, who first utters the name "Godzilla" while watching his people reel in empty fish nets (another reference to the *Lucky Dragon*) and the rational presence of Dr. Yamane (Takashi Shimura), who urges the military to refrain from killing the incredible creature so that man can learn how it could have possibly survived irradiation by the Bomb. Heroic march music plays as the navy litters the bay with depth-bombs, but Japan pays the ultimate price for attacking Godzilla when the monster comes ashore twice and wipes out Tokyo. In the end, the mysterious Dr. Serizawa unveils his Oxygen Destroyer and Godzilla is liquefied at the bottom of Tokyo Bay. The military and the Japanese people see Godzilla as their enemy, but is the monster really an evil villain? Only Yamane realizes Godzilla's larger implications, and as the picture ends he is left wondering whether man did the right thing. So long as nuclear testing continues unabated, will Nature unleash more Godzillas?

The second, more personal story line is a soap-opera love triangle in which the professor's daughter, Emiko Yamane (Momoko Kochi), wants to cut off her arranged marriage to Serizawa and instead wed the sailor Ogata (Akira Takarada), but the monster's appearance intrudes upon their plans at every turn. The focus of this three-way relationship is Serizawa who, despite the fact that he is rarely seen and has comparatively few lines, is the film's most well-drawn character, a man living in darkness in an upper-class European-style house and mysteriously clad in a lab smock and eye patch. This is not a jealous rivalry between two men courting the same woman; Ogata clearly respects Serizawa and regrets inflicting any pain upon him — at one point, Ogata refers to the scars on Serizawa's face (they unfortunately do not show up well on camera, but are clearly visible in publicity photos), which were inflicted during World War II — while Serizawa is so preoccupied with the implications of his research that at first he doesn't seem to notice that Emiko is leaving him. Both men clearly love Emiko, although Serizawa subtly expresses his feelings by revealing his darkest secrets to the girl. "My character was scarred from the war," Hirata said in an interview published in *Toho SF Special Effects Movie Series Vol. 3*. "I didn't want to bring that out with sentiment. I didn't think that would be interesting. . . . Dr. Serizawa didn't speak much in the movie. I think that's why it worked."

The conflict between the two men is on a symbolic level — Emiko and Ogata represent hope for

Japan's future and a break from old pre-war values, evidenced by their joint decision to terminate Emiko's betrothal, while Serizawa is a brilliant yet disillusioned man from the generation that lost the war (in Shigeru Kayama's original story, Serizawa was 40 years old and Ogata 30, but actors Hirata and Takarada were considerably younger). When Ogata bravely and blindly insists that Serizawa use his invention to save Japan, the conflict escalates into a fistfight. In this deeply moving scene, the camera pans to Serizawa's aquarium, the place where the horrible power of the Oxygen Destroyer was first unveiled, while the men's blows are only heard, not seen, a great metaphor for the power struggles that weapons of mass destruction inevitably bring, and which Serizawa is so afraid of. Serizawa wins the fight, but as Emiko bandages Ogata's head wound, Serizawa finally realizes he has lost the girl, his only connection to the outside world. In an instant, his fate crystallizes: he decides to uphold the old code of honor and pass the torch along to the next generation. As Godzilla dies on the sea bottom, Serizawa bids goodbye to Emiko and Ogata; his tragic suicide puts an end to the current menace (Godzilla), a potentially greater menace (the Oxygen Destroyer), and his inner torment, while neatly allowing the lovers to unite without shame. The requiem that plays at the film's end is for both Godzilla and Serizawa, two misunderstood characters.

Honda skillfully creates an eerie, bleak atmosphere throughout the film, accentuated by the grainy, documentary-like photography of Masao Tamai. The story takes place during late summer, and the blazing sun is palpable as the actors often sweat profusely, but several scenes are actually chilling. As the Odo villagers perform their ceremonial ritual, donning eerie *tengu* (devil) masks and dancing to strange paganish music, the old fisherman tells the reporter Hagiwara (Sachio Sakai) about the Godzilla legend. All of a sudden a typhoon strikes and a series of booming noises shakes the village. This is Godzilla's first appearance, and the fact that he is never seen (except for a tiny glimpse of his leg as he plows past Shinkichi's crushed house) lends the monster an air of the supernatural. When the scientific investigators arrive on the island, Dr. Yamane makes an awesome discovery, a perfectly preserved trilobite imbedded in a gigantic footprint on the beach, and death hangs in the air as the entire area is discovered to be tainted with radiation.

After Godzilla's terror raid, the camera pans across the smoldering remains of Tokyo, then switches to a hospital where people lie dead and dying everywhere. A doctor tests a child for radiation and the Geiger counter goes wild. A little girl wails as she watches her mother die of terrible burns. The suffering overwhelms Emiko and compels her to reveal Serizawa's secret. Finally, the scene in which Ogata and Serizawa deploy the Oxygen Destroyer in Tokyo Bay is artfully creepy, with the two divers floating in the depths like some weird death ballet set to Akira Ifukube's requiem theme and Godzilla watching them from a distance, as if accepting his fate. Godzilla's death is gut-wrenching: the Oxygen Destroyer bubbles the sea violently and the monster writhes in pain, poking his head above the surface (splashing water on the camera lens) and bellowing his death-cry before sinking and dissolving to a skeleton, then to nothingness.

Arguably the most memorable scene in *Godzilla*, however, derives its power from something the camera *doesn't* show. In his dungeon-like basement laboratory filled with beakers and scientific gizmos, Serizawa drops a small metallic pellet into a large fish tank. Accompanied by Akira Ifukube's discordant musical sound effects (violins screeching uncontrollably and the crash of a dissonant piano chord), Serizawa holds Emiko close and she suddenly screams in terror. Serizawa exacts a vow of secrecy from the girl, and she is so disturbed by what she has seen that she is unable to terminate their engagement, the purpose of her visit in the first place.

GODZILLA STEPPED HERE: The star of the show is Godzilla, of course, and the highlight is his maiden mission of mayhem. The city of Tokyo is divided into 23 wards (called *ku* in Japanese), and Godzilla trampled many of them during his first two nights on the town back in 1954, in an orgy of Eiji Tsuburaya's special effects.

The scene in which Godzilla peers over the ridgeline on Odo Island and roars mightily is a classic in monster-movie history — perfectly executed via an old-school in-the-camera matte shot combining footage of actors running down the slope and the Godzilla puppet peering over a miniature mountain (the melding together of the model trees and the real-life hillside is virtually indistinguishable). When the monster departs, Dr. Yamane and the others look down from the hill and see a trail of gigantic footprints leading from the beach into the surf, another brilliant matte fusing footage of the ocean with a painting of the sand. By only hinting at Godzilla's immense size in the early going, Tsuburaya saves the knockout punch for Godzilla's arrival in the city. It is well worth the wait.

The monster's rampage is divided into two parts, the first a showcase for the masterful composite photography work supervised by Hiroshi Muka-iyama. In the film's most stunning visual sequence, Godzilla lands on eastern Tokyo Bay and makes his approach onto dry land, towering above the Tokyo streets as scores of tiny people flee in the foreground. This is the first time that the original Godzilla suit, known in fan circles as the *Shodai-Goji*, is shown in all its glory, and it is breathtaking. Silhouetted against the black night sky, Godzilla is like a giant spirit, with a mammalian face and beady, dead eyes peering out from under his thick, scarred brow, surveying his targets methodically and unemotionally. The illusion of Godzilla's size is enhanced by Tsuburaya's low-angle camera place-ment, rapid back-and-forth edits between the SFX and live-action footage, and the use of very fast cuts so as not to betray the miniatures and the monster effects. At the Shinagawa rail station (a major trans-portation hub between Tokyo and the suburbs of Kawasaki and Yokohama), the monster walks right into the path of a speeding train whose passengers and crew are unaware of the death-drama unfold-ing outside. In a series of quick cuts, the monster's feet are seen approaching the tracks from the con-ductor's point of view as the train passes underneath a bridge (a nice, rolling dolly shot). In a meticulous shot filmed by cameraman **Teisho Arikawa** (who had to lay flat on his stomach), Godzilla steps on the tracks and the train collides with his mighty foot at full speed, jackknifing the cars and sending bodies flying. As the passengers jump out the train windows, Godzilla claws through electrical wires, trying to reach the locomotive, then picks up a train car in his mouth and flings it (another classic moment, utilizing the hand-manipulated Godzilla puppet).

Godzilla retreats to the sea, but Japan instinctively knows the monster will soon return and a massive evacuation of Tokyo is orchestrated, the first and biggest of many panicking-crowd scenes that Honda would direct in his genre career. To prevent the monster from re-entering the city, the authori-ties erect high-tension electrical wires carrying 50,000 volts along the shoreline, strung between 100-foot-high towers. At night, Godzilla seems to sense he is being dared. He comes ashore in pre-cisely the right place, but as everyone now knows,

the joke's on Tokyo. Here, Godzilla's white-hot atomic breath is first revealed, melting the barrier to molten metal. (The towers were constructed of white wax, and the melting effect was achieved by aiming hot lights at them.) From there, Godzilla embarks on a destructive tantrum spanning a full 13 minutes of screen time, leveling many landmarks and giving viewers a Tokyo sightseeing tour in the process. Godzilla stomps through Minato-Ku, Shimbashi, and other wards en route to Ginza, Tokyo's internationally famous, upscale shopping district, where he torches the Matsuzakaya Depart-ment Store, one of Tokyo's oldest and priciest retail establishments. A clock tower atop the roof of the nearby K. Hattori and Co. clock shop (known today as the Wakko Building) begins to chime and Godzilla responds by tearing down the famous timepiece.

Heading northeast, Godzilla crosses the Sukiya Bridge (a matte shot that wobbles a bit, accentuat-ing the monster's weight), trashes the commuter train overcrossing (the site where he would later destroy the bullet train in *Godzilla 1985*), and with his tail knocks in the side of the famous Nichigeki Theater (now called the Tokyo Marion Building, a venue owned by Toho and located near the company's corporate headquarters). The monster then crosses into the Akasaka district, where major government buildings are located, and smashes a wing of the Diet Building. Reporters broadcasting live from a tower in Akasaka's "TV Village" (an area concentrated with broadcast stations) attract Godzilla's attention with their flash bulbs and the monster chomps down on the tower, sending the newsmen hurtling to the ground in a brilliant shot, filmed from the victims' perspective. Godzilla smashes the Kachidoki Bridge at the mouth of the Sumida River before fighter planes finally chase him back to the ocean.

Even before the monster comes ashore, the gloomy stage is set by the searchlights eerily fan-ning across the bay. As Godzilla marches through the streets, a few hangers-on who ignored the evac-uation order pay the price for their curiosity as they are crushed under his huge feet in a wonderful matte shot. Tanks confront Godzilla at an inter-section, but Godzilla is merely annoyed by their pesky gunfire and swiftly does away with them with a blast of his death-breath. With Tsuburaya's high-speed photography heightening the illusion of a slow-moving giant, Godzilla plows through buildings with ease, stopping only to peer over the rooftops and occasionally incinerate a police car or other target. Glimpses of the monster's animalistic nature appear when Godzilla snarls at a cage full of frightened-to-death birds in a rooftop aviary (a scene hinting that man, not Godzilla, is the real animal) and again when he tears down the clock tower.

As the rampage builds to a crescendo, fire engulfs all of Tokyo. An oil refinery is decimated, flames curl out of windows and lick the sides of buildings, and long shots of the miniature city — which were filmed outdoors on the Toho lot because the special-effects soundstage was not big enough to contain the expansive set — reveal gigantic sheets of fire and smoke rising into the sky in slow motion. The fires rage all the way to the shoreline, illustrated by a nice matte shot of flames rising behind the crowds of people gathered there. The scope of *Godzilla's* disaster has never been equaled on film, in terms of both the damage toll and the atmosphere of pathos and death that accompanies it.

★ ★ ★

Godzilla is not a perfect film. The arduous constraints of time, money, and technology under which it was made are occasionally evident in mismatched jump cuts that should have been reshot, or unconvincing special effects like the model helicopter that tips over during the Odo Island storm and the wire-guided rockets that visibly collide with the sky backdrop in Tokyo Bay. In one scene, the wire manipulating Godzilla's tail is clearly visible. The Oxygen Destroyer is a brilliant metaphor for the Bomb, but nitpickers might wonder why a weapon that disintegrates oxygen in water does not merely leave behind hydrogen gas, as textbook chemistry suggests it should. But this rough-hewn, virtually handmade work of art has a visual impact and underlying prophecy of the world's self-inflicted doom that remain stunning and socially relevant today.

Outside Japan, *Godzilla* remains an underrated and somewhat misunderstood film, usually lumped alongside Western giant monsters of the same period. Bomb-birthed creatures like *The Beast from 20,000 Fathoms* evoked America's fears of a Soviet nuclear attack, and could only be killed by new and more powerful American nuclear weapons; thus, there is a tendency to interpret *Godzilla* as the flipside of this motif, with Godzilla standing in for America, the Oxygen Destroyer a symbol of Japanese resolve, and its inventor's suicide representing Japan's denouncement of nuclear weapons. Film pundits have long tried to define what Godzilla means, often concluding that the monster is a symbol of Japanese postwar shame, guilt, anger, and other repressed emotions stemming from the atomic bombings. While there is some truth in such interpretations, it may be impossible for non-Japanese to fully fathom what the filmmakers were trying to say. Not only did Japan have the uniquely horrifying experience of suffering a nuclear attack, but *Godzilla* seems to tap into mythology and cultural history not shared by the West, especially in such a young country as America. Still, something bigger is at work on a subconscious level in *Godzilla*. Producer Tanaka and director Honda clearly created the monster in the image of the Bomb, but the metaphor is universal. Godzilla's hell-born wrath represents more than one specific anxiety in the modern age — it is the embodiment of the destruction, disaster, anarchy, and death that man unleashes when he foolishly unlocks the forbidden secrets of nature, probes the frightening reaches of technology and science, and, worst of all, allows his greed and thirst for power to erupt in war.

The initial reaction to *Godzilla* among Japanese critics was mixed. Joseph Anderson and Donald Richie, in *The Japanese Film*, relate that *Godzilla* was lauded by some reviewers for "intellectual content usually lacking in foreign pictures of the same genre." Richie himself reviewed the film in *The Japan Times*, calling it "vastly entertaining" and praising the special effects as "much more realistic" than those employed in other big-monster movies, yet criticizing it nonetheless. "The implicit fault in the method used in 'Gojilla' [sic] is that no matter how well made the miniatures are they still look unreal," Richie wrote. "Here they are extremely well done and look precisely like extremely well done miniatures. If a film is strong enough, one willingly suspends logic and agreeably refuses to believe that what one sees is false. 'Gojilla' . . . is not that strong. There are so many long talky scenes that the monster's appearance becomes positively welcome. It's fun to watch the man walking on the toy buildings."

Godzilla was praised by some members of the Japanese intelligentsia, including novelist Yukio Mishima. However, the reviews that stuck in Ishiro Honda's mind were those that called the film a crass attempt to capitalize on Japan's nuclear nightmares. "They called it grotesque junk, and said it looked like something you'd spit up," director Honda told *Tokyo Journal* decades later. "I felt sorry for my crew because they had worked so hard." Over time, however, *Godzilla* has come to be regarded as a classic of the Japanese cinema. In 1984, the prestigious film journal *Kinema Junpo* rated *Godzilla* among the top 20 Japanese films of all time. In 1989, a published survey of 370 Japanese movie critics, *Nihon Eiga Besuto 150* (*Best 150 Japanese Films*), ranked Godzilla the 27th-greatest Japanese feature ever made.

Director Honda once said he believed the film's enduring popularity is owed, paradoxically, to the fact that he did not completely succeed in scaring people as he intended: "Many young viewers didn't have any first-hand knowledge, or only dim memories, of the war. As strange as it may sound, I think the film succeeded because I didn't completely succeed as a director. . . . It represents only 65 percent of what I wanted to achieve. Since I fell 35 percent short, audiences could see it wasn't a real story."

GOD⟨ZILLA⟩FATHERS

The Founders of Toho's Monster Cinema

The Idea Man: TOMOYUKI TANAKA

Godzilla's birth was a collaboration of many talented people, but only one man was truly the monster's father. Godzilla was the brainchild of Tomoyuki "Yuko" Tanaka, without whom Japan's *kaiju* cinema likely would never have become a worldwide phenomenon, and perhaps may never have transpired at all. Tanaka came up with the idea to make *Godzilla* and later assembled the Honda-Tsuburaya-Ifukube triad, the creative nucleus of Toho's sci-fi epics. In turn, *Godzilla*'s success catapulted Tanaka to become one of the most prolific producers in Japanese film history, with over 200 movies to his credit, including all 22 Godzilla movies and more than 80 special-effects pictures overall. Nevertheless, he was always a somewhat unsung hero, particularly outside Japan.[8]

Tanaka was born April 26, 1910, on the outskirts of Osaka, in Yamanashi Prefecture, to a wealthy family. As a boy, he fell in love with silent movies, and often walked miles to the nearest theater to spend afternoons watching adventures, ninja stories and tragedies. At 14, he saw the American film *The Covered Wagon* (1923, directed by James Cruze, an early western about the plight of settlers on the Oregon Trail) and was so impressed by the film's vivid cinematography that it remained his all-time favorite. During his youth, he was once disowned by his parents for paying more attention to his passions, films and acting, than his studies. He majored in economics at Kansai University, but his real dream was always to become a stage and film actor. At the university, Tanaka hooked up with a drama troupe, and he later joined the *Shingeki* ("modern drama," a Western style of theater

Producer Tomoyuki Tanaka, circa 1982.
ASAHI SHIMBUN/WIDE WORLD PHOTOS

founded in the early 1900s that broke away from *Kabuki* and other traditional Japanese drama) movement in Osaka. But he soon realized he had "only average dramatic skills," and turned instead to producing and directing plays in the 1930s.

Tanaka entered the film industry in 1940 when he was hired by the Taisho Film Company, a small Tokyo outfit acquired by Toho the following year.

From then on, his rise was meteoric: After working in Toho's literature department briefly, Tanaka was groomed by studio chief Iwao Mori to be a film producer. The first movie he produced was a war drama, *Until the Day of Victory* (1944); this was followed by a handful of films before the end of World War II. After the war, from 1945 to 1948, he made at least a half-dozen movies, including *Those Who Make Tomorrow* (co-directed by Akira Kurosawa, 1946) and *Over the Silvery Peaks* (a.k.a. *Snow Trail*, 1947); the former was a controversial pro-union propaganda film sanctioned by the Allies to bolster Japan's labor movement, the latter a melodrama about bank robbers who escape into the Japan Alps, featuring early appearances by superstar Toshiro Mifune and *Godzilla* star Takashi Shimura, and was the first film scored by *kaiju* composer Akira Ifukube. In 1948, Tanaka was among a group of producers, actors, and other employees who left Toho to protest the purging of 1,200 supposedly communist workers and its crumbling relations with the labor unions. For the next few years he worked with the Society of Film Artists, led by exiled directors Kajiro Yamamoto and Akira Kurosawa, who had also left Toho. Tanaka returned to Toho in 1952, wooed back by his old friend Iwao Mori. Two years later, he created a monster.

Although he gave directors free reign during the moviemaking process, Toho's special-effects films were Tanaka's domain and he made pivotal decisions concerning scripting, marketability and other matters. In the genre's heyday, Tanaka introduced "monster-vs.-monster" movies in *Gigantis: The Fire Monster*; he capitalized on Russia's 1957 launch of the Sputnik satellite and the ensuing interest in space travel with *The Mysterians* and *Battle in Outer Space*; he developed Toho's "mutant films" (*The H-Man*, *The Human Vapor*, *Secret of the Telegian*) — a cross between mystery and sci-fi that focused on humans disfigured by radiation. Tanaka got the idea for *Rodan* from a dream, and hired professional sci-fi novelist Takashi Kuronuma, to pen an original story upon which the screenplay was based (he was fond of commissioning stories from writers — other examples include *Godzilla*, *The Mysterians*, *Battle in Outer Space*, *Mothra*, and *Attack of the Mushroom People*). Seeking to broaden the *kaiju eiga*'s audience, Tanaka in 1961 made *Mothra*, a "modern fantasy," complete with tiny twin singing women to add a feminine appeal.

Tanaka's aim was to keep Toho ahead of its competitors in special-effects filmmaking, and his influence over the genre was all-encompassing. At the same time, he produced other types of films, including works by directors Akira Kurosawa (including the acclaimed *Yojimbo*, *Sanjuro*, *High and Low*), Kihachi Okamoto, and Hiroshi Inagaki. He worked hard to export Toho movies, traveling abroad and helping arrange co-productions that infused foreign capital and American actors, increasing the overseas marketability of several features. Not coincidentally, Tanaka's films have been seen around the world more than those of any other Japanese film producer. Tanaka also had a few miscues in his long career — it was his idea to make Godzilla a hero and to increase his appeal to children, a move he later regretted ("This character change was responsible for his decline. It was a mistake," he told *People* magazine in 1985), but he atoned for it years later when he resurrected the beast as an infernal villain in *Godzilla* (1984), and insisted that the monster become a serious threat once again.

Colleagues described Tanaka as a workaholic and a voracious reader of newspapers and magazines, from which he often gleaned ideas for films. "I am not sure how to describe it, but he is just amazingly diligent, or I guess earnest," special-effects director Teruyoshi Nakano said. "I once heard this story about an episode where Mr. Tanaka went to see Mr. Masumi Fujimoto (a high-ranking Toho producer) to get some project authorized. Mr. Fujimoto glanced at the proposal . . . then went right to bed. You know what Mr. Tanaka did? He patiently waited at the corner of the room! Mr. Fujimoto woke up several hours later and found Tanaka still sitting there in the corner. 'What in the world are you doing? I can't even take a leak!' Mr. Fujimoto said. Then Tanaka answered, 'I won't move until you OK that project.' What persistence!"

Tanaka remained active in the movie business in his later years, holding the title of executive producer on all the 1990s Godzilla movies. However, his frail health forced him to hand most of the actual production chores over to his successor, producer Shogo Tomiyama — who, by comparison, is grossly lacking in original ideas and tends to throw everything but the proverbial kitchen sink into his monster films, hoping to please everyone (usually failing). The latter-day Godzillas were among the most successful domestic films in Japan (both *Godzilla vs. Mothra* [1992] and *Godzilla vs. Destoroyah* [1995] topped the yearly box-office charts), concluding Tanaka's long string of monster box-office hits that began more than four decades before.

Tomoyuki Tanaka died of a stroke at age 86 on April 2, 1997, in Tokyo, just 16 months after Godzilla perished in *Destoroyah*. During the last few years of his life, Tanaka was reportedly eager to see his monster-child remade in grand style, in a big-budget Hollywood movie. His dream came true a year after his death, but although TriStar Pictures' *Godzilla* (1998) was dedicated to Tanaka's memory, perhaps it is better that he never saw the picture, which fell far short of his own vision and spirit.

The Storyteller: ISHIRO HONDA

Perhaps no one deserves more credit for Godzilla's longevity than the man whose epic cinematic style and sensitivity to the human condition are the enduring signatures of Toho's *kaiju eiga*. Ishiro Honda will always be remembered as a director of monster movies, having helmed 25 special-effects pictures, including eight of the first 15 Godzillas. But he was much more than that. He was a visionary filmmaker who, with Eiji Tsuburaya, transcended the limitations of the genre to create films that remain thoroughly entertaining, even today.[9]

Honda (whose first name is often erroneously transliterated as "Inoshiro") was born May 7, 1911, in Yamagata Prefecture. His interest in movies began as a youth, when he was fascinated with the *benshi* silent-film narrators. "I was more interested in them than what was happening on the screen," Honda told *Tokyo Journal* in 1991. "My father was a Buddhist priest and didn't go to the movies. I'd come back and, as kids do, I'd tell him the entire story of whatever I'd seen. . . . I watched movie theaters being built and regular theaters being turned into movie theaters and eventually I realized there could be a pretty well-paying future for me in the business. It all came together: I enjoyed telling stories and could find work in an industry that was financially successful and artistic to boot."

After high school, Honda studied film at Japan University's art department. During his college years, he entered PCL Studios' apprenticeship program (the group was supervised by Iwao Mori, who two decades later would be the executive producer to green-light *Godzilla*, and its members included Senkichi Taniguchi, another future Toho director). In August 1933, even before completing his studies, Honda was already an accomplished cameraman, and landed a job in PCL's production department; eventually, as PCL was absorbed into Toho, he ascended the ranks to become an assistant director. But Japan's conquest of Asia interrupted Honda's career. He was drafted into the Imperial Japanese Army in 1936, and over the next eight years he

served three tours as a foot soldier in China and Manchuria. In between his military duties he would return to Toho, working mostly as an assistant director under Kajiro Yamamoto, who directed many of Toho's epic war films. In 1937, Honda first met budding director Akira Kurosawa, another Yamamoto protégé, with whom he forged a lifetime friendship and creative alliance. Also during this period, Honda met and married his wife, Kimi, a Toho script girl.

In 1942, while stationed in China, Honda saw *The War at Sea from Hawaii to Malaya* and was wowed by Tsuburaya's special effects for the Pearl Harbor sequence. One year later, in December 1943, while working as an assistant director on Yamamoto's *Kato's Flying Falcon Forces*, Honda met and worked with Tsuburaya for the first time. But the legendary partnership between the men would take years to develop — in fact, that first meeting proved a difficult experience for the young Honda. In a memoir published in 1983, he recalled preparing for a scene wherein a squadron of model fighter planes were to be filmed flying in formation over a bank of clouds made of white cotton. When Tsuburaya inspected how Honda had set up the shot, he wasn't pleased, and immediately complained to Yamamoto about it. "I could tell Eiji was not happy with the width of the stage, the cloud material or the method used to operate the model [plane]," Honda wrote in *The Complete History of Toho Special Effects Movies*. "I couldn't help feeling like a failure, but Yamamoto was very reassuring and helped soothe my feelings."

In 1945, while stationed along the Yangtze River in central China, Honda was captured and held as a prisoner of war for about half a year; it was during his incarceration that he learned of the atomic bombings and Japan's surrender. After the war, Honda returned to Japan and to moviemaking, working with different production companies due to labor strife at Toho. In 1949, he was chief assistant director to Kurosawa on *Stray Dog*, the story of a young Tokyo cop (Toshiro Mifune) whose gun is stolen and used in a series of crimes. In 1949 and 1950 he directed two documentaries, *The Story of a Collaborative Union* and *The Legend of Ise-Shima*; this led to his return to Toho and his first feature film as a director, *The Blue Pearl* (1951), a movie about female pearl divers.

Over the next two years, Honda directed five features, including *The Man Who Came to Port* (1952), starring Toshiro Mifune and Takashi Shimura as Japanese whalers. This was the first time Honda

Director Ishiro Honda, circa 1991.
KYODO NEWS AGENCY/WIDE WORLD PHOTOS

collaborated directly with Tsuburaya, who used rear-screen projection to make the Japanese actors appear as if they were at the South Pole. Honda's big break came with the 1953 film *Eagle of the Pacific*, a war drama with an all-star Japanese cast that became a box-office hit and which, according to many sources, included some of Tsuburaya's most impressive war effects work. Honda then made *Farewell, Rabaul*, a love story set amid the Pacific War, released in February 1954. His next scheduled assignment was a film called *Bokushi Sanshiro* (*Sanshiro the Priest*), but thankfully it was canceled and Honda was instead chosen to direct the film that would forever change the world of science-fiction cinema: *Godzilla*.

Honda approached *Godzilla* more like it was a war drama, with documentary-like straightforwardness, than a monster or science-fiction movie. Above all, the idea that Godzilla represented the Bomb was foremost in his mind: After the war, Honda had visited devastated Hiroshima and was haunted by its images, and he wanted the monster to convey the same horrific, destructive power.

"Most of the visual images I got were from my war experience," Honda said in an interview published in *Toho SF Special Effects Movie Series Vol. 3*. "After the war, all of Japan, as well as Tokyo, was left in ashes. The atomic bomb had emerged and completely destroyed Hiroshima. . . . If Godzilla had been a big ancient dinosaur or some other animal, he would have been killed by just one cannonball. But if he were equal to an atomic bomb, we wouldn't know what to do. So, I took the characteristics of an atomic bomb and applied them to Godzilla."

Among the 44 feature films he directed, Honda considered *Godzilla* his best work. Honda hoped, perhaps naively, that his monster movie could help bring an end to nuclear testing, but *Godzilla* generated more monster mania than nuclear phobia and its success shaped the rest of his career. After *Godzilla*, Honda made a variety of melodramas and light comedies, but he was increasingly called upon to work on Toho's growing *kaiju* cinema; by the mid-1960s, he was exclusively a monster-movie director, the lone exception being *Come Marry Me* (1966), a romantic comedy-drama starring youth idol Yuzo Kayama. Honda was not a maverick artist of the Kurosawa school, but a skilled craftsman and company man who did as Toho asked, even if it meant sacrificing other career dreams.

Still, Honda sometimes declined to work on certain films if he did not like the script or had other objections. In an interview with *Cult Movies* magazine shortly before his death, Honda explained his absences from the Godzilla series in 1966–67 and 1970–74 this way: "There were scheduling problems, and also, Toho decided that they did not want people to feel that monster films had to be directed by me. . . . Frankly, I was having a hard time humanizing Godzilla the way Toho wanted anyway." He said the scene where Mothra intercedes between feuding Rodan and Godzilla in *Ghidrah: The Three-Headed Monster* particularly bothered him, and he would have found it "difficult" to direct *Son of Godzilla*. In a 1995 interview, Honda's wife told the magazine that Honda preferred sci-fi sagas like *The Mysterians* and *Gorath* that focused on the need for nations to unite in the face of world destruction, and he was worried about being pigeonholed. "I'm not sure if the success of the Godzilla movies was a good thing or not," Kimi Honda said. "They were so popular that Mr. Honda became trapped. He had to work on them." Even so, Honda repeatedly delivered sci-fi spectacles of epic scale, with startling visuals; he was loved and respected by crew members, and his smooth, relaxed demeanor on the set enabled him to get more engaging performances from his casts than any other Japanese genre-movie director. "He was a very interesting man," the great character actor Eisei Amamoto told Guy Tucker in *Ultra-Fan* magazine. "He was a romantic, but he didn't like to express his own nature too much. The company made him into the director of special effects movies, and that was all; he didn't get to show much of his own personality."

Honda took a hiatus from film directing after *Yog: Monster from Space* (1969). In the late 1960s and early '70s, he supervised the re-editing of eight monster films, reducing them to matinee length — a process he described as "destroying" himself — or the Toho Champion Festivals, a series of re-releases to exclusively kiddie audiences; he also forayed into television, directing episodes of three sci-fi/superhero programs for Tsuburaya Productions, *The Return of Ultraman*, *Mirror Man*, and *Fireman*, plus other series called *Thunder Mask* and *Urgent Command 10-4, 10-4* (apparently a documentary-style show about rescue workers). His last film as a director was the strange and uneven *Terror of MechaGodzilla* (1975), but his film career was far from over; reuniting with Akira Kurosawa, his friend of nearly 60 years, Honda contributed to the screenplays and directed scenes for five films, on which he was billed as associate director: *Kagemusha: The Shadow Warrior* (1980), *Ran* (1985),

Akira Kurosawa's Dreams (1990; directed "The Tunnel" segment), *Rhapsody in August* (1991; directed the Buddhist ceremony), and *Madadayo* (1992).

Ishiro Honda died at 11:30 PM on February 28, 1993, at Kono Hospital in Setagaya, Tokyo, at age 81, of respiratory failure brought on by heart problems. Hundreds of friends and colleagues attended a memorial service in Tokyo on March 6. Sadly, Honda didn't live long enough to see his dream of nuclear disarmament begin to come true, with the mutual destruction of nuclear warheads by the U.S. and Russia in recent years. It may have helped him rest easier.

"It is sad that the number of atomic bombs hasn't been reduced even by one since [1954]," Honda once said. "We'd really like to demand abolition of nuclear weapons to both America and Russia. That is where Godzilla's origin is. No matter how many Godzilla movies are produced, it is never enough to explain the theme of Godzilla."

Master of Illusion: **EIJI TSUBURAYA**

In 1964, *Famous Monsters of Filmland* magazine asked special-effects master Eiji Tsuburaya how his film career began. "When I was a youngster I 'borrowed' coins from my father's shop," Tsuburaya said, "to buy a movie projector I had seen in a store window. I realized that if I were caught with the camera I would be punished, so I took it apart, examined it and threw it away. Then I built my own."

This story has been repeated countless times over the years, and whether or not it is true, it illustrates the ingenious, make-it-from-scratch ethic underlying Tsuburaya's huge body of work. Blessed with a talent for "creating something from nothing," as he liked to say, Eiji Tsuburaya dedicated 50 years of his life to inventing wonderful illusions for the film and television screen, ranging from epic war battles to gigantic monsters and superheroes, yet utilizing resources and techniques that were paltry and crude compared to today's computer-driven standards. If not always realistic, they were never less than fantastic, and that was the magic of the father of *tokusatsu*, the art of Japanese special effects.

Tsuburaya was born July 7, 1901, in Sukagawa City, Fukushima Prefecture. Fascinated by airplanes, he longed to become a pilot and at age 14 enrolled at the Japan Aviation Academy, but the school soon closed and he studied electrical engineering instead. At 18, Tsuburaya entered the film industry (curiously, starting out as a scenario writer, according to some sources), and for the next 18 years he worked stints at a number of studios, ascending to the position of cameraman and learning early special-effects techniques. His career was interrupted, however, from 1921–23 when he was drafted into the military, serving on the Imperial Army's correspondence staff.

Tsuburaya landed his first job with a major Japanese film studio in 1925 at the Shochiku Motion Picture Co., where he worked with critically acclaimed impressionist filmmaker Teinosuke Kinugasa. Tsuburaya was an assistant cameraman on Kinugasa's *A Page of Madness* (1925), a movie film historians describe as a dark, brooding examination of depression. During this period, Tsuburaya earned his first credit as a cinematographer on *Baby Kenpo* (1927); he also began working with miniatures for the first time.

Sometime in the mid-1930s, Tsuburaya saw RKO's *King Kong* when it was imported to Japan, and it became the inspiration for his career and ultimately for *Godzilla*. "The change in my life came . . . when I saw *King Kong*," Tsuburaya said in 1961. "That inspired me. At that time, Japanese trick photography

THE MAN: Eiji Tsuburaya at Toho Studios c. 1961, wearing his trademark soft hat, coat and tie.
ASAHI SHIMBUN PHOTO/AP WIDE WORLD PHOTOS

Eiji Tsuburaya checks a miniature pilot's ejection seat used in the
plane in the foreground. This photo was taken for a February 2, 1961
article by Associated Press syndicated columnist Bob Thomas.
AP/WIDE WORLD PHOTOS

was very backward. I started working in that field and by 1937 I began to accomplish some of the things I wanted to do."[10]

Tsuburaya's career accelerated in 1935 when he was hired by JO Studios in Kyoto, where studio head Yoshio Osawa encouraged him to develop his talents for film trickery. In *Princess of the Moon*, a fantasy based on "The Tale of the Bamboo Cutter," a Japanese folk story, Tsuburaya photographed a miniature model of the city of Kyoto, superimpos-

ing a crowd of people and a cow-drawn carriage in the foreground, and he devised an effect to simulate angels descending from the sky. This film, apparently long lost, solidified Tsuburaya's interest in special effects as a new art form, and he was grateful to Osawa for spending the money needed to tinker with new techniques. Around this time, Japan and Germany had signed an anti-communist pact, which led to Japan's first international coproduction, the Japanese-German film *The New Land*

The Summit: Frank and Eiji. Eiji Tsuburaya (far left, with eyeglasses) confers with director Frank Sinatra (center) on location in Hawaii, over the aerial dogfight scene and plane crash in *None But The Brave* (1965). Tsuburaya directed special effects for the war drama, a Japanese-American co-production.

COURTESY A.C.E. PHOTOS

(1937). By then, Tsuburaya had developed a process for the still-tricky art of rear-screen projection photography that surpassed similar techniques being used in Europe; his method was employed extensively in the movie, bringing his inventive talents to the fore at last. From then on, he blossomed.[11]

Tsuburaya joined PCL in 1937, and two years later, after the company became Toho, he was appointed head of its new special photographic techniques department. It was basically a one-man operation at first, but the staff of model-makers and craftsmen grew as special effects became integral to Toho's popular war films in the early 1940s. From 1939 to the end of World War II, Tsuburaya spearheaded the first boom in Japanese special effects, working on nearly 40 films, most notably a trio of war blockbusters directed by Kajiro Yamamoto: *The War at Sea from Hawaii to Malaya* (1942), *General Kato's Falcon Fighters* and *Torpedo Squadrons Move Out* (both 1943). Devoted Tsuburaya fans should seek out *The War at Sea*, which was released on home video in Japan and may be found in some specialty video outlets in the U.S. The film, which follows a naval cadet from boot camp to the Pearl Harbor attack, has gone down in Japanese film history as an amazing piece of wartime propaganda. "It . . . marked the greatest use of special effects and miniature work ever seen in a Japanese film up to that time," Joseph Anderson and Donald Richie said in the book *The Japanese Film*, and its re-creation of Pearl Harbor was so convincing that after the war, the Occupation authorities mistook some scenes for actual newsreel footage. "It was gigantic in every sense of the word and cost over \$380,000 to make, when the average first-class film was budgeted for \$40,000."

After the war, Tsuburaya left Toho amid the studio's feuding with labor unions (although, according to some sources, he was forced to quit the film business when the General Headquarters of the Occupation purged everyone who had made war movies), and worked with acclaimed directors Kinugasa, Kon Ichikawa, and Mikio Naruse before establishing an independent company, Tsuburaya Special Effects Laboratory, in 1948. Although he produced the effects for Daiei Studios' *Invisible Man Appears* (1949), Japan's first modern sci-fi film, work was scarce in the movie business and Tsuburaya dabbled in other endeavors including mass-marketing the "Auto-Snap," a camera controlled by a foot pedal enabling a person to take self-portraits. Music composer Akira Ifukube tells an amusing anecdote about meeting Tsuburaya for the first time, during these lean years. Ifukube and a friend who worked in the film industry were drinking *sake* at a Tokyo inn when a down-on-his-luck man happened by and, recognizing Ifukube's friend, stopped to bum a few drinks. Ifukube never saw the man again until 1954, when he was hired to score *Godzilla*. The man was Tsuburaya, now almost unrecognizably upbeat and successful.

Tsuburaya returned to Toho as a freelancer in 1950, and as a staff member in 1952. When production began on *Godzilla* in 1954, he was already in his fifties, but he was about to launch Japan's second special-effects boom, the most productive and creative period of his life. He worked hard to earn respect for special effects within the movie industry, and it was a long time coming — his first screen credit as special effects director was on *Gigantis: The Fire Monster* (1955), but even then his line of work was looked down upon. "Mr. Tsuburaya was well known for *The War at Sea from Hawaii to Malaya*, but there were few people who acknowledged his talent," said Teisho Arikawa, who took over as Toho's main special-effects director in the late 1960s. "It was a hard time for him."[12]

From *Godzilla* until his death, Tsuburaya worked on 56 feature films, mostly science-fiction or war movies. The Honda-Tsuburaya works, in particular, were among the biggest moneymakers of Toho's golden age, so Tsuburaya's trickery began to receive the recognition he had hoped for. He won five technical-achievement awards from the Japan Movie Association (roughly the equivalent of an Oscar for SFX) for *Godzilla* (1954), *The Mysterians* (1957), *The Three Treasures* (1959), *The Lost World of Sinbad* (1963), *Monster Zero*, and Seiji Maruyama's war film *The Retreat from Kiska* (both 1965). In 1957, Tsuburaya officially established Toho's Special Effects Techniques Department, and oversaw its operations as it grew to include more than 200 personnel. In 1963, after visiting Hollywood to observe the special-effects workings of major American studios, Tsuburaya opened an independent company, Tsuburaya Special Effects Productions (later called simply Tsuburaya Productions), which soon pioneered the production of SFX programs for Japanese television. Its first series was the popular *Ultra Q* (1966), a Japanese *Outer Limits*-meets-*The X-Files* which unfortunately has never aired in the U.S. This was followed by numerous, increasingly child-oriented superhero programs featuring weekly match-ups between the protagonist and a giant monster. Tsuburaya wielded considerable power at Toho then, enabling him to retain his job as the studio's special-effects director even while launching his own production company, a maverick move in those days.

Bespectacled and given to wearing soft hats, suits, and ties at work despite grueling filming conditions and work schedules, Tsuburaya was a consummate professional known for his innovative spirit, his fierce determination, and dedication to his work. And despite the unrelenting demands he often made of his crew members, he was looked upon with reverence and respect by colleagues, many of whom were younger than him and referred to him as a mentor, an "uncle," or simply "The Old Man" (director Ishiro Honda, for example, was 10 years his junior). He was known for a quiet yet intense style, and when brainstorming ideas for a new film he would often withdraw inside his own head. "I heard about this episode when Mr. Tsuburaya was returning home from work one day and he ran into this woman who kind of looked familiar to him," said special-effects director Teruyoshi Nakano, another Tsuburaya protégé. "So he said, 'Hello, it's been a long time.' Do you know who that woman was? It was his wife! Mr. Tsuburaya was so deep into his own thoughts, he kind of lost himself sometimes."

In 1969, doctors advised Tsuburaya to reduce his workload due to deteriorating health, but he took on more projects than ever, dividing his time between Tsuburaya Productions and directing special effects for two films, *Latitude Zero* (his last picture with Ishiro Honda) and Seiji Maruyama's *Battle of the Japan Sea*, his final film. In addition, Tsuburaya was hired by Mitsubishi to oversee a special exhibit at Expo '70, the World's Fair in Osaka. Amid these activities, he died of a heart attack in Tokyo on January 25, 1970.

Tsuburaya's legacy was shaped not only by his determination and drive, but also his fertile imagination and a soft spot in his heart for children. The latter became increasingly evident in his monster films of the 1960s, where he refused to show bloodletting and gore, and was prone to touches of humanism and lighthearted humor. Despite Godzilla's origin as a nuclear allegory, Tsuburaya felt the films failed if they did not connect with kids the way his own inspirations had affected him in his youth. "My heart and mind are as they were when I was a child," Tsuburaya told *Caper* magazine in a 1962 article (reprinted in *Japanese Fantasy Film Journal*). "Then I loved to play with toys and to read stories of magic. I still do. My wish is only to make life happier and more beautiful for those who will go and see my films of fantasy."

Music composer Akira Ifukube at his home in Tokyo, 1995.
COURTESY WINTERGARDEN PRODUCTIONS

The Maestro: **AKIRA IFUKUBE**

In the history of motion pictures there is perhaps no better pairing of a music composer and a fictional character than Akira Ifukube and Godzilla. Ifukube's signatory monster music and military marches, characterized by his distinctive Eastern tonalities and brash instrumentation, are so uniquely identified with Toho's science-fiction cinema that from the first thunderous note, the listener knows Godzilla is near. Messrs. Tanaka, Honda, and Tsuburaya created the *kaiju eiga*, but Ifukube breathed life into it with his music.

Unknown to many monster-movie fans, Ifukube is an internationally acclaimed composer who has amassed a large body of classical music during the past 60 years. His works, ranging from orchestral pieces to ballets to music for solo piano or guitar, have been performed by orchestras in Europe and the U.S. for decades. Meanwhile, he has scored more than 200 feature films, including several classics of the Japanese cinema (*The Burmese Harp*, *Chushingura*, many installments in the popular

Zatoichi film series among them), and although he is best known for his sci-fi film music, it represents only a small part of the Ifukube canon.

A self-described "country boy," Ifukube was born May 31, 1914, in the tiny village of Kushiro, on the northernmost island in the Japanese archipelago, Hokkaido. He was raised in the rural Tokatsu Plain, an area heavily populated by the Ainu, an aboriginal people racially and culturally distinct from the Japanese. In his youth, Ifukube was influenced by Ainu folklore, especially the improvisational style and spirit of their music and dance, which freed him of the restrictions of music theory and made composition easy for him. Though self-taught in music, Ifukube had such an aptitude for it that he became a concert master in high school, and by the time he reached the University of Hokkaido, where he majored in forestry and studied music, Ifukube was performing as a soloist on the violin, accompanied by his friend, pianist Fumio Hayasaka (1914–1955, who later became director Akira Kurosawa's primary composer in the 1940s and '50s). He wrote his first classical piece, "Piano Composition," in 1933 at age 19, and two years later his first orchestral piece, "Japanese Rhapsody," won a competition held by renown Russian composer Alexander Tcherepnine. Tcherepnine, in turn, became a major booster of the young Ifukube, tutoring him in formal composition and orchestration, publishing many of Ifukube's first classical works and premiering them for European audiences.

Despite his early musical success, Ifukube still considered forestry a more practical career choice. "Japanese musicians were thought to be 'less than a man,'" Ifukube told *G-Fan* in a definitive 1995 interview. "Much less composers, who were but semi-insane to common people in Japan. So the profession of composer would almost never function in society. Knowing this, I had never imagined becoming a professional composer in the Pre-War period." Upon graduating from the university, Ifukube worked for the Hokkaido Municipal Forest in the rural countryside and composed in his free time. Around 1940, he relocated to Sapporo, the capital city of Hokkaido, to become more active in music. Then, during World War II, the Imperial government recruited Ifukube, using his knowledge of wood (he had written a thesis at the university on the vibrations of wooden musical instruments) to help study a wooden British warplane the Japanese had captured, and using his musical talents to compose marching hymns for the Japanese army and navy. Ifukube's studies of the plane left him bedridden with radiation sickness from exposure to X-rays. While hospitalized, he was listening to the radio one day and was stunned to hear his naval march performed at a ceremony for Gen. Douglas MacArthur's arrival in Japan to begin the postwar Occupation.

After the war, Ifukube switched to music full-time, teaching composition at Tokyo Art University and establishing himself as a concert composer. But it was a struggle to make a living in the arts, so, like many of his music peers, Ifukube began writing motion-picture scores to support himself and his family. Still, according to historians, Japanese film composers were grossly underpaid; Hayasaka, an A-list film composer, was considered "handsomely compensated" with the equivalent of about $1,000 (in 1954 U.S. funds) for writing the music to *The Seven Samurai* (1954), and it's safe to say that Ifukube was paid much less in his early movie career. In 1947 Ifukube wrote his first score, for Toho's *Snow Trail*; from then until 1954, he scored more than 60 films, including the anti-bomb movies *Children of the Atom Bomb* and *Hiroshima*, and director Josef Von Sternberg's Japanese-made *Saga of Anatahan* (1953). Ifukube scored one movie for Akira Kurosawa, *A Quiet Duel* (1949), the story of a physician stigmatized by syphillis. Unlike many in the film community who dared not stand up to Kurosawa, Ifukube bluntly told the director that he thought the story was "illogical." The two men never worked together again.

Even today, Ifukube considers the original *Godzilla* his finest film score. Despite budgetary, scheduling, and technical limitations that forced him to write the music before ever seeing the film and to record it with a much smaller orchestra than he was accustomed to conducting (this was common in Japanese films, as the musical score was often secondary in the planning process), Ifukube created a masterwork that cast the mold for his many science-fiction scores to come.

As music historian Randall Larson documented in his book *Musique Fantastique*, it was in *Godzilla* that Ifukube introduced the march, the horror theme, and the requiem — three motifs that form the foundation of his genre movie music. The *Jietai* (Self Defense Force) march, which plays over the opening credits in the Japanese version of the film and again when the military retaliates against the monster, has become so synonymous with Godzilla over the years that even Ifukube refers to it as "Godzilla's Theme." This piece, played by fast-moving strings and hard-pounding drums and characterized by repetitive three-note phrases that seem to sing "Go-Dzi-La, Go-Dzi-La," was supplanted in future films by increasingly complex, nationalistic marches, the best of which are heard in *War of the Gargantuas* and *Destroy All Monsters*.

The horror theme of *Godzilla* is a slow-moving piece played by low brass, piano, and strings that conveys the monster's incredible size and invincibility, heard during the final, annihilating rampage through Tokyo. The music most commonly associated with Godzilla-on-the-loose, however, was not fully realized until 1964, when Ifukube wrote *Gojira no Kyofu* ("Horror of Godzilla"), the piece heard when Godzilla first appears in *Godzilla vs. The Thing* (an early, slightly different version of this theme is heard in the Japanese version of *King Kong vs. Godzilla*). Beginning with a long, sustaining note followed by a dissonant, cascading short phrase, this eerily beautiful piece has come to epitomize the Godzilla spirit so definitively that it was even used in Godzilla movies scored by other composers (*Godzilla vs. Biollante*, *Godzilla vs. Space Godzilla*).

The horror theme is an important element of all Ifukube's sci-fi scores, particularly in films featuring monster-vs.-monster battles; for these, he composes a distinct theme for each creature, and during the climax a *magnum opus* combining the two (or more, depending on the number of monsters fighting) is often heard, as in *King Kong vs. Godzilla, Godzilla vs. The Thing*, and *Frankenstein Conquers the World*.

The requiem, a slow, mournfully melodious theme, is Ifukube's most profound statement in film music and the device he inevitably uses to underscore a tragic ending. Randall Larson quoted Ifukube as saying his requiems are inspired by the Japanese "traditional sense of beauty," and their distinct sound is owed to his use of Japanese music scales, which are uniquely different from Western major and minor keys. "When Westerners hear my music, they think of church music of the Middle Ages," Ifukube said. "When Japanese hear it, it sounds like Japanese [music] but its tempo is slow and sounds like a requiem." The requiem at the conclusion of *Godzilla* is a prayer for the future of mankind, and it endures as the finest piece Ifukube has written of this type.

In January 1995, a concert titled "SF Symphonic Battle: Akira Ifukube vs. John Williams" was performed in Tokyo by the Shinsei Japan Symphonic Orchestra. It was an appropriate match-up since, like Williams', Ifukube's trademark sound immediately brings countless film images to memory. But comparisons between Ifukube and his Western contemporaries end there. Although he employs compositional riffs common to 20th-century composers — the 12-tone scale, chromaticism (extensive use of half-step intervals between notes), shifting accents (i.e., moving the "downbeat" around), and clusters (three or more intervals of 2nds played simultaneously, resulting in dissonant chords) — Ifukube says his sensibilities are rooted in eastern modal systems. In classical music, Ifukube was influenced by Europeans like Stravinsky, Manuel De Falla, and Mussorgsky, rather than Beethoven or Mozart. In film music, Ifukube was heavily influenced by the Russian Sergei Prokofiev (*Ivan The Terrible*, 1943), the Frenchman Jacques Ibert (Orson Welles' *Macbeth*), and Polish composer Alexander Tansman. The trademarks of Ifukube's distincitive scoring style are *Ostinato* (a technique of using short, repeating phrases to construct a motif, which he learned from Ainu music) and his manipulation of motifs for dramatic effect. Often, Ifukube reworks a single theme throughout the course of the film, using it to convey contrasting emotions; he does this by increasing or decreasing note values (creating the illusion of tempo change) or changing the instrument arrangement. A good example is the playful Drats melody in *Godzilla vs. King Ghidorah*, which later becomes King Ghidorah's thundering theme. Ifukube also amplifies the impact of his music by placing it only beneath scenes that require it; by leaving entire portions of a film without music, his score becomes more striking and forceful when it finally blares out.

The music of Akira Ifukube lent the Honda-Tsuburaya films a sense of continuity and commonality, and it is no coincidence that this creative trio was responsible for the biggest box-office successes of Toho's golden age of genre pictures. In a very real sense, Ifukube is just as responsible for the birth of Godzilla as Tomoyuki Tanaka, Ishiro Honda, and Eiji Tsuburaya, for without his music, without his ingenuity in the creation of the monster's roar and footsteps, Godzilla's thundering power and awesome horror — the very essence of the character — might never have been fully realized.

In the 1970s, as the *kaiju eiga* went into decline, Ifukube's epic music lost lustre in films that clearly lacked the epic scale of bygone days. In *Yog: Monster from Space, Godzilla on Monster Island* (in which library tapes of his old scores were used), and *Terror of MechaGodzilla*, Ifukube's music seems bombastic and ill-at-ease when paired with a giant squid, a flea-bitten King Ghidorah, and a punch-drunk Godzilla. Ifukube retired from scoring films and turned his attention instead to teaching, becoming president of the Institute of Ethnomusicology of the Tokyo College of Music Institute. Later, in 1991, Toho coaxed him out of retirement to score four of the last five Godzilla films. Though pushing 80, he hadn't lost his magic. *Godzilla vs. MechaGodzilla* (1993) proved to be one of the finest science-fiction scores of his career, and the requiem accompanying Godzilla's death in *Godzilla vs. Destoroyah* is truly emotional.

Like director Ishiro Honda and many other artists and craftsmen associated with the Godzilla series, Ifukube is a true perfectionist who has felt compromised by the tight scheduling, small budgets, and other demands of working in Japanese films. But he has never shied away from his association with the monster. "I am not satisfied with my film music because of a lot of the limitations," he told *Soundtrack!* magazine in a 1994 interview. "So, I try to express my ideas in concert music. But my film music is popular with people, while my concert works are not so well known."

HOLLYWOOD MON-STAR

THE AMERICANIZATION

> "This agreement made the 27th day of September, 1955, by and between International Toho Inc., a corporation organized under the laws of the State of California, United States of America, having its principal offices at 369 E. First Street, Los Angeles, California (hereinafter referred to as 'licensor') and Edmund Goldman, having his principal office at 922 S. Robertson Boulevard, Los Angeles, California (hereinafter referred to as 'licensee'). Licensor hereby sells all its rights, title and interest in and to the motion picture 'Godzilla' for a period of five years commencing from the date the licensee receives from the licensor one fine-grain print of the picture, a print of the sound and music track and effects track, for use in the territory of the United States of America, all its possessions, and including the dominion of Canada, for the sum of Twenty-Five Thousand Dollars ($25,000), and the licensee hereby purchases all rights of said motion picture, payable as follows: Dollars which licensor has already received from licensee on June 1, 1955, and which licensor hereby acknowledges receipt of. . . .
>
> "It is further agreed by the licensor and licensee that the motion picture 'Godzilla' will be narrated, dubbed in English and completed in accordance with the revisions, additions and deletions which have been submitted by licensee to licensor and which have been forwarded to Toho Co. in Japan for final approval, and which approval has been received in accordance with the letter to licensee dated September 6, 1955. . . ."
>
> — *From the original contract for the U.S. rights to* Godzilla, *courtesy Edmund Goldman*

On his way to an assignment in Cairo, Steve Martin, a foreign correspondent for United World News, makes a stopover in Tokyo for a social call. One helluva lucky reporter, he arrives in Japan just in time to cover the story of the century, as the nation's capitol is leveled by "a force which, up until a few days ago, was entirely beyond the scope of man's imagination."

Much has been written over the decades about the remaking of *Godzilla* into *Godzilla: King of the Monsters!* Most critics point out that the American film is inferior to the original, which is indeed true, but they often overlook the fact that the U.S. version bridged the gap between Honda's somber, nightmarish film and the atomic-monster genre that was so popular in 1950s America. It is the U.S. version, much more than the original, that launched Godzilla's global assault and has been seen around the world. Godzilla was born in Japan, but his ascent to international stardom began in

America, thanks to his discovery by a handful of savvy Hollywood types who knew a moneymaker when they saw one, and how to exploit it.

In 1955, Hollywood was swept up in an era of exploitation-movie madness, as so wonderfully depicted in Tim Burton's film *Ed Wood* (1994). Literally hundreds of pictures were cranked out every year by small-time and big-time dealmakers striving not for art, but for the almighty dollar. At the same time, Japanese movies were just starting to be released in the U.S., mostly to art-house cinemas and Japanese-language movie houses in the major cities. Toho International, a subsidiary created to distribute Toho films abroad, opened a small office in the Little Tokyo section of Los Angeles. One of the first people to inquire about Toho's product was **Edmund Goldman**, owner of a small film distributing company called Manson International.

A lot of people have claimed credit for discovering Godzilla, but Goldman (b. 1906) can prove it — he

GODZILLA - KING OF THE MONSTERS!

Alive! Surging up from the depths of the sea on a tidal wave of terror to wreak vengeance on mankind!

GODZILLA — KING OF THE MONSTERS!

It's alive! A gigantic beast! Stalking the Earth! Crushing all before it in a psychotic cavalcade of electrifying horror! Raging through the streets on a rampage of total destruction!

GODZILLA — KING OF THE MONSTERS!

Incredible titan of terror! Wiping out a city of six million in a holocaust of flame! Jet planes cannot destroy it! Bombs cannot kill it! All modern weapons fail! Is this the end of our civilization? Can the scientists of the world find a way to stop this creature?

For the answer, see **GODZILLA — KING OF THE MONSTERS!**

You may wish to deny it, but your eyes tell you it's true! A tale to stun the mind! More fantastic than any ever written by Jules Verne! More terrifying than any ever shown on the screen! Awesome! Incredible! Unbelievable! A story beyond your wildest dreams!

DYNAMIC VIOLENCE! SAVAGE ACTION! SPECTACULAR THRILLS!

GODZILLA — KING OF THE MONSTERS!

Fantastic beyond comprehension! Gripping beyond compare! Astounding beyond belief!

See **GODZILLA — KING OF THE MONSTERS!**

— *From Trans World's theatrical trailer for* Godzilla: King of the Monsters!

still has the contract showing he paid a measly $25,000 for the theatrical and TV rights to the picture. "It was a very low figure, even at that time," he recalled in 1995. "First of all, the value of films was about one-tenth of what it is today, or less. And this was (Toho's) first venture in the U.S. and they were anxious to get into the American market. They had shown me some advertising materials and I thought it [*Godzilla*] looked interesting, so I asked them to screen it for me. I made them an offer, and they accepted it rather quickly. I didn't know at the time that Raymond Burr was going to be in it, or that it would be dubbed into English. I just thought it was something we could put subtitles on. It turned out to be a bonanza." Although Goldman insists that he alone discovered Godzilla, Samuel Arkoff of American International Pictures claims that he, too, made a bid for the picture. "The whole situation was ridiculous," Arkoff told the *Los Angeles Times* in 1998. "We were dickering with (Toho) for about three months, then came to find the rights were already sold."

Goldman's main line of work, however, was selling American-made films in the Far East; he had little experience in distributing foreign films in the U.S., and didn't really know what to do with *Godzilla*. So, he turned for help to **Harold Ross** (a.k.a. Harry Rybnick) and **Richard Kay**, who had produced a number of low-budget pictures under the banner of Jewell Enterprises, most notably *Untamed Women* (1952), a story of military men marooned on an island inhabited by cavewomen. "They [Ross and Kay] saw all the possibilities," Goldman said. "It was all their idea to dub it, and to get the services of Raymond Burr." Shortly thereafter, Goldman sold out his interest in the film to Jewell.

Seeking more capital to finance the project, Ross and Kay turned to movie mogul extraordinaire **Joseph E. Levine,** whose Boston-based Embassy Pictures had distributed *Untamed Women*. Levine (1905–1987), still pretty much a small-time film distributor at the time, had already developed his knack for exploiting gimmick films and was well on his way to the big time (years later, he produced *The Graduate* and many other pictures). Ross and Kay arranged a screening of *Godzilla* for Levine in Los Angeles. Levine immediately became excited about its possibilities and paid more than $100,000 to enter a partnership wherein the rights to *Godzilla* were split between Embassy and Jewell. Under this arrangement, Ross and Kay supervised the revamping of the picture for its American release, while Levine brought in additional partners like Edward Barison of Cinema Distributors Corp. in Los Angeles, and created a new company, Trans World Releasing Corp., to distribute the movie. Terry Turner, a producer brought on board by Levine, developed outlandish promotional strategies and blitzed the media, even getting Steve Allen to mention the film on *The Tonight Show*, whetting the nation's moviegoing appetite. After briefly considering the title *Godzilla, the Sea Beast* (according to a report in *Variety*), Levine and Turner instead coined the suffix "King of the Monsters," an overt invitation for comparisons to *King Kong*.

"We were in the States-rights business," Kay (b. 1921) said. "We had done *Untamed Women* and a couple of werewolf and prehistoric pictures at the time. Joe was in the States-rights business as well, operating on the East Coast, and when he saw *Godzilla* he liked it a lot and offered us a tremendous amount of money for half the rights. They used to call him '$100,000 Levine,' because he paid $100,000 for everything he bought, whether or not it was any good. A lot of the success of *Godzilla* had to do with Joe, and the advertising campaign that he and his people came up with. They did a great press book, and took out large newspaper ads, which was quite unusual at that time."

To write and direct *Godzilla: King of the Monsters!*, Ross and Kay hired **Terry O. Morse**, an accomplished film editor and sometime director. Morse (1906–1984) began his career in 1934 at Warner Bros., where he edited many B-movie crime thrillers, most less than 70 minutes long and with no-star casts. Warners elevated him to the director's chair, but relegated him to the same low-brow movies (including *Smashing the Money Ring*, starring Ronald Reagan, in 1939). Dissatisfied with the crumbs the studio was throwing him, Morse became an independent in the 1940s, working steadily as an editor and director for two decades. Other than *Godzilla: King of the Monsters!*, Morse's best-known films as a director are the thriller *Fog Island* (1945), several Charlie Chan pictures, and *Young Dillinger* (1965), a cheapie gangster flick with Nick Adams that was shot in 10 days. "The Godzilla movie is his most famous film, even though he only directed parts of it," said Morse's son, Terry Morse Jr., himself a producer of children's films (*Kiss Meets the Phantom of the Park*, *Teenage Mutant Ninja Turtles II* and *III*). "He was a very good editor, but he just never made it as a director."

Another key player in the Americanization was **Paul Schreibman**, a business associate of Edmund Goldman's who assisted in the acquisition of the film. A Los Angeles entertainment attorney, deal-maker, and former owner of a small distribution company called Topaz Films, Schreibman (b. 1904) is a throwback to the old Hollywood, where cigar-smoking men once ruled. He agreed to be interviewed twice for this book, but only by telephone, while he was lunching at the Friar's Club in Beverly Hills — on one of those occasions, with his good friend Milton Berle. It was Schreibman who contacted Raymond Burr's agent Lester Salko and arranged for the burly actor to appear in the film, and he claims to have flown to Tokyo to arrange Goldman's purchase of *Godzilla* (this may or may not be true, as the contract was clearly drawn up in Los Angeles). Edmund Goldman, Richard Kay, and others involved in the discovery of Godzilla all

Thrill-filled "Godzilla" Out-Monsters "King Kong"
Hollywood, which has long prided itself on its technical know-how, gets some pretty keen competition from a spectacular science-fiction thriller, "Godzilla: King of the Monsters!" which bears the trade-mark "Made in Japan." . . .

The new science-fiction pulse-pounder is said to make such hair-raisers as "The Creature," "The Thing," and "King Kong" seem like "Peter Pan" by comparison. . . .

Filmed entirely on location in Japan, the Trans-World release has Burr playing an American newspaper correspondent in Tokyo, who happens to be on hand when the monster first makes its presence known. He stays to cover the story and nearly pays for it with his life. . . .

Also in the cast of *Godzilla: King of the Monsters!* is the willowy, almond-eyed beauty Momoko Kochi, whose romance with a naval officer has a direct bearing on the monster's eventual destruction. . . .

Scenes showing the mammoth trampling and burning of Tokyo and the awesome, breathtaking climax when Godzilla is finally liquidated, are among the most realistic and spinetingling ever offered fans.

— *From Trans World's publicity materials for* Godzilla: King of the Monsters!

describe Schreibman as a consummate promoter with a flair for talking up any project, and credit him with being a key intermediary in their discussions with Toho and Embassy Pictures. But to hear Schreibman tell it in his colorful way, it was he — and he alone — who truly discovered the monster.

"Nobody had ever heard of Toho before, and neither did I until this picture. *Rashomon* and *Gate of Hell* were the only two Japanese pictures previously that had meant anything in the U.S., but they didn't do much business, because they were art films with a narrow appeal," Schreibman said. "*Godzilla* was the first picture that I felt would have mass appeal, so I decided to launch it as a general release picture, and it worked. . . . My launching it really launched a whole industry." After the success of *Godzilla: King of the Monsters!*, Schreibman was kept on retainer by Toho from the 1950s through the early 1970s, and helped negotiate the U.S. distribution of monster movies and other films. He was also U.S. counsel for Toho's sister company, Tsuburaya Productions, for many years.

Producers Ross and Kay and writer-director Morse did an admirable job of inserting a new story line — with Burr playing the American newsman who gets caught in the Japanese Juggernaut's path of destruction — into Honda's film while preserving the theme and tone of the original. Co-starring as security official Tomo Iwanaga, Martin's interpreter and principal news source, was **Frank Iwanaga** (d. 1963 of lung cancer), a Los Angeles insurance salesman, part-time actor, and former USC track-and-field star, who had played Japanese soldiers in World War II pictures like *The Frogmen* (1951). Rather than simply dub the entire movie into English, Morse alternated between having Burr narrate the picture and Iwanaga translate the dialogue from the Honda version, which allowed a lot of scenes to remain in Japanese. In addition, Burr "talks" to Dr. Yamane, Emiko, Ogata, and Serizawa through clever editing and the use of body doubles, clad in costumes matching the Japanese actors', who were filmed over-the-shoulder with their faces deftly concealed (in the case of Serizawa, the actor's face was hidden behind a bank of lab equipment). There were also a few Asian-American pseudo-actors hired to play minor parts (Dr. Serizawa's attache, a policeman, and the Odo islander who wears a Mexican straw hat), all of whom speak *really* bad Japanese. The new footage of Burr, Iwanaga, and the other actors was shot in three days (or five, depending on who you talk to) on a rented soundstage at Visual Drama Inc., a now-defunct production facility on Vermont Avenue in Hollywood. For rewriting and directing the picture, Terry Morse was paid $10,000. Raymond Burr received the same amount for spending one day — yes, one day — on the set. As legend has it, Burr had to work nearly 24 hours to finish all his scenes. In most scenes, he does little more than talk while standing, sitting, or looking out a window, but Morse did add one "special effect" of his own, in the scene where Burr and Iwanaga are nearly blown away by the typhoon on Odo Island.

There were also several scenes from the original *Godzilla* that remained intact in the American print and therefore required English-speaking voices, but the method used was far different from the cartoony dubbing that would become a goofy trademark of later Godzilla movies. Little effort was made to match the dubbed voices to the actors' lip movements, and in some scenes, one or more lines of Japanese dialogue were left untouched — for example, the senators bickering in the Japanese parliament, and Ogata and Serizawa's fistfight at the film's climax. It's almost like eavesdropping on the Japanese conversations: only the important information is translated (dubbed) for the audience's benefit. This strengthens the documentary-style feel of the picture, but as it turns out, it wasn't done that way to preserve the movie's authenticity — it was done because it was cheap.

"We dubbed the entire picture in about five hours, in just one session. We did it really fast. I think I got paid just a couple hundred bucks for that," said veteran character actor **James Hong**. Hong (b. 1929), who has appeared in over 300 TV shows and feature films, was just beginning his Hollywood career when he landed the one-day gig dubbing voices for *Godzilla: King of the Monsters!* in late 1955.

"We didn't know Raymond Burr was going to be in the picture. We weren't told anything about what was going on," Hong said. "The director just locked us up in a little room and had us read all the roles. He'd say, 'A little faster,' or 'A little slower.' We recorded each line at several different speeds, and then they just used the one that best matched the action on the screen. We never saw the movie. We dubbed the whole thing sitting at a table, with a microphone in front of us.

"I and Sammee Tong (a character actor from the teleseries *Bachelor Father*, 1957–62, and *Mickey*, 1964–65) dubbed all the Asian roles. There was one woman, and the two of us. I played the lover [Ogata], plus the scientist that was his adversary

[Serizawa]. If you listen to the scene close enough, you can tell I'm talking to myself." Indeed you can — at times, it is difficult to tell whether it's Ogata or Serizawa who's speaking, and the voices performed by Tong (Dr. Yamane and many others) all sound alike.

Hong, who is Chinese-American, said a number of Japanese actors auditioned for the voice-over work, but he and Tong got the jobs because of their versatility. "I had the ability to adjust my voice. This was a very, very low-low-budget production, and by hiring us, they could get their money's worth. Sammee did about six voices, and I did about seven. He did all the old men roles, and I did the younger guy roles — we took care of them all. And amazingly, even though we couldn't see the film, or the characters we were playing, everything fit perfectly."

CONTINENTAL DIVIDE: GOJIRA vs. GODZILLA

Until the 1980s, few Americans had ever seen Honda's original, unadulterated *Godzilla*, so critical comparisons of the Japanese and U.S. versions were both moot and virtually impossible. But in 1982, an English-subtitled print of *Godzilla* was screened in New York, Chicago, and other cities; in the 1990s, several subtitled editions of the film became available on the "bootleg" home-video market. For the first time, fans in the West could see for themselves what drastic alterations this elusive Japanese classic of the horror cinema underwent en route to becoming its own bastard American cousin.

For the record, here are the major differences between *Godzilla* and *Godzilla: King of the Monsters!*:

"When I think back, only a few days ago I was en route to Cairo. . . ." While the drama of *Godzilla* proceeds chronologically, beginning with the first shipping disaster, *Godzilla: King of the Monsters!* unspools in flashback format. The American film opens with Burr sloughing through the rubble, with scenes of a smoldering city and a disaster hospital filled with trampled Tokyoites. These images are taken from the aftermath of Godzilla's final rampage in Honda's movie. While this approach

strengthens the documentary-like style of the original film and heightens the feeling of dread, it also steals some of Godzilla's ultimate thunder. By revealing the extent of the monster's damage toll at the outset, the film leaves little wonder as to what lies ahead.

Making way for Ray. The U.S. version clocks in at about 80 minutes long — 18 shorter than the Japanese original. Subtract about 20 minutes of new American footage with Raymond Burr, and only about 60 minutes of Honda's film is left intact. The inevitable result of such tampering was the weakening of the film's dramatic and thematic underpinnings, and the elimination of some necessary character development.

The most severe damage was inflicted upon the role of Dr. Daisuke Serizawa, with the partial deletion of several crucial scenes from the original film. The first occurs when Dr. Yamane and his research party set sail for Odo Island. Standing silently among the throng of well-wishers on the pier is Serizawa, wearing dark shades and an expressionless stare. This is the first glimpse of the scientist in Honda's version, and it is immediately clear he will play a pivotal role in the drama. Serizawa is not only concerned about the ominous disasters besetting Japan, his heart is breaking because his betrothed Emiko has fallen for Ogata. Also deleted is a later scene, in which Hagiwara, the newspaper reporter (cut almost entirely from the American version), tries to question Serizawa about rumors emanating from a source in Germany who says the scientist is working on a device that could save Japan from Godzilla. Serizawa flatly denies this and sends the reporter away, but it's obvious the scientist is hiding something. Although this scene does raise interesting questions about Serizawa, critics in the West have tended to read too much into it, some going so far as to speculate that the scientist may have collaborated with the Nazis on some weapons research. This is nonsense; Hagiwara's mention of an alleged "German contact" is a bluff to get Serizawa to talk (an old reporter's trick). Still, in Honda's film Serizawa was a dark figure with suspicious motivations who sequestered himself in his lab and secretly suffered a heavy heart, but in Morse's picture he's just a weirdo scientist and supposedly a college friend of Steve Martin's — hard to believe, since Serizawa keeps postponing his meetings with the American, an impolite gesture toward a friend who's come halfway around the world to see him.

Less severe, though still significant, are a few deletions that undermine the drama of the Ogata-

Emiko-Serizawa love triangle in the American version, and ultimately lessen the emotional impact of Serizawa's sacrificial suicide at the climax. The first is a scene at the beginning of Honda's film where Ogata receives a phone call at his office at the South Seas Shipping Co., informing him that one of the firm's vessels has been sunk. Emiko is there, too; the couple were planning to attend a performance of "The Budapest Quartet," but instead Ogata rushes off to the Coast Guard offices and Emiko attends the show on her own. In this scene, cut entirely from the American print, Ogata is seen toweling himself off after a shower. Although hardly erotic, this is a rare instance when the two lovers are alone together and not engrossed in disasters unfolding around them, and it provides some insight into their intimacy, compared to the more formal, arranged relationship between Emiko and Serizawa. Later, aboard the ship en route to Odo Island, Ogata grows impatient to make the courtship public and warns Emiko they will inevitably be caught if they continue to sneak around. This scene is included in the U.S. version, but the dialogue remains untranslated. Instead, Raymond Burr smokes his pipe and tells the audience that the lovers' quandary — "the usual triangle" — will somehow play a pivotal role in the survival of the world.

There is yet another character whose back story is gelded: Godzilla himself! Shortly before the reporters arrive on Odo Island for the first time, there is a scene in the Japanese version where an old man (the great character actor Kokuten Kodo of *The Seven Samurai* fame) watches as the villagers pull their empty fishing nets onto the beach. The shipping disasters, the dearth of fish in the waters — all these maladies must be a sign of the evil Godzilla, the old man says, and the younger islanders scoff at his old-fashioned beliefs. The scene is not only funny, it helps establish the Godzilla mythos, the sense that this monster is a force of nature that has struck before, and will again. Later, after the great hurricane on the island, the reporters and the island natives are taken to Tokyo to testify before government officials. In the American version, their testimonials are cut very short, but in the Japanese version there is talk of missing cows and other livestock, evidence that a great animal may be responsible for the damage. One islander says the hurricane was no ordinary storm, but caused by "a force from above."

Messing with the message? Movie critic Danny Peary, in his book *Cult Movies 2*, accuses the American distributors of *Godzilla: King of the Monsters!* of

making "deletions that arouse suspicions regarding the covering up of references to damage done by the A-Bomb." Peary is not alone in his theory — for years, many film fans and pundits have accused Terry Morse & Co. of having a hidden Cold-War agenda, and deliberately excising anti-nuclear messages from Honda's version. It is undeniable that deletions were made and that the American film is watered down as a result, but it seems doubtful the filmmakers were engaged in some sort of personal conspiracy.

There are several major scenes in which Godzilla's ties to the Bomb are discussed that Morse either altered or excised:

- The first occurs upon Dr. Yamane's return from Odo Island, when he addresses a meeting of the Diet about the discovery of Godzilla. When Yamane reveals his theory that Godzilla is a creature spawned by H-bomb tests, a pompous senator stands up and declares that this bit of information should be kept secret, to avoid a crisis of international relations. A female senator challenges him, saying the truth must be made public, and a heated argument on the senate floor ensues; Yamane, realizing the most significant scientific discovery in history is already buried by politics, lowers his head in disgust. This scene is one of Honda's best moments in the original film: not only is it a realistic enactment of the kind of political posturing that occurs in the face of a major crisis (and, incidentally, Honda's way of acknowledging the growing influence of women in Japanese politics at that time), but it also hints at the enduring rage and disgust over the Hiroshima and Nagasaki bombings brimming just beneath the surface of the Japanese psyche. But in the American version, this scene is reduced to a few seconds of squabbling among the politicos, with no dialogue translation, leaving the viewer to believe only that the government is panicking amid the crisis.

- The second and perhaps most profound Bomb reference in the film occurs when commuters aboard a subway train are chatting about the day's Godzilla headlines. One woman bemoans the news, saying she doesn't want to face another tragedy: "I hope I didn't survive Nagasaki for nothing." A man chimes in, "I hope we don't have to evacuate the city again," an apparent reference to the firebombing of Tokyo during the war. This scene, which makes it all too clear that Honda intended Godzilla as a direct stand-in for a nuclear holocaust, was entirely deleted from

Reverse Import

Godzilla: King of the Monsters! was released in Japan, with Japanese subtitles, on May 29, 1957, as *Kaiju o Gojira* ("Monster King Godzilla," a literal translation of the English-language title). For this release, the film was reformatted to the wide-screen aspect ratio, recently introduced in Japanese cinemas. Why this was done is anyone's guess, since the movie had to be blown up to fill the wider frame, causing the top and bottom of the picture to be cropped. Thus, both Raymond Burr's and Godzilla's heads are sometimes chopped off! Footage from this uniquely weird version of the film was included on the *Godzilla* 40th-anniversary special-edition Laser Disc, released by Toho Video in Japan in 1994.

Morse's version. So was another, heart-wrenching scene in which a mother clutches her little daughter close amid the flaming nightmare of Godzilla's Tokyo attack. The mother says, "We'll see daddy in Heaven. In just a little while, we'll be by his side," then the pair is crushed by falling debris. The inference is clear: the Bomb and the war left thousands of Japanese families fatherless; now, Godzilla has come to claim the lives of the survivors.

- The military consults Dr. Yamane, asking his advice on how to destroy Godzilla. But Yamane is confused and angered by their inquiries. Godzilla, he insists, should not be killed, he should be scientifically studied to learn how he survived the devastating effects of the hydrogen bomb. In Morse's film, this scene occurs earlier in the picture, and it is completely rewritten. While Steve Martin and other reporters observe, Yamane consults with the military officials, telling them they should question the natives of Odo Island, which is located close to where the shipping disasters occurred. The dialogue is supposedly translated by Martin's attache, Iwanaga, but the meaning is changed entirely. If you listen closely, you can clearly hear Dr. Yamane say "Gojira," a curious reference, since Godzilla hasn't even been discovered yet!

- A direct comparison of the Bomb and Godzilla, omitted entirely from the American print, occurs in a tense scene at the Yamane house in the moments right before Godzilla's final rampage. Ogata and Emiko are waiting for Dr. Yamane, hoping to break the news of their engagement to the old man. But when Yamane returns, he is upset by the military's foolish insistence on killing the monster. The strident Ogata objects: "We can't just do nothing. [Godzilla is] a menace to all Japanese, like the H-bomb."

- The ending was significantly altered for the film's American release. Although Godzilla is dead, Honda's version ends on a definitely pessimistic note as Dr. Yamane wonders aloud whether continued nuclear testing might bring about another Godzilla. Morse cut this somber speech out of the film, ending on a more upbeat note as Martin says the world can now "wake up and live again." This is perhaps Morse's most ill-advised change of all, for it reduces the film to a typical American atomic-monster movie — a genre wherein nuclear-spawned bugaboos were inevitably defeated with new and more powerful weapons (in this case, the Oxygen Destroyer).

Even with so many nuclear references relegated to the cutting-room floor, the American version makes it clear that Godzilla is a child of the atom. When Dr. Yamane spells out his theory about Godzilla's existence, he declares that the monster is tainted with Strontium 90, one of the most dangerous by-products of a nuclear explosion. And although Steve Martin never explicitly makes the same connection, he is constantly hinting at it: Those who come in contact with Godzilla die of "shock and strange burns," and in his wake, the monster leaves the "odor of human flesh," and a devastated city that is now "a smoldering memorial to the unknown."

Still, the question remains. Did Terry Morse et al. deliberately downplay the monster-as-atomic-bomb theme to make Godzilla a standard movie monster? Did they whitewash the picture to make it more politically palatable?

"No," said producer Richard Kay. "We weren't interested in politics, believe me. We only wanted to make a movie we could sell. At that time, the American public wouldn't have gone for a movie with an all-Japanese cast. That's why we did what we did. We didn't really change the story. We just gave it an American point of view."

When judged against its Japanese counterpart, the flaws inherent in *Godzilla: King of the Monsters!* are obvious. But on its own merits, the film is one of the best American atomic-monster movies of the 1950s, on par with — or even better than — the classic giant-ant thriller *Them!* Its scripting, direction, and special-effects achievements are far superior to those of American-made giant-monster movies of the same period, like *Tarantula* (giant spider), *It Came from Beneath the Sea* (giant mollusk), and *The Deadly Mantis* (giant insect). And although Ray Harryhausen fans may disagree, *Godzilla: King of the Monsters!* is far more entertaining than the film that inspired it, *The Beast from 20,000 Fathoms*.

Goldman, Levine, Ross, Kay, Morse, and all those responsible for the American production deserve a great deal of credit, not only for taking a gamble on a Japanese monster picture — something no major studio had dared do — but also for their effective reworking of the film for Western viewers. Whether Raymond Burr is standing on the sidelines watching the action, "talking" to characters from the original film via the use of body doubles, phoning his editor in Chicago, or wiping the sweat from his brow as Tokyo goes up in flames, the new and rescripted scenes effectively transform the film from a uniquely Japanese disaster drama into a mass-market American monster epic. Still, the success of the film is really a testament to Ishiro Honda and the folks at Toho, as all its truly memorable moments were filmed in Japan. The incredible first glimpse of the monster on Odo Island, the scenes of widespread city destruction, the massive military mobilization, Godzilla emulsifying in Tokyo Bay — these images dwarf other American monster movies of its time period in visual and emotional impact.

Godzilla: King of the Monsters! opened on April 4, 1956, at Loew's State Theater, a 3,450-seat cinema in New York City. This was a major feat for a Japanese-made feature — heretofore, Japanese films had strictly been art-house fare, relegated to theaters with 300 or so seats. Joe Levine engaged in "saturation booking," first in the Boston area, where the film opened simultaneously at 283 theaters, then in other major cities. According to *Variety*, the movie grossed more than $2 million during its initial run.

In those days, that was impressive box office for a low-budget picture, and even moreso considering it was purchased from Toho for chump change and independently distributed. By comparison, *The Beast from 20,000 Fathoms* grossed about $5 million in 1953, but it had the advantage of distribution by Warner Bros., a major studio. In a 1998 interview with the *Los Angeles Times*, producer Richard Kay said *Godzilla: King of the Monsters!* earned about $200,000 in profits for its producers. The TV rights were later sold to RKO, and in 1959, the film's broadcast premiere on KHJ-TV in Los Angeles was watched by one out of every two viewers, according to reports in the entertainment trade press.

While the original *Godzilla* is regarded in Japan as one of the best films of all time, in much the same way that *King Kong* is beloved in America, its sibling *Godzilla: King of the Monsters!* hardly receives the same sort of reverence. Nevertheless, the U.S. version has endured through the decades as a stalwart on television and home video, to become an essential "camp classic" — a designation which, unfortunately, makes it equally attractive both to aficionados of classic horror and sci-fi and those who take pleasure in ridiculing films they perceive as cheap or substandard. The difference between Japanese and Western views of the film is obviously due to the discrepancies between the two versions, but there are other factors. *Godzilla* was a landmark achievement in Japanese cinema — nothing like it had ever been attempted before, and it remains the godfather of a uniquely Japanese motion-picture genre. But *Godzilla: King of the Monsters!* arrived in American cinemas amid a swarm of big bugs, dinosaurs, and other atomic monsters, and it is forever associated with a bygone era when films were made fast, frightening, furious (and, usually, flimsy). What is often overlooked, however, is that *Godzilla: King of the Monsters!* did give birth to an entirely new Western genre, the imported, dubbed-in-English Japanese monster movie. Seeing what profits Joe Levine and his partners reaped hawking Godzilla, other wheelers and dealers in Hollywood were salivating to get hold of their own foreign-born monsters. And Toho, having done well with its domestic release of *Godzilla*, was ready to oblige. In fact, by the time *Godzilla: King of the Monsters!* was playing America, the first Godzilla sequel had already been completed in Japan, and other monsters were on the way. . . .

The Heavy: RAYMOND BURR

**Raymond Burr, the man without whom Godzilla might
never have achieved such great international stardom.**

Whether you consider it a stroke of Hollywood genius or the bastardization of a classic film, one thing is clear: *Godzilla: King of the Monsters!* enabled Toho's *Godzilla* to be marketed worldwide, a major feat for a Japanese film in the 1950s. Key to its success was the tall, deep-voiced star and narrator, Raymond Burr.

Though best known as the altruistic defense attorney who inevitably outsmarted prosecutors in the TV series *Perry Mason* (1957–66, CBS, for which he won two Emmys), Burr began his Hollywood career as a character actor, mostly playing hoodlums or heavies in films like *Meet Danny Wilson* (1952), as a Chicago mobster extorting a singer (played by Frank Sinatra), and Hitchcock's *Rear Window* (1954), as Thorwald, the wife-dismemberer with bleached-blond hair. Though reporter Steve Martin was hardly a villain — and hardly a protagonist either, depending on your interpretation of the film — Burr gave the character an understated, convincing performance that never descends into campiness or schlock. He may not have had much to work with, but Burr delivered nonetheless.

Raymond William Stacy Burr was born in British Columbia in 1917, the son of a Canadian hardware dealer and American organist, and was raised in Vallejo, California. He began acting in his youth, toured England with a repertory theater group, worked in radio and sang at a Paris nightclub — all before World War II. After serving in the navy during the war, he made his film debut in Gordon Douglas's *San Quentin* (1946). With his trademark massiveness and resonating voice, he worked in more than 50 films before making the transition to television. After *Perry Mason*, he was the tough, wheelchair-bound San Francisco detective *Ironside* in the late '60s and early '70s. Burr had three marriages, two of which left him a widower; his first wife died in a plane shot down by the Nazis in World War II. He had one child, a son who died of leukemia at age 10.

In his later years, Burr continued to grow — physically, that is. In a 1986 interview, the *Washington Post* described him as "gigantic . . . [with] a wing span like the Spruce Goose." It was this larger-than-life man that reappeared in *Godzilla 1985*. Around the same time, *Perry Mason* was revived for a series of TV movies, and Burr's career was on the upswing again. He also collected fine art and took retreats on his private island, Naitamba, in the Fiji chain (he sold it in 1983 for about $2 million). Burr died of liver cancer at age 76 on September 12, 1993, at his sprawling vineyard and ranch in Northern California.

Over the years, few journalists bothered to ask Burr about his work on the two Godzilla movies. That's a shame, because in what few on-the-record comments he made, Burr seemed to have a genuine affection for the creature. According to *Raymond Burr: A Radio, Film and Television Biography* by Ona L. Hill (McFarland, 1994), Burr once said:

> The first *Godzilla* was done in the U.S.A. The producers bought the rights to the Japanese picture, cut it, edited it and shot my scenes in a tiny studio on Los Angeles' Vermont Avenue. We had every scene in that small studio, including the mountains, the climbing scenes. The hospital scenes, the hotel scenes, with me looking out the window watching Godzilla destroying Tokyo. It was all done in that one little studio.

Hill's book also quotes Burr as saying, "I wanted them to give me part ownership of [*Godzilla: King of the Monsters!*], but they refused."

As for reprising the Steve Martin role nearly 30 years later in *Godzilla 1985*, Burr told the *Washington Post* he welcomed the role, although he was clearly displeased with the way the film turned out. "When they asked me to do [*Godzilla 1985*], I said, 'Certainly,' and everybody thought I was out of my mind. But it wasn't the large sum of money. It was the fact that, first of all, I kind of liked Godzilla, and where do you get the opportunity to play yourself 30 years later?"

Two

YOU CAN'T KEEP A BAD MONSTER DOWN

"I sped through a bank of clouds that made my vision difficult and momentarily impossible. Then, as I flew through the haze, I looked anxiously below - searching, searching, searching . . ."

— Tsukioka, describing his every move

GIGANTIS: THE FIRE MONSTER

RATING (OUT OF FIVE STARS): ★★

JAPANESE VERSION: GOJIRA NO GYAKUSHU (REVENGE OF GODZILLA). Released on April 24, 1955, by the Toho Motion Picture Company. Academy ratio, black-and-white. Running Time: 82 minutes.

U.S. VERSION: Released on June 2, 1959, by Warner Bros. Pictures Inc. Running Time: 78 minutes.

STORY: A new Godzilla and a second monster — the quadrupedal, spike-backed reptile Angilas — engage in deadly combat in the streets and harbors of Osaka, destroying much of the city before Godzilla finally kills his foe with a bloody bite to the neck. The Japanese military, aided by two spotter pilots from a local fishing cannery, chases Godzilla to a snow-covered island north of Japan; fighter planes bombard the ice-capped hills and bury the monster in an avalanche.

RETURN TO GROUND ZERO

In November 1954, a few weeks after *Godzilla* opened in Tokyo, a "welcome home" party was held for executive producer Iwao Mori, who had been overseas working on an Italian-Japanese coproduction of *Madame Butterfly*. Although Mori was gone when the monster smashed the Tokyo opening-day box-office records, he was pleased that his gamble on *Godzilla* had paid off in spades. At the party, he approached producer Tomoyuki Tanaka and gave him these instructions: Make another one.

Five months later, in April 1955, Toho released *Gojira No Gyakushu* (titled *Godzilla Raids Again* for the English-speaking world by Toho's foreign-sales department) in Japan. Like most American genre-movie sequels (e.g., *King Kong*/*Son of Kong* and *The Amazing Colossal Man*/*War of the Colossal Beast*), it was made more quickly and apparently somewhat more cheaply than the first, and as a result it lacked much of what made *Godzilla* so special, except for Tsuburaya's special effects, and even they failed to fully meet expectations. The film fared well commercially but had little impact in Japan, making the viability of a continuing Godzilla franchise seem unlikely. In the U.S., its distributor came up with the spectacularly stupid idea of changing Godzilla's name to *Gigantis: The Fire Monster*, a decision that limited the film's commercial potential. As a result of all this, *Godzilla Raids Again* has always been a somewhat overlooked entry in the Godzilla series.

After completing *Godzilla*, Ishiro Honda returned to directing standard fare like melodramas and young love stories. When *Godzilla Raids Again* was conceived, Honda was already working on his next film, *Love Tide*, which was released a few months later, in January 1955. It is unclear why Tanaka and Mori chose not to wait until Honda was available to helm the second Godzilla movie, although some Japanese texts indicate that Mori was afraid of losing the momentum created by *Godzilla*'s success. At any rate, Tanaka instead assigned the project to **Motoyoshi Oda**, a director who, despite having made more than 50 movies in his career, has gone down in Japanese movie history as a mostly undistinguished studio hack. It was an unfortunate choice, for Oda displays little of the war-torn conviction or penchant for monster mayhem that Honda expressed so well in *Godzilla*.

Oda (1910–1973) joined Toho's precursor, PCL Studios, in 1935 and, like Honda and Akira Kurosawa, began as an assistant director and protégé of the great Kajiro Yamamoto. One of his best-known films was *Lady from Hell* (1949), a drama about postwar corruption in Japan which featured a script by Kurosawa. It's likely that he was chosen for *Godzilla Raids Again* because he had just completed *Invisible Man* (*Tomei Ningen*, released December 1954, with effects work by Eiji Tsuburaya), the story of a — what else? — invisible man, who poses as a clown to help solve a murder. Another key change in the creative lineup is the absence of Akira Ifukube, who was an increasingly sought-after film composer at that time, scoring about a half-dozen films or more per year. Tanaka and Mori apparently underestimated the connection between Godzilla's terror and Ifukube's crushing music, and chose instead to use an up-and-coming musical talent, **Masaru Sato**.

Just as Tokyo served as a stand-in for Hiroshima in *Godzilla*, Osaka becomes a faux Nagasaki in *Godzilla Raids Again*, but direct parallels between Bomb and monster are fewer and less striking. A powerful visual metaphor is created when Hidemi, left alone at her father's home in the mountains for safety, looks down upon a flaming Osaka, from which smoke rises like a mushroom cloud, and a TV newscaster suggests, "For the good of us all, we should consider the idea of using a hydrogen bomb against Godzilla." This is the only truly chilling moment in the film, as it serves as a eulogy for the victims of nuclear (or, in this case, monster) holocaust and a prayer for the survivors left behind to rebuild. Earlier in the film, Dr. Kyohei Yamane (Takashi Shimura, all-too-briefly reprising his role) theorizes that Godzilla and Angilas were revived by H-bomb tests in the hemisphere and suggests that flares might remind Godzilla of his nuclear roots.

In Honda's *Godzilla*, every aspect of the monster's invasion was depicted on an epic, wartime scale: The confusion over the ship disasters, the press scrambling for answers, the scientific inquiry, the military mobilization, the political posturing. But director Oda, working from a script fashioned by returning screenwriter Takeo Murata (who co-wrote with Shigeaki Hidaka) and based again on an original Shigeru Kayama story, chose to make a sequel that was narrower and more personal in scope. *Godzilla Raids Again* focuses on a small group of family, friends and co-workers, and the ordeals they endure as a result of Godzilla's return. Much more time is spent with the characters and their sappy stories than in the previous film. There is the protagonist of sorts, the young fish-scouting pilot Tsukioka, who struggles with doubts about his worthiness to marry the company president's daughter; Kobayashi, the only one who really seems to have a gusto for living in this picture and whose foolhardy, very un-Serizawa-like self-sacrifice tragically ends his life just after he's found a woman to love; and the cannery owner and his cohorts, who struggle to keep their fishing operations afloat despite Godzilla's nasty habit of torching their factory and sinking their boats. In a sense, *Godzilla Raids Again* is really two different films. One is an all-out, man-vs.-giant-monsters movie, with epic action and some great effects. The other is a downbeat, drawn-out melodrama that leaves the viewer constantly wishing the monsters will show up again soon. Luckily, they do.

FIGHT TO THE DEATH: While wading back out to sea, Godzilla's attention is caught by an explosion at a nearby refinery. As he slowly makes his way to the shore, the creature is bombarded with tank, cannon, and fighter-plane gunfire, but he is unswerved. Suddenly, Angilas surfaces in the harbor, and the two gigantic beasts immediately resume their war on the landing dock. They stalk, lunge at, tackle, and bite one another, their fierce battle decimating entire sections of Osaka. Angilas is momentarily flipped over on his back, but this is no helpless turtle — he swiftly kicks Godzilla away and rights himself, and the battle continues raging. Eventually, the fight moves to the Osaka Castle, where Godzilla finally sinks his teeth into his spiny foe's neck. Both monsters fall onto the crumbling castle and Godzilla delivers the bloody *coup de grâce*, sucking the last bit of life from Angilas and sending the creature's carcass over the dock and into the harbor, then burns it to a crisp.

Unlike the original Godzilla, who plundered Tokyo slowly and deliberately, the monsters in *Godzilla Raids Again* move with an animalistic swiftness and predatorial fury more akin to the *Jurassic Park* dinosaurs. This change is intensified by the fact that much of the special-effects footage of the Godzilla-vs.-Angilas battle was not shot in the high-speed (72 frames per second) mode, but at a slower speed (probably 18 frames per second). Thus, the monsters alternate between slow, heavy movement and lightning-fast fighting. This discrepancy has long been a source of confusion. Was it an error? If so, why didn't Tsuburaya order the footage reshot? Teisho Arikawa, the head special-effects cameraman, recalled the incident in the book *Godzilla Days*: "There were three cameras — A, B and C — and it was ordinary to shoot Godzilla at high speed. But camera C wasn't set in high speed. I don't know if he meant to do it, or he forgot to set it, we still don't know. But when we saw the dailies, cameras A and B were on the right setting, but camera C's Godzilla moved quicker than A and B. Mr. Tsuburaya said, 'What is this?'" After watching for a while longer, Arikawa recalled that Tsuburaya said, "'Wait a minute. That movement's not that bad. maybe we can use it.' . . . Ever since that incident, we've used different [camera] speeds in different scenes." Although Arikawa did not name the cameraman culprit, some Japanese texts have identified him as Yoichi Manoda. However, other sources have listed the offender as another cameraman, Koichi Takano. It seems odd that a trained cameraman would fail to notice that his camera was set wrongly, for the noise generated by the motor varies according to speed. Nevertheless, the true identity of the guilty party is unknown.

The athletic monster stunts performed by Godzilla (Haruo Nakajima) and Angilas (Katsumi Tezuka) in this film were made possible by constructing the costumes from lighter materials than the previous Godzilla suit, and by casting the suits from plaster molds designed to fit the stunt actors' bodies. The new Godzilla design (called *Gyakushu-Goji*) created by sculptor Teizo Toshimitsu is patterned after the original but more slender throughout, particularly in the lower body and legs, making the monster appear less powerful than before. In addition, the costume's arms, claws, and tail betray the fact that it was constructed with a cloth base over which latex was applied, for the material tends to bunch up like a baggy shirt at times. The head is slightly redesigned, with Godzilla sprouting more prominent teeth and the fangs jutting out over the lower lip. From a profile view, the beast looks quite menacing, but when viewed head-on, it has large ears and thick eyebrow ridges that detract from Godzilla's menace. Nevertheless, the costume was much lighter than before and Nakajima turned in one of his most physical performances as Godzilla, but in some ways the suit was more cumbersome than the first. It had a motor for moving Godzilla's eyes and mouth mounted in the head, and batteries located between Godzilla's legs, at the base of the tail. "When I jumped, it was such a pain," Nakajima said.

Angilas, meanwhile, is an inspired creation. Its most fearsome attributes are its head, with prominent spikes on its crown and a long, horned snout with dagger-like teeth lining its jaw, and the intricate spikes covering its back (which serve no purpose other than to look dangerous). To help hide the human proportions of the actor inside the costume, the special-effects crew photographed Angilas mostly from angles that showed little or none of its hind legs, and miniature buildings, trees, and other obstacles were placed in between the camera and monster to conceal the fact that Tezuka had to walk around on his knees, with the bottoms of his feet exposed. Toho would create many more quadrupedal monsters in future films, but never again would the illusion of a four-legged creature be so effectively done. In addition to the monster suits, hand puppets of Godzilla (again using a spray to depict his radiation breath in some scenes) and Angilas were utilized in close-up shots, but the puppets are obviously less detailed than the suits, and not very convincing.

There are some great visuals in this film, and much care was taken to make the monsters appear huge by filming them from low camera angles. During the Osaka monster battle, there are at least three beautifully executed shots that zoom by quickly, yet deserve mention. The first is a long shot of the monsters wrestling amid the city rubble, with flames and smoke rear-screened into the shot, slowly rising high and bright into the air; the second is a brief, yet very imaginative shot of Angilas snarling at Godzilla, viewed through the twin pillars of the entranceway to Osaka Castle Park, reminiscent of the "conductor's-eye view" of Godzilla's foot coming down in the previous film; the last is a great matte shot of the monsters fighting around the Osaka castle, with throngs of tiny people fleeing for their lives in the foreground.

Although there is considerably less miniature work here than in *Godzilla*, the two-meter-tall Osaka castle model, the Yodoyabashi bridge, Osaka Bay and the entire city set are nicely detailed and well photographed. With *Godzilla*'s success, the SFX crew was given more ample work space this time around, and the miniature Osaka was erected in Toho's newly constructed soundstage No. 8. The Osaka castle, like the Diet Building in the last film, was the focus of the miniature work, and also like the Diet Building, it failed to crumble as planned during the shoot. Because of the model's heavy construction, wires were installed inside the castle and run underneath the platform, and when the monsters collided with the structure, several crew members pulled the wires. Somehow, the building withstood both the monsters' impact and the crewmen's pulling; Tsuburaya yelled, "Cut!" but the stagehands didn't hear him and kept yanking, and the model came tumbling down after the cameras stopped rolling. The castle had to be partially rebuilt and the scene reshot.

The best effects sequence in the film, however, is Godzilla's battle with the pilots on the icy island. Partially shot on an outdoor set, this scene includes innovative views of Godzilla, shot from low angles with the snow-covered peaks towering over him, that show both the monster's immensity when compared to man (e.g., the fighter planes) and his relative smallness in the scheme of Nature. The entire battle is masterfully edited, with overhead shots of Godzilla zooming by, seen from the pilots'

perspective, and fine wire manipulation of the model planes. The optical animation of Godzilla's ray (one of few times the technique is used in the film) becomes more steamy in the cold Arctic air, an impressive effect, and the planes' bombardment of the hillsides and the ensuing snowslides, filmed in slow motion, is well staged. Godzilla's white blanket was created with real ice, using an ice machine borrowed from a Tokyo skating rink and an ice crusher. This is one of the most inventive means of monster-disposal ever conceived in a Toho movie, and its only drawback is that the ice boulders sometimes appear incredibly large and should have been ground into smaller pieces — at one point, it looks like Godzilla is trapped in a huge party cooler, searching for a beer. And this scenario also begs the question: Why doesn't Godzilla simply use his radiation breath to melt the ice and free himself?

What prevents *Godzilla Raids Again* from rising above its mediocrity is Murata and Hidaka's halting, unevenly paced script and Oda's static, dispassionate directorial style. When Tsukioka and Kobayashi discover the monsters, they are immediately imperiled and the excitement begins; then they go back to Osaka and everything is calm; the monsters show up and engage in a ferocious battle; everyone packs up and leaves for Hokkaido; and worst of all, during the air raid on Godzilla, the squadron pilots fly all the way back to base to reload their planes with bombs, putting the action on hold in the heat of battle!

The dramatic structure seems forced, perhaps because the script was written under tight deadlines. The entire cast's relocation to Hokkaido, in particular, bisects the film and seems pointless. Godzilla — in a gigantic coincidence — follows them there and attacks one of Yamaji's ships. Obviously, Hokkaido was thrown into the story to bring Godzilla into snowy territory and set up the film's great finale, but there seems to be an underlying theme as well. Oda seems to say, although rather weakly, that Godzilla is a harbinger of doom that cannot be fled; in order to conquer its fears of nuclear war and other demons, Japan must stand up to Godzilla. It's a lesson Tsukioka learns from his friend Kobayashi in the bittersweet end.

Also hampering the film is Oda's lack of imagination and stiff staging of the human drama. In nearly every scene the characters sit and talk, or stand and talk. The only characters in the movie who move around much are the monsters, the rare exception being the convicts who escape from the paddy wagon and flee through the streets of Osaka. Screenwriter Takeo Murata said he originally wanted to show the widespread mayhem and looting that would occur if a disaster like the monster battle erupted in the city, but time and budget restrictions limited him to this one scene, and it is somewhat botched by Oda's handling of the material. These hardened criminals, who had the guts to overcome armed guards, suddenly become the Keystone Kops when loosed on the streets, stumbling and falling over themselves as they run. The thugs are eventually swallowed up in a flooded subway tunnel (a nice matte shot), making it hard to tell whether Oda intended this sequence for laughs or not.

The cast of *Godzilla Raids Again* is serviceable but unspectacular. The only real standout is Minoru Chiaki (Kobayashi), a fine actor from Akira Kurosawa's company who is famous for his roles in *The Hidden Fortress* and other films, and who won a Japanese academy award in 1985 for his role as an Alzheimer's patient in *Grey Sunset*. Hiroshi Koizumi (Tsukioka) is rather dull, and Shimura, playing the lone continuing character from the first Godzilla film, seems bored rather than dismayed by Godzilla's return. He can be seen visibly playing with his pen as he speaks, and of course he has nothing to do but sit and talk, like everyone else.

Dr. Yamane makes it clear in *Godzilla Raids Again* that this monster is not the Godzilla that died in Tokyo Bay, but a new monster of the same type which, along with Angilas, was probably also revived by nuclear testing. Since the first Godzilla surfaced near Tokyo and the second off Osaka, it's a wonder that dozens of other Godzillas didn't appear in Japan over time. Then again, they did — but they took on different forms and had different names, like Rodan and Mothra. And it was this second Godzilla that would go on to star in a series of (usually) self-titled epics, co-starring many of his nuclear-bred brethren, over the next two-plus decades.

MUSHROOM CLOUD
The Japanese
Monster Explosion

Godzilla Raids Again drew 8.3 million ticket buyers, significantly less than the original *Godzilla* but still a respectable business. However, the film failed to generate the enthusiasm of its predecessor among the public, the press, or even Toho staff. Tomoyuki Tanaka wrote years later, "We didn't have much preparation time and it would be difficult for me to say the production was successful." Special-effects cameraman Teisho Arikawa noted, "Something was missing when we wrapped *Godzilla Raids Again*. At the [staff prerelease] screening, people were talking about the first Godzilla movie."

Thus, Tanaka put Godzilla on the shelf and would not find the right vehicle for the monster's return for seven years. But Godzilla's sophomore jinx did nothing to slow the exploding growth of the *kaiju eiga* (Japanese monster movie). In the latter half of the 1950s, although rival studios began making their own sci-fi and monster films (Daiei released *Warning from Space* in 1957, while Shin-Toho launched its *Starman* serials), Toho boldly took the lead in this field by pouring money and talent into its productions — by 1957 Toho had formally established its own special-effects department with Eiji Tsuburaya at the helm, and most of its genre films were in color and Toho Scope.

Just as *Godzilla* borrowed elements from *The Beast from 20,000 Fathoms*, the entire Japanese monster and sci-fi movie crop adopted the basic elements of American movies of the same type: Monsters created or reawakened by atomic tests or other environmental disturbances, futile attempts by the authorities to defend the populace, and the usual character archetypes and relationships (a scientist, a hero, a romantic entanglement). Toho's genre pictures, particularly those directed by Ishiro Honda, also addressed certain Japanese themes, particularly the idea of self-sacrifice and atonement, which was present in *Godzilla*, *Godzilla Raids Again*, *The Mysterians* (1957), *Battle in Outer Space* (1959), and *The Human Vapor* (1960). Toho also introduced its own sub-genre of mutant movies, sometimes called "body transformation" films, which focused on people mutated by radiation into monsters. These included Honda's *The H-Man* (1958; an atomic blob transforms men into liquid creatures), *The Human Vapor* (a radiation experiment gone awry turns a man into a gas cloud), and Jun Fukuda's *Secret of the Telegian* (1960; a deranged man teleports himself as an electromagnetic signal and seeks revenge on his enemies). And, unlike American sci-fi/monster movies of the 1950s, which were predominantly independently produced, low-budget affairs, the Japanese pictures were major studio movies with an abundance of expensive effects work and well-known actors, often A-list stars.

Beginning with the spectacular *Rodan*, Honda directed all of Toho's giant-monster movies of the late 1950s, the lone exception being Hiroshi Inagaki's *The Three Treasures*, a mythical fantasy featuring a giant, eight-headed serpent. Although it lacks the stark anti-nuclear subtext of *Godzilla*, *Rodan* is one of Honda's best films and a masterpiece of Japanese horror moviemaking. Even more than *Godzilla*, *Rodan* is closely patterned on the American monster-on-the-loose mold. It begins in a small coal-mining town, where a miner's mysterious disappearance is soon attributed to man-sized bugs that manage to scare the hell out of everyone. There are other familiar American horror-movie riffs, including a protagonist stricken with amnesia, eerie caverns, and swampy water. *Rodan* is often truly chilling, and it is certainly the best "flying monster" movie of its generation (consider *The Giant Claw*), thanks to Tsuburaya's incredible effects work, some of the best of his career, with the two gigantic Rodans outrunning supersonic jets and blowing away entire sections of the city of Fukuoka (changed to Sasebo in the U.S. version, probably for fear that the original name would incite snickers from the audience).

The Mysterians was the first of several Toho space-opera extravaganzas, an attempt at an alien-invasion epic on the order of *The War of the Worlds* or *Earth vs. The Flying Saucers*. The film introduces two major themes that Honda would repeatedly touch upon in his science-fiction films: the need for nations to cooperate for the survival of the planet and the dangers of allowing science and technology to overshadow human emotion and rational thought. The latter idea is played out via the tragic character of Ryoichi Shiraishi (Akihiko Hirata), the scientist who joins the aliens in hopes of surpassing the limits of Earth's technology, only to find that the aliens are using their knowledge for evil purposes; in the end, Shiraishi atones by sabotaging the aliens' plans. The film also has many great Tsuburaya effects, although the final battle between Earth's "Markalites" (huge electrical dishes that shoot rays) and the aliens is overlong. There is also a giant monster thrown in for good measure, the alien robot Mogera, an inspired creation that briefly wreaks havoc on a remote town. Even in movies where it was uncalled for, producer Tomoyuki Tanaka realized the box-office value of including a new monster on the bill, a trick he would continue to pull in future science-fiction films like *Gorath* (1962), *Atragon* (1963), and *Latitude Zero* (1969).

The Mysterians was followed two years later by a similar film, *Battle in Outer Space*. Between those two films, Honda made the lackluster *Varan the Unbelievable* (1958), a mostly dull yarn about a legendary gigantic monster resembling a crossbreed of Godzilla, Angilas, and a giant squirrel, which revives to terrorize rural villagers. The film is obviously cheaper than other Toho efforts; it was shot in black and white, the miniature work is sparse, the cast is second-rate, and the film utilizes stock footage of attacking jets and city destruction culled from *Godzilla*. *Varan* eventually turned up in U.S. cinemas in 1962 in an inept, heavily re-edited version with additional scenes of Myron Healey as a scientist conducting water desalination experiments in Japan. Curiously, the U.S. version deleted all scenes of Varan dilating his wing-like membranes and flying through the air.

The *kaiju eiga* cycle hit its stride at about the same time that American giant-monster movies began petering out. In the late 1950s, there were still a few giant creatures terrorizing U.S. audiences in movies like *The Black Scorpion*, *The Deadly Mantis*, *The Amazing Colossal Man*, and *The Giant Claw*, but U.S. exploitationists gradually downsized to man-sized monsters brought to life with men in suits. By 1960, the American monster movement was pretty much over with, although there were still a few of these films being made in Europe, like *Konga*, *Gorgo*, and *The Giant Behemoth*. Thereafter, the Japanese were more or less the sole producers of giant-monster fare. Competition among the Japanese studios for a piece of the *kaiju eiga* pie would not only bring Godzilla back, but force the genre to evolve in even more outlandish directions and keep it going strong until the late 1960s, when economic factors would inevitably take their toll on Godzilla and friends.

MISTAKEN IDENTITY
How Godzilla Became Gigantis

Godzilla was released in Japan, sold to a U.S. distributor, re-edited with new American-made scenes, and thundered into cinemas as *Godzilla: King of the Monsters!* all in a span of less than 18 months. But it took a full four years for the sequel, *Godzilla Raids Again*, to show up on Western movie screens, and when it did, the picture was strangely re-titled

Look out, they're coming! Not one, but two . . . of the most terrifying creatures ever loosed on man! Each a raging unkillable horror! Both on a rampage to stun your every sense! "GIGANTIS THE FIRE MONSTER" Born to destroy each other. . . . But first they'll destroy the world!

Here's motion picture adventure and excitement to stagger the imagination. The fantastic fire monster, raging out of the flaming bowels of hell. Mighty Gigantis, crushing whole cities in his wrath. And deadly Anguirus [sic], screaming its challenge of mortal combat. The battle of the ages! Scenes and sights and sensations beyond anything the screen has ever shown.

GIGANTIS THE FIRE MONSTER . . . THEY'LL MAKE YOU SCREAM TWICE AS LOUD!

— *From Warner Bros. theatrical trailer for* Gigantis: The Fire Monster

Gigantis: The Fire Monster. The long delay and the confusing name change form one of the great mysteries of Godzilla lore. The prevailing theory is that Warner Bros., which distributed *Gigantis* in the U.S. and elsewhere, could not obtain the rights to use the "Godzilla" name from Joseph E. Levine and the other owners of *Godzilla: King of the Monsters!*, or that Warners was unwilling to pay Levine or Toho for said rights. Although the exact sequence of events leading up to *Gigantis* is hard to trace (many of the players have since died, or their memories have become fuzzy with age), evidence suggests there was no compelling legal or financial reason to drop the name "Godzilla." The people who acquired *Godzilla Raids Again* from Toho were members of the same group of small-time film mavens who bought *Godzilla*: Harry Rybnick (a.k.a. Harold Ross), Richard Kay, Edward Barison, Paul Schreibman, and Edmund Goldman chief among them. In a gross underestimation of Godzilla's marquee value, these men changed his moniker to bamboozle the public into believing this was an "all-new" monster. It was a stupid mistake, and it backfired.

In late 1956 or early '57, Rybnick and Barison struck a deal to distribute *Godzilla Raids Again* in the U.S. With Rybnick, who had coproduced (with Richard Kay) the Americanization of *Godzilla*, acting as the "idea man" and Barison the "money man," plans were made to revamp the new Godzilla film even more drastically than the first one, cannibalizing the picture's special-effects footage and incorporating it into a new, American-made movie called *The Volcano Monsters*. Rybnick hired two screenwriters, Danish-born **Ib Melchior** (then a budding film and television writer, who later wrote *Reptilicus* and directed *Angry Red Planet*, *The Time Travelers*, and many other films) and his then-roommate and writing partner **Edwin Watson**, who jointly developed an original story in which a volcanic eruption in Japan unveils two gigantic monsters encased in rock. The monsters are subsequently shipped to the U.S. for scientific study but they unexpectedly revive from suspended animation and battle in San Francisco. Although the project involved the near-complete decimation of *Godzilla Raids Again*, Toho was eager to further develop a foothold in the American marketplace. It not only approved the deal, it agreed to ship Godzilla and Angilas costumes to Hollywood so that Rybnick could film additional monster scenes, just as Toho had sent an Abominable Snowman costume to Hollywood in 1956 so that Distributors Corp. of America (DCA) could film additional scenes of the monster laid out on a morgue slab for its butcher-job release of Honda's *Half Human*.

To underwrite *The Volcano Monsters*, Rybnick and Barison made a deal with AB-PT Pictures Corp., a small, newly established production company headed by executives from the American Broadcasting Company and the Paramount Theaters chain. AB-PT was formed to produce a package of 20-plus low-budget movies in the late 1950s and early '60s. The plan was to release the films through Republic Pictures, which would distribute them to Paramount's movie houses and other theaters, and then subsequently show them on the ABC television network (at the time, "new" movies were still a novelty on TV, even low-budget ones). However, as it turned out, AB-PT released only two films, both bargain-basement sci-fi pictures: director Bert I. Gordon's *The Beginning of the End*, in which Peter Graves battles monster grasshoppers in Chicago, and *The Unearthly*, a mad-scientist movie starring John Carradine and Myron Healey. The two pictures were released on a double bill in July 1957, and AB-PT folded not long after, when principals in the company decided to abort the scheme, for unknown reasons. Several films were in development when

AB-PT shut down, one of which was *The Volcano Monsters.*

Preproduction was in its advanced stages when the plug was pulled. Melchior and Watson, after spending many hours watching *Godzilla Raids Again* on a Movieola and cataloguing the special-effects shots, completed a 129-page shooting script (dated May 7, 1957), complete with specific instructions to the film editor as to which shots of Godzilla, Angilas, the military mobilization, fighter jets flying in formation and attacking, and crowds fleeing were to be used, and where they were to be inserted into the picture. "We used everything," Melchior recalled in a 1993 interview. "We watched the movie and we took notes of all the effects stuff, then we sat down and thought about how we could build our story around it, an American story. It wasn't easy. The idea was that we didn't want anyone to know this was a Japanese film, so we eliminated the entire Japanese story and cast. This was my first feature film (screenplay), so I worked very, very hard on it, but of course the movie was not made and it's hard to say how it would have turned out. The Japanese film that we were given to begin with wasn't very good, and I think they [AB-PT] were working on a small budget. But we tried hard to turn it into something different."

Indeed they did. First off, Melchior and Watson stripped Godzilla and Angilas of their monster identities, reducing them to gigantic dinosaurs — Godzilla was referred to only as a female tyrannosaurus, Angilas as an ankylosaurus. For unknown reasons (presumably, because real dinosaurs did not spew fire), all shots of Godzilla breathing his radioactive ray were to be eliminated — on page 74 of the script, there is even an instruction to the film editor that says, "Note: Cut before back of tyrannosaurus lights up!" Thus, several special-effects shots went unused, including Godzilla's cremation of Angilas in Osaka Bay and all shots of Godzilla blasting the planes on the ice-covered island. Instead, several new shots were to be filmed of the tyrannosaurus (Godzilla) swiping its hand outside the frame; these were to be intercut with shots of the planes slamming into the mountainside, making it appear as if the creature swatted the planes from the sky.

The Melchior-Watson script called for quite a few new special-effects scenes. These included matte shots of the scientists and the dormant gigantic monsters inside the Noshiro Volcano cave; an elaborate sequence wherein bulldozers and explosives are used to enlarge the mouth of the cave, then the monsters are pulled out of the cave with steel cables and loaded onto an aircraft carrier; during the trans-Pacific voyage, there were to be numerous rear-projection shots of crew members standing in front of the huge dinosaurs, strapped down on deck (large prosthetics of the tyrannosaur's foot and the ankylosaurus' spikes were apparently going to be constructed); a storm sequence at sea, wherein the cables holding the tyrannosaurus are snapped and the monster rolls overboard; a matte shot combining stock footage of the Golden Gate Bridge and the aircraft carrier entering San Francisco Bay, with the ankylosaurus on board; and several shots of the ankylosaurus awakening and freeing itself from its harnesses on the ship.

This was followed by the tyrannosaurus-vs.-ankylosaurus battle. Since the entire monster battle takes place at night, Melchior and Watson simply pretended that Osaka was actually San Francisco — when the monsters battle near the Osaka Castle, the script refers to the locale as the city's "oriental quarter" (i.e., Chinatown). Most all footage from the Osaka monster battle was to be used, although the script indicates that much of the monster action was going to be re-edited. Interestingly, the panic and disaster scenes were to be included, including the Caltex truck crashing into the refinery (with the preceding prison break and police chase snipped away), the nightclub patrons fleeing (using only the portion where all the Japanese faces are turned away from the camera or shrouded in darkness), and long shots of the metropolis, with entire city blocks shutting off their lights (this was rewritten so that the blackout is caused by the monsters stepping on a power plant, not as a result of a civil defense order). The monster battle was to be augmented by splicing in stock newsreel footage of army troops leaving their barracks, tanks being manned, fleeing crowds, and fire engines and military trucks mobilizing. There were also new shots to be filmed of the tyrannosaurus stepping on buildings and roaring.

To enable filming of the new effects footage, sometime in early 1957 Toho shipped one Godzilla costume and one Angilas costume to Los Angeles. The footage was to be filmed at Howard A. Anderson's special-effects studio, which at that time was a successful "insert house" that shot optical effects, titles, miniature work, and other trick photography for independent and studio productions. In or around May 1957, special-effects artist Bob Burns (who has worked on *Aliens* and dozens of other movies) and the famous creature creator Paul

Blaisdell (designer of many classic monsters for AIP) were working at Anderson studios on the AIP sci-fi/comedy *Invasion of the Saucermen*. While filming a scene in which a Martian spaceship is blown to bits, Burns made an unusual discovery, which he remembered in a 1996 interview.

"We were there doing all the *Saucermen* inserts that day, and we were going to blow up the saucer. The [pyrotechnics] guy kept loading more and more powder into it, and we were getting a little worried about the explosion. So, we decided to hide behind these crates at the far side of the sound-stage. So they blew up the saucer, and I started looking at these crates and I noticed they had a lot of Japanese writing, but somebody had written 'Godzilla' in English on one of them, and it said 'Toho' all over the box. The crates had already been opened, they weren't nailed shut anymore, so I asked Howard [Anderson Jr.] if we could look in there and he said, 'Yeah, sure.' And it turned out to be the original Godzilla suit. It looked like it was made of a canvas base underneath, with rubber layered on the outside. The head appeared to be over some sort of wire armature. He was sort of dark gray color. He had a little green in him, but he was basically a dark gray color. The suit was in really bad shape, it looked like they were going to really have to patch it up, because it had burn holes all over it — you could really see where they had shot that thing up, and where they had run lines when they were shooting fireworks into it.

"I used to wear monster suits, and I'd have hated to be the guy in that thing! There was actually a hole on the inside where it had burned through. I'm sure the actor who was inside that thing got burned. They didn't really fix it up at all. So we hauled the suit out of the box, and it looked pretty cool. I'm not that tall, I'm like five-foot-eight, and there was no way I could even fit in it, it was pretty small. He didn't have a zipper up the back, it opened and closed with snaps along the dorsal, a lot like the costume Paul [Blaisdell] built for *The She-Creature*. It was a one-piece suit, the head was attached, and there was this sort of gauze material on the neck where the actor inside looked out, but God, you could hardly see anything through it. And then we opened the other crate, although we didn't take the other suit [Angilas] out, we just saw him sitting there with his spikes on his back and his head. The Angilas suit had more color, he had blue, a little red. At that time, Howard Jr. didn't know what they were going to do with the suits. He told me, 'We just got those in, we're going to be shooting some inserts.' I never knew what happened to those suits."

The origin of the Godzilla and Angilas suits shipped to America for *The Volcano Monsters* is curious. Burns clearly remembers damage to the costumes that indicates they were previously used for filming, and his description of the Godzilla suit, made with rubber over canvas, matches that of the lighter costume built for *Godzilla Raids Again*. However, in the mid-1990s, a photograph of the Godzilla and Angilas suits (and the three men who built them: Teizo Toshimitsu, Kanji Yagi, Eizo Kaimai) that Toho sent to the producers of *The Volcano Monsters* in 1957 appeared in several Japanese-language Godzilla books, and the costumes clearly appeared to be different than those used in *Godzilla Raids Again*. The Godzilla costume in the photograph is closer in appearance to the suit used later in *King Kong vs. Godzilla*: Fat in the middle, with thunder thighs, a thick tail, and a long snout and menacing stare, a sharp contrast to the lean, lighter costume with fanged teeth of *Godzilla Raids Again*; what's more, the suit in the photo has no ears and only three toes, whereas the *Raids Again* costume had ears and four toes. The Angilas costume is partially obscured in the photograph, but its head is clearly visible and it, too, is different from the suit used in the film.

HOT LAVA

Synopsis: <u>The Volcano Monsters</u>
by Ib Melchior and Ed Watson

A massive eruption at the Noshiro volcano in Japan unveils a huge cave opening in the mountainside. American geo-paleontologist Dr. Roy Carlyle, joined by his young assistant Marge and several Japanese scientists, surveys the cave for fossils. Carlyle finds pristine prehistoric stalactite and stalagmite formations and, better yet, the gigantic forms of an ankylosaurus and a female tyrannosaurus rex, apparently swallowed up in molten lava while deadlocked in battle millions of years ago. The monsters are several hundred feet long (much larger than actual dinosaurs) and although they appear to be dead, their bodies are in perfect condition. The scientists surmise that the volcanic gases preserved the beasts through the ages.

One of the Japanese crew members warns the Americans not to disturb the "monsters of Noshiro," believing the creatures are the fulfilment of an ancient prophecy, but his protests are dismissed as silly superstition. Carlyle plans to transport the dinosaurs to San Francisco to study them at a special laboratory. At a conference in Tokyo with military officials and scientists, he postulates that the two behemoths are gigantic cousins of the ankylosaurus and tyrannosaurus, two natural enemies that roamed the Earth during the Cretaceous Period and were prone to engage in a "sudden, frightening struggle" whenever they met.

Navy Sea Bees use dynamite charges to blast the mouth of the cave, clearing the way for the monsters to be removed. A bridge is built between the cave mouth and an aircraft carrier docked at the shore, and the dinosaurs are pulled onto the ship using cables and a steam-powered winch. During the trans-Pacific trip, an attraction develops be-

tween Marge (described as bookish, but "all woman" beneath the surface) and Navy Commander Steve McBain (a man of "personal strength and straight-forwardness"), while Corvin, another scientist, begins to fume with jealousy and behaves erratically. McBain is skeptical of the scientists' motives and resents being assigned to transport the beasts; he is also a bit of a chauvinist, referring to Marge (only half-jokingly) as "lady-scientist" and asking, "How do you expect a guy to tell you how pretty you are and everything when you always change the subject to dinosaurs?"

During the trip, it is discovered that the dinosaurs are not dead but merely dormant, and the scientists titter with joy over the prospect of discovering the secrets of suspended animation. McBain immediately wants to throw the animals overboard, fearing they will reawaken and cause untold problems, but he agrees to keep them on. Then, during a violent storm, one of the cables harnessing the tyrannosaurus snaps (it had been foolishly loosened by Corvin, who feared it was so tight it would damage the creature) and the beast rolls across the deck, killing a sailor, then falls overboard. The ship sails on, successfully delivering the ankylosaurus.

Once arrived, McBain and Marge go out on the town for the evening, and while they are away from the ship, the tyrannosaurus surfaces in the bay. The ankylosaurus awakens and breaks out of its harness, and the two monsters do battle at the shoreline, trampling through a power station and cutting off electricity to part of the city. The driver of a CalTex truck is startled by the monsters and crashes at a nearby oil refinery, igniting a huge fire. The monsters make their way to Chinatown and battle fiercely among the Oriental-looking buildings. Carlyle, realizing what a mess he's caused, suffers a stroke, and when McBain and Marge visit him at the hospital he implores them to "destroy them . . . for me!" Before the heroes leave, Carlyle's doctor reads them a sermonic diagnosis: The Volcano Monsters must be stopped, but they cannot be killed; if they are, Carlyle will lose his chance at a Nobel Prize for research and surely die of depression. Martial law is imposed as the battling monsters move to the heart of the city, then make their way to the shoreline again. The tyrannosaurus kills its enemy with a fierce bite to the neck. The military's top brass rack their brains for a plan to rub out the remaining menace.

The tyrannosaurus heads toward the university, where Marge and a team of scientists are working to re-create the volcanic gas formula in hopes of putting the tyrannosaurus back to sleep (this, she hopes, will save mankind *and* her beloved professor). Despite the approaching monster, Marge and the scientists insist they are on the verge of cracking the formula, and they refuse to leave the building. McBain arrives to rescue his girl, but when she refuses to leave with him, McBain "lets loose a short jab to Marge's chin; she sags limply in his arms." McBain carries ko'd Marge away just before the tyrannosaurus crushes the lab, killing the others. The monster heads back out to sea, unscathed by a barrage of tank, rocket, and jet firepower.

The Navy sends planes and submarines after the sea-faring tyrannosaurus, which is unharmed even by repeated bomb blasts and depth charges. Aboard a naval destroyer, McBain and Marge follow the creature but lose track of it somewhere in the Arctic Ocean, then relocate it as it heads for an island that remains mysteriously warm and tropical in the polar region. Mitchell, another scientist, deduces that the beast wants to lay her eggs there, and fears if that happens, "we'll have her brood to contend with." McBain considers nuking the dinosaur with an atom bomb, but then hits on another plan that will, as Marge had hoped, succeed in both stopping the monster and preserving it for study. The navy places a ring of oil drums around an ice canyon, but before ship gunners and fighter planes can seal the monster inside with a ring of fire, there is a tense scene where McBain rescues another seaman trapped under one of the barrels, just yards away from the approaching monster. The two men just make it out in time, and McBain ignites the oil drums with a grenade. Then jets bombard the hills around the dinosaur, causing an ice avalanche, but the creature frees itself before it can be completely buried. The jets swoop down again and hit the slopes more heavily until the creature disappears under the ice. Scientists say the cold-blooded reptile will be placed permanently in suspended animation, so Carlyle can examine the specimen anytime he wants.

The story ends at the Noshiro volcano, where a claw probes out the cave opening. . . .

FOR GODZILLA FANS, *The Volcano Monsters* remains a great "what if." While it certainly would have been interesting to see Godzilla, even if reduced to the role of "tyrannosaurus," as shot by an American studio, chances are that the new SFX scenes would have paled in comparison to Toho's footage — the effects work produced at Howard Anderson's studio for other low-budget monster movies at that time isn't exactly Tsuburaya caliber. It's also worth noting that AB-PT Pictures' two lone productions have gone down in the annals of SF movie history as forgettable junk, and it's a safe bet *The Volcano Monsters* would have fared no better. As written, Melchior and Watson's screenplay is a pretty typical 1950s American giant-monster movie, the main difference being an abundance of special effects and monster scenes, and that's only because most of the effects work was bought for a song. The story is pretty routine for a film of its type and era, but Melchior and Watson did a good job of fashioning a credible script around pre-existing monster footage, which is no simple task. Inevitably, some elements of the story seem forced, such as the linking of the monsters' fate with that of Professor Carlyle, the tyrannosaurus's sudden flight to the Arctic island and the unconvincing explanation that the monster wants to breed there, and McBain's ingenious solution to save both the dinosaur and the professor by burying the tyrannosaur in ice (in American giant-monster movies, the monster is always killed at the end!).

It is not known whether any attempt was made to revive *The Volcano Monsters* with another production company after AB-PT Pictures closed shop. However, in 1958 the rights to *Godzilla Raids Again* were picked up by three investors, the venerable Paul Schreibman, Edmund Goldman, and Newton P. Jacobs. Jacobs, the former head of Favorite Films (and who later established Crown International distribution in 1959), helped Schreibman finance the production of a modest Americanization of the film by dubbing it into English and making other modifications. Around the same time, Schreibman also acquired a low-low-budget, independently produced science-fiction film called *The Boy from Out of This World* that was written, directed, and produced by Tom Graeff (who was also its star). Searching for a gimmick to get these two pictures into wide release, Schreibman approached the late Bill Foreman, then-president of Pacific Theaters, a chain of mostly drive-ins in the western states. Schreibman convinced Foreman to buy the theatrical and TV rights to both pictures, then turned around and helped Foreman peddle the theatrical rights to Warner Bros. In the deal that was struck, Foreman agreed to show the two movies on a double bill in all his theaters, and Warners would distribute them to other theaters. Warners received two complete motion pictures, with no production-related expenses, and was given all theatrical rights in the U.S. and Latin America for four years. In May 1959 the films hit theaters as *Gigantis: The Fire Monster* and *Teenagers from Outer Space*.

"Warners paid substantially nothing for it. The only real investment they had in it was [theatrical] prints and advertising," Harry B. Swerdlow, Foreman's attorney, said in 1997. Swerdlow became "designated owner" of the rights to both movies because Foreman did not want his own name to appear on the copyright notices. "I am proud to say that I have never seen either one of these 'epics.' They are even worse than what's on television today," he said.

After *Gigantis* and *Teenagers* ran their course in the U.S. and other countries, *Gigantis* was syndicated to television in the early to mid-1960s. After the films reverted back to Foreman and Swerdlow, however, no attempt was made to continue selling the TV rights. Swerdlow said, "I don't think we ever put *Gigantis* on television. Nobody asked to buy it, and we weren't advertising it." In the mid-1980s, after *Gigantis* had seemingly disappeared for two decades, the rights reverted to Toho and the film was subsequently released to U.S. television and home video, bringing a "lost" Godzilla movie out of retirement.

BANANA OIL: If the dubiously talented director Edward D. Wood Jr. had been allowed to make a Godzilla movie, it would have been something like *Gigantis: The Fire Monster*. Compared to the great care taken to preserve the integrity of Honda's *Godzilla* even while greatly altering it, the doctoring of this picture is thoughtless, uninspired, and of bargain-basement quality. The primary goal behind the Americanization of *Gigantis* seems to be to quicken the pace, add more visual stimuli, and lighten the tone of what is admittedly a slow-moving, static, and somber movie, but the end result is sadly comic.

Hugo Grimaldi, a film editor who had worked for *Gigantis* associate producer Edmund Goldman on the war film *Surrender, Hell!* (1957) and later directed the science-fiction dud *The Human Duplicators* (1965, starring Richard Kiel) and a few other films, was hired to oversee the English dubbing of

Gigantis and to re-edit the film. Grimaldi parroted DCA's Americanization of *Rodan* (released in U.S. 1957), using the same voice actors in the principal roles (character actor Keye Luke, voice impresario Paul Frees, and George "Star Trek" Takei) and even recording the English dialogue at the same facility, Ryder Sound. Like *Rodan*, *Gigantis* is narrated by the main character, voiced by Luke. But *Gigantis* is over-narrated, with Tsukioka describing every thought in his head and nearly every action played out on screen. This is not only unnecessary, it's downright annoying after a while. The dialogue is elementary school-level English and is marred by a number of awkward and arcane expressions, probably due to Grimaldi's ignorance (he is a non-native English speaker). Some dialogue lowlights include Tsukioka's famous retort, "Ah, banana oil!" — a saying that was already way out-of-date in 1959, and which brought ridicule from more than one reviewer; and when Tsukioka suggests Kobayashi buy a present for the radio dispatchers who aided in his rescue, Kobayashi responds: "Down, boy! I guess I wouldn't honestly know what to buy," to which Tsukioka answers, "Ha-ha-ha-ha. Trying to please a woman is like swimming the ocean."

These lines are surpassed in their ineptitude only by the conference of military officials and scientists, in which Dr. Tadokoro sums up the proceedings: "Oh, this is bad! This *is* bad! Every lesson we've ever learned has told us this." Later, he pulls out a dinosaur book, the inane title of which is *Anguilla-saurus, Killer of the Living*.[13] Grimaldi's newfound rationale for the monsters' existence, which says they are from a common family of "fire monsters" that "can wipe out the human race" makes little sense. Gigantis, the "fire monster" himself, is afraid of fire. Apparently, Grimaldi and Company failed to watch the final reel, where the military traps Gigantis on the Arctic island by igniting fuel drums around him and the monster is too timid to step over the puny flames.

The dubbing wouldn't be so bad if it weren't for the incessant narration, the stupid script, and the fact that the actors speak in mock Asian accents and cartoony characterizations. Paul Frees can be heard doing an early version of his Boris Badenov character in some scenes, while the actor playing Kobayashi (possibly Frees again) sounds a lot like Daws Butler's Yogi Bear.

Compounding this insanity is the melange of stock footage inserted into the picture. Whereas *Godzilla Raids Again* opens with a main title sequence over a puffy white cloud bank backed by Sato's main title theme, *Gigantis* begins with a hackneyed, run-of-the-mill opening copied from *Rodan* and many U.S.-made giant-monster films of the 1950s. First, there is an oceanic nuclear test, then various rockets launching (including an embarrassing contraption that leaves a trail of white cigar smoke in its wake) while a narrator intones ominously about the dangers of atomic weapons and the exploration of space. After the opening credits, there is more stock footage of ships and fishermen emptying their nets as Tsukioka talks about his job as a spotter pilot. After Gigantis is believed to "bypass Osaka," as a faux newspaper headline says, there's yet more stock film of Japanese neon signs, geisha girls, and nightclub acts; some of this was probably culled from old war newsreels, as swastikas or some other sort of religious symbols appear to have been (rather sloppily) masked from the frame. At the end of the picture, after Gigantis has been buried alive, there is yet more stock footage of crowds praying for peace outside Shinto shrines, a shot of Tsukioka and Hidemi at their rooftop haunt taken from earlier in the film (with both actors looking uneasy, not relieved), and a stock shot of an ocean sunset for the dénouement. The latter changes attempt to give the film a happy ending, whereas the Japanese version ends with Tsukioka flying home in his plane, shedding tears for his dead friend.

By far the most insulting use of stock footage in the film occurs during the military-scientific conference. In the Japanese version, the shades are drawn and Dr. Yamane shows a film of Godzilla's first rampage in Tokyo the previous year. The film is silent — there is no music, no commentary by Yamane, nothing — giving it an eerie weight. But Grimaldi reworks this scene, inserting a prologue called "the formation of the world" showing Earth's dramatic evolution from a blob of fiery matter to a haven for prehistoric animals (luckily, a camera crew was there to record this for posterity). This is pieced together from old special-effects footage, some recognizable, some derived from unknown sources. A shot of several guys romping around in the desert in cardboard tyrannosaurus rex suits appears to have been lifted from *Unknown Island* (1948), while a couple of lizards pretending to be dinosaurs apparently came from *One Million BC* (1940). Adding insult to injury, nearly all of Masaru Sato's original film music was thrown out (the exception being Godzilla's arrival in Osaka Bay, and the Godzilla-vs.-Angilas battle, until the three convicts duck into the subway tunnel) in favor of themes by composers Paul Sawtell and Bert Shefter from *The Deerslayer*, *Kronos*, and *It! The Terror from Beyond Space*. The music change appears to be an attempt to quicken the film's staid pacing. For instance, when Kobayashi goes out on his maiden flight in Hokkaido, Mr. Shibeki looks wistfully out the window at the snowy bay. Grimaldi adds zippy, fast-paced music here, switching the mood from melancholy to adventurous. The sound effects were also toyed with. In several scenes where Godzilla's lips are sealed, Grimaldi added monster roars. The problem is, he stuck Angilas's roar in Godzilla's mouth, making it sound as if both monsters have the same voice.

NAME GAME: Nearly 40 years after the release of *Gigantis*, the question still looms large: Why was Godzilla's name dropped, first for *The Volcano Monsters* and subsequently for *Gigantis*?

Producer Paul Schreibman claims to have no knowledge of *The Volcano Monsters*, but he takes full "credit" for subsequently changing the monster's name to *Gigantis*, which sounds more like a glandular disorder than a monster. In fact, the producer's attempts to deceive the public went beyond merely changing the title and the name of the monster. In January 1959, when Schreibman announced the forthcoming release of *Gigantis* in a *Variety* report, he falsely told the newspaper that the film's original Japanese title was *Angirus* [sic].

"That was the second [Godzilla movie]," Schreibman said. "We called it *Gigantis* because we didn't want it to be confused with *Godzilla*." Why the hell would Schreibman *not* want people to think this was a Godzilla movie, seeing as the first one was such a hit? Moreover, surely no one who was paying attention was fooled by this silly gimmick. "I went to see *Gigantis* in Chicago in 1959, when it first opened," said Don Glut, author of *Classic Movie Monsters*, one of the first English-language books to intelligently analyze the Godzilla series. "I just thought it was another monster movie, but as soon as Gigantis showed up, I knew it was really Godzilla. There was no mistaking it. I just couldn't figure out why everyone was calling him Gigantis."

There is one final clue that further shrouds the title of *Gigantis* in mystery. Back in the 1950s and '60s, movie studios distributed hundreds of black-and-white movie publicity stills to cinema owners for hanging in theater lobbies and other purposes. In the bottom corner of these stills was usually written an abbreviation of the film title. Several publicity stills issued for *Gigantis* bear the abbreviation "GRA" (i.e., *Godzilla Raids Again*) with a line crossed through it and the letters GFM (*Gigantis: The Fire Monster*) written instead. This shred of evidence, however slight, indicates Schreibman and/or Warners at one time considered releasing the film under its proper title.

This was the only time Godzilla would be robbed of his own name in the U.S. Unfortunately, it was not the last time American distributors would tamper heavily with a Godzilla movie. Just a few years later it would happen again, to an even greater and more damaging degree. . . .

CITY-SMASHING TO THE BEAT

MASARU SATO, composer extraordinaire

If Akira Ifukube's music epitomizes the dark, ponderous, and god-like aspects of the Godzilla mythos, then composer Masaru Sato best captures the other half of the monster's character, a side that is lighter, more lively, and personalized. Sato's and Ifukube's starkly contrasting musical styles are the *yin* and *yang*, respectively, of the Godzilla series and Toho's sci-fi fare of the 1950s through the 1970s.

Unlike Ifukube, who has divided his time among films, classical music, and teaching, Sato has essentially devoted his entire career to movie music. He has written more than 300 scores over the past four-plus decades, and remains one of Japan's foremost film composers in the late 1990s. Sato hasn't exactly embraced his association with sci-fi and fantasy movies, which is understandable, for they comprise only a fraction of his life's work and have brought him little critical praise; his work for Akira Kurosawa and other A-list directors, on the other hand, made him one of the world's premiere film composers. Nevertheless, the first monster score Sato wrote was *Godzilla Raids Again*, and he has made memorable contributions to the genre with his upbeat, jazz-instilled musical stylings ever since.

Sato was born May 29, 1928, in Toru City, Hokkaido, and studied at the National Music Academy. Upon graduation, he was tutored in film composition and orchestration in Tokyo by Fumio Hayasaka, Kurosawa's principal composer during the late 1940s and early '50s. Though still a young protégé, his career accelerated rapidly in 1955; early that year, Toho gave him the nod to score the second Godzilla movie, and after Hayasaka suddenly died of tuberculosis in October, Sato completed his master's work on the scores to Kurosawa's *Record of a Living Being* and Kenji Mizoguchi's *New Tales of the Taira Clan*.

Music composer Masaru Sato in Tokyo, circa 1996.
COURTESY STUART GALBRAITH IV

In an article published in 1993 in *Toho SF Special Effects Series Volume 8*, Sato said he was honored to be chosen as the composer of *Godzilla Raids Again*. "I knew I could not do the same thing that Mr. Ifukube did [in the previous film], I had to do something unique. . . . I felt that I could express Godzilla's passion in a way that was different from Mr. Ifukube's musical style. Later on, the director [Motoyoshi Oda] praised me, saying, 'Your music sounds American.' . . . The company tried me out, but they came to the conclusion later that Mr. Ifukube's music was better suited [to the genre]."

Sato received advice from his mentor, Hayasaka, while writing the score, but he looks back on the film as one of his lesser works. "It's like listening to a kid, trying to learn," he told Stuart Galbraith IV in a 1996 interview. Even so, Sato's characteristic style was already emerging. His music for the battle between Godzilla and Angilas, which begins on Iwato Island and resumes in Osaka, is reminiscent of a duel between two archenemies rather than a giant-monster rampage. (Sato said, "I didn't think the music should suggest they were trying to kill each other. I felt that the atmosphere of a game, or competition, was needed.") Other musical cues, like the heroic march during the opening titles, are somewhat inappropriate, probably due equally to Sato's inexperience and to the lackluster quality of the film itself.

Although Sato's output in the genre is small, it still shows his wide-ranging, versatile musical talent. His music for Honda's *The H-Man* (1959), particularly in the nightclub scenes, bridges the gap between this unique film's twin genres of detective mystery and monster thriller (this music turns up again in Kurosawa's *High and Low*); the score for Senkichi Taniguchi's *The Lost World of Sinbad* (1963) is a wild ride; and his work on Jun Fukuda's two "island" Godzillas, *Godzilla versus The Sea Monster* (1966) and *Son of Godzilla* (1967), is underrated, probably because those films are widely thought to signal the start of Godzilla's decline. His score for Fukuda's *Godzilla vs. The Cosmic Monster* (1974) is also quite good, especially the theme for the three-way standoff involving Godzilla, King Seesar, and MechaGodzilla, in a style similar to Ennio Morricone's spaghetti-western themes. Unfortunately Sato, like Ifukube, has suffered the insult of having several of his scores obliterated by American distributors. Hardly any of his music for *Godzilla Raids*

Again remained in the American version of the film; the same is true for *Half Human*, and in *Godzilla versus The Sea Monster*, his wonderful main title theme was cut.

Sato proudly boasts that, at the height of the Golden Age of Japanese movies, he wrote 18 film scores in one year, an output none of his American contemporaries could ever match. Yet, despite heavy scheduling, tight time deadlines (he routinely had only one week to write music for a picture), and other constraints, Sato has produced many gems. The apex of his career is the much-imitated score for Kurosawa's *samurai* saga cum *yakuza* thriller, *Yojimbo* (1961), widely recognized as one of the best scores ever.

Although Sato never developed a strong camaraderie with director Ishiro Honda, he was a favorite of Jun Fukuda, who handpicked Sato to score many films including several outside the sci-fi and fantasy realm (Sato once remarked that Fukuda's participation in the musical score was "more sophisticated" than Honda's). Just as Ifukube's music seems perfectly matched to Honda's epic cinematic style, so Sato's music rightly suited Fukuda's fast-paced, lighthearted, and action-oriented pictures. The "Sato sound" is a combination of jazz and contemporary music à la Quincy Jones and Henry Mancini (both of whom Sato admired), incorporating modern instruments and musical idioms: it's Godzilla with a *beat*. Sato has long gone underappreciated by genre buffs who believe only Ifukube's music can accompany Godzilla, but comparisons of the two composers are unwarranted, as their styles are completely different.

Still, Sato has admitted he never quite grasped the monster the way Ifukube does. In the *Toho SF Special Effects Series* interview, he said, "I personified animals. The [monsters] started to have human personalities and characteristics. . . . Mr. Ifukube succeeded because he didn't personify Godzilla. I turned the beast into a person."

Part 2

GOLDEN AGE

The 1960s

"For a people who love the delicate beauty of flower arranging and tea ceremonies, the Japanese can dream up some of the most nightmarish monsters ever projected on movie screens. The reasons are simple: monster films are hits and great moneymakers."

— *From an Associated Press wire story, July 25, 1967*

"Japanese monster films have all the signs of catchpenny productions — faded American stars in featured roles, abysmal dubbing, uneven special effects."

— *John Baxter,* Science Fiction in the Cinema, *1970*

Three

CLASH OF THE TITANS

"Godzilla has a brain about this size."

— Dr. Arnold Johnson, holding up a children's marble

KING KONG vs. GODZILLA

RATING (OUT OF FIVE STARS): ★ ★ ★ 1/2

JAPANESE VERSION: KING KONG TAI GOJIRA. Released on August 11, 1962, by the Toho Motion Picture Company. Toho Scope, in color. Running Time: 98 minutes.

U.S. VERSION: Released on June 26, 1963, by Universal-International Inc. Premiered in New York. Running Time: 90 minutes.

STORY: The publicity-crazed advertising director for a major pharmaceuticals corporation kidnaps King Kong from his home on Faro Island in hopes of using the big ape as the company's mascot, but Kong escapes and runs wild through Japan. Meanwhile, Godzilla bursts out of an iceberg and likewise begins trampling the country; the military tries to dispose of both creatures by pitting them in a battle to the death at the foot of Mount Fuji, and after a titanic struggle, both monsters tumble into the sea.

MONKEY BUSINESS

In 1954, Godzilla was stirred from his prehistoric slumber on the ocean floor by a hydrogen-bomb test and promptly laid waste to Tokyo in a symbolic acting-out of Japan's — and all the world's — fears of mass destruction. The great monster was a harbinger of mankind's ultimate, self-inflicted doom, a mythical dragon made flesh in the modern world to issue a warning that the nuclear age may close the book on human history.

But, despite his ominous origins, Godzilla has undergone drastic personality changes over the years. In 1962, when Toho finally woke Godzilla from hibernation to face off with his most famous and most formidable foe, the Monster King resembled his old self only in the physical sense. Seven years inside an iceberg had given the surly saurian a newfound sense of humor. Oh, sure, he still trashed Japan with abandon, and still rassled roughly with his enemies, but now he did so with a wink in his eye and a comic bravura. Meet Godzilla, the Movie Star.

King Kong vs. Godzilla marked a number of firsts for the Godzilla series. It was the first entry filmed in the Toho Scope wide-screen format (Toho's version of Cinemascope), the first in Eastmancolor, and the first with a stereophonic (Perspecta Sound) soundtrack. Perhaps most importantly, it was the first Godzilla movie to be produced in cooperation with an American company, a practice Toho would engage in often during the 1960s to make its films more salable abroad. This film is unique, however, because at its inception it was not a Godzilla movie — far from it. The genesis of *King Kong vs. Godzilla* was not, as might be suspected, the brainchild of Eiji Tsuburaya but of an American special-effects genius, the great **Willis O'Brien**. The final product notwithstanding (some people consider the film a classic, others call it a travesty), the story of how one of O'Brien's last filmic ideas evolved into this picture is tragic, and shows how readily the cigar-smoking Hollywood deal-makers of the 1950s and '60s would disregard the hopes and dreams of a great filmmaker to make a buck for themselves.

O'Brien (1886–1962), affectionately called "Obie" by his fans, is best known for creating the stop-motion animation effects made famous in *The Lost World* (1925), *King Kong*, *Son of King Kong*, and *Mighty Joe Young*. By 1960, however, O'Brien's glory days were behind him, although he was still working in the special-effects field as a technical advisor on *The Black Scorpion* (1957), *The Giant Behemoth* (1959), a remake of *The Lost World* (1960), and other pictures. In 1960, no doubt inspired by the plethora of monster-on-the-loose movies released in the 1950s and by *King Kong*'s successful TV revival, O'Brien decided to try and bring America's most famous monster back to life in a color production called *King Kong vs. Frankenstein*.

According to Don Shay, publisher of *Cinefex* magazine and an authority on O'Brien's work, O'Brien wrote a brief story outline in which a descendant of the Frankenstein clan creates a new monster in a laboratory hidden deep in an African jungle. The monster escapes, kills its creator, and destroys the laboratory, and when news of the creature makes its way to America, several savvy promoters set out to capture it and bring it back to San Francisco to put it on display. Simultaneously, another group sets out to Skull Island to capture King Kong. Worldwide attention focuses on San Francisco as plans are made to show off the two monsters, side by side, in a huge stadium. The creatures (of course) break free from their cages and instead fight to the death in the streets, wrecking much of the city's renowned architecture in the process. The story reportedly ended with the Frankenstein monster riding a cable car.

To help sell his story, O'Brien made dozens of watercolor illustrations and sketches of the two monsters, some of which are reprinted in Steve Archer's *Willis O'Brien: Special Effects Genius* (McFarland, 1993). The Frankenstein monster in this story bore no resemblance to the creature portrayed earlier by Boris Karloff — it had elephantine skin, a stubby, bald head, and long, ape-like arms, and, standing over 20 feet tall and weighing 34 tons, it was capable of going toe-to-toe with Kong. O'Brien showed his story and illustrations to Daniel O'Shea, an attorney at RKO Radio Pictures, hoping to obtain the rights to use Kong in the film. O'Shea liked O'Brien's idea and not only gave it his blessing, he introduced O'Brien to **John Beck**, a producer. O'Shea probably thought he was doing O'Brien a favor, and that Beck could help bring the project to fruition. As it turned out, Beck ultimately sacrificed O'Brien's ideas for the sake of cash. O'Brien got screwed, but *King Kong vs. Godzilla* would not have happened otherwise.

Beck (1910–1993) had something of a storied career in Hollywood, although he was hardly a major film producer. His most famous film is *Harvey* (1950), starring James Stewart, and his other productions include *One Touch of Venus* (1948) with Ava Gardner, *The Singing Nun* (1966) with Debbie Reynolds, and *The Private Navy of Sgt. O'Farrell* (1968) with Bob Hope. Born in Pomona, California, Beck went to New York while still a youth and became a talent agent under the tutelage of Vaudeville impresario Harry Weber. Beck became general manager of International Pictures in 1942, at the young age of 32, and supervised that company's merger with Universal Pictures to form Universal-International, which released many monster pictures in the 1950s, including *Creature from the Black Lagoon* and *The Deadly Mantis*. It was under the U-I banner that *King Kong vs. Godzilla* was later produced, although Beck was working as an independent producer by that time.

Beck's first task was to find a proven science-fiction screenwriter to flesh out O'Brien's story into a full treatment that could be pitched to the studios for financial backing. He hired George Worthing Yates, who penned an impressive list of sci-fi and monster classics like *Them!*, *It Came from Beneath the Sea*, *Earth vs. The Flying Saucers*, and *War of the Colossal Beast*. Yates renamed the Frankenstein monster "Prometheus" and changed the title of the story to *King Kong vs. Prometheus* (a reference to Mary Shelley's classic novel *Frankenstein, or The Modern Prometheus*). On November 2, 1960, a blurb in *Variety* announced that Beck and O'Brien had signed a contract for production of a sequel to *King Kong*, titled *King Kong and Prometheus* (sic).

The newspaper said Beck had talked to a director named Jerry Guran (possibly a pseudonym for Nathan Juran, director of *The Deadly Mantis* and others) about the possibility of making the picture the following summer.

After failing to sell the film in Hollywood, Beck looked overseas for a backer and talked to studios in Italy and other countries before eventually striking a deal with Toho in Japan. The deal, of course, had little to do with *King Kong vs. Prometheus*; Toho was merely interested in acquiring the use of the King Kong character from RKO and Beck. While these negotiations were going on, Beck "neglected to keep Obie informed of the progress," according to Don Shay. "Obie phoned him regularly and was repeatedly assured that he would be notified when anything developed." In the meantime, O'Brien was busy supervising the special effects for the famous fire-escape sequence at the end of Stanley Kramer's *It's a Mad, Mad, Mad, Mad World* (1962). While O'Brien was working on that film, Shay says, the trade papers reported that "Beck, who had not contacted Obie for many months, was at the Toho Studios in Tokyo putting the final touches on *King Kong vs. Godzilla*. . . . Obie was heartbroken. All the time, effort, and expense of developing his story had come to less than nothing."

On November 8, 1962, O'Brien died at his home in Los Angeles at age 76. In Archer's book, a nephew of O'Brien's says a lawsuit was filed (however, it is not known when or against whom, although the defendant was presumably John Beck) over the use of O'Brien's ideas in *King Kong vs. Godzilla*, for which he was neither credited nor paid. The case was dropped due to attorney costs.

COMIC RELIEF: A flea-bitten monkey costume passed off as the great King Kong. A narrator/newsman who interrupts at every opportunity, slowing a fast-paced action film to a halt. A clowning Godzilla who joyfully flails his arms, making a silly "clackety-clack" sound, every time he singes Kong's hairy hide. An ominous quote from Shakespeare's *Hamlet* ("There are more things in Heaven and Earth, Horatio . . .") that inexplicably opens the film.

At first glance, it's easy to see why *King Kong vs. Godzilla* doesn't show up on many critics' lists of the all-time greatest monster movies — on the contrary, it has been featured in books like the Medved brothers' *Golden Turkey Awards* and Michael Sauter's *The Worst Movies of All Time*. Devotees of the original *King Kong* usually dismiss the film for obvious reasons: Willis O'Brien's Kong was a masterwork of stop-motion techniques, and portraying the monster via the man-in-suit method is, in their view, unforgivable. But, like many Japanese monster movies, *King Kong vs. Godzilla* has suffered the ill repute of a low-class production in the Western world primarily because its U.S. distributor tampered heavily with it prior to its English-language release. Admittedly, that sub-par King Kong suit has a lot to do with the film's negative reputation. But it was John Beck who botched the film and sucked nearly all the fun out of it, because there was one simple thing he apparently did not understand. *King Kong vs. Godzilla* is a satire, and a clever one at that.

It's too bad the original, Japanese version of the film has never been (and likely, never will be) shown in America, for it would become very clear why some Japanese fans consider it the apex of the Godzilla series. Filmed in glorious wide-screen, with an abundance of special-effects scenes, a great ensemble cast, and a booming musical score by maestro Akira Ifukube, the film was, in its day, a first-class, big-budget Japanese production. It was released as part of Toho's 30th-anniversary celebration, alongside films like Akira Kurosawa's *Sanjuro* and Hiroshi Inagaki's *Chushingura*, both considered classics today.

By the early 1960s, the postwar gloom that hung over Japan during Godzilla's first rampage was replaced by newfound economic prosperity and guarded optimism under Prime Minister Hayato Ikeda's reform programs. Just as director Ishiro Honda captured Japan's uneasiness about nuclear testing in the first Godzilla movie, he now seized upon another current social dilemma: Rampant commercialism. Television was still a relatively new phenomenon in Japan in 1962 (the first broadcasts occurred in 1953), and ratings wars were turning the medium into a circus. Honda and screenwriter **Shinichi Sekizawa**, authoring the first of several great Godzilla scripts, deftly fashioned intersecting story lines to create two movies within one: The first is a great parody of Japanese corporate greed and ruthlessness in the advertising age, symbolized by Mr. Tako, the foolhardy publicity man willing to risk the safety of an entire nation to hype his company's products through a TV program; the second, lesser half is a stock giant-monster scenario, with the hero rushing to save his girl from the two beasties and the government and military trying to restore order. Ingeniously, Honda used Ichiro Arishima

(Tako), Tadao Takashima (Sakurai), and Yu Fujiki (Furue), three actors well-known in Toho's wildly successful *salaryman* comedies (a type of film popular in the late '50s and early '60s, satirizing Japanese corporate life and focusing on sly mid-level employees outsmarting their dimwitted bosses) for the funny elements, while the monster-movie plot features *kaiju eiga* stars like Kenji Sahara (Fujita) and Akihiko Hirata (as the defense minister). These dueling themes cause the tone of the film to shift wildly at times, making it hard to take the picture seriously. But then, *King Kong vs. Godzilla* wasn't intended to carry the thematic weight of the original *Godzilla*, or even *King Kong*. As Honda said, "The main thing I wanted in this picture was enjoyment." On that level, the picture is a success — though flawed, it is wildly entertaining.

King Kong vs. Godzilla was made just two years after the Security Treaty between the U.S. and Japan was revised (in 1960), prompting widespread political demonstrations in Japan, and it has been speculated that the film was Honda's veiled treatise on the state of relations between the two nations at that time. This theory has even been offered by people who worked on the film. In the book *Godzilla Days*, Teisho Arikawa says a fundamental conflict emerged between Honda, who saw Kong as a stand-in for America and Godzilla for Japan, and Eiji Tsuburaya, who "didn't care about the relationship between America and Japan, [and] just wanted to show the spectacle of these two big monsters fighting." According to Arikawa, *King Kong vs. Godzilla* was the first film in which Tsuburaya made a conscious effort to appeal to children's sensibilities and broaden the genre's audience, an approach that was favored by the front office and inevitably won out. Even members of the special-effects crew, Arikawa says, thought Tsuburaya had gone "overboard" with his new, lighthearted approach to monsters, and during the shoot, many of them "couldn't believe" some of the things Tsuburaya asked them to do — such as the scene where Godzilla and Kong volley a boulder back and forth.

Honda, the faithful company man, bowed to the whims of the marketplace and witnessed his infernal monster reduced to a slapstick saurian. Nearly 30 years later, Honda recalled his dilemma in an interview with *Tokyo Journal*. "There was a huge fall in the average age of Godzilla fans, so Toho decided it would be a good idea to make him more heroic and less scary. I didn't like the idea, but I couldn't really oppose it. . . . We didn't have many rights

then. Once you made a film, it became company property."

Ironically, Toho's dumbing-down of Godzilla in this film mirrors the very things that Honda and Sekizawa were criticizing in the television industry. The timely, underlying message was, Honda said, that "nothing good" will come from television programming designed only to out-hype the competition rather than entertain and inform. "All a medicine company would have to do is just produce good medicines, you know?" he told another interviewer. "But the company doesn't think that way. They think they'll get ahead of their competitors if they can use a monster to promote their product. Mr. Sekizawa satirized social conditions well. That was his specialty."

Ichiro Arishima has such a romp portraying Tako that it's easy to forget that he, not Godzilla, is the true villain of the story. Arishima (1916–1987) was a great comic actor whose career on stage and screen spanned five decades. In an obituary in *Markalite* magazine, Guy Tucker said Arishima "had an uncanny aura of pathos about him which invariably won him tremendous audience sympathy. . . . He was even likened to the great Charlie Chaplin in his deft ability to evoke both laughter and tears. . . ." Throughout the film, Arishima steals the show as the goofball, media-crazed publicity pusher. In Tako's mind, Kong is not a god, a monster, or even a gigantic animal, but strictly a marketing device — in one scene, he discusses how he'll get Kong to smile so he can use the monster's hairy mug in advertisements promoting the company's products. One of the script's shortcomings, though, is that Tako never pays for his brazenness. As the monsters literally chew up the scenery, Tako seems oblivious to the fact that he is responsible for a catastrophic loss of property (and lives, although human casualties are unmentioned), and at the end of the picture, when Kong and Godzilla float away, you get the idea that Tako will probably just go back to his office and dream up some other new stunt. It's as if, in Honda and Sekizawa's opinion, corporate publicity hounds and TV mavens are unredeemable.

This is a much faster-moving film than the first two Godzillas and most of Toho's early *kaiju eiga*. Orchestrated by Ishiro Honda's taut direction and the brisk pacing of film editor Reiko Kaneko (who later worked on Akira Kurosawa's *Dodes'ka-den*), the action is fueled not only by the monsters but also by the human cast, who constantly find themselves chasing after or running away from gigantic creatures. As in virtually all Japanese genre films, it has an abundance of characters, many of whom have relatively little to do with furthering the plot. Thus, the star and hero of the film, Tadao Takashima (as Sakurai), has only slightly more time onscreen than anyone else and shares much of it bantering with his comic sidekick, Yu Fujiki (Furue). Having worked together as a comedic duo in films since the late 1950s, actors Takashima and Fujiki have a brilliant onscreen chemistry and easy rapport that contrasts well with Arishima's frantic energy.

By comparison, the subplot involving young lovers Fujita (Kenji Sahara, star of *Rodan* and *The H-Man*, reduced here to a supporting role) and Fumiko (Mie Hama) seems rather obviously inserted into the story to provide Godzilla with an identifiable near-victim and Kong with a requisite female love interest. When Kong snatches Fumiko out of a subway train (what a coincidence!), the human-ape-human love triangle is broken not by some heroic rescue performed by Fujita, but by Fumiko's brother, who has the smarts to put the giant to sleep; Fujita uses his super-wire to transport Kong away to Mount Fuji, but he is a mere accessory to the heroics, not the hero himself. Why Honda and Sekizawa chose such a contrived scenario is anyone's guess. This being a King Kong movie, it seems obvious that Sakurai and Fumiko should have been lovers rather than siblings, and that Fumiko should have accompanied the expedition to Faro; there, the gigantic gorilla's unrequited love for her would begin, building to a more effective dramatic climax. Nevertheless, Hama and Eiko Wakabayashi (as Tamiye, Fumiko's pie-dropping, sandwich-eating friend), both rising young sexy starlets at the time, are enjoyable, though mere cogs in the plot machinery.

Merian C. Cooper's *King Kong* was a warning against mankind's desire to harness Nature for his own personal gain, but in this picture the great beasts are mere prehistoric palookas. Still, there are numerous homages to the RKO Kong. Faro Island is, of course, a stand-in for Skull Island, but it pales in comparison, with nearly all the action taking place on a rather obvious indoor soundstage. Kong breaks free from his captors and goes off on a rampage, just as in Cooper's film, and peers through the windows of Fumiko's subway car (a tip of the hat to Kong peeping into Fay Wray's window in the original). Hama is outstanding in the damsel-in-distress sequences — she is believably delirious with fear as she splashes through a stream bed, trying helplessly to escape Godzilla; later, while in Kong's grasp, she belts out some very respectable

screams, comparable even to Wray's immortal shrieks. The Diet Building, Kong's obligatory, scalable skyscraper, hardly matches up to the Empire State Building, though. Not only is it too small to present a serious climb for this new, supersized Kong (just a few steps, and he's on top of it), but it is just unbelievable that the building would support the immense creature's weight without crumbling to bits. In fact, there is no mention of how Kong grew to be so big (his height was boosted to 45 meters in this film, while Willis O'Brien's original stood just four stories tall), or where he came from, and little sense of the majestic, mysterious beast that was the RKO Kong. By the time *King Kong vs. Godzilla* was made, the Toho universe had developed its own mythology, and monsters were an everyday fact of life — a rationale for their existence was rarely offered.

Godzilla fares much better than Kong in this picture, retaining his mean streak if not his atomic allegory. The scene where Fumiko and the other passengers aboard the express train frantically disembark and flee the oncoming monster, ending with Godzilla's huge feet trampling the locomotive, is both a reference to the original *Godzilla* and a classic scene in genre history. Godzilla's ponderous plundering of the Arctic military base and the Japanese countryside contrast nicely with his swift-moving, agile fighting tactics against Kong in the finale. There is one bit of revisionist G-history in the film, however, that is never explained: Somehow, the military succeeds in preventing Godzilla from entering the heart of Tokyo with an electrical barrier. Hey, wait! Just eight years earlier, Godzilla *incinerated* another high-voltage roadblock en route to demolishing the downtown. What gives?

BATTLE OF THE CENTURY: As his jungle sleeping potion wears off, King Kong is Dumbo-dropped onto the slope of majestic Mount Fuji. Waiting below is his ultimate enemy, a gigantic reptile instinctively stalking him across Japan. The battle royal begins as soon as Kong hits the ground, colliding with Godzilla and sending the dragon rolling downhill. Godzilla rights himself and gives chase as Kong scales the mountainside. Ducking underneath a giant cavern, the great ape hides from his foe, then launches a sneak-attack, grabbing Godzilla by the tail, briefly rendering the lizard helpless. Kong hurls a gigantic boulder at Godzilla, who returns the volley with a smack of his tail. Godzilla keeps his enemy at bay with his white-hot breath, but Kong body-slams him and the two beasts tumble downhill, with Kong slamming his head into a rock, knocking himself unconscious. Godzilla begins building a burial mound on his vanquished foe, but Kong awakens and charges Godzilla, who quickly repels Kong with a head butt and a mighty, two-footed kick to the gut. Kong again seems down for the count, and Godzilla celebrates by torching the forest to ignite a funeral pyre. But an electrical storm erupts, recharging the mighty ape, whose fingertips glow with new-found energy. Kong grabs Godzilla by the tail and swings him mightily through the air. The battle rages through the city of Atami, and ends only when the monsters, deadlocked in mortal combat, tumble over a cliff into the Pacific.

The special effects in *King Kong vs. Godzilla*, particularly the stupendous slugfest at the climax, are a veritable symphony of Tsuburaya techniques — suitmation, miniatures, pyrotechnics, wire works, optical effects, and even a bit of stop-motion animation thrown in for good measure.

The monster costumes, to begin with, show both the best and worst of Akira Watanabe and Teizo Toshimitsu's suit designing and building abilities. The *Kin-Goji* Godzilla suit is one of the best in the entire series — more bulky, ominous, and powerful than the streamlined suit deployed in *Godzilla Raids Again* and recapturing the monolithic proportions of the first Godzilla, while still flexible enough to allow suit actor Haruo Nakajima to perform full-body rolls and other very physical stunts. This being the first Godzilla movie in color, the monster is painted a slightly darker shade of gray than in the first two films. He has a long, slinky tail (used to great effect throughout), large, prominent dorsal fins, and an enlarged head with thick eyebrow ridges and a pronounced snout. When viewed from a profile or three-quarter angle, Godzilla looks absolutely menacing; however, when glimpsed from the front in a few shots, the monster has mumpy cheeks and a rounded muzzle that are less striking. This particular incarnation of Godzilla has remained a worldwide fan favorite throughout the decades, and its design was the basis for a popular Godzilla model kit sold in the U.S. by Aurora for many years.

King Kong, on the other hand, leaves much to be desired. Tsuburaya had wanted his suitmation Kong to match or even surpass the image of the stop-motion original, but according to Teisho Arikawa, the sculptors had a hard time coming up with a Kong design that pleased Tsuburaya. Their first Kong model was fat, with coarse hair and long legs and arms, looking more cute and cuddly than Willis O'Brien's horrific beast. Several more were made before Tsuburaya approved the design ultimately used in the film, from which two Kong costumes were built, each of which can be easily identified from scene to scene by the attentive viewer. One suit had a flat head, short, human-length arms that enabled the actor inside to scratch his head, throw boulders, and wrestle with Godzilla at close range, and perpetually open white eyes. The second one had a triangular head, elongated ape arms for chest-pounding, and moving eyelids that flutter and close whenever Kong is knocked cold by the soma-berry juice. The problem with "Kyoto Kong," as he was dubbed by *Famous Monsters of Filmland*, is that he is just plain unconvincing. His shabby fur looks unkempt like an old rug; his dopey face, with bushy eyebrows and crooked teeth, hardly instills fear; worst of all, his dumpy physique resembles an out-of-shape, middle-aged man, with a sagging chest and pot belly.

In addition to the costumes, models of Kong and Godzilla, both about one meter high, were built. The Kong model was used for the scene where Kong is airlifted by balloons, and both models were used for Godzilla's famous kung-fu kick to Kong's stomach (achieved with stop-motion animation rather than suit acting). Small hand puppets of Kong and Godzilla, with movable arms, were also used for long shots of Kong entering Tokyo and of the monsters battling atop a ridgeline. Finally, a puppet of Godzilla's head was created for several tight shots of the monster emitting his ray (done, as in the first two films, with a liquid mist sprayed from a nozzle in his mouth), but these shots were excised from the final film and appeared only in the prerelease trailers.

In keeping with the film's over-the-top antics, the final, titanic struggle between Godzilla and Kong is staged as the World Heavyweight Monster Championship. But unlike the fighting tactics used by Godzilla and Angilas in the previous film — stalking, charging, biting — here the monsters freely borrow their moves from professional wrestling, a sport gaining popularity in Japan at the time. Nakajima and Shoichi "Solomon" Hirose, the actor inside the Kong suit, choreographed the final battle sequence themselves. "I used the elements of pro wrestling, as well as the movements of the original Godzilla," Nakajima recalled years later. "I modified the way he moved, so it was quite difficult. None of the staff, including Mr. Tsuburaya, knew anything about staging a fight." Katsumi Tezuka, the stuntman who worked inside the Godzilla suit briefly in *Godzilla* and then portrayed Angilas in *Gigantis*, also has a minor part in this film, playing Godzilla in the scene where the monster breaks out of the iceberg.

Though Godzilla and King Kong are the mon-stars of this film, one other creature must be mentioned, for it is more realistic and horrifying than the titular beasts. The gigantic octopus, which attempts to sneak a nip of the Faro Island berry juice and nearly feasts on a native boy and his mother in the process, is a slimy, loathsome creature and one of Tsuburaya's best creations. The monster was actually created with three different effects: Several live octopi were employed for the shots of the mollusk attacking the bamboo shack, while a rather obviously fake rubber one (looking as if it's coated with Saran Wrap) was used where the creature attacks Kong "face-hugger" style, and a very well-executed stop-motion animated model of a tentacle was created for the shot where the octopus grabs a hapless Faro native. Tsuburaya's crew went to a beach near Tokyo, to shoot the sequences requiring a live animal. There they constructed the miniature set of the shack on a small platform, and waited for fishermen to arrive with the requested octopus. The crew actually spent several days trying to get the right shots, as the weary octopi, having just been plucked from the drink, were none too eager to act for the cameras. The frustrated filmmakers poked the animals with sticks and blew warm wind on them to get them to move in the right direction, but in the end, the miniature shack was taken back to the studio and filming was completed there. Teruyoshi Nakano, a member of the effects team, recalled in an interview with *Cult Movies* that after the sequence was completed, Tsuburaya ate one of the octopi!

Unlike the first two Godzillas and other early Toho monster pictures, there are few scenes of urban destruction in this film, but there is lots of miniature work nevertheless. Some fine examples include the freighter that transports King Kong to Japan, which was actually a 10-meter-long model propelled through the water tank by a built-in motor (and complemented nicely by a full-scale set of the ship's rear deck, left over from a Toho war movie); the earthmovers and other construction vehicles that dig a gigantic Godzilla-trap; the miniature Tsugaru Express train, complete with silhouettes of the passengers inside; the Koraku-En amusement park, which Kong gleefully flattens; the Japanese countryside around Mount Fuji, serving as the final battleground, complete with dense forestry that goes up in a glorious display of pyrotechnical fire as the monsters struggle; and the great miniature of the Atami Castle, a roughly two-meter-tall model that crumbles when Kong and Godzilla face off on opposite sides, and which was constructed and filmed on an outdoor set next to the big pool on the Toho back lot. Two shots involving miniature people — a stiff doll of Tako in safari outfit, lowered onto the deck of the freighter and a Fumiko doll with moving arms and legs, which Kong clutches in his hand — fail miserably, however.

By the early 1960s, Tsuburaya had greatly improved his ability to produce complex composite shots, now that color film was the standard and the blue-screen traveling matte process had replaced the old-school in-the-camera matte process used in the first two Godzillas. Unfortunately, for reasons unknown, the composite work in *King Kong vs. Godzilla* is nothing amazing, and there are several shots wherein the telltale blue matte lines are visible. The best composite shots occur when Kong breaks through the rampart on Faro Island and a gaggle of tiny natives flee at his feet, and during the *Gulliver's Travels*-like scene when the soldiers (actually hollow cel-animation silhouettes composited into the picture) strap harnesses onto the sleeping, subtly breathing Kong, preparing him for airlifting. The worst ones are seen when the Faro Islanders fling spears and torches at the gigantic octopus, a scene apparently botched in the planning process. When the spears and other projectiles fly through the air, they cast obvious shadows upon the background plate — apparently, the shot was done with rear-screen projection rather than blue-screen matte photography. What's worse, the camera errantly pans from side to side in the octopus footage, making it look like the octopus, the trees, and the earth are swaying back and forth in front of the natives. Finally, even though there are no fighter jets or flying monsters, the wire-works crew gets its share of the work in the scenes of Kong's balloon ride, the monsters' boulder toss, and — most impressively — Kong's swinging-around of Godzilla by the tail (interestingly, it appears that the Godzilla suit is empty in this shot, but Haruo Nakajima has said in published interviews that he was indeed inside the suit, hanging from wires).

Since setting the standard for *kaiju eiga* musical scores with *Godzilla*, Akira Ifukube had gone on to become Toho's premier composer in the genre, having perfected his trademark military marches, horror themes, and requiems in *Rodan*, *The Mysterians*,

IT'S CATACLYSMIC!!!
IT'S CATASTROPHIC!!!
THE TITANIC TERRIFYING BATTLE BETWEEN
THE MIGHTIEST MONSTERS OF ALL TIME
KING KONG VS. . . . GODZILLA!

The great Godzilla, blazing a trail of terror to his Japanese homeland! Roaring defiance to the only enemy on Earth strong enough to challenge him — the unconquerable King Kong! Giant gorilla god of this tropical south seas paradise, where sensuous maidens offer themselves in ritual sacrifice to his brute embrace!

King Kong vs. Godzilla! Heading for their colossal collision! Shattering every obstacle that stands between them in the most fantastic rampage of annihilation ever recorded on film!

See King Kong stamp Tokyo to the ground, holding a beautiful girl in his grasp. See Godzilla destroy an entire army! See King Kong trapped by the blazing barrier of a billion volts! But nothing, nobody can stop the great showdown, when King Kong and Godzilla meet to fight for survival of the fittest!

SO GIGANTIC IN SCOPE
IT DWARFS EVERY WONDER THE SCREEN HAS EVERY SHOWN BEFORE
DON'T MISS THE BATTLE OF THE CENTURIES!
KING KONG VS. GODZILLA!

— *From U-I's theatrical trailer for* King Kong vs. Godzilla

Battle in Outer Space, Varan the Unbelievable. Here, his return to the Godzilla series is triumphant. It was in this film that Ifukube introduced Godzilla's horror theme, a new variation of the monster's motif from the original film that begins with a thunderous, dissonant 12-tone passage. His Faro Island chant, which plays under the opening credits and also serves as Kong's motif, sets the picture's adventurous pace and is a fine example of Ifukube's musical instincts and versatility. His music for the appearance of the gigantic octopus is also fittingly grotesque and eerie. Unfortunately, nearly all of Ifukube's music would be obliterated from the soundtrack when the film was imported to America.

RESTORING A CLASSIC: For a long time it seemed the original, uncut Japanese version of *King Kong vs. Godzilla* was never again to be seen in its full glory. When Toho Video released the film to home video in 1985, something seemed dreadfully wrong. Entire segments of the movie, many running several minutes in length, had apparently faded badly to a brownish-red hue and suffered from severe scratching and wear.

Was this the best print of the film available from the Toho archives?

As recounted by *kaiju eiga* historian August Ragone in *Video Watchdog Special Edition #2*, the Toho Video release of *King Kong vs. Godzilla* was pieced together from a mint-condition 35-millimeter print of the Champion Festival (a series of Toho kiddie matinees in the late 1960s and early '70s) version of the film, which was edited down to about 70 minutes. To restore the film to its original running time, the edited-out footage was replaced, using another print that was badly faded — resulting in the inconsistent quality of the video. Later, in the mid-1990s, Toho Video reissued the film on VHS tape and Laser Disc, with mint-condition image quality from beginning to end. According to Ragone, Toho Video used a new telecine (film-to-video transfer) technology to digitally enhance the faded-out parts of the movie; other sources indicate that Toho simply discovered, at long last, a full-length, good-quality print of the film in its archives. Whichever is true, *King Kong vs. Godzilla* was restored to its original luster once and for all.

GOING A.P.E.

The Americanization of King Kong vs. Godzilla

Perhaps the most well-known "fact" about *King Kong vs. Godzilla* is that there are supposedly two different endings, depending on where you see the movie. In the U.S. version, the story goes, the American ape King Kong wins the battle, and in the Far East the Japanese Juggernaut Godzilla gets the nod. It's not known exactly where this falsehood originated, although it was published in *Famous Monsters of Filmland* as far back as the early 1960s. What's even more amusing is how widespread the double-ending myth is. For example, the "Genus III" edition of *Trivial Pursuit* asks, "Who won the Japanese version of *King Kong vs. Godzilla*?" and claims that "Godzilla" is the correct answer. The erroneous legend has even been misreported by writers for reputable news organizations — in the 1980s a *Los Angeles Times* columnist recounted seeing the film on late-night TV in a Tokyo hotel room and, much to his surprise, Godzilla emerged victorious. He must have been drinking some good *sake*, for as many latter-day Godzilla fans have (perhaps disappointedly) come to find out, the ending is the same in both versions: King Kong swims back toward Faro Island, and Godzilla sinks to the ocean's depths. Kong appears to be the winner, although the outcome of the monsters' fight is somewhat ambiguous. At best, Godzilla settles for a draw.

What *is* different about the Japanese and U.S. versions of *King Kong vs. Godzilla* is not the ending, but most everything else.

The exact details of the deal between Toho, John Beck, and RKO are elusive, but several things about it are clear. The only money exchanged in the deal appears to have been paid by Toho to the Americans, not vice versa, for the studio had to scale back the production in order to afford its end of the bargain. "RKO had the rights [to Kong], and Toho leased the rights to the character, with a guarantee of 80 million yen [about $200,000]," actor Yu Fujiki told Stuart Galbraith IV in a 1996 interview. "King Kong was a really expensive actor! We planned to shoot the film on location in Sri Lanka, but because of RKO's guarantee, we couldn't afford to let Kong leave Japan! It was decided to shoot the island scenes on Oshima, an island just outside of Tokyo. King Kong took all the money!"

Thus, John Beck apparently had no financial stake in the production of *King Kong vs. Godzilla*. Furthermore, he had no input in the script, for when he first saw the completed film he didn't know what to make of it. On August 1, 1962, 10 days before the picture opened in Japan, Beck attended a private screening on the Toho Studios lot accompanied by two representatives of Warner Bros. Pictures who were interested in acquiring the theatrical distribution rights from Beck. This was the second time Beck saw the movie, and according to a letter one of the Warners men, J.E. Dagal, sent to his superiors in America, "Johnny Beck was not quite enthusiastic from the first screening, probably because he does not understand the Japanese language."[14] Beck was "more enthusiastic after the second screening," after hearing an interpretation of the Japanese dialogue.

Toho was so eager to get King Kong that it not only paid for the character, it agreed to give John Beck the lucrative theatrical and television distribution rights to *King Kong vs. Godzilla* in the U.S., Canada, Alaska, the U.K., and Israel, while Toho retained the Far East rights. Beck also obtained permission to produce his own American version of the film via re-editing, as was done with the first two Godzillas. Upon returning home to Hollywood, Beck continued to shop the picture to interested distributors and eventually sold it to his old cronies at Universal-International, as reported in *Variety* on April 29, 1963. Even though it had no involvement in the making of the film, Universal engineered a sweetheart deal under which it has retained copyrights to the U.S. version of *King Kong vs. Godzilla* for nearly 40 years. As of 1998, the picture's U.S. rights had not reverted to Toho, as they had with every other film in the Godzilla series. A similar deal was struck when Universal distributed *King Kong Escapes* in 1968; that film, too, is still copyrighted by Universal in the U.S.

In early 1963, months before the Universal deal was announced, Beck set to work on his American version of the film. Following the successful example set by *Godzilla: King of the Monsters!*, he wanted to give *King Kong vs. Godzilla* an American frame of reference, with a U.S. newsman interpreting the story for the audience, but Beck lacked the ingenuity and (apparently) the financial resources to match the quality of the original film. His first move was to hire two struggling Hollywood writers, **Paul Mason** and **Bruce Howard**, both of whom were at low ebbs in their respective writing careers, to work up an American script. Mason, a dramatic writer, had received his first feature film credit as a co-screenwriter on *Angel Baby* (1962) starring George Hamilton, but was having no luck finding further movie assignments. Howard was a stand-up comic from Brooklyn who had written for Jonathan Winters, Sid Caesar, Carl Reiner, and Victor Borge and was a onetime roommate and writing partner of Woody Allen's (he was best man at Allen's first wedding). In the years since, both went on to successful Hollywood careers: Mason became a producer, and later an executive vice-president at Viacom Entertainment, while Howard became a member of Sherwood Schwartz's clan and wrote for most every major TV sitcom in the 1960s and '70s including *Gilligan's Island*, *The Brady Bunch* (including the "Jan needs glasses" episode), *Good Times*, and *The Dukes of Hazzard*.

While awaiting better days, Mason and Howard became temporary partners and supported themselves by contributing ideas to Mort Walker's *Beetle Bailey* comic strip, earning $50 for each one. "One day, Paul came to me and he said, 'I got an assignment,' but he seemed reluctant to tell me about it," Howard said in a 1996 interview. "He had been introduced to the producer, John Beck, by a friend who knew he needed work. So he told me, 'They've got this *King Kong vs. Godzilla*, it's made in Japan, and they want to put an American story to it.' I said, 'Hey, great! It sounds like fun!' But he wanted to do it himself because it didn't pay that much. He told me, 'It only pays $3,500 for five weeks' work,' and I said, 'Hey, we're partners! You have to let me in on it!'"

Mason and Howard split the fee, taking $1,750 apiece, but they ended up working on the film longer than expected. "With all the time I spent on that, I probably made something like $40 a week, but I was very excited about it because it was my first feature-film assignment," Howard said. "We didn't really change the story, we just added the idea that everything was being reported on a newscast. I remember that I named the reporter Eric Carter, after an old friend of mine named Goldstein from Brighton Beach who wanted to be an actor — Eric Carter was his stage name. I got in other aspects of the production too, and even dropped in when they were recording the dialogue and did some of the voices in the picture. I'd be hanging around the recording studio and if they needed an extra voice for a soldier or a police officer — "Hey, move that truck along," that sort of thing — they'd have me do it because I had experience as a performer. It was a tremendous education, and a blast."

To film the new scenes scripted by Mason and Howard, Beck hired a director named **Thomas Montgomery**, which is likely an Alan Smithee-like pseudonym for someone who didn't want his name attached to the production. If so, it's understandable, because the American footage incorporated into *King Kong vs. Godzilla* is nothing to put on a director's résumé. A quartet of low-rent thesps were tapped to essay the men who relay the story's earth-shaking events to the world: Michael Keith, who has no other feature-film credits, played the narrator-reporter Eric Carter; James Yagi, a bit player who portrayed Japanese soldiers in several early-1960s war movies and had a nonspeaking part in *The Manchurian Candidate* (1962), plays Tokyo correspondent Yutaka Omura; the late character actor Harry Holcombe, best known as "grandpa" in commercials for Country Time lemonade during the 1970s and 80s, shows up as Arnold Johnson, head of the Museum of Natural History in New York; and an unbilled actor suffers the indignity of playing Ricardo Enfanta, a news correspondent in Chile, without screen credit. The newscast scenes were shot over a few days on a rented soundstage at Samuel Goldwyn Studios in Hollywood, but they could just as well have been shot in a garage. The production values are bare-bones, with Keith spending all his time sitting behind a desk or standing in front of a blackboard. The few props and set dressings include a telephone, a United Nations flag and a map of Japan, both of which are dime-store variety and have visible creases and folds, and a children's dinosaur book that Holcombe displays while expounding his theories on Godzilla's origins. When Eric Carter refers to "the UN newsroom and all its facilities," it's downright laughable. Yutaka Omura has a female news assistant lurking in the background, played by a Japanese woman to give the scene "authenticity."

Peter Zinner, a veteran music editor who had worked at MGM for more than a decade and had recently formed his own editing company, was hired by Beck to meld the new footage with the Japanese original. Although he has never thought highly of *King Kong vs. Godzilla* (Zinner, after all, went on to edit such great films as *In Cold Blood*, *The Godfather*, and *The Deer Hunter*, for which he won an Oscar), he has strong memories of the film because it was one of his first jobs as an independent. "John Beck knew of my company's existence, and one day he gave me a call," Zinner said in 1996. "He had a deal with Universal, but he still had to Americanize the film and put it into English. And then he would sell it, I later found out, to Universal for $200,000, which was a lot of money in those days. We got very little, about $12,000 to do everything, which was ridiculous. We re-cut it, we added the music, which was a compilation of things from several different composers, things in the public domain. They [Beck] didn't like the original music, they felt it should be sort of Westernized, and that's what I was told to do. I supervised the dubbing and lip-synching as well.

"John Beck gave me carte blanche. He trusted me, and of course he OK'd everything I did in the end. Then, he sent it to Universal and they bought it. As I remember, it didn't come out too bad. It was sort of tongue-in-cheek. It did very good business, and I was very thankful to work on it because it came at a time in my career when I had just set out on my own."

MONKEYING AROUND: It's understandable why John Beck believed *King Kong vs. Godzilla* needed more than a simple job of English-dubbing for its American release. In its original form, the movie is a broad parody of the Japanese media culture in the early 1960s, and much of its humor would probably not have been appreciated by Western viewers. However, the picture was subjected to an unforgivable hack job, reducing one of Toho's best monster movies to third-rate American junk. The newscast scenes, with reporter Michael Keith smiling glibly even as the world seems to be coming apart at the seams, add absolutely nothing to the story, and the haphazard deletion and re-shuffling of Japanese footage and the near-wholesale elimination of Akira Ifukube's musical score are dumbfounding. Nevertheless, this is the way most of the world has seen *King Kong vs. Godzilla*, and somehow the wonderful things about the Japanese version shine through the dreck just enough to make the film an international cult favorite.

The major differences between the Japanese and U.S. versions of *King Kong vs. Godzilla* can be broken down into the following categories:

• **Added scenes**

The American version opens with a shot of Earth rotating in space as a narrator reads the afore-mentioned *Hamlet* quote (read by character actor Les Tremayne, who dubbed Jun Tazaki and several other actors in the film), then proceeds to a United Nations news report about a massive earthquake in Chile. From there, reporter Eric Carter segues into another story about the discovery by Dr. Makino (who, in this version, is "winner of last year's Nobel Prize for medicine") of the red narcotic berries and the legend of the Faro Island god, which sets the stage for Sakurai and Furue's meeting with Tako. The implication is that some great environmental disturbance has caused the earthquake, the warm ocean currents north of Japan, and ultimately the appearance of Godzilla, but this idea is never pursued — the earthquake is not mentioned again. Bulletins constantly interrupt: Yutaka Omura talks to the captain of the Seahawk; Godzilla appears, and Eric Carter says there is "no explanation"; Godzilla heads for Japan, and Yutaka Omura reports on the evacuations; Fumiko heads for Hokkaido, and Omura announces Godzilla is heading there, while Carter and Dr. Johnson waste time talking about the improbability of Godzilla's existence, citing a re-animated prehistoric frog in Mexico and flowers blooming from 3,000-year-old seeds in Japan; King Kong is discovered, and Dr. Johnson cites the differences between the two monsters, holding up a marble and declaring, "Godzilla has a brain about this size. He is sheer brute force": Godzilla lands in Hokkaido, and Omura says, "The eyes of the world have turned to Japan." And again, and again.

The reporters are so detached from the monster action that their appearances are increasingly irritating — whenever the film picks up steam, another news flash brings it to a halt. What's more, the U.S. version adds typical pseudo-science that is completely unnecessary and often erroneous. The U.S. helicopter pilot, while searching for the Seahawk, screams "Godzilla!" when the monster breaks free from the iceberg (in both versions), but Eric Carter and Dr. Johnson act as though the monster has never appeared before. Carter says, "The world is stunned to discover that prehistoric creatures exist in the 20th century," and Johnson theorizes that Godzilla is a dinosaur awakened from suspended animation, a cross between the tyrannosaurus rex and stegosaurus. Johnson is the "first" to know that Godzilla will head for Japan, since fossils resembling the monster were found there, and that the two monsters will instinctively try to destroy one another. The most hilariously stupid moment occurs when Johnson bleats, "As a reptile, Godzilla might shy away from electricity," thus taking credit for the Japanese military's subsequent plan to shock the monster. Johnson somehow also knows that Kong will derive strength from electricity, even before the big ape comes in contact with the power lines.

• Removed scenes

The addition of so much new material required lots of footage to be cut from the film, mostly involving interplay between Mr. Tako and his staff (Ichiro Arishima's role is more substantial in the Japanese version). The globe that appears at the beginning is *not* supposed to be Earth floating in space as the U.S. version suggests, but actually a prop from the *Mysteries of the World* TV show. Mr. Tako is watching the program in his office at Pacific Pharmaceuticals, frustrated with the show's dullness and its poor ratings. The film's comic tone is established from the start, as Tako complains about the company's sponsorship of the program to his incompetent assistant, Obashi, and receives a scolding phone call from his boss. From there, the action switches to a TV studio, where Sakurai is playing drums on a commercial for one of Pacific's products and Furue comes to summon him to a meeting with Tako. After Sakurai and Furue are assigned to go to Faro Island, a farewell-party, where Tako frustratedly learns that Obashi neglected to invite the press corps, is deleted. Later on, another deleted scene shows Tako meeting with his subordinates, complaining that all the media attention is going to Godzilla and concocting the ultimate publicity stunt, a fight between the monsters. Throughout the rest of the film, other scenes were trimmed short.

On the other hand, several scenes were re-edited for the U.S. version with positive results. In the Japanese version, the action shifts back and forth between Tokyo and the Seahawk submarine, culminating in the sub's crash into the iceberg; in the U.S. version the submarine episode unspools in one long, continuous sequence ending in Godzilla's appearance, which is more effective and compelling than the Japanese version's choppy editing. The army's efforts to trap Godzilla in a gigantic ditch are similarly reworked. In the Japanese version, the ditch-digging is stalled when Godzilla and Kong battle on the Nasu plain, but in the U.S. version it is not.

• Dubbing flubs

"My corns always hurt when they're near a monster." No, Furue does *not* really have corns, just a severe case of jungle fever and, in the U.S. version, the ignominy of having someone put stupid words in his mouth. In attempting to add humor to what was already a funny movie, John Beck's version resorts to infantile jokes and phrases, like Furue calling Tako a "dumb bell," and Tako declaring, "King Kong can't make a monkey out of us!"

Even stranger are the mistakes made in the dubbing process that are apparent even if you haven't seen the original Japanese version. Furue, the TV sound man, points his microphone toward the fighting monsters and says, "I'd better get a light check"; Fumiko is informed that her boyfriend's plane has crashed, but the newspaper article clearly shows a ship (in the Japanese version, he was traveling by sea); several characters' names are haphazardly changed in midstream — Gen. Shinzo becomes Gen. Kenzo, Fumiko becomes Tamiko, Defense Minister Shigezawa becomes Premiere Shigezawa; and when Konno the interpreter speaks to the Faro islanders (in a mixture of pidgin English and rudimentary Chinese), only his English dialogue is dubbed, making it sound as if he has two different voices.

As mentioned before, *King Kong vs. Godzilla* features one of Akira Ifukube's greatest monster scores, but all that remains in the U.S. version is the Faro native dance that plays when Kong falls asleep on the island and again in Tokyo, and some faint jungle music heard when Sakurai and Furue search for Kong. The replacement themes are not only inferior, they come from so many different sources that the film no longer has an underlying musical motif, and in some cases the recordings are so old that the audio quality is noticeably tinny. Godzilla and Kong both appear to Henry Mancini's horror theme from *Creature from the Black Lagoon* (1954), and according to *Video Watchdog*, some of the music comes from films as old as *Frankenstein Meets the Wolf Man* (1943).

While Universal-International apparently contributed much of the library music to the film, RKO also gave John Beck some stock footage from *The Mysterians*, which RKO had released in the U.S. several years before. The "international communications satellite" is really the Mysterians' space station; the foreign officials arriving in Japan for a security conference, and the floods and landslides that suddenly erupt when Kong and Godzilla tumble into the water and cause an earthquake at the end, are all culled from Toho's space opera.

Monster Marketing

The release of *King Kong vs. Godzilla* was ballyhooed on both sides of the Pacific, with both Toho and Universal-International waging major publicity campaigns characterizing the meeting of the world's two greatest gigantic monsters as the all-time world-title match.

In a bilingual press release issued by Toho, both monsters predicted victory. "Seven years have passed since I rose from the bottom of the southern seas and raved about in Japan, leaving destruction behind everywhere I crawled," Godzilla said. "It is most gratifying for me to have the privilege of seeing you again after breaking through an iceberg in the Arctic ocean where I was buried. At the thought of my engagement with King Kong from America I feel my blood boil and my flesh dance. I am now applying myself to vigorous training day and night to capture the world monster-championship from King Kong."

Kong responded, "I may be a stranger to the younger people here, but have quite a number of fighting adventures to my credit. I will fight to the last ditch in the forthcoming encounter with Mr. Godzilla, for my title is at stake. . . . Hearing that the world-renowned special effects director Eiji Tsuburaya is to act as referee I am going to return to the screen in high spirits."

For the U.S. release, Universal's Exploitation Department, based in New York, published a handbook for a "Mighty Monster Showmanship Campaign" full of silly ploys that cinema owners could use to lure "the whole family — baby to great-grampa" to the ticket booth. Some highlights:

- Theater owners were advised to send a telegram to the sports editors of their local newspapers, with two tickets to "the biggest match in a million years," inviting them to cover the bout for their sports pages. Sports commentators on radio and TV were also to be targeted. "The idea of two science-fiction monsters treated as a sports event should be off-beat enough to give you the plug."

- Posters, lobby cards, cutouts, and stickers were to be plastered in "every key location in town and on the highways," actors wearing Godzilla and King Kong costumes were to be sent into the streets ("the costumes should be easy to prepare . . . use red electric bulbs to simulate atomic fire . . . for a gag, let King Kong carry a jug of 'King Kong Juice' which he drinks lustily from time to time, getting hilariously drunk as he does in the picture!"). Universal offered theaters large cutouts and models to create a parade-style float on the back of a flatbed truck with Godzilla and Kong fighting amid a cardboard city, and encouraged proprietors to paint huge monster footprints on the street, leading a path to the theater.

- Other suggested stunts included getting kids to "walk along Main Street" carrying signs reading "King Kong will win," "we're for Godzilla," etc., and getting the local soda fountain to make a special "double monster" ice-cream sundae to promote the film.

In Japanese publications, producer Tomoyuki Tanaka often failed to mention John Beck's involvement in *King Kong vs. Godzilla*, implying that the impetus for the film was his own. It's understandable why he might want to take all the credit. Released at the height of the Japanese movie industry's Golden Age, *King Kong vs. Godzilla* sold more than 11.2 million tickets during its initial theater run in Japan, making it one of the highest-grossing films of 1962 and the biggest box-office draw of the entire Godzilla series, a distinction it retains today. Despite its incredible success, the film remains an anomaly in genre history, as it was Toho's only *kaiju* film made as an outright comedy. For the most part, future films would be played straight, but comedic elements would remain a staple of the genre. The monsters would take a cue (at the urging of Toho's front office, of course) from *King Kong vs. Godzilla* and gradually assume more anthropomorphized and silly behavior for the small-fries whom Toho — in the face of increasing competition from television and declining production budgets — would target as its main genre audience.

But before that, Godzilla would revisit his mean streak once more, for old time's sake. . . .

MONSTER SCRIBES

Screenwriters Shinichi Sekizawa and Takeshi Kimura

King Kong vs. Godzilla features the first of many Godzilla screenplays by Shinichi Sekizawa, a remarkable writer whose flair for adventure, humor and fantasy left an indelible mark on Toho's *kaiju eiga*. Sekizawa was an integral member of the creative team behind the genre in the 1960s and '70s, authoring 10 of the first 15 Godzilla movies and helping make the King of the Monsters' transition from mortal enemy to saurian hero a smooth and successful one.

Sekizawa (1920–1993) is actually best known as a screenwriter for critically acclaimed director Kihachi Okamoto, for whom he wrote *The Big Boss* (1959), *Westward Desperado* (1960), and other films, and as a lyricist for hit pop songs and television theme songs during the 1950s and '60s (in the 1970s, he also wrote "theme songs" for several Godzilla movies). Science-fiction and monster movies formed only a small part of his career, but he was arguably the most thoroughly entertaining scenarist in the genre's history. *King Kong vs. Godzilla* contains all the characteristics of Sekizawa's best monster screenplays: A mysterious South Pacific island locale, dancing natives, a "jungle potion" that acts as an elixir, witty banter among the main characters, and a central love triangle or romantic entanglement. In a genre where concept often takes precedent over characterization and plot development, Sekizawa's scripts usually produced memorable characters and engaging stories. Above all, they were *fun*.

Sekizawa's diversity as a writer is owed to his varied personal and professional interests. Before World War II, he joined an association of *manga* cartoonists in his native Kyoto, a group whose members also included Osamu Tezuka, who later pioneered Japanese animation. "Drawing comics back then probably helped me imagine all the stories

in my head, to visualize stuff," Sekizawa said in an interview published in *Toho SF Special Effects Movie Series Vol. 2*. Sekizawa was drafted into the Japanese military in 1941 and fought in the South Pacific, where he became intrigued by the tropical islands and their peoples. His sense of adventure was nurtured through his love of American westerns like *Stagecoach* and *Rio Grande*, and he was fascinated by locomotives.

Sekizawa began his film career in 1948, joining Beehive Productions as an assistant director. His first screenplay was a film called *Profile of the City* in 1953, and he directed one movie, an obscure sci-fi picture called *Fearful Invasion of the Flying Saucers*, for Shin-Toho in 1955. Although he was always an independent, he began his relationship with Toho in 1958, co-scripting *Varan the Unbelievable*, and worked steadily for the studio for a decade and a half. After the great success of *Mothra* (1961), in which Sekizawa fashioned a screenplay from an original short story attributed to three different writers, he became Toho's main monster scripter. His Godzilla screenplays include *Godzilla vs. The Thing, Ghidrah: The Three-Headed Monster, Monster Zero, Godzilla versus The Sea Monster, Son of Godzilla, Godzilla's Revenge*, and *Godzilla on Monster Island*. His other genre films include *Battle in Outer Space, The Secret of the Telegian, Atragon, The Lost World of Sinbad, Dagora: The Space Monster*, and *Latitude Zero*. In all, Sekizawa wrote 18 of Toho's SFX movies. All the while, he was busy working on many other kinds of films and related projects, writing as many as six screenplays a year during the 1960s. He wrote war movies, *salaryman* comedies, episodes of Tsuburaya Productions' *Ultraman* and *Kaiju Booska* (a kids' show about a talking alien critter, similar to *Alf)*, and animated feature films like *Gulliver's Travels Beyond the Moon* (1965) and

Jack and the Beanstalk (1967). "I once kind of got sick of writing screenplays for monster films like Godzilla," Sekizawa said. "So when I got an offer to write animation feature screenplays, I accepted it."

The lighthearted Sekizawa shared most of Toho's SFX movie writing chores in the 1960s with **Takeshi Kimura**, a man who, by comparison, was a dark, enigmatic soul. Relatively little is known about Kimura's personal life. Beginning with *Frankenstein Conquers the World* in 1965, Kimura wrote all his screenplays under the pseudonym **Kaoru Mabuchi**, further shrouding himself in mystery. Accordingly, Kimura was assigned to write movies that were more somber, sometimes even pessimistic in tone.

Kimura (1911–1988) broke in as a writer at Toho in the early 1950s and penned one of Ishiro Honda's first features, *Farewell, Rabaul* (1954). He wrote only two Godzilla pictures, *Destroy All Monsters* and *Godzilla vs. The Smog Monster*, both of which were co-written with the director, and these are not his most significant contributions to Toho's sci-fi and monster genre. Far more compelling are his screenplays for *Rodan* (co-written with Takeo Murata), *The Mysterians*, the sci-fi/detective meller *The H-Man*, the tragic story of *The Human Vapor*, and the apocalyptic *The Last War* and *Gorath*. Kimura's lesser works include *Varan the Unbelievable* (co-written with Sekizawa) and the more simplistic *King Kong Escapes*.

Kimura's scripts are moody and usually characterized by dour themes, notably Armageddon and unrequited love (between man and woman, or sometimes monster and woman). Unlike Sekizawa, Kimura usually portrayed monsters as tragic, pitiable figures and victims of mankind's disrespect for Nature, as in *Frankenstein Conquers the World* and *War of the Gargantuas*. His masterpiece is *Attack of the Mushroom People* (1963), a *Lord of the Flies*-like story in which a group of castaways are done in by temptation and lust.

"Mr. Sekizawa and Takeshi Kimura were completely different," director Ishiro Honda told *Cult Movies*. "If the story was very positive, or even childish, it would go to Mr. Sekizawa. If it was negative, or involved politics, it would go to Mr. Kimura. I really can't compare the two because they were so different."

THE KING'S COURT

Famous faces of Toho's classic monster movies

It's easy to assume that the men and women who shared the screen with Godzilla, Mothra, and company during the glory years of Toho's sci-fi and monster movies were second- and third-rate actors and actresses, relegated to roles in B-movie productions in which lesser talents would suffice.

Not true.

During the late 1950s to early 1960s, each of the major Japanese studios (Toho, Toei, Shochiku, Nikkatsu, and Daiei) kept a stable of contracted actors who worked constantly in myriad studio features, much as their Hollywood counterparts once did. It was not unusual to see Akira Takarada, Takashi Shimura, Kumi Mizuno, and other headliners of Toho's monster cinema also appear in period dramas (by Akira Kurosawa), gangster and spy movies, comedies like Toho's long-running *Shacho* ("company boss") series, dramas, love stories, war films, and other staples of the Japanese moviegoing diet. Far from a B-list cast, these were the stars and supporting actors of Toho's mainstream, commercial movie crop. It was only when the industry began its decline in the late 1960s and early '70s that lesser actors began taking center stage, in monsterdom and all Japanese moviedom.

THE MEN OF MONSTERLAND

The concept of the protagonist in Japanese films is often different than in American cinema. Japan's group ethic has traditionally dictated that even top-billed movie stars share the running time almost equally with an entire ensemble of actors. In the second half of the century, Akira Kurosawa and other directors have introduced a more Westernized,

egocentric style of screenwriting, but the practice has remained the norm in Japanese monster movies. The "hero" of these movies is often a central male figure (a reporter, scientist, pilot/astronaut, policeman/authority figure, or other archetype) who mostly reacts to the unfolding events rather than propelling the action himself, and who is surrounded by an assembly of second-tier characters who move the story along incrementally. Thus, the genre doesn't always afford center stage to its leading actors, which makes it all the more remarkable what indelible impressions these men have left upon their fans worldwide — impressions that transcend the cultural barriers, the English dubbing, and other factors that denigrate their work.

AKIRA TAKARADA: Mr. Handsome

He appeared in only four installments of the original Godzilla series and just a handful of Toho's other science fiction and fantasy exploits, but Akira Takarada always played the leading man, making him the most recognizable actor in the genre. A major star at Toho during the 1950s and '60s, Takarada has appeared in more than 180 films during his long career, at the height of which he was known as "Mr. Handsome" and his popularity rivaled that of mega-stars like Toshiro Mifune.

Like many of his generation, Takarada was raised in Japanese-occupied East Asia after Japan's invasion of Manchuria in 1931. Born April 29, 1934, in Korea, he also lived in Manchuria before his family returned to Japan in 1948. In April 1953, at age 19, he joined Toho's New Face program and trained at the studio's acting institute (alongside future fellow *kaiju eiga* stars Yu Fujiki and Momoko Kochi), and later that year he debuted with a small role in *And Then the Liberty Bell Rang*, a biographical film

Akira Takarada in Tokyo in 1996.
COURTESY STUART GALBRAITH IV

about Yukichi Fukuzawa, a leading educator who introduced Western ideas to Japan during the Meiji era. Takarada was groomed for stardom quickly: After playing a young lover in *Bride in a Bathing Suit*, Takarada was elevated to the leading role in *Godzilla*, still with less than a year's experience in front of the cameras.

As the forthright sailor Ogata, Takarada was somewhat overshadowed in *Godzilla* by supporting actors Takashi Shimura and Akihiko Hirata, both portraying scientists with the weight of the world (and a giant monster) on their shoulders. It took several years for Takarada to develop his trademark screen persona, the cocky, slightly cynical urban male; by the time he starred in *Godzilla vs. The Thing*, this image was well established. Godzilla fans have come to identify Takarada best with his character in that film, the edgy, yet good-hearted reporter Sakai. His other standout genre roles include the similarly dispositioned astronaut Fuji in *Monster Zero*, and Yoshimura the bank robber in *Godzilla versus The Sea Monster*. In real life, however, the actor is said to be far more relaxed and easygoing than his movie characters.

Even though Takarada's face is familiar in Toho's monster movies, the genre has comprised only a fraction of his career, and has tapped only a fraction of his acting talents. Takarada has a flair for physical comedy and action, as evidenced in films like *100 Shot, 100 Killed* (1965), a rollicking spoof of James Bond and Japanese spy movies directed by Jun Fukuda and co-starring Mie Hama, Akihiko Hirata, and Ichiro Arishima.

Takarada still has a soft spot in his heart for monster movies, especially the original *Godzilla*. He remembers watching Tsuburaya's war pictures as a child, including *The War at Sea from Hawaii to Malaya*, and recalls his surprise when, years later, he was cast in Tsuburaya's first giant-monster epic. "The fact that they had chosen me to play (Ogata) when I had just debuted as a hopeful of Toho's future gave me great encouragement," he told an interviewer in *Toho SF Special Effects Movie Series Vol. 7*. "I will be forever grateful that they gave me a chance. I owe that feeling to everyone concerned with Godzilla films."

Takarada is still a celebrity in Japan today, appearing regularly in TV dramas, on quiz shows, and in commercials. In the early 1990s, the late director Juzo Itami (*Tampopo*, *A Taxing Woman*) slyly cast Takarada in two comedies, *A-Ge-Man* (*Tales of a Golden Geisha*) and *Minbo, or The Gentle Art of Japanese Extortion*. In *Minbo*, which is available on home video in the U.S., Takarada is wonderful as a nervous hotel manager besieged by *yakuza* gangsters; in one scene, he briefly appears nude, although it's hardly a flattering moment. In 1992, Takarada returned to the Godzilla series as a government official in *Godzilla vs. Mothra*.

GENRE CREDITS: *Godzilla, Half Human, The Three Treasures, The Last War, Godzilla vs. The Thing, Monster Zero, Godzilla versus The Sea Monster, King Kong Escapes, Latitude Zero* (speaking English), *Godzilla vs. Mothra*.

AKIHIKO HIRATA: the tragic hero

Although he was almost always a supporting player, Akihiko Hirata's ability to fully immerse himself in his characters made him a perennial fan favorite in both the East and West. During a career that spanned 30 years, Hirata became Toho's top contract supporting actor, playing virtually every type: military man, elite businessman, scholar, entrepreneur, politician, and scientist. But he will always be remembered best as the tormented young genius Dr. Daisuke Serizawa.

Born December 16, 1927, in Japanese-occupied Korea, Hirata (real name: Akihiko Onoda), like many of his Toho cohorts, took a roundabout route to an acting career. As a youth in the 1940s, he attended military schools in preparation for enlistment, but the war ended before he was drafted. He enrolled at Tokyo University's law school, and during his studies took a part-time job as an assistant director trainee at Shin-Toho Studios, working under his older brother, director Yoshiki Onoda. In 1950, Hirata graduated law school and took a job with a major import-export firm in Tokyo, but at the urging of a friend, actress Shigeko Yamaguchi, he took a stab at acting, joining Toho Studios' New Face program in 1953. His first film appearance was in *The Last Embrace* (1953) starring Toshiro Mifune, and his first starring role came soon after in *Even the Mighty Shed Tears* (also 1953). After playing the romantic lead in Honda's war movie *Farewell, Rabaul* (1953), he was cast in *Godzilla*.

It has been rumored that Honda originally cast Akira Takarada as Dr. Serizawa, and Hirata as Hideto Ogata, but pulled a switcheroo just before filming began. In interviews shortly before his death in 1993, Honda was unable to confirm or deny this, but in 1996 Takarada told Stuart Galbraith IV that he indeed was supposed to play the tortured scientist. This role-reversal was a wise move, for only Hirata could have given Serizawa his contradictory mixture of youth, maturity, hope, and tragedy. Although Hirata's screen time was limited, the actor embodies the scientist's loss of his work, his love, and ultimately his life not via maudlin histrionics, but with subtle words and expressions.

Hirata had many other monster-movie roles, but his acting talents were hardly limited to genre films. In the 1950s and '60s he appeared in many of acclaimed director Hiroshi Inagaki's films, including *The Three Treasures* (1959), *Tale of Osaka Castle* (1961), and *Whirlwind* (1964), in Akira Kurosawa's all-star *samurai* blockbuster, *Sanjuro* (1962), and many comedies. Hirata is also remembered for his roles on Tsuburaya Productions' *Ultraman* (1966–1967, as Dr. Iwamoto, an inventor who aids the Science Patrol against aliens) and *Ultra Seven* (1967–1968, as Dr. Yanagawa). He also played recurring villains in Toho's *Rainbowman* teleseries (1973–74) and Toei Television's *Giant Ironman 17* (1977–78). In his later years, he appeared as a panelist on game shows.

Hirata's monster and sci-fi roles are many and varied, and he usually played supporting parts that required him to exert only a fraction of his acting talents, but were memorable nonetheless. His last two Toho SFX pictures were *The War in Space* (1977) and *Sayonara Jupiter* (1984), in which he had minor parts. What lingers in memory, however, is his last major role as the tormented Dr. Mafune in Honda's *Terror of MechaGodzilla* (1975). Hirata's performance is unfortunately his least effective, a sadly inappropriate swan song to a great career.

During Godzilla's screen hiatus from 1975–84, Hirata was an active spokesman for the monster's return. He appeared at a Tokyo press conference to officially announce the production of *Godzilla* (1984) on the studio's behalf, but unfortunately his failing health prevented him from appearing in the movie. Hirata died in Tokyo of lymphatic cancer at age 56 on July 25, 1984.

GENRE CREDITS: *Godzilla, Rodan, The Mysterians, The H-Man, Varan the Unbelievable* (his part was edited out of the U.S. version), *Mothra, The Secret of the Telegian, Gorath, King Kong vs. Godzilla, Atragon, Ghidrah: The Three-Headed Monster, Godzilla versus The Sea Monster, Son of Godzilla, Latitude Zero, The Last Days of Planet Earth, Godzilla vs. The Cosmic Monster, The War in Space, Sayonara Jupiter.*

KENJI SAHARA: jack of all trades

Kenji Sahara's tortured throes as the sight of a hatching chick brings back the suppressed, horrible memory of a prehistoric monstrosity in *Rodan* remains one of the most powerful and lasting images in all of Toho's science-fiction classics. Likewise, Sahara himself has long been one of the most beloved actors in the genre, both by director Honda (who cast Sahara in nearly every SF film he helmed) and by fans on both sides of the Pacific. Sahara, in turn, calls the *kaiju eiga* "my genre."

Sahara has appeared in more than 30 sci-fi and monster films, including four of the last five entries in the *Heisei*-era Godzilla series, playing virtually every role imaginable along the way. In his early days, he was the handsome, upstanding young hero in films like *Rodan, The Mysterians, The H-Man,* and *King Kong vs. Godzilla,* but he was equally effective when cast against type as a slimy villain, as in *Attack of the Mushroom People, Atragon,* or *Yog: Monster from Space.* Indeed, Godzilla fans perhaps know Sahara best as villain Jiro Torahata, the cigar-smoking, brandy-sipping financier of Mothra's egg in *Godzilla vs. The Thing.*

Born May 14, 1932, in Kawasaki, Sahara won a magazine-sponsored modeling contest and, using his real name Tadashi Ishihara, made his Toho debut in 1953. Unknown to many, Sahara had a minor nonspeaking role in *Godzilla* as one of the party-goers startled by the monster on a boat; Sahara can be seen briefly, seated at a table with a girl, smoking. He began using the pseudonym Kenji Sahara in *Rodan*, and over the next decade and a half he appeared in more than 100 films, ranging from comedies to war dramas like *Tokyo Bay on Fire* and *The Retreat from Kiska*. In 1965, he played one of the Japanese soldiers marooned on a South Seas island with a band of their American counterparts in the Toho-Warner Bros. coproduction of Frank Sinatra's *None but the Brave*.

In 1966, Sahara made the transition from movies to Japanese science-fiction television, accepting the leading role in Tsuburaya Productions' first teleseries, *Ultra Q*. At a time when the small screen was considered a step down for Japanese movie actors, Sahara took a gamble that paid off: the role of heroic pilot and science-fiction writer Jun Manjome cemented his popularity among genre fans in Japan for generations to come. He also had a recurring role as Chief of Staff Takenaka in the spin-off series *Ultra Seven*.

Through the decades, Sahara has continued to appear on TV shows and occasionally in films, including a 1982 feature, *Callgirl*, directed by Shosei Kotani. In 1991, he added to his record-setting number of *kaiju eiga* appearances, playing the prime minister in *Godzilla vs. King Ghidorah*; two years later he returned in *Godzilla vs. MechaGodzilla* as Segawa, chief of anti-Godzilla military operations for G-FORCE — a man who in real life would surely be fired for wasting billions of taxpayers' yen on ineffective mecha-junk!

GENRE CREDITS: *Godzilla, Rodan, The Mysterians, Mothra, Gorath, King Kong vs. Godzilla, Atragon, Attack of the Mushroom People, Godzilla vs. The Thing, Ghidrah: The Three-Headed Monster* (bit as editor of TV program), *Frankenstein Conquers the World, War of the Gargantuas, Son of Godzilla, Destroy All Monsters* (bit part as SY-3 navigator), *Godzilla's Revenge, Yog: Monster from Space, Godzilla vs. The Cosmic Monster* (bit as ocean liner captain), *Terror of Mecha-Godzilla, Godzilla vs. King Ghidorah, Godzilla vs. MechaGodzilla, Godzilla vs. Space Godzilla*.

TAKASHI SHIMURA: the elder

Though he made fewer sci-fi and fantasy film appearances than other Toho actors, Takashi Shimura's contributions to the genre are immeasurable. Shimura's understated manner and perfect on-screen poise, developed during his years working with Akira Kurosawa, elevated Honda's *Godzilla* beyond mere monster-movie status. As the sensitive-yet-rational Dr. Kyohei Yamane, Shimura was more than just believable in his own right; he made Godzilla believable too.

Takashi Shimura

Born March 12, 1905, in Hyogo Prefecture, Shimura first was a stage actor, then made *chambara* ("swordplay") movies at Nikkatsu before joining Toho in the early 1940s. He had a small role in Kurosawa's directorial debut, *Sanshiro Sugata* (1943), and played minor parts in several of the master director's films over the next few years. From *Drunken Angel* (1948) forward, Shimura was one of Kurosawa's principal players along with Toshiro Mifune and Tatsuya Nakadai. He received worldwide acclaim for his roles in many Kurosawa films, including the woodcutter in *Rashomon* (1950), the dying bureaucrat in *Ikiru* (1952) and Kambei, the ascerbic warrior-for-hire in *The Seven Samurai* (1954). He also appeared in *Throne of Blood* (1957), *The Hidden Fortress* (1958), *The Bad Sleep Well* (1960), *Yojimbo* (1961), *Sanjuro* (1962), *High and Low* (1963), and *Red Beard* (1965). Unlike most other actors familiar to the genre, Shimura was not a Toho contract player but a freelancer who worked for many studios.

Shimura reprised the Yamane character in Oda's *Gigantis: The Fire Monster*, and during the 1950s and '60s he played occasional supporting parts in Honda's science-fiction films. Shimura died at age 76 on February 11, 1982. Later that year in New York, the Public Theater's Summer In Japan film festival was dedicated to his memory, a testament to his international legacy in film. The program featured, for the first time in decades in America, a screening of Ishiro Honda's original, uncut *Godzilla*.

GENRE CREDITS: *Godzilla*, *Gigantis: The Fire Monster*, *The Mysterians* (Dr. Adachi), *Mothra* (newspaper editor Amano), *Gorath* (Dr. Kensuke Sonoda), *The Lost World of Sinbad*, *Ghidrah: The Three-Headed Monster* (Dr. Tsukamoto), *Frankenstein Conquers the World* (scientist who gets nuked at Hiroshima).

HIROSHI KOIZUMI: the professor

Whether Mothra's egg washes ashore, King Ghidorah's meteoric fireball crash-lands in Japan, or ancient Okinawan writings must be deciphered to save mankind, all-purpose scientist Hiroshi Koizumi will probably be there to investigate.

Although one of the least charismatic of Toho's genre actors, Koizumi nonetheless played key parts in several of the studio's science-fiction classics, beginning with the leading role in *Gigantis: The Fire Monster*. Koizumi was not exactly compelling as Tsukioka, the fish-spotting pilot, but it's due more to the film's lackluster scripting than his performance. Director Honda later put Koizumi to better use by casting him as rational, concerned-yet-stoic types, usually scientists. The first of these was Dr. Nakazo in *Mothra*, a wooden, straight-man character to Frankie Sakai's playful reporter. Essentially the same character, renamed "Professor Miura," was reprised by Koizumi in *Godzilla vs. The Thing* (1964) and again (this time as "Professor Murai") in *Ghidrah: The Three-Headed Monster*.

Born August 12, 1926, in Kamakura, Kanagawa Prefecture, Koizumi worked as a radio announcer for the NHK network after graduating from university in 1948. He left that position to learn acting in Toho's New Face program in 1951, and made his screen debut the following year. Known for his good looks, Koizumi was groomed as a star at Toho in the mid-1950s and appeared in films by major directors like Mikio Naruse and Hiroshi Inagaki, mostly tear-jerker love stories. But by the 1960s his

Hiroshi Koizumi

popularity had tapered off and he was cast mostly in supporting roles. He later moved to television acting and hosted a game show.

Koizumi returned to the genre for the Big G's 20th-anniversary film, *Godzilla vs. The Cosmic Monster* (1974), and on the occasion of Toho's 50th-anniversary he appeared at the studio's Half Century Greatest Hits Fair in Tokyo in 1982, where several of his monster films were screened. Two years later, graying at the temples but retaining his trademark good looks, he returned to the series one last time, as Dr. Minami in *Godzilla* (1984). He eventually gave up acting.

GENRE CREDITS: *Gigantis: The Fire Monster*, *Mothra*, *Attack of the Mushroom People*, *Atragon*, *Godzilla vs. The Thing*, *Dagora: The Space Monster*, *Ghidrah: The Three-Headed Monster*, *Godzilla vs. The Cosmic Monster*, *Godzilla* (1984).

OTHER FACES

Another leading actor in Toho's genre films was **Akira Kubo** (b. Dec. 1, 1936, in Tokyo), a handsome, charismatic type who, like Akira Takarada, made only a handful of sci-fi and monster films but usually played the hero. Kubo began acting in his teens and achieved notoriety when, at age 17, he was cast in *The Surf* (1954), a filmic adaptation of Yukio Mishima's famous novel *The Sound of Waves*.

Akira Kubo in Tokyo in 1996, still retaining those trademark good looks of his genre movie days 30 years earlier.

PHOTO BY THE AUTHOR

A star of "angry young man" films at Toho during the 1950s and '60s, he is best known to Godzilla fans as Goro Maki, the pesky reporter who makes an uninvited visit in *Son of Godzilla* and Katsuo Yamabe, the top-gun interstellar rocket pilot in *Destroy All Monsters*. Kubo also had prominent roles in *The Three Treasures* and Honda's *Attack of the Mushroom People*, *Gorath*, and *Yog: Monster from Space*. He has appeared in few films over the past three decades, switching to TV and stage instead, but he made a great cameo as a ship captain in Daiei's *Gamera, Guardian of the Universe* (1995).

Jazz drummer-turned-actor **Tadao Takashima** (b. July 27, 1930, in Kobe) is yet another talent who has made only a few appearances in the Godzilla series yet is well remembered for his charm and presence. Takashima and his comic sidekick, actor **Yu Fujiki** (b. Jan. 8, 1931, in Tokyo), appeared together in several *salaryman* comedies in the late 1950s, and were perfectly cast as the bumbling television crew in *King Kong vs. Godzilla* (they reprised essentially the same roles — this time, as centerfold photographers — in *Atragon*). Takashima showed up in two more monster films, although his comic abilities were not tapped in either one: In *Frankenstein Conquers the World* he played a scientist unable to see the humanity in the Frankenstein boy and determined to dissect the monster; in *Son of Godzilla* he was Dr. Kusumi, another character devoted to scientific advancement despite the alarming consequences of his research. Fujiki, meanwhile, was memorable as the egg-eating reporter Nakamura in *Godzilla vs. The Thing*. Takashima's two sons, Masanobu and Masahiro, are actors as well, and both have played major roles in the 1990s *Godzilla* movies. As an aside, in the Japanese version of *King Kong vs. Godzilla* Takashima can be seen playing drums in a television commercial. The scene was edited out of the U.S. version, making it seem strangely convenient when he later lulls Kong to sleep with a bongo drum.

With his tough and gruff screen presence, **Jun Tazaki** (1910-1985) was a favorite character actor of director Ishiro Honda. Tazaki's best genre roles were Jinguji, the nationalist naval commander in *Atragon*, and Sonoda, the spaceship captain who bravely pilots his rocket even as it crashes into a meteor in *Gorath*. In the Godzilla series, Tazaki was a military commander in *King Kong vs. Godzilla*, the newspaper city editor in *Godzilla vs. The Thing*, World Space Authority leader Dr. Sakurai in *Monster Zero*, the leader of the evil Red Bamboo terrorists (the man seen only on the TV monitors) in *Godzilla versus The Sea Monster*, and Dr. Yoshida, the head of Monsterland operations in *Destroy All Monsters*. His other genre films include *The Three Treasures*, *Dagora: The Space Monster*, *Frankenstein Conquers the World*, and *War of the Gargantuas*. He also appeared in a variety of war movies and other pictures, including several of Kurosawa's works.

GODZILLA
GIRLS

Much like their counterparts in American sci-fi movies, the female characters in Toho's classic genre films played second fiddle to the men, but similarities end there. Toho's monster maidens may have appeared to be the usual damsels in distress, scream queens, or romantic diversions, but beneath the surface were often strong, vibrant characters who acted as the moral fulcrum to the drama. In many of Toho's best sci-fi and monster films, especially those directed by Ishiro Honda and penned by either Shinichi Sekizawa or Takeshi Kimura, the fate of society or even the world hinged on one woman's act of conscience — consider, for instance, *Godzilla*, *Attack of the Mushroom People*, *Monster Zero*, *Terror of MechaGodzilla*. The memorable women of the *kaiju eiga* ran the gamut from heroines to tragic villains, and in their best moments they infused the genre with a certain sensuality and eroticism even while remaining at an arm's distance from their lovers, another tradition in Japanese films (count the number of kisses in the entire Godzilla series: One — *gaijin* Nick Adams broke the taboo in *Monster Zero*, and even then, the kiss is seen only fleetingly). As an added bonus, they were portrayed by beautiful, captivating actresses.

KUMI MIZUNO: queen of outer space

Kumi Mizuno's performance as Miss Namikawa, the alien interloper-turned-lover in *Monster Zero* encapsulates all the qualities that make her the Godzilla series' most alluring actress: Flirtatiousness, wit, vulnerability, mystery. Mizuno transcended the genre's conservative limitations and turned in daring performances, igniting the screen with her vivacious looks, her acting talent, and above all her star quality. Even when clad in a body-hugging latex spacewoman suit and jet-black wig, Mizuno looked glamorous, not silly. Director Ishiro Honda once said, "My movies . . . have more Westernized females than traditional Japanese women characters," and he preferred "a type of actress who actually transform themselves into the characters emotionally." Mizuno's ability to delve into her roles made her one of Honda's favorite performers.

Mizuno (b. January 1, 1937, real name: Maya Igarashi), like many of her contemporaries, spent only a small part of her career in monster movies. She made her film debut in 1957 and soon appeared in her first SFX film, *The Three Treasures*, directed by Hiroshi Inagaki who, like Honda, appreciated Mizuno's intense style and cast her in several features, including the classic *Chushingura* (1962). Honda used her prominently in several of his best genre movies: Mizuno was Ari Sonoda, whose astronaut lover is killed aboard the ill-fated spaceship in *Gorath* (a film in which Mizuno is seen taking a bath!); Mami Sekiguchi, the brassy, bitchy starlet who succumbs to temptation and seductively eats the allegorical "forbidden fruit" in *Attack of the Mushroom People* (Mizuno sings a wonderfully ditzy song during the film's opening); and a sympathetic scientist who becomes a giant monster's love object in both *Frankenstein Conquers the World* and *War of the Gargantuas*. Apart from *Monster Zero*, Mizuno appeared in only one other Godzilla film. In *Godzilla versus The Sea Monster* she played the similarly strong-willed native girl Daiyo, a savage beauty who cunningly escapes her Red Bamboo captors.

Mizuno worked in dozens of movies during the 1960s; sadly, the most widely seen of these outside Japan is Woody Allen's looped-and-loopy reworking of a Toho spy flick, *What's Up, Tiger Lily?*, where Mizuno can be seen showering behind an opaque glass window while "Phil Moscowitz" (Tatsuya Mihashi) has a showdown with the bad guys in the next room. Mizuno's film work tapered off in the '70s but she continues to appear on Japanese soap operas and other TV programs. She is still beautiful, and she still looks back fondly upon her work in monster movies. In 1993, she appeared alongside Toho stalwarts like Haruo Nakajima and Teruyoshi Nakano in a tribute program to the late director Ishiro Honda on Japanese television.

The jury is still out as to whether Mizuno and Nick Adams, her leading man in three films, really had a romantic affair (see chapter 6). One thing's for sure: If they didn't, it wasn't because Adams wasn't interested.

YURIKO HOSHI: Toho's cub reporter

If Kumi Mizuno was the *kaiju eiga*'s reigning sexy starlet, Yuriko Hoshi was its sassy charmer. A member of a Brat Pack-style group of young Toho actors in the mid-1960s, Hoshi was popular in Toho's "Young Guy" (*Wakadaisho*) movies and her youthful enthusiasm carried over into her handful of sci-fi movies. Born December 6, 1943, Hoshi began her film career in the early 1960s and appeared in dozens of comedies, dramas, and war movies. As the photographer Junko in *Godzilla vs. The Thing*, she provided a delightful, lightly comical and naive counterpoint to Akira Takarada's edgy reporter, and in *Ghidrah: The Three-Headed Monster* her spunkiness as reporter-sister Naoko Shindo compensated for policeman-brother Yosuke Natsuki's blandness. With her good looks and smile, she even succeeded in brightening up the bleak doomsday film *The Last War*. Hoshi continues to act today, mostly in television roles.

THE PEANUTS: diminutive divas

Some fans claim they can tell the difference between **Emi Ito** and **Yumi Ito**, the identical twins who make up the singing duo the Peanuts, but it's probably just empty boasting. For the record, Emi is the elder of the Ito sisters, who were born in January 1941 in Nagoya. The pair debuted with a hit single on the Japanese pop charts in 1959 and rose to fame with the novelty of their twin-sister act and on the strength of their alluring vocal harmonies. The Peanuts became a premier talent for Watanabe Productions, Japan's answer to the William Morris Agency, and in 1961 they appeared as the *shobijin* ("little beauties") in *Mothra*, introducing elements of fantasy to Toho's monster cinema and broadening the genre's appeal to women and children.

Although probably due more to their speaking-in-unison shtick and Eiji Tsuburaya's trick photography than their singing and acting talents, the Peanuts are undoubtedly Toho's most widely recognized monster-movie women outside Japan. After *Mothra* was released overseas, the Peanuts had their proverbial 15 minutes of fame in the U.S., performing on *The Ed Sullivan Show* and other programs, and according to some reports they recorded an album of English-language pop songs, including "Raindrops Keep Falling on My Head" and "Do You Know the Way to San Jose?" The duo reprised their role as Mothra's little channelers in *Godzilla vs. The Thing* and *Ghidrah: The Three-Headed Monster* and made life-size appearances in a number of non-monster films including the Crazy Cats' *Las Vegas Free-for-All* (1966). By the end of the 1960s, their film work had petered out, but they continued as a singing and recording act, eventually retiring in 1975 after Emi Ito married Kenji Sawada, a Japanese pop singer. Since then, they have reunited for periodic performances and appearances.

MIE HAMA: beauty and brains

Sexy and sophisticated, Mie Hama ranks alongside Kumi Mizuno as a queen among the monster starlets of Toho's golden age. Hama is best known in the U.S. as Kissy Suzuki, James Bond's love interest in the final third of *You Only Live Twice* (1967), but she was far better in Toho's two King Kong films, playing the big ape's love interest in *King Kong vs. Godzilla* and Madame Piranha, Dr. Who's mysterious financier, in *King Kong Escapes*. She made one other SFX film appearance, as Princess Yaya in *The Lost World of Sinbad*.

Mie Hama, one of Toho's most alluring and talented actresses of the 1960s, in a publicity still for the James Bond film *You Only Live Twice* (1967), in which she married agent 007.

Mie Hama

Hama (b. November 20, 1943, in Tokyo) joined Toho in 1959 and became a major star, appearing in more than 75 feature films in the 1960s. She was best known in Japan for her leading roles in comedies opposite Hitoshi Ueki (sometimes called "the Bob Hope of Japan") and the Crazy Cats, with whom she made more than a dozen movies. These days, Hama's interest in acting has tapered off drastically; she has not made a movie since 1989.

Hama is the only female *kaiju eiga* star to have posed nude for a major American men's magazine. In the June 1967 issue of *Playboy*, a photo spread on the "Asian beauties" of *You Only Live Twice* featured Hama, looking coyly over her shoulder, in a Maynard Frank Wolfe photograph that reveals just enough of her sexy female physique, including great tan lines on her fanny. "Mie has earned the sobriquet 'the Brigitte Bardot of Japan' and a reputation as the most photographed girl in the Orient," the magazine said. Hama also appeared nude throughout much of Katsumi Iwauchi's *Night of the Seagull* (1968), a film which unfortunately was only briefly released in the U.S.

Four

MADAME BUTTERFLY

"You, there! Don't touch that egg. You might damage it, and I certainly don't want that to happen."

— Mr. Kumayama

GODZILLA vs. THE THING

RATING (OUT OF 5 STARS): ★ ★ ★ ★

JAPANESE VERSION: MOSURA TAI GOJIRA (MOTHRA VS. GODZILLA). Released on April 20, 1964, by the Toho Motion Picture Company. Toho Scope, in color. Running Time: 89 minutes.

U.S. VERSION: Released August 26, 1964, by American International Pictures. Premiered in Los Angeles. Running Time: 90 minutes.

STORY: Amid a fierce typhoon, Mothra's gigantic egg is dislodged from Infant Island and floats all the way to Japan, while — unbeknownst to anyone — a dormant Godzilla (possibly ko'd by King Kong in their underwater battle) washes ashore and is buried under tons of mud; greedy promoters exploit Mothra's egg for profit, ignoring the pleas of Mothra's twin fairies to relinquish it. Godzilla awakens, goes on a rampage in the city of Nagoya, destroys the promoters' scheme and heads instinctively for the egg; the adult Mothra dies defending its offspring, but two Mothra caterpillars hatch and engage Godzilla in the battle royal, coating the lizard in a disabling silk cocoon.

BUG OFF

The success of *King Kong vs. Godzilla* kicked Toho's *kaiju eiga* into high gear. From 1963 to 1965, the studio produced six giant monster pictures and one "mutant" film (*Attack of the Mushroom People*), all directed by Ishiro Honda and with SFX by Eiji Tsuburaya, and most of which are among the studio's best output. After pitting Godzilla against America's favorite giant monster, Toho next chose one of its own creations for the infernal beast's next opponent: Mothra, a gigantic insect whose self-titled 1961 feature film debut, laced with fantasy and musical themes unique in the genre, cost about 200 million yen to make — about twice as much as *Godzilla* — and was a great domestic success. With both Honda and Tsuburaya at the top of their game, *Mothra vs. Godzilla* (originally released in the U.S. as *Godzilla vs. The Thing*) stands indisputably as the greatest of all the Godzilla sequels, with a fast-paced story and likable characters, the most

At the height of their popularity in the mid-1960s, Japanese monster movies routinely played in first-run American movie theaters. A marquee display for *Godzilla Vs. The Thing* at the Embassy Theater in New York City, 1964.

impressive Godzilla design ever, two of the Big G's most spectacular battles, and an abundance of special-effects "money shots" that evoke the thrills of the 1954 original.

The story is essentially a direct sequel to both *Mothra* and *King Kong vs. Godzilla*, and re-visits a theme that director Ishiro Honda and screenwriter Shinichi Sekizawa covered in both of those films: The dangers of greed and extreme commercial exploitation. However, unlike its predecessors, *Godzilla vs. The Thing* completely side-steps the subject of Japanese-U.S. relations.

Mothra is usually dismissed in the West as an outlandish, mindless Japanese monster spectacle but Honda and Sekizawa expressed a serious concern about Japan's reliance upon America for military protection. In the story, a group of shipwreck survivors are rescued from Beiru Island, a South Pacific outpost left barren and decimated by H-bomb tests. Although the island is believed uninhabited, the men say the natives gave them a red juice to drink, which somehow protected them from radiation exposure. When a scientific expedition is sent to the island, a pair of tiny twin girls are found living there. Clark Nelson, a ruthless promoter from the country Rolisica (read: America) kidnaps the girls and forces them to work as a singing act on a Tokyo stage, but soon Mothra, the giant caterpillar-god of the Infant Islanders, swims to Japan and plunders through Tokyo seeking to rescue the twins. The Rolisican government comes to Japan's aid with its newest version of nuclear weapons technology, blasting Mothra with atomic heat-ray guns. Nelson flees home to Rolisica, but the adult Mothra — an elegant, gigantic moth with smoothly fluttering wings and a color scheme reminiscent of a traditional Japanese wood-block painting — hatches and flies across the Pacific and, in a stunning display of wing-flapped windstorms, literally blows away much of Newkirk City. Faced with Nature's mighty retribution, Nelson turns into a stark-raving madman, pathetically grabbing a cane out of an old man's hands as he tries desperately to escape, only to die in a gunfight with police.

As originally conceived, *Godzilla vs. The Thing* was to have picked up where *Mothra* left off, with the Rolisicans once again cast as the villains (see accompanying sidebar following). However, this idea was dropped and a pair of Japanese slickster promoters was substituted instead. The story is a mostly standard monster-movie scenario, with an ensemble of three stock heroes — the cynical reporter Sakai (Akira Takarada), the altruistic and somewhat naive female photographer Junko (Yuriko Hoshi), and the rational scientist Miura (Hiroshi Koizumi) — more or less carried over from *Mothra*, albeit with different character names and, except for Koizumi, played by different actors. It is a classic good-versus-evil standoff, raising philosophical issues about the brotherhood of mankind and the ability or inability of enemies to put aside their differences for the greater good, with the specter of nuclear annihilation (in the form of Godzilla) casting its shadow over the drama.

With the adult Mothra aging and near death, the Infant Islanders fear losing their deity and protector. Mothra's tiny twin fairies appear in Japan pleading for the return of Mothra's wayward egg, but the shifty Kumayama, his conniving financier, Torahata, and the authorities are powerless to intervene. Disappointed at man's inhumanity to man, the fairies fly home atop Mothra's head. Soon, the tables of trouble are turned and it is Japan that is in need of help when Godzilla awakens, dusts himself off, and sets about trampling Nagoya.

With the military fruitlessly laboring to stop the giant reptile, the three heroes ask Mothra to take on Godzilla and save Japan from obliteration. The Infant natives understandably refuse — what has Japan done for them lately, anyway? — and the tribal leader condemns the outsiders to face their fate, just as his radiation-scarred people have suffered. Japan, once a victim of nuclear attack, now pays again for its mere association with the forces that despoil the earth through nuclear proliferation. Only after Junko makes an impassioned appeal for mercy and understanding (with an assist

from Sakai) do the tiny twins relent and send Mothra to the Japanese mainland, although their decision is probably also motivated by the fact that Godzilla is making a beeline for Mothra's egg.

Sekizawa's screenplay for *Godzilla vs. The Thing* strikes a nice balance between emphasis on the visuals (which are always the focus of attention) and the human drama. The characters are well-sketched for a film of this type, and this is perhaps the finest all-around cast in the entire Godzilla series. Although Akira Takarada (by this time a major star at Toho) lent the film his marquee value, the real scene-stealer is Kumayama (**Yoshibumi Tajima**), a wonderfully devilish yet somehow likable villain who falls victim to his own greedy nature and lack of smarts. Tajima (b. 1918) was a second-string character actor at Toho during the 1950s and '60s who worked in many of the studio's B-movies, but he was a favorite of director Honda, who cast him in nearly all his science-fiction pictures. Tajima has played many recognizable roles in the genre, usually a small part as an authority figure — he was a ship captain in *King Kong vs. Godzilla* and again in *Ghidrah: The Three-Headed Monster*, a detective in *The H-Man*, an investigator in *War of the Gargantuas*, and a military commander in *Destroy All Monsters* — but perhaps his finest role is that of Kumayama, "the great entrepreneur," who swindles the local fishermen out of Mothra's egg by offering to pay 1,224,560 yen, a price equal to the wholesale cost of 153,820 chicken eggs![15] This blowhard talks like a wheeler and dealer, but in truth he's just a field agent for Torahata (Kenji Sahara), who lets Kumayama do his dirty work while he sits in a posh hotel room sipping brandy with a doting concubine. When the fishermen demand that Kumayama pay for the egg, Torahata coerces his underling to put up half his stock in the company as collateral for a loan to pay off the debt. Kumayama isn't inherently evil, but rather unethical; Torahata, however, is a joyously unrepentant crook who doesn't think twice about ripping off his own business associate. Sahara, who usually played stand-up characters, thrives in the role, lending Torahata a blunt gruffness and a sinister smirk. Unlike Tako, the foolhardy promoter of *King Kong vs. Godzilla*, Kumayama and Torahata ultimately pay for their mistakes with their lives, with Godzilla standing in symbolic moral judgment. As the monster lumbers toward Torahata's hotel, the now-penniless Kumayama bursts in and demands his money back and the two men get into a physical struggle. Torahata shoots Kumayama dead, but he

© 1994 BY MATT GROENING

COPYRIGHT 1994 BY MATT GROENING. ALL RIGHTS RESERVED. REPRINTED BY PERMISSION OF ACME FEATURES SYNDICATE.

gets his just desserts: Godzilla smashes the hotel before he can escape.

Godzilla vs. The Thing is a pure entertainment picture, and while Ishiro Honda hints at the antinuclear message and other serious themes, he does not try to re-create the somber tone of the original *Godzilla*. There are elements of humor throughout to keep the atmosphere from becoming dark, from the edgy banter between Takarada and Hoshi, to the wonderfully goofy reporter Nakamura who's always eating hard-boiled eggs for comic effect, to the caricature-like portrayal of the villains, especially Kumayama. There's also a recurring bit wherein a shifty-eyed politician who's all smiles (Kenzo Tadake) tries to reassure reporters that despite the terrible damage inflicted by the typhoon, a massive industrial development project on the coast will continue. Although the politician is amusing, this is one of several plot threads that either goes nowhere or just appears without warning. The film opens with huge hydraulic pumps siphoning water from the land and workers pulling debris out of the water, but the industrial project only surfaces again as a plot device to get Sakai and Junko back to the site for Godzilla's unexpected entrance. Then there is the fluorescent piece of debris that Junko finds afloat in the water. There is no explanation as to what it is, although it can be surmised that it has something to do with Godzilla (a piece of his skin? his excrement?), for it turns out to be highly radioactive. Sakai and Junko, having been exposed to the blob, are also radioactive, but pseudo-scientist Miura cures them by placing them in steam chambers and de-nuking them (a far, lighthearted cry from Toho films like *The Human Vapor* and *The H-Man*, where radiation exposure was a deadly curse). And in a contrivance that puts the heroes in the path of danger during the last reel, a group of schoolchildren are trapped on the island where Godzilla and the twin Mothras are battling, but the rescue sequence is hardly terrifying.

GOD OF THUNDER: The rampaging Godzilla finally reaches his target: Mothra's egg. He smashes at Kumayama's giant incubator with his tail, but Mothra arrives just in time to protect her offspring and fells Godzilla with wing-induced whirlwinds. A fierce battle ensues, with Godzilla clearly outmatched as Mothra emits a poisonous yellow pollen from her wings, blinding the big lizard. Godzilla haphazardly breathes fire in all directions until he finally hits his foe with a deadly blast. Mortally wounded, Mothra rests upon the eggshell and dies.

Abandoning the hot-blooded cunning of *Godzilla Raids Again* and the comic high jinx of *King Kong vs. Godzilla*, Godzilla is once again the cold, unsympathetic, and deadly destructive force he was in his 1954 debut, and his dark, fearsome nature is heightened in contrast to Mothra, the mythical and vaguely beautiful monster. The new Godzilla costume, known as the *Mosu-Goji* ("Moth-Godzi") design, was made by sculptor Teizo Toshimitsu with more input from suitmation actor Haruo Nakajima than ever before. The costume-making process took about two months prior to filming with Nakajima visiting the workshop often, and the result is a lighter costume that allows for more fluid movement. *Mosu-Goji*, widely regarded as the best Godzilla suit in the entire series, is colored a deep gray that personifies the beast's dark side. God-

zilla's head is more articulated than before, with a rubbery upper lip that trembles[16] when the monster roars and sinister, staring eyes. The body is slightly more slender than the *Kin-Goji*, but Godzilla seems all-powerful nonetheless as Nakajima constantly assumes the "attack posture" — walking upright, slightly bent forward, with Godzilla's talons extended in front — and Tsuburaya's use of high-speed photography once again creates the illusion of a monolithic, slow-moving creature. Nakajima's input also resulted in another costume improvement that goes largely unnoticed: Reinforced heels were added to the feet, allowing Nakajima to do flips and rolls without losing his footing (this was especially important in the two titanic battles with the adult and larval Mothras, as Godzilla was constantly falling and getting up again). "After I retired, they didn't put heels in the costumes anymore," Nakajima said.

In addition to the Godzilla suit, virtually all the effects work in *Godzilla vs. The Thing* is impeccable. The miniature cityscapes and model tanks and helicopters, the mechanical props and puppets that bring Godzilla and Mothra to life, and the wind and water effects used in the storm sequence are among Tsuburaya's best. The film also includes a unique effects scene in which oversized furniture, wallpaper, carpeting, and other props were built eight times their actual size to make the twin fairies appear to be just 30 centimeters tall as they flee from Kumayama and Torahata in the hotel room. But most impressive is the marked improvement in composite photography. Gone are the telltale blue matte lines that marred the effects work in *King Kong vs. Godzilla* and other previous Toho genre pictures in color. The great strides made in this area are immediately apparent in the first full-view shot of Mothra's egg on the beach, as the joining of the live-action footage (a crowd of people standing in a circle around the egg) and the special-effects footage (the egg) is virtually undetectable. In another breathtaking scene, the human heroes watch from a hillside, in a corner of the screen, as Godzilla and Mothra battle in the distance.

The techniques utilized to make the monsters appear gigantic were likewise used to make the *shobijin* ("tiny beauties") appear small. In *Mothra*, made just three years earlier, the tiny twins were often surrounded by glowing halos, or the bars of the cage in which they were imprisoned appeared to quiver. Here, if not for logical thought, it might be quite easy to forget the little women are a special effect. When the girls first reveal themselves to the three heroes in the woods, actresses Emi and Yumi Ito (wearing cute, furry hats and shawls) are super-imposed onto a real tree branch. Even better is the scene wherein Sakai, Junko, and Miura present the tiny twins to the honchos of Happy Enterprises in hopes of getting the egg back: When the cover and front flaps of the wooden case are opened, revealing the little girls inside, the effect is seamless. The improved composite work is owed to an Oxberry 1900 optical printer Tsuburaya had seen while touring American movie studios the previous year and then pressured the studio heads to purchase. The Toho brass were reportedly reluctant to lay out the expenditure at first; the machine was pricey and, according to some reports, one of only two in use at that time, the other one at Walt Disney Productions in Hollywood. The investment paid off, as the blue-screen matte photography in Toho's monster and sci-fi pictures of the mid-1960s is excellent.

Godzilla's entrance in this film is a classic — first, his gigantic, scaly tail whips out from beneath the rumbling earth, and the monster rights himself, shakes off the dirt, and embarks on a rampage through Nagoya. The composite work here, too, is nearly perfect as Godzilla attacks an oil refinery at Yokkaichi, with frightened workers fleeing in panic. As Godzilla enters the heart of the city, real-life streetscapes are used in lieu of miniatures in several shots, with Godzilla looming realistically in the distance. The monster destroys two landmarks in clumsy accidents: First, his tail gets caught in the Nagoya Tower, causing the structure to crash onto the monster's back, at which he whips his head around in anger. Soon thereafter, Godzilla stumbles and falls onto the historic Nagoya Castle, crumbling the upper part of the building. This is one of the most memorable moments in G-history, but it didn't go exactly as planned during filming. In *Unused Toho Special Effects Footage*, a documentary released on home video in Japan in the mid-1980s, the first take, which was deemed an NG ("no good"), can be seen. In it, Godzilla smashes into the castle but only slight damage is inflicted. Haruo Nakajima tried to salvage the scene by improvising a roar, as if Godzilla were enraged by the castle's strong fortification, but in the end the model had to be repaired and the scene shot again.

The first fight between Godzilla and Mothra is the ultimate Toho face-off between a suitmation monster and a mechanically controlled puppet. Like the original Mothra prop in *Mothra*, the newly built adult Mothra utilized in *Godzilla vs. The Thing* flies through the air controlled by wires attached to a Y-shaped brace that opens and closes, causing the wings to flap up and down. An additional feature to the new Mothra puppet is radio-controlled legs that twitch constantly, making the creature more lifelike. The entire battle sequence is impressively staged, despite the complex combination of suits, props, wind effects created by high-powered fans, and the optical animation of Godzilla's ray (better conceived in this than in any Godzilla film, a glowing bluish white-hot gas). When Mothra buzzes Godzilla at close range, there is rapid crosscutting between close-up shots filmed with a hand-operated Godzilla puppet and medium shots using the suit, utilizing a slow-speed photography technique similar to the accidentally revved-up action in the Godzilla-vs.-Angilas fight in *Godzilla Raids Again*, lending the action a kinetic frenzy that looks as if it were done with stop-motion animation. The scenes of Mothra dragging Godzilla by the tail, pulling him away from the egg, were done with the Godzilla suit in medium shots (with Haruo Nakajima inside, scratching furiously at the dirt) and a Godzilla prop in long shots.

The Japanese military's three-prong plan to dispose of Godzilla is also impressively staged. In Plan A, the army bombards Godzilla with napalm bombs and tank gunfire, luring the monster into an "artificial lightning" field where giant electrodes zap him with rays, but Godzilla knocks over one of the towers. In Plan B, choppers drop huge metal nets from the sky, ensnaring Godzilla while more electrical rays are fired from all sides. Godzilla appears vanquished, but an overzealous commander orders the jolt increased to 30 million volts and the generator blows. Godzilla incinerates electrical towers and the tank fleet, and the military switches to Plan C, which apparently is "Let's get the hell out of here."

As the action builds to a climax and Godzilla seems unstoppable, the fairies serenade Mothra's egg. Not one but two giant caterpillars emerge and head to Iwa Island, where their foe continues his assault. Godzilla taunts the seemingly puny insects, igniting an entire village with his breath, but the worms are undaunted. The Mothra larvae in *Godzilla vs. The Thing* are considerably smaller than their caterpillar parent who smashed through Tokyo in the original *Mothra*. In that film, the larval Mothra was a suitmation prop operated by six stunt actors who crouched together in single-file inside. The original Mothra had leathery skin, and its smooth movement made it a somewhat convincing creature; in contrast, the baby caterpillars in *Godzilla vs. The*

Mothra, "The Mysterious Thing"

What is the thing? Born to defy . . . The world's most terrifying monster! GODZILLA!

GODZILLA VS. THE THING

It looks innocent as a gigantic egg. But its unseen powers are so great that its worshippers beg The Thing's indulgence in self-abasing ceremonies.

GODZILLA VS. THE THING

The War of the Giant Monsters!

That Makes the Very Earth Tremble!

Will man's inventions defeat their unknown powers?

Will humanity survive their battle?

A shattering soul-shocking experience!

In eye-jolting color and Terror-Scope!

GODZILLA VS. THE THING

— From AIP's theatrical trailer for Godzilla vs. The Thing

American International Pictures' advertising campaign for *Godzilla vs. The Thing* was an amusing attempt to pull the wool over moviegoers' eyes. The theatrical trailer clearly showed glimpses of Mothra, yet created an air of mystery by asking, "What is The Thing?" Advertising materials showed Godzilla battling a monster hidden behind a panel labeled "censored," with the disclaimer that "the producers of this motion picture take this precaution to spare those who cannot take its full horror . . . for those who can . . . see the film from the beginning!" Protruding from behind the panel were a number of tentacle-like appendages that looked like they belonged to the monsters in *The Day of the Triffids*.

It's hard to imagine exactly what the publicity men at AIP were thinking when they decided to keep Mothra's ID secret. Perhaps AIP believed Mothra was too wimpy an opponent for Godzilla, and that a title like *Godzilla vs. Mothra* would inspire laughs rather than anticipation. It is also possible (perhaps likely) that AIP was wary of legal action by Columbia Pictures, which released the original *Mothra* in the U.S. two years before.

Thing are a combination of motor-driven mechanical props that crawl across the landscape and hand-operated puppets (used in close-ups of the bugs spraying their sticky silk, which was an oil-based compound concocted by the effects crew).

The effects work in the final battle, set amid the island's barren rocks, relies on fast-paced editing and derives much of its power from the incredible score by Akira Ifukube, who weaves Godzilla's and Mothra's themes into a thundering climactic musical piece that begins when the Mothras swim across the sea and spans more than eight minutes, ending only after a fully cocooned Godzilla, kicking and screaming, tumbles into the water. This opus, which incorporates the beautiful melody of *"Mosura no Uta"* ("Song of Mothra") from Yuji Koseki's score to the original *Mothra*, is the highlight of one of Ifukube's best genre scores. Ifukube also composed "Holy Spring," the mournful and touching piece sung by the twin fairies in front of a spring on Infant Island, the last spot of lush greenery on their otherwise despoiled home.

THE NEW FRONTIER (MISSILES): Just a few weeks after the film was released in Japan as *Mothra vs. Godzilla*, *Variety* reported on May 6, 1964, that the U.S. theatrical and television rights had been acquired by Henry G. Saperstein, an upstart Hollywood producer. Saperstein would eventually become a major figure in Godzilla's stateside career (*see Chapter 6*) but at this stage he did not have the apparatus to launch a wide theatrical release on his own, and after boasting to *Variety* that *Godzilla vs. the Giant Moth* (Saperstein's proposed English-language title for the picture) had earned "a whopping $217,000 gross in [its] first three weeks in eight theaters in metropolitan Tokyo," he sold the rights to Samuel Z. Arkoff's American International Pictures, a company known for releasing such disparate pictures as *I Was a Teenage Werewolf* and Fellini's *La Dolce Vita*. Arkoff handled the picture admirably, re-titling it *Godzilla vs. The Thing* for promotional value and launching an impressive publicity campaign. Most importantly, he avoided the butchering that both *Gigantis* and *King Kong vs. Godzilla* had suffered and left the film virtually intact, with only a few minor adjustments, most notably the truncation of the twin fairies' song on Infant Island and the excision of a very short scene at the end of the picture in which Sakai, Junko, Miura, and Nakamura (the egg-eating, hardhat-wearing reporter) wave goodbye as the Mothras swim home. Also deleted was a brief shot of Kumayama handing out leaflets to attract visitors to the giant egg incubator, and

when Torahata shoots Kumayama during their fight in the hotel room, the Japanese version shows Kumayama, bleeding from the forehead, slumping over dead.

The English-language version of *Godzilla vs. The Thing* includes a sequence in which U.S. military officials come to Japan's aid against Godzilla, deploying a new superweapon called the Frontier Missile fired from a Destroyer located offshore, but the missile does little harm to Godzilla and succeeds only in creating a huge smokescreen. The sequence is superfluous to the story, and the effects involved (thick smoke clouds, fake-looking missiles) are unimpressive. In the Japanese version of the film, there are no American military men; instead there is a brief scene in which the Japan Self Defense Force commander (Susumu Fujita, a famous movie star in the 1940s, now playing small character parts) lays out the battle plan against Godzilla.

For many fans on both sides of the Pacific, *Godzilla vs. The Thing* is the last great Godzilla film. It marks the final installment in which Godzilla is unrepentantly sinister throughout; from hereon, humor and human characteristics would pop up in the monster's motif with increasing frequency. In many ways, Mothra also remains Godzilla's greatest adversary, using finesse and intelligence rather than strength to send Godzilla to the only resounding defeat in his movie career.

MOTH HOLES

The evolution of the Godzilla vs. The Thing screenplay

Shinichi Sekizawa's screenplay for *Godzilla vs. The Thing* underwent drastic alteration from its original form before being filmed. The villainous Torahata did not exist in the original story and reporter/hero Sakai was joined by two scientists, one his college friend and the other his friend's mentor. Originally it was Godzilla's body, thought to be lifeless, rather than Mothra's egg that washes ashore and draws the interest of a shifty businessman. Mothra's egg was ultimately substituted, a more sensible choice for commercial exploitation than a huge, immovable, and highly radioactive carcass.

The visit to Infant Island to plead for Mothra's help against Godzilla was basically unchanged, though the first idea was that the heroes would offer themselves up as hostages. Honda's hand in rewriting was evident here, as the finished film's impassioned plea for cooperation and the brotherhood of mankind is one of his signatures. Godzilla was to attack Rolisica (the country where the orig-inal *Mothra* took place), the Rolisicans using Frontier Missiles to defend themselves. (The scene was eventually cut from the Japanese script and filmed only for international versions, with "Rolisican" references omitted. Instead, the Americans use the missiles to defend Japan.)

The geography of Godzilla's attacks was a bit different in the original story, with Himeji Castle (the only major castle in Japan never destroyed and rebuilt) being trampled and Godzilla moving east across the country until arriving near Tokyo. The idea for artificial lightning is conceived when Godzilla is repelled from Tokyo by special electrical towers that attack the monster, but eventually he develops an immunity to the tactic, and at that critical moment, Mothra comes to the rescue. As Godzilla stalks the human heroes at a beach, the adult Mothra (not the caterpillars) faces off against Godzilla in the climactic battle.

— *Jay Ghee*

111

Five

ENTER THE DRAGON

"Oh, Godzilla! What terrible language!"

— Mothra's twin fairies

GHIDRAH: THE THREE-HEADED MONSTER

RATING (OUT OF 5 STARS): ★ ★ ★ 1/2

JAPANESE VERSION: SAN DAIKAIJU — CHIKYU SAIDAI NO KESSEN (THREE GIANT MONSTERS — THE GREATEST BATTLE ON EARTH). Released on December 20, 1964, by the Toho Motion Picture Company. Toho Scope, in color. Running Time: 92 minutes.

U.S. VERSION: Released on September 29, 1965, by The Walter Reade Organization and Continental Distributing. Premiered in Dallas. Running Time: 85 minutes.

STORY: A princess from the tiny Asian kingdom of Selgina heads for Japan to escape an assassination plot; when her plane explodes over the Pacific, she is believed dead, but the princess (apparently suffering amnesia) soon reappears in Japan claiming to be a prophetess from Venus (Mars in the U.S. version) and foretelling the world's destruction by King Ghidorah, a three-headed space dragon, and other monsters. Her predictions come true: A gigantic meteorite crashes into the Japan Alps and Ghidorah is born in a fireball, and it's up to Godzilla, Rodan, and Mothra to settle their petty differences and unite to save the world.

TRIPLE THREAT

By the mid-1960s, giant monsters were virtually extinct in American movies, save for the occasional dinosaur such as Ray Harryhausen's stop-motion tyrannosaur in *The Valley of Gwangi*. But Toho continued to experiment in the genre. After *Godzilla vs. The Thing*, Ishiro Honda and Eiji Tsuburaya teamed up on *Dagora: The Space Monster* (released August 1964), a sort of spoof of the *yakuza* gangster movies that were popular in Japan at that time, in which a running battle among a group of jewel thieves, the police, and an intrepid insurance investigator is constantly and inconveniently interrupted by the appearance of a gigantic alien creature that hovers in the sky. *Dagora* is one of Toho's lesser efforts, but the creature itself, a glowing, jellyfish-like apparition brought vividly to life through a combination of wire-manipulated puppetry and optical effects,

Beautiful actress Akiko Wakabayashi, one of Toho's sexy starlets of the 1960s, portrays the alternately regal and frumpy Princess Salno in *Ghidrah: The Three-Headed Monster*. She is shown here in publicity stills for the James Bond film *You Only Live Twice* (1967), in which she played a Japanese spy who assists James Bond.

exemplifies the boldly inventive spirit of Tsuburaya and his craftsmen during this period. Amid this highly creative atmosphere, Toho's SFX men gave birth to perhaps their most inspired monster (second only to Godzilla, of course): King Ghidorah, the galaxy-roaming, golden, three-headed flying dragon.

With giant monsters continuing to score well at the box office, Toho pushed its second Godzilla picture and third Honda-Tsuburaya film of the year into production in late summer 1964. Despite the filmmakers' frenetic workload, the resulting film, *San Daikaiju — Chikyu Saidai No Kessen* (*Three Giant Monsters — The Greatest Battle on Earth* — a strange title, since there are *four* giant monsters in the picture), known in the West as *Ghidrah: The Three-Headed Monster*, is an extravaganza of sorts, with a far-fetched and fantastical story and a four-way

climactic monster battle unprecedented in terms of visual scope. The effects work is abundant and impressive, utilizing the Godzilla suit and one of the Mothra larva props from the previous movie, an awe-inspiring King Ghidorah costume that is operated both by a stunt actor inside, and a crew of wire-works technicians who manipulate its heads, twin tails, and huge wings, and a new and slightly redesigned Rodan, Toho's famous flying pteranodon, which returns to the big screen eight years after its 1956 debut (this is one of the original twin Rodans believed to have died in the eruption at Mount Aso; it emerges from the same mountain).

On the negative side, the tight production schedule is evident in some of the effects work — for example, the all-too-obvious explosion of a model plane, the Godzilla and Rodan puppets that hardly match their respective costumes — and the monsters again resort to silly antics (like Ghidorah blasting Godzilla in the butt) and anthropomorphized behavior; at one point, Godzilla, Rodan, and Mothra *talk* to one another in a "monster Esperanto" understood by all three, despite their differing species. And although Godzilla is still portrayed as a force of anarchy and destruction, this is where he begins his inevitable transition from evil monster to Japan's titanic superhero.

The story, which seems to have been partly inspired by the popularity of the James Bond film series, weaves international intrigue, a beautiful woman, casebook detective work, prophetic psychic powers, and alien invasion with the monster scenario, and high-brow issues like nuclear weapons and commercialism are abandoned in favor of pure, fast-paced escapism. Princess Salno (Akiko Wakabayashi), heiress to the throne of a small, exotic Asian country called Selgina, where all men wear harlequin suits, is believed killed, but an identical-looking woman (clad not in her highness's royal garb, but in a fisherman's jacket and cap) subsequently appears in Tokyo, claiming to be from Venus (Mars in the U.S. version) and prophesying with great accuracy the appearances of monsters. The rest of the film concerns the efforts of Shindo (**Yosuke Natsuki**), a young detective, to figure out whether the prophetess is really the princess and, if so, to try and cure her of her apparent amnesia and delusions, all the while protecting her from the knife- and gun-wielding Selginan thugs who have come to Japan to finish the job that the plane bomb could not. Meanwhile, Shindo's sister Naoko (Yuriko Hoshi), a reporter for a radio program about strange phenomena, takes care of the wayward Venusian in hopes of getting a good scoop. Amid all this, King Ghidorah bursts out of a meteorite in a fiery birth rite. Other plot threads focus on Naoko's vague involvement with Professor Murai (Hiroshi Koizumi), a geologist studying the huge meteorite that has crashed into the mountains. Naoko and Murai team up with Mothra's twin priestesses, who come to Japan to guest-star on a TV program (willingly this time, as opposed to being kidnapped as in *Mothra* four years before) to bring Mothra to Japan.

With so much going on at once, there are some inevitable loose ends. The story opens amid a terrible heat wave in the middle of winter, an apparent premonition of the disasters awaiting, yet the abnormal climate is never mentioned again. The members of a UFO club are seen scouting the heavens, hoping to contact aliens who may know why

the Earth is out of whack — there seems to be some connection here to the disembodied voice that lures the princess out the escape hatch just before her airplane goes ka-boom, but it is never explained. And King Ghidorah, having wiped out the civilizations of Venus, now appears on Earth without much of a rationale. It has been wisely speculated in *G-Fan* magazine that because Ghidorah acts under control of space aliens in all subsequent film appearances, it can be assumed that his maiden visit to Earth was engineered by the Controller of Planet X, who orchestrates Ghidorah's rampage in the sequel *Monster Zero*.

The cast is an assembly of Toho's then-new and veteran talent led by Natsuki and Wakabayashi, who also starred in Honda's previous film, *Dagora*. Natsuki, a popular leading man in Toho war pictures like *I Bombed Pearl Harbor* (1960), is somewhat bland compared to Akira Takarada and some of the studio's other front-line talent, and he is overshadowed by Hoshi, who plays his spunky reporter sister. On the other hand, Wakabayashi, a popular starlet who joined Toho after an unsuccessful audition for the role of Princess Yukihime in Kurosawa's classic *The Hidden Fortress* (1958), is perfectly cast as the clairvoyant amnesiac princess. The actress's good looks and exotic features, coupled with her deadpan delivery and blank stare, lend the prophetess a sense of mystery and vulnerability. The great Takashi Shimura fills in as Dr. Tsukamoto, the shock-therapy-happy scientist who, while trying to "cure" the princess, almost unwittingly kills her when the Selginan thugs sneak into the lab and crank up the voltage. The assassins, led by the poker-faced Malmess (Hisaya Ito, a frequent Toho character actor in the late 1950s and '60s) and another henchman with a pencil mustache (Susumu Kurobe), are more comic than threatening, tooling around the city in white and black gangster suits, hats, and sunglasses. Every time these tough guys seems to have the princess in their hands, their plan is thwarted — the twin fairies shut out the lights, Godzilla and Rodan crash onto the power lines, or Ghidorah buries their car in a landslide. In the end, a bleeding, wounded Malmess grazes the princess with a bullet, but before he can put her away another monster-induced rockslide drops a foam-rubber boulder on him, which he impossibly catches, then falls to his death. The assassin's fate was probably meant to be funny, but it plays out embarrassingly. There are also two Toho bit players in the film who steal their brief scenes: Ikio Sawamura (1905–1975), the wide-eyed old fisherman, was a perennial member of Ishiro Honda's sci-fi casts, and Senkichi Omura (b. 1923), best known as Konno the translator in *King Kong vs. Godzilla*, retrieves another man's hat from the crater at Mount Aso, only to be greeted by Rodan emerging from the mountainside.

THE BROTHERHOOD OF *KAIJU*: This time it is the monsters, not the human cast, who must put aside their differences to join forces against a common enemy. Godzilla is a malevolent badass throughout most of the picture, as is Rodan, but the two monsters spend more time sparring with each other than attacking cities, thus shifting the focus of villainy onto the evil Ghidorah, which more than makes up for the other monsters' new indifference to Japanese metropolises, strafing Yokohama with its wonderfully erratic energy bolts and cackling gleefully, with each of its three heads emitting a slightly different-pitched roar. Mothra fully assumes her role as monster intermediary here, willfully responding to the Japanese government's plea for assistance in the fight against Ghidorah. As Godzilla and Rodan taunt and tackle each other at the base of Mount Fuji, Mothra breaks up the melee by spraying her sticky silk at them to get their attention. A three-way "monster summit" is held, with translation provided by Mothra's female channelers, in which the two giant reptiles refuse to aid in the battle.[17] It takes only a moment for Godzilla and Rodan to relent, for when Ghidorah blasts Mothra with a dose of its lightning-breath, the little caterpillar goes sailing through the air. In the mother of all monster fights, King Ghidorah clearly seems to have his three foes out-dueled as his rays send Rodan cowering behind a rock and cause Godzilla to shimmy in pain as the blasts hit his neck and tummy. Only when the Earth monsters truly combine their strengths, with Mothra perched atop a hovering Rodan's back and coating the three-headed dragon with silk (while Godzilla, the odd-monster-out, is relegated to holding Ghidorah's tails) do they succeed in driving the enemy back to outer space.

Eiji Tsuburaya's special-effects crew again makes some great strides, particularly in the staging of Ghidorah's hatching from the meteorite. The sequence combines a miniature meteorite prop, a shower of pyrotechnics when the space rock cracks open, and a stunning series of rapidly edited explo-sions that segues into a beautiful hovering fireball created by optical animation, finally revealing the monster's entire form. Ghidorah's attack on Yokohama is a showcase for the optical animation of the dragon's rays, one of Toho's most well conceived monster weapons, which dance across the cityscape at crisscrossed angles, with wire-rigged explosions sending up columns of debris and fans simulating the powerful winds unleashed by the hydra's huge wingspan. Godzilla's entrance in the harbor is also a classic moment, with the monster surfacing offshore and blasting an ocean liner, with the optical animation of his dorsal fins and radioactive breath glowing brilliantly against the dark night sky. The composite photography is even more impressive than in *Godzilla vs. The Thing*, not only in the near-flawless execution of the tiny twin fairies, but also several great shots incorporating people into the monster action. In one example, a crowd of people run toward a Shinto shrine for safety, only to be startled by the marauding Ghidorah, seen through the shrine's wooden *torii* (entranceway); in another, the Godzilla-vs.-Rodan battle rages in the distance as people flee, seen from a long-distance vantage.

Godzilla and Mothra look more or less the same as in the previous film, with slight modifications to the *Mosu-Goji* costume's face (it no longer had the trembling rubber lip) and one of the larval Mothra props (its eyes were changed from blue to red), but the new Rodan costume hardly matches the awesome sight of the 1956 original, with a redesigned and goofy-looking face, a thick, oddly modeled neck that betrays the presence of the stuntman's head inside, and triangular wings. The real awe-inspiring monster is Ghidorah, the 100-meter-tall, 30,000-metric-ton dragon with a 150-meter wingspan that fills up the entire screen. The monster is reminiscent of the *Yamata no Orochi* (a legendary dragon that appears in the *Kojiki*, the mythical tale of the birth of Japan), Chinese dragons, the Hydra in Greek mythology, and legendary sea serpents, but it is more fearsome than any of those. The monster was brought to life by stunt actor Shoichi Hirose, who spent hours upon hours hunched over inside the costume, holding on to a crossbar for support (the suit had no arms), and a team of wire-works puppeteers who operated the wings, the necks, and the tails. At times, there were six or seven men in the rafters over the soundstage, looking something like a trapeze act, SFX cameraman Teisho Arikawa said in *The Complete History of Toho Special Effects Movies*. "There were times when all three necks got tangled up, or the piano wires would reflect the studio lights, or the wires would get caught in [Ghidorah's] scales. It was an agonizing operation."

DO THE CONTINENTAL: Within a few months of its release in Japan, the U.S. distribution rights to *The Greatest Battle on Earth* were acquired by Walter Reade-Sterling Inc., a New York company that operated a chain of movie theaters and distributed art house and low-budget films through its subsidiary, Continental. Continental inexplicably shortened the spelling of King Ghidorah's name to "Ghidrah" [sic], retitled the picture *Ghidrah: The Three-Headed Monster*, and opened it in 83 theaters in Boston on a double bill with a James Bond spoof called *Agent 8 3/4*, and later in other areas with the Elvis Presley vehicle *Harum Scarum*. Continental officials proudly boasted in *Variety* at the time that *Ghidrah* earned more than $200,000 in film rentals in its first five days of release and more than $1.3 million overall.

But it was blood money! Unlike the mostly hands-off approach that American International Pictures took with *Godzilla vs. The Thing*, Continental subjected *Ghidrah* to an array of unnecessary, annoying, and sometimes incompetent editorial changes, including the removal of scenes, the shifting around of scenes, the replacement of some of Akira Ifukube's marvelous score (including a great theme for the Godzilla-vs.-Rodan sequence, with unique motifs for each monster) with nondescript film library music, and the truncation of the twin fairies' second rendition of the lovely "Cry For Happiness," sung just prior to Mothra's departure from Infant Island. The English dubbing by Joseph Belucci (a former voice actor and director at Titra Sound in New York, who had formed his own dubbing studio) is adequately scripted but dully acted, the lowlight being an off-camera starlet named "Annie Sukiyaki" reading a rough translation of the fairies' song.

Continental's sloppy editing is exemplified by the scene in which Godzilla surfaces and makes his landing on Yokohama. While Godzilla is wading in Sagami Bay, a shot of Rodan flying overhead, his angular body brilliantly silhouetted against the night sky, was snatched from a later sequence and inserted here, making it seem as if Godzilla spies Rodan above and follows him onto the mainland; in the Japanese version, Rodan does not appear in the sky until Godzilla has come ashore. The American version jumbles several scenes around during Godzilla's approach from the water into the city — the monster is seen onshore, then offshore, then on land again. Another major change involves the re-working of Dr. Tsukamoto's examination of the princess and King Ghidorah's blitz on Yokohama. In the U.S. version, Ghidorah attacks the city even as the princess is still prophesying the monster's imminent arrival to destroy the planet, as if no one had seen the creature yet. In the Japanese version, the princess is taken to Tsukamoto's clinic before Ghidorah's first appearance, and she warns everyone that the monster is coming. In the next scene,

Something to Wear at Capote's Masked Ball

Walter Reade-Sterling's publicity campaign for *Ghidrah: The Three-Headed Monster* featured one of the greatest pieces of paraphernalia ever created in a *kaiju* promotion: The Ghidrah full-color mask!

This cardboard mask, which depicted the monster's three faces side-by-side, is surely a collector's item today, if any are still in existence. Walter Reade-Sterling's *Ghidrah* pressbook showed a drawing of some kid in a schoolboy uniform (complete with knee-high stockings) wearing the mask and flailing his arms outside a cinema, and stated that the masks were to be given to local television hosts who, in turn, would give them out to viewers, thereby generating free publicity for the film.

Ghidrah!

Nothing the screen has ever shown before can surpass the thrills of *Ghidrah! The Three-Headed Monster!*

Created from an atomic fireball hurled from outer space, Ghidrah: The Three-Headed Monster, threatens man's very existence on Earth!

Ghidrah: The Three-Headed Monster, battles Godzilla, Mothra, and Rodan, for mastery of the world.

Men quake before the terror of their unleashed fury!

All new! All never to be forgotten! A new high in screen terror!

GHIDRAH! THE THREE-HEADED MONSTER!

— From Continental's theatrical trailer for *Ghidrah: The Three-Headed Monster*

Ghidorah hatches from the meteorite and launches its attack — much more logical. Numerous other scene switcheroos and minor deletions are more subtle and certainly unapparent to anyone who has not seen the original Japanese version of the film, but have the combined effect of making *Ghidrah* more confusing and disjointed. The only positive change introduced in Continental's version of *Ghidrah* is the re-editing of several sound effects. While Malmess and Shindo are waging their gun battle in the hills, the U.S. version has the cries of the monsters battling in the distance superimposed over the shoot-out, a nice touch.

With so much action and so many plot elements rolled into one package, *Ghidrah* can be a confusing film at times, with the human drama and the monster scenario playing out almost independent of each other. But it is a hell of a thrill ride, a thoroughly enjoyable escapist Japanese monster movie with lots of visual knockouts. It was one of the last Godzilla movies to be released theatrically in the U.S. relatively shortly after its Japanese debut; from here on, the dwindling popularity of these films in America would make them more and more scarce in theaters. But its reputation in the U.S. has suffered due to fact that most present-day fans have only seen the film on television, in panned-and-scanned format, which does no justice to the vistas of the monsters fighting at Mount Fuji, Ghidorah gloriously spreading his wings, and other sights only enjoyed in the original Toho Scope widescreen format.

In October 1964, while *Ghidrah: The Three-Headed Monster* was in production at Toho, a reporter from *Newsweek* visited the set and reported his experiences watching the filming in a brief article. "The monster [Godzilla] climbed out of the Toho studio tank. With the help of two men, he got untaped and unzipped, and from the Godzilla suit an arm with a wristwatch emerged, followed by a perspiring figure in a white sweat shirt." The reporter described Godzilla as "half gorilla and half whale," and said Toho had recently announced its next giant monster film, *Frankenstein vs. Godzilla*.

GODZILLA CONQUERS THE WORLD

Frankenstein vs. Godzilla (circa 1963)

Toho tried for several years to make a film with the Frankenstein monster in the early 1960s. The first story to be developed was written by Shinichi Sekizawa in February 1963, pairing Frankenstein with an established Toho character, Mizuno (from *The Human Vapor*). In Sekizawa's treatment of *Frankenstein vs. The Human Vapor*, the monster's body is stolen from Baron Von Frankenstein's graveyard by a mad scientist who intends to revive the creature and vindicate the work of the German scientist. Meanwhile, the tragic Vapor Man, who has survived the theater blast which took the life of the actress he loved (at the end of *The Human Vapor*), learns of the scientist's plans and tracks him down, hoping to resurrect his dead lover. The story treatment submitted by Sekizawa was incomplete, and, lacking inspiration to finish it, he dropped the idea and moved on to other projects.

Enter Kaoru Mabuchi (a.k.a. Takeshi Kimura), who had an idea to link the Frankenstein monster with Toho's most proven commodity, Godzilla. For some time, Mabuchi had pondered the matchup, and finally produced a finished screenplay for *Frankenstein vs. Godzilla*. This story was written to follow *Godzilla Raids Again*, and began with Godzilla still encased in ice in the Bering Sea. The monster is constantly monitored by the JSDF, who keep his location secret. (Mabuchi developed this idea despite the fact that *King Kong vs. Godzilla*, in which Godzilla escapes from his icy tomb, had already been made. With Godzilla having disappeared into the ocean at the end of *Godzilla vs. The Thing*, Mabuchi thought the idea could still work.)

While the screenplay was rejected as a vehicle for Godzilla, Toho felt strongly enough about its potential to retain major portions of it for what would eventually come to the screen as *Frankenstein Conquers the World*. The human protagonists remained the same in both versions: Dr. Bowen, a physician specializing in radiation illnesses, his assistant Sueko, and Kawachi. Nearly all of the opening act remained the same from Mabuchi's original screenplay: The transfer of the monster's heart to a lab in Hiroshima at the end of WW II, the mysterious street child foraging food in the city, Sueko befriending the monster upon its capture, the monster's escape, the misguided fear that the monster would eat people, the cat-and-mouse game as Frankenstein eludes the military. Curiously, Frankenstein is given little sympathy as a human being by the main characters, even his caretaker Sueko who reluctantly agrees to perform a regeneration test where the monster's finger is severed. From start to finish, Frankenstein is regarded more as a specimen for study than as a human being.

Since Frankenstein's growth rate is directly related to his ability to feed, the authorities' concern over Frankenstein's behavior is far more exaggerated in the original story, so the military tries to use Godzilla to kill Frankenstein (like staging the battle in *King Kong vs. Godzilla* to rid Japan of Godzilla). As a result, Godzilla is freed from the ice. A military attack baits Godzilla into following a destroyer to Suruga Bay, and heat-ray projectors set atop a series of towers on land are activated in sequence to anger and guide Godzilla from the ocean to the Fuji area, where Frankenstein was last reported. This strategy was the story's major downfall. Since mankind never had any success in dealing with Godzilla (except for the Oxygen Destroyer, which was no longer an option) and Godzilla was far more powerful than Frankenstein, such a tactic seemed nonsensical.

Godzilla exhibits some uncharacteristic behavior, spotting a group of humans and chasing them, picking up Sueko in his claw, perhaps as if to eat her — this is unexplained. Frankenstein, who has badgered Godzilla while staying out of sight to this point, finally battles Godzilla to save Sueko. Without any special powers or defense other than his cunning, Frankenstein is ridiculously overmatched by Godzilla, but curiously Godzilla seldom uses his weapons. Thanks to convenient geologic instability in the area, the fight never amounts to much as Godzilla spends most of his time stumbling into faults and fissures, eventually tumbling into a raging river current which washes him away while Frankenstein disappears into a magma flow — monsters disappearing from sight and convenient natural disasters, the staple devices for ending several films of the era. With a seemingly faulty premise and a less than spectacular conflict, this is one Godzilla film best left on paper.

— Jay Ghee

Six

VOYAGE INTO SPACE

"Double-crossing finks!"

— Astronaut F. Glenn

MONSTER ZERO

RATING (OUT OF 5 STARS): ★ ★ ★ 1/2

JAPANESE VERSION: KAIJU DAISENSO (THE GREAT MONSTER WAR). Released on December 19, 1965, by the Toho Motion Picture Company. Toho Scope, in color. Running Time: 94 minutes. English-dubbed version released internationally as *Invasion of the Astro-Monsters*.

U.S. VERSION: Released on July 29, 1970, by Maron Films on a double bill with *War of the Gargantuas*. Premiered in Houston. Running Time: 94 minutes. MPAA Rating: G.

STORY: The people of Planet X, a newly discovered celestial body beyond Jupiter, ask to borrow Godzilla (Monster Zero-one) and Rodan (Monster Zero-two) from Earth to help repel King Ghidorah (Monster Zero) from their planet, offering in exchange a "miracle drug" that wipes out all diseases; soon the truth is revealed — the wonder drug is a hoax, and the aliens (whose planet is short on H2O) take control of the three monsters and set out to conquer Earth and its bountiful water supply. Two heroic astronauts, Glenn and Fuji, save the day with help from Glenn's self-sacrificing alien girlfriend and a geeky gizmo freak, whose new invention (a purse alarm for women) emits a hideous buzz that disables the aliens' computers and frees Godzilla and Rodan to battle Ghidorah.

GODZILLA'S MAN IN AMERICA

In May 1965, *Variety* reported an unprecedented development in Toho's *kaiju eiga* history. **Henry G. Saperstein** of United Productions of America in Hollywood announced he had entered into a deal to co-produce five motion pictures with Toho, including three giant-monster films, a war movie, and a spy thriller, plus a television show that would be filmed in Japan and air on U.S. stations. Thus began Toho's long relationship with a self-made Hollywood mogul whose contributions to Godzilla's career have been sometimes heroic, sometimes dubious. It was Saperstein who first brought American "stars" to Japan to increase the overseas marketability of Toho's science-fiction films, resulting in a trio of genre classics: *Frankenstein Conquers the World*, *War of the Gargantuas*, and the sixth Godzilla movie, *Monster Zero*.

Saperstein (1918–1998) began his career in Chicago as the head of a small theater chain inherited from his father, and later produced training films for the Air Force. After dabbling in film distribution, in 1959 he took over UPA, the cartoon studio that created Mr. Magoo and Gerald McBoing Boing, and began acquiring films for television syndication. When business associates advised Saperstein that he could make a surefire profit by getting into the monster-movie business, he inevitably wound up on Toho's doorstep.[18] Saperstein says his interest was piqued when, sometime in the early 1960s, he saw the Japanese version of the original *Godzilla* at the now-defunct Toho La Brea theater in Los Angeles, and he takes much credit for convincing Toho to turn their terrible tyranno into a Herculean hero. "I sat in the audience and I saw that although they were depicting him as a villain, the audience saw Godzilla as a hero and was cheering for him," Saperstein told a Los Angeles newspaper in 1994. "That's when I went to Tokyo to talk to Toho about playing him as the hero he was, rather than cloaking it in a metaphorical message. I told them that if they did that, Godzilla would become a worldwide phenomenon." Despite Godzilla's nightmarish origins, Saperstein unabashedly prefers the monster as a do-gooder. "Godzilla is the guy in the white hat, who comes forth reluctantly to save the day when somebody's messing things up," he said. "It's the classic morality play."

Saperstein says he provided 50 percent of the funding for his three giant monster co-productions, the first of which was the aforementioned *Frankenstein Conquers the World*. Released in August 1965 and starring Nick Adams, it was a wonderful fusing of Mary Shelley's Frankenstein myth with the giant-monster motif. During the dwindling days of World War II, the immortal heart of the Frankenstein monster is shipped from Germany to Japan for research purposes, arriving in Hiroshima just in time to be nuked on August 6, 1945. The irradiated heart survives the blast and over the course of about 20 years grows into a full-sized mutated human being resembling a young Japanese rendition of the Frankenstein monster. Like Shelley's original, the Japanese Frankenstein is a sensitive soul who is basically harmless until provoked, but the press, the authorities, and a rogue scientist (Tadao Takashima) who is convinced the monster is a menace do nothing but provoke him. And, this being a Tomoyuki Tanaka production, Frankenstein spends much of the time battling a gigantic, horn-snouted, ray-spitting quadrupedal reptile called Baragon,

which shows up in Japan without a hint as to its origins, and the two creatures eventually die when a volcano conveniently erupts nearby, swallowing them in lava. The film is a perennial curiosity in the genre because publicity stills published in *Famous Monsters* and elsewhere showed Frankenstein battling a gigantic octopus similar to the one in *King Kong vs. Godzilla*, yet the scene never appeared in either the Japanese or U.S. version of the film. Turns out that the octopus battle *was* indeed scripted and filmed specifically to be included only in the U.S. version, at Saperstein's request. But for reasons unknown, the footage was excised from the final cut (perhaps because the mollusk — a rubbery prop whose tentacles were controlled by wires — was unconvincing). The octopus footage is included as supplemental material on Toho Video's Laser Disc release of the film, available in Japan.

MON-STAR WARS: In *The Mysterians* and *Battle in Outer Space*, intergalactic invaders were portrayed similarly to their counterparts in American films like *War of the Worlds*, as coldhearted conquerors bent on taking over the planet and exploiting its natural resources. In *Monster Zero*, Toho's first real fusing of the alien and giant-monster genres, director Ishiro Honda and screenwriter Shinichi Sekizawa update the space-invader formula for the transistor age by casting the aliens as a Huxley-like technological cult, a society where individualism is nonexistent (everything, and presumably everyone, is assigned an impersonal number rather than a name, and all women look exactly alike), human emotions are outlawed, and all actions are "controlled by electronic computers" to preserve order. Honda has suggested in many of his films that blind faith in science poses a serious threat to mankind's spiritual and physical survival, and the people of Planet X are a full-scale realization of his concern. This premise provides an interesting thematic backdrop for one of the most thoroughly enjoyable Japanese monster movies of all. *Monster Zero* is more or less a direct sequel to *Ghidrah*,[19] with three of the previous film's four monster stars — Godzilla, Rodan, and King Ghidorah — combining forces under alien control to threaten Japan like never before. The story is simpler and less convoluted, the cast and characters more captivating, and the visuals are a tour-de-force of monster action, outer-space locales, imaginative props and models (the P-1 rocket and the A-Cycle light-ray cannons chief among them), swiftly moving flying saucers, and cool-looking alien costumes. At the same time, there are vague but telltale warnings of the imminent decline of the Godzilla series: This is the first Godzilla movie in which stock footage from previous films is used to pad the special-effects sequences, and Eiji Tsuburaya's penchant for monster humor rears its silly head in the infamous victory jig that Godzilla performs after he and Rodan win their first battle with King Ghidorah on Planet X.

Despite the techno-supremacy of its people, Planet X is deficient in one serious regard: It lacks water. Even with King Ghidorah at their disposal, the X-Seijin know that Godzilla and Rodan have previously teamed up to drive their monster away (curiously, there is no mention of Mothra, who had a major role in this), and so an evil plan of double-crossing and deceit is hatched in order to seize control of Earth and its bounty of H_2O. Why the aliens simply do not steal Godzilla and Rodan from Earth is anyone's guess — they probably could have done so undetected, since no one seems to notice their flying saucers submerged in Lake Myojin until they reveal themselves — but the spacemen's conniving, manipulative ways make them a more mysterious breed of villain. It is interesting to note that instead of launching a direct attack on Earth, the X-Seijin set an interplanetary trap by sending out magnetic wave signals; these attract the attention of Dr. Yoshida, head of World Space Authority, who launches an expedition to the new planet. At first, Planet X appears to be a friend in need, albeit a cold and stand-offish friend, but in truth these computerized, unfeeling aliens are preying upon what they perceive as mankind's greatest weakness, its compassion and sympathy.

Amid all the galaxy-trotting and monster-swapping, a love triangle develops between astronaut F. Glenn (played with gusto by Adams), the alien interloper Miss Namikawa (alternately played with slyness and vulnerability by Kumi Mizuno), and the conformist mores of Planet X, which imprison Namikawa's heart. A subplot focuses on the nerdy inventor Tetsuo (Akira Kubo) and his girlfriend Haruno (Keiko Sawai), who want to marry despite the disapproval of Haruno's older brother who, by sheer Toho coincidence, is Kazuo Fuji, Glenn's astronaut partner. The goofy Tetsuo wants desperately to impress Fuji so he can get his blessings, and the aliens twice give Tetsuo his chance. First, under the guise of a fictitious toy company, they offer him

a wad of cash for his newest creation, the Lady-guard. But the aliens have no intention of marketing Tetsuo's product; indeed, they want to prevent it, for the Ladyguard is the X-Seijin's Achilles Heel, emitting a high-frequency sound that both causes the aliens to recoil in unbearable physical pain and makes their godlike computer equipment go haywire. Namikawa, in a final act of love and redemption (slipping a handwritten note into Glenn's pocket just before she is executed), reveals this secret, and Glenn and Tetsuo save the day by broadcasting the Ladyguard's buzz over an entire nation of radios, sending the aliens to their demise and allowing Godzilla and Rodan to send King Ghidorah packing. Sekizawa's script is freewheeling and easy to follow, and allows for easy suspension of logic and disbelief. Its only major faux pas is Glenn and Fuji's discovery of a reservoir full of gold on Planet X — a scene meant to show how the aliens, despite their immense riches, desperately need water, but it is childish and unnecessary.

PLANET X MARKS THE SPOT: What sets *Monster Zero* apart from Toho's other Godzilla and sci-fi efforts of the mid-1960s is its great attention to art direction and visual detail in both the dramatic and special-effects scenes — of the studio's genre films of this period, only *Atragon* was more ambitious. In the post-*Star Wars* era, the notion of what aliens, spacecraft, and faraway planets might look like has made the world of *Monster Zero* old hat, but even today the film retains a certain audacity and kitschy style that is irresistible fun. The minimalist set representing the surface of Planet X is a dark, barren wasteland, dwarfed by the huge figure of Jupiter hovering on the horizon (a beautiful backdrop painting). The X-Seijin's underground base is a labyrinth of interconnecting tunnels with a huge presidential suite where the Controller holds court, with a video screen on the wall that monitors Ghidorah's above-ground attacks and a variety of electronic panels and gizmos (including a globe-like orb that glows when the Controller speaks — possibly an interplanetary language translating device). Planet X's old-school flying saucers are impressive, glowing from within, flying in perfect formation with agility and able to submerge under water — the scene in which the lake bubbles violently and the saucers emerge, hovering above the surface, is both spectacular and creepy, and hints at the aliens' ulterior motives. The spaceships fire destructive ray beams capable of blasting open a mountainside and melting the WSA's radar dishes (an effect similar to the "tower melting" scene from the original *Godzilla*, created by blowing hot wind on a polystyrene miniature prop) and they transport Godzilla and Rodan to Planet X using a capture ray created by optical animation. These flying saucers are represented by wire-manipulated models and a stellar composite shot at Lake Myojin, similar to the landing of Mothra's egg on the beach in *Godzilla vs. The Thing*. Also noteworthy are the alien costumes, with form-fitting latex body suits, head-mounted antennae, and wraparound shades (perhaps an inspiration for Levar Burton's getup in *Star Trek: The Next Generation*). The futuristic restaurant where Tetsuo first meets Miss Namikawa is another nice touch.

"OUR COMPUTERS ARE ALWAYS INVINCIBLE!": The Ladyguard's ugly noise sabotages the computers aboard the invaders' flying saucers. The A-Cycle light-ray cannons break the aliens' control over Godzilla, Rodan, and Ghidorah. Rather than concede defeat, the Controller and his minions commit *hara-kiri*, and their sputtering spacecraft explodes. Godzilla and Rodan instinctively turn against Ghidorah and a battle royal erupts. Deadlocked in close combat, the three creatures eventually tumble together over a cliff and into the ocean.

The coordinated rampage of the monsters and the Planet X flying saucers, and the battles pitting Godzilla and Rodan versus Monster Zero (first on Planet X, then in Japan), are more impressively staged than in *Ghidrah*. King Ghidorah benefits from a number of improvements in his second screen foray, particularly some revisions to the monster costume, which appears to be a darker shade of gold, making the creature more striking and sinister. The wire-works crew has also learned from experience, as Ghidorah flies through the air and walks on land with more agility, and his three heads titter more nervously and menacingly than before. A new Godzilla costume, called the *Daisenso-Goji* (a.k.a. "Zero-Godzi"), was built for this film, but its design is certainly the weakest of all Godzillas up to this point. It has a roundish head with wide eyes and a broad, frog-like mouth, and the body of the suit is rather baggy, with an underdefined musculature — from certain angles, it looks as though Haruo Nakajima is wearing a potato sack. Godzilla is also more fleet-footed in this film than before; in addition to the aforementioned dance (known as the Godzilla *"Shie,"* and reportedly adopted from a Japanese comic-book character that was popular at the time), Godzilla also hits King Ghidorah with a flying body slam during the first battle, and during the second fight he shuffles his feet à la Muhammad Ali. These silly monster mannerisms were introduced by Tsuburaya, whose power at the studio was at an all-time high, and who was increasingly conscious that the movies should appeal to small children, despite protests from his staff and colleagues. "When Tsuburaya-san talked about Godzilla doing the 'Shie' pose, I was totally against it," said SFX cameraman Teisho Arikawa. "But Mr. Tsuburaya said, 'Never mind, it will make children happy.' . . . I shot the scene real reluctantly. The actor in the Godzilla suit [Haruo Nakjima] didn't want to do it either. . . . Mr. Tsuburaya had more lenient ideas about Godzilla's character, compared to our ideas. When we all saw the rough cut of the movie, people were snickering, saying, 'How far will Godzilla go with stuff like this?' Even director Honda was snickering. . . . Later on, fans told us that after the 'Shie' pose, Godzilla movies had changed in quality."[20] The *Shie* pose is indeed funny as a stand-alone joke, but it is out of place in this film, an awe-inspiring alien-invasion epic, thus it sticks out like a sore thumb and downgrades the film.

A new Rodan costume was constructed for *Monster Zero* and it is a definite improvement over the suit employed in the previous film, with more rounded wings and an angular, sleek face that restores some of the flying monster's lost menace. King Ghidorah appears more all-powerful in *Monster Zero* than in any of his other appearances in the Godzilla series: At the climax, although acting on his own volition and without the guiding hand of an alien force, Ghidorah holds his own against Godzilla and Rodan. The film's ending is ambiguous, with neither Godzilla nor Rodan surfacing from the ocean, which suggests that Ghidorah scored an undersea knockout punch on one or both of his foes before surfacing and flying away into the stratosphere. By now, the practice of culminating monster battles by having the warring beasts disappear into the ocean or swallowed up by a volcanic eruption or some other natural phenomena was a Toho standard, and perhaps a signal that the genre was starting to tire.

Monster Zero's most serious shortcoming, however, is the use of stock footage from *Rodan*,

"From a planet 50 million miles beyond the stars came a strange message: lend us your Rodan and Godzilla to fight our Monster Zero. The stage is set for the mightiest battle ever seen with the most dreaded creatures in the universe. What started as a call for help from space turns into a nightmare of terror on earth: *Monster Zero*!"

   — From UPA's TV spot for Monster Zero *and* War of the Gargantuas

Mothra, and *Ghidrah: The Three-Headed Monster* during Ghidorah's and Rodan's rampage scenes. Although it is only briefly used, this cost-cutting method portends the budget-conscious moves that were on the horizon, and which were about to cause the Godzilla series and all of Toho's monster movies to suffer a serious and steady decline in production values. Even director Ishiro Honda took this development as a harbinger of bad things to come. "It was a vicious cycle of time and budget," Honda said in an interview published in *Toho SF Special Effects Movie Series Vol. 4.* "If we recycled scenes from previous movies, we could cut the effects budget. But then we received complaints from our fans saying, 'It looks weird, it's not fresh.' We could fool the audience for a little while, but eventually they would know the trick and stop coming to see the shows. Then the studio would think that special effects films don't sell anymore. It's no wonder we could not make anything good around that period. . . . It is a sad story."

LOST IN SPACE: *Monster Zero* was not released in the U.S. until 1970, when it opened on a double bill with *War of the Gargantuas*, playing mostly in drive-in theaters, and it was subsequently syndicated to television stations. The inexplicably long gap between the two pictures' Japanese releases (*Monster Zero* was released in 1965, *Gargantuas* in 1966) and their joint American debut is one of the great mysteries of Godzilla's career, especially in light of the fact that the pictures were co-produced by a U.S. company and featured imported American actors to make them more marketable in the West. Henry Saperstein has never fessed up to what really happened. In a 1995 interview with *G-Fan* magazine, he gave this very improbable explanation for the delay. "Toho doesn't always put a picture into quick release internationally. . . . There's a lot of technical work to be done: Sending in interpositives, soundtracks, effects and music tracks, and then there's the things that we have to do with them

here. . . . So if they [Toho] drag their feet . . . it just impacts on how much longer down the road it gets pushed."

And now, a dose of reality: It appears that Saperstein planned to release *Monster Zero* to American cinemas sometime in 1966. On June 1 of that year, *Variety* reported that Saperstein had just wrapped up postproduction (i.e., English dubbing) of the film and that he was "currently negotiating a distribution deal" for the picture.[21] Because Saperstein did not have a distributorship of his own, it is likely he originally envisioned releasing *Monster Zero* through American International Pictures, as he had done with *Frankenstein Conquers the World, What's Up, Tiger Lily?* (Woody Allen's spoof-dubbed Toho spy film, which apparently replaced the all-new detective thriller Saperstein had planned to make with Toho), and other films. It is possible that Saperstein and Samuel Z. Arkoff had some sort of falling-out around this time, for *Tiger Lily*, released in November 1966, was Saperstein's last release through AIP. According to a September 1970 *Variety* article, *Monster Zero* and *War of the Gargantuas* "sat on the shelf at [UPA] because [distributors] figured they had no potential" until 1970, when Saperstein struck a deal with a small distributor, Maron Films. The newspaper said Maron did brisk business with the two Toho films, with a projected box-office gross of $3 million.

The Americanization of *Monster Zero* is respectful to the original Japanese version, and only slight modifications and deletions were made. Several sentences of "Planet X language" spoken by the Controller (improvised by actor Yoshio Tsuchiya) were cut from scenes occurring on Planet X, and a few brief shots were excised from scenes involving the flying saucers at Lake Myojin. Some sound effects were added to the American version (including booming footfalls when Godzilla does his *Shie* dance) and several pieces of Akira Ifukube's incredible music score were re-arranged. The Japanese version of *Monster Zero* begins with opening credits set to Ifukube's main title music, a reworking of the *Kaiju Daisenso March*, one of his most recognizable military battle themes. During the opening credits of the U.S. version, the eerie music from the flying saucers' capture of Godzilla and Rodan is substituted. This is actually an improvement — he new music better establishes the film's uneasy, spooky tone from the beginning.

A third version of *Monster Zero* also exists. Toho's international English-dubbed version, which was released in the United Kingdom in 1966, is called *Invasion of the Astro-Monsters*. This version also contains minor editing changes but is closer overall to the original Japanese cut.[22]

THE CONTROLLER SPEAKS!

Yoshio Tsuchiya: Actor, UFO-watcher, and Godzilla's ally

Yoshio Tsuchiya (b. 1927) is well-known in Japan as one of Akira Kurosawa's best-loved supporting actors, having played key roles in *The Seven Samurai*, *Red Beard*, and other films. But to fans of Toho science fiction, he is remembered for portraying sinister aliens (the leader of *The Mysterians* and Controller of Planet X in *Monster Zero* — fitting roles, since the actor claims to have seen several bona fide UFOs in his lifetime) or characters who were always teetering on the edge of a nervous breakdown, such as the sun-stroked scientist Furukawa in *Son of Godzilla*, and the alien-possessed Dr. Otani in *Destroy All Monsters*. Tsuchiya was also originally cast as Malmess, the Selginan assassin in *Ghidrah*, but due to his work on *Red Beard* he was unavailable and the part went to Hisaya Ito instead.

The eccentric, venerable Tsuchiya has always been proud of his association with *kaiju* movies — in the 1960s, he frequently visited the special-effects sets and became a friend of Eiji Tsuburaya. In 1991, he triumphantly returned in *Godzilla vs. King Ghidorah*, portraying Shindo, a military officer whose garrison is protected from U.S. invaders during World War II by a pre-atomic Godzilla.

Yoshio Tsuchiya, circa 1996.
PHOTO BY THE AUTHOR

Around the time that you were making The Seven Samurai *with director Akira Kurosawa*, Godzilla *was also being made at Toho. What was the atmosphere at the studio like back then?*

Everyone was saying a strange movie is being filmed, and I was very interested. I liked stuff like that, you know, science fiction. Back then, people thought something like *Godzilla* was unknown, weird stuff. It was the first movie of its kind, although special effects had been done during the war. Well, I was real curious, so after I wrapped *The Seven Samurai*, I joined the production of *Godzilla Raids Again* as a character named Tajima on the firefighter bombardment team. While we were

shooting, of course I couldn't see the monster, I had to pretend it was there. But after everything was completed, it was very exciting. I thought, SFX movies are great, and I began my association with them.

You made three movies with Nick Adams — Monster Zero, Frankenstein Conquers the World, *and the obscure film* The Killing Bottle. *What was he like?*

Nick and I were very close. He had a great sense of humor, and we were always trying to pull practical jokes on one another. Nick was constantly asking me, "How do you say this or that in Japanese?" One time he asked me, "What should I say when I come to the studio in the morning?" So I told him how to say, "I'm hungry" in Japanese. He had no idea what he was saying. So the next morning, he comes into the studio and says, "I'm hungry!" and everybody just stared at him. He also asked me a good greeting for a woman, so I taught him how to say, "Are you making a profit?" in an Osaka dialect, which sounds quite funny. Once, when we were on location for *Monster Zero*, Nick asked the owner of a hotel, this pretty woman, "Are you making a profit?" It was hilarious. Everyone was saying, "Who's teaching Nick all these weird things?"

You spent a significant amount of time with Eiji Tsuburaya. How did your friendship with him come about?

Mr. Tsuburaya approached special effects like an art form, and we communicated on that level. Whenever they were getting ready to shoot a scene on the special-effects set, Mr. Tsuburaya would send an assistant director to come and get me. I was working on the principal-shoot soundstage, and I would make an excuse to the cameraman like, "I have to go to the restroom." I would sneak off to the special-effects set, and Mr. Tsuburaya would be waiting. Then he would say, "Stand by . . . action!" I was really into how Godzilla moved, his movement was usually like slow-motion, so I thought to myself, "Why can't he move a little faster sometimes?" I always offered suggestions to Mr. Tsuburaya, saying that sometimes Godzilla needs to act a little more humanlike, especially as his popularity increased and he became a hero. That's what led to the famous *Shie* [Godzilla's victory dance on Planet X in *Monster Zero*] and Minya's spartan education in *Son of Godzilla*.

In 1965, you appeared both in Kurosawa's Red Beard *and in Honda's* Monster Zero, *two wildly different kinds of films.*

Right. Most actors get comfortable with a certain kind of role or genre, and they stick to that. But as far as I was concerned, it was equally prestigious to appear in science-fiction films or in Kurosawa movies. Back then, there were many people who looked at special-effects movies as weird things, but I once said those kind of people weren't really intelligent, because movie fans were just dying to see our films. I remember going to the dentist once, and I sat down and opened my mouth and he said to me, "Tsuchiya-san, I saw your movie today." He was an older man, but he really loved SFX stuff.

What was director Honda like?

Mr. Honda and Mr. Kurosawa were the same, as far as their approach to moviemaking. Mr. Honda cared deeply about the meaning of Godzilla, and he tried to preserve that. He doesn't receive the same kind of recognition that Mr. Kurosawa does, but he was every bit as talented and dedicated. Those are my memories of him.

After Yog: Monster from Space *(1970) you did not appear in another science-fiction movie until 1991. Why did you return to the Godzilla series in* Godzilla vs. King Ghidorah?

Mr. Shindo is my all-time favorite movie role, believe it or not. I was chosen for that role because I am the only one who can talk to Godzilla. I understand where he comes from, and what is in his heart, just like Shindo does. Even though Godzilla is only a fictional character, he is very real to me. I have an affinity for him that is difficult to describe.

THE REBEL: NICK ADAMS

Nearly a decade after the Raymond Burr-ized *Godzilla: King of the Monsters!* was released, Toho finally realized its sci-fi films could be even more successful overseas if a Western actor were included in the cast. From 1965 to 1969, the studio collaborated with Hollywood producers to import second-tier American stars to Japan: Russ Tamblyn starred in *War of the Gargantuas*, Rhodes Reason in *King Kong Escapes*, Joseph Cotten, Cesar Romero, and Richard Jaeckel in *Latitude Zero*. But the first actor to make this eastbound trip was Nick Adams, remembered best in this country as Johnny Yuma, the wayfaring ex-confederate solider and would-be novelist in the early 1960s ABC-TV series *The Rebel*.

Nicholas Aloysius Adamshock was born July 10, 1931, in Nanticoke, PA, the son of a Ukranian coal miner. He was raised in New Jersey, and during his last year of high school he got his first role in a New York play with the help of his friend, actor Jack Palance. According to legend, Adams hitchhiked to Hollywood in 1950, hoping to become a movie star, but when success eluded him, joined the Coast Guard instead. While on leave, he would hang around the movie studios; he landed his first part, in *Mr. Roberts*, while still enlisted. A succession of films followed, but despite his intense drive, Adams never fulfilled his dream to be a leading man.

By the time Adams headed for Japan, both his career and his personal life had descended into turmoil. After *The Rebel* went off the air Adams appeared in several films, but he quickly became *persona non grata* in Hollywood after he mounted an obnoxious campaign for an Academy Award for his role as an accused killer in *Twilight of Honor* (1963), a box-office dud. Adams spent about $10,000 of his own money to place ads in the trade papers and managed to secure a Best Actor nomination; he was so confident he would win that he and his wife, former child star Carol Nugent, arrived early at the 1964 Academy Awards ceremony so Adams could practise walking up to the stage to

Nick Adams, as he appeared in *Die, Monster Die!* (1965). After finishing that film, which co-starred Boris Karloff, in England, Adams went to Japan to make *Frankenstein Conquers The World* and *Monster Zero* at Toho.
AMERICAN INTERNATIONAL PICTURES © 1965

accept his golden statue! Around this time, Adams also got on a soapbox and railed against Hollywood producers who were casting foreign actors in domestic productions or cutting costs by shooting movies overseas. "Runaway production is killing us," the actor said, and he pledged: "I will never make a picture abroad."

He didn't keep his promise long. After his Oscar debacle, Adams began fielding offers to make films in Israel, Italy, England, and Japan. His first foray was to England to make *Die, Monster, Die* with Boris Karloff in early 1965 (it was also his first horror movie), followed by a trip to Japan to make two films at Toho. Adams was effective, if unremarkable, in *Frankenstein Conquers the World* as Dr. James Bowen, a sympathetic American physician researching the aftereffects of the atomic bombs on Japan's people. But fans perhaps love him best as the heroic, galaxy-trotting astronaut F. Glenn in *Monster Zero*, a role he put his heart and soul into. Adams apparently enjoyed working in Japan so much that he returned in 1966 to star in a spy thriller, *The Killing Bottle*, which he also coproduced under the banner of Nick Adams Enterprises Inc. As an interesting side note, *The Killing Bottle* was dubbed into English at Titra Sound Studios in New York around late 1967 or early 1968. Adams' dialogue tracks were apparently lost, and his voice was re-recorded by Jack Curtis (Pops Racer from the *Speed Racer* cartoon series). However, the picture was apparently never released in the U.S., for reasons unknown.[23]

In each of his three Toho pictures, Adams' love interest was played by the beautiful Kumi Mizuno, leading to speculation that Adams and Mizuno had a romantic affair. (In the book *Monsters Are Attacking Tokyo*, producer Henry G. Saperstein confirms that Adams and Mizuno were lovers, while Mizuno reveals that Adams once proposed to her, but says she declined because she was engaged to another man.) At the time, Adams and Nugent were having marital problems: In January 1965, Adams had announced on a TV talk show that he was filing for divorce, which came as a shock to his wife, whom he hadn't yet told. But a few months later, Adams reconciled with Nugent — in fact, she and their two small children accompanied him to Japan for the shooting of *Frankenstein Conquers the World*. But after Adams' shenanigans in Tokyo, Nugent filed for divorce.

"Yes, they [Adams and Mizuno] had an affair. That's one of the reasons my parents were divorced," said Adams' daughter, playwright Allyson Lee Adams. "My dad had a penchant for becoming infatuated with his leading ladies. It was a way for him to take on the role he was playing at the time. After the movie [*Frankenstein*] was shot, Saperstein threw a party in Tokyo and all the people from Toho were there, and we were invited. My dad was obviously infatuated with Kumi, to the point where the Americans there were embarrassed for my mother."

Adams was great in *Monster Zero*, exuding a confident, easy familiarity with his fellow actors. At first, Adams' swagger seems drastically out of place with the subdued Japanese cast and the film's pseudo-scientific countenance, but it wouldn't be the same wild, woolly ride without him. Speaking in English while the other actors spoke Japanese, Adams apparently embellished a few lines with Americanisms like "baby," "I got big news for you, pal," and "a hill of beans." His performance builds to a crescendo as Glenn begins to suspect the X-lings of ulterior motives, finally learning of their plans to conquer Earth. When Glenn confronts Namikawa over her secret alien identity, Adams' tough guy and Mizuno's *femme fatale* seem straight out of classic Hollywood. Pulling Mizuno close to his face, Adams seethes contempt for the hostile invaders who imprison his woman's heart, then he explodes in rage when she is destroyed for having loved him. Moments later, he gets to exact his physical revenge, beating up on a few wimpy aliens. "Being a good actor was the most important thing in my father's life," says Allyson Adams. "He would never have phoned in any performance."

After finishing *Frankenstein Conquers the World*, Adams wrote a piece for the *Los Angeles Times* (August 22, 1965) titled "A Kind Word for Those Monster Movies," in which he shed light on his feelings about working in the *kaiju* realm: "I then discovered the film was going to be directed by Ishiro Honda and the special effects wizard was to be Eiji Tsuburaya. These two geniuses have earned the well deserved title of the world's greatest directors of science fiction films. . . ." Adams praised producer Tomoyuki Tanaka, and boasted that *Frankenstein* had a budget of $5 million (an exaggeration — most of the Toho sci-fi films of the 1960s cost about $1 million to $1.5 million).

Over the next few years, Adams appeared in a string of minor pictures, mostly shot overseas. His last American film was the 1965 cheapie *Young Dillinger*, which was shot in 10 days (ironically, it was also the last film directed by Terry Morse of *Godzilla: King of the Monsters!* renown).

Nick Adams was just 36 when he died February 6, 1968, of an overdose of a prescription drug used to treat alcoholism. Because the actor had been on an emotional roller-coaster, his death was assumed a suicide, but Allyson Adams believes her father may have been killed. She says Adams had just returned from making a film in Mexico and was working out (he was an avid weight lifter) for another Hollywood comeback, and that the coroner's office changed the official cause of death from "natural causes" to "homicide" before finally ruling it suicide. Adding to the mystique is the fact that Adams' body was discovered by his attorney Irvin Roeder, who was gunned down in broad daylight on Wilshire Boulevard several years after Adams died. In the years since, Hollywood columnists have raised the specter of a plot to kill Adams, but it's a mystery that appears will never be solved.

Despite his dubious reputation in Hollywood, Adams' serious approach to films other actors might have taken for granted (just look at Russ Tamblyn in *War of the Gargantuas*) earned him great admiration on the Toho set, and his contribution to Godzilla lore continues to delight fans of Japanese science fiction to this day. But in perhaps the ultimate show of disrespect, Saperstein and Maron Films gave Adams no billing in promotional advertising when they released *Monster Zero* in the U.S. in October 1970. Five years had passed since the film was shot, and three since the actor had died, and the distributor apparently feared Adams' name would date the picture. "This is a shame, because Adams' tongue-in-cheek playing adds to the film's appeal," wrote a reviewer for *Box Office* magazine. "The whole approach is light-hearted."

Seven

It Came from Beneath the Sea

"You must be losing your sight!"

— Red Bamboo leader, without a hint of irony, chastising his eyepatch-wearing subordinate

---

GODZILLA VERSUS THE SEA MONSTER

RATING (OUT OF FIVE STARS): ★ ★ ★

JAPANESE VERSION: GOJIRA, EBIRA, MOSURA: NANKAI NO DAIKETTO (GODZILLA, EBIRAH, MOTHRA: GREAT BATTLE IN THE SOUTH SEAS). Released on December 16, 1966, by the Toho Motion Picture Company. Toho Scope, in color. Running Time: 87 minutes. English-dubbed version released internationally as *Ebirah: Horror of the Deep*.

U.S. VERSION: Distributed to television stations in 1967 by the Walter Reade Organization. No U.S. theatrical Release. Running time: 82 minutes.

STORY: A persistent teenage sailor, accompanied (reluctantly) by two friends and a stowaway bank robber, sails to the South Seas on a stolen yacht, searching for his shipwrecked older brother; the boat is attacked by a gigantic crab-like monster and the foursome washes ashore on Letchi Island, the secret base of a terrorist group manufacturing nuclear bombs. Hunted by gun-toting militarist thugs, the castaways retaliate by awakening a sleeping Godzilla, who battles the gigantic crustacean Ebirah and destroys the terrorists' military compound, allowing the heroes and a group of enslaved natives to escape (with help from Mothra) before the island is destroyed in a nuclear blast.

GODZILLA AND THE ACTION MAN: Jun Fukuda

Godzilla versus The Sea Monster marks a major turning point in the Godzilla series. By the mid-1960s, television was fast overtaking movies as Japan's primary form of family entertainment, and Godzilla and friends were attracting fewer and fewer ticket buyers to each new film. Toho began streamlining the series, cutting back on special-effects costs by setting the action in island locales that eliminated the need for the construction of intricate miniatures and scenes of widespread pandemonium involving large crowds. *Sea Monster* is also the first entry in

Director Jun Fukuda, who brought action and adventure to the Godzilla series but was constantly hampered by lower budgets, circa 1996 in Tokyo.
COURTESY OF STUART GALBRAITH IV

the series since *Godzilla Raids Again* not directed by Ishiro Honda, whose visual and narrative style had defined the *kaiju eiga* genre over the previous 10-plus years.

Instead, the directorial chores were handed to **Jun Fukuda**, who had worked mostly on Toho's "underworld" films like *The Weed of Crime* (1963)

and *The White Rose of Hong Kong* (1965), and comedies including several entries in the popular "Young Guy" series. Fukuda has been held in low esteem by Godzilla fans who feel his contributions to the series pale in comparison to Honda's work, but such comparisons are really unwarranted, for Fukuda never tried to imitate Honda's broad-brush, epic style. His movies are more gritty and action-oriented, with hints of violence and sometimes pessimism. It is true that Fukuda's five Godzilla movies — especially the three he made in the 1970s, *Godzilla on Monster Island*, *Godzilla vs. Megalon*, and *Godzilla vs. The Cosmic Monster*, are among the poorest in the series; however the blame cannot be entirely placed on the director. As production budgets and schedules continued to shrink, Fukuda was a devoted company man who did the best he could with the resources he was given.

Born February 17, 1923, in Japanese-occupied China, Fukuda returned to Japan by himself at age 16 to attend high school, and later studied at Japan Art University for a while before being drafted into military service during World War II. In 1951, he was hired by Toho as an assistant director and worked under many top names including Hiroshi Inagaki, Senkichi Taniguchi, Kajiro Yamamoto, and Ishiro Honda (Fukuda was an assistant director on *Rodan*). He made his directorial debut in 1959 on a film called *Playing with Fire*, but he is better known in America for his second film, the sci-fi thriller *The Secret of the Telegian* (1960). His other genre movies include ESPY (1974), a successful film about secret agents gifted with ESP, and the forgettable *The War in Space* (1977). Unlike Honda, who was almost strictly reduced to directing monster movies by the mid-1960s, Fukuda directed a wide variety of commercial movies. But later, in the '70s, he too became pigeonholed as a monster movie and sci-fi director during the most forgettable years of Toho's genre movies, and he is often unfairly held responsible for movies that are bad for reasons he had little or no control over.[24]

Fukuda is a modest man who, in published interviews, does not speak highly of his own work. He does not share Ishiro Honda's affinity for the Godzilla series, either — it is clear that he probably resented having to work on science-fiction movies under conditions that were more and more obstinate. In an interview published in 1995 in *Cult Movies*, Fukuda recalled his experiences working on *Godzilla versus The Sea Monster* this way:

> All I can remember is that making *Godzilla versus The Sea Monster* was like pouring two cups of water into one. I had to cut one sequence after another. My memories . . . are not very clear because I was working on a script for a television drama while we were shooting the film. As soon as we completed it, I . . . confined myself so I could finish the script. . . . Toho sent me a copy of the VHS tape edition of *Godzilla versus The*

Sea Monster when it was released. It was like opening up an old wound. I didn't watch the tape. . . .

According to reports in *Godzilla Magazine* and other Japanese texts, *Godzilla versus The Sea Monster* was originally planned not as a Godzilla movie, but as a vehicle for the return of Toho's rendition of King Kong, to be titled *Operation Robinson Crusoe*. Although details are elusive, sometime in 1965 or '66 Toho struck a deal with Rankin-Bass Productions, the animation studio famous for *Rudolph the Red-Nosed Reindeer* and other Christmas TV specials, to co-produce a feature film starring the great ape. The movie was to be promotionally tied to Rankin-Bass's new cartoon series *The King Kong Show*, which premiered on Saturday, September 10, 1966, on the ABC-TV network, and which was one of the first cartoons animated in Japan (by Toei's animation division) for U.S. network presentation. However, Rankin-Bass reportedly turned down the script to *Operation Robinson Crusoe*; in 1967 Toho and Rankin-Bass instead produced *King Kong Escapes*, which was loosely based on the animated series (the villain Dr. Who and a character named Susan appear in both the movie and the cartoon).

Toho decided to push *Operation Robinson Crusoe* into production anyway, substituting Godzilla for King Kong but otherwise making few script changes. The absence of American co-funding may account for the scaled-down production values, and the fact that King Kong was originally the leading monster actor probably explains Godzilla's brief flirtation with a native woman, a very uncharacteristic bit of behavior for the Big G. The title was changed to *Nankai No Daiketto* (*Great Battle in the South Seas*), and the film was later released in the U.S. as *Godzilla versus The Sea Monster*. The story is a sort of James Bond adventure without a Bond-like character, with a gaggle of cunning teenagers, a safecracker and a tough island girl substituting smarts and perseverance for the British secret agent's bravado and high-tech weapons and devices. Like all good Japanese monster movies, the story is far-fetched, fun, and often pleasantly humorous, but Shinichi Sekizawa's screenplay is unique because it is based not on the global threat of monsters attacking a major city, but on a series of chase scenes and near-misses in which an isolated group of characters must avoid being killed by Ebirah, Godzilla, the Red Bamboo thugs and, finally, a nuclear bomb (the Red Bamboo, which goes unnamed in the U.S. version of the film, is an apparent stand-in for the People's Republic of China and its nuclear proliferation).

The cast is outstanding, led by Akira Takarada as Yoshimura the criminal and Kumi Mizuno as Daiyo, an Infant Island native girl who escapes enslavement by the Red Bamboo and is befriended by the castaways. A quartet of younger Toho actors rounds out the principal characters, including Toru Watanabe as Ryota, the boat-stealing teen who gets everyone into this mess, and Toru Ibuki (a tall, odd-looking actor who usually played villains) as his shipwrecked older brother. The real standout, however, is Akihiko Hirata as the villainous captain of the Dragon Squadron. Hirata, clad in an eye patch and military garb, is a real badass throughout, and it's fun to watch him marshal his goons into the jungles or up the hillsides, shooting their guns haphazardly in all directions as they hunt down the interlopers.

Although Eiji Tsuburaya is credited as the special-effects director of *Godzilla versus The Sea Monster*, the actual directorial chores were given to Teisho Arikawa, who by this time had been promoted to Tsuburaya's first assistant director. Tsuburaya had final say on the effects sequences, but he was more of a supervisor than a hands-on director. The reasons for this staffing change are twofold. On the one hand, Tsuburaya was by now dividing his time between Toho and his own company, Tsuburaya Productions, which was making a string of highly successful "Ultra" television series. On the other hand, Tsuburaya had become a powerful figure at Toho and it was easier for the brass to impose budget restrictions on Arikawa than on the Old Man. In *Godzilla Days*, Arikawa expressed frustration about making *Godzilla versus The Sea Monster*, saying he was told from the beginning to avoid expensive composite shots. "There were major limitations on the budget from the studio," he said. "The movie industry wasn't doing too well back then. Maybe it was because of this lack of funding that I [was promoted]. Toho couldn't have made too many demands about the budget if Mr. Tsuburaya had been in charge. The studio knew I was also doing TV work then, so they must have figured I could produce the movie cheaply."

Although the effects sequences in *Godzilla versus The Sea Monster* are visibly pared down compared to earlier films, Arikawa keeps things interesting by photographing the monsters from a variety of new angles. The low camera angles that made Godzilla appear gigantic in *Godzilla*, *Godzilla vs. The Thing*, and other films are abandoned, but the Big G's size is illustrated in other ways. In one scene, Daiyo is frozen with fear at Godzilla's feet and the monster's gigantic toenail can be seen in the background; in another, Ninda (Hideo Sunazuka) sneaks into the Red Bamboo base at the lower right-hand part of the screen, with Godzilla's gigantic foot matted into the background. Other camera work that lends the film a fresh feel includes a shot of Ebirah emerging from the ocean, viewed from over Godzilla's shoulder; a Godzilla's-eye-view of Daiyo; and a head-on view of Godzilla blasting his radiation breath into the camera lens. When Mothra rescues the Infant Islanders by airlift, there are several nice wide shots of Mothra flying overhead (filmed with a weird, slow-motion effect) and landing, with the natives on the ground scurrying to board their makeshift gondola. Of all Mothra's film appearances, this is perhaps the best shot ever to demonstrate the creature's size.

UNDER THE SEA: Lightning strikes! Godzilla's dorsal fins glow with an electric charge, and his toes twitch. Then, one eye opens. Godzilla is awake! Bursting out of the mountainside, Godzilla is greeted by his crustacean foe and immediately lobs a boulder at him, inducing a game of monster catch. Ebirah drags Godzilla to the sea bottom, and Godzilla pounds the shellfish with a rock, forcing its retreat.

Godzilla versus The Sea Monster is the first movie since the 1954 original in which Godzilla is shown underwater. These scenes were mostly filmed on an indoor soundstage, with Godzilla (played again by Haruo Nakajima) and Ebirah (Hiroshi Sekita) filmed through the glass of a water-filled aquarium (there are also brief shots of the Godzilla costume being tugged underwater, with air bubbles flowing from its mouth, that were shot in a real water tank). Arikawa paid much attention to detail, adding luminescent sparkles to the foreground and background to simulate the sun's rays striking the water's surface. Godzilla's roar is nicely muffled during these scenes, reinforcing the illusion.

Even though Godzilla and Ebirah's sea battles are brief, Nakajima had to labor hard because the Godzilla suit was constantly soaking up water, making it heavy and hard to maneuver. "The same pool was used in *War of the Gargantuas* and *Sea Monster*," Nakajima said. "It took at least a week to wrap up the water-related filming. I worked overtime until about eight o'clock every day. I lived in the water! Even though I wore a wet suit under the costume, I got cold. But I never got sick, because I was so tense during the filming."

Godzilla versus The Sea Monster

In Color

"The titanic hero-ape [sic], Godzilla, fights the battle of his life with the most gigantic and ferocious sea monster the world has ever known. The huge-scaled filming of the amazing South Seas adventure is a marvel of technical achievement in which courageous humans are dwarfed and terrorized by the size, strength and deeds of super creatures."

— Text of promotional materials issued by the Walter Reade Organization in 1967; the film's director was misidentified as "Jun Fukuenda"

The Godzilla costume from *Monster Zero* was re-used in this film, and the wear and tear on it is evident, especially in the final reel when Godzilla tramples the Red Bamboo base. This was probably one of the last special-effects scenes filmed, because the rubber on Godzilla's face is badly warped and the body of the costume shows burn marks from pyrotechnics. Ebirah, a 50-meter-long, 23,000-metric-ton cross between a shrimp and a crab (its name is derived from "*ebi*," Japanese for "shrimp") with 15-meter-long claws, is portrayed via a waist-up costume worn by stuntman Sekita during the water battles, to which a tail was attached for shots of Godzilla judo-flipping Ebirah or dragging the crustacean underwater. Ebirah is hardly one of Godzilla's most formidable foes — its inability to fight on dry land and its lack of special powers ensure that Godzilla will soon turn the creature into broiled seafood. Nevertheless, the monster manages to generate some unusually good terror here. The gigantic crab claw rising ominously from the ocean, which involves both miniature work and composite shots, is a masterfully chilling effect, and Ebirah is one of few Toho *kaiju* shown eating humans (actually, some rather unconvincing dolls). The adult Mothra prop from *Godzilla vs. The Thing* was also recycled in this film and it, too, suffers from apparent heavy use — most of its brilliant colors have become dull, and Mothra's head has become fuzzy and unkempt, her wings rag-tag.

After Godzilla defeats Ebirah for the second time, he wades ashore and instinctively pursues his arch-rival Mothra (seems he's forgotten their 1965 team-up in *Ghidrah: The Three-Headed Monster*). The brief encounter between Godzilla and Mothra is a half-baked rehash of their titanic fight in *Godzilla vs. The Thing*, with Mothra kicking up dust and choking the giant lizard. Mothra adds one new and rather

humorous trick to her play book, knocking Godzilla down with a wing slam to the shoulder. There is one other monster in the picture, a gigantic condor that swoops down out of nowhere and attacks Godzilla when he's trying to take a nap. Although there is some impressively filmed combat at close quarters (with a hand puppet standing in for Godzilla's head — the last time a Godzilla puppet was utilized in the original *Godzilla* series), the monster is poorly detailed and moves unrealistically. Fittingly, Godzilla quickly roasts the bird with a breath blast, sending it crashing into the sea. Another impressive effects sequence is the nuclear blast that destroys Letchi Island, which starts off with a series of low-level explosions and culminates in a gigantic mushroom cloud (however, Toho Video's letter-boxed version of the film reveals that the studio klieg lights protrude into the shot).

Another key staffing change is the presence of composer Masaru Sato, who returns to the series for the first time since *Godzilla Raids Again* (1955). Although it lacks the all-out power of Akira Ifukube's work, Sato's contemporary-style music for *Sea Monster* underscores the film's tropical setting and its sense of high adventure. During the battles between Godzilla and Ebirah, Sato combines sparse orchestrations with heavy use of sound effects created with an electric guitar (with the reverb cranked up on the amplifier). There are Dick Dale-like surf-rock themes during the dance contest and Godzilla's first face-off with the giant shrimp, a piece that sounds like Carl Stalling's frenetic music for Warner Bros. cartoons during the Dragon Squadron's gun-shooting search for the castaways, and a wonderful vocal piece for the Infant Island fairies, who are played this time by the Bambi Pair, another singing duo comprised of identical twins (it is not known why the Peanuts did not reprise their roles in this film; perhaps the Bambi Pair commanded a lower fee). The most curious element in the soundtrack is the oddball go-go music that plays when Godzilla is attacked by the Red Bamboo fighter jets. This inappropriate music sticks out like a sore thumb, and it is possible that it was not composed by Sato (as evidence of this, the *Godzilla versus The Sea Monster* soundtrack, released on CD by Toshiba/EMI in Japan, does not include this cut). Interestingly, in the Japanese theatrical trailer for *Sea Monster*, the "Godzilla-vs.-the-jets" scene was set to "Night on Bald Mountain." In the U.S. version of the film, the music was wisely removed from this scene.

The picture was syndicated directly to U.S. televisions beginning in 1967, without a theatrical release, by the Walter Reade Organization, which had successfully released *Ghidrah* to theaters two years before. The film was dubbed into English at Titra Sound in New York. Compared to the heavy editing job that *Ghidrah* was subjected to, the U.S. version of *Sea Monster* is, thankfully, almost completely intact. The only major deletions occur at the beginning of the picture: The entire opening credits sequence, featuring a nice main title theme by Sato, was cut out, as were two scenes of Ryota asking officials at the Maritime Safety Agency and then a newspaper reporter for help in finding his brother. At the newspaper offices, Ryota sees a poster on the wall for a dance marathon contest where a sailboat will be given to the winner. He rips the poster off the wall and heads for the contest.

The U.S. version opens with what is supposed to be Yata's boat being trashed at sea by Ebirah's claw; this scene was swiped from later in the picture — look closely and "Yahlen" — the name of the yacht that Ryota later steals — is emblazoned on the boat's side.

Although marked by symptoms of the continuing downturn of the series, *Godzilla versus The Sea Monster* is an underrated entry in the Godzilla canon. Its unusual scenario and director Fukuda's fresh approach to the material are welcome changes. And although Godzilla had already begun his ascent to Japan's dinosaur do-gooder, he remained a very real threat in this picture, feared equally by both the heroes and villains; although Godzilla's actions ultimately aid the castaways and the slaves in their escape, Godzilla would just as soon step on them as save them. Even though there are a few touches of silliness — Godzilla and Ebirah tossing boulders, Godzilla ripping off Ebirah's claw and making clackety-clack noises with it to taunt his foe, Godzilla scratching his nose (a tribute to Yuzo Kayama, star of Toho's "Young Guy" movies) — Godzilla's sense of humor was well established by now and these moves are hardly as outlandish as some of the stunts the monster pulled in *King Kong vs. Godzilla*.

Like many Godzilla movies, *Sea Monster* has only been seen in the West on television. Most TV prints aired in the U.S. are badly scanned and worn out, reducing the film to but a shadow of the viewing experience it was intended to be.

Eight

ALL IN THE FAMILY

"This shirt's not yours, it's a girl's shirt.
Unless maybe you're a girl."

— Saeko (a.k.a. Reiko) Matsumiya, to her soon-to-be boyfriend Goro

SON OF GODZILLA

RATING (OUT OF FIVE STARS): ★ ★ ★

JAPANESE VERSION: KAIJU TOH NO KESSEN: GOJIRA NO MUSUKO (SHOWDOWN ON MONSTER ISLAND: SON OF GODZILLA). Released on December 16, 1967, by the Toho Motion Picture Company. Toho Scope, in color. Running Time: 86 minutes.

U.S. VERSION: Distributed to television stations in 1969 by the Walter Reade Organization, Inc. No U.S. theatrical release. Running Time: 84 minutes.

STORY: A secret weather-control experiment conducted by United Nations scientists on Sol-Gel Island in the South Pacific goes awry, unleashing radioactive rainstorms and intense heat that causes a species of large mantises to grow into gigantic insects, called Kamakiras ("Gimantis" in the U.S. version). A baby Godzilla hatches from a huge egg, and Godzilla defends the tyke from these mantises and the Kumonga ("Spiega" in the U.S. print), a gigantic, poisonous monster-spider; as the warring monsters threaten to wipe them out, the scientists (aided by a beautiful, orphaned Japanese girl living in the jungle) successfully freeze the tropical island and escape, leaving Godzilla and son to hibernate on a snowy beach.

BOOM TIME

In the history of Japanese monster movies, 1967 is known as the first "monster boom," a year in which each of the four major Japanese movie studios released at least one *kaiju eiga* and the genre reached its productive pinnacle, if not its creative zenith. Toho's principal rival, Daiei Co. Ltd., released *Gamera vs. Gyaos*, a.k.a. *Return of the Giant Monsters*, the third in a series of films launched in 1965 starring Gamera, a gigantic turtle and obvious Godzilla knockoff. The Nikkatsu studio released *Monster from a Prehistoric Planet*, a.k.a. *Gappa*, a Japanese reworking of the British giant-monster film *Gorgo*, in which a baby monster is nefariously stolen from a tropical island and its two giant-sized parents trample Japan in the course of rescuing their pup; the film featured special effects by Akira Watanabe, formerly Eiji Tsuburaya's SFX art director

Son of Godzilla

In Color

A science fiction thriller set in a wildly futuristic, man-created world of mammoth creatures. The famed Godzilla engages in exciting combat to protect his infant son and save the lives of the research team imperiled by their own experiments. . . .

A United Nations research team on uninhabited Sollgel Island in the South Seas has performed experiments to control the atmospheric temperature. Because of a damaged control unit the temperature soars to an abnormal high causing all life on the island to grow to gigantic proportions.

A giant reptile egg hatches and out pops a peculiar being, which turns out to be Godzilla's son. The baby is threatened by monster animals and Godzilla engages them in ferocious combat to save his offspring.

The research team is also endangered and after many harrowing escapes manages to correct the control unit and plunge the temperature down to the point where the island is transformed into a land of snow and ice.

As the scientists leave the island by submarine, everything is frozen solid including Godzilla and his son, both of whom will undoubtedly reappear again when the snow and ice melt away.

— *Text of publicity materials for* Son of Godzilla, *issued in 1969 by the Walter Reade Organization*

at Toho and a veteran of the original *Godzilla* and other films. The Shochiku studio came out with *The X from Outer Space*, a wonderfully outlandish film directed by Hiroshi Nihonmatsu and featuring the monster Guilala, spawned from radioactive blobs that attach themselves to the hull of a spaceship and grow to giant size, resembling a mixture of Godzilla, a gigantic chicken, and Kermit the Frog.

For its part, Toho released two giant-monster films that year, the aforementioned co-production with Rankin-Bass of *King Kong Escapes* and the eighth installment in the Godzilla series, *Son of Godzilla*. Probably due to the infusion of American capital, the Kong film was staffed with Toho's front-line genre talent, with Ishiro Honda in the director's seat, Eiji Tsuburaya directing the effects (not merely acting as a supervisor, as he did on *Sea Monster*), Akira Ifukube writing the music score, and popular actors Akira Takarada and Mie Hama headlining the cast. Meanwhile, *Son of Godzilla* was staffed with basically the same second-string crew that made the previous film: Director Jun Fukuda, special-effects man Teisho Arikawa, and composer Masaru Sato. Although it is often maligned as a "kiddie movie" because of Godzilla's increasing anthropomorphization and the introduction of the Big G's pug-nosed tadpole Minya, or dismissed as a cheapie due to its island setting and the absence of

miniature work, *Son of Godzilla* is actually an undervalued gem. It features a great ensemble of Toho's best genre actors, a very good script by Shinichi Sekizawa, an engaging Sato musical score, and an abundance of effects work, some of which is quite innovative for a Toho film of its era.

ASCENDING THE THRONE: *Son of Godzilla* is the first Toho giant-monster movie in which Eiji Tsuburaya did not direct the special effects. Although Tsuburaya was credited as SFX supervisor, the directorial duties were officially given to Arikawa, Tsuburaya's top protégé and most trusted cinematographer. Arikawa (sometimes billed as Sadamasa Arikawa) was born in June 1926 in Tokyo and graduated from Japan University's engineering department with a degree in machinery before joining the Japanese navy's aviation corps during the war, where he flew anti-submarine patrols in the Pacific, narrowly escaping death several times. He joined Toho in August 1945, immediately after the war ended, and worked as an audio engineer, but he longed to learn about the special-effects field. During the war, Arikawa had seen *The War at Sea from Hawaii to Malaya* and other SFX-laden war movies while stationed at a Japanese military base in Taiwan.

Disillusioned by the constant feuding between the movie studio heads and left-wing union leaders in the late 1940s, Arikawa left Toho and knocked on the door of Eiji Tsuburaya, who was then working independently at his special-effects institute in Tokyo. With the young man's experience as a wartime flyer and Tsuburaya's own personal love of aviation, the two men bonded quickly and Tsuburaya soon took Arikawa under his wing. "Mr. Tsuburaya and I enjoyed talking about planes all night long," Arikawa said. "When I was about to leave, Mr. Tsuburaya asked me, 'Why don't you join us?' . . . I excitedly replied, 'Yes.' With that word, my history in special effects had begun."[25]

After several years at Tsuburaya's institute, working on a variety of special-effects projects for various film production companies, Arikawa and most of Tsuburaya's staff followed the Old Man when he rejoined the Toho staff in the early 1950s. Over the next decade and a half, Arikawa was Tsuburaya's lead cameraman on nearly every SFX film, from giant-monster movies to war pictures to the Crazy Cats' comedy *Daiboken* (*The Great Adventure*, 1965) and other genres. He also directed special effects for Tsuburaya Productions' pioneering television programs including *Ultra Q*, *Ultraman*, *Ultra Seven*, and *Mighty Jack*. Arikawa's promotion to the position of SFX director at Toho in 1967 was the fulfillment of a long cycle of study under his great mentor; unfortunately for him, it lasted a short time. Arikawa directed special effects for just three pictures — *Son of Godzilla*, *Destroy All Monsters* (1968), and *Yog: Monster from Space* (1970). After Tsuburaya's death in 1970, and with the studio's increased pillaging of effects budgets, Arikawa became dissatisfied with movie work and left Toho to join Houei International, where he directed special effects for television programs like *Century of the Emperor* and *Rainbowman*. In the 1970s, Arikawa worked as an SFX director and as a producer on several television shows and movies jointly produced by Japan and Hong Kong.

FIRST BORN: Toho's decision to introduce Godzilla's son to the series was almost certainly inspired by competition at the box office from Daiei's Gamera movies, which catered more directly to the small-fry audiences. In nearly every movie, the gigantic, walrus-tusked turtle saved kids from monsters or aliens, and sometimes flew them home on his back. "We wanted to take a new approach. So, we gave Godzilla a child. We thought that it would be a little strange if Godzilla had a daughter, so we instead gave him a son. We focused on the relationship between Godzilla and his son throughout *Son of Godzilla*," director Fukuda told *Cult Movies* in 1995.

Thankfully, child characters were kept out of the mix at first (although they would take center stage in forthcoming movies) and, thankfully, Toho refrained from humanizing Godzilla to point of interacting with the human cast — that role was left to his tike Minira ("mini-Godzilla"), known as "Minya" in English.[26] With his wide eyes, upturned snout, pot belly, and chubby thighs, Minya resembles a cross between Godzilla and a human baby, and he behaves more like the latter. He is friendly (taking a quick liking to Saeko the island girl), playful (skipping rope over his napping daddy's twitching tail), hungry (chowing down lots of jungle fruits which Saeko, with a Joe Namath throwing arm, launches into his mouth), curious (always getting into trouble), and afraid (always emitting a pathetic cry for help from Dad: "WAAA-GWAAAA!"). Minya is undeniably comical and charming, but his impact upon Godzilla's characterization is troublesome. Although Godzilla remains a threat in *Son of Godzilla*, endangering the research scientists and reigning as the "king of Sol-Gel Island," the monster nevertheless assumes a personified parental role that is a radical departure from the mean, sometimes clowning monster of previous films. Godzilla is constantly bailing his son out of trouble, or teaching him how to breathe fire in the infamous scene in which Minya can only exhale puny smoke rings until Dad steps on his tail. This look inside the Godzilla family is fun and funny in its own right, providing some laughs for kids and adults alike, but it detracts from the straightforward and serious sci-fi story.

Son of Godzilla's theme of environmental depletion is just as relevant today as when the film was made. Faced with the threat of global overpopulation and dwindling natural resources, Dr. Kusumi and five assistants conduct weather-control experiments which may eventually enable arid deserts to be converted to fertile lands. Kusumi's intentions are good, but his experiments have a dangerous air about them: The climate-control system involves the use of Zonde, a synthetic radiation, and the entire operation is kept top-secret for fear that it could be used as a weapon if acquired by hostile nations. Ultimately, Kusumi's headstrong attitude and the blind devotion of his scientists leads to a classic man-versus-nature confrontation. The radiation balloons explode too early, unleashing enormous amounts of energy that cause the island's temperature to quickly skyrocket. For three straight days the island is flooded with boiling rain, and when the torrent breaks, the island's already large insects have grown into gigantic, radiation-induced mutations. From this point forward, the story turns into a sort of monster-on-the-loose scenario with the hideous gigantic spider Kumonga playing the villain as it preys upon the other monsters and pursues the human heroes. There is also some standard fare for a "jungle movie" — the scientists are afflicted with tropical fever, and the only cure for the disease is the liquid from a Red Water Lagoon which, of course, is located in the path of monsters. As in the past three films, Godzilla is the hero by coincidence. When he rescues his son from the Kumonga he helps clear the way for the scientists — now watching their experiments come to successful fruition — to escape the island.

The cast features Tadao Takashima of *King Kong vs. Godzilla* fame as Kusumi. Here, Takashima is stoic and stern, smoking his pipe and displaying none of the witty banter he is known for, but he is perfect for the role. Akira Kubo is likable as the pesky freelance reporter who parachutes, without an invitation, onto the island in hopes of getting a story, only to be given the job of chief cook and bottle washer, and starlet Beverly Maeda (known for appearances in films like *Judo Champion* [1967], a "Young Guy" movie starring Yuzo Kayama) is passable as the cunning orphaned girl who grew up alone on the island after the death of her scientist father. Toho genre stalwarts Akihiko Hirata and Kenji Sahara show up in supporting roles, but the real standout is Yoshio Tsuchiya as Furukawa, the researcher driven to madness by sun stroke

and cabin fever. The film appropriately opens with Furukawa complaining about the swelter, and soon he's bitching that the experiments are taking too long. Then he grabs a gun and runs to the beach, determined to go home even if he has to swim to Japan. But offshore, in the distance, something is stirring . . . Godzilla has come to rescue his young!

Godzilla's entrance in *Son of Godzilla* is one of the most impressive in the entire series. Godzilla swims facedown toward the beach, his back fins creating a column of water until the monster finally rises up. "I had a mouthpiece in my mouth, connected to an oxygen tank that easily weighed 10 kilograms, located in the stomach of the Godzilla suit," said Haruo Nakajima. "I had the crew place a movable cart underwater, because it was so heavy it wouldn't move an inch. I was holding on to the cart while I was standing by under the water. My back fins were barely above the surface. They tied a rope to my foot and pulled on it when the camera started to roll, because I couldn't hear if they yelled 'action' above the water. I was pulled by this heavy-duty vehicle, like a jeep. When I knew it was time to rise out of the water, I used all of my energy to spring out, but the water pressure was tremendous and the mouthpiece was about to fall out of my mouth. It was a pain in the neck."

Nakajima only played Godzilla for two scenes in the movie, both utilizing the *Monster Zero* costume again: The monster's entrance at Sol-Gel Island, and a brief prologue prior to the opening credits in which a weather observation plane crew spots Godzilla swimming for Sol-Gel (he's attracted by the magnetic signals generated by Minya's egg). All other Godzilla scenes were performed by Seiji Onaka and Hiroshi Sekita, both of whom were taller than Nakajima — the Godzilla suit was built larger this time to accentuate Godzilla's size compared to that of his 18-meter-tall, 2,800-metric-ton son

Ciao, Bambino Godzilla

In Italy, *Son of Godzilla* was released on home video retitled *Il Ritorno di Gorgo* (*The Return of Gorgo*). But Godzilla's name was just one of several that were lost in the translation.

According to the film's opening credits, the cast of *Il Ritorno di Gorgo* includes actors named John Wembley, Dick Kennedy, and Charles Simon.

Weirdest of all, the Italians translated the name of the film's director, Jun Fukuda, as . . . *Ishiro Honda!*

(according to an interview with Nakajima in *G-Fan* #22, Onaka was slated to do most of the Godzilla scenes, but midway through filming he broke his fingers, so Sekita completed the assignment). This is by far the worst Godzilla costume to date, and perhaps the worst design in the entire series. Godzilla has a large head with big, forward-mounted eyes, a matronly midsection with ill-defined musculature and big dorsal fins that appear misshapen. It appears that Arikawa's intent was to create a Godzilla that bore a strong physical resemblance to his guppy-faced offspring, but how much more satisfying it would have been if Minya had been designed to resemble Godzilla! "Marchan the dwarf" turns in a nice little performance as Minya, performing lots of jumps, pratfalls, and rolls and invoking a pitiable "little boy lost" quality despite the costume's simplistic, doughboy look.

What really makes *Son of Godzilla* more than a run-of-the-mill effort is the execution of the gigantic preying mantises and the Kumonga, both of which involved numerous overhead wires and required large teams of puppeteers to work together in unison. Particularly difficult was the Kumonga, with multiple joints on each of its eight legs, requiring two or three technicians to control each leg. When filming the insect monster scenes, Arikawa often had more than 20 puppeteers working the wires from a platform mounted over the stage. Although the Kumonga doesn't look all that scary from a distance (it's a rather obvious hairy puppet), the close-up shots of the monster's mandibles quivering as it hunts its prey and its sticky webbing spinning from its mouth are positively gruesome, and the sound effects for the giant spider are creepy. A large, hairy spider talon was also built for the scene where Kumonga probes into Saeko's cave, looking for a people-snack, and the prop is very well articulated. There is one effect in the picture guaranteed to incite laughs: When the monster battle causes the earth to quake, foam boulders shake loose from the rafters inside Saeko's cave. The men cower in fear from these large, but very obviously fake rocks that bounce like playground balls when they hit the floor.

As with the last film there are few miniatures, but there are an impressive number of optical effects in the film, some of which are well executed, such as the gigantic insects walking through the trees past the research base, Kumonga peering into the crevice where Goro and Saeko are trapped, or the shards of burning preying mantis body parts that fly through the air and crash into the trees when Godzilla blasts one of the huge bugs with his breath.

As with *Sea Monster*, the U.S. rights to *Son of Godzilla* were acquired by the Walter Reade Organization. Again, there was no theatrical release, and the picture was syndicated directly to television in 1969. The U.S. version begins with Godzilla inexplicably walking into the camera lens amid a rainstorm; as the picture fades to black, the title card appears on the screen. Reade cut out the prologue in which Godzilla is sighted at sea during a rainstorm, resulting in the rather strange beginning of the U.S. version. The rest of the film is virtually uncut. Curiously, the main title sequence (scenes of the scientists walking the beach and jungles, shot on location in Fiji and backed by the strains of Masaru Sato's adventurous music score) was left intact, but no English-language credits are supered over the film.

Nine

WAR OF THE WORLDS

"The question is, who will be first? Godzilla? Rodan? Angilas? Which of these giant creatures will lead the others in the attack? Ah, they're coming now! I believe I see something stirring there beyond the trees!"

— A newscaster, in AIP's release of *Destroy All Monsters*

DESTROY ALL MONSTERS

RATING (OUT OF FIVE STARS): ★ ★ ★ 1/2

JAPANESE VERSION: KAIJU SOSHINGEKI (MONSTER INVASION). Released on August 1, 1968, by the Toho Motion Picture Company. Toho Scope, in color. Running Time: 88 minutes.

U.S. VERSION: Released on May 28, 1969, by American International Pictures. Premiered in Cincinatti. Running Time: 88 minutes. MPAA Rating: G.

STORY: Japan, 1999: Futuristic science has conquered all of Earth's once-dangerous monsters, which are now safely corralled at "Monsterland" on Ogasawara Island for study. But a technologically advanced race of alien women from Kilaak, a small planet between Mars and Jupiter, seizes control of the monsters and dispatches them on a worldwide assault campaign, demanding mankind's surrender; United Nations scientists eventually take possession of the invaders' mind-control transmitters and send the monsters to attack the Kilaaks' secret base beneath Mt. Fuji, and the spacewomen counter by unleashing King Ghidorah, resulting in an epic battle.

TOHO UTOPIA

As the 1960s began drawing to a close, Toho's once-booming science-fiction movies were slowly but surely fading from view. *Son of Godzilla* attracted less than 2.5 million ticket buyers during its Japanese theatrical run, the lowest attendance of any Godzilla film, and the two most recent Godzillas had failed to get a theatrical release in the U.S., signaling the waning of the genre's popularity abroad. The Toho brass sensed their mightiest monster was slipping into a creative and commercial void. "They were going to end the Godzilla series then," SFX director Teisho Arikawa recalled

145

in *Godzilla Days.* "Producer [Tomoyuki] Tanaka figured that all the ideas had just run out."

Destroy All Monsters was originally planned to be the last Godzilla movie, a whiz-bang extravaganza to end the series on a high note. To that end, director Ishiro Honda and composer Akira Ifukube were brought back and a noticeably higher budget was expended for special effects than on the previous two films. The focus is the mother of all battles, a face-off between King Ghidorah and 10 — that's TEN! — of Earth's gigantic monsters: Godzilla, Minya, Rodan, Angilas, Mothra, Gorosaurus (the dinosaur from *King Kong Escapes*), Manda (the sea serpent from *Atragon*), Baragon (of *Frankenstein Conquers the World*), Varan (of *Varan the Unbelievable*), and Kumonga (the spider from *Son of Godzilla*). Set on the eve of the millennium, with a lightweight, comic-book-level story and some of Akira Ifukube's best genre music lending the awesome monster spectacle a sense of freewheeling fun, *Destroy All Monsters* has gone down in history as a classic that marks the end of an era. It is the last Godzilla film made by the four "Godzillafathers" who were the genre's creative cornerstones — Tanaka, Honda, Ifukube, and Eiji Tsuburaya (once again acting as special effects supervisor, while Arikawa directed); after this film, the series would begin hurtling into a void, for a variety of reasons. Even here, symptoms of the emerging regression are evident in some shoddy effects work, the use of stock footage (Ghidorah's first appearance is a rehash of his fiery birth in *Ghidrah*, and the destruction of the Kilaak base includes snippets of the Red Bamboo complex blowing up from *Godzilla versus The Sea Monster*), sloppy scripting, and the near-complete hero transformation of Godzilla, who acts as chieftain of the monster squad and, for the first time ever, saves the day by willfully defending the Earth from a hostile force. Still, these are but minor gripes and overall the film is highly diverting.

Screenwriter Takeshi Kimura (using the pen name Kaoru Mabuchi), a veteran of Toho's science-fiction fare, takes on his first Godzilla assignment here, and his approach is markedly different than that of Shinichi Sekizawa, who had written every film in the series since *King Kong vs. Godzilla*. Kimura's script is an ultrasimplistic contest between good and evil that eschews most of the themes that had become standards of the series (i.e., nuclear weapons, science gone awry, and commercialism). Instead of dooming mankind to some terrible fate, the futuristic technological strides of the late 20th century have instead created a certain peace and harmony on Earth. All the monsters that once terrorized Japan have been corralled at Ogasawara Island, where they are well-fed and kept under high-tech lock and key to prevent further city-trashing. The United Nations has assumed a prominent role in international security and worldwide scientific advancement, man can now create new species of fish (and presumably other animals as well, helping maintain the global food supply), and travel to and from the moon is an everyday occurrence (although its purpose is not really explained). In short, life on planet Earth is just swell until one day when a legion of invading space ladies from the planet Kilaak (located between Mars and Jupiter), wearing shimmering silver skull caps and frocks, show up and use yellow knockout gas to subjugate the monsters and turn them loose against mankind in a global assault, threatening to wipe out the species unless the world surrenders. If there is any subtext whatsoever, it is Ishiro Honda's (who collaborated on the script with Kimura) concerns about the dangerous possibility of mind control and what might happen if some members of a conformist society like Japan were made to turn on one another. But enough of all that — this is a monster movie, dammit!

MONSTER MASH: Under Dr. Yoshida's supervision, the U.N. scientists descramble the Kilaaks' radio-control system. The monster army, now following orders from Earth's authorities, assembles at the base of Mount Fuji to attack the alien base. Suddenly King Ghidorah appears in the sky and circles the other monsters from above, then lands smack-dab in the middle of the monster posse, ready to battle. A titanic, all-versus-one fight rages, during which Ghidorah drops Angilas from high in the air, the impact causing a landslide that exposes the alien base, which Godzilla soon destroys. Cold air seeps into the underground cavern and the alien women, who can survive only in intense heat, lose their human visages and shrivel up into disgusting black snake-rocks.

The climax of *Destroy All Monsters* is one of the most memorable fights in Toho history, an impressively staged battle in which a parade of monsters fill the screen. The battle is a wonderful ballet of men in monster costumes and wire puppeteers moving Ghidorah's wings and heads from above, and due to the logistics of operating and filming

Shout It Out Loud

AIP's publicity campaign for *Destroy All Monsters* is famous in fan circles for three reasons:

1. The weirdly inaccurate artwork that shows a gaggle of Toho monsters converging on a city, with Godzilla looking like a bat-ghost, Minya resembling a giant troll, and Gorosaurus sporting a horn on his nose (Ghidorah, however, was very well drawn).

2. The slogan "The Battle-Cry That Could Save The World!"

3. The theatrical trailer, in which that acronym "DAM" is used.

so many monsters at once, the Earth beasts take on Ghidorah individually or in small groups rather than ganging up on the space monster, avoiding total pandemonium on the screen. Godzilla rassles with Ghidorah's necks, Gorosaurus gets in an athletic kangaroo-kick, Minya administers asphyxiating smoke rings, and Angilas heroically clamps onto one of Ghidorah's necks, pit-bull style. In the end it is once again the sticky silk of Mothra (joined by Kumonga and its webbing) that straitjackets Ghidorah and leads to the demon's defeat, its carcass sinking into a crevice in the Earth.

Several new monster costumes were constructed for the film, including Godzilla and Angilas, while most of the other suits, as well as the Mothra and Kumonga props, were pulled out of Toho's storage shed and recycled from previous movies. Both the Rodan and Ghidorah suits are noticeably modified since last seen in *Monster Zero* (1965). Ghidorah is not as well detailed and looks less fearsome than before, especially in the face, and his huge wings are more simplified, looking like a children's kite. Rodan has a more sleek, bird-like head and crudely designed wings and chest plate; a small Rodan prop was also used for filming scenes of the monster plucking a dolphin out of the water at Ogasawara and chasing after the Moonlight SY-3 rocket. The Angilas costume is much improved over the spike-backed dinosaur's first and only previous appearance in *Gigantis: The Fire Monster*, retaining basically the same design but with thick, scaly skin and a ribbed neck. The new Godzilla costume is perhaps the most widely recognized incarnation of the monster ever, even though it surely is the most friendly looking Godzilla to date with its wide eyes, large mouth, slightly longer snout, and a body with more human proportions than before. This G-suit

would be re-used in an unprecedented three more movies, with only slight modifications, over the next four years. The *Monster Zero* Godzilla costume also appears briefly in the film during Godzilla's attack on New York. Interestingly, Minya looks exactly the same here as he did in *Son of Godzilla*, even though this movie is set in 1999, 31 years into the future. Seems those Godzillas don't grow too quickly.

What makes *Destroy All Monsters* unique among giant-monster movies is its pretense of global annihilation, even if it is only briefly explored. When the Kilaaks dispatch the monsters on a worldwide assault, each of the creatures takes a "solo," with Rodan destroying the Kremlin, Godzilla blasting the United Nations building with his breath, and Gorosaurus uncharacteristically burrowing out from under the Arc de Triomphe. Although these scenes show great imagination on the part of the filmmakers, the limitations on the special effects are evident here, especially when Godzilla visits a very poorly detailed representation of the Big Apple, standing in what looks like a big bathtub. Incidentally, the famous *faux pas* committed by the newscaster (Saburo Iketani) who says Paris is being destroyed by Baragon rather than Gorosaurus is *not* an error committed by the film's U.S. distributors in the English dubbing. According to *The Pictorial History of Godzilla Vol. 2*, Baragon was supposed to take a more prominent role in *Destroy All Monsters*. In the original script it was Baragon, not Gorosaurus, that was to attack Paris. However, the Baragon costume from *Frankenstein Conquers the World* had been loaned to Tsuburaya Productions for use in a television series; when the costume wasn't returned to Toho in time for filming, Gorosaurus (a creature that could not possibly tunnel underground, except in the Toho universe) was substituted. Varan, too, is seen only fleetingly, in a long-distance shot and a glimpse at the end of the film, when the monster leaps into the air. According to Japanese texts, a new small-scale Varan model was built for this film (hard to believe, since it looks so crummy) but not a costume, which explains why Varan doesn't take part in the big battle.

There are other, non-monster effects that are memorable too: The Moonlight SY-3 was actually three different models built of wood and putty, one small model with a rocket booster for the docking-in-space sequence early in the film, and two complete models (one large, one small) for flying scenes. The launching of the Kilaak flying saucers is also impressive; it was filmed with a model of the spaceship measuring 80 centimeters in diameter and made of FRP (a type of plastic). Piano wires were stretched through a miniature model of the aliens' docking tunnel, and the ship was pulled through the tube by winding a winch. Also noteworthy is the Kilaak-orchestrated monster attack on Tokyo, which features some imaginative camera angles (at one point, the serpent Manda curls around a monorail in the foreground while Godzilla is seen rampaging in the rear of the frame) and an interesting if unconvincing confrontation between Godzilla and the Japanese defense forces, who launch some rather unthreatening rockets and fire guns from batteries mounted atop skyscrapers. The *Unused Toho SFX Footage* video reveals a very interesting scene shot during the raid-on-Tokyo sequence, in which Godzilla and Manda suddenly engaged in a fight while decimating the metropolis. Arikawa wisely cut the footage, for it is a lackluster fight and incongruous to the script. But still, the idea of Godzilla fighting a giant snake seems intriguing . . . .

Like *Sea Monster*, this film differs from the typical giant-monster format in that the action centers on a series of chases and obstacles, which keeps the pace moving quickly but also results in some pointless and boring meandering. For example, when Yamabe and his crew storm the Kilaaks' moon base, they expend several minutes disconnecting the aliens' transmitter device with common power tools and a ray gun, and the scene seems to go on forever, backed by a maddeningly frenetic "worker bee" theme by Akira Ifukube. There is little characterization in this movie, but the actors do what they can with their parts. Akira Kubo is particularly good as astronaut/all-purpose hero Katsuo Yamabe,

and Yoshio Tsuchiya stands out again as the alien-possessed Dr. Otani, who unfortunately is killed off early (via a stiff dummy plummeting out a window) and undergoes an unusually graphic and queasy surgery to remove a transmitter from behind the ear of his corpse. Kyoko Ai is wonderfully mean as the Kilaak queen, but Yukiko Kobayashi is rather flat in the leading-lady role as Yamabe's alien-captured girlfriend, Kyoko.

In May 1969, *Destroy All Monsters* benefited from a prompt and wide-scale theatrical release in the U.S. by American International Pictures. Just as it had done with *Godzilla vs. The Thing* five years before, AIP hired Titra Sound to dub the English dialogue and it devised an effective ad campaign to draw audiences to theaters. As a result, *Destroy All Monsters* received notices in many of the major U.S. newspapers, even if they weren't exactly rave reviews. The only noticeable deletions made by AIP are the opening credits sequence, including Akira Ifukube's stirring main title theme (his *Destroy All Monsters* march, an anthem backed by snare drums that plays several times throughout the picture, notably when the SY-3 is in flight) and a brief shot of Minya shielding his eyes when King Ghidorah drops Angilas from high in the sky.

Destroy All Monsters continued to appear occasionally on U.S. television stations until the early 1980s, when it mysteriously vanished. For more than a decade, this was truly the lost Godzilla movie — despite the advent of the home video phenomenon, which saw all other films in the series from *Godzilla: King of the Monsters!* to *Godzilla vs. Biollante* become easily available on VHS tape and/or Laser Disc as of 1992, *Destroy All Monsters* remained unreleased. In 1996, the film finally resurfaced in a series of broadcasts on the Sci-Fi Channel, and it was subsequently released to home video by ADV Films in 1998. Thankfully, the new print utilized in the TV broadcasts and the video was presented in glorious widescreen; regrettably, it featured a completely "new" English-dubbed dialogue track. For reasons unknown (although probably due to copyright issues), the nostalgic American International version of *Destroy All Monsters* has now been supplanted in the U.S. by Toho's own "international" English version, which was dubbed by Frontier Enterprises in Japan in the late 1960s but heretofore released only in English-speaking territories outside the U.S.

Special Section

GODZILLA TALK

English Dubbing in Japanese Monster Movies

It has become a cliché as old as Godzilla himself: Japanese monster movies are known for the cartoonish voices, out-of-sync lip movements, and sub thespian dialogue that result when foreign films are re-dubbed into English.

Ever since he first appeared in the U.S., Godzilla has been synonymous with "bad dubbing" among

critics who revile the genre. In 1959, a reviewer for the *Los Angeles Examiner* called *Gigantis: The Fire Monster* "unintentionally hilarious" and singled out the infamous "banana oil" line as evidence of the film's ineptness. Mocking parodies featuring Japanese people speaking stilted English have appeared in recent years on *The Tonight Show*, the MTV movie awards, and other programs. Even an early draft of TriStar Pictures' *Godzilla* remake featured a scene in which an actor's mouth movements didn't match his speech — a "tribute" to old Godzilla movies. It's a bad rap that Godzilla can't live down.

Admittedly, English-dubbing is an imperfect practice and it leads to lots of unintended laughs. But it's hard to imagine a theater full of teens sitting through a subtitled screening of *Ghidrah: The Three-Headed Monster* in 1965. The fact is, dubbing enabled Godzilla movies — and many foreign movies now considered classics, for that matter — to be shown in America during the genre's heyday. If not for the men and women who performed the thankless job of voicing Godzilla's human co-stars, the monster might never have become so popular.

Peter Fernandez, the voice of Speed Racer, as he appeared in the mid-1960s, when he lent his vocal talents to Godzilla and other foreign movie stars at Titra Sound Studios in New York.

COURTESTY OF PETER FERNANDEZ

GODZILLA MEETS SPEED RACER

Perhaps the most famous voice in Japanese monster movies is that of **Peter Fernandez**, best known for portraying *Speed Racer* in the self-titled animated series (he also wrote the lyrics to the zippy "Go Speed Racer, Go!" theme song). Fernandez's inimitable vocal cords (which still retain that raspy "Speed" sound today, nurtured by years of smoking) are heard in most every *kaiju* movie dubbed during the 1960s at Titra Sound Corp. studios in New York, a facility favored by American International Pictures, the Walter Reade Organization, and other distributors who imported Godzilla films for U.S. release. Among Fernandez' many performances are Ryota, the teen who searches for his shipwrecked brother in *Godzilla versus The Sea Monster*; Goro, the pesky reporter in *Son of Godzilla*; and Yukio, the young rebel in *Godzilla vs. The Smog Monster*.

It's no coincidence that Titra (TEE-tra) produced what is widely accepted as the best examples of dubbing in all Godzilladom. The company, founded in Paris as a subtitling business, occupied three floors in the National Screen Building at 1600 Broadway between 48th and 49th streets in Manhattan, with re-recording studios operating 'round the clock. Titra dubbed more movies than any other facility of its kind, for clients ranging from the major studios to minor distributors. The voices were supplied by professional actors, most of whom worked in the New York theater scene, and the entire dubbing process was orchestrated by highly trained writers and directors who took their work seriously.

Fernandez (b. 1927 in New York) is one of the most experienced voice actors in the U.S., with credits ranging from Goodyear tire commercials to arthouse movies. Having began his career as a child actor in Broadway plays, on radio programs, and in films, he found success in the 1950s writing scripts for television programs in New York, but as television production moved west to Los Angeles, Fernandez found himself searching for a new line of work. In the late 1950s he found his niche in dubbing, first as an actor and later, in the mid-1960s, as a writer and director. Japanese monster movies are just blips on Fernandez' long resume, which includes more than 500 films as an actor and about 350 as a writer or director.

"The Godzilla movies were always fun to do, as I recall. I can remember doing *Ultraman*, which I wrote, directed, and acted in. That was like doing a whole series of Godzillas — every half hour, a different part of Japan was being destroyed by a monster. The miniatures were terrific, and I liked doing that one very much. The individual films I don't remember too well. I do remember *Mothra* — I acted in that one, and it was quite an elaborate picture."

One of the main gripes against the way Japanese movies were dubbed in the old days is the actors' use of faux Asian accents. In today's atmosphere of political correctness, the producers might be accused of racial insensitivity for doing it that way but Fernandez says the intent at Titra was to make the films sound as natural as possible.

"We found that doing a Japanese film without a slight accent doesn't work." (He adopts an Asian accent:) 'You just need to get a little bit of *that* in there.' That seems to help overshadow the fact that the Japanese tend to end their sentences with open-mouth sounds, whereas we usually don't. When you're writing the lip-sync script, hopefully you can find a word to end the sentence that doesn't end with a labial — a B, M, or P, the three letters that you close your lips on — and still make it sound like normal English."

According to Fernandez, Titra's dubbing procedures in the 1960s weren't much different from today's methods, although technological advances have replaced 16mm and 35mm film with videotape. Back then, the films were cut up into short "loops" consisting of just a few lines of dialogue (the genesis of the term "looping"). As these loops were projected onto a screen in the recording studio, the actors watched the action and spoke into a microphone. Often, many takes were needed before the actor matched his character's lip movements correctly.

"A loop was literally that: a very short strip of film connected into a loop using 'leader,' or blank film," Fernandez said. "In the projector, the loop would run continuously, coming past the lens every few seconds. After a few rehearsals, recording would begin — there were no advance rehearsals, and the actors had never seen the script before! An electronic signal, three beeps spaced two-thirds of a second apart, would be heard in the studio. The actor would pick up the timing and then speak as if cued by a fourth beep.

"Seventy to 80 loops was considered a good amount to accomplish on any given day. By then, the actor would be exhausted, because each script loop had to be memorized instantly so that the actor could watch the lips on the screen and project himself into those lip movements, act with as much emotion as necessary, and be in dead-on sync! As soon as one loop was done, the actor would forget it and start learning the next one."

Dubbing scripts were written from a literal translation of the dialogue, not the original shooting script, provided by Toho or whichever studio had made the film overseas. The translations from Japanese studios, compared to those from other countries, were "particularly meager," Fernandez says, and required creative writing to liven up the dialogue. "We practically had to create the entire translation in the dubbing process," he says. "We tried to be faithful to the original dialogue, to preserve the original story and whatever nuances we could. Of course, we Americanized it, but we didn't use slang."

Perhaps the best-known actor to have graced the Godzilla series with his voice is Hal Linden, TV's *Barney Miller*, whom Fernandez hired for dozens of dubbing roles during the Titra era. Linden supplied the voice of Yoshimura the bank robber (Akira Takarada) in *Godzilla versus The Sea Monster* and Katsuo the astronaut (Akira Kubo) in *Destroy All Monsters*. Norman Rose, a deep-voiced actor, was the narrator in *Destroy All Monsters* ("The year is 1999 . . ."), among other roles.

Other names are not so easily recognized, though they played (unwittingly, perhaps) an important part in the development of the genre: Larry Robinson played voices in nearly all the dubbed *kaiju* films, including the egg-loving reporter in *Godzilla vs. The Thing*; Terry Van Tell and Paulette Rubinstein spoke in unison as the Infant Island twin fairies in the same film; Bret Morrison, also a dubbing director for Titra, played Dr. Yoshida (Jun Tazaki) in *Destroy All Monsters*, among others; Jack Curtis, one of Fernandez's *Speed Racer* cohorts, played dozens of voice roles, including Takashi Shimura's elderly scientist in *Frankenstein Conquers the World* and the TV newscaster who reads the infamous "Paris by Baragon" faux pas in *Destroy All Monsters*; Lucy Martin was Saeko, the orphaned girl on Sol-Gel Island, in *Son of Godzilla*; and William Kiel voiced Tadao Takashima (Dr. Kusumi) in the same movie.

In 1967, Fernandez left Titra to work on *Speed Racer* and other projects, although he returned for freelance dubbing jobs. Sometime in the late 1960s or early 1970s, Titra became Titan Productions due to administrative changes, and around 1980, the studio stopped dubbing films. The last *kaiju* movies to be dubbed there were *Godzilla vs. The Smog Monster* in 1971, *Infra-Man* in 1975, and *Message from Space*. The genre, it seems, hasn't been able to speak English quite so well ever since.

As for the widespread bias against English-dubbing, Fernandez isn't fazed. "In other countries, people are used to dubbing and it doesn't bother them if the mouths don't close on the labials, or don't open on the 'O' sound. In Germany, for instance, if there is an American film dubbed into German, they're not very critical of the lip sync. But you can't show a dubbed film here that way. Everything's got to match the lips, as if it were shot in English."

OTHER VOICES

Even before Fernandez and his colleagues were dubbing Godzilla movies on the East Coast for AIP at Titra Sound, other distributors were doing the same thing in Hollywood, using actors with varying degrees of radio, film, and television experience. As chronicled in Chapter 1, Asian actors were hired in the beginning to give the films an "authentic" sound. While James Hong worked on *Godzilla: King of the Monsters!*, films like *Rodan* and *Gigantis: The Fire Monster* featured Keye Luke (1904–1986, Master Po from TV's *Kung Fu*) voicing the main characters, and George Takei of *Star Trek* fame in minor roles.

Titra's counterparts on the West Coast included Ryder Sound, where *Gigantis* and *King Kong vs. Godzilla* were dubbed (years later, *Godzilla 1985* was also dubbed there), and Glen Glenn Sound, which remains one of the top film sound recording facilities in Hollywood today. Henry G. Saperstein's United Productions of America contracted with Glen Glenn to dub most of the Toho films it distributed, including *Monster Zero*, *War of the Garantuas*, and *Godzilla's Revenge*; Rankin-Bass's release of *King Kong Escapes* was also re-recorded there. The recording was usually overseen by the late postproduction supervisor Riley Jackson, and often included the voices of Marvin Miller (1913–1985), a character actor best known as the voice of Robby the Robot in *Forbidden Planet* and as the faithful male secretary on CBS-TV series *The Millionaire* in the 1950s, who supplied Akira Takarada's voice in both *The Last War* and *Monster Zero*, and Paul Frees (1920–1986), who dubbed Eisei Amamoto (Dr. Who) in *King Kong Escapes* and many, many other voices. Frees was one of the most talented voice-over actors in Hollywood history, with an incomparable knack for imitation and capable of a wide range of characters. He was Boris Badenov in the *Bullwinkle* cartoons, the Pillsbury Dough Boy, Professor Ludwig Von Drake for Walt Disney Studios, and dubbed actors as disparate as Humphrey Bogart and Toshiro Mifune.

THE EASTERN FRONTIER

In January 1996, the Sci-Fi Channel "premiered" two Godzilla movies that had seemingly been long lost: *Destroy All Monsters* and *Godzilla vs. Hedora*. Although the films were presented in glorious

William Ross, founder of Frontier Enterprises, in Tokyo c. 1994.
PHOTO BY THE AUTHOR

wide-screen format and appeared to be mastered from brand-spanking-new celluloid, something was amiss — the voices sounded different than before. The dialogue had changed slightly, and the song "Save the Earth" wasn't translated into English!

The source of this confusion can be traced to about 1966, when Toho began contracting with Frontier Enterprises, a Tokyo-based company, to dub many of its science-fiction films and other movies into English for export. For reasons that remain unclear, AIP and other U.S. distributors sometimes chose not to buy these dubbed-in-Japan versions, opting to produce their own English-language versions at Titra. Most likely, it was cheaper to do it this way, although it's possible AIP simply felt the Frontier dubs weren't up to snuff or even that Toho did not make these versions available to U.S. distributors.

Thus, for the past 30 years, alternate English-language versions of several Toho classics, sometimes referred to in fan circles as the "international versions," have been floating around the United Kingdom and Europe. In addition to *Destroy* and *Hedora*, they include *Ebirah, Horror of the Deep* (the international version of *Godzilla versus The Sea Monster*), *War of the Gargantuas* (in this version, even Russ Tamblyn's voice was dubbed by another actor, and the film is a direct translation of the original Japanese version, with the references to "Frankenstein" intact), and *Son of Godzilla* (also unedited, and includes the prologue wherein Godzilla is spotted by a weather plane).

Frontier Enterprises was founded by **William "Bill" Ross** (b. 1923), a Cincinnati native who went to Tokyo after serving in the Korean War, hoping to learn Japanese and join the State Department. Instead, Ross ended up getting involved with the

Japanese movie industry, appearing in more than 80 Japanese films and playing recurring roles on several television shows. Ross entered the dubbing business in 1959 on a referral by So Yamamura, a popular Japanese actor. On his first day on the job, Ross showed such a knack for working with the other dubbing actors that the Japanese director quit, leaving him in charge. Soon thereafter, he was hired as a director by Asian Films, a company that dubbed Japanese pictures into English for distribution across Asia.

One by one, the other dubbing companies in Tokyo folded, and in 1964, Ross founded his company and was working for all the major studios: Toho, Toei, Shochiku, and so on. Since then, he has dubbed about 465 live-action and animated feature films and countless Japanese TV shows, working as dialogue writer, dubbing director, and voice actor. In addition to his dubbing-related work, Ross was an associate producer on Toei's *Terror Beneath the Sea* and the MGM-Toei coproduction *The Green Slime* (he was also an assistant director to Kinji Fukusaku on this film). He continued to act occasionally, and appeared in *Message from Space* (as a pilot), *The Last Dinosaur* (as a scientist), and *The War in Space* (as an evil alien disguised as a scientist).

While Titra employed trained actors, Ross was forced to rely on whatever native English speakers he could find in Tokyo back in the 1960s. Most of the lip-synching was done by businessmen, musicians, students, and other Anglos who had little or no acting experience; still, Ross held auditions and made sure he hired the best people available, and he trained them thoroughly. Perhaps the most "famous" voice to work for Ross belonged to actor-stuntman Robert Dunham, best known as insurance agent Mark Jackson in *Dagora: The Space Monster* and the King of Seatopia in *Godzilla vs. Megalon*.

In the 1960s, and especially the 1970s, Toho and other Japanese studios began sending films to Hong Kong for English dubbing. Compared to the work done by Titra Sound in the U.S., and even by Frontier Enterprises in Japan, the Hong Kong dubs are noticeably inferior — the dialogue is often poorly scripted, and the voice actors (most of whom were transplants and expatriates from U.K., western Europe, Australia and the U.S.) speak in an array of mis-matched English dialects. In the '70s, all the Godzilla films from *Godzilla on Monster Island* to *Terror of MechaGodzilla* were dubbed in Hong Kong, as were other Japanese sci-fi films like *The Last Days of Planet Earth* and *The War in Space* (interestingly, these films feature voices also heard in popular "chop-socky" martial arts films like *The Chinese Connection* and *Five Fingers of Death*). And, because the Godzilla movies were almost strictly matinee and drive-in fare in the U.S. by this time, American distributors like Cinema Shares spared themselves the expense of recording new dialogue tracks, and simply used the sing-songy HK dubs. This, along with Godzilla's comic antics of the period, reinforced the monster's reputation abroad as more of a camp icon than a serious sci-fi character.

In the 1980s and '90s, Toho continued to use Hong Kong dubbing companies like Omni Productions to produce the English tracks for *The Return of Godzilla* (Toho's "international" version of *Godzilla 1985*), *Godzilla vs. Biollante* and all subsequent entries in the series; these films have featured a number of notable faux pas, including a character who keeps saying "Godziller" in *Biollante* and the grammatically challenged twin fairies ("We are the Cosmos, my friends") of *Godzilla vs. Mothra*.

Ten

UNKNOWN ISLAND

"Godzilla says we have to fight our own battles and not be cowards."

— Minya

GODZILLA'S REVENGE

RATING (OUT OF FIVE STARS): ★ ★

JAPANESE VERSION: GOJIRA, MINIRA, GABARA: ORU KAIJU DAISHINGEKI (GODZILLA, MINYA, GABARA: ALL MONSTERS ATTACK). Released on December 20, 1969, by the Toho Motion Picture Company. Toho Scope, in color. Running Time: 70 minutes.

U.S. VERSION: Released on December 8, 1971, by Maron Films on a double bill with *Island of the Burning Damned* (a British horror movie starring Christopher Lee). Running Time: 69 minutes. MPAA rating: G.

STORY: Ichiro, a latchkey kid growing up in a blighted industrial city, escapes the dreariness of his lonely, bullied life by collecting junked electronics parts from abandoned factories and by dreaming of Monster Island, the imaginary home of Godzilla, Minya and other creatures. Kidnapped by a pair of bumbling bank robbers, Ichiro remembers watching Godzilla teach Minya how to stand up for himself, and he heroically fights off the crooks; instilled with new self-confidence, the boy takes his revenge on a gang of kids that have been terrorizing him.

A BOY AND HIS MONSTER

Toho's commitment to ending the Godzilla series with *Destroy All Monsters* didn't last long. On the eve of the monster's 15th birthday, Tomoyuki Tanaka conceived a new film that would employ unprecedented cost-cutting measures. Probably inspired by Daiei Co. Ltd.'s *Destroy All Planets* (1968), the fourth installment in the Gamera series, which utilized heavy doses of stock footage from the giant turtle's prior films to beef up the running time and the special-effects content, Tanaka chose to take precisely the same tack. As further evidence that Toho was feeling Gamera's breath on its neck, the new Godzilla film was made expressly for young children, with a little boy in the starring role and introducing a talking Minya who helps the kid learn valuable life lessons, monster-style. Signaling the direction in which the genre was de-evolving, *Godzilla's Revenge* opened as the main attraction of the first Toho Champion Festival, a periodic program of kiddie films.

One of the tradeoffs of Japan's economic growth during the 1960s was the rise of the two-income family, and many Japanese children, like their American counterparts, were living the latchkey life. *Godzilla's Revenge* is director Ishiro Honda and screenwriter Shinichi Sekizawa's treatise on the breakup of the Japanese nuclear family, seen through the eyes of a child suffering the consequences. Set against the backdrop of the belching smokestacks of a heavily industrialized Tokyo suburb, the story takes place in vacant dirt lots, dilapidated buildings, and the cramped quarters of the apartment where little Ichiro spends most of his time alone, waiting for his parents to arrive home (his father is a railroad conductor, his mother works at an inn) and escaping the dreariness of his life by dreaming of a better place: Monster Island! With Godzilla reigning over a gaggle of beasts including Angilas, Gorosaurus, Kumonga, and others, Ichiro envisions this place as a utopia where he can meet his favorite kid *kaiju*, Minya, but he soon finds out that fantasy worlds are as messed up as real life. Just as Ichiro is always getting picked on by creeps who are bigger than he, Minya is also a small-fry suffering from an inferiority complex, constantly harassed by a taunting monster-thug with a gruesome grimace and a sinister hyena's laugh, a symbol of boyhood fears made flesh. With the aid of Minya and Shinpei Minami, a kindly toy inventor who lives next door and always has time to spare for the boy, Ichiro learns to be a man at a very early age — by the film's end, he's quit cowering and is standing up for himself, earning self-respect and the respect of others.

When compared to everything else that has come before in the Godzilla series, the cheapness of *Godzilla's Revenge* can be downright depressing. The film suggests that the monsters, after all, were never meant to be taken as real creatures — it's as if Ichiro saw *Destroy All Monsters* the previous year and based his fantasies on Ogasawara Island. But on its own merits, this is a well-made and effective children's movie with a message relevant even today.

DEJA VU: *Godzilla's Revenge* suffers from a much-deserved dubious reputation not only because of its kiddie theme but also due to the preponderance of monster footage cannibalized from other movies. Most of the monster stuff is from the two recent "island" Godzillas, *Godzilla versus The Sea Monster* and *Son of Godzilla*, but there

are snippets taken from *King Kong Escapes* (a shot of Gorosaurus standing near the trees) and *Destroy All Monsters* (a shot of Manda the serpent) as well. A lot of running time is burned up with Ichiro and Minya watching Godzilla battle with other monsters, which is apparently his way of setting an example for his kid. Godzilla's fights with the giant condor and Ebirah, plus his face-off with the Red Bamboo fighter jets from *Sea Monster* are all rehashed, as is the battle with Kumonga from *Son*. In addition, a few monster scenes were newly filmed, utilizing the Godzilla costume from *Destroy All Monsters* (looking the same as it did before, with slight modifications to the face and eyebrow ridges). Curiously, the scene in which Godzilla administers a lesson in fire-breathing to his son was shot specifically for this film, even though it is basically a note-for-note replay of Minya's education in *Son of Godzilla*, right down to Minya's smoke rings and his inability to shoot a stream of flame until Dad steps on his tail. The other new SFX scenes involve the sadistic troll monster Gabara, an ugly, upright-walking green-warted thing with a pug nose and a tuft of red fuzz on his crown. According to some reports, Gabara is supposed to represent a mutated bullfrog, but he hardly looks that way, and is one of Toho's most laughable monster creations. There are two confrontations with the gigantic ogre, who can give paralyzing electromagnetic shocks by placing his hands atop Minya's head and onto Godzilla's body.

The final monster battle among Godzilla, Minya, and Gabara takes place as Ichiro drifts off to dreamland, even while he is held hostage by the bank robbers (seems the boy's not too scared to miss his beauty sleep). Pushing a boulder off a cliff and onto Minya's tail, Ichiro helps his friend blast radiation breath into his foe's face. Ichiro helps Minya knock Gabara for a loop by jumping onto the see-saw end of a fallen tree, sending the evil monster flying off the opposite side, and Godzilla puts an end to matters by flinging Gabara across the miniature jungle. Because the Godzilla costumes in the stock film from *Sea Monster* and *Son* and the new monster scenes all have drastically different designs, the constant crosscutting between old footage and new footage is jarring even to the untrained eye, as Godzilla's face seems to be shape-shifting from scene to scene.

In a departure from the now established tradition of dividing the work on giant-monster movies between the principal and special-effects teams, Ishiro Honda directed not only the dramatic scenes but also the new special-effects sequences for *Godzilla's Revenge*. The reasons for this are likely twofold: On the one hand, much of the new SFX work involved interaction between the junior-sized Minya (played again by "Marchan the dwarf") and Ichiro (**Tomonori Yazaki**) on the Monster Island sets. On the other hand, Toho may have been reeling in costs on the film, for not even second-string SFX director Teisho Arikawa was tapped. Instead, **Teruyoshi Nakano**, then a first assistant director of special effects, aided Honda in staging the monster scenes. Even though Eiji Tsuburaya's name appears in the credits, he was not actively involved in the film because of commitments to other projects and his deteriorating health (Tsuburaya died just a few weeks after *Godzilla's Revenge* opened).

In a 1993 interview with *Cult Movies*, Honda described his experiences directing giant monsters for the first time in *Godzilla's Revenge*:

> Mr. Tsuburaya was given credit simply out of respect. . . . I directed almost all of [the special effects]. The two main reasons why I did were the budget and time constraints. Also, a very small studio was used for the shooting of the film, so it was decided not to separate the filming of the special effects and the regular actors as was usually done.

Honda handles the remainder of the drama very well also, maintaining a light and simple tone for the kids while touching a few nerves that the adult viewers can relate to — namely, the guilt and worry parents feel when they can't spend enough time with their kids. Honda seems to be mildly preaching to adults and children alike here, admonishing parents to put the kids first but also telling the youngsters they must learn to be more independent, because times are tough and families must work hard to survive.

The acting is fine if unchallenging, with a few standout cast members, including Yazaki, a natural child actor who actually has a great deal of screen presence for a boy his age, and **Eisei Amamoto** (a.k.a. Hideyo Amamoto) as the bearded and bespectacled toy inventor. Amamoto, an odd-looking character actor with an angular face and twisted teeth, often played villains (like Dr. Who in Honda's *King Kong Escapes*) but here he is cast against type as Ichiro's surrogate dad. Amamoto apparently disliked the role. "I felt out of place in *Godzilla's Revenge*," Amamoto told Guy Tucker of *Ultra-Fan*

magazine. "Directors never asked me to do that kind of role. That was my weakest part!" Kenji Sahara plays Ichiro's dad (a role probably shot in one or two days) and Toho stalwarts Yoshibumi Tajima, Ikio Sawamura, and Sachio Sakai show up as a policeman, a noodle-shop owner, and the mean-spirited bank robber, respectively.

Lastly, another huge difference between *Godzilla's Revenge* and its predecessors is the music soundtrack, composed by **Kunio Miyauchi**, who previously wrote the score to Honda's mutant film *The Human Vapor* and, more importantly, wrote the great theme music for Tsuburaya Productions' *Ultra Q* and *Ultraman* TV series. Rather than a booming orchestral score à la Ifukube or a jazzy soundtrack à la Sato, Miyauchi opts for a small combo playing jazz-tinged music befitting a cartoon soundtrack, ranging from fast-paced and furious (e.g., the music that plays when Gabara chases Ichiro through the forest) to creepy sound effects (the musical effects heard when Ichiro falls into a hole) to cheerfully naive and playful (like when Minya rescues Ichiro and the two first meet).

Henry G. Saperstein's UPA Productions originally announced the film in the U.S. sometime in 1971 with the title *Minya: Son of Godzilla*, but after realizing (a little too late) that Continental was already showing *Son of Godzilla* on U.S. television stations, he apparently feared the new film would be mistaken for the old one. It is not known how extensively *Minya: Son of Godzilla* was released (if at all); however some collectors of Godzilla memorabilia have unearthed advertising posters indicating that at least a very limited release occurred. "There was a confusing thing there. Toho had already released a *Son of Godzilla* made in 1967, so we released it as *Godzilla's Revenge* instead," Saperstein told *G-Fan* magazine in a 1995 interview.

The U.S. version of *Godzilla's Revenge* is almost indistinguishable from the Japanese version, except for Minya's voice (dubbed by a girl in the Japanese version, and a goofy Barney Rubble type in the U.S. print) and the music that plays under the opening credits. The Japanese version opens with a song called "*Kaiju* March" as the main title theme, which is scream-sung by an annoyingly loud child (not by Yazaki, the actor who plays Ichiro). In the U.S. version, this Japanese-language song was replaced by a groovy, 1960s-style garage-band number reminiscent of *The Munsters* theme, with a blaring saxophone solo and distorted Hammond B-3 organs. This song is unfortunately unnamed and uncredited in the opening titles.

With the death of Eiji Tsuburaya in 1970 and the headlong spiral now engulfing all Japanese movies, the Godzilla series entered a transition period. Perhaps unfortunately, Toho decided to forge ahead with the series, despite the fact that special-effects movies were the most expensive pictures to make in Japan. To overcome this stumbling block, the Toho brass would deploy cost-cutting moves over the next few years that would make *Godzilla's Revenge* seem lavish by comparison.

Part 3

DARK DAYS
The 1970s

"In the first Godzilla film, I think Godzilla himself is used symbolically. He represents death. But in the Godzilla films that were produced in the 1960s and certainly during the 1970s, is there much you can read into that, is there some sort of subtext? No. Not at all."

— *David Milner, staff writer for* Cult Movies *magazine, interviewed on CNN International, 1995*

"As part of a drive for new stories, Godzilla became more human. He was called upon to perform more, to play a role. And as time passed, he became a force for justice."

— *Film director Jun Fukuda, in a BBC-TV documentary, 1998*

Eleven

TOXIC AVENGER

"Don't lose your courage. One place where there is no pollution's in our hearts. Come on now. All of us. Our message is loud and strong. We're going to send it up higher."

— Yukio, the youth movement leader, in AIP's release of *Godzilla vs. The Smog Monster*

GODZILLA VS. THE SMOG MONSTER

RATING (OUT OF FIVE STARS): ★★

JAPANESE VERSION: GOJIRA TAI HEDORA (GODZILLA VS. HEDORAH). Released on July 24, 1971, by the Toho Motion Picture Company. Toho Scope, in color. Running Time: 85 minutes.

U.S. VERSION: Released in April 1972, by American International Pictures. Running Time: 85 minutes. MPAA rating: G.

STORY: An amorphous alien creature is carried aboard a meteorite to Earth, where it feasts upon the rampant air and water pollution along the Japanese coastline and grows from a sea-faring, boat-sinking monster into a gigantic, land-roving blob that sucks on smokestacks and can morph into a flying disc. The slimy monster's toxic emissions overpower Godzilla, but a scientist convinces the military to construct two giant electrodes and kill Hedorah by dehydration; the smog monster is lured into the deadly trap, but the electrodes malfunction and Godzilla — employing his newfound ability to fly — saves the day.

THE LOWER DEPTHS

The 1970s is a decade that Godzilla would probably like to forget. The mighty nuclear monster that once invoked Japan's greatest fears and faced an assembly line of worthy adversaries was powerless against the economic forces that were destroying the once proud Japanese movie business, and with it the careers of many talented filmmakers, technicians, writers, and actors. In a sense, Godzilla was one of the lucky ones: in the first half of the decade his career continued unabated, and he starred in a new feature each year. But in order to keep his job, Godzilla had to pull out all the stops and try anything and everything to maintain the interest of the ever-dwindling audiences, now comprised mostly of small children. This is the decade when Godzilla

161

tucked his tail 'tween his legs and took flight, "talked" to his buddy Angilas in growling English, shook hands with a gigantic robot, and performed flying kung-fu kicks.

To illustrate the severity of the film industry's swoon, here are some numbers. According to the *International Motion Picture Almanac*, there were 4,694 movie theaters in operation in Japan in 1965, the last year of the Showa 30s (1955–1965, the period associated with Japan's greatest and most prolific film output). There were 483 feature films released by Japanese studios, and the total number of tickets sold exceeded 372 million. Fast-forward to 1975, the year that *Terror of MechaGodzilla*, the most poorly attended Godzilla film and the precursor of the monster's involuntary retirement, was released. Although the industry's output was still high, with 405 domestic feature films released,[27] there were now only 2,530 theaters operating in the country and the annual attendance figure had plummeted by nearly half, to 187 million.

The "oil shock" of 1973 and the accompanying recession are often blamed for the destruction of the Japanese movie business, but even before then, television had firmly supplanted film as the country's preferred visual entertainment medium and the studios were reeling from declining revenues. Employees were laid off, guaranteed union contracts were discontinued, studio real estate was sold away, and business was restructured to cut costs (in Toho's case, the studio established the subsidiary Toho-Eizo, which operated as an independent TV and film production unit and was not beholden to Toho's labor agreements). The hardest-hit studio was Daiei Co. Ltd., one of Japan's oldest and (formerly) mightiest film companies, which went bankrupt and ceased production, putting an end to — among other things — the infamous series of Gamera movies, the last of which was *Gamera vs. Zigra* (1971).

The popularity of television had a particularly severe impact on the *kaiju eiga*. With a plethora of Japanese superheroes battling it out with aliens and monsters on TV every week, monster movies were something of an anachronism, and with their shrinking budgets and declining production values they had nothing to offer that the TV shows could not match or surpass. It is ironic that when the second *kaiju* boom erupted in the early 1970s with an unprecedented number of superhero programs, the original Japanese monster medium that Eiji Tsuburaya launched with *Godzilla* in the 1950s was now overshadowed by the type of programming

that the Old Man had helped to pioneer in the 1960s with *Ultra Q*, *Ultraman*, and the rest.

Two months after the release of *Godzilla's Revenge*, Toho's most cost-conscious monster film to date, and just weeks after the death of SFX master Tsuburaya, Toho officially closed its special-effects department on March 1, 1970. The last feature film completed by the Toho special effects department was *Yog: Monster from Space*, with SFX directed by Teisho Arikawa. One month later, on April 1, Toho Eizo (Toho Vision) Inc., also known as the "visual production department," was established with Tomoyuki Tanaka as president, employing many former members of the special-effects team. With the film business in decline, Toho's new offshoot put the techniques, equipment, and personnel of its SFX group to more profitable use, working on not only films but farming out crews and equipment for TV commercials and programs, visual presentations at conventions and expos, and other non-film uses. Around this time, many veterans of the Tsuburaya years were retiring or making the jump to TV work. Fewer films were being made, fewer people were working at the studio, and hardly any money was spent on new equipment or techniques. It was the end of one era and the start of the lean years.

SOYLENT GREEN: In the late '60s and early '70s, Japan was plagued by the by-products of its own industrial growth, modernization, and dependence on cheap energy: the heavy pollution of its urban areas, air, and water. Pollution-related illnesses were now considered a serious threat and legislation was enacted to control emissions and dumping. Things were so bad in some cities that oxygen tanks were installed on street corners to prevent pedestrians from passing out, and children went to school wearing face masks to filter out photo-chemical smog.[28]

It was against this bleak backdrop that *Godzilla vs. The Smog Monster*, the most bizarre Godzilla movie ever, was conceived. This picture is drastically different in tone from all the previous entries in the series, owing to the recent death of Tsuburaya and the absence of veterans Ishiro Honda and Akira Ifukube. Taking their places were three men of lesser distinction and arguably lesser talent — longtime Tsuburaya understudy Teruyoshi Nakano took over the special effects, first-time director **Yoshimitsu Banno** took charge of the production, and the music score was penned by **Riichiro Manabe**, known best for his jazzy scores to the

Purveyors of Fine Filth

The publicity campaign for AIP's release of *Godzilla vs. The Smog Monster* featured some of the most creative devices ever devised to generate ticket sales for a Godzilla flick. It's unknown, however, whether any theater owners tried any of this stuff:

- "A figure of Godzilla as a fighter against pollution might be promoted just as Smokey the Bear symbolizes the campaign against forest fires. An anti-pollution drive could be set up centered around the symbol of Godzilla, with the backing of local boy and girl scout headquarter officials and Four-H clubs. Rallying their membership to clean up streets and alleys and delivering bottles and cans to recycling centers . . .

- "A very pertinent and eye-catching three-dimensional display can be created in your lobby by setting up cut-outs of the monster figures from poster over a mound of rubbish, tin cans and bottles so that the Smog Monster rises up from the heap. Effectiveness depends on the effort in making a realistic display of the pollution. A good accent would be to use a red scrim over the eyes of the monsters, with back lighting shining through, illuminating them. . . .

- "*Godzilla vs. The Smog Monster* presents a smart case against smog and pollution in language especially suited to grammar school age children. Screen the film for members of the local board of education, principals and teachers to arrange for group showings to their young students. . . .

- "Godzilla Cocktail: Have local bar owner create a new mixed drink called the Godzilla Cocktail — "it clears that five o'clock smog from your brain" — for use in promoting his cocktail hour offerings. picture title and play date can be plugged in as advertising. Gag should be of interest as a humor item to local newspaper columnists and radio and television commentators.

- "Natural Gas Promo: Make a tie-up with local natural gas supplier and municipal and state agencies which have converted their vehicles to natural gas fuels as part of the anti-smog effort. theme of the campaign would link Godzilla's battle against the smog evil on the screen and the agency's battle for air purity on the streets.

early films of new-wave director Nagisa Oshima (e.g., *Night and Fog in Japan*, *The Cruel Story of Youth* [both 1960]), animated features, and a trio of vampire movies made by Toho in the 1960s and '70s (*The Vampire Doll*, *Lake of Dracula*, *Evil of Dracula*). Many fans profess a certain love for *Smog Monster*, and some may argue that the film's antipollution stance is a serious attempt to make the series socially relevant again. The problem is that its treatment of pollution is visually didactic and dramatically childish, and the tone shifts wildly from preachy ecological messages to kiddie cartoon segments to alternately silly and grotesque monster action to rock 'n' roll rebellion. Grim images of scum and trash floating on the ocean's surface, sulfur-belching smokestacks and the flesh melting off the bones of Hedorah's victims are hammered over the viewer's head with no subtlety, but in the end, the issue of pollution is reduced to terms a child can understand (a monster)

and its root causes are never discussed, making it hard to take the picture seriously. Nevertheless, *Godzilla vs. The Smog Monster* contains some entertaining moments and some very cool music. Today, the film is best viewed as a piece of camp nostalgia.

Director Banno (b. 1931), who joined Toho in 1955 and had worked as a production assistant to Akira Kurosawa, Mikio Naruse, and Eiji Tsuburaya, took inspiration for *Smog Monster* from Rachel Carson's *Silent Spring*, the landmark book credited with launching the environmental movement. Banno said he came up with the idea for the movie after visiting a beach near Yokkaichi (the site of the oil refinery attacked by Godzilla in *Godzilla vs. The Thing*), which was polluted with gross bubbles and smelled like rotten eggs, and he felt he could return the series to its roots by substituting the threat of an environmental catastrophe for nuclear war. "There was a message in the original *Godzilla*,"

Banno said in *The Complete History of Toho Special Effects Movies*. "I wanted to have him battle not with something like a giant lobster, but the most notorious thing in current society."

However, Teruyoshi Nakano tells a different version of events, saying it was he who wanted to make a serious film while Banno was concerned about catering to children's sensibilities, because *Smog Monster* was to be released as part of the Toho Champion Festivals, a series of movies packaged for kids. "We made Godzilla fly in that movie," Nakano said. "That was outrageous, we probably shouldn't have done that. But Mr. Banno was looking for something extraordinary, and even though there was no flying sequence in the script, we added it. Looking back, the movie seems kind of cruel and heavy-handed. I was trying to show the serious threat of pollution with scenes of Godzilla's eyes being burned and people dying. I guess I became uncomfortable with it, even while we were filming — that's why we added the comical scenes."

Hedorah (whose name is derived from *hedoro*, Japanese for "sludge") is a smokestack-toking, car-eating menace — a mucky monster that cannot be vanquished by Godzilla's radiation breath, punching power, and other usual fighting tactics, making him a most formidable and interesting opponent. When Godzilla slugs the creature, his hands pass through its amorphous body without harming it; his death ray bounces off Hedorah's body, producing sparks but little else. Hedorah has an arsenal of horrific weapons: it spews globs of acidic muck from glands located below its pupils, fires a squiggly red ray from its vertical-mounted eyes, farts asphyxiating fumes, and, worst of all, secretes a thick bodily mud-fluid that drowns Godzilla in a disgusting dirt bath.

Despite the fact that Hedorah is anything but agile on dry land, the huge blob-beast nonetheless proves to be one of Godzilla's most challenging adversaries. The battle is divided into three rounds: Round 1, at the docks in Fuji City, is easily won by Godzilla as he swings the Smog Monster around like a mace, dazing the creature. Hedorah lunges hard at Godzilla but misses its target, slamming into the pavement and stunning itself (so severely that it excretes a sickening, diarrhea-like fluid) and then retreats to the sea. Round 2, staged near an oil refinery (a nice miniature), goes to Hedorah when Godzilla, clutching his throat, is rendered unconscious by the flying orb's noxious gases. Round 3, the rubber match, takes place at the foot of Mount Fuji, and it is the Big G's most gruesome battle ever.

Godzilla, blinded in one eye by Hedorah's acid mud, retaliates by punching the sludge-demon in the face, causing its eyes to bleed. Hedorah gains the upper hand by dropping Godzilla into a crater and burying him in mud-crud; now completely blinded, Godzilla haplessly fires his ray in all directions, and appears doomed. Godzilla escapes from the crater, although it is unclear exactly how — in the next scene, the monsters are suddenly tumbling down a hill, then they resume their struggle. In the end, Godzilla takes the final step in his long conversion to superhero status. The monster teams up with mankind to fry Hedorah in the gigantic electrode sandwich, saving Japan and all the world from the disgusting evil.

Godzilla vs. The Smog Monster is Toho's first monster movie to depict graphic scenes of death, and if not for its prevailing juvenile attitude, this could have been a very chilling film. Most Toho monsters are oblivious to the human population as they trek through cities, creating widespread death and destruction on a very impersonal level, the main exception being the Tokyoite-eating Gaira (green gargantua) in *War of the Gargantuas*. But much time is spent showing the extent of Hedorah's human casualty toll, from Dr. Yano's facial scar to the bones and burned flesh left behind when the smog monster flies by. In one scene, a loosed chunk of Hedorah's body buries a group of Mah-Jong players; in another, Ken runs home through the streets, encountering dead bodies everywhere; and there is a great scene where Hedorah flies past the frame of an under-construction building. A worker screams and falls off the structure, and by the time he hits the pavement he's reduced to bones. Even the steel girders warp due to Hedorah's emissions. And although Hedorah doesn't eat people, it displays a certain curiosity about them when it probes into a psychedelic nightclub with a long, oozing tongue of mud (curiously sparing the life of a kitten that apparently didn't taste good) or when it interrupts the teenagers' mountaintop party. These grim moments are undermined, however, by Godzilla's goofy antics — he scratches his nose like Japanese pop star Yuzo Kayama, strikes an Ultraman-like "beam pose" only to have his hand burned by Hedorah's ray, and takes his aforementioned maiden flight, first spreading his arms at his sides, holding his tail to steer himself and blasting his breath at the ground, somehow jet-propelling himself through the air. Hedorah gets in on the silliness, shaking with laughter when Godzilla is suffering.

The Godzilla costume from *Destroy All Monsters* was used again, with some slight modifications (it has a longer neck here). Hedorah was brought to life via several props and a large, heavy, nearly immobile costume worn by stuntman Kengo Nakayama, better known today as Kenpachiro Satsuma, who would go on to play Godzilla from 1984–1995. This was Nakayama's first monster-acting experience, but because of the costume's incredible bulk (it was made of sponge rubber), he really doesn't get to do much in the way of acting. Most of the action relies on the work of Haruo Nakajima, who turns in his most animated performance as Godzilla to date. At times it seems like the Godzilla suit really is emoting — the famous scene wherein Godzilla plucks two eggs out of Hedorah's carcass and holds them out, one in each hand, is a testimony to Nakajima's skills. Godzilla truly looks disgusted.

To help keep costs down, Toho again avoids using big-name actors. **Akira Yamauchi**, a veteran actor of Toei and Daiei productions, is serviceable as Dr. Toru Yano, a small-time scientist who figures out what makes Hedorah tick and (with the help of son Ken) how to kill it, but he spends most of the picture lying in bed with a head wound, which doesn't make for exciting viewing. **Hiroyuki Kawase**, known for his role in Akira Kurosawa's *Dodes'ka-den* (1971), in which he played a bum's son, is fine, if somewhat bland, as Ken, the young boy who writes poems about Godzilla and has a clairvoyant ability to sense the monster's presence. The cast also includes Toshio Shibamoto (star of a superhero TV series called *Silver Mask*) as Yukio, Ken's 20-something uncle and organizer of the psychedelic rock party that almost no one shows up to — a weird, oddly interesting scene that begins with some eerie guitar music and vistas of the area around Fuji in black-and-white, then smash-cuts back to color when Yukio bolts upright and urges his dejected friends to start partying (which they do — curiously, the band plays electric instruments in the middle of nowhere). In one of the script's strange miscues, Hedorah kills Yukio with a mudball, but no one ever mentions his death, not even his girlfriend.

Manabe's soundtrack music is bizarre, to say the least, and a bit out of place in a giant-monster picture. However, the main title theme (called "Bring Back Nature" in Japanese, known as "Save the Earth" in English) is a fast-rocking psychedelic number with electric guitars and wah-wah effects, nicely sung by the film's female star, Keiko Mari. Manabe's theme for Godzilla, with trumpets blar-

ing maddeningly and often, is pretty bad, and must be heard to be believed.

Yoshimitsu Banno had visions of a sequel to *Godzilla vs. The Smog Monster*. At the end of the Japanese version, after Godzilla walks off into the sunrise, there is a title card with a picture of Hedorah and a message suggesting the monster will return ("And yet another one?" in Toho's international English-language print). But producer Tomoyuki Tanaka would have none of it. "Mr. Tanaka was hospitalized while we were filming the movie," Teruyoshi Nakano said. "He was much older and more restrained than Mr. Banno and I, so we were kind of happy to be able to make the movie freely. We decided to go for it. But after he returned from the hospital, Mr. Tanaka saw the movie and he wasn't pleased. He told Mr. Banno, 'You ruined the Godzilla series.'" Fittingly, Banno never directed another feature film, although he did work on a few documentaries. He co-scripted Toho's *The Last Days of Planet Earth* but later moved to the production side of the business.

American International Pictures released *Godzilla vs. The Smog Monster* in the U.S. in 1972, in a practically uncut version. The English dubbing was well done by Titra Sound again, although it contains some wonderfully funny lines like Ken's nonsensical "Superman beats them all" (in Toho's international version, he says, "and Superman, too," which makes more sense) and Dr. Yano's reference to the planet Hedorah came from as "gooey." In an unprecedented step for a Godzilla movie, English lyrics were written and recorded for the song "Save the Earth," adding a nice touch. The song was recorded at a Los Angeles recording studio and supervised by Guy Hemric, a producer and music arranger who had worked on many of AIP's "beach party" movies in the 1960s, including *Muscle Beach Party* (1964). Hemric wrote the lyrics (a loose but faithful translation of the Japanese lyrics) with **Adryan Russ**, an aspiring singer who was then working at AIP as a secretary. Russ also performed the song, and her voice nicely matches (and is superior to) that of Mari, the original singer. "For a long time, I never told anyone that I did the Godzilla movie because I was embarrassed about it," Russ said in a 1996 interview. "Later on I learned that the movie has kind of a cult following. Now I think it's cool and I'm glad to be associated with it." Today, Russ is better known as co-author of *Inside Out*, a musical play that had an award-winning off-Broadway run in 1994.

Orion Home Video released AIP's version of *Smog*

Monster, but Orion's distribution rights to the picture lapsed sometime in the early 1990s and the picture has been supplanted in television syndication by Toho's international English-dubbed version, called *Godzilla vs. Hedorah*, which is uncut and in widescreen but, unfortunately, has an inferior English dub and no translation of song lyrics. It seems that "Save the Earth," a battle hymn for Western Godzilla fans who grew up during the 1970s, may be lost forever.

SUCCESSOR TO THE THRONE

Teruyoshi Nakano, Special Effects Director

In the annals of Godzilla history, there are at least two schools of thought about the work of Teruyoshi Nakano. Critics may consider him an unworthy successor to Eiji Tsuburaya and accuse him of eroding the quality of the genre with his work in films like *Godzilla on Monster Island* and *Godzilla vs. Megalon*, both of which contain lots of notoriously obvious stock footage to pad the paltry effects sequences. On the other hand, a new generation of Godzilla fans, both in Japan and the U.S., was weaned on the *kaiju* films of the 1970s, wherein the King of the Monsters checked his atomic-bomb allegory at the door and assumed the simplistic role of superhero and Earth-defender. Sure, the monster costumes became flimsy, the miniature sets became more sparse, the wires more visible, and the optical effects more rare, but many fans would argue that the freewheeling films of the 1970s — which saw Godzilla fly, judo-flip his opponents, and perform running jump-kicks — are the most purely entertaining entries in Toho's giant-monster canon.

Nakano (sometimes billed as Akiyoshi Nakano or Shokei Nakano) — who assumed the duties of special effects director (although not credited as such) on *Godzilla vs. The Smog Monster* (1971) and was officially granted that job title two years later after the disaster film *Submersion of Japan* (1973) was a blockbuster success — seems keenly aware of his peculiar position in Godzilla lore. Born in 1935 in Japanese-occupied China, he graduated from the film department of Japan University in 1959 and quickly joined Toho Studios, working as a low-level assistant director (a go-for job, more or less) under Akira Kurosawa, Hiroshi Inagaki, and other A-list directors. By 1964, he had been handpicked by Eiji Tsuburaya to become a first assistant director of special effects (a title he first held on *Godzilla vs. The Thing*), a job that enabled him to work immediately

under Tsuburaya more or less until the old man's death in 1970.

To this day, Nakano regards Tsuburaya as his ultimate mentor, not only in special effects techniques and filmmaking, but also in his work ethic and his approach to the creative process, although Nakano seems to realize that his own work did not always measure up to the standards set by his teacher. Still, it must be pointed out that Nakano inherited the helm of Toho's special effects movie-making at the most inopportune time, when Japan was reeling from high inflation and deep economic recession, and its once-thriving film industry was but a shadow of its former self. Afforded less money and time than his predecessors, and faced with the fact that Godzilla's dwindling audience was comprised mostly of children, Nakano dutifully accepted his role as a challenge to keep the series alive, trying to defy such limitations any way he could. In 1984, he was repaid for his diligence when Toho resurrected Godzilla after a nine-year hiatus, giving Nakano the studio's biggest special-effects budget to date, with which he erected elaborate miniatures of Tokyo's new towering skylines and built perhaps the studio's biggest special effects boondoggle, the five-meter-tall Godzilla Cybot.

One delightful surprise about Nakano is his personality. He is warm, funny and articulate, with real passion for films and filmmaking. And, while he is unabashedly proud of his contributions to Japanese science-fiction cinema, his appraisal of his own work is realistic.

How did you become interested in movies?

I was born in Manchuria, and I came to Japan for the first time in 1945, after the war ended, with my mother. My father was a prisoner of war in Siberia, so in that situation, my mother had to work to

Special Effects Director Teruyoshi Nakano, circa 1996.
PHOTO BY THE AUTHOR

support us. We lived in Niihama on Shikoku Island, and my mother . . . was able to get discount movie tickets from [her] company. There were four movie theaters in Niihama, and the program changed every week, so I went to the movies four times a week. The only entertainment we had back then was movies. Everybody went to see movies, but I think I went more often than anyone. I remember, back in my junior high period, there was a screenplay in a Japanese textbook . . . I think it was *Spring on Lepers' Island*, written by Shiro Toyoda. The textbook showed an entire scene from the script,

and used the words "fade in," "fade out," "overlap." My classmates didn't even know something called a screenplay even existed, they had no idea what that meant. My teacher didn't know either, so I was so proud to be able to explain what they were. That's when I started writing screenplays and became interested in movie-making.

What kind of movies did you enjoy?

I lived in Niihama from 1945 to 1948, and because I had these discount tickets, I saw every single movie that was shown in Japan, all the Japanese films and even the American ones. I especially liked westerns, the Tarzan films with Johnny Weissmuller, and slapstick comedies.

Was it your intention to become a dramatic film director?

I entered Toho in 1959. I was young and ambitious, just starting my career in the movie business, and I favored artistic movies, and I wanted to devote my work to those kinds of films. At first, I worked as an assistant director to both principal photography and special effects teams. One of my first assignments was *The Three Treasures* (1959). I was basically an intermediary between the special effects team and principal team on that film. My job was to schedule the actors. It was the height of Mr. Tsuburaya's career, he had 90 people on the special effects staff. It was a happening work environment, but it was a very hard job. They used to use the term "3-K" for the crappiest jobs. "3-K" stands for *Kitsui*, a hard job, *Kitanai*, a dirty job, and *Kurushi*, a stinky job. But special effects work was more like a 7-K or 8-K job! The crew was covered with mud, covered with sweat, and they were just running around . . . I was worked very hard.

My first real encounter with special effects was during the making of *Submarine I-57, Never Surrender!* (1959, a war movie directed by Shue Matsubayahsi). This was a black-and-white movie, but the special effects sequences were shot on color film, using the blue-screen traveling matte process. I was fascinated by this and wanted to find out how it worked. . . . I wanted to make my own movies, but in order to do that, I thought I had better learn about every field, such as artistic films, special effects, everything. So that's how I decided to get involved in *tokusatsu* and learn about it.

What was it about special effects that attracted you?

In movies, actors are playing what the director wants them to play. It's as if they are doing it instead of the director. But in special effects, the director can portray his ideas using visual images, without words. That's what attracted me. I don't have to use actors to express myself, I can express myself using SFX. I believe movies have to express something, even without words. The visual image itself has say something or address something.

What was Eiji Tsuburaya like?

Many things come to mind. I would describe Mr. Tsuburaya as a poet. In Japanese society, we tend to divide people into two categories. One is the scientific people, and the others are more like poets, the artistic type. But I would describe Mr.

Tsuburaya as someone who fit into both types, he was scientific and he was artistic as well.

King Kong vs. Godzilla was your first experience on a Godzilla movie. What was it like working on that film?

I was a snobby movie buff back then, so when I read the script I wasn't impressed with this movie. The first *Godzilla* had such a social impact, because Godzilla was the aftermath of the bomb. I wasn't sure if it could be transformed into something that was entertaining and comical. But commercially, it was very successful, and after that the Godzilla series became one monster-vs.-monster movie after another. But it was totally opposite to what the first film was about. It was a little confusing to me. After that particular film, the flow of Godzilla movies and *kaiju eiga* completely changed. It had been hard, but after that, Godzilla movies became soft.

Godzilla vs. The Thing was the first film in which you were credited as an assistant director. What are your memories of that film?

There were four assistant directors and one director. The assistant directors were classified as first, second, third, and fourth rank. When I became first assistant director, then I received credit on the screen. . . . I don't remember much (about making the film) now. Do you remember the scene where Godzilla was buried underground, and he raised himself up from beneath the Earth? It was my idea to have him shake the dirt off his body. I think that was the best shot in that movie!

How did you feel about the changes in Godzilla's character during the 1960s and '70s?

That's a difficult question. I believe that without any changes to Godzilla's character, the series would not have been able to continue. If Godzilla had remained a villain, probably only hardcore Godzilla fans would have watched the movies, and not the general audience. I think it was correct to change Godzilla's character . . . it was a reaction to the times and the changes in the audience. But myself, I basically like a scary Godzilla, rather than a good Godzilla.

What were your impressions of director Ishiro Honda?

Mr. Honda's first film was *The Blue Pearl*, a semi-documentary about the lives of pearl divers. Before then, he had worked on documentaries, which is why his films had such a strong connection with nature, and with people's daily lives. For example, do you remember the scene where a woman is taking a bath and she sees a monster through the window (*The Mysterians*)? That illustrates his basic approach to making movies. Even if the movie was about something as unrealistic as monsters, he wanted to show how it would affect people's lives.

Yet, in spite of the fact that Mr. Honda cared about nature and about daily life, he also tried to create the most exciting kinds of scenes, that other directors usually are embarrassed to show. For instance, in the first *Godzilla*, there is a scene where a newscaster is broadcasting from a tower as the monster is approaching him. Godzilla destroys the tower, and the newscaster screams something like, "Now Godzilla is destroying the tower! What am I going to do!" In real life, the newscaster would try to run away, he would not stay. Mr. Honda cared about reality, but he also wanted to make the movie fun. I love that scene very much.

Mr. Honda believed that nature was the strongest force on Earth, and that nobody could resist nature's will. Mr. Tsuburaya believed this also.

Mr. Tsuburaya did not direct the special effects for Godzilla's Revenge. *What was it like working on that film without him?*

Well, in the fall of 1969, Mr. Tsuburaya's condition worsened and he was in and out of the hospital. That's when *Godzilla's Revenge* was in development. Mr. Tsuburaya's doctor ordered him to stop working, so Mr. Honda directed the special effects. I was first assistant director of special effects. . . . Director Honda told me he wasn't sure of the details of the special effects, so he would look to me. I drew the storyboards, and I added the flavor of fantasy to it. Come to think of it, maybe it was *Godzilla's Revenge* that Mr. Tsuburaya would have most wanted to be involved with, because he loved children. Because of that, this movie was one of my most memorable projects. I got along with Mr. Honda. However, I didn't expect Mr. Tsuburaya to pass on like that. It came so fast, too soon. Mr. Tsuburaya died in January 1970. He had seemed very tired of late. . . . I think the most difficult time for him was during production of *Battle of the Japan Sea* (*Nihonkai Daikaisen*, a war film directed by Seiji Maruyama, released August 1969). Mr. Tsuburaya was going back and forth between Toho and Tsuburaya Productions. He was so busy. He was also handling a big special exhibit for Mitsubishi at Expo 1970 [the World's Fair] in Osaka. In the middle of everything, he passed on.

Mr. Tsuburaya had a very strong sense of pride and professionalism. He always told me, make movies as a professional — don't make something

you'll have to apologize for. When we had planning meetings between the principal and special effects teams, the principal director would ask Mr. Tsuburaya, "Do you think this kind of effect is possible?" It would be something totally new, and which even an expert photographer would have had a hard time to film. But Mr. Tsuburaya would say, "Of course we can do it." When he said that, he had no idea how he was going to do it, so I asked Mr. Tsuburaya why he said that, and he answered, "Unless you say you can do it, you won't get any new good ideas. You can think about how you'll do it later on, until your stomach starts hurting from nervousness." I learned techniques from Mr. Tsuburaya, but on top of that I learned professionalism from him. There are always all kinds of limitations in this field: no time, not enough budget, impossible projects that you have to do. Every time I have to face a situation like that, I remember what Mr. Tsuburaya used to say.

I once heard about this episode where Mr. Tsuburaya was on his way home and he ran into this woman who looked familiar. So he said, "Hello, it's been a long time." Do you know who that woman was? That was Mr. Tsuburaya's wife. Mr. Tsuburaya kind of lost himself and was so deep into his own thoughts.

Were the budgets of the 1970s films much less than those of the 1950s and '60s films?

That's right. I was a "poor director," because I had to continue making the films during this difficult time.

What were the budgets of the 1970s films, in comparison to the earlier films?

Damn! Usually a director is not good at calculation or mathematics. So, probably I guess there was an extreme difference in the budgets and expenses from what they had been before. That's why we were forced to use our brains, not money.

How did you feel about using so much stock footage for the special effects sequences in Godzilla on Monster Island?

I hated it, but there was no choice. Of course it hurt me when I had to re-use those scenes, but there was no other way — we did not have the time or the money to film new scenes. So, I tried to confront this situation as a challenge: how could I creatively edit the footage to create a completely new scene? I tried my best, but of course if you watch the movie you will recognize that these are scenes from previous films. When we edited the footage, we tried to make the old film look new, and the new film look old, so it would match and flow together smoothly.

What was your working relationship with director Jun Fukuda like?

Mr. Fukuda was a skilled craftsman, someone who could do many types of things very well. He was equally skilled at directing *kaiju eiga*, action films, comedies. We also worked together on ESPY (1974), which was written by Sakyo Komatsu, who also wrote *Submersion of Japan*. It's about a group of spies with psychic powers. It was the first Japanese movie about psychic phenomena, so I had a hard time trying to visualize the special effects for this film.

How did Mr. Fukuda feel about directing monster movies as opposed to other types of movies?

I'm not sure, but he was a craftsman, so *kaiju eiga* was just one of the many types of films he was good at. Some of his most famous movies were from the "Young Guy" series. He also made *100 Shot 100 Killed* (1965, a James Bond–style spy spoof starring Akira Takarada). I guess he didn't like *kaiju eiga* all that much. But I think sometimes the greatest movies we make are ones we don't necessarily like. Whether or not we like something has nothing to do with making a great movie.

After Terror of MechaGodzilla, *were you surprised that Toho discontinued making Godzilla films for nearly a decade?*

I really thought the series would continue, because nobody lets a big star like Godzilla die. But I did feel that he could use some time off. From *Godzilla vs. The Smog Monster* to *Terror of MechaGodzilla*, that was a very busy time for the special effects staff. That's why the studio decided to take time off for Godzilla, because we had been so busy. I always knew he would come back, though, and next time, we would make Godzilla even more powerful than before.

If you were given the money needed to make the ultimate Godzilla movie, what would it be like?

Even if I had the federal government budget, there would always be something I could not accomplish. There are certain things that are just impossible. I don't think a bigger budget automatically means a better movie. It depends on the director's creativity. I would prefer a big budget in my imagination.

If you look at the eras of Godzilla history, there is the period of Mr. Tsuburaya, the period of Mr. Arikawa, my era, and afterwards. I think mine was the toughest period of all time in Godzilla history.

SPECIAL EFFECTS BY TERUYOSHI NAKANO: *Godzilla vs. The Smog Monster* (1971); *Godzilla on Monster Island* (1972) *Sumbersion of Japan* (a.k.a. *Tidal Wave*), *Godzilla vs. Megalon* (1973); ESPY, *The Last Days of Planet Earth, Godzilla vs. The Cosmic Monster* (1974); *Terror of MechaGodzilla* (1975); *The War in Space* (1977); *Deathquake* (1980); *Imperial Navy* (1981); *Godzilla* (1984); *Princess of the Moon* (1987); *Tokyo Blackout* (1987). Nakano is retired from motion pictures and now helps create effects-oriented rides for children's amusement parks.

Twelve

TWILIGHT OF THE COCKROACHES

"I think it stinks!"

— Comic book editor

GODZILLA ON MONSTER ISLAND
a.k.a. GODZILLA vs. GIGAN

RATING (OUT OF FIVE STARS): ★ 1/2

JAPANESE VERSION: CHIKYU KOKEGI MEIREI: GOJIRA TAI GAIGAN (EARTH ATTACK MISSION: GODZILLA VS. GIGAN). Released on March 12, 1972, by the Toho-Eizo Company. Toho Scope, in color. Running Time: 88 minutes.

U.S. VERSION: Released in August 1977, by Cinema Shares International/Downtown Distribution. Running Time: 88 minutes. MPAA rating: G.

STORY: Gengo, a cartoonist hired to design monsters by the developers of an amusement park called World Children's Land, senses trouble when he meets the company chairman — a teenager whom, he later learns, is supposedly dead! As it turns out, his employers are really alien cockroaches (disguised in the bodies of dead people) from a planet despoiled by pollution, now hatching an evil plan to take over resource-rich Earth; Gengo, with help from his *karateka* girlfriend, a fat hippie and a woman trying to rescue her brother (a kidnapped computer scientist forced to repair the aliens' electronic gizmos), foils the invaders' plans and Godzilla and Angilas swim forth from Monster Island to confront the customary "bad guy" monsters, Gigan and King Ghidorah.

ALIEN INVASION ON A SHOESTRING

The alien invaders in *Monster Zero* and *Destroy All Monsters* were admirably evil, using advanced tech-nology and deceptive double-crossing to manipulate Japan's monsters in their bid to take over Earth. But, like everyone else, space aliens were hit hard by economic recession in the 1970s. Forced to tighten their belts, they seldom tooled around in spaceships anymore and they plotted their takeovers in rented office suites rather than stealthy underground bases. And their plans for intergalactic conquest were carried out under cover of laughable schemes, like the development of children's amusement parks.

At least, that's the impression one gets when watching *Godzilla on Monster Island*, a film which, on its surface, pretends to be space-invader spectacle in the classic Toho style, but upon closer inspection is in fact a mostly uninspired, low-rent update of this motif for the silly 1970s. With a paper-thin and mostly unengaging story and a cast of nobodies (the lone "exception" being Gen Shimizu, a Toho bit player from the 1960s who shows up here as a commander at a tiny military outpost), this film expends much energy building up to the final, four-way monster showdown between Godzilla and Angilas in one corner, and King Ghidorah and the cyborg-bird Gigan in the other (staged like a wrestling match, with both monster teams retreating to their corners and discussing strategy), but the payoff isn't worth the wait.

Godzilla on Monster Island is padded to the hilt with stock footage from other Toho monster spectacles, much of it tinted with optical printers so that day scenes are turned to night. Special effects are culled from *Ghidrah: The Three-Headed Monster*, *Monster Zero*, *War of the Gargantuas*, *Destroy All Monsters* and even *Godzilla vs. The Smog Monster* — if *Godzilla: King of the Monsters!* had been in color, Teruyoshi Nakano and Company might have cannibalized that film, too. Further cheapening the proceedings is the re-use of the *Destroy All Monsters* Godzilla costume, which is now literally falling apart in front of the camera (scales peel visibly from the body, and in one scene, a tear can be seen under Godzilla's armpit). Lastly, although the soundtrack is credited to maestro Akira Ifukube, he really had nothing to do with the picture: producer Tomoyuki Tanaka, in another belt-tightening move, utilized library tapes of previous Ifukube scores, from films as old as *Battle in Outer Space*; some of the music was originally written by Ifukube for the Japanese exhibit at the World's Fair in Osaka in 1970.[29] While some of the music fits the monster action well, several cuts sound positively bombastic and even ironic when used to underscore the human drama. When the heroes go to City Hall to conduct research on the World Children's Land group, a mid-tempo Ifukube military march plays as they walk up and down the steps of office buildings, and the mismatching of music and visuals is unintentionally hilarious.

The cast of characters in Shinichi Sekizawa's script is interesting only because it seems to be a calculated attempt to appeal to the widest variety of children, but it fails miserably. There is a bumbling comic-book artist (who goes for laughs by slipping on a large globe and is always pushing the bangs out of his eyes), his karate-expert girlfriend, and an overweight "star child" type whose headband can't hide the fact that his long hair is a wig. The aliens profess to be a group building a children's amusement park with a monster theme and who seek to establish a "perfect peace" in the world, but even when they reveal their true identity as aliens from Star M in the Hunter Nebula, their sinister plans, and their insect alter egos (this via the unimpressive effect of casting shadows in the shape of a cockroach on the wall), they are hardly threatening.

A race of scavengers who inherit planets from dominant life forms doomed to self-extinction by pollution, these "body snatchers" use the corpses of dead Japanese men to blend into society and chart their computerized takeover of the world, but their methods are rather unimpressive. Their hideout is the crudely fashioned Godzilla Tower, where security is lax: Machiko, the woman whose brother has disappeared there, easily sneaks in and steals a computer program tape, and Gengo and his girlfriend slip inside and snoop around. The aliens' most impressive piece of gadgetry is a pack of cigarettes with a built-in transmitter that helps them track Gengo to his house (apparently, they did not ask for his address on his job application), and their goon squad is a wimpy bunch who quickly retreat at a few punches and kicks from Gengo's girlfriend. These inept invaders have plans of wiping out all of Earth's monsters, but it's a wonder they thought they could pull it off.

The one ray of hope for monsterkind in all this is Gigan, a 65-meter-tall, 25,000-metric-ton half-creature, half-robot alien equipped with a rotating saw in its belly (useful for cutting pesky buildings in half) and huge, sickle-shaped hands, pincers flanking its beak, and a wraparound single eye. Portrayed by Kengo Nakayama, the stunt actor who played Hedorah in the previous film, Gigan moves a little awkwardly at times, owing to the costume's heavy bulk and the strange shape of its hands and feet, but its sleek appearance and menacing look are at times awe-inspiring. The King Ghidorah and Angilas costumes, left over from *Destroy All Monsters*, appear to be in decent shape, although little care was taken to avoid filming the bottoms of Angilas's feet, and Ghidorah's wings remain stationary throughout much of the action, like two huge

From beyond the stars came the most fearsome monsters in the galaxy! Only Godzilla stands in their way in *Godzilla on Monster Island*! Is even Godzilla strong enough to defeat the invaders! Matching unbelievable strength! Exchanging incredible detonating rays! Don't miss *Godzilla on Monster Island*!

— *From TV spot for Cinema Shares' release of* Godzilla on Monster Island

fans filling the frame. The film's most embarrassing moment, monster-wise, occurs when the aliens summon Gigan and Ghidorah from outer space: the two monsters appear in the stratosphere, trotting across the universe encased in glowing crystals that explode to reveal the monsters when they enter Earth's atmosphere. Stiff, immobile wooden puppets of Gigan and Ghidorah circle the Godzilla Tower, and because Nakano films these props in revealing tight shots, they are ineffective and fake-looking. This is the first film in which Monster Island is matter-of-factly referred to as Godzilla's home, and although the island's exact location is not mentioned, it's likely somewhere in the South Pacific, a place where Godzilla, now comfortable with his role as Earth's dinosaurian defender, has his own piece of real estate where he can get some needed R&R between monster battles.

Godzilla on Monster Island is the last film in which Haruo Nakajima climbed inside the Godzilla suit, and unfortunately his monster career ends on a sorry note. Godzilla's characterization suffers another indignity in this film as Toho now gives the monster the ability to "talk." In the Japanese version, Godzilla and Angilas's communication is illustrated with comic-book-style thought bubbles, accompanied by squeaky sound effects much like somebody "scratching" on a stereo turntable, which is bad enough. The English-dubbed version one-ups this injustice by actually giving the monsters distorted, growling voices that are somewhat hard to understand, especially Angilas, who seems to be suffering an inferiority complex and mutters everything under his breath.

The silliness of the recent Godzilla films continues, with Angilas back-slamming King Ghidorah during the final battle and Godzilla delivering the *coup de grace* by judo-flipping the three-headed dragon. For the first time, there is blood and gore in the monster battles as Gigan slices open Godzilla's shoulder, a break with Eiji Tsuburaya's tradition of avoiding graphic violence. Amid all this wildly uneven action and the preponderance of stock footage linking the monster scenes together, there is one sequence in the film that is well staged. The four-way monster battle that takes place at an oil reserve is a showcase of one of Teruyoshi Nakano's main strengths, pyrotechnic explosions. Huge columns of fire rise up in the air as the monsters ignite the refinery, and the battle is filmed in slow motion to accentuate the monsters' size. The Toho Scope format is well utilized to create a panoramic, almost three-dimensional perspective.

In the 1970s, Godzilla movies arrived in the U.S. rather erratically, sometimes with long delays. Released in Japan as *Earth Attack Mission: Godzilla vs. Gigan* in 1972, this film did not show up in the U.S. until 1977, when Cinema Shares International renamed it *Godzilla on Monster Island* (a somewhat nonsensical title, since all the action takes place on the Japanese mainland). Strangely, *Monster Island* reached America after *Godzilla vs. Megalon*, even though *Megalon* was released in Japan one year later.

Although Cinema Shares had heavily promoted *Megalon* and reaped a nice return on it (see Chapter 13), unfortunately the company did not put as much effort behind *Monster Island*. The picture remained in circulation for more than a year, playing sporadically across the nation, mostly at matinee showings. Cinema Shares left the movie virtually uncut for its U.S. release — the most noteworthy change is the deletion of the word "bitch." Early in the film, when Gengo is being teased by his girlfriend, he mutters, "you're a hard bitch"; Cinema Shares clipped this sentence to "you're a hard." When the film was released to home video in the 1980s it was retitled simply *Godzilla vs. Gigan*.

THE EVIL BRAIN FROM OUTER SPACE

Godzilla vs. the Space Monsters (circa 1972)

The 1970s was the era of monster tag-team matches, and one of the earliest story ideas was *Godzilla vs. the Space Monsters — Earth Defense Order*, a script by Kaoru Mabuchi which would eventually evolve into *Godzilla vs. Gigan*. While little reference material on this script is available, Kodansha's *Godzilla Encyclopedia* offers a brief synopsis of Mabuchi's story which shows a prototypical 1970s Toho monster script — evil aliens controlling several monsters in an attempt to conquer Earth, only to be repulsed by Godzilla and friends. *Godzilla vs. the Space Monsters* introduces Gigan and Megalon, teaming them with King Ghidorah against the duo of Godzilla and Angilas.

Several elements of what would eventually become *Godzilla vs. Gigan* are in evidence here — the mind-controlled space-monster team (minus Megalon, who would have to wait another year to make his screen debut) versus the Earth monsters, Godzilla Tower located in an international exhibition park called Science Land (changed to Children's Land for the film). The nemesis in this story is an alien named Miko, a living brain with designs on subjugating the Earth's population. Using the space monster team, Miko terrorizes the planet and threatens to annihilate the world unless control of the planet is turned over to him. Godzilla and Angilas appear to repel the invading monsters whenever they attack, but Miko pulls back his minions each time to minimize the damage to the planet which he covets so much. Finally his patience wears thin and Miko issues an ultimatum

— surrender or be destroyed. Wishing to assume a less unsettling yet imposing physical appearance before his future subjects, Miko decides to have the monsters place his life support unit inside the giant statue of an ancient Incan god, Majin Tuol, which is located in Tokyo's Science Land. When the space monsters arrive in Science Land to carry out the fiendish plot, Godzilla and Angilas arrive to do battle, and this time the alien monsters spark a fierce battle. When Gigan's buzz saw attempts to slice into the statue of Majin Tuol to carry out Miko's plans, the idol begins to bleed. . . . With a tremendous rumble and flash of light, the statue moves. Brought to life by the invaders' attack, Majin Tuol helps to turn the tide against Miko and his forces. Godzilla vaporizes Miko as his monsters flee for their lives back into space. The invaders vanquished, Majin Tuol returns to its pedestal next to Godzilla Tower, a scar on the stone surface a reminder that the idol stands ever vigilant to defend the planet again should the need arise.

Shinichi Sekizawa took this script and reworked it under the title *The Return of King Ghidorah*, the idea being that King Ghidorah's name provided a better hook to the audience. Sekizawa's story used different monsters than Mabuchi's (King Ghidorah, Gigan, and a new monster named Mogu challenging Godzilla, Rodan, and Varan), but contained nearly all the same elements. Sekizawa later reworked the script into *Godzilla vs. Gigan*.

— *Jay Ghee*

MONSTER FOR HIRE

Tsuburaya Productions' proposed Godzilla vs. Redmoon (1972)

In the early 1970s, with the movie industry in a deep financial and creative void, Toho began farming out its giant monsters for use in other productions. It is well known that Godzilla, King Ghidorah and Gigan all made appearances on the *Zone Fighter* TV series (see *Ultra-Goji*, Chapter 13). Unbeknownst even to many Japanese fans, the studio also agreed to loan Godzilla to Tsuburaya Productions for a juvenile feature film which, fortunately, was never made.

Kodansha's *Encyclopedia of Godzilla* (*Godzilla vs. MechaGodzilla* edition) reveals that after Tsuburaya co-produced the children's monster film *Daigoro vs. Goliath* as part of its 10th-anniversary celebration in 1972, the commercial success of this project prompted the studio to hatch a new feature film for small children. The idea man behind this new film was producer **Noboru Tsuburaya**, who wanted his father's most popular creation to star in a film for his own company. The timing of this kind of project coincided with Godzilla's ever-emerging role as superhero defender of the planet. With Tsuburaya as Japan's premier producer of live-action superhero fare, such a film seemed a logical step for the monster star.

Tsuburaya Productions commissioned the writing team of Inoue Mitsuda and Tetsuo Kanoshiro with developing a tentative screenplay, the result being *Godzilla vs. Redmoon*. In celebration of its reunification with Japan on May 15, 1972, Okinawa was chosen as the setting for the film. In this story, a series of mysterious tremors on the surface of the moon culminates with the emergence of Redmoon, a terrible beast which had hibernated for many years beneath the moon's surface. Without explanation, the creature immediately takes off for Earth.

Almost at the same time, the prehistoric monster Erabus awakens from eons of slumber on Habu Island in Okinawa Prefecture. With two monsters suddenly appearing in the vicinity of Japan, the authorities decide the best course of action would be to lure the monsters into a battle with each other, hoping that one or both would perish in the ensuing struggle. But the plan goes badly awry when instead of fighting, the two monsters proceed to mate! The sudden appearance of the two creatures is actually part of their instinctive migration to a mating grounds, and the humans find out too late they have unwittingly lent a hand to the process. The seemingly ferocious monsters become docile and eventually give birth to a baby monster known as Hafun.

The monster family's tranquil existence on Habu Island is shattered when a ruthless opportunist seizes Hafun with the intent of turning the creature into a public attraction. When Hafun resists, the humans accidentally kill the infant, causing Redmoon and Erabus to become violently angry. As the vengeful parents lash out against mankind, Godzilla appears on the scene. The hero monster must fight the angry parents to tame their anger and stop them from laying waste to the planet.

Producers Noboru Tsuburaya and Toyowaki Awa planned this film with the cost-cutting intention of reusing/redressing some of the monster costumes from *Daigoro vs. Goliath*, along with one of Toho's Godzilla costumes. The project nearly went before the cameras with Shokei Tojo as director and Kazuo Sakawa as special-effects director, but the reasons for its abandonment are unknown.

— *Jay Ghee*

GODZILLA IN THE FLESH

Haruo Nakajima, the man inside "the suit"

Perhaps no one deserves more credit for Godzilla's enduring international popularity than the man who brought the monster to life on screen, Haruo Nakajima. Between 1954 and 1972, Nakajima was Toho's main man inside the Godzilla suit, portraying the King of the Monsters in 12 films and also tackling the roles of other noteworthy creatures including Rodan, Varan, Baragon (of *Frankenstein Conquers the World* fame), Mogera (the alien robot in *The Mysterians*), King Kong in *King Kong Escapes*, and Gaira, the mean, green monster in *War of the Gargantuas*. As if that weren't impressive enough, he also worked as a monster actor and stunt choreographer on Tsuburaya Productions' *Ultra Q* and *Ultraman* teleseries.

Nakajima was born January 1, 1929, in Sekita city, a small town known for its rice and fish in Yamagata prefecture. As a boy, he worked fetching seaweed out of the ocean after school, and at the tender age of 14 he entered the Japanese Imperial Navy during World War II as a pilot trainee. After the war, he worked in a meat shop owned by his parents and later worked as a truck driver at an occupation forces camp before finally enrolling in 1949 at the International Film Acting School in Tokyo. There, an instructor who was a contract player at Toho helped Nakajima land a job at the studio in 1950. For his first few years, Nakajima was assigned to mostly stunt-action roles for *samurai* films, including many minor pictures and even a few made by major directors like Akira Kurosawa and Hiroshi Inagaki. In 1953, he worked for director Ishiro Honda for the first time, playing a zero fighter pilot whose plane is bombed in *Eagle of the Pacific*. The following year, he played one of the bandits who is killed by swordsman Seiji Miyaguchi in the famous "field of flowers" scene in Kurosawa's masterpiece *The Seven Samurai*.

Nakajima says he does not know exactly why he was picked to play Godzilla, but he remembers one day in 1954 when he was approached by the head of the actors division at Toho, who told him about an unusual new project at the studio that he might be suited for.

"I still remember when I was first assigned to play Godzilla," Nakajima says. "At first I was told there was this new science-fiction film — it was called 'Project G' during preproduction, since they had not revealed the monster's name yet — and I was introduced to Mr. Tsuburaya. There was a screening on the Toho studios lot of *King Kong*, of a print that Mr. Tsuburaya personally owned, and from that I began to study the way a monster should move. Tsuburaya told me it would take years to make a movie like *King Kong* in Japan, with stop-motion animation. Instead, he said this new movie would be made with monster suits." In preparing for his role, Nakajima says he also packed a sack lunch and spent afternoons at the zoo in Tokyo's Ueno Park, studying the movements of gorillas and other animals.

"I have an incredible memory of the first time I ever tried on a Godzilla suit. It was the very first suit every constructed, and it was on Stage 3 of the studio lot. I and [Katsumi] Tezuka tried on the suit in front of Mr. Honda, Mr. Tsuburaya, Mr. Tanaka, and members of the staff. But the suit was so heavy, so stiff — I was able to walk about 10 meters, but Mr. Tezuka could only walk about three meters and then he fell down. I thought, 'This is going to be impossible.' "

Nakajima's skills as a monster man grew. He was so good at it that on most films, Tsuburaya gave him a free hand to choreograph the monster battles himself. "Mr. Tsuburaya just told me where to finish at the end of each scene. In other words, I created

Haruo Nakajima, photographed during a 1996 interview.
COURTESY OF WINTERGARDEN PRODUCTIONS

all the monster fights. My fighting scenes were never the same — that's how good my acting skills were,'' he recalls. His admirers included not only Godzilla fans, but Hollywood types as well. Nakajima says that during the filming of *King Kong vs. Godzilla*, he was approached by an American producer (possibly John Beck) and invited to come to Tinseltown to work for a year, but ultimately he declined the offer.

"I told Mr. Tsuburaya about the offer, but he said to me, 'I cannot make Godzilla movies without you,' so I stayed with Toho. I was very proud of my work and took it seriously. This was a very prestigious type of job in the Toho company. I had realized early on that I would not become a big movie star, but inside the Godzilla suit I felt I had a very important role to play."

Asked which of his monster roles is his favorite, Nakajima cites both the original *Godzilla* and *War of the Gargantuas*. In *Gargantuas*, Nakajima played a very different monster compared to Godzilla and his other creatures. Gaira is a fleet-footed humanoid, and because the costume had a more expressive face, he succeeded in lending the creature a thoroughly demonic quality that is chilling.

It may be every Godzilla fan's dream to step inside the monster costume and take a stab at knocking down a miniature reconstruction of the Tokyo metropolis, but Nakajima can attest that it's no day at the playground. With the thick costume providing little air circulation, the heat from the studio lights bearing down upon the thick rubber skin, the immense weight of the costume, the poor vision through the tiny holes in Godzilla's neck, and the complexity of staging a realistic fight with other monsters that are mechanically or remotely controlled and often involve wire works, explosions, and other mechanisms, the work of a suitmation actor can be grueling and intense.

It can also be risky. Nakajima doesn't like to complain about the intense discomfort and near-injuries he suffered inside the suit, but he admits that he was hurt at least one time. "When we were filming *Varan the Unbelievable*, I was inside the monster costume and a truck loaded with explosives crashed into me. My 'important spot' was burned, but I never told anybody about it. I didn't want them to worry about me."

After Tsuburaya's death, Nakajima's enthusiasm for working in monster movies began to wane. His feelings, along with a massive layoff of actors by Toho, led to his retirement after *Godzilla on Monster Island*, capping a career of monster-mashing inside asphyxiating rubber suits and under hellacious studio lights.

"When Mr. Tsuburaya died, I lost the will to continue. I was persuaded by [Teisho] Arikawa and [Teruyoshi] Nakano to keep on, and I played Gezora [the alien squid creature in *Yog: Monster from Space*] and two more Godzilla movies before I finally retired. Another reason I left was because the Japanese movie industry was in terrible condition. Toho had 350 actors under contract, but because of the economy they laid people off to reduce expenses. Around 1972, they released all 350 actors, all at once, including me. It was a very difficult time for all of us, although the company tried to accommodate us by finding jobs for us. After *Godzilla on Monster Island* I worked in a bowling alley. I was 43 when I retired, but it wasn't because of my age. I was physically fit, and I felt I could keep doing it."

Even today, Nakajima embodies the fearsome fighting spirit of the classic Godzilla movies. Others have tried to fill his shoes, including several stunt actors who played Godzilla after his departure in the 1970s and Kenpachiro Satsuma, Toho's latter-day Godzilla actor, but none has ever matched the intensity, spirit, and personable qualities that Nakajima brought to the rubber-clad role. Godzilla has never been the same without him, and he knows it.

"In the *Heisei* Godzilla series [the films made after *Godzilla 1985*], the monsters just stand there and blast rays at each other. In my time, it was hand-to-hand combat. It was real action," he said. "The choreographed monster battles that we filmed in those days were exhausting. Every time we would finish a scene, I would come out of the suit, drink gallons of water, and squeeze cupfuls of perspiration from my sweatshirt. If Mr. Tsuburaya asked me to do something, I would do it, no matter how difficult. But I always enjoyed what I was doing."

As an interesting side note, Nakajima also had bit parts in the dramatic segments of several monster movies. He was a military officer at the strategy center in *Destroy All Monsters* and the prime minister's chauffeur in *Tidal Wave*. It has been rumored that in *Godzilla: King of the Monsters!*, Nakajima was the power plant worker who throws the switch that (ineffectively) electrocutes the monster, but this is incorrect.

In recent years, Nakajima has helped to further the cause of Godzilla fandom abroad. In 1996, '97, and '98 he and fellow monster-actor Kenpachiro Satsuma traveled to the U.S. to attend Godzilla fan conventions in Chicago and New York. Though in his late sixties, Nakajima retained an enthusiasm and pride for his association with the monster that made fans fall in love with him.

Thirteen

LOST CONTINENT

"Megalon! Megalon! Wake up, Megalon! Come on,
rise up now, to the Earth's surface! Destroy the Earth!
Destroy our enemies! Rise up! Go on! MEGALON!"

— Antonio, King of Seatopia, beseeching the big bug

GODZILLA vs. MEGALON

RATING (OUT OF FIVE STARS): ★

JAPANESE VERSION: GOJIRA TAI MEGARO. Released on March 17, 1973, by the Toho Motion Picture Company. Toho Scope, in color. Running Time: 81 minutes.

U.S. VERSION: Released July 21, 1976, by Cinema Shares International/Downtown Distribution. Running Time: 78 minutes. MPAA Rating: G.

STORY: After their aquatic nation is nearly wiped out by a series of underwater nuclear tests in the Pacific Ocean, the enraged people of Seatopia dispatch their monster-protector, Megalon, to take revenge on the surface-dwellers; meanwhile, Seatopian field agents steal Jet Jaguar (a colorful, remote-controlled, flying robot created by a young Japanese inventor) and use it to guide Megalon on its destructive course across Japan. The inventor regains control of the robot and sends it to retrieve Godzilla from Monster Island, and a four-way tag-team match between the goodies (Godzilla and Jet Jaguar) and the baddies (Megalon and Gigan) takes place.

CHILD'S PLAY

With Godzilla continually losing ground at the box office and the Japanese superhero phenomenon reaching its apex, Toho's next Godzilla movie is essentially a feature-length television program with a juvenile script and production values only marginally better than most of the genre shows that were popular in Japan at the time. *Godzilla vs.*

Megalon is universally regarded as the worst of all Godzilla movies, reducing the monster to a punch-drunk do-gooder with a cute, puppy-dog face and a penchant for ridiculous fighting tactics and stunts, and pitting him against perhaps the worst-designed monster in Toho history, a gigantic, upright-walking beetle with drill-bit arms and a daisy-shaped horn atop its head. As if the bare-bones production values of *Godzilla on Monster Island* were not bad enough, here the quality drops

181

yet another notch. Ironically, this is one of the most widely seen Godzilla movies in the Western world, owing to a wide and successful theatrical release in summer 1976 and the film's subsequent prime-time premiere in summer, 1977 on the NBC-TV network, hosted by comedian John Belushi wearing a Godzilla costume used in Joe Dante's comedy *Hollywood Boulevard* (1976).

The subject of lost continents and undersea worlds had long fascinated screenwriter Shinichi Sekizawa, who explored the subject matter in *Atragon* (1963) and *Latitude Zero* (1969, as a script adviser only). Whereas those films incorporated the legends of Mu and Atlantis, respectively, the undersea dwellers in *Godzilla vs. Megalon* hail from the nation of Seatopia, located on what was once the continent of Lemuria, which supposedly existed 700,000 years before Atlantis and was located in the south-central Pacific, stretching from what is now India to South America. The Seatopians, a race of idol-worshipping Caucasians dressed in flowing white gowns and smocks, are understandably upset at the damage inflicted on their land by undersea nuclear testing. But rather than appeal to the world above for a reprieve, they simply unleash their pet monster Megalon to the Earth's surface, inflicting death and destruction even worse than what they have suffered. Despite the nuclear theme, there really is no subtext — the Seatopians go from being innocent victims to ruthless war-mongers in the bat of an eye. Even more perplexing is the fact that, despite their lack of ties to the other residents of planet Earth, the Seatopians are good friends with the aliens from the faraway Hunter Nebula, who send their monster Gigan to aid in the battle. If there is any moral to the story, it must be that nuclear testing, after all, is a good thing, for in the end Megalon cowardly retreats to his subterranean world and Godzilla's heroics have extinguished any threat to the arms race's continued vitality.

Despite lending his name to the title for marquee value, Godzilla really plays second fiddle throughout most of the movie to Jet Jaguar, the silvery robot with a big grin that looks like the front grill of an American muscle car, and who is gifted with the ability to transform himself to gigantic size whenever gargantuan monsters threaten the world. Obviously inspired both by *Ultraman* and Toei TV's *Giant Robot* series (known in the U.S. as *Johnny Sokko and his Flying Robot*), Jet Jaguar is based on the results of a nationwide contest held by Toho soliciting designs for Godzilla's robot sidekick. The winning entry, originally called Red Arone, was

drawn by an elementary school student,[30] and its giant-transformation powers were introduced to the script by director Jun Fukuda, who wrote the screenplay based on Sekizawa's treatment. Like many things in the movie (the dolphin water cycle, the model planes, etc.), the robot is part of the parade of visual stimuli for young boys. Brought to life with a small, stiff prop for flying scenes and a costume fashioned out of a wet suit and an angular head cast from FRP plastic, Jet Jaguar represents the ultimate dream of every nine-year-old Japanese kid in the early 1970s, a friendly, toy robot with a heroic heart, who rushes headlong into battle with marauding alien monsters whenever the world is endangered, but he seems out of place in the Godzilla universe. Thankfully, Jet Jaguar fills the role of little Rokuro's object of monster friendship, preventing Godzilla from descending once and for all into the completely humanized realm of the Gamera series.

Then again, the Godzilla that appears in this film hardly seems like the same monster, either. He runs, strikes karate poses, unleashes Muhammad Ali-like punching combinations, and emits the most poorly animated atomic ray ever, the trajectory of which often bends because the monster's mouth and the ray's target are incorrectly aligned. Godzilla is also a bit cowardly in this film — at one point, Megalon imprisons the Big G and Jet Jaguar in a rather unimpressive ring of fire. Instead of walking over the puny flames, Godzilla recoils from them and is saved only when Jet Jaguar airlifts him out of the trap on his back. And let us not forget the ultimate blemish on Godzilla's career, even worse than his breath-blown flight in *Smog Monster*. Borrowing from Angilas' reverse-slamming technique in the previous film, Godzilla executes a flying, two-footed karate kick to a prone Megalon's sternum (he enjoys it so much, he does it twice), sliding across the landscape on the base of his tail. And in a move introduced in *Smog Monster* and often repeated in the 1970s films, Godzilla grabs Megalon by the tail and slams his body into the ground repeatedly, dazing the insect — an effect enabled, rather obviously, by wire operators located in the rafters who bounce the Megalon costume up and down.

While an insect monster is an interesting idea, Megalon is designed in the Tsuburaya Productions tradition rather than classic Toho style, and is suited more to the smaller and less revealing confines of a television screen. The monster possesses some impressive powers, including geothermal napalm shells fired from its mouth and the ability to burrow underground with its power-tool forearms, but when viewed in its totality the creature is absolutely gawky, with tree-trunk legs and the deadweight of the heavy rubber drill bits making it difficult for the stunt actor to keep the arms upright. Although undiscerning viewers might not care, Megalon's attack on Tokyo is unimpressive due to the mere fact that all of the destruction shots are taken from *Ghidrah* and *Monster Zero* — Megalon's daisy-stem ray is, fortunately for Toho, a carbon-copy of Ghidorah's ray, enabling the old footage to be substituted easily. Also shameless is the use of stock film from *Godzilla on Monster Island* during the fighter-jet attack on Megalon — when the monster swats away the planes in close-up, it's actually Gigan's sickle arms that are knocking down the planes.

The Godzilla costume built for this film is positively insulting to the monster's legacy — a simplistic, puffy rubber sack with a friendly grin on its face. This design would become the standard for the remaining films in the original Godzilla series, although (thankfully) the suit would undergo some changes to make it look a little more respectable in subsequent appearances.

The cast is again filled with mostly unknowns, although Hiroyuki Kawase of *Smog Monster* fame returns in the little-boy role, spending most of the film clad in shorts and a Snoopy sweatshirt. **Katsuhiko Sasaki**, son of actor Minoru Chiaki (Kobayashi in *Gigantis*), is adequate as Rokuro's inventor-brother, Goro Ibuki, but the real star of the cast is the hilariously hairy-chested, toga-wearing King of Seatopia, humorlessly played by **Robert Dunham**, a veteran Caucasian bit player in Toho films. With his truck-driver sideburns and Megalon-shaped tiara, Dunham steals the show as he invokes mighty Megalon to come forth and save his people. Adding to all the unintended hilarity is Riichiro Manabe's musical score, which features a breezy and pleasant rock theme for the main title (cut from the U.S. version, it is an instrumental rendition of the "Godzilla and Jaguar Punch-Punch-Punch" song that plays at the film's end), but otherwise is marked by the same wacky, blaring oddball themes that plagued *Godzilla vs. The Smog Monster*.

Yet, for all its shortcomings, it is impossible to blame *Megalon* squarely on Fukuda and the other filmmakers. The film had an extremely tight budget and was made under arduous conditions, making their task unenviable. "I remember it was a very short shoot, probably about three weeks," said SFX director Nakano. "It went into production without enough preparation. There was no time to ask Mr. Sekizawa to write the script, so Mr. Sekizawa kind of thought up the general story and director Fukuda wrote the screenplay. The screenplay was completed right before crank-in."

The original Japanese version of *Godzilla vs. Megalon* contains several violent scenes (albeit tame by today's standards), and even a brief glimpse of nudity. According to Brian Culver, a historian of Japanese monster-movies who has written for *Kaiju Fan* and other publications, much of this "offensive" material remained intact when Cinema Shares first released the film to U.S. cinemas in 1976. However, while *Megalon* was still in theaters, Cinema Shares apparently replaced it with a substantially edited version, perhaps due to concerns about maintaining a G rating from the Motion Picture Association of America. This truncated edition (or, slight variations of it) has been utilized for nearly all American TV showings and home-video releases of *Megalon* from the late 1970s until today — one known exception being NBC's aforementioned 1977 national broadcast, for which *Megalon* was hacked down even further, to fit into a one-hour time slot!

Thus, as seen in the U.S. for the past 20 or so years, *Megalon* contains numerous baffling deletions.

"Robotman" vs. "Borodan"

If you've got one, it's a collector's item: the four-page color comic given away as a freebie at theaters during the U.S. release of *Godzilla vs. Megalon*. It's not known who wrote and drew this dubious classic (it included no credits), which was purportedly a short adaptation of the film story. However, the author apparently did not watch the film, or perhaps didn't watch it very closely, before writing the comic, for the names of two major characters were flubbed. Jet Jaguar is called "Robotman," and Gigan is dubbed "Borodan"!

> A once proud civilization now had to place its trust and hope in Godzilla and his powerful ally, Robotman! In concert they would fight this evil in a duel to the death. Battling by day, battling by night. It was more than a race against time. This war was an all out effort whose ultimate purpose was to save our planet from total destruction. Now came the moment of truth . . . the ultimate battle! Titan against titan! Giant against giant in the most spectacular battle yet! You'll see it all in *Godzilla vs. Megalon*!"
>
> — *From Cinema Shares' theatrical trailer for* Godzilla vs. Megalon

These include: the opening credits; the rough-stuff kidnapping of Rokuro (in the Japanese version, the Seatopian agents are seen throwing the kid into the back seat of a car, while in the U.S. print, the scene ends with the kidnappers driving alongside the kid as he tools around on his Baby Rider cycle); the two truck drivers beating up the bearded Seatopian and dumping his body over a cliff (in the U.S. print, the bearded man disappears without explanation); and another Seatopian being crushed to death by a giant boulder. Also snipped were the opening credits, and a brief view of a nude centerfold hanging inside the cab of a truck.

The U.S. rights to *Godzilla vs. Megalon* apparently fell into the public domain sometime in the late 1980s, and for several years the film was available from a plethora of home video labels; these videotapes ranged from ghastly to so-so quality, all utilizing old, faded pan-and-scan prints. Toho has since reclaimed copyright control over the film, and officially licensed videos have appeared in the 1990s but, unfortunately, these are virtually identical to the old "bootleg" editions. Admittedly, *Godzilla vs. Megalon* will never be a classic, but (believe it or not) the movie is substantially better when viewed in vivid color and widescreen, as with the Japanese-import Laser Disc and videocassette from Toho Video.

WHITE GUY IN MONSTERLAND

Robert Dunham, the King of Seatopia

In the Toho Universe, every evil monster answers to a higher authority, usually a gang of aliens hailing from futuristic places in galaxies yet unknown. But Megalon's puppetmaster is of a different pedigree: Antonio, King of Seatopia, is a cross between Greek God and Teamsters truck driver, a deity decked out in a graceful white gown, yet wearing sideburns and tattoos befitting a hardware store clerk in Jersey. What gives?

Meet Robert Dunham, actor, stunt driver, and an all-around *bon vivant* of the Japanese movie scene. During the 1960s, Toho regularly hired Caucasians to play villains or foreign diplomats — examples include Jerry Ito, the evil Mr. Nelson in *Mothra*, Andrew Hughes, who played Dr. Stevenson in *Destroy All Monsters* and appeared in dozens of non-monster movies, and Harold S. Conway and George Furness, two elderly gents who routinely played Western officials. But Dunham (b. 1931 in Maine) is perhaps the best known of all the white guys who populated the *kaiju eiga,* for he was usually cast in meatier roles than his peers. In *Mothra* (1961), he played an official of the Rolisican government; in *Dagora: The Space Monster* (1964) he was Mark Jackson, an insurance agent tracking stolen jewels; in Toei's *The Green Slime* (1968) he was a space station worker. Monster movies comprised only a small fraction of his film work, but as it turned out, *Godzilla vs. Megalon* was the last film Dunham made in Japan before returning to the U.S.

Each of these guys had a unique story as to how they got involved in the Japanese movie business — Hughes, for example, was an import-export businessman based in Tokyo, while Furness was an American attorney who had defended a Japanese cabinet minister in the war crimes tribunals after World War II, and remained in Japan as a celebrity of sorts. There were women, too (like Linda Miller of *King Kong Escapes* fame), many of whom came to Japan to work as models or in nightclubs. What all these people had in common was that none were professional actors. But their lack of thespian talents hardly mattered; most of them spoke Japanese so poorly that their dialogue had to be over-dubbed later by a "real" actor anyway. Dunham, however, stood out among the crowd because he spoke fluent Japanese — in almost none of his films, he boasts, were his lines re-recorded by someone else.

Dunham first visited Japan as a U.S. Marine during the Korean War, and he returned in the late 1950s to marry a Japanese girl (the first of several wives) and soak up the culture. After appearing in a few plays with the Tokyo International Players (a stage troupe consisting of foreigners living in Japan), he was approached by the Kokusai Agency, a small company casting *gaijin* actors for the major Japanese studios. Over the next decade and a half, Dunham lived in the fast lane of sorts in Tokyo, working as an actor in films and television, as a voice-dubbing actor for Frontier Enterprises, as a professional race car driver for Toyota, and as a stuntman and stunt driver (in addition to playing the King of Seatopia, he was also the guy on the motorcycle during the chase scene in *Godzilla vs. Megalon*). Since returning to America, Dunham has been writing for stag magazines like *Swank* and *Titter*, writing screenplays, and acting in community theater groups in Florida, where he now resides.

Your first monster movie was Mothra. *What was that like?*

I had a small part in *Mothra*. Frankie Sakai and the Peanuts, those were the little girls that they reduced in size, were the main characters, and Jerry Ito was the bad guy, the promoter that kidnapped them

Robert Dunham as Antonio, King of Seatopia, in *Godzilla Vs. Megalon*.
FROM THE PERSONAL COLLECTION OF ROBERT DUNHAM. USED BY PERMISSION.

from the island. Jerry Ito is Eurasian, his father was Japanese, his mother was French, I think, and so he was brought up in Japan and spoke perfect Japanese and excellent English — he did quite a few films in Japan and he also did nightclub work and so forth. But he was a little ticked that they were bringing other foreigners in the field, because he thought he was a big fish in a small pond. So, we didn't get along too well personally, but he and I didn't have scenes together directly. Frankie Sakai, the newspaper reporter, he's a fun guy, I had a lot of fun with him. He's basically a comedian and he does most of his parts that way, so he had fun doing the picture.

The Peanuts were just cute little things. They were just starting out, and I believe that they built the story around their singing. Most of their scenes were done with special effects so there wasn't any direct contact, other than behind the scenes when you'd be sitting around waiting for the next shot. I worked on *Mothra* probably for about a week. *Dagora* was the first film that I really had a major part.

Did you develop any friendships with Japanese actors?

Akiko Wakabayashi. In *Dagora*, she was the bad gun moll, trying to steal the diamonds away from the gang she was working for, and they finally ended up killing her. We dated a few times during filming. That film took a longer time, I would say about six to eight weeks, because we had locations. It was not done in the studio at all, so that took quite a bit of time because of weather conditions. I think we spent about two weeks in a place called Shimbara, where they did the beach scenes and chase scenes. So I got to know her pretty well, unofficially [laughs]. But she was another one of these Japanese stars that they were trying to build up. She wasn't a great actress, but she did have a great body.

How did you get the part in Megalon*?*

This was one where there was no interview, there was nothing as far as an audition is concerned. As I recall, Johnny Yusef said, "Can you come out to the studio tomorrow morning?" He says, "We got a film and I think you'll be terrific for the part, and the director just wants to refresh his memory of your face and so forth." As I recall, I went out and we talked about 10 minutes and he [director Jun Fukuda] says, "Sign him up. Get out there in wardrobe and get everything fixed up with his toga and his tiara." Within two or three days we started shooting. There was one other foreigner in that film, a guy named Rolf Jessup, a German, who was standing there with me at the control panel. I worked about five days on that movie, that's about it.

What did you think about that outfit?

I got a lot of kidding on that one. They had at least a dozen sound stages, and when you were going for lunch at the commissary you wouldn't take your makeup off. You just go and have your lunch and go back on the set and touch your makeup up, and you're ready to roll again. So, I got a lot of ribbing about wearing this uniform.

You also did the motorcycle chase.

Well, actually I did all the stunts on the motorcycle, but I'm not the one who gets the paint dumped all over him, or whatever that was. I did the stunt work, and then I switched with a Japanese guy who put the helmet and the face mask on, and he laid the bike down and they poured that whitewash on him. The reason was, I had an appointment to film a TV commercial that afternoon, and I was looking at my watch the whole time and saying, "Jeez, I've gotta get out of here." I wasn't going to get paint spilled all over me — I would have never been able to get cleaned up and make it in time to shoot the commercial!

By the way, there were rumors about you and the lovely Linda Miller.

Yeah, she was in a lot of films, and we had a torrid love affair for a while. A nice-looking girl really. The type of girl if you walk into a restaurant and she's on your arm, everybody's head turns — they think she's a movie star. Anywhere you went it was, "Wow, how did he get that lucky?" But she came back to the States and the last I heard she was in Vegas singing in a bar. We exchanged a few letters after she got back to the States, but I lost trace of her.

Were most of the foreigners working in Japanese movies Americans?

Actually, I would say they were mainly Turks. There were a lot of Turks in Japan, because there had been a revolution in Turkey before World War II and a lot of them just fled the country rather than serving in the army. They fled across China to Japan, and ended up mostly in Tokyo. They had their own little community there, and they went to Japanese schools and learned Japanese perfectly. After [World War II] when the Japanese wanted foreigners in the movies, they used a lot of these Turks. They could speak perfect Japanese, so they could read their own dialogue. This is how Johnny Yusef [Nelson's henchman in *Mothra*, and one of the principals in the Kokusai Agency] got started, because he could negotiate with the directors and producers of the Japanese major studios.

In films like Monster Zero *and* War of the Gargantuas, *Nick Adams and Russ Tamblyn are speaking English while the other actors speak Japanese, which seems like a very difficult thing to do. Did you ever do that?*

No, because I spoke fluent Japanese. By the way, I have an interesting story about Nick Adams. When I had the part in *Dagora: The Space Monster*, Toho wanted to make a series of movies using my character. Toho sent me to Hollywood with a print, to negotiate with some guy and sell the film for distribution and to proposition him about doing a series with me as Mark Jackson, and the rest of the cast would be Japanese actors. The guy said he liked the film, and of course he wanted to steal it and gave a real lowball offer. And as far as I was concerned, they said it was difficult to judge the performance because it wasn't my voice [Dunham spoke Japanese in the film, and his voice was dubbed in the English-language version]. And they said, "This guy doesn't have a name in the States, so it's going to be difficult to make a deal." So they picked up Nick Adams, who had a name here because he had done *The Rebel* [TV series]. He made *The Killing Bottle*, which I don't think was very successful, then he came back to the States.

ULTRA-GOJI

Godzilla teams up with Japanese TV superheroes.

While the popularity of Godzilla movies and *kaiju eiga* in general began to wane in the 1960s and declined even more rapidly in the 1970s, live-action super-hero programs loaded with special effects, giant monsters, and nonstop action were thriving on Japanese television. It's no wonder the kiddies stopped spending their allowances to see Godzilla & Co. at the local movie house, for there were many more — and far more outlandish — *kaiju* to be watched for free on the boob tube. By 1972, a second monster boom had occurred, and Japan's airwaves were overrun with incredible super-men clad in brightly colored costumes and otherworldly helmets with luminescent eyes, and gifted with wild weapons to combat a new gigantic monster each week. Toho, following the lead of Tsuburaya Productions, Toei, and others, joined the superhero business first in 1972–73 with its *Rainbowman* series; then, from April to September 1973, Toho-Eizo produced *Meteor Man Zone* (*Ryusei-Ningen Zon*, unofficially known as *Zone Fighter*). It was on *Zone Fighter* that Godzilla swallowed his pride and guest-starred in five episodes, as Toho attempted to reintroduce the monster to the small-fry set and resurrect his flagging career.

Superhero programs originated on Japanese television during the late 1950s, but they became a phenomenon only after Eiji Tsuburaya put his stamp on the genre. In April 1963, Tsuburaya established an independent production company, Tsuburaya Special Techniques Productions (shortened, in 1968, to Tsuburaya Productions, and often referred to simply as "Tsuburaya Pro"), to produce special-effects-for-hire for various movie studios and to launch its own brand of SFX-oriented television programming. The company's first TV venture was *Woo*, a series about a space creature marooned on Earth, which was scheduled to air on Fuji TV in 1964 but was canceled right before it went into production. Next, Tsuburaya sold another program to TBS (Tokyo Broadcasting System — *not* the Turner network!) called *Unbalance*, an *X-Files*-like series that underwent several changes before it finally premiered in January 1966, with the new title *Ultra Q*. Although not really a superhero program, *Ultra Q* set the stage for *tokusatsu* on TV for the next 30-plus years. There was no hero or character called "Ultra Q" — the name, according to some sources, originally stood for "Ultra Question." The show focused on the adventures of a pilot and science-fiction writer (Jun Manjome, played by Kenji Sahara), his photographer girlfriend, and his humorous pilot sidekick, who investigate various weird phenomena and monsters terrorizing Japan. Shot in black and white on 35mm film (later reduced to 16mm for TV airing), this incredible series was loaded with great monsters and elaborate effects, and marked by great stories and a great cast. Unfortunately, it was never shown in the U.S.

Although it aired for only a half-season (28 episodes), *Ultra Q* was a great success. Tsuburaya immediately followed it in July 1966 with *Ultraman*, a new series incorporating ideas from its abandoned *Woo*. *Ultraman* told the story of an alien soldier from the Land of Light, a planet located in Nebula M78, who came to Earth by accident while transporting an evil monster ("Bemlar") to the Grave-yard of Monsters. When Bemlar breaks free and heads for Earth, the soldier gives chase and crashes into an air-vehicle piloted by Hayata (Susumu Kurobe, who appeared in many a *kaiju* movie), a member of the Science Patrol, an organization that investigates strange phenomena. Hayata is killed, but the alien brings the man back to life by combining his life-force with the human's. He gives Hayata the Beta Capsule, a pen-like solar device that

Eiji Tsuburaya on the set of *Ultra 7,* one of the first TV programs
about giant costumed super-heroes to come out of Japan.

COURTESY TSUBURAYA PRODUCTIONS CO., LTD.

enables him to change into Ultraman, a sleek, red-and-silver metallic-suited giant resembling an android with an array of super-weapons and powers, most notably the "specium beam," an energy ray emitted from either arm whenever Ultraman strikes his "beam pose" (a flashy Kung-Fu-ish stance). In each episode, Hayata and the other Science Patrol members try to thwart hostile aliens' efforts to take over Earth; inevitably, the invaders unleash a savage, gigantic monster upon the world (with names like Baltan, Red King, Gomora, Gavadon, etc.) and Hayata must assume the role of Ultraman to save the day.

Though obviously formulaic, this incredible show is great entertainment and it was a big hit in Japan. An English-dubbed version was shown on US TV during the 1970s, but the show has unfortunately never been more than a cult favorite in the West. *Ultraman* became a huge cultural and merchandising icon of "Superman" proportions in its homeland,

and as the granddaddy of all Japanese superhero shows it introduced the model for a never-ending series of spin-offs and imitations: futuristic super-heroes, wrestling and martial-arts-style fighting, audacious monsters, and fantastic secret agents toting ray guns and flying spaceships. The best of the "Ultra" follow-ups is *Ultra Seven* (1967), which was revived in a dumbed-down, English-dubbed form on the Turner network in the early 1990s. Under the guidance of Tsuburaya's sons, Hajime Tsuburaya and Noboru Tsuburaya, Tsuburaya Productions has produced an endless Ultra lineage including Ultraman Taro, Ultraman Ace, Ultraman Leo, and so on. The "Ultra" name was even farmed out to overseas productions, with Caucasian actors: *Ultraman: Towards the Future* (c. 1990) was made in Australia, and *Ultraman: the Ultimate Hero* (c. 1994) was shot in Los Angeles, but neither measured up to the original, not by a long shot.

Besides the Tsuburaya connection, *Ultra Q* and

Ultraman are of interest to Godzilliacs because the Big G made appearances in both shows, albeit disguised and renamed as a new monster each time. In episode 1 of *Ultra Q* ("Defeat Gomess!" aired January 2, 1966), the subterranean monster Gomess — in actuality, the *Mosu-Goji* costume from *Godzilla vs. The Thing* and *Ghidrah*, embellished with walrus-like tusks, a horn atop its head, a chest plate, and Ghidrah-like scales on its body — terrorizes workers in a mining shaft. According to an ancient prophecy, the only thing that can kill Gomess is Ritora, a legendary vulture-bird-thing, which shows up at the end of the episode and shoots a ray from its mouth, killing the pseudo-Zilla. The following year, it was the *Daisenso-Goji* costume from *Monster Zero* and *Godzilla versus The Sea Monster* that was spruced up for *Ultraman* episode 10 ("The Mysterious Dinosaur Base," aired September 18, 1966). In this one, a mad scientist named Dr. Nakama creates a prehistoric monster, Jirass ("Kira" in the

Ultraman faces off with the monster Jiras (Kira or Keyra in the U.S. version) in Episode 10 of *Ultraman*, directed by Kazuho Mitsuta. The Jiras costume was made from the body of the *Mosu-Goji* Godzilla costume from *Godzilla Vs. The Thing* and the head of the *Daisenso-Goji* costume from *Monster Zero*. The colorful frill was attached to the neck to conceal the place where the two costumes were joined, as well as to *disguise* Godzilla (which was not very effective).

COURTESY TSUBURAYA PRODUCTIONS CO., LTD.

Not even those pointy teeth, that horny head and that chest plate can hide the fact that this monster is Godzilla in disguise. Gomess, as seen in Episode 1 of *Ultra Q* ("Defeat Gomess!").

COURTESY TSUBURAYA PRODUCTIONS CO., LTD.

English-dubbed version), which he keeps in the depths of Lake Kitiyama. When some kids dump poison into the lake, the enraged Jirass surfaces and goes on the warpath, only to be stopped eventually by Ultraman. In this one, Godzilla's appearance isn't masked nearly as well as it was in *Ultra Q*. The only modifications to the costume were some yellow paint and a large, colorful, scaly dinosaur frill attached at the base of the neck, which Ultraman rips off during the final battle (this scene was edited out of the versions shown on US TV, probably considered too violent). Even though it's not "really" Godzilla, this episode is considered a genre classic, as it is the only time that Japan's two greatest science-fiction icons ever appeared on-screen together.

During the early 1970s, at the tail end of the first wave of *tokusatsu* television, *Zone Fighter* was Toho's attempt to capture a piece of the "Ultra" pie, albeit a little too late. The 26-episode series, which ran from April 2 to September 24, 1973, was produced by Tomoyuki Tanaka and featured the creative talents of Godzilla series veterans like directors Ishiro Honda and Jun Fukuda and SFX directors Teruyoshi Nakano and Koichi Kawakita. The series follows three refugees from the planet Peaceland, which was destroyed by the evil Baron Garoga, leader of a renegade band of aliens out to conquer the universe. The three refugees are taken in by the Sakimori family, an average Japanese household, and they adopt the human alter egos of Hikaru, a.k.a. Zone Fighter (the main character, a man in his early 20s), his teenage sister Kei, a.k.a. Zone Angel, and his little brother, Akira, a.k.a. Zone Junior. Every week, the Baron Garoga and his minions make yet another vain attempt to vanquish Earth by unleashing one or more destructive monsters, called "Terro Beasts." The Zone Family members shout "Zone . . . Fight . . . Power!" and strike a corny martial-arts stance to transform themselves into superhero form (signified by a skin-tight costume, a metallic helmet, and a face mask). All three heroes have super weapons and ninja-like fighting skills (although Zone Junior's most wily tactic is to run between the villain's legs, which he seems to do in each episode), but Zone Fighter also has the special ability to become a gigantic Ultraman clone whenever the need arises. The Zone Family also has at its disposal a spaceship, called "Smokey," which is always concealed in a cloud of smoke until they decide to use it. The series is action-packed with human fights, monster fights, and car chases (Hikaru, when not defending Earth, also enjoys a career as a race-car driver, a frequent plot device), but on the whole it is an obvious and inferior imitation of *Ultraman*, from the premise ("Peaceland" sounds suspiciously like *Ultraman*'s "Land of Light," among other similarities), to the audacious monsters to Zone Fighter's arsenal, which includes the Comet Kick, the Proton Beam, and the Monster Missiles, which he fires from wrist bracelets to deliver the *coup de grace* to his foes.

It's kind of weird to see Godzilla fighting alongside a humanoid superhero and against all sorts of bizarre, anything-goes, 1970s-style *kaiju*, as it demonstrates how the monster that started it all had fallen out of step with the times. Still, Godzilla does his best to get into the act. If you thought his antics in *Godzilla vs. Megalon* were silly, you'll be sad to know that the monster falls yet another notch on the dignity scale in *Zone Fighter*. Then again, if you like your Big G wild and woolly, his five appearances on this series might be considered classics. Also noteworthy are two appearances by King Ghidorah (these episodes are actually better than the Godzillas) and one by Gigan. The Gigan costume seems none the worse for wear, but King Ghidorah, which had already been used in four feature films, was clearly falling apart and could have used a trip to the cleaners.

Zone Fighter made its TV debut just one month after *Godzilla vs. Megalon* was released. The Godzilla costume from that film was dusted off and used here, taking a severe beating with all the physical stunts and pyrotechnics it is subjected to. By Episode 25, Godzilla's last *Zone Fighter* role, there are various signs of wear, including rubber scales peeling off. It's hard to believe this suit was refurbished and re-used in two more Toho films. Overall, the special effects in *Zone Fighter* are on par with, and often superior to, those in *Megalon*, especially the miniature work. Godzilla rarely uses his atomic breath in the show, and when he does, it's bluish in color and poorly animated; in one episode, the breath is created by the old-school method of shooting smoke or steam from a nozzle mounted in the mouth of the Godzilla suit, not optical animation.

Zone Fighter was never distributed in the U.S., but it was released to home video in Japan and bootleg tapes of the show have found their way into American fans' hands in recent years. What follows is a guide to the episodes featuring Godzilla, King Ghidorah, and Gigan, in the order in which they originally aired:[31]

EPISODE 4
"Onslaught! The Garoga Army Attacks — Enter Godzilla"
April 23, 1973
Directed by Ishiro Honda, written by Jun Fukuda.

Zone Angel is reunited with an old boyfriend from Peaceland, named Tetsuo, who has a mysterious air about him . . . little does she know that he is now working for the Garogas as a spy. After gaining the Zone Family's confidence, Tetsuo tries to kill them by unleashing a battery of toy tanks and planes that fire real missiles in their home, but the heroes escape alive. Kei shoots Tetsuo, but the boy turns into Spilar, a gigantic monster with a robotic head. Spilar and another monster, Wargiglar, beat the hell out of Zone Fighter until Zone Angel and Zone Junior send out a call for help from Godzilla, who saves the day.

EPISODE 5
"The Arrival of King Ghidorah"
April 30, 1973
Directed by Jun Fukuda.

Baron Garoga summons King Ghidorah to help him recover the Dark Prism, a magic crystal that has been swiped by the Zone Family. The climax features a great fight between Zone Fighter and the three-headed demon.

EPISODE 6
"King Ghidorah Strikes Back!"
May 7, 1973
Directed by Jun Fukuda.

Ghidorah returns and gives Zone Fighter a tough fight; the superhero outwits the *kaiju* by luring him into outer space, then evading him. In the end, the three Zones fly into space in a rocket and locate King Ghidorah, forcing him to leave the galaxy.

EPISODE 11
"By a Thread — The Roar of Godzilla!"
June 11, 1973
Directed by Jun Fukuda.

The Garogas kidnap Hikaru by programming his race car to drive into the back of a freight truck, then they haul him off to the junkyard to be killed in a huge car-crusher. Godzilla arrives to save Hikaru, but the Garogas send Gigan to stop him. Godzilla defeats Gigan, but then he leaves, apparently forgetting that he came to save Hikaru.

No problem — Hikaru manages to get out of his car before it's pulverized, just in time to change into Zone Fighter and battle Gigan, who has revived. Zone downs Gigan with his Monster Missiles, and the *kaiju*, foaming at the mouth, explodes!

EPISODE 15
"Submersion! Godzilla, You Must Save Tokyo"
July 9, 1973

Zandolar, a ridiculous-looking, rubbery mushroom-monster, causes havoc by burrowing underneath Tokyo (an impressive effect). Zone Fighter and Zone Junior are buried underground by Zandolar, and Godzilla shows up to engage the alien monster in battle. The Godzilla-vs.-Zandolar battle causes earthquakes that allow Zone Fighter, trapped below, to escape. Then, Godzilla and Zone team up to defeat the baddie, and they celebrate their victory by shaking hands. A most unusual episode, with Osman Yusef (*Mothra*, *Gorath*, many others) portraying a mysterious, *Yakuza*-like Garoga agent clad in black.

EPISODE 21
"Invincible! Godzilla's Violent Charge"
August 20, 1973

This one opens with an unexpected sight: Godzilla and Zone Fighter, deadlocked in a fierce battle. Turns out it's only a friendly sparring match, and afterward Godzilla goes back to his cave, complete with retractable doors. Garoga sends a capsule containing an amoeba-like monster to his agents on Earth, but the capsule is intercepted by the Zone Family. The Garogas kidnap Zone Junior and demand their capsule for his release; once the exchange is made, the aliens unleash the glob-monster Jurah. Godzilla tears off one of Jurah's tentacles, which grows into a second monster! In the end, Godzilla and Zone triumph over the two creatures.

EPISODE 25
"Bloodbath! Zone and Godzilla vs. the United Terro Beast Army"
September 17, 1973

At a secret base, Garoga's agents shrink an army of monsters and put them into small capsules. Then, they plant the capsules all over the Zone Family's neighborhood — in trash cans, etc. — and prepare to hatch them for an all-out attack. The Zone Family figures out the plan and stamps out most of the monsters, but two of them, Spideros and Garobug, team up against Zone Fighter. Never fear, Godzilla is near.

Fourteen

ROBOT MONSTER

"Damn Godzilla. You're mistaken if you think your powers are a match for MechaGodzilla."

— Kuronuma, the alien leader

GODZILLA vs. THE COSMIC MONSTER a.k.a. GODZILLA vs. MECHAGODZILLA

RATING (OUT OF FIVE STARS): ★ ★

JAPANESE VERSION: GOJIRA TAI MEKAGOJIRA. Released on March 21, 1974, by the Toho Eizo Company. Toho Scope, in color. Running Time: 84 minutes.

U.S. VERSION: Released in March 1977, by Cinema Shares International/Downtown Distribution. Running Time: 80 minutes. MPAA rating: G. Originally released briefly as *Godzilla vs. The Bionic Monster*.

STORY: An ancient doomsday prophecy, inscribed on the wall of an Okinawan cave, comes true when Godzilla (acting uncharacteristically vicious) emerges from an exploding meteorite and tramples the island countryside; soon, however, the monster (literally) sheds its skin and reveals its true identity: MechaGodzilla, a cyborg built by Earth-conquering aliens from a black hole in space. The Okinawans summon their dog-like monster god, King Seesar, from hibernation to aid the real Godzilla in battling his titanium twin.

TIN MACHINE

You're the evil military commander from a mighty alien race. Your people are determined to conquer Earth, but there's a slight problem: Godzilla. You've got the budget, the technology and the special effects to create the ultimate weapon to accomplish your goal. So, what do you build? A futuristic laser beam? A gigantic battle-tank? An atomic bomb? No, stupid. This is a Japanese monster movie. You build a robot, a BIG robot. And, what the heck, just to piss off Godzilla a little, make it look just like him!

After two creative disasters in a row, Toho managed to restore some of Godzilla's lost dignity in his 20th anniversary film, pitting the monster against one of his most brilliantly conceived foes: Mecha-Godzilla, a titanium evil twin invented by alien

195

The Bionic Monster. A menacing giant, an awesome machine. Unleashed with a deadly task. Godzilla: the only hope for our Earth's survival. *Godzilla vs. the Bionic Monster!* Godzilla strives to win supremacy in a fight to the end. Will Godzilla triumph? Will the Earth survive? *Godzilla vs. the Bionic Monster!* An Earth-shaking movie!

— *From TV spot for Cinema Shares' release of* Godzilla vs. the Bionic Monster

invaders as the ultimate weapon with which to dispose of Godzilla and thereby take the planet for themselves. Infused with a slightly larger budget than recent films, and with the musical talents of Masaru Sato lending an air of adventure and Western-style showdown to the action, *Godzilla vs. The Cosmic Monster* is fast-paced, at times visually inspired, and boasts an array of new effects work with no stock footage to mar the effort. Still, this film is not up to the level of the Godzilla classics of the 1960s, and it once again rehashes the well-worn premise of an alien invasion. It also treads a not-so-fine line between an adult-level script (a spy-movie type theme, mythological prophecies, violent fights, and hints of long-standing resentment between the Okinawans and the mainland Japanese) and kiddy fare (monster fights with blood and guts, Godzilla's "Aw, shucks!" move when he misses Mecha-Godzilla with his ray, aliens with green *Planet of the Apes*-like visages beneath their human masks). Thankfully, there are no child characters in sight and director Jun Fukuda handles the material in a straightforward manner.

In a throwback to the style he displayed in *Godzilla versus The Sea Monster*, Fukuda constructs the film as a series of pursuits, with the spacemen "from the third planet of the Black Hole, Outer Space" (this is how their leader recites his home address) in hot pursuit of the statue of King Seesar in a bid to prevent the unfolding of an ancient prophecy that stands in the way of their invasion ambitions. The aliens, despite their technological sophistication, are nonetheless reliant on the backward methods of Earth scientists, as they kidnap a mechanics expert, Dr. Miyajima (Akihiko Hirata, in his first Godzilla film since *Son of Godzilla*) and threaten to kill his daughter unless he helps repair the damaged head-control of MechaGodzilla. INTERPOL agents show up out of nowhere and save the heroes from the would-be statue-stealing aliens and the prophecy is fulfilled, with the legendary monster King Seesar (a gigantic cross between a lion and a dog, resembling the *komainu* statues that stand guard outside Shinto shrines in Japan) revived in time to aid Godzilla in the final battle for Earth's survival.

The real star of this film is MechaGodzilla, which stands 50 meters tall, weighs 40,000 metric tons and is made of an interstellar alloy called Space Titanium. The robot is equipped with finger missiles, a space beam that fires from its eyes, the Cross Attack Beam fired from its chest, and a repellent force field created when the monster whirls its head around at supersonic speed, deflecting Godzilla's attacks and burning the Big G's knuckles. Under the aliens' remote-controlled operation, MechaGodzilla displays cunning fighting ability and pulls off stunts no other monster can match. When Godzilla and King Seesar attack it from both sides simultaneously, MechaGodzilla appears defenseless — its body faces Godzilla, but its backside is exposed. Quickly, the robot rotates its head 180 degrees and fires its Space Beam at King Seesar while shooting finger missiles at Godzilla, and both opponents drop to the ground. The robot monster shines throughout, but there are some shoddy effects here as well. In the scenes where the disguised Mecha-Godzilla attacks the countryside and later faces off with Godzilla along the waterfront, a Godzilla costume constructed for promotional appearances (and *not* film work) was utilized in certain shots. The costume is so cheaply built and its features so poor that, even with rapid cross-cutting, the obvious changes in Godzilla's appearance are jarring. There are also some rather obvious wires intruding on the monster fights, particularly when the disguised MechaGodzilla drop-slams Angilas repeatedly to the ground, and when Godzilla uses his newfound magnetic powers to pull the flying MechaGodzilla out of the air. And the sight of Godzilla forcing MechaGodzilla's darts out of his bloody wounds, accompanied by a pinball-game sound effect, is unintentionally hilarious. The Godzilla costume from *Godzilla vs. Megalon* was re-used here, but improved with a new head, a fierce stare, and sharp teeth.

The main cast members, including blank-faced **Masaaki Daimon** as the architect Shimizu and

Shin Kishida (best known as the Dracula character in Toho's vampire movies), are acceptable if not outstanding. Lending the film a bit of nostalgia and credibility are Hirata, looking fit and healthy 20 years after playing the classic Serizawa character, and Hiroshi Koizumi as the archaeologist Professor Wagura (in an unintended funny moment, Wagura cowers in the background while Shimizu wrestles violently with an alien intruder). Kenji Sahara also shows up in a bit part, as captain of a cruise ship.

With the presence of *kaiju eiga* veterans, the fantastic design of MechaGodzilla, plus Masaru Sato's fine score (which features a great Godzilla theme, and memorable music for the three-way monster showdown at the film's end), *Godzilla vs. The Cosmic Monster* has much to recommend it, especially compared to the dreck in the previous two movies. Overall, however, the film is terribly uneven — even though there is no stock footage, there are numerous symptoms of the penny-pinching, creative drought and overall silliness that pervaded these films in the 1970s. Some examples:

- The Azumi princess has a psychic vision of King Ghidorah attacking a city, but this is shown in a still-frame photograph rather than live-action footage and, inexplicably, Ghidorah is never mentioned again.

- Like the aliens in *Godzilla on Monster Island*, the Black Hole invaders don't use space ships (at least, not on camera, for that would require miniature work). They spend most of their time holed up in their underground base, which isn't very impressive.

- The alien leader has sadistic tendencies. Rather than simply shoot Dr. Miyajima and his daughter, he locks them in a steam chamber to scald them to death (of course, they are rescued).

- In a plot device reminiscent of *Monster Zero*, the aliens' conquest is sabotaged by a little electronic gizmo invented by one of the main characters. Tetsuo's Ladyguard alarm helped knock down a fleet of flying saucers, but Dr. Miyajima's metal pipe is a pale imitation. The heroes separate the pipe into two halves, causing it to emit magnetic waves that make the MechaGodzilla console go haywire.

- Close-ups of the intrepid Interpol Agent Nanbara dragging deeply on his cigarette, backed by strains of sinister music, are intended to create an air of mystery and intrigue, but the effect is hilarious.

BIONICALLY COSMIC: Originally titled *Godzilla vs. MechaGodzilla*, this film was released in Japan in March 1974. Nearly three years later, Cinema Shares International, on the heels of its money-making release of *Godzilla vs. Megalon*, snatched up the U.S. distribution rights and announced plans to release the film as *Godzilla vs. The Bionic Monster* in March 1977 (as reported in *Variety* on December 6, 1976). What subsequently happened is the stuff of Godzilla legend, and a source of some confusion over this movie's actual title. In July 1977, *Variety* reported that Universal Television, which owned the highly successful teleseries *The Six Million Dollar Man* (which followed the exploits of Steve Austin, the first "bionic" man) and *The Bionic Woman*, had threatened legal action against Cinema Shares, claiming its usage of "bionic" in the title was an infringement of Universal's trademark and merchandising rights. Cinema Shares and Lancair Films (the film's distributor in the United Kingdom) capitulated and changed the title of the film to *Godzilla vs. The Cosmic Monster*.

As it had with *Megalon*, Cinema Shares edited some violence out of *Cosmic Monster*, most of it occurring in the fist-fights between the heroes and the aliens. The most significant deletion was the opening credits sequence, which features an exotic theme by Masaru Sato; unfortunately, Cinema Shares also cut out Toho's imaginative title sequence (in which Godzilla's name, flashing repeatedly on the screen, is supered over a volcanic eruption). In the late 1980s, Toho officially licensed the film to home video in the U.S., utilizing its uncut "international" English-language edition in lieu of the Cinema Shares cut; since then, the film has been known in America simply as *Godzilla vs. MechaGodzilla*. However, several unlicensed, low-quality videos bearing the *Cosmic Monster* title have been issued by disreputable distributors.

Godzilla vs. The Cosmic Monster was the best entry in the Godzilla series since *Destroy All Monsters* — but then, that's not saying much. Although it restored some lost luster to the King of the Monsters, it was hardly enough to prevent his inevitable box-office death. But before that happened, the great Ishiro Honda would take the director's chair one last time.

Fifteen

BRIDE OF
THE MONSTER

*"[Sinister laughter] Come on and shoot.
You can't kill me anyways [sic], so what do
your bullets matter? [more sinister laughter]"*

— Mugar, the alien leader, just before jumping off a cliff

TERROR OF MECHAGODZILLA
a.k.a. THE TERROR OF GODZILLA

RATING (OUT OF FIVE STARS): ★ ★ 1/2

JAPANESE VERSION: MEKAGOJIRA NO GYAKUSHU (REVENGE OF MECHAGODZILLA). Released on March 15, 1975, by the Toho Motion Picture Company. Toho Scope, in color. Running Time: 83 minutes.

U.S. VERSION: Released theatrically in Summer 1978, by Bob Conn Enterprises as *The Terror of Godzilla*. Running Time: 78 minutes. MPAA rating: G. A longer version was distributed to U.S. television stations in Fall 1978 as *Terror of MechaGodzilla*; all subsequent U.S. television and home-video releases have kept this title.

STORY: The black hole aliens construct a new MechaGodzilla from the wreckage of the original cyborg, enlisting deranged biologist Dr. Mafune (inventor of a device that controls the actions of Titanosaurus, a gigantic dinosaur) to work on the robot. When Mafune's daughter Katsura is killed, alien surgeons install the MechaGodzilla controller inside her body and resurrect her as a cold-hearted cyborg; MechaGodzilla and Titanosaurus attack Tokyo and Godzilla defends his turf, but the King is overmatched until the military disables Titanosaurus with a supersonic-wave gun and Katsura (in a final act of compassion to save the Earth and a young biologist whom she secretly loves) kills herself, rendering MechaGodzilla defenseless and enabling Godzilla to triumph.

HONDA'S LAST HURRAH

Godzilla's 20th-anniversary movie, *Godzilla vs. The Cosmic Monster*, attracted 1.3 million ticket buyers, a far cry from the huge crowds of the Golden Age but nonetheless an improvement of about 350,000 over the dismal business of *Megalon*. A somewhat more mature tone and better production values appeared to sway the momentum in the right direction, even if only slightly. Tanaka decided to forge ahead with the beleaguered series, summoning the talents of four key contributors to the monster's 1954 genesis and giving them the unenviable (and nearly impossible, given the circumstances) task of restoring some of Godzilla's lost credibility. Director Ishiro Honda, working on several teleseries since his last feature film, the disappointing *Yog: Monster from Space* (1970), was brought out of semi-retirement. Akira Ifukube, who lately had scored several acclaimed movies — including *Sandakan No. 8* (1975), an Academy Award nominee for Best Foreign Film — also was wooed back to the genre. **Mototaka Tomioka**, an assistant effects director on the original *Godzilla*, and one of Eiji Tsuburaya's main SFX cameramen on many pictures, was tapped as Director of Photography for both the human drama and SFX scenes.

After the release of *Godzilla vs. The Cosmic Monster*, Toho held a story contest, seeking ideas for a sequel. The winning entry was written by a woman, **Yukiko Takayama**, a student at a Tokyo screenwriting school. Producer Tanaka not only chose Takayama's story as the basis of the new film, he commissioned her to write a full script, and although her scenario was altered somewhat by Honda, Takayama received full credit as the film's screenwriter. She remains the only female author of a Godzilla movie to date.[32] The result was *Terror of MechaGodzilla*, a somewhat bizarre film combining giant monsters, handlebar helmet-wearing aliens and a beautiful cyborg girl. While it was obviously a publicity stunt to tap an unknown talent rather than a series veteran like Shinchi Sekizawa or Takeshi Kimura, it was also a way to infuse some new energy into the creatively zapped genre. Takayama's script is a welcome change of pace, a full-blown monster-action thriller melded with a character-driven story.

The 15th and final film in the original Godzilla series aspires to a level of greatness not attained since *Destroy All Monsters*. But, unfortunately, conflicting forces at work in front of and behind the camera lens undermine the effort. Even with a bigger budget than the recent Godzilla entries (evidenced by the major Toho talents involved, more elaborate effects work, and the lack of stock-footage padding), there is a shabbiness that pervades the production — for instance, in an early scene, Captain Mugar outlines his plan for an alien-occupied Neo-Tokyo on a cheap, drugstore-variety map of the city, complete with folds and creases. Also apparent is the friction between Honda's desire to return the series to the more straightforward style of the 1960s films and the prevailing view at Toho that Godzilla be geared toward the kiddies.

WHEREFORE ART THOU, ICHINOSE?: On the surface, *Terror of MechaGodzilla* is a routine Toho tale of aliens using mind-controlled monsters to conquer mankind. What elevates this film above the last few Godzillas is the underlying themes of mankind's (or, in this case, womankind's) free will and the classic struggle of good versus evil, which unfold in the unrequited attraction between the altruistic hero Ichinose and the tragic female Katsura — two unlikely lovers from warring sides of an Earth-threatening conflict. Katsura's once-virginal soul is claimed by the dark side, devoted to her revenge-maddened father and the marauding aliens who twice revived her dead body. Ichinose stirs the last remaining traces of human compassion within Katsura, allowing her to redeem herself with one final, fateful act, killing herself to foil the Black Hole Three aliens' evil plan. *Terror of MechaGodzilla* has a more powerful dramatic premise than any Godzilla movie since *Monster Zero*, of which it is very reminiscent (e.g., the alien Namikawa sacrifices herself to save Glenn and Mankind from Planet X). There are also parallels to the original *Godzilla*: MechaGodzilla 2 is an allegory of sorts, a machine sent to annihilate a polluted, overpopulated and abused Tokyo by aliens who want to replace the city with a utopian civilization. Whatever subtext may be at work here, *Terror of MechaGodzilla* is a Toho giant-monster movie after all, but it rises above the studio's otherwise brain-dead 1970s output.

Katsuhiko Sasaki of *Godzilla vs. Megalon* fame returns in a more substantial role, and despite his slightly awkward screen presence the actor does a nice job as the love-blinded biologist Ichinose (comically pronounced "itchy-nosy" in the English-dubbed version). The highlight performance in the film, however, is given by 20-year-old actress **Tomoko Ai**, making her feature film debut as Katsura. Sexy yet icy cold, a mechanical-hearted woman given to flashes of true human emotion, Katsura is a conflicted, complicated character and Ai perfectly captures her wide range of emotions, from quiet sadness to panic and vengeful rage. Sadly, the same cannot be said for Akihiko Hirata's portrayal of the disgraced biologist Dr. Mafune. Perhaps the blame should be placed on director Honda for expending Hirata's fine acting talents in such a frivolous way. Mafune offers an opportunity to update the Dr. Serizawa character from the original *Godzilla*, but instead of a scientist haunted by his own theories and forced into seclusion by an ignorant world, Mafune comes off as a sheer deluded madman. The fact that Hirata wears a white lab coat and cheeseball "old man" getup — complete with a gray wig and mustache, with barely concealed spirit gum and tape holding everything in place — and spends much of his screen time cackling and gesticulating wildly does not help matters. The ensemble also includes Goro Mutsu as alien leader Mugar (essentially the same character as "Kuro-numa," whom Mutsu played in the last film — apparently, all Earth-invasion commanders from Black Hole Three look the same!), who revels in evil, wearing his sunglasses indoors (a frequent Honda riff that visually equates the aliens with *yakuza* gangster thugs) and horse-whipping disobedient troops before executing them. Toru Ibuki, the tall, odd-looking actor who played Yata in *Godzilla versus The Sea Monster*, is well cast as Tsuda, the bearded alien henchman. The rest of the cast is serviceable, if not remarkable, including Katsumasa Uchida as Murakoshi, the INTERPOL agent whose sole purpose is to bail his buddy Ichinose out of trouble; long-time Toho actors Tadao Nakamaru and Kenji Sahara show up as the INTERPOL chief and the defense forces commander, respectively.

"NOW, KATSURA. MECHAGODZILLA!": Katsura's eyes blaze with green light! MechaGodzilla 2 launches from its hidden hangar inside a mountain. Together, MechaGodzilla 2 and Titanosaurus march on Tokyo, the former blowing up entire city blocks with its awesome rainbow eye-ray and the latter striking a karate stance, dilating its fishtail membrane and unleashing hurricane-force winds that blow buildings off their foundations. Godzilla appears, ready to defend Japan! The King charges Titanosaurus but is thrust backward by a gust of tail-wind and Mecha-Godzilla 2's rays. Titanosaurus punts the downed Godzilla, football-style, and the monster's limp body sails across the valley, defying the laws of physics. Titanosaurus tackles Godzilla, the two beasts fight at close range, and in another gravity-defying stunt, Godzilla lifts Titanosaurus over his head. Total chaos erupts, with Godzilla taking a mighty licking from his foes. Titanosaurus bites down on Godzilla's upper lip and punches his lower body, sending Godzilla's dazed frame floating up and down. Like Bruce Lee with a pair of nunchakus, MechaGodzilla 2 flashily flips his mighty hand and fires its finger-missiles into Godzilla's stomach (smoke pouring out of the monster's mouth as a result), knocking him out. Titanosaurus again kicks Godzilla for a field goal and MechaGodzilla 2 bombards the surrounding terrain, burying the King in a ravine.

Teruyoshi Nakano's special effects are, for the most part, executed with flash and are well-edited to create fast-paced action sequences. They are also plentiful — for the second consecutive film there is hardly any reliance on stock footage, the exceptions being the recap of Godzilla and Mecha-Godzilla's previous battles during the opening credits (which doesn't really count) and Mecha-Godzilla's all-out assault with rays and missiles during the final battle — a snippet from the previous movie, flip-flopped so that MG2's weapons appear to be firing in the opposite direction, thereby masking the fact that it's a stock shot. Godzilla looks basically the same as in the last movie, but modifications to the costume's head give the monster a more stunted snout and a meaner, snarling look. A new MechaGodzilla costume was built, with roughly the same design but a taller and thinner body, some modifications to the chest plate making the robot look more angular, a new "MG2" insignia on its upper arms, and a darker, tarnished finish compared to the sleek and silvery original. The monster marvel of the film, however, is Titanosaurus, a bipedal marine dinosaur with colorful skin markings and a well thought-out physiology. Brought to life via both suitmation and a head prop with moving eyes and mouth for close-ups, Titanosaurus is deep coral red, peppered with yellow and black spots, its body covered with dark amphibian warts. Its lower body is more dinosaur-like than most Toho monsters: thick at the thighs but with slender legs and feet. The neck, chest, and lower abdomen are defined by a ridged exoskeleton, and its spine is lined with a flashy, frilly crest. Viewed from the front, Titanosaurus is quite impressive, its pronounced snout, narrow eyes and twin antennae creating a monster image that, while fantastical, is almost logical. The sound effects for the monster add to its believability — Titanosaurus has a hyena-like cackle-roar and it snorts loudly and constantly, like a gigantic horse. Finally, Titanosaurus fires no silly rays from its mouth or eyes, a welcome departure from the anything-goes Toho monsters of the era. Whereas MechaGodzilla 2 is pure, unadulterated evil, Titanosaurus is a sympathetic creature, a "gentle dinosaur" that, like Katsura, is forced to fight against its will. Yet, also like the girl, the monster has a sinister quality that makes the creature both pitiable and fearsome.

In an interview with David Milner in *Cult Movies #12*, Takayama said her screenplay underwent several major changes prior to filming, but her main concern was that the integrity of Katsura, the cyborg girl, be preserved. "Even after [Katsura] had been altered, she had emotions. As long as this idea was not removed from the script, I didn't care that much about what was done with it." Most of the screenplay revisions, Takayama said, involved special-effects sequences that were trimmed to cut production costs. The original draft contained two monsters, both called "Titan," which fused together into one, more powerful creature, but this idea was scrapped in favor of a singular Titanosaurus. The final monster battle, as originally written, was also more ambitious. "All of Tokyo was originally going to be destroyed. . . . However, Toho limited the scope of the destruction in order to save money," Takayama told the magazine.

Even if the city-destruction scenes in *Terror of MechaGodzilla* were cut back, there is still more all-out Tokyo trashing than in any film since *Destroy All Monsters* SFX director Nakano sets the stage for the final battle effectively. The two baddies slowly enter the heart of Tokyo, MechaGodzilla 2 hovering menacingly above the skyline and Titanosaurus marching deliberately. Both monsters strike kung fu poses as they wreak havoc. This somehow accentuates their inherent evil rather than dragging the event into the realm of camp. MechaGodzilla 2's rainbow ray is animated just as well as in the previous film, and combines with decent miniature work (utilizing leftover buildings constructed for *Tidal Wave* and *The Last Days of Planet Earth*) and impressive pyrotechnics, to make the cyborg's wholesale obliteration of entire city wards rekindle the spectacle of older Toho monster pics — rivaling,

if not equaling that of *Godzilla* and *Rodan*. There is also an impressive shot wherein MechaGodzilla 2, standing at the far end of a city street, with smoke and flames rising all around, uses his revolving hand missiles to shatter the pavement, sending cars and debris hurtling into the air.

By now, there is little suspense about what Godzilla looks like or what he'll do when he shows up, so Nakano changes the pace slightly by having the King appear without warning, even more suddenly than he did in *Godzilla vs. The Cosmic Monster*. Godzilla's first arrival, with his head silhouetted against the city skyline at night, his figure illuminated by a distant explosion, is a classic, but his second entrance — springing out of nowhere to rescue a couple of brats, Gamera-style — begs credibility. "I could have had Godzilla appear after giving the audience a hint that he was going to pop up, but a sudden appearance sometimes has greater impact," Nakano said. "I always try to think extra hard how we should make Godzilla appear, how it can be more visually effective."

There are some fine effects in the final three-way battle. Enraged, Godzilla slams Titanosaurus into an apartment building under construction! Godzilla rips off MechaGodzilla 2's head, revealing a ray-shooting electronic brain (a glass sphere with red "blood vessels") inside! Yet, despite the slow, calculated warfare of the opposition, Godzilla still seems to be reading out of the *Godzilla vs. Megalon* rule book, and the finale becomes another silly slugfest, although better staged than in the recent films. Portrayed by **Toru Kawai** (who previously played Godzilla on the "Zone Fighter" teleseries), Godzilla runs, body-slams his opponents, unleashes punching combinations, and comically dusts himself off — but thankfully avoids grabbing one of his foes by the tail and slamming his body against the ground, a stunt performed in each of the past four movies. Unfortunately, some equally poor effects were substituted: Godzilla once lifts Titanosaurus into the air, and Titanosaurus twice kicks Godzilla's prone body a mile, then clamps down on Godzilla's face and illogically slaps his body high into the air with body punches. The former effect looks incredibly awkward, with an obviously empty Titanosaurus suit hanging from wires; the latter effects, probably intended to be funny, are just embarrassing, as the slightest kick or punch sends limp-Zilla air-sailing. An overhead shot of Godzilla tangling with MechaGodzilla 2's tail looks like a "view from the balcony" from Busby Berkeley's *The Gold Diggers of 1935*. There are several composite

Will the powerful serpent Titanosaurus's cyclone tail, and the robot monster MechaGodzilla's lethal rays destroy our Earth? See this ultimate test of power! *The Terror of Godzilla!* Rated G!

— *From TV spot for Bob Conn Enterprises' release of* The Terror of Godzilla

shots of Titanosaurus and MechaGodzilla 2 in Tokyo, wherein the background and foreground plates don't match, making the monsters look drastically out of scale. The ultimate insult is Godzilla's parting glance, the victorious monster roaring into the camera before swimming out to sea. A big-toothed "promotion suit," never intended for filming, was rather obviously — and embarrassingly — used here. By including these substandard effects, Nakano mars his otherwise fine work on the film.

DR. STRANGE: Despite Akihiko Hirata's over-the-top performance as Mafune, director Honda still succeeds in creating the creepy aura of a mad scientist. The run-down exterior of Mafune's mansion on Manazura Island, with the foreboding screeches of invisible birds emanating all around it, the mansion's darkened interior, Mafune's laboratory, and the looming presence of the mute chauffeur/gardener (played by Ikio Sawamura) have the cumulative effect of a chilling dream. Sawamura, a longtime Honda bit player, died shortly after the film was made, having been, according to some reports, quite ill during filming. Strangely gaunt and dressed in disheveled clothes, Sawamura is a haunting, silent figure in the film, particularly when he's spying on Katsura from his car — a sequence edited with a series of odd, quick cuts.

The somber tone of Honda's direction is accentuated by Akira Ifukube's ominous musical score. Much more than the haphazardly used stock themes in *Godzilla on Monster Island*, Ifukube's music is well suited to both the monsters and the human characters here. Ifukube's MechaGodzilla theme is comparable to his traditional Godzilla and King Ghidorah motifs in the way it captures the cyborg's awesome size and power, and is far more imposing than Masaru Sato's themes for the robot. The Titanosaurus theme is both powerful and mysterious, and Ifukube's music for the Katsura and the Mafune house is subtle and eerily dark. In all, it is

one of the Maestro's better genre scores, but one of his most underrated.

But despite the strong horror motif, there are many shortcomings that downgrade the film. This is the last Godzilla picture in Toho Scope widescreen format, but unfortunately the use of smaller, modest sets and meager locations do not allow Honda to capture the glorious vistas that his best monster movies are known for. There are also some haphazard continuity glitches in the scripting. At the end of *Godzilla vs. The Cosmic Monster*, Godzilla dumps his cyborg double into the sea off Okinawa; but as the sequel opens, INTERPOL is searching for its wreckage in the sea off the Bonin Islands — on the other side of Japan. Katsura sends Titanosaurus to destroy the submarine . . . but why? She and her father do not become conspirators with the aliens until much later in the film. Kusugari, the INTERPOL agent aboard the destroyed submarine, is apparently killed, yet he turns up later as the prisoner who escapes the alien base and is shot. Why are the aliens holding prisoners, and why do they cut their throats? These plot holes seem to indicate something cut from the script. The time frame and sequence of events leading to the weird alliance between Mafune, Katsura and the Black Hole Three aliens is also puzzling. In a flashback, it is revealed that Katsura was mortally injured years ago in one of Mafune's experiments, only to be saved on the aliens' operating table. But Mafune apparently had no idea that the financiers who underwrote his research and saved Katsura's life were from another galaxy; when he is taken to the alien base, these facts strike him as surprising.

There are also several elements that seem out of character for a Honda picture. Mafune's descent into madness is recounted in a series of black-and-white photos that show the scientist throwing temper tantrums. During Katsura's final surgery, her breasts are fully exposed (well, plastic falsies anyway) and her electronic heart is a contraption made of silly-looking wires and springs. The supersonic wave oscillator, while an effective weapon against Titanosaurus, is a dime-store device compared to the classic Toho *meka* weaponry. And, as sexy as Tomoko Ai is in her body-hugging jumpsuit, the silver alien costumes are old hat, reminiscent of films like *Plan Nine from Outer Space* and *Queen of Outer Space*, and inspire more giggles than awe.

OH, HENRY

In the April 30, 1976 issue of *World Cinema*, a now-defunct movie trade newspaper published in Los Angeles, Toho placed a half-page advertisement for *Terror of MechaGodzilla* that included four movie stills — one showing Katsura on the operating table, fake tits exposed — and a synopsis of the film (which, interestingly, referred to Godzilla as "the Earth's guardian"). The advertisement invited interested distributors to contact Toho's offices, an apparent contradiction to latter-day assertions by Henry G. Saperstein that his UPA Productions not only distributed *Terror of MechaGodzilla* in the U.S., but also co-financed the film with Toho. Saperstein's name, nor that of his company, does not appear in the movie's Japanese credits (as it had on previous Toho-UPA films); there were no American actors sent to Japan to beef up the marquee value and no creative contribution from a Saperstein-hired writer (again, as in previous films); therefore the extent of Saperstein's actual role in the production, if any, is unclear. Nevertheless, as with the three previous Godzilla movies, much time elapsed before *Terror of MechaGodzilla* received wide exposure in the U.S., and when it did, Saperstein was responsible. Unfortunately, he also presided over a series of haphazard editorial decisions that have caused lingering confusion about differing versions of the movie, and even about its title.

Although rival distributor Cinema Shares had staged an impressive release of *Godzilla vs. Megalon* just two years earlier, Saperstein realized that the theatrical market for Japanese monster films was basically all washed up, and he focused instead on selling *Terror of MechaGodzilla* into television syndication. At the same time, perhaps seeking a little more bang for his buck, Saperstein made a deal with Bob Conn Enterprises, a small Beverly Hills-based independent distribution firm founded by a former sales executive for 20th Century Fox and Warner Brothers. In the summer of 1978 Saperstein and/or Conn re-named the picture *The Terror of Godzilla* (probably to make it clear to the kiddies that this was a Godzilla movie) and edited out all profane dialogue (e.g., characters exclaiming, "damn!") and several scenes of semi-graphic violence (people getting shot and strangled to death) to gain a G rating from the Motion Picture Association of America. Conn then launched a small-scale, roadshow-style theatrical release, with the film sporadically appearing in different U.S. cities at matinees, usually only for a few days. In Los Angeles, for example, *The Terror of Godzilla* played for just four days, from February 22 to 25, 1979. Strangely, the film continued to play in theaters well into 1980, even after Saperstein released it to television, in more complete form, under its actual title *Terror of MechaGodzilla*.

Thus, some U.S. fans had the odd experience of seeing *Terror of MechaGodzilla* first on television, then later going to the cinema to see *The Terror of Godzilla*, believing it to be a different film, only to discover an edited-down version of the same picture. Confusing? Yes. But that's only the beginning of it.

When *Terror of MechaGodzilla* started showing up on U.S. television stations in Fall, 1978, a nearly complete print of Toho's English-language international version was used, the only noticeable excision being the shot of Katsura's prosthetic breasts on the operating table. What makes this version uniquely weird is that Saperstein actually produced "new" footage for the film, in the form of a six-minute prologue telling the story of Godzilla's "origins." Opening with the sound of Godzilla's pounding footfalls (culled from the soundtrack of *Godzilla: King of the Monsters!*), the prologue consisted of clips pieced together from two other UPA Godzilla titles, *Monster Zero* and *Godzilla's Revenge*. Reading from a kindergarten-level script, a narrator tells the story of Godzilla's first appearances, his destructive rampages, and finally — after "invaders from other planets and galaxies decided this was the opportunity to take over the Earth," employing "frightening monsters of their own" to accomplish this — how Godzilla became Earth's defender. Bizarrely, this added footage makes it appear that the Planet X aliens from *Monster Zero* are the creators of MechaGodzilla! Why Saperstein felt it necessary to add material to the film is unknown. The most plausible explanation is that he was simply padding the running time, for the "prologued" version of *Terror of MechaGodzilla* clocked in at 89 minutes — six minutes longer than the Japanese original. When the film was first shown on TV, it played in two-hour time slots, with dozens of commercials sandwiched into the half-hour breaks.

Compounding this confusing situation is the fact that, sometime in the early 1980s, the 89-minute version of the film was withdrawn from circulation, and disappeared. For unknown reasons, it was supplanted in television circulation (and, subsequently, on home video) by the shorter, G-rated theatrical version known as *The Terror of Godzilla*, with the title corrected to *Terror of MechaGodzilla*. The end result of all this nonsense is that the film, less-than-perfect to begin with, has suffered added ill repute in the U.S. because most people have unwittingly only seen the chopped-up, kiddy version.

Although the "Americanization" (such as it is) of *Terror of MechaGodzilla* is less severe than that of other Japanese genre films, several notable alterations were made. Most significantly, the ending was trimmed, creating unnecessary confusion about Katsura's fate. For the record, here are the major differences between the Japanese version and the prevailing U.S. television and home video version:

- During the opening sequence, there is a visual recap of Godzilla and MechaGodzilla's battle from the previous film. The Toho version superimposes the main title and credits over 13 freeze-frame shots of the monsters. The U.S. distributors, either too lazy to do a complete translation of the credits, or merely trimming the running time, used only eight such freeze-frames and edited out the final five, resulting in five noticeable "blips" in Akira Ifukube's main title music, jarringly annoying to the ear.

- When INTERPOL agent Kusugari flees the alien base, he is surrounded in the woods by aliens. In the Japanese version, the scene concludes with the aliens shooting Kusugari, who dies in a weird, slow-motion shot.

- After Ichinose and Murakoshi narrowly escape capture outside the alien hideout, the Japanese version shows alien commander Mugar horse-whipping three minions and sentencing them to death for letting the humans get away.

- When Katsura is spotted near the Supersonic Wave Oscillator, she is chased by soldiers into the nearby hills and shot. In the Japanese version, Katsura is seen clutching her neck as if wounded, and as she falls over a cliff and into the ocean below she cries out, "Father!" In the U.S. version, Katsura seems to disappear after being shot, and the soldiers and Murakoshi peer down at the crashing waves.

- In the operating-room scene, the aforementioned shot of Katsura's breasts was snipped.

- As Titanosaurus and MechaGodzilla invade the city, two curious boys approach the monsters. Titanosaurus springs upon them, stomping the kids dead as they cry out, "Godzilla!" before the King of the Monsters suddenly arrives to defend Tokyo. In the U.S. version, the shot of Titanosaurus' foot is excised, making it appear as if Godzilla saved the boys.

- During the final human showdown in the aliens' command center, a scene of Ichinose strangling the alien Tsuda with a rope, and another where Tsuda removes his rubber "human face" mask to reveal an ugly, subhuman alien face underneath as he lay dying on the floor, were removed.

- Who shot Katsura Mafune? Who shot Dr. Mafune? The most critical questions concern the death of the madman and his robo-daughter. In the Japanese version, as Katsura threatens to shoot Ichinose with a laser pistol, Murakoshi bursts into the room and shoots Katsura in the right shoulder, and the girl faints. Through clever (!) re-editing — including the insertion of a still-frame shot of Katsura's back — to piece together the mismatched action, the U.S. version makes it appear as if Murakoshi's gunshot mortally wounds the girl. Next, Mugar enters the room and fires his gun at Murakoshi, who fires back. A shot of Dr. Mafune being struck by a deadly bullet in the crossfire was cut out, making it appear that Dr. Mafune is still alive at the picture's end. When Katsura cries out, "Father!" the U.S. version makes is appear that she is calling for help. Actually, Dr. Mafune lies dying on the floor across the room.

- Tragic end: An emotional exchange between faithful Ichinose and his meka-bride was entirely cut from the U.S. print. Cradled in Ichinose's arms, Katsura weeps for her father and for the mess she's gotten into. Ichinose professes his love for the girl and tries comforting her, saying, "You aren't to blame . . . You shed tears . . . You have a human heart like anyone else." To atone for her misdeed, Katsura realizes she must sacrifice her own life. She reveals that the MechaGodzilla controller is inside her chest, and begs Ichinose to shoot her; when he refuses, Katsura picks up a gun and blasts herself in the side. As the monster battle unwinds, Ichinose carries Katsura's body outside and places it on the ground. By removing all these scenes, the U.S. version does away not only with graphic violence but with the most moving moment in the film — Katsura's final redemption — and gives the false impression that

Katsura and Ichinose probably went on to get married and buy a house in the 'burbs.

Overall, *Terror of MechaGodzilla* is a diamond in the rough, an uneven movie with enough truly memorable moments to justify its status as a quasi-classic and cult favorite among fans in both the East and West. Watching the film today, the feeling is bittersweet: although this is by far the best Godzilla movie of the 1970s — and arguably the best entry in the series since *Monster Zero* — it is a less-than-glorious ending to the directorial career of the great Ishiro Honda. Fortunately, Honda would continue to work, rekindling his working relationship with Akira Kurosawa in the 1980s to collaborate with him on several films; but sadly, Honda's days as master of monsters were over, and Godzilla has never fully recovered from the loss.

Although it was not Toho's intention to retire its mighty monster after *Terror of MechaGodzilla*, economic factors, a creative void, and other circumstances brought the first cycle of the Godzilla franchise to a merciful end before it could spiral downward any further. But Godzilla was never known to sit at home by the phone. With his popularity at an all-time low in Japan, Godzilla found employment overseas . . . so to speak.

THE ELECTRIC KOOL-AID KAIJU TEST

Luigi Cozzi's Colorized Godzilla (1977)

It's too bad most fans will never get to see the most bizarre, yet least known of all Japanese monster movies: *Cozzilla!*

Years before Ted Turner became infatuated with colorizing (i.e., bastardizing) American film classics, an Italian film mogul named **Luigi Cozzi** tried to put the colors of the rainbow into *Godzilla: King of the Monsters!*, using a crude, if somewhat interesting process called Spectrorama 70. But colorization (if what he did can really be called that) was actually just one of Cozzi's many transgressions. He also heavily re-edited the film, removed entire scenes, and added lots of stock footage of graphic death and destruction. Cozzi obviously intended to intensify the movie's antinuclear themes, but his overkill approach obliterated what made both the Japanese and American versions of the first Godzilla movie so great.

According to Max Della Mora, a noted genre movie buff from Italy who has written for many European and American fanzines, Cozzi began his film career in Rome in the early 1970s, directing thrillers and dramas, writing books and magazine articles on sci-fi (he was even published in *Famous Monsters of Filmland*), and organizing movie festivals. He is best known in the U.S. by the pseudonym Lewis Coates, the name he used when he costarred alongside the beautiful scream queen Caroline Munro in his *Star Wars* ripoff, *Starcrash* (1979). Many of his other films have made their way to the U.S., and before the advent of home video, some were released theatrically, including *Contamination* and *Hercules*, the latter starring Lou Ferrigno.

Cozzi's Godzilla movie opens with "Hiroshima, 6 Agosto 1945" superimposed on the screen, fol-lowed by depictions of a day in the life of the fated Japanese city. Suddenly, it's ground zero: there is a blast and a mushroom cloud, then a long series of aerial fly-by shots of the decimated city's charred ruins. After the opening credits (with titles against an odd, smokey background), Cozzi fast-forwards to Tokyo nine years later, where a disaster of identical scale has just occurred. Here, finally, is the first trace of the original film, as Raymond Burr sloughs familiarly through the rubble. Throughout the film, Cozzi hammers home his message more strongly (and less tactfully) than Ishiro Honda ever could — although the basic story remains unchanged, it is interrupted at every turn with World War II newsreel footage, mostly showing bombed buildings and scorched human bodies. The effect is startling for its lack of subtlety, if not exactly chilling the way Cozzi intended it to be.

Consider these sights: Real military planes attack Godzilla, and they appear to blow up in midair, even without a blast of his breath! When Godzilla pokes his head above water in the bay and scares a shipload of dancing party-goers, night suddenly turns to day and scores of people jump into lifeboats while the ship burns! And when Ogata and Serizawa dive to deploy the Oxygen Destroyer, they watch a shark eat an octopus (in a scene surreptitiously culled from *The Beast from 20,000 Fathoms*)! Curiously, during Godzilla's second rampage, there is also a snippet of the scene in *Gigantis: The Fire Monster* where the escaped convicts are swallowed in a flooded subway tunnel.

To make room for this new material, Cozzi edited out much of the human drama. Raymond Burr's role as Steve Martin remains more or less intact, but the characters of Dr. Yamane, Ogata, Emiko, and especially Dr. Serizawa were all trimmed. Gone is any sense of the tormented scientist sequestering himself in the lab — instead, Serizawa's just a weirdo inventor. The order of many scenes is shifted around, there is heavy re-editing of music and sound effects (raging wind and horrible screams are added wherever possible), and in various scenes the film speed is altered to create a jittery slow-motion effect. The oddest sequence by far takes place after Godzilla devastates Tokyo for the second time. The song "Oh Peace, Oh Light" is heard over documentary footage of cities smoldering and bodies burned beyond recognition, intercut with close-ups of Godzilla breathing fire.

By far the strangest aspect of Cozzi's Godzilla, however, is the radioactive-like glow permeating every scene. Forget Turner's computers that color-by-numbers. "Spectrorama 70 is just a process where color gels are put on the original black-and-white film to add a sort of weird colorization, something like Angry Red Planet's Mars scenes," says Della Mora. "The colorization was executed by Armando Valcauda, a special-effects technician who also worked with Cozzi on Starcrash and Hercules,

later doing stop-motion and model effects. He's quite good, a sort of Italian Ray Harryhausen in some ways. Cozzi never used the colorization effect again, either before or after Godzilla."

The film is also interesting for its "Futursound" soundtrack, which was just Sensurround with a new name. Della Mora reports that when the film was shown in theaters, the effect was truly amazing, causing the seats to shake every time Godzilla roared or one of his mighty footsteps hit the ground. Also noteworthy is the new theme music composed for the opening Hiroshima sequence, which is like nothing ever heard in a Godzilla film before or since. Reminiscent of an early techno-rave tune, the synthesizer-heavy theme was recorded by Magnetic System, which consisted of three composers named Bixio, Frizzi, and Tempera, according to Della Mora.

Cozzilla, as it is called by fans and the filmmaker himself, was released in Italy in 1977. Apparently it did quite poorly, for it has never been officially released on video and has been shown only a few times on Italian television. Today, Della Mora says, it is considered merely "a freak and an oddity."

GODZILLA, AMERICAN-STYLE

Hanna-Barbera's cartoon series (1978)

Godzilla once had the power to radiate laser beams from his eyes. What's worse, he vaguely resembled Barney, the purple bane of all Godzilla fans' existence.

Long before TriStar Pictures began talking about an American-made, high-tech Godzilla movie, there was the first-ever U.S. production starring the Japanese giant — a low-tech, animated version courtesy of Hanna-Barbera Productions. This cartoon rendition of *Godzilla* was an overgrown, green, poorly-detailed T-Rex, looking nothing like the real monster and lacking any trace of the Big G's personality. Like Marvel Comics' mid-'70s Godzilla adaptation, the cartoon series also flopped with longtime fans because it excluded any of Godzilla's Toho foes, substituting a series of new, ludicrous Earth-threatening aliens and beasts.

In the short-lived show, which ran for two 13-episode seasons in 1978 and 1979 on NBC, Godzilla was the guardian of the four-member crew of the *Calico*, a seafaring scientific research ship. As they traversed the globe, the crew found themselves investigating some new, strange scientific phenomena each week and inevitably facing the brink of world destruction. Using a special electronic device, the crew could immediately summon Godzilla from the ocean's depths to defend them. In addition to his laser eye-beam, Godzilla exhaled a stream of crackling flame that couldn't hold a candle (pun intended) to Toho's radioactive breath.

Artistically speaking, the 1970s were bad times for Godzilla. Even so, the monster's popularity among the small-fry set was at an all-time high, and animation kingpin **Joseph Barbera** saw an opportunity.

"My job back then was to dig up new characters, new ideas, new shows, and I had wanted to do Godzilla for a while — I liked the monster thing, and the way it looked, and I thought we could do a lot with it," says Barbera, the show's co-executive producer with BIll Hanna. "So I contacted Hank Saperstein, who was a very good friend, and we got talking about it. Then, there was an executive at the network who wanted to get into the act, and urged us to lighten the story line up. So, I came up with the character Godzooky, who was like his son. The show had a sort of father-son relationship, which we had done before on shows like *Auggie Doggie* and *Jonny Quest*."

Godzilla purists have long maligned this show, but it may come as a surprise that Barbera says he originally wanted to do *Godzilla* more or less as a straight adaptation of the movie series, rather than a watered-down dinosaur serial barely resembling its inspiration. But the powers-that-be at the network would not allow it, he says.

"The problem with the show was simply this: When they start telling you in Standards and Practices, 'Don't shoot any flame at anybody, don't step on any buildings or cars,' then pretty soon, they've taken away all the stuff that he represents. That became the problem, to maintain a feeling of Godzilla and at the same time cut down everything that he did," Barbera says. "We managed to get a fair show out of it. It was OK. Godzooky kind of got the kids going."

The *Calico*'s crew consisted of Captain Carl Majors, his assistants Brock (the show's token African-American) and Pete (token annoying, idiotic white kid), and Dr. Quinn Darian (token female scientist). They were inexplicably joined by Godzooky, their cowardly, clumsy mascot — a 10-foot-tall junior Godzilla with bat-like wings whose groaning and whimpering were performed by Don Messick, the voice of Scooby Doo. According to publicity material, Godzilla became the ship's grateful protector after the crew rescued Godzooky from a coral reef, but this was never shown on the program. Godzilla, whose voice was acted by Ted Cassidy ("Lurch" from the *Addams Family* television series), sounded like a man roaring into a microphone. The show opened with a catchy title song by Hoyt S. Curtin, composer of the themes of *Scooby Doo*, *The Flintstones*, *The Jetsons*, and all Hanna-Barbera's classic toons.

"I think the real inspiration for the show was *Jonny Quest*," says Duane Poole, who, with then-partner Dick Robbins, developed the show for TV. "Every episode was a serious science fiction piece, with Godzooky as the occasional fool to lighten it up. Each episode had a major monster taken from the Godzilla series for inspiration, but not literally — there were no Smog Monsters or whatnot. The trick was finding some villain or a situation big enough that Godzilla was needed to come in and handle it. That was usually a monster, or a massive tidal wave, and frequently a combination of both. We really crammed a lot of action into it."

At first, the idea of doing the first-ever *Godzilla* animated series created a rush of excitement at Hanna-Barbera. "What was different about *Godzilla*, compared to the all-out comedies, the adventure hours and the lighter things we had done before," says Poole, "was that it was a real action piece with serious antagonists in a science fiction format. It seemed different, and I do remember a lot of the artists trying to find new ways to do things, trying to find a new style that would represent Godzilla and this approach, so the kids wouldn't mistake it for a Scooby."

Ultimately, though, kids were tiring of the mostly uninspired, limited-animation Saturday morning fare of that era, and they began switching channels for other programming. And many kids probably wondered why the King of the Monsters was hanging around with the dorks on that ship.

Hanna-Barbera's half-hour *Godzilla* cartoons premiered on Saturday, September 8, 1978, on NBC as *The Godzilla Power Hour*, featuring one episode each of *Godzilla* and *Jana of the Jungle*, a show about a female Tarzan. In November 1978, *Jonny Quest* joined the lineup and the show was renamed *The Godzilla Super 90*. A second season of new *Godzilla* episodes aired in 1979, and the show continued in reruns over the next two years as *The Godzilla Show*, *The Godzilla-Globetrotters Adventure Hour*, *The Godzilla-Dynomutt Hour*, and *The Godzilla-Hong Kong Phooey Hour*. The last show was broadcast September 5, 1981.

EPISODE GUIDE

Season 1
(originally aired September–December 1978)

1. THE FIRE BIRD
A long-dormant Alaskan volcano erupts and looses a mysterious Fire Bird that emits fierce heat and threatens to melt the polar cap. The *Calico* crew sicks Godzilla on it to stop a global meltdown.

2. THE EARTH EATER
The Earth Eater is eating San Francisco! Our seafaring friends come ashore to turn Godzilla loose on him.

3. ATTACK OF THE STONE CREATURES
A sacred Egyptian pyramid is guarded by mysterious creatures. The crew helps an archaeologist in his attempt to exploit the ancient ruin by sicking Godzilla on the creatures.

4. THE MEGAVOLT MONSTER
Monsters living in an undersea desert loose aquatic lightning bolts that sink ships. The *Calico* kids and Godzilla show them what's what.

5. THE SEAWEED MONSTER
A kelp mutant terrorizes islanders in the West Indies. Godzilla kills it by exposing it to the sun's rays.

6. THE ENERGY BEAST
The title monster comes to Earth via a meteor and proceeds to suck electricity from a dam. The creature replicates Godzilla's appearance, but the real G arrives to send it back into space.

7. THE COLOSSUS OF ATLANTIS
Atlantis was a spaceship! The undersea kingdom is rediscovered after an earthquake. Godzilla helps free its people from the control of a monster, then the Atlantians fly off into space.

8. THE HORROR OF THE FORGOTTEN ISLAND
The evil Cyclops is released when a magnetic storm deactivates a force field created long ago by space visitors to contain the monster.

9. ISLAND OF THE LOST SHIPS
The crew is trapped on a mythical island that appears only once every 1,000 years.

10. THE MAGNETIC TERROR
This monster terrorizes an Antarctic oil-drilling outpost, but explodes when it consumes more energy than it can handle.

11. THE BREEDER BEAST
This beast is a threat to both the nation's safety and economy: it harbors nuclear energy and it wants to eat all the gold and silver in the U.S. mint.

12. THE SUB-ZERO TERROR

On a scientific expedition to the Himalayas, the crew is attacked by Watchuka, a giant snowman.

13. THE TIME DRAGONS

Godzilla catches a falling satellite, which somehow causes he and the crew to be transported through time to a prehistoric age. Listen as Pete exclaims, "Godzilla's holding it in!"

Season 2

(originally aired September–December, 1979)

1. THE GOLDEN GUARDIAN

Godzilla is turned into a gold statue by this nemesis, but is eventually freed by the ingenious crew.

2. CALICO CLONES

An evil scientist clones the *Calico* crew in hopes of learning the location of a secret oil field. Godzilla battles the madman's giant squid.

3. MICROGODZILLA

Inspired by *The Fly*. Godzilla and a fly are exposed to a pink gas that causes each creature to assume the other's size.

4. GHOST SHIP

Godzilla and the gang discover a World War II submarine trapped in an iceberg and free the long-dormant crew. A missile accidentally goes off and awakens a giant octopus.

5. THE BEAST OF STORM ISLAND

Axor, a lizard beast, turns Majors, Quinn and Brock into zombies, but Godzilla saves the day.

6. VALLEY OF THE GIANTS

On another expedition, the crew discovers a valley inhabited by giant insects.

7. THE CYBORG WHALE

Pete and Brock take a ride on a robot whale, which gets struck by lightning and heads on a collision course with Honolulu Harbor.

8. THE CITY IN THE CLOUDS

A cyclone sends the crew and Godzilla to a futuristic city in the sky. The evil leaders try to get them to trade Godzilla for their safe return.

9. THE MACRO-BEASTS

A volcanic eruption causes fish to grow to giant size.

10. MOONLODE

A lunar eclipse sends a monster to earth. Its gravity threatens to suck the *Calico* into a whirlpool.

11. PACIFIC PERIL

A massive quake traps Godzilla in the Earth's crust, beneath the ocean floor. The gang discovers a space rocket and uses it to propel their friend back to the surface.

12. ISLAND OF DOOM

Terrorists known as the Cobra Council threaten Earth with nuclear missiles. Godzilla and friends locate their base and destroy their nuclear reactor.

13. THE DEADLY ASTEROID

The Ice People of Frios try to create a new Ice Age on Earth. Godzilla turns the invaders' spaceship upside down, reversing the freezing process.

PART 4

RESURRECTION

The 1980s

"In 1975, Tanaka put his reptile out to pasture. But that move did not sit well with the lizard's many Japanese fans. [In 1983] the 10,000-member Godzilla Resurrection Committee gathered 40,000 plus signatures on a petition demanding a rebirth of the great monster. By then, the nuclear arms race had heated up again and Tanaka thought the world was ready for another reptilian allegory."

— *From an article in* People, *January 14, 1985*

Sixteen

THE LEGEND IS REBORN

*" . . . and just for the record, 30 years
ago they never found any corpse."*

— "Steven" Martin, author of *Cairo Via Tokyo*

GODZILLA (1984)
a.k.a. GODZILLA 1985

RATING (OUT OF FIVE STARS): ★ ★ 1/2

JAPANESE VERSION: GOJIRA (GODZILLA). Released on December 15, 1984, by the Toho Motion Picture Company. Widescreen, in color. Running Time: 103 minutes. English-dubbed version released internationally as *The Return of Godzilla*. Screened at the Cannes Film Festival May 11, 13, and 15, 1985.

U.S. VERSION: Released on August 23, 1985, by New World Pictures. Running Time: 91 minutes. MPAA rating: PG.

STORY: When a Soviet submarine is destroyed, the U.S. is blamed for the attack and World War III is averted only when Japan reveals the mishap was caused by Godzilla, who has reappeared after a 30-year absence. The monster attacks Tokyo, accidentally causing the launch of a Soviet nuclear missile aimed directly at the metropolis; Godzilla is nearly killed by the military's Super-X flying battle tank, but he is revived when the Soviet missile explodes above the stratosphere, and Tokyo is saved when a scientist uses bird sounds to lure Godzilla into the volcano at Mount Mihara.

THE COMEBACK TRAIL

Godzilla went into a nine-year retirement after the dismal response at the Japanese box office to *Terror of MechaGodzilla*, the worst-attended of all the Godzilla films and only the second in the series to sell less than a million tickets during its theatrical run. However, the monster's long absence from the screen wasn't intentional, for Toho tried and failed to rejuvenate Godzilla's movie career a number of times in the late 1970s and early '80s.

In 1977, Toho announced plans for *The Rebirth of Godzilla* (*Gojira No Fukkatsu*), a color remake of the original *Godzilla*, which never materialized. Not

215

long thereafter, reports surfaced in Japan (and were transmitted to the U.S. in the fanzine *Japanese Giants #5*, published in 1978) that Toho and Henry G. Saperstein's UPA Productions would jointly produce *Godzilla vs. the Devil* (*Gojira Tai Debiru*), to be released sometime in 1978. Although details were sketchy, it was said the film had a $4 million budget, its script would be written by an American (presumably, Saperstein's longtime associate Reuben Bercovitch) and its proposed running time was 110 minutes. *Japanese Giants* described the plot of *Godzilla vs. the Devil* like this: "The evil in the world gives birth to a number of monsters, among them a gigantic spider, fish, and bird, all of whom do battle with Godzilla. The climax supposedly will involve a confrontation between Godzilla and Satan himself." At a time when it typically took three or four years for one of Toho's Godzilla films to be released in America, fans of the genre welcomed the American involvement in the project, believing it might guarantee a quick stateside release. Not so. The picture was never made. Neither was *Godzilla vs. Gargantua*, supposedly proposed by Saperstein in the late 1970s, in which Godzilla was to fight a creature similar to the feuding Frankenstein siblings of *War of the Gargantuas*. This project was said to have a whopping budget of $6 million, and also based on a story written by Bercovitch. A two-part short story called *A Space Godzilla* (no relation to Toho's 1994 film *Godzilla vs. Space Godzilla*), written by Nobuhiko Obayashi, published in the Japanese edition of *Starlog* magazine in 1977, ignited more Godzilla movie rumors, but nothing developed.

In August, 1979, as Godzilla's 25th birthday (on November 3) approached, the Associated Press reported that Godzilla would "Make a comeback [in 1980] as the hero of a nuclear power plant accident." Spurred by world interest in the March 1979 disaster at the Three Mile Island power plant in Pennsylvania, and by renewed Japanese enthusiasm for Godzilla (according to news reports, a 25th-anniversary retrospective of all 15 G-movies, held in August 1979 in Tokyo, sold 60,000 tickets and sales of Godzilla toys in Japan from 1975–79 pulled in $4.5 million), Toho sought to make Godzilla relevant in the modern era by updating his nuclear symbolism: Whereas the monster once invoked fears of the Bomb, now he would raise the specter of a Meltdown.

Once again steering Godzilla toward his destiny was producer Tomoyuki Tanaka. "It will be a serious film, just like the first movie, which was a reaction to uncontrolled atomic bomb testing," Tanaka told the AP. "We are in the middle of scriptwriting. The Japanese are now fearful of the future, much as at the time of the 1954 film. . . . The oil shortage, the prospects of World War III, food shortage and the possibility of another giant earthquake are now beginning to preoccupy the Japanese, much like the atom bomb did 25 years ago." Tanaka added that Godzilla "Shows the Japanese attitude toward the atom," but when asked by a reporter whether the new Godzilla film would address all these societal fears, he replied, "I don't think we will be all that logical."

The story that was subsequently written, titled *The Return of Godzilla*, authored by **Akira Murao**, and completed in 1980, promised to be one of the most exciting Godzilla sequels ever. The story had a savage Godzilla pitted against Bagan, a monster capable of changing its shape. The monster battle was set against a dramatic backdrop of illegal nuclear-waste-dumping at sea, the destruction (by Godzilla) of a nuclear power plant, and the development of a new element that safely produces nuclear energy but is capable of becoming a super-weapon of mass destruction if it falls into hostile hands. The finale had Godzilla's body washing ashore on the coast of the United States. The Associated Press indicated that Ishiro Honda would direct the new film, and he pledged to avoid the mistakes Toho committed during the 1970s. "We went downhill in the last five or six pictures," Honda told the AP. "The first film was pacifistic in intent." But, like every other Godzilla project rumored or announced during this period, *The Return of Godzilla* never went before the cameras, with no explanation given.

Why did Toho struggle for so long to bring Godzilla back? Very likely, it was a combination of Tanaka's insistence that any new Godzilla film be nothing less than a first-class effort, with production values that would restore the monster's lost luster, and the fact that Toho and the Japanese movie industry in general was still trying to figure out how to bounce back from years of economic woes and the public's defection to television and American movies as its staple entertainment. Tanaka wanted to resurrect the monster, but he couldn't come up with the right project and the financing, not even on Godzilla's 25th anniversary.

Still, Toho continued to make special effects pictures, most notably *The War in Space* (*Wakusei Daisenso*, 1977), a shabby space opera directed by Jun Fukuda. In this film, Toho attempted to update its classic film *Atragon*, casting Ryo Ikebe (*Battle in*

Outer Space) as a Jinguji-like character developing the Gohten, a submarine-shaped spaceship which, of course, aliens are trying to seize control of. The film came out less than a year after *Star Wars* and it featured a Wookie-like alien creature, leading to accusations that Toho had ripped off George Lucas' masterpiece, even though the two stories are hardly similar. However, complaints about the film's effects sequences, heavily padded with stock explosions from *Tidal Wave* and *The Last Days of Planet Earth*, were justified. So were snickers about the obvious *Star Trek* influence, the sappy story, the terrible musical score and the hapless aliens, especially "Dr. Schmidt," portrayed by English-dubber impresario William Ross. In an anti-classic Toho moment, the heroes discover Ross to be an alien impostor and shoot him. Ross jumps through a plate-glass window and spontaneously combusts on the pavement. "Due to budget constraints we . . . had to work within confined parameters," Tanaka later recalled. "Thankfully, we were able to create an entertaining work but received severe criticism from our fans." (From memoir published in *The Complete History of Toho Special Effects Movies*, 1983) Other Toho SFX productions from this period include *Imperial Navy* (1981), a war movie directed by Shue Matsubayashi, and the disaster movie *Deathquake* (1982). Both featured Teruyoshi Nakano's work, but neither recaptured the studio's glory days.

Out of nowhere, a man appeared in 1983 with an unprecedented proposal that seemed to solve all Toho's protracted Godzilla-related problems. **Steve Miner**, a young Hollywood director, wanted to produce the first-ever Americanization of the Godzilla legend, envisioning it as a big-budget affair with a story set in the U.S. and utilizing top-name American actors and high-priced American special effects. All the financing, talent and other resources would come from the U.S., and Toho would hardly need to spend a dime or lift a finger. The picture, if well done, would surely be a huge hit in both the U.S. and Japan and generate millions of dollars in ticket sales and merchandising. Toho had literally nothing to lose and everything to gain, so the studio quickly gave Miner its blessing to develop a concept for the film and to begin seeking backing from American movie studios.

In the 1990s, Miner has made a name for himself with dramas and comedies like *Forever Young*, with Mel Gibson, and *My Father the Hero*, with Gerard Depardieu. But back in the early 1980s he was cutting his teeth on horror movies such as *Friday the 13th Part 2* (1981) and *Friday the 13th Part 3-D* (1982). Miner began by hiring **Fred Dekker**, a 22-year-old graduate from UCLA film school who had just landed a placement with a screenwriting agent at the prestigious International Creative Management (ICM) in Beverly Hills (in the intervening years, Dekker has directed *Night of the Creeps*, *Monster Squad*, and *Robocop 3*). In just a few weeks, Dekker had completed the first draft of a screenplay that had Godzilla attacking San Francisco in a story that mixed a nuclear accident, a *Gorgo*-esque mother-baby monster relationship and a Cold War-era, James Bond-style subplot wherein an American secret superagent and his longstanding Russian rival fight for control of Soviet nuclear missiles, with the fate of the world hanging in the balance. Miner also hired **William Stout**, an artist who had done storyboards for *Conan the Barbarian* and *First Blood*, and who, more importantly, was the author of an acclaimed illustrated book, *The Dinosaurs* (1981) that was widely credited with starting a "dinosaur renaissance" during the 1980s. Using prototypes created by Steve Czerkas, a noted paleontologist who builds full-scale dinosaur dioramas for natural-history museums, Stout designed a "dinosaurized" version of Godzilla that basically looked like a mutated Allosaurus with large dorsal fins along its spine. He painted a full-color "teaser" poster, showing Godzilla blasting the Golden Gate Bridge, that Miner used when making presentations to studio officials.

Throughout 1983 and '84, Miner tried endlessly to obtain backing from one of the Hollywood majors, but there were several stumbling blocks. First off, Miner wanted to use the best people in the SFX business. He contacted Rick Baker, the legendary makeup and mechanical effects man, to develop a cable-controlled, large-scale Godzilla head, capable of realistic expressions, for use in close-up shots. He requested bids from the top two special effects houses in the business, Industrial Light and Magic (ILM) and Dream Quest. He wanted top people to do the stop-motion animation and other complex effects. Further complicating matters, Miner wanted to make the film in 3-D, which would require dual camera setups for every effects shot. Miner estimated that to make the film "his way" he needed a budget of about $30 million, a price tag that sounds measly for a major SFX film today, but was considered gargantuan at the time.

THE ONE THAT GOT AWAY

An oral history of GODZILLA: KING OF THE MONSTERS IN 3-D (circa 1983)

This section comprises excerpts from interviews with producer-director Steve Miner, screenwriter Fred Dekker, and production designer William Stout, conducted by the author in 1994–95.

The origins of the project . . .

MINER: I had always been a fan [of *Godzilla*] since I was a kid. Once seeing it as an adult, I realized that this could be remade as a good movie. My original idea was to do it in 3-D. I had just done *Friday the 13th* in 3-D, and wanted to do a good movie in 3-D, and I thought the miniatures would lend themselves to doing good 3-D effects. So it was a combination of trying to do a really good monster movie and doing it in 3-D. I had to get the rights, so I went to Japan and made a deal with the Toho people to co-finance the development of the project — myself and Toho. I hired Fred Dekker sort of on a fluke, and he turned out a really good script. I hired Bill Stout, and he did some storyboards as well as some concept art. Then, with the script and the art, we started going to the studios, and we got very close at a lot of places. But to make it was just very expensive. Everyone was saying they wanted to make it for $10 million, but it clearly was going to cost $25 million or $30 million at that time, because of the special effects. At that time it was pretty much the *Star Wars* type of technology. There wasn't any computers at that point. We were going to use miniatures, stop-motion animation, and probably some guys in suits. But the idea was to do it so it didn't look like that.

DEKKER: I had just written a script called *Forever Factor*, which was a science-fiction thriller — sort of a cross between *Marathon Man* and *Back to the Future*. Steve Miner liked it a lot. I had always been a big monster fan. I loved the Universal *Frankenstein*, *Dracula*, *The Wolf Man*. Science fiction, horror, and fantasy were a big deal for me when I was a kid. So I was familiar with Godzilla and felt I could do it, but one of the reasons that Steve liked my approach to it was I was not a Godzilla fan. I loved the Ray Harryhausen films, I loved dinosaurs, but I always thought the Japanese films were really pretty cheesy. He did not want to make a cheesy film, and I wasn't interested in just special effects and knocking buildings down. The first thing I said to Steve was, "If all this movie is about is this big monster destroying buildings, we're screwed."

The script . . .

STOUT: I was so excited by the script. I thought it was a great idea. Because usually people will try to remake classics, and you start out with three strikes against you. As soon as you announce you're about to remake a classic, the public hates you, because they cherish the memory of the film. But Steve was taking a film that had a great idea but wasn't executed particularly well, and doing it state-of-the-art. So, if you do it right, you end up with a low public expectation — the audience is expecting another cheesy Godzilla film — and you go in and knock their socks off with a Steven Spielberg-like effects extravaganza. I think that's much smarter than remaking a film that was done really well.

DEKKER: The Toho movies really weren't influential to me at all, I really thought they were cheesy movies. I'd never seen any of the Godzilla movies all the way through. I was familiar with them: I knew Mothra, Ghidorah, I knew Honda. I was familiar with the *oeuvre* but I wasn't a fan at all. I was much more influenced then — and still am — by Spielberg and by the James Bond films. So, my take on it was to do a story that would still be interesting, even if Godzilla wasn't in it. I thought of it as an action adventure that had Godzilla in it. He was the engine that drove the thing, but we had to care about the people. It almost had a Irwin Allen quality — it had a lot of characters and it was really epic.

MINER: The premise was, this was the first Godzilla movie. We acted as if all the previous ones didn't exist. Our plan was to make Godzilla mean, scary,

| SHOT #: | BACKGROUND: | P.P.#: | PAGE #: 93 |
| OPTICAL: | | | FRAME COUNT: BOARD #: TE24 |

DESCRIPTION: GODZILLA REACHES DOWN   ROTO.

DIALOGUE:

GODZILLA: KING OF THE MONSTERS in 3-D

| SHOT #: | BACKGROUND: | P.P.#: | PAGE #: 105 |
| OPTICAL: | | | FRAME COUNT: BOARD #: TE178 |

DESCRIPTION: ROTO:

DIALOGUE:

GODZILLA: KING OF THE MONSTERS in 3-D

Production designer William Stout created hundreds of storyboards, completing
about 80 percent of the special-effects sequences, hiring several artists (including
Johnny Quest creator Doug Wilder, according to some reports) to help complete
the huge job. Stout envisioned a more dinosaur-like Godzilla, which director
Steve Miner planned to bring to life with stop-motion effects by David Allen.

STORYBOARDS USED BY PERMISSION OF WILLIAM STOUT AND STEVE MINER ferocious. The action focused on a group of characters, and was told from the point of view of a little boy, whose father is the hero of the film. We borrowed a little bit from *Gorgo* by putting a baby monster in the story, which personalizes the story and gives Godzilla a purpose. But Godzilla was not going to be a good monster. He was going to wreak havoc all over San Francisco.

DEKKER: The hero of the story was Peter Daxton, a colonel. He wore an eyepatch, and I wanted to do this very "Snake Plisskin" take on him, and also there was a character in the original *Godzilla* [Dr. Serizawa] that had an eyepatch, so it was a reference to that. Daxton's nemesis is this KGB agent, whom he once fought aboard a helicopter. Daxton had cut off the KGB agent's hand with a helicopter blade, so now he's missing a hand and he has this detachable hand and a blade sticking out of it. He kills people, very similar to the [Lawrence] Olivier character in *Marathon Man*. Daxton had cut off his hand, and he had taken out Daxton's eye, so they have this history together. Then there was this paleontologist character at [UC] Berkeley, who we always saw as Jeff Goldblum — very wacky, very Bill Murray, irreverent and goofy. Our other main character was Dana Martin, a young upstart reporter based on the Steve Martin character in the original *Godzilla*. One of the secret service agents was named Honda. There were lots of little Japanese touches.

I was very high on Powers Boothe to play Daxton. We talked about Demi Moore for the part of the newspaper reporter; even though she wasn't a big star yet, I was a fan of hers in the early days. Those were the prototypes. We also wanted to give Raymond Burr a cameo.

Revamping Godzilla . . .

DEKKER: I think our origin for him essentially was the origin from the Toho films, nuclear testing creating this freak of nature. In the Toho series, you started out with a very spiritual allegory for splitting the atom and the Japanese losing World War II at the hands of the atomic bomb. From there, the films gradually became Saturday morning cartoons with guys in big costumes, swatting at each other, and cheesy miniatures. There's so many films in the series, but I think they degenerated fairly quickly. I wasn't interested in anything after the original *Godzilla*.

My take on Godzilla was to address it all in very scientific jargon. Ballinger had this wacky theory, which is that based on the "big bang" there was

the possibility that some of the earliest dinosaurs were, in a sense, nuclear powered. It was kind of a far-fetched science-fiction premise, but what it bought was Godzilla's radioactive breath, and it also bought a way to kill him at the end, using these missiles the Soviets developed.

STOUT: For reference, we screened the first *Godzilla*, the Japanese version, without Raymond Burr. And I was shocked at how slow that sucker was. But it still had that one scene that I remembered as a kid, which was still real effective and scary, with Godzilla popping out over the hill. To me, that was the essence of the film. If we could retain that sense of wonder and excitement, and the horror factor, I felt that was what we should shoot for.

We had hired Steve Czerkas to sculpt an initial concept of Godzilla that was much more dinosaur-like. I didn't have a lot of input in that. We worked with that for a while, but then we realized it was more important to pull back a little bit toward the original concept of Godzilla — a little less dinosaur-like — so I redesigned it. But I used dinosaurs as an analog. I wanted to get away from something you could obviously tell was a man in a suit, and deliver a creature that people could either completely believe, or if they doubted it at all, they'd go, "How in the hell did they do that?" I gave him a more dinosaur-like configuration in the legs, to begin with, so it didn't look like there was just a guy in there with human legs. Then I began to develop a muscular structure that was believable. It was based on an Allosaurus, which has arms that actually function, as opposed to those of a T-rex, which are basically useless.

We had thought about [using the man-in-suit method]. I had worked with Tony Gardner (an SFX makeup expert) who had developed these leg extenders that made it possible for a guy wearing them to sort of walk like a dinosaur, with the same sort of leg configurations. It was not out of the question. I was not leaning toward that, but I especially liked anything that we could shoot in real time. With destruction scenes, if there was water and stuff, obviously we would build big miniatures. One of the big problems with miniatures is recreating the natural effects of water, smoke and fire. And I had an idea of how to do miniature water — basically to sculpt and cast miniature water out of resin, then create the illusion of movement with shifting light. So, you have the translucence of the water, and then you have the lights set up so the lights change constantly, undulating the highlights on the water.

Godzilla: King of the Monsters in 3D screenwriter Fred
Dekker, on the set of his film *The Monster Squad* (1987).

I thought, here is this gigantic creature, big as a building, and he's been under the sea for all this time, so I wanted to show close-ups of his skin, showing coral growing on his skin, maybe some lost pirate treasure, crabs. He would be this gigantic living reef. According to the script, he had been dormant for a long time, and that would have allowed things to grow on him.

DEKKER: Steve was very interested in making Godzilla look reptilian, more believable and more realistic. In all of the design work that Bill [Stout] did, he was basically a tyrannosaurus rex. In retrospect, I wouldn't go that way. It didn't look like Godzilla. If you're going to do a Godzilla movie, he'd better look like Godzilla.

Godzilla as an icon . . .

MINER: I've always been a big *Godzilla* fan, but I only like the original one. I think the sequels are all horrible. They have a certain charm, but it stems from the original film. If you've seen the Japanese version, it's really a beautiful movie. It has larger implications to society in general, and how we're the victims of our own reach, unleashing technologies and weapons without knowing really what the consequences are. That's really what it was about, that's what was the beauty of the whole story. When you see the American version with Burr cut in, you can see how badly shot the inserted American footage is.

DEKKER: It's an interesting character, but for me, it was a gig. I was offered the assignment and I was tremendously flattered. It was my first paid [screenwriting] job and I really enjoyed it. [But] I'm not a fan of the character. He's a walking spectacle, and unless there is a humanity, unless there is some kind of emotional hook, it's just special effects.

Making a Godzilla movie in 3-D . . .

STOUT: Nobody had ever done it, and there may be a good reason for that! 3-D was intriguing for us, because it's such an in-your-face special effect. Quite frankly, it's a gimmick, but I think it's a gimmick that the public enjoys, if it's done well. Wouldn't you like to see Godzilla come right out of the screen?

The project's demise . . .

DEKKER: Toward the end, [Miner] talked to me about writing another version that was much cheaper. He said, "You know, maybe our version is too big." And for all I know, I may have fucked it up for Steve by writing this giant movie, whereas if it were a little more manageable he might have gotten it off the ground. But it's a big character and a big story, and it would seem kind of silly to have a movie about three kids who befriend Godzilla. That wouldn't be a Godzilla movie. And what I liked about the script was, it was the movie you would expect it to be and more — as opposed to just fulfilling the most fundamental obligations.

STOUT: It fell through every couple of months, because it was going from studio to studio to studio, and finally Steve ran out of studios. I felt bad for Steve because he had spent a lot of time and money on the project without it bearing fruit. . . . If the film was successful, we were going to do *Rodan* next. Steve was going to let me direct, and he was going to produce. That excited me, because I was a bigger fan of *Rodan* than of *Godzilla*. There was a lot of cool stuff in *Rodan* — volcanoes, these big flying creatures, the eggs. For me, it had a lot more stuff in it.

DEKKER: If Steven Spielberg or Sidney Pollack or Jim Cameron said, "I want to make Godzilla," they'd give it a green light in a minute. Steve had a moderate hit with *Friday the 13th Part 3*, a picture that cost maybe $5 or $6 million. I just think that he

William Stout compares his "new" Godzilla (at left, a badly decaying wire-and-foam-rubber model) to the "old" Godzilla (at right, a Bandai action figure toy).
PHOTO BY RICHARD TRIMARCHI.

just wasn't enough a player at the time, and they weren't willing to put up the money. It was a very ambitious movie and it was eight steps beyond what he had done before.

MINER: Most of the studios were pretty interested. I almost got it made at Warner Bros., but it was too expensive for everybody. I was a bit of a neophyte and didn't understand how the business side worked. If I knew then what I know now, I think I could have gotten it made by partnering and bringing someone in. Eventually, the rights reverted back to Toho, because I couldn't get the American financing, and then they came out with that New World *Godzilla 1985* or whatever, which put a big hold on the whole thing.

GORGO-ZILLA

Today, in the post-Cold War era, Fred Dekker's *Godzilla: King of the Monsters in 3-D* screenplay is pure anachronism. In the classic James Bond tradition, Dekker distills a tug of wills between the two great nuclear powers into two comic-book foes with superhuman intuition and physical abilities. A dissection of the screenplay's politics is moot, but this much is clear: This is a fast-paced, well written script, but it's certainly not a traditional Godzilla movie. As Dekker himself said, the story would function perfectly well even if Godzilla were taken out of it.

Often, Godzilla is a mere accessory to the drama, not the focus of it. It's as if Godzilla were errantly walking through the set of some big-budget spy movie, and the actors barely cast a glance at him. Further weakening the film's dramatic punch are the lack of any real ties to the Japanese Godzilla legend, the introduction of a Baby Godzilla, and the idea that Godzilla has "maternal instincts," causing it to search for its young. Worse yet is Godzilla's new origins — a pseudoscientific mishmash in which Godzilla is said to be a pre-dinosaurian life form, hailing from an era when such creatures had nuclear fission occurring in their bodies (this accounts for Godzilla's atomic breath, which is his fatal weakness, enabling the heroes to kill him by firing missiles down his throat, causing a nuclear implosion). Rather than just stomping everything, with no regard for man, this Godzilla behaves like a wild animal, snapping his jaws and claws at planes and vehicles, and even grabbing telephone wires and swinging them around like a lariat, knocking a fighter plane from the sky. Still, the special effects alone — particularly, the sight of a gigantic reptile laying all-out waste to a major American city — would have been reason enough to see the film. William Stout's redesigned Godzilla, while a far cry from Toho's beast, was more realistic- and animal-looking than anything done previously in Japan. Could stop-motion animation, motion-control model photography and other SFX tricks of the *Star Wars* era pull off a giant-monster movie on this scale? Sadly, we will never know.

Even as Miner struggled to put together his epic version of Godzilla, Toho was resuming its own attempts to bring the monster back. On July 13, 1984, *Variety* reported that "a pair of Godzilla productions in the works will depict the monster as an atrocious, fearsome beast, a truly hair-raising character." The newspaper said that Universal Pictures was "heavily in negotiations" with Miner and Toho, and an agreement was being drawn up in which Toho would distribute Miner's film in Japan and the Far East, while Universal handled the rest of the world. A "formal announcement" was expected within a week, and the production was expected to go before the cameras in late 1984. Although no one knew it at the time, *Variety* was describing one of Miner's last Godzilla-related flirtations with a Hollywood studio. The director had already compromised on several key points: The idea of doing the film in 3-D had been scrapped, and its estimated budget was now down in the $10-$15 million range. As late as October, 1984, *Variety* again reported that Miner's U.S. version of Godzilla was "being talked up but has not yet gone into production."

Meanwhile, Japanese fans were pressuring Toho to bring Godzilla back. A 10,000-member group calling itself the Godzilla Resurrection Committee had gathered more than 40,000 signatures demanding the monster's return. Tanaka revived the *Rebirth of Godzilla* concept, first conceived back in 1977, and was now actively putting together an all-new G-feature that according to news reports would be "strictly for domestic consumption" while Miner's film would play globally. But unlike the Godzilla movies of the 1970s, Toho's new effort would be snatched up rather quickly by a U.S. distributor — a move which cemented the fate of Miner's project once and for all.

GODZILLA VERSUS
. . . CLEVELAND?

In the early 1980s, a struggling young comedian and screenwriter in Hollywood named **Dana Olsen** was trying hard to sell a script he'd been working on for several years. *It Ate Cleveland* was a spoof of horror and sci-fi movies, with the Godzilla series as its main inspiration. In the story, a dinosaur-like beast (which is *not* called Godzilla, or any other name, in the script) is spawned in the depths of Lake Erie by toxic pollution. It rises from the murk and rampages through (you guessed it) Cleveland, wreaking comedic havoc as it takes a crap on the highway, falls in love with a female reporter, battles the military and ultimately retreats back into its cesspool of a home. Along the way, there were numerous sight gags, like obvious wires manipulating the model tanks and planes, and an overhead shot of the monster revealing the bare ass of a stuntman hanging out the open back of the rubber dinosaur suit.

In 1984, Olsen presented his script to **Menahem Golan**, one half (with Yoram Globus) of the infamous Golan-Globus producer duo that made lots of bad movies (and a few good ones, like 1987's *Barfly*) as heads of the now-defunct Cannon Group. But Golan wanted to turn *It Ate Cleveland* into *Godzilla vs. Cleveland*, thinking the name would attract more attention.

"Gene Quintano (director of *Loaded Weapon* and *Honeymoon Vacation*), who was going to direct the film, and I were having dinner with Menahem to discuss the project one evening," Olsen said. "I described it to him as a cross between *Godzilla* and *Ghostbusters*, because that was the hot comedy at the time. And he said, 'you have to use Godzilla in the title.' We tried to explain to him that Godzilla is owned by Toho, and you can't just do that."

With Cannon's backing, Olsen and Quintano made preparations for filming. A studio in the San Fernando Valley was secured for shooting the special-effects sequences, and monster costumes were being made. But then, to Olsen's surprise, Golan published two-page advertisements in the Cannes Film Festival issues of *Variety* and *The Hollywood Reporter* in March 1985, seeking backers for *Godzilla vs. Cleveland*. The ad showed a goofy caricature of the Big G stomping through town, wearing a big pair of Converse hi-top sneakers, with the caption, "He's a Man Eater and a Lady Killer."

"We thought, this is it. We've had it. And, sure enough, Toho's lawyers came knocking, practically the very next day," Olsen says. Olsen isn't sure if Cannon paid any damages to Toho, but the two parties reached some sort of out-of-court agreement. "In short, it made it impossible to make the film. We would have needed their approval every step of the way," he says.

Olsen continued trying to resell the *It Ate Cleveland* script for a few years, without success. He went on to more successful projects, and his screenwriting credits now include *The 'Burbs, Memoirs of an Invisible Man*, and *George of the Jungle*.

A revised teaser poster for *It Ate Cleveland*, formerly known as *Godzilla vs. Cleveland*. The original poster showed a monster that was decidedly more Godzilla-like before Toho threatened the producers with legal action. Dana Olsen and The Cannon Group used this version to try and generate new interest in the film, but they never got far. Interestingly, a similar fate befell a film called *Star Godzilla* several years earlier. In the May 7, 1980 issue of *Variety*, a poster with cartoon-like renditions of Godzilla, Angilas, and King Kong announced the film as an upcoming release from First Distributors Ltd. of Hong Kong, with the tag line, "Where the old world and the new world meet — STAR GODZILLA." The movie was apparently never made, probably due to legal pressures from Toho, and no one seems to know exactly whether it was supposed to be a straight monster movie, a parody, or something else altogether.

FROM THE PERSONAL COLLECTION OF DANA OLSEN. USED BY PERMISSION

BEGIN THE BAGAN

The Return of Godzilla by Akira Murao (circa 1980)

Having allowed his anti-nuclear monster to become a humanized kiddy hero, producer Tomoyuki Tanaka sought to correct this fatal mistake and bring Godzilla back as a no-nonsense atomic monster. In 1980, Tanaka commissioned a new story from writer Akira Murao, who eventually turned in a 47-page treatment called *The Return of Godzilla*. To gain support for the project from the Toho studio brass, Tanaka wrote an introduction to Murao's story, in which he explained his rationale for bringing back the King of the Monsters. "Godzilla is a world famous character, on a par in terms of notoriety with *Superman* and *Star Wars*," Tanaka wrote. "Unfortunately, we had to close down the Godzilla film series once, because ideas had become so weak and the costs were too much. Despite this . . . Godzilla is loved by several generations, so I think it is a good idea to bring him back for a new film to celebrate Toho's 50th Anniversary . . . Since we had a problem in making Godzilla just for younger ages, we now think that Godzilla must be for a general audience, both older and younger people. By introducing more new super weapons and using the fear of nuclear power as a basic theme, we can broaden the audience."

The Return of Godzilla was curiously based on the premise that Godzilla himself was not sufficient to carry the story. As a result, the enemy monster Bagan — a name which would continue to resurface in several story proposals through the 1980s and '90s — was created to challenge Godzilla. In Bagan, Murao actually created three enemies (and a lot of the costs with which Tanaka was so concerned); the monster was a shape-shifter that adopted unique visages on land, in the water, and in the sky. Unable to wean Godzilla completely from his 1970s personality (again in curious contrast to Tanaka's introduction), Murao wrote the first act to have Godzilla rid the planet of Bagan

before getting down to the real business of providing mankind with a nuclear-fueled nemesis. Murao introduced a bevy of super weaponry, but it is Bagan rather than Godzilla that is attacked (ineffectively, of course). Godzilla's battles with Bagan are mostly one-sided, with Godzilla inflicting damage time after time, and Bagan regenerating itself by assuming a new form. Only after Godzilla renews his strength by destroying a nuclear power plant and absorbing its full radioactive output does he defeat Bagan.

After the monster-vs.-monster portion of the scenario concludes, the next act becomes a none-too-subtle rehashing of the original *Godzilla*. A scientist has discovered a new element called "Reiconium," which possesses super nuclear energy. Far more powerful than conventional nuclear energy, its potential as a weapon is so enormous that the scientist refuses to allow it to be used against Godzilla. Only after witnessing Godzilla's aftermath, and with furtive pleas from his daughter, does the man finally relent, only to sacrifice himself to detonate the device which defeats Godzilla. Radiation seems omnipresent in the story: covert nuclear-waste-dumping in the ocean revives Godzilla and brings him to Japan; the monster feeds on radiation in power plants; radiation is used as bait to lure Godzilla to his demise; and the beast is seemingly defeated by a super nuclear-energy weapon.

The message of the original *Godzilla* about the evils of the nuclear age is replaced by a new and more contemporary theme, summed up in the final line of the story after Godzilla's lifeless body washes ashore near a nuclear power plant months later, and suddenly revives: "As long as nuclear energy exists on Earth, Godzilla will live." In other words, whatever its purpose, nuclear energy will always present a catastrophic danger.

— *Jay Ghee*

GODZILLA: KING OF THE MONSTERS IN 3-D

Synopsis

A falling meteorite crashes into an orbiting U.S. "Star Wars"-type defense satellite, accidentally launching a cruise missile with a live warhead toward Earth. The missile lands in the South Pacific, and its detonation stirs a long-dormant reptilian creature on the ocean floor.

A Japanese fishing trawler mysteriously disappears en route to San Francisco. The badly burned and damaged boat is found and towed to port for examination, and is kept under heavy guard by the authorities. Dana Martin, a snoopy, 22-year-old female reporter for the San Francisco *Chronicle*, sneaks aboard the vessel and finds a perfectly preserved prehistoric trilobite, but she is startled by a mutilated, dying Japanese fisherman who lurches out of the shadows, moaning, "Gojira, Gojira." Martin takes the trilobite to Gerald Balinger, a paleobiologist and dinosaur expert, who is at first skeptical of its authenticity. Meanwhile, on faraway Oto Island in Tahiti, American Special Forces troops witness the destruction of a native village by a huge creature (still not revealed onscreen) that flattens thatch huts and breathes sheets of fire.

Off the coast of Mexico, Navy Colonel Peter Daxton, a military super-agent, leads the investigation of a sunken Russian nuclear submarine. Unknown to Daxton, he is being watched from a nearby boat by his arch-rival, Russian secret agent Boris Kruschov (who suffered a trademark maiming in a fight with Daxton years ago, and now has a fiendish, retractable steel blade where one hand should be). The Russians want two top-secret nuclear missiles that sank with the sub, but Daxton recovers them and takes them back to the U.S., where they are held by the military pending nego-

tiations between the two countries and the United Nations. Also recovered from the sub is a videotape, recorded by external cameras, showing how the ship sank: it was attacked by a reptilian monster.

Daxton returns home to San Francisco and his young son Kevin (who is fond of lizards and is a wiz at Houdini-esque escape tricks — plot devices that figure prominently later). But as soon as he arrives home, G-men summon Daxton to yet another mission. Daxton, little Kevin and the scientist Balinger are taken to Baja, Mexico, where a dead reptile "roughly the size of a house" has washed ashore. This is the creature that attacked the Russian sub; it was killed when the crew fired missiles, desperately trying to save themselves. Balinger deduces it is a dinosaur, but the military brass and scientists pooh-pooh his theories, insisting the creature is from another planet and ordering the incident be swept under the rug. As the military prepares to ship the giant carcass to the Presidio, a depressed Balinger tells Kevin the story of a Japanese mythical dragon called Godzilla. Little Kevin, a geeky misfit, begins to empathize with the huge, dead creature, which seems lost in time. Meanwhile, off the California coast, another giant monster, this one several hundred feet tall, surfaces and destroys an oil derrick and a tanker.

The dead Baby Godzilla is stored in a huge warehouse at the Embarcadero pierfront for study. Balinger becomes alarmed when the researchers begin fainting from radiation sickness; he theorizes that the monster is a living atomic reactor, with regenerative properties predating the dinosaurs. And, since the sea disasters have continued even after the Baby Godzilla's death, Balinger believes another, larger creature is heading for the city by the Bay, but the military again scoffs at his ideas.

As Godzilla nears San Francisco Bay, Kruschov kidnaps Kevin and demands Daxton return the missiles as ransom. Using his Houdini tricks, Kevin escapes his captors' hideaway beneath the Golden Gate Bridge, but just then, Godzilla rises in the bay and, with a swipe of his tail, appears to kill the boy and Kruschov. Godzilla toys with cars on the bridge, causing a gigantic traffic jam and sending the entire city into panic. The military dispatches tanks and begins bombarding the beast heavily, which only angers him. Godzilla smashes the massive bridge with his fists and lumbers ashore, trampling Ghirardelli Square and heading for the heart of the city. Blackhawk Cobra helicopters and F-16 fighters are summoned to attack the monster, while Daxton and Balinger plan to lure Godzilla out of the city and kill him with the two Russian missiles. The city is reduced to rubble as the jets confront Godzilla at Union Square; during the skirmish, the monster swings a cable car through the air like a mace, batting a fighter plane out of the sky and sending it hurtling into the *Chronicle* newspaper building. On Market Street, a wino drinking from a paper bag laughs hysterically as Godzilla crushes him like a bug.

Dana and Balinger head for Alcatraz Island, where they plan to blast a recording of the Baby Godzilla's roar (taken from the Russian sub's videotape) over the PA speakers and lure Godzilla out to sea, where it can be nuked. Daxton readies the two Russian missiles onto a helicopter, but before he can take off, Kruschov appears, demanding the missiles be returned. Kevin is alive too, but before Daxton can rejoice, he and his nemesis are locked in a slugging match aboard the whirlybird as it flies over the city. Soon, Daxton is hanging out of the copter and about to be slashed by the Russian's blade-hand, but Daxton somehow knocks Kruschov out of the helicopter. The Russian agent lands in Godzilla's palm and, in the first on-screen display of the monster's nuclear breath, is incinerated. Then, Daxton's helicopter spirals out of control and goes down.

Godzilla goes on an awesome rampage of destruction, melting tanks with its ray and tearing the roofs off buildings, as if searching for something. Finally, it arrives at the warehouse where the Baby Godzilla is stored and, realizing that its offspring is dead, emits a fearsome roar. At that moment, Dana and Balinger turn on the decoy recording at Alcatraz, and the heartbroken monster begins heading out to the bay. Daxton, having survived the helicopter wreck, drags one of the Russian nuclear missiles back to the command post and loads it onto the Scorpion-78, a military battle-copter prototype.

Daxton's co-pilot falls out of the chopper as it takes off, and it is little Kevin who must save the city by dealing the monster's death knell while his father pilots the helicopter. Daxton nears Godzilla, and as the monster opens wide to roar, Kevin says, "I'm sorry," and fires the missile down the beast's throat. Godzilla drops to his knees, then collapses in mortal pain. Kevin falls out the side of the banking helicopter, but Godzilla catches the boy in his giant claw and saves him. Kevin weeps as the majestic monster takes its final breath.

RESURRECTION:

The Making of GODZILLA (1984)

"Personally, I prefer Godzilla to have a mean streak."

— *Producer Tomoyuki Tanaka, in the* Detroit Free-Press, *December 19, 1984*

Tokyo, 1984: The Big Brother of George Orwell's nightmare novel is nowhere in sight, but after 30 years, Japan is once again visited upon by the Big Other. Tomoyuki Tanaka's unflagging, nine-year-long effort to bring his monster-child back to celluloid life finally came to fruition in *Godzilla*, a movie which, despite its title, is not a remake of the 1954 original but a direct sequel to it. In a stroke of brilliance, Tanaka erased all 14 previous series entries, from *Godzilla Raids Again* to *Terror of MechaGodzilla*, from the Godzilla timeline, creating a new continuity wherein the monster somehow survived his apparent death in Tokyo Bay and now reappears, jarred awake by a volcanic eruption. This revisionist mytho-history allowed Tanaka to avoid addressing the monster's illogical villain-to-hero transformation and his increasingly anthropomorphized behavior in the 1960s and '70s. As far as this movie is concerned, stuff like *Godzilla vs. Megalon* was pure fantasy; *this* Godzilla is the real thing, and he's back to kick ass. Based on an original story idea conceived by Tanaka himself, *Godzilla* (1984) faithfully attempted to return Godzilla to his origins at the flashpoint of a mushroom cloud, with the monster serving as the catalyst for a threatened U.S.-Soviet nuclear conflict that could unleash World War III. "We wanted to show how easily an (atomic) incident could occur today," Tanaka told *People* (January 14, 1985). "But vivid images of nuclear war are taboo. Godzilla, on the other hand, can bring the message to light and still be entertaining." The full potential of this high concept was unfortunately not attained in the finished film, but it formed the basis for an entirely new series that would re-launch Godzilla's career at the dawn of the next decade.

As further evidence that Toho intended to makes its own new Godzilla movie, whether Steve Miner's American-made version panned out or not, pre-production work on *Godzilla* began in late 1983, when screenwriter **Shuichi Nagahara**, whose previous credits included co-writing the aforementioned dud, *The War in Space*, was chosen to flesh out Tanaka's concept into a full script. The resulting screenplay borrowed Godzilla's attack on a nuclear power plant from Akira Murao's aborted *The Return of Godzilla* story (1980), and stole numerous ideas from *Godzilla: King of the Monsters in 3-D* — even while Miner was still shopping that script around in Hollywood! These include: the Cold War scenario and heightened superpower tensions; the accidental launch of a nuclear missile from an orbiting satellite; the use of a secret flying military weapon that fires antinuclear missiles into Godzilla's mouth, poisoning the monster; Godzilla's attack on a Soviet nuclear submarine; and even Godzilla stepping on a wino for comic effect.

Why does Godzilla suddenly reappear? The monster's return is a warning against the proliferation of nuclear weapons and energy, a point hammered home by his immediate attack on a Russian nuclear submarine and subsequent feasting on a power-plant reactor core. Nagahara's screenplay is certainly ambitious, and Tanaka's decision to abandon the monster-versus-monster motif for a Godzilla-versus-mankind showdown is an opportunity to revisit the terror missing from these movies since the late 1950s. Ultimately, however, the script lacks both the commitment to develop what good ideas it contains and the pathos to create a true horror-drama. Despite occasional flourishes of wanton destruction, Godzilla fails to unleash the full-blown instinctual rage that once motivated him, therefore never inspiring a sense of true awe. No one seems to question how or why Godzilla, long suspected dead, has been resurrected, and other than Professor Hayashida, who compares Godzilla to a living nuclear reactor, the human characters aren't much

**Producer Tomoyuki Tanaka clowns around with three of his
closest friends, on the occasion of the opening of *Godzilla* (1984).**
PHOTO BY GREG DAVIS, © PEOPLE WEEKLY

interested in what makes him tick. Also undermining Godzilla's on-screen power is the subplot about his "homing instinct," which is revealed just half way through the picture to give the heroes an all-too-easy, unimaginative solution to their titanic problem and — even worse — reveals the film's ending far in advance. A dim-witted Godzilla, displaying none of the cunning or fighting spirit that the monster is known for, is lured into the mouth of the volcano without the slightest protest. Hardly terrifying, he's just a monster-sized chump.

As for the human drama, it's almost nonexistent, save for the prime minister's engaging struggle to do what is right for Japan and for world peace. Trapped among the U.S., the Soviets and Godzilla,

the prime minister must first diffuse a global political crisis, then decide how best to defend his country from annihilation — first by Godzilla, then by an unintentional nuclear strike — all the while maintaining Japan's anti-nuke moral high ground. The other characters spend more time on screen, but are far less compelling. Professor Hayashida's parents were killed in Godzilla's 1954 rampage, yet although the scientist once sought revenge he is now content to study the monster. This Dr. Yamane-like premise would work if given a counterpoint — for example, a government official or other character bent on killing Godzilla — but the government quickly signs off on Hayashida's volcano-burial plan. Okumura, the young sailor, initially swears retribution for the death of his fellow seamen (this would make better sense if Godzilla had actually destroyed the fishing boat *Yahata Maru*; all the crewmen, however, were killed by Godzilla's insect parasites), but quickly aids in Hayashida's bird-brained plan, without a single objection. How much more interesting it would have been had he tried to sabotage the plan, or to kill the monster single-handedly. Goro Maki, the main character, is introduced as a cold-hearted, story-motivated reporter, but he has absolutely no role in propelling the plot toward its ultimate resolution. His true purpose is to redeem his unscrupulous self amid Tokyo's flaming ruins, while becoming a hero and providing a love-interest for Naoko, who looks about half his age, and whose role in the drama is equally marginal. The main problem with the picture is that no one is passionate about much of anything — not even Godzilla, who seems bored clambering through Tokyo, as if following some city-smashing textbook diagram. Finally, there is the Super-X flying tank, another good idea poorly integrated into the story. There is no suspense or dramatic buildup surrounding the Super-X — a government official suddenly announces the weapon's existence mid-way through the film — and there is no character (a pilot, etc.) identified with it. When Godzilla destroys Super-X, no one cares.

The filming of *Godzilla* began in late July, 1984. There were rumors that Ishiro Honda declined a request from Tomoyuki Tanaka to direct the movie, although this is unconfirmed. The job was instead given to **Koji Hashimoto**, who began his career with Toho in the late 1960s and worked as an assistant director on more than 70 films including Akira Kurosawa's *Dodes'ka-den* (1970), and under several top directors, including Hiroshi Inagaki and Toshio Masuda (working on the latter's *The Last Days of Planet Earth*). More importantly, Hashimoto had worked as an AD under Ishiro Honda on several monster movies, and he was now being groomed as Toho's next great science-fiction director.[33] Hashimoto had just finished work on *Sayonara Jupiter* (released December 1983), an adaptation of a 1960s novel by popular Japanese sci-fi writer Sakyo Komatsu (who also wrote the story upon which Toho's *Tidal Wave* was based). *Sayonara Jupiter* was Toho's most expensive special-effects picture to date, a 140-minute-long yarn about space colonization that featured lavish sets, elaborate miniatures and effects work that entailed motion-control photography, and composite work rivaling then-current Hollywood standards. The fact that Toho entrusted *Sayonara Jupiter* to Hashimoto, a first-time director, can be interpreted in one of two ways: Either Hashimoto was believed to be the second coming of Ishiro Honda, or he was a competent director who would toe the line of Toho's front office brass. Watching *Jupiter*, it appears the latter was true. The film is padded with long and uncompelling sequences that do little but show off the sets and the special effects, making the movie lethargic and often boring. If Hashimoto left any directorial stamp on his first film, it was his inability to strike a balance between effective storytelling and visual scope. He displayed the same shortcomings in *Godzilla*, although to a lesser degree.

Perhaps the problem is Hashimoto's interpretation of Godzilla himself. On the one hand, the director professed a very Honda-esque vision for the film. "The antinuclear weapons movement is on the rise all over the world, and I personally think Japan should get involved more," Hashimoto told an interviewer in *Toho SF Special Effects Movie Series Vol. 1*. "America and Russia, their attitude is more nuclear weapons, more peace. . . . I didn't want my movie to end up just being entertaining, but to throw some questions at people and make them think about the nuclear problem." On the other hand, Hashimoto's view of the monster is more sympathetic than his predecessor's. "I wanted viewers to feel sorry for Godzilla, and I think I succeeded," he said later in the interview. "The existence of Godzilla itself is a dilemma. Godzilla is a living conflict of evil and sadness." Honda's Godzilla was a doomsday creature, but Hashimoto's is a pitiable beast that merely strayed out of his undersea dominion. Mankind's challenge is not to destroy the monster and save itself, but merely to send the poor creature away so he'll stop bumping into the real estate.

Another distinction between this picture and the classic Honda-Tsuburaya SFX entries is the lack of distinctive visual and dramatic styles. Even when working with subpar material (as in *Terror of Mecha-Godzilla*) or with less than A-list crews and casts, Honda had a way of dazzling the eyes and getting memorable performances from his actors. Hashimoto's choices of sets and locations, his staging of the human action (such as it is — most of the time, everyone is sitting and talking), and his framing of the actors are mostly nondescript, and some shots seem claustrophobically tailored to the dimensions of a TV screen rather than a feature film.

The actors in this film are difficult to evaluate because their characters are sketchy. The most memorable performances are given by Toho veterans

Keiju Kobayashi as Prime Minister Mitamura and Yosuke Natsuki as Professor Hayashida. Kobayashi, a popular Japanese character actor since the 1950s, with over 200 films to his credit (including Toho's *The Three Treasures* and *Tidal Wave*) is convincing as the stoic, introspective head of state who stands firm in the face of disaster. Natsuki, known for his roles in Honda's *Ghidrah: The Three-Headed Monster* and *Dagora: The Space Monster*, makes the best of a part that seems to have been under-written. Tomoyuki Tanaka had originally wanted Akihiko Hirata to play Hayashida, but the veteran actor was too ill to take the part and he died just before filming began. "We really wanted Mr. Hirata to be in the movie, even in just one scene as a scholar — an easy scene — but he passed on. It was really too bad," said Hashimoto. Two popular comic actors, Kohji Ishizaka and Tetsuya Takeda, make cameos in the film as a power-plant worker and a scavenging wino, respectively, both of whom are stomped to death by Godzilla.

THE PRICE OF PROGRESS: *Godzilla* (1984) surpassed *Sayonara Jupiter* to become Toho's most expensive genre production to date, due to unprecedented expenses for miniature construction and the creation of a "first" in Godzilla SFX history: The Godzilla Cybot, a 16-foot-high, cable-controlled robo-zilla designed to perform a wide range of facial expressions and upper-body movements not possible with traditional *suitmation* and puppetry. Perhaps inspired by the 40-foot prosthetic ape and the huge mechanical arms that attracted much publicity to Dino De Laurentiis' *King Kong* remake nearly a decade earlier, Toho spent a reported $475,000 to build the Cybot, which contained 3,000 computer-controlled mechanical parts, weighed 1.2 tons and was operated by hydraulic pressure. At a July 1984 press conference, Toho hyped the Cybot heavily and generated advance interest in the new Godzilla movie, calling it a huge advancement for the series and claiming that the majority of Godzilla's scenes would utilize the robotic prop. This caused some reporters (particularly in the West) to mistakenly marvel, as the Associated Press did, at this "technological *tour de force*, rolling its eyes, baring its fangs and belching flames" when in fact the Cybot was only employed for close-ups of Godzilla's head — the majority of monster scenes were still accomplished with the traditional man-in-suit techniques.

Composed of a mechanical skeletal structure covered by a urethane rubber skin, the Cybot had moveable eyes, a mouth capable of opening and shutting, moving lips, a head that tilted upward and side-to-side, and arms capable of limited movement; although built in "full size," the monster was cut in half and the upper body placed among miniature sets for filming. Although capable of more animated expressions than any Godzilla suit, the Cybot betrays a "muppet"-like appearance from certain angles — not a very threatening image — and its design doesn't match the Godzilla suits used in the film, making for some awkward back-and-forth cuts. Although it rears its head and snarls and roars mightily, the robot wobbles a bit at times, making it look fragile; as a result, the Cybot was used sparingly. Still, the prop was a valuable publicity tool. In the months leading up to *Godzilla*'s release, Toho put the Cybot on display in Osaka, Tokyo, and elsewhere; in the years since, it has been dusted off for periodic public appearances.

Regardless of the Cybot's shortcomings, Godzilla looks better in this film than he has since 1964's *Godzilla vs. The Thing*. The 1984 costume is an original design that evokes features of two previously popular Godzillas: the thick-browed, menacing face of the 1964 (*Mosu-Goji*) suit and the familiar look of the 1968 (*Soshingeki-Goji*) suit; also, this was the first suit since the 1955 (*Gyakushu-Goji*) model to have ears and to have four toes — not three — on each foot. The suit has three rows of jagged dorsal fins along the spine — the most well-executed fins on any Godzilla costume to date — and a long, well-articulated tail. When viewed in profile, this Godzilla is truly awesome; when seen from a frontal perspective, however, the face has a stunted muzzle and ping-pong ball eyes that are decidedly less threatening. As detailed in the book *The Making of Godzilla 1985*, and in an extensive article in *Japanese Giants #7*, Toho's costume-making process for *Godzilla*, under the direction of long-time suit builder **Noboyuki Yasumaru**, was more elaborate and detail-oriented than on previous films. Just as Teizo Toshimitsu began the first Godzilla suit 30 years earlier, Yasumaru started by building a one-meter clay model, taking design suggestions from SFX director Teruyoshi Nakano, producer Tomoyuki Tanaka, and others. When the final design was approved, Yasumaru sketched the figure of the monster actor, viewed from front and profile angles, on a wooden panel for sizing purposes. Yasumaru then built a statue (constructed of a wire-and-wood frame covered with plaster) standing two meters —

the costume's height — from which body-part molds were cast. Each part of the body was then cast separately in urethane foam, the costume was assembled from these individual parts, with a tail cast in a large, solid foam piece, rather than in a series of consecutive pieces as before. Work on suit construction began in February and took two months.

Unlike previous Toho efforts, wherein separate phases of the suit-building process were handled by different craftsmen with different skills, Yasumaru supervised the entire project. The result was a costume that is one of Toho's most visually striking, but one that was very demanding on the actor inside. "[The suit] was constructed from the outside in, and weighed about 110 kilograms," **Kenpachiro Satsuma** said in an interview published in *Markalite #1*. Satsuma, formerly known as Kengo Nakayama, was no stranger to acting in cumbersome monster costumes — as noted in Chapter 11, he was Hedorah in *Godzilla vs. The Smog Monster*, and Gigan in *Godzilla on Monster Island* and *Godzilla vs. Megalon*, two costumes also

The 13-foot-tall, 1.2-ton Godzilla cybot on display at a department store opening in the Ginza district of Tokyo, on October 8, 1984. Although this real-life "MechaGodzilla" hardly appeared in the film, it has become handy as a publicity attraction for Toho.

PHOTO BY SADAYUKI MIKAMI, AP /WIDE WORLD PHOTOS

designed by Yasumaru. "[Yasumaru] only wanted to make a monster. He doesn't build it based on concern for the person who will get inside of it," said Satsuma. "So, he collides with people like me . . . For instance, we argue about various aspects, such as, 'Because this part presses against my body, it's difficult to move,' or, 'It's hard to raise the elbow.' Then he replies, 'I made it so, because if it raises at the elbow, he becomes a human being.'"

In addition to the Cybot and the suit, Godzilla was brought to life in this film with several props, some of which involved effects never before attempted by Toho. A full-size (1/1 scale) foot, measuring 15 meters from front to back, was built for high-impact scenes of Godzilla crushing cars and slamming into the pavement. This huge prop was operated by a crane and filmed on an open set, with actors Ken Tanaka and Yasuko Sawaguchi fleeing in the foreground in an eerie, flaming, red-hued sequence during Godzilla's rampage. While it moves stiffly, the foot prop provides more interesting and more convincing ways of demonstrating Godzilla's immense size compared to traditional composite shots. Another foot prop, this one constructed in 1/20 scale, appears in several close-ups, smashing miniature buildings constructed to the same scale. Both foot props are far more effective than several close-ups of the costume's feet colliding with the pavement and stomping the Shinkansen train: The rubbery toes are wobbly, and when Godzilla is crushing the railway he seems awkward and off-balance.

SFX director Nakano, finally afforded a budget comparable to those of the Tsuburaya years, makes the most of it. There are several outstanding views of Godzilla in this movie that surpass anything done before. The monster's first appearance at the nuclear power plant is a triumph, a fine showing of special effects, cinematography, music, and sound effects, all working together seamlessly. It begins with a flock of birds, disturbed by something approaching, fluttering out of the brush. Then, through the clouds a monster's-eye view of the power plant emerges, and Godzilla's growling voice is heard against an eerie musical backdrop, while gargantuan footsteps — BOOM! BOOM! — echo in the distance. A night watchman emerges to see what's going on, and suddenly the ground splits open in front of him! Here, for the first time, is Godzilla, in all his outsize glory. The rest of the scene is very effective, with Godzilla approaching the heart of the reactor as blue-screened extras flee in the foreground. Godzilla rips out the reactor core (a fine miniature) and absorbs radiation until his feathered friends lead him away. As Godzilla exits, his tail flicking in his wake, a foreboding piano melody tingles with dissonance. Pure monster poetry.

Godzilla's confrontation with the military in Tokyo Bay is also stunning. As a helicopter surveys the water's surface, Godzilla suddenly bolts out of the drink, startling the pilot! Nakano illustrates Godzilla's size by showing the monster from several new points of view (here, through the cockpit windows of the helicopter and the fighter jets), making the otherwise routine man-vs.-monster action more interesting. After withstanding the assault of the military might assembled before him — tanks, rocket launchers — Godzilla's fins crackle with light (the only time in the film this effect is used) and he unleashes a mighty, long-sustaining stream of radiation breath wiping out the entire weapons fleet. However, Godzilla doesn't use his breath weapon very much in this movie, and when he does, the optical animation isn't nearly as well-done as in Tsuburaya pictures like Godzilla vs. The Thing, despite the advancement of SFX technology in the preceding 20 years. Godzilla's protracted battle with the Super X, interrupted briefly when Godzilla is TKO'd by the cadmium bombs, is the most suspenseful sequence in the entire movie, a fierce struggle in which Nature finally prevails over man's mighty machine. Only the ending of the battle, wherein Godzilla comically knocks over a skyscraper (which lands with a dull "thud") on top of Super X, is unsatisfying.

According to an October 24, 1984 report in Variety, the budget for miniature work on Godzilla went out of control, pushing the cost of the entire movie up from $5 million to $6.25 million, an increase of 25 percent. The miniatures of Tokyo's Ginza shopping district and Shinjuku skyscraper district took eight months to design and build, the newspaper reported, and involved the work of 160 employees. Despite the greater expense, the miniature work in Godzilla has less detail, and therefore less realism, than Toho's early sci-fi efforts. This is due to a decision, attributed to Tomoyuki Tanaka, to increase Godzilla's height from 50 meters to 80 meters (264 feet, about 99 feet taller than before) so that the monster would not be dwarfed by Tokyo's skyline, which had grown since 1954 to heights rivaling the Sears Tower. Obviously, the size of the Godzilla costume cannot change; to make Godzilla appear larger, the miniatures were downsized to 1/40 scale. "If this had been 30 years ago, [1/25 scale] would have been fine," said director Hashimoto. "The buildings in Ginza were about 30 meters high back then, about seven or eight stories. But nowadays, [1/25 scale] isn't tall enough. . . . We wanted to make Godzilla appear bigger, more powerful, with more scale." Tokyo's modern skyline is so tall that even this new, bigger Godzilla seems small by comparison. The enlarged size of the model buildings also made it difficult to create a sense of depth-of-field. Thus, the miniature photography has a flat quality to it, detracting from the illusion. Moreso than the buildings, the drop to 1/40 scale really hurts the miniature tanks, maser cannons and trains, which are smaller than ever before. The miniature model of the Super-X is worst of all, although this is due more to is oversimplified design than to its size.

Teruyoshi Nakano shot more than 700,000 feet of special effects footage for *Godzilla* equal to roughly 13 hours of viewing time.[34] Knowing that, it's hard to imagine why he resorted, as he always does, to the use of stock footage. Thankfully, there are no mismatched shots of Godzilla from *Terror of MechaGodzilla*, or other films, to jar the eye; but there are a few destruction shots pulled from the 1970s Toho disaster movies *Tidal Wave* and *The Last Days of Planet Earth*, the most annoying of which occurs when Godzilla blasts a helicopter from the sky and the debris hits the ground, igniting a chain-reaction explosion as a row of cars goes up in huge flames. The latter half of this sequence is grainy and the miniature work is of obviously poorer quality. Other stock shots include explosions, building debris falling on a crowd, and the destruction of a highway ramp

Last but not least, *Godzilla* is a feast for the ears. The sound effects, including Godzilla's roar (which is returned to the primeval, low-pitched growl of the 1954 original) and footsteps, are loud and thundering. Although Akira Ifukube passed on Tomoyuki Tanaka's request to score the film, the music soundtrack is at times marvelous, if uneven. Reijiro Koroku (b. 1949), a longtime composer of television themes and pop songs, delivers a Western-style score somewhat reminiscent of John Williams' work. By far the best cut is the Godzilla's theme, an ominous, rumbling piece played by a full orchestra accented with low-end brass. There are several renditions of this theme, played at varying tempos with different instrumentation.

Critical reaction to Godzilla's return to the screen was lukewarm. Box office returns were less than expected, but according to some reports, Toho raked in a whopping $33 million in merchandising

tie-in revenues after the film's release. While this financial windfall virtually guaranteed that a sequel would be forthcoming, two men instrumental in *Godzilla* (1984) would not be back. This was Teruyoshi Nakano's last Godzilla movie, although he would work on two more films, the fantasy *Princess of the Moon* and the independently produced disaster film *Tokyo Blackout* (both 1987). This was only Koji Hashimoto's second film as a director, but it was his last: He entered Toho's front offices and became a producer.

"SAYONARA, SUCKER!"
The Americanization: GODZILLA 1985

If Toho really intended *Godzilla* (1984) as a movie strictly for domestic audiences, it quickly changed its mind once the film was released to Japanese theaters. The movie didn't exactly knock 'em dead at the box office, earning a reported gross of roughly $6.8 million (reported in *Variety*, May 7, 1985), which afforded Toho a slim profit margin but was far less than the $12 million the company had hoped for. An overseas release would recoup some of the cash that Toho failed to reap in domestic ticket sales. Meanwhile, the time seemed right for a new Godzilla film to play in American theaters, as the 30th anniversary of the U.S. debut of *Godzilla: King of the Monsters!* was fast approaching.

Almost immediately after *Godzilla*'s domestic release, Toho began shopping the picture around in Hollywood. In early 1985 the trade papers reported that Toho was asking several million dollars for the North American distribution rights, and that discussions had taken place with MGM/United Artists and other studios. At one point, a Toho spokesman complained that the best offer ponied up (by an unnamed Hollywood studio) was in the $2 million range. It's doubtful that he was telling the truth, for the bidding war, such as it was, didn't last long, and Toho wound up getting far less money. By May, the new Godzilla movie had been passed over by the majors and fallen instead into the hands of New World Pictures, the modern-day equivalent of the kind of low-budget, exploitation movie producers and distributors that gobbled up Godzilla movies

The incredible shrinking *kaiju*? The suit from *Godzilla* (1984) presses the flesh at Rockefeller Center to promote the release of the U.S. version, *Godzilla 1985*.
PHOTO BY MARTY LEDERHANDLER, AP /WIDE WORLD PHOTOS

during the 1960s and '70s, such as American International, Continental, and UPA. New World was founded by cheesy-movie impresario Roger Corman, who produced classics with titles like *Piranha*, *Big Bad Mama*, and *I Escaped from Devil's Island*. Corman sold the company in 1983 to two lawyers, Harry Sloan and Lawrence Kuppin, who tried to improve New World's image, proclaiming their company "the rising star in Hollywood," moving away from exploitation films and increasing production budgets to the $4 million to $7 million range (Corman typically spent $1 million or so). Sloan and Kuppin's expenses for the new Godzilla movie were more Corman-esque, however. They paid Toho a measly $500,000 for the rights, then spent roughly $200,000 more to film new English-language insert scenes, plus $2.5 million for advertising and promotion and to strike theatrical prints. In July 1985, New World issued promotional materials announcing that the film would be released as *The Return of Godzilla*, its international title.

Anthony Randel, a postproduction director who had been with New World since the Roger Corman years, was elevated to the position of producer and put in charge of revamping the movie for U.S. audiences. Randel, who now goes by "Tony Randel" and has since directed *Hellraiser II*, *Children of the Night*, and other pictures, said the company believed from the start that the best way to sell the picture to Americans was to stress its inherent campiness. "Because this was going to be dubbed from Japanese, there's no way it wasn't going to be funny," Randel said. "There was so much goofy stuff in it that we had to take a lighter approach, otherwise it wouldn't work." New World's plan, Randel said, was to dub the Japanese footage into English in a straightforward manner, and splice in newly filmed "linking scenes" with American actors; the inserted footage would provide the comic relief to the otherwise dead-serious monster drama. Working with film editor Michael Spence, Randel studied the film to determine where the new scenes could be interjected, and he hired two screenwriters — Lisa Tomei, who wrote the script to be used for dubbing the Japanese footage, and Strom Weisman, who wrote the new American scenes. He chose a longtime colleague, film editor **Robert "R.J." Kizer**, to direct the new material, and eventually decided to rename the picture *Godzilla 1985*, inspired by the Boris Karloff film *Frankenstein 1970*, a childhood favorite of Randel's.

"At first, it was all very tongue-in-cheek," Kizer said. "The thinking was that we'd get someone like Leslie Nielsen to be the 'star,' so to speak. There was all this silly dialogue, and it was very ambitious. We were going to have a sequence of a general arriving in a helicopter, landing on a heliport. We were trying to track down stock footage from the Air Force of B-52 planes being scrambled and fighter pilots reacting to a scramble horn and hopping in their jets, missiles being readied, all sorts of stuff. But all of that went by the wayside because of lack of time and money. We had a contact at the Department of Defense who was trying to push it through for us, but military channels take forever to push these things through. We were doing this in July, for a picture to be released at the end of August."

When New World began looking for the film's leading man it was not Nielsen but Lorne Greene whose name was suggested. But Randel had a better idea. "The head of marketing remembered that Roger Corman had released a Japanese movie called *Tidal Wave* a few years back and had added some new scenes with Lorne Greene to make the movie more marketable. So he said to me, 'Why don't you get Lorne Greene?' And I thought, if we're going to do that we should try to get Raymond Burr, because the same thing had been done with him in the first Godzilla movie. I don't think anyone at New World even realized that Raymond Burr had been in the original. Luckily, we contacted him and he was enthusiastic about doing it."

But as soon as Burr came aboard, his representatives were quick to tell New World that for the actor, Godzilla was no laughing matter. Burr took "very seriously" the idea that Godzilla was an anti-nuclear allegory; thus, the filmmakers revamped the script to make sure Burr's lines were played straight. Then, when character actor Warren Kemmerling was hired to play the general, New World was informed that he, too, refused to do anything comical (although not due to his Godzilla convictions). Thus, all the supposedly funny lines were given to the junior military officer (Travis Swords). "He carried the brunt of the silliness, or what little silliness we were able to keep," Kizer said.

The new scenes featuring Burr, Kemmerling, and the other actors were shot in three days, two at Raleigh Studios on Sunset Boulevard, the same place where scenes for *Citizen Kane* were shot (leading a *Los Angeles Times* writer to ask: "Is nothing sacred?"), and one at a house in Malibu. Burr was on the set only the first day, and he was adamant that he not work longer than eight hours, recalling how, 30 years earlier, he agreed to work just one day on *Godzilla: King of the Monsters!* but ended up pulling a 24-hour shift to finish all his scenes. To accommodate Burr's demands, Kizer worked feverishly the first day, shooting nothing but Burr — all the reverse angles and reaction shots of other actors were saved for the second day. For his services in *Godzilla 1985*, Burr was paid $50,000. At the time, Burr was also producing the first of many Perry Mason TV movies, and during breaks in the shoot he was constantly making phone calls about his other project. Despite the distraction, Kizer and Randel describe Burr as a consummate pro.

"What also threw us for a loop was that he insisted on using TelePrompTers," Kizer said. "He wouldn't necessarily memorize the script. He would do a run-through, and we would figure out where his eyeline was going to be during the scene. Then he would tell the TelePrompTer guy, 'Put a monitor here, here, and here.' He worked it out so that you're not aware when you watch him that he's reading off the TelePrompTer. I asked him why this was necessary, because it meant a lot more logistical stuff on our part and I was kind of irritated by it. He said he learned it on *Perry Mason* — there was an episode that got bounced by the censors at the last minute and there was no time to learn the new lines, so he used prompters and found he liked working that way."

Burr provides a dramatic link to the first Americanized Godzilla by reprising his role as reporter Steve Martin, although here the character is called simply "Mr. Martin," to avoid references to the popular actor and comedian ("If we called him Steve Martin, everyone in the theater would start going 'Excuuuuuuse me,'" Kizer said). Another nod to *Godzilla: King of the Monsters!* that Kizer cleverly added is a book titled *Cairo Via Tokyo*, which can be glimpsed on Martin's desk — a reference to the fact that Steve Martin was en route to Cairo when he stopped off in Tokyo and found himself in the monster's path back in 1956.

Although the "war room" scene in *Godzilla 1985* looks somewhat impressive, it was actually created with stock footage from another New World movie. "What I basically did was, I took the shot of the big war room from *The Philadelphia Experiment* and built our Godzilla set behind it," said Randel. "We shot all the scenes with Raymond Burr and the military guys in reverse, so when we cut to the war room, it looked as if we were in this huge place, but it was really another movie! There were these three big monitor screens on the wall, and we optically matted various elements into them — footage from the original *Godzilla*, maps of Japan, and other stuff."

As an interesting aside, Kizer had actually planned to add one "special effect," so to speak, to the film. After the bum [Tetsuya Takeda] is squished by Godzilla's foot, there was to be a quick shot of his bloody hand sticking out of the asphalt rubble. "We were going to move in on the hand and his wristwatch would be broken, and the hands were stopped at precisely the time that the Hiroshima bomb went off. That was going to be our little homage of sorts. We actually shot that, but we couldn't get it to work editorially because the watch was too small in the frame. [For Godzilla's foot], we had this painted piece of cardboard — it was just going to be a very quick sense of something brushing past the lens. It was not wonderfully articulated, because it was largely going to be out of focus."

The Super Loopers, whose claim to fame was the U.S. version of *The Gods Must Be Crazy*, dubbed *Godzilla 1985* at Ryder Sound in Los Angeles. The dubbing job is one of the best in the entire G-series, as well-synched as possible and eschewing the phony Asian accents of yore. The music soundtrack, however, did not fare quite so well. Several of Reijiro Koroku's music themes were needlessly rearranged to accompany different scenes in the U.S. version, and several cuts were replaced entirely by stock music from composer Chris Young's scores for other New World films like *Def Con 4*. (The substitute music, which doesn't mesh well with the original score, can be heard during Godzilla's attack on the Soviet sub, the military's mobilization and elsewhere.) Worse yet, due to the heavy re-editing of the film, New World was forced to release the film with a mono soundtrack, whereas the Japanese version was in Dolby stereo. "There was not enough separation between the music and sound effects tracks for us to do a stereo dub," Kizer lamented. "Toho also had sent us separate elements of just the music, just the sound effects, and just the Japanese dialogue — all in mono — and that's what we ended up using."

BRAVE NEW WORLD: *Godzilla 1985* is the third Godzilla movie to feature inserted American footage. In terms of the amount of damage done to the original version, the "Burrization" of this film falls somewhere between John Beck's reworked *King Kong vs. Godzilla* (the most severely re-edited Godzilla movie) and *Godzilla: King of the Monsters!* (the most respectful of the full-blown Americanizations). New World tampered more heavily with the sequence of events, the character relationships, the music soundtrack, and even the story subtext, than did Terry Morse's 1956 effort; but *Godzilla 1985* is far less ambitious by comparison. Less new footage was shot and there was no attempt to integrate the new material into the story: No body doubles, no telephone calls to the Japanese actors, no Iwanaga-like interpreter. "When you look at the finished film, you can tell that Raymond Burr is just commenting on the action, he's not propelling the story in any way," said Randel. "His scenes absolutely don't need to be there, but somehow it all fits."

The nature and extent of New World's scene-shuffling, particularly in the second half of the movie (i.e., everything after the press conference scene), is mind-boggling. For an exhaustive, scene-by-scene comparison of *Godzilla* (1984) and *Godzilla 1985*, interested readers should hunt down a copy of *Video Watchdog Special Edition #2* (published 1995). What follows here is a condensed analysis of the major differences between the two versions:

- Goro's battle with the sea louse aboard the *Yahata Maru* is cut short in the U.S. version. In the original version, the big bug seems to fly through the air in pursuit of its victim, a silly-looking effect that was wisely omitted. The sea louse's voice, which originally sounded like the Gimantises from *Son of Godzilla*, was also altered.

- In the Japanese version, whenever one of the major government officials (prime minister, defense minister, etc.) appears for the first time, his name and title (in Japanese characters) appears on the screen.

- Early in the Japanese version, Professor Hayashida visits Okumura in the hospital and shows him some photos from Godzilla's 1954 rampage. This explains how the government knows that Godzilla has shown up again, and why everything is being kept secret. Hayashida's photos are the only visual reference in the Japanese version to Honda's *Godzilla*, whereas the U.S. version includes actual footage from the 1954 film.

- In the U.S. version, the reporter Maki tells Naoko that her brother is being confined in a hospital because he saw Godzilla, and the girl rushes to Okumura's room. But the last part of the scene is omitted, showing Maki and a photographer snapping photos of the brother-sister reunion for a newspaper story. The Japanese version makes it clear that Maki, at first, is only interested in the others for their news value.

- In the Japanese version, the Japanese prime minister listens to appeals from the U.S. and Russian ambassadors to allow a nuclear strike against Godzilla offshore. In the U.S. version, this sequence is condensed into a succinct scene in which the prime minister rebuffs the button-happy diplomats. There are pros and cons to this — on the one hand, the original sequence had a very "Japanese" feel and illustrated the prime minister's philosophical dilemma (i.e., which is the greater evil, Godzilla or the Bomb?), but it was too long and dull for an American audience. On the other hand, the U.S. ambassador (Walter Nicholas) had many more lines in the Japanese version, and the U.S. re-editing mercifully cuts out most of his awful acting. Also sliced was a short, but meaningful scene in which the prime minister explains how he convinced the ambassadors that nukes are not the answer. "I asked them, if Godzilla appeared in Moscow or Washington, would you have the courage to use nuclear weapons? . . . They finally understood," he says. In the Japanese version, the meeting between the prime minister and the diplomats takes place after Godzilla's attack on the nuclear power plant, but in the U.S. version, the meeting takes place first.

- Godzilla's rampage is heavily restructured in the U.S. version, with Godzilla first appearing in the harbor, then suddenly in Shinjuku (the business district) and then again advancing toward the center of the city. (In the original version, Godzilla comes ashore at Harumi, then marches to Yurakucho, the Ginza, then Shinjuku).

- In the Japanese version, Godzilla picks up a Shinkansen (bullet train) car and peers inside at the passengers. A shot of a long-haired Christian priest smiling at Godzilla — a bit of intended humor that doesn't translate well to non-Japanese audiences — was thankfully cut out of the U.S. print. Next, Godzilla walks past the Yurakucho Marion building (former site of the Toho Nichigeki Theater, which Godzilla destroyed in 1954), a structure with a mirrored glass exterior that impressively reflects the monster's image. Inexplicably, this wonderful SFX shot (which was a tribute to a painting by Yuji Kaida on the cover of the CD *Godzilla Legend Chronology 1*, released by King Records in 1986) was eliminated.

- Later, when Godzilla passes the window of Hayashida's office, and the sonic-wave amplifier is turned on, New World inserted a piece of footage (taken from later in the film, during Godzilla's

He's Not a Pepper

Over the years, many Japanese consumer products have been prominently featured in Godzilla movies. As the monster waltzed through Tokyo he often passed huge signs for Bireley's soft drinks, Morinaga confectioneries and other products erected among Eiji Tsuburaya's miniature cityscape. But the most shameless product placement in the entire Godzilla series took place in *Godzilla 1985*, via the positioning of a Dr. Pepper machine in the Pentagon set, with brand-name soda cans in view of the camera.

Shortly after New World Pictures acquired *Godzilla 1985*, Rusty Citron, the studio's promotion director, learned that Dr. Pepper had recently made a deal to feature Godzilla in TV commercials airing around the same time the picture would be out. Dr. Pepper produced two commercials featuring Godzilla, both filmed in black and white, the second featuring a female Godzilla called "Newzilla." In both commercials, Godzilla rampages through the city until his rage is quelled by a sip of Dr. Pepper.

Citron immediately met with Dr. Pepper officials in Dallas, offering to put the soda in the movie in exchange for a piggyback ride on its $10 million advertising campaign. According to a *Los Angeles Times* story, in less than three hours Dr. Pepper had agreed to promote the film in all its Godzilla ads during the weeks right before and after *Godzilla 1985*'s release.

"We were told by the New World marketing department in clear and unambiguous terms that we should try to get Dr. Pepper in the picture as often as we could without compromising the integrity," said director R.J. Kizer. "The Pentagon is an office building, so we thought we'd just put a Dr. Pepper vending machine there and have someone walk by it, and that would take care of it. But then, they said they wanted someone to be drinking a Dr. Pepper in the film, and they desperately wanted Raymond Burr to do it. I had to ask Burr about that, and he fixed me with one of these withering glares and just said nothing. The marketing guy persisted and said, 'You've got to get him to do it,' and I said, 'Why don't you get him to do it?' And then they backed off. Instead, we had the smart-aleck major taking a sip of Dr. Pepper in one shot."

fight with Super X) making it appear that Godzilla is roaring and advancing toward Hayashida and the others. In the Japanese version, the monster just stands there, vexed by the sonic generator, until the maser tank attacks him and he whirls around, his tail smashing the building. Naoko and Goro are trapped inside the damaged office building for a much longer time in the Japanese version.

- During the Godzilla-vs.-Super X battle, the Japanese version had Godzilla using his breath weapon only after being shot in the mouth with cadmium bombs. New World re-edited the passage so that Godzilla goes on the offensive, firing his radiation breath as soon as the battle-tank approaches him.

- Two actors well-known to Godzilla fans, Yoshibumi Tajima (Kumayama from *Godzilla vs. The Thing*) and Kunio Murai (Takeshi Shima from

Godzilla on Monster Island) make cameos in the Japanese version, but their scenes were excised from the U.S. version.

- The opening credits sequence to *Godzilla 1985*, wherein a series of slash marks slowly carves out the main title against a flaming background, is more imaginative than the rather standard opening of Toho's original version. To accompany the closing credits, New World pieced together a medley of Reijiro Koroku's soundtrack music and substituted it for "Godzilla," the awful pop song (with lyrics like "take care now, Godzilla, my old friend") sung by Star Sisters, which plays under the Japanese version's ending credits,

- All theatrical prints of *Godzilla 1985* (and, subsequently, all home video versions) opened with Marv Newland's 1969 animated short-short, *Bambi Meets Godzilla* which, for the uninitiated, is a supposedly humorous parody wherein a fawn, grazing in the grass, is suddenly stomped flat by a huge G-foot.

THE RUSSIANS ARE COMING: By far the greatest transgression New World committed, however, was to rework the scene in which Captain Kathren, the Russian naval officer, tries to stop an ICBM from accidentally launching toward Tokyo, making it appear that he is actually *launching* the missile! New World's owners Sloan and Kuppin were known for injecting their right-wing, Reagan-era politics into films like the nuclear holocaust yarn *Def Con 4*, and Godzilla — the pacifist, antinuclear monster — was not exempt. "Everybody who was working for New World at that time learned very quickly that this management group was decidedly conservative in its political outlook," said director Kizer. "Toho had given us an English-subtitled videotape of [the Japanese version] for reference, and after I watched it I read the script that had been written for the re-cuts that we were doing. And I said to Tony [Randel], 'Wait a minute, why are we having the Russian trying to blow everything up?' And he just turned to me and said, 'This is the company we're working for.' We just left it at that." In the Japanese version, Godzilla's appearance in the bay knocks the Soviet ship against the pier, accidentally setting off the launch mechanism for a satellite-based missile, and the injured Captain Kathren valiantly crawls toward the control panel to try to cancel the launch, but is killed in an electrical fire. To complete the bastardization of this sequence, New World inserted a newly filmed shot of the Russian officer's finger pressing a button, dispatching the missile.

Although New World adopted the tag line "the legend is reborn" from Toho's original English-language publicity materials for *Godzilla* (1984), the advertising and promotion for *Godzilla 1985* signaled that the film was a campy comedy. A theatrical trailer announced Godzilla's return by paying him a mock tribute, proclaiming, "The greatest star of all time has returned!" New World produced a music video for a tie-in song called "I Was Afraid to Love You," which played once or twice on MTV and was never seen again. In an unprecedented move, Toho sent one of the actual Godzilla costumes used in the movie to the U.S. to aid in New World's publicity stunts. Brad Garfield, a 28-year-old Los

Angeles actor, was hired to don the 200-pound suit in Los Angeles (where Godzilla walked down Hollywood Boulevard) and New York (where he visited the Staten Island Ferry, the Museum of Natural History, Grand Central Station and the Empire State Building). At every event, a registered nurse with two bottles of oxygen trailed the monster in case the actor inside passed out. "It takes all my energy to walk 30 steps in this thing," Garfield complained to *People* magazine. "I'm an actor, though I don't regard this as one of my finer parts. It gets sweaty in here, and my wife sometimes wonders why I come home smelling like rubber." Press coverage of Godzilla's U.S. tour was plentiful, including mentions on *Good Morning America*, *Entertainment Tonight*, and local news programs. The *Chicago Tribune* conducted an "interview" with Godzilla in which the monster answered 24 questions with "AAARRRGGGGHHH!" At a press conference covered in *The Hollywood Reporter* (August 25, 1985), Godzilla proclaimed *Godzilla 1985* a "grudge match" between himself and Raymond Burr, striking a "Mr. T" pose and saying, "I pity the fool. I've decided to fight fire with fire, and in my case, radioactive fire."

While it is obvious why New World felt it necessary to re-edit *Godzilla* (1984) for its U.S. release (the original being too long and talky for the short attention spans of young Americans), the company's approach to the Americanization turned the film into a half-hearted, half-assed parody. If New World had wanted a comedy, perhaps it should have gone the *What's Up, Tiger Lily?* route; if it wanted a good Godzilla movie, perhaps it should have opted for a simple, straightforward dubbing job while trimming some scenes to quicken the pacing. Instead, what it ended up with was a dead-serious Japanese monster movie, interrupted every ten minutes or so by pointless vignettes featuring (mostly bad) American actors, including a wise-cracking military punk who should be shot. Here, Raymond Burr is hardly the expository narrator/commentator he was in *Godzilla: King of the Monsters!* Burr does the best he can with the feeble part written for him, intoning seriously about the dangers of nuclear weapons and Godzilla's symbolic immortality. But the truth is that Burr has no good reason to be in this film, and the actor at times appears uncomfortably aware of this.

Furthermore, the radical re-editing of the film weakens character relationships, creates continuity problems and — worst of all — undermines the antinuclear message that Tanaka wanted to convey in the Japanese version. The end result is that *Godzilla 1985* isn't funny and isn't compelling. Mostly, it's just boring. *Godzilla 1985* was universally panned by the American critics (except Joel Siegel of *Good Morning America*, who likes everything), whose view of the movie was so obscured by New World's hack job that they could not appreciate Toho's worthwhile, although flawed, attempt to return Godzilla to his role as Mother Nature's doom beast.

"We thought we did an incredible job, given the circumstances," said director Kizer. "No matter what we had done with the film, though, I don't think it was ever going to be a huge hit. This was already the mid-1980s, and special effects were changing quite a bit. The American public was accustomed to films like *Terminator* and *Aliens*. At that time, I felt that an American audience was ripe for a really good Godzilla movie, but this one wasn't quite it. However much they redesigned the Godzilla monster, it was still a guy in a rubber suit and some aspects about it were still corny. When *Godzilla 1985* came out I was working in New York and I saw it in a theater there. At the beginning, there was a vibe in the theater, the audience was really excited. But when Godzilla finally appeared, there was this big letdown."

Despite all the media attention, *Godzilla 1985* generated scant viewer enthusiasm and word of mouth, thus doing only modest box-office business, earning $4.1 million in grosses, according to *Variety*. "Actually, that's a little misleading," said producer Randel. "It was one of the most successful films that New World ever did. It was very profitable for them." The profit margin was boosted with the December, 1985, home-video release, complete with a promotion campaign that included TV commercials, ads in magazines like *National Lampoon*, *Circus*, and *Rolling Stone*, inflatable Godzillas in retail stores, and a toll-free telephone number allowing fans to "talk" to Godzilla.

POP MONSTER

Everywhere you look, it seems, Godzilla rears his ugly head in American pop culture. References to and parodies of Godzilla routinely appear in movies (everything from *Cooley High* to *The Bad News Bears Go To Japan* to *Honey I Blew Up The Kid*), TV shows ("Saturday Night Live," "Animaniacs," "The Critic," "The Tonight Show" and endless others), in adver-

tising campaigns (for soft drinks, athletic shoes, and other products) and even in public service announcements (Godzilla has been an anti-smoking spokesman; more recently, high-fat buttered popcorn was called "The Godzilla of snacks").

What follows is a selective overview of Godzilla sightings in various pop-culture media.

Go, Go, Rockzilla

Blue Oyster Cult's 1977 hard-rock anthem "Godzilla" is one of the greatest tributes ever paid to the monster. By now, everyone knows the lyrics and tune (written by guitarist Donald "Buck Dharma" Roeser), but here are some interesting factoids about the song (*acknowledgments to the Blue Oyster Cult Internet FAQ:* ftp://ftp.spc.edu/boc-l/boc_faq-2_2.txt):

- The Japanese chatter heard in the song (*Rinji news o moshiagemasu! Rinji news o moshiagemasu! Gojira ga Ginza hoomen e mukatte imasu! Daishkyu hinan shite kudasai! Daishkyu hinan shite kudasai!*) translates roughly as "Attention, emergency news! Attention, emergency news! Godzilla is going toward the Ginza area! Immediately [take] shelter please! Immediately [take] shelter please!"

- B.O.C. paid royalties to Toho for use of Godzilla's name, but the amount is unknown.

- The band used two Godzilla models onstage, one 20 feet tall, the other (for larger venues) 40 feet tall. The monster's eyes would light up and smoke spewed from its mouth.

- In concert, drummer Albert Brouchard began wearing a Godzilla mask during his drum solo.

- Donald Roeser later wrote an instrumental track called "Gamera is Missing" on a music-instruction album released by *Guitar* magazine.

- "Godzilla" first appeared on *Spectres* and has been released, in various versions, on at least seven B.O.C. albums.

Blue Oyster Cult's is the most famous Godzilla-inspired rock song of all, but the Big G has been honored by many pop and rock musicians. In Japan, there have been too many Godzilla-inspired songs to mention. Here are a handful of Godzilla-related songs and bands from the West:

Michael Sembello, known for the hit "Maniac" from the *Fame* soundtrack, recorded a song called "Godzilla" on *Bossa Nova Hotel* (Warner Bros., 1983); Praxis, an industrial-funk-hardcore band featuring Bootsy Collins of Parliament/Funkadelic, recorded a song called "Godzilla" on *Transmutation* (Axiom, 1992); American Music Club, an alternative rock band, recorded "What Godzilla Said to God When His Name Wasn't Found In the Book of Life," on *Mercury* (Warner Bros., 1993); Soundgarden included samples of Godzilla's roar and Raymond Burr's dialogue on the 1990 EP, *Screaming Life/Fopp*; Flaming Lips, an alternative rock band, recorded "Godzilla Flick" on *Hear It Is* (1985); Godzilla Volume, a U.K. techno group, featured sampled roars, sounds and dialogue from *Godzilla vs. Megalon* and included pornographic artwork with Godzilla sporting a huge penis, in its self-titled CD (Temple Records, 1994); Neil Norman and his

Cosmic Orchestra recorded a rock version of Akira Ifukube's "Godzilla theme" on *Greatest Science Fiction Hits* (GNP Crescendo, 1979); Guttermouth, a punk band, put Godzilla on the cover of the CD *Teri Yakimoto* (Nitro, 1996); Destroy All Monsters was an experimental rock band formed in Detroit in the mid-1970s by former members of The Stooges. The band published its music under the banner of Megalo (i.e., Megalon) Music.

Godzilla 101

Perhaps the greatest evidence that Godzilla is more than just kid stuff is the way the King of Monsters has crept into literature. The novel *Gojiro* by Mark Jacobson (Atlantic Monthly Press, 1991) is Godzilla's autobiography set in a surreal world, haunted by perpetual fears of nuclear holocaust. Gojiro (an alternation of "Gojira," probably to avoid reprisals from Toho) is a lizard irradiated by atomic testing into a gigantic monster, and a disillusioned movie star living on Radioactive Island. The Vonnegut-esque book isn't for everyone, but the author demonstrates true understanding of the Godzilla mythos (interestingly, Jacobson wrote an obituary for producer Tomoyuki Tanaka in the *New York Times Magazine* in 1997).

The short story *Elvis Meets Godzilla* by Michael Reaves appeared in the anthology *The King Is Dead: Tales of Elvis Postmortem* (Delta Press, 1994). A producer of low-budget horror films is saved from financial ruin when his partner returns from Japan with the last surviving print (and all distribution rights) of a long-lost movie wherein Elvis battles Godzilla in Tokyo. The film was shot shortly before Elvis's death, but never released. Elvis plays a singer whose Japanese concert tour is interrupted by Godzilla's rampage; a team of Japanese scientists administer rays that cause Elvis to grow into a gigantic, jumpsuit-wearing lounge act monster. But after some politically correct soul-searching, the producer realizes it's not right to exploit a fat, dead rocker and a punch-drunk prehistoric beast. Using scissors, he cuts the film into little pieces, destroying it forever. Not as good as it could have been. Noteworthy quote: ". . .The distinctive battle-cry of Godzilla . . . always sounded to Lex like an elephant being butt-fucked by a diesel locomotive."

Godzillas, real or imagined, also make appearances in the following American novels: *Rim*, a cyberpunk detective yarn by Alexander Besher (HarperPrism, 1994); *An Artist of the Floating World* by *Remains of the Day* author Kazuo Ishiguro (1986); *A Genuine Monster* by David Zielinski (Atlantic Monthly Press, 1990); *Monster Makers* by Laurence Yep (Arbor House, 1986); *Sunsmoke* by James Killus (Ace Books, 1985).

The Incredible Skulk

By the mid-1970s, Godzilla had been appearing in Japanese comics, or *manga*, for more than a decade. These unavailable-in-America publications (except, on occasion, in Japanese bookstores) run the gamut from direct adaptations of the Godzilla movies, to children's stories featuring "super-deformed" versions (short, pudgy caricatures) of Godzilla and other Toho monsters, to all-original stories written for teens and adults with themes ranging from humorous to serious.

Thus, it was probably inevitable that Godzilla should have his own comic book in America as well. In 1977, Marvel Comics, creators of *Spiderman*, *Fantastic Four*, *The Incredible Hulk* and other classic titles, acquired the rights to produce an all-original book, *Godzilla: King of the Monsters*. Although generally regarded as a blemish on Godzilla's long resume, the comic book was the first Americanization of the Japanese giant in any entertainment medium, a milestone in G-history. And, although Marvel's approach to the material was flawed, the book paved the way for future, more successful Godzilla comics in the 1980s and '90s.

Marvel's Godzilla book arrived at a time when the U.S. comics scene was at a low ebb, after a huge boom in the 1960s. To spice things up a bit, Marvel and its main competitor, D.C. Comics, began publishing books based on popular, action- and fantasy-oriented movies and television shows, like *Star Wars*, *Battlestar Galactica* and *The Six Million Dollar Man*. In an editorial in *Godzilla: King of the Monsters* #1, editor Archie Goodwin said Marvel had sought the rights to do a Godzilla book for nearly five years before Toho finally agreed. Once the deal was made, "the big question was how to handle the character," Goodwin said. Goodwin contended that Marvel chose not to do adaptations of the Toho movies because that would be "monotonous," but legalities were no doubt a factor; apparently, Marvel could use only Godzilla in its book, and not Rodan, Mothra, Ghidorah, or any other monsters. Thus, Godzilla was placed into the "Marvel Universe" where he was constantly pursued by the military super-force SHIELD, and sometimes battled Marvel super-heroes. Marvel's monster is an "alternate Godzilla" that follows its own time and story line, with no ties to the Toho films.

In issue #1, written by Doug Moench (creator of forgotten 1970s titles like *Werewolf By Night* and *Moon Knight*) Godzilla is introduced as a prehistoric reptile-amphibian hybrid asleep for eons on the ocean floor off Japan, and re-animated by a 1956 undersea nuclear test. A Japanese scientist, Dr. Yuriko Takiguchi, tried to stop the U.S. government from conducting the test, but was rebuked; Takiguchi was the lone survivor when Godzilla rose from the sea and demolished a ship carrying the researchers monitoring the blast. Godzilla terrorized Japan for the next 20 years before being was trapped in an iceberg; now, off the coast of Alaska, an unusually warm winter thaws the iceberg and frees Godzilla, and the monster destroys an oil pipeline construction project and heads south down the west coast of North America. Dr. Takiguchi, his assistant Tamara, and his 12-year-old grandson Robert Takiguchi head for America to assist SHIELD in battling Godzilla. Young Robert becomes Godzilla's friend, and saves the monster several times during the series.

Marvel said its Godzilla was designed after the 1954 original, but there were great differences. First off, this Godzilla was bright green! It had a long, horse-like head, stalactite teeth, flat, red eyes, and three toes (not four, like the original G). Worst of all, it exhaled a stream of crackling fire, rather than a radioactive ray. In fact, after its nuclear-bomb awakening in the premier issue, little mention was made of Godzilla's radioactive properties. Even so, Marvel-zilla behaved something like the original Toho version, as an unsympathetic, fearsome creature bent on destroying all in its path. In tone, the comic was like the Toho films of the late '60s and early '70s, with crazy scientists, conquesting aliens, and a host of zany "villain" monsters. Marvel's *Godzilla: King of the Monsters* was published for 24 issues, from August 1977 to July 1979.

In the 1980s, with a resurgence in the comics trade and the rise of the independent comics publishing scene, Godzilla got another chance. Following the stateside release of New World's *Godzilla 1985*, Dark Horse Comics, a company with a niche in movie tie-in comics (*Aliens*, *Predator*, *Species*, *Robocop*, *The Mask* and many others), published an all-new Godzilla "origin story" that deviated from Toho's original Godzilla genesis, but nonetheless treated Godzilla in a straightforward manner. This was followed in 1988 by a historic event, the first English-language translation of a Japanese Godzilla *manga*, when Dark Horse published Kazuhisa Iwata's adaptation of *Godzilla* (1984) as a six-issue series. Over the next decade, Dark Horse produced a sporadic output of Godzilla material that varied in quality. Its most valiant effort was the monthly series *Godzilla: King of the Monsters*, which ran from issue #0 (May 1995) to issue #16 (September 1996). Like Marvel, Dark Horse was straightjacketed by its inability to use other Toho kaiju in its books and instead substituted its own monsters, with mixed results.

The Godzilla Underground

For the past 30 years, the lifeline of Godzilla fandom in the West has been the rag-tag world of fanzines, ranging in quality from mere gibberish crudely printed on mimeographed-and-stapled paper to insightfully written, beautifully designed works that rival professional magazines. They fill a void by providing information that mainstream publica-tions (like *Famous Monsters* and *The Monster Times* in the old days) simply cannot.

The first significant *kaiju* fanzine to appear in the U.S. was *Japanese Fantasy Film Journal*, which premiered in 1968. Published in Ohio by founder-editor Greg Shoemaker, *JFFJ* is the granddaddy of all Godzilla zines, the first publication to approach the

genre in a serious way. Shoemaker's skills as a writer and graphic artist gave the zine a credibility beyond mere fan-rag and, at its peak, its circulation was in the low thousands. With an emphasis was live-action SFX films, *JFFJ* was the "thinking fan's" zine, characterized by the skillful analysis of Shoemaker and other writers. *JFFJ* was published once a year for 15 years, but by 1983, Shoemaker's interest in the subject matter had diminished and, sadly, he shut down *JFFJ* with issue #15.

Japanese Giants, founded by Mark Rainey in the early 1970s and published in Chicago (since issue #5, 1978) by editors Ed Godziszewski and Bill Gudmundson, focuses on in-depth background infor-

mation on all things Toho. Over the years *JG* has published thorough "making-of" articles on several films (*Latitude Zero*, *Godzilla* [1984], and *Godzilla vs. Biollante*) and the *Godzilla vs. Barkley* TV commercial. *JG* comes out sporadically (probably to help preserve the editors' sanity); as of 1998, eight issues had been published.

In the late 1980s and early '90s, spurred by the stateside release of *Godzilla 1985* and the dawn of an all-new Godzilla series of the 1990s, a new mini-"Godzilla boom" took shape in the U.S., bolstered by the 1990 debut of *Markalite, the Magazine of Japanese Fantasy*. Named after the Markalite heat-ray projectors from *The Mysterians*, the magazine's premiere issue covered the making of *Godzilla vs. Biollante*. *Markalite*, with its broad coverage of the genre, authoritative writing, and slick production values, was a fan's dream come true but, unfortunately, after issue #3 (Fall 1991), the San Francisco-based magazine suddenly disappeared.

In 1992, a high school teacher in Manitoba, Canada named J.D. Lees placed a small ad in *Starlog* seeking to connect with interested Godzilla fans. The result was *The Daikaiju Society of North America*, a four-page, photocopied newsletter first published in February, 1993. Five years, two name changes (for a short time, it was known as *G-Force*), and 30 issues later, *G-Fan* proved to be the most successful, long-running and prolific (with each new issue running about 60 pages long) Godzilla fanzine. Featuring articles written by fans around the globe, covering everything from interviews with Toho personnel, fan fiction, info on Godzilla-related toys, and models, *G-Fan* appeals to a wide array of sensibilities, from hard-core to casual fan, small-frys to adults. In 1996, a few key contributors broke away from the magazine and founded a similar publication called *Kaiju Fan*.

Other noteworthy fanzines contributing to Godzilla lore in the U.S. include *The Kaiju Review*, published in New York in the 1990s; *Nippon Rando no Yumei Kaiju* (*Famous Monsters of Japanland*),

published by author Stuart Galbraith IV; *Henshin Newsletter*, published by former *Markalite* editors; and *Monster Attack Team*, a Texas-based fanzine.

The "Godzilla boom" has also seen an increase in genre coverage by magazines and books. From 1993 to 1997 *Cult Movies* magazine ran a series of unprecedented interviews with filmmakers, actors, and others Japanese monster movie personalities, by David Milner. Stuart Galbraith IV's *Japanese Science Fiction, Fantasy and Horror Films* (McFarland, 1993) was the first book of its kind; the author followed this with *Monsters are Attacking Tokyo!* (Feral House, 1998), an oral history of the genre. Two excellent books were also published on a limited basis in 1996 and sold in fan circles: *The Illustrated Encyclopedia of Godzilla* by Ed Godziszewski and *Age of the Gods: A History of the Japanese Fantasy Film* by Guy Tucker. Also noteworthy are *A Critical History and Filmography of Toho's Godzilla Series* by David Kalat (McFarland, 1997) and *An Unofficial Guide to Godzilla Collectibles* by Sean Linkenback (Schiffer, 1998). Toho has initiated legal action that successfully removed two unauthorized Godzilla books from the marketplace: the dubious *Godzilla: King of the Movie Monsters* by Robert Marrero (Fantasma, 1996) was available for a short time, while *Godzilla! The Complete Guide to Moviedom's Mightiest Monster* by Frank Lovece (Quill/Morrow, 1998) was nixed before publication.

Godzilla Goods

Godzilla merchandising is vast and varied. Literally thousands of licensed products bearing Godzilla's name and/or likeness have been sold in Japan and abroad. Action figures, model kits, board games, candy, soft drinks, plush toys, coloring books, LPs and CDs and more — you name it, Godzilla has probably endorsed or emblazoned it.

According to Sean Linkenback, author of *An Unauthorized Guide to Godzilla Collectibles*, the first-ever Godzilla toy was a gun-and-target game sold in Japan in 1955, when *Godzilla Raids Again* was released. But the first significant Godzilla items were actually manufactured in America to coincide with *King Kong vs. Godzilla* in 1963, notably a Godzilla board game by Ideal and a Godzilla model kit by Aurora (released in 1964), patterned after the *Kin-Goji* Godzilla suit. The model, packaged in a box featuring classic artwork by James Bama, has become a coveted collector's item.

In the mid-1960s, a Japanese manufacturer called Marusan released cartoonish-looking Toho monster vinyl figures, the first such toys. When Marusan closed in 1970, its toy molds were bought by Bullmark, which continued and expanded the line until ceasing production in 1975 (Ken Yano can be seen playing with Bullmark toys in *Godzilla versus The Smog Monster*). Around this time, several Godzilla-related items appeared in the U.S., including new Rodan and Ghidrah (King Ghidorah) model kits by Aurora, and large action figures of Godzilla and Rodan by Mattel.

Godzilla merchandising increased exponentially in Japan with the release of *Godzilla* (1984), and especially with the success of the 1990s Godzilla movies. Bandai's finely detailed vinyl monster figures, introduced in 1983, became the most widely sought-after line of Godzilla toys, and a wide array of *kaiju* "garage kit" models were produced by myriad companies; however, all these goodies were scarce in America, available only through import dealers.

In 1995, St. Louis-based Trendmasters launched the first-ever full line of U.S.-made Godzilla toys, which included action figures and play sets featuring Godzilla and many of his monster comrades, even some (like Battra, Space Godzilla, and Mogera) from movies that, at that time, were not yet released in America! In 1998, Random House published *Godzilla Returns*, first in a continuing series of all-new Godzilla fiction for kids and teens. In 1998, Trendmasters and hundreds of companies unleashed a huge assortment of tie-in merchandise for TriStar Pictures' *Godzilla*.

Part 5

SECOND COMING

The 1990s

"As always, the '90s Godzilla films offer precise miniature models of big cities for the trashing. Much of the fascination for Japanese fans is seeing familiar urban areas reduced to rubble. Hardly a prominent new structure can be raised in Japan — the Tokyo City Hall and the Yokohama Landmark Tower are recent examples — before Godzilla turns it to dust."

— *From an article in the* International Herald Tribune, *September 23, 1994*

"The samurai spirit is to obey one's overlord no matter what, always moving forward and never looking back. And I saw that as similar to the spirit of Godzilla — he always rushes ahead to attack and never retreats, no matter how dangerous."

— *Kenpachiro Satsuma, Godzilla suitmation actor, in a Reuters wire story, July 26, 1994*

Seventeen

THE NAME OF THE ROSE

*"If we don't produce this bacteria, then sure
as eggs is eggs someone else is gonna do it."*

— Mr. Okochi

GODZILLA vs. BIOLLANTE

RATING (OUT OF FIVE STARS): ★ ★ 1/2

JAPANESE VERSION: GOJIRA VS. BIORANTE. Released on December 16, 1989, by the Toho Motion
Picture Company. Widescreen, in color. Running Time: 104 minutes. Screened at the Cannes Film
Festival on March 13 and 16, 1990.

U.S. VERSION: Released directly to home video by Miramax/Dimension Films on December 9, 1992.
Running Time: 104 minutes.

STORY: A grieving biologist tries to keep the spirit of his dead daughter alive by combining her DNA
with a rose, creating haunted flowers; enlisted to develop Anti-Nuclear Energy Bacteria (ANB, a
substance poisonous to Godzilla), the scientist secretly combines Godzilla Cells with the roses and
unwittingly creates Biollante, a reptile-plant monster with feminine traits. Godzilla, unleashed from
Mount Mihara by terrorists, kills Biollante and, although infected with ANB, Godzilla's low body
temperature prevents the poison from taking effect; the military tries to lure Godzilla into the
Thunder Beam (an "artificial lightning" field) and heat him up but a resurrected, hideously
morphed Biollante reappears and the monsters fight, Biollante eventually vaporizing into a
glowing mist and Godzilla, finally suffering the ANB's effects, sluggishly returns to the sea.

A NEW BEGINNING

After *Godzilla 1985* came and went without much
impact, Godzilla fans in the West may have thought
that Japan's thunder lizard had finally faded into
obscurity forever, but this was hardly the case.
Seven years later, in 1992, a new Godzilla movie
suddenly appeared, without fanfare, on the shelves
of video-rental stores, and thanks to new and

improved special effects and a throwback to the
glory days when Godzilla was an unapologetic badass, *Godzilla vs. Biollante* succeeded not only in
reviving the Godzilla legend but also updating it
for the 1990s.

In its Japanese release, *Godzilla* (1984) was only a
marginal success, but producer Tomoyuki Tanaka
nonetheless believed his monster-child's screen
career should continue. Tanaka quickly set about

Godzilla battles a final-stage Biollante that looks like it was made out of hamburger, in a model diorama displayed at a Godzilla exhibit in 1994 in Tokyo.
PHOTO BY MERRILL GOOZNER/CHICAGO TRIBUNE

putting together a sequel in the classic monster-vs.-monster vein, pitting Godzilla against an all-new opponent but, due to a series of stumbling blocks, *Godzilla vs. Biollante* took four years to complete. The film reached Japanese theaters in December 1989, and although it wasn't a runaway hit either, *Biollante* recaptured some of the awesome power of the original *Godzilla* (1954) and other early Japanese giant monster movies. Most importantly, it launched a new Godzilla series (unofficially known as the *Heisei* series, because it began in the first year of the *Heisei* Era, the reign of Emperor Akihito) made by a new generation of filmmakers. In all, six new Godzillas were made in Japan in the 1990s, culminating in the King of the Monsters' tragic death in *Godzilla vs. Destoroyah* (1995).

Godzilla vs. Biollante is a direct sequel to *Godzilla 1985*, and begins in the burning rubble of the aftermath of the monster's attack on Tokyo. The story concerns a battle for the possession of "Godzilla Cells," precious samples of the monster's tissue, which are coveted for their self-reproductive properties. The Japanese government is using the G-cells to develop Anti Nuclear-Energy Bacteria (ANB), a weapon that is poisonous to Godzilla. The Republic of Saradia, a fictional Middle Eastern nation, wants to use the cells to develop a new, genetically engineered wheat that can grow in the deserts, ending worldwide dependence on the U.S. for grain exports. A long-haired Saradian terrorist spends much of the film battling with several secret agents from Bio-Major, an American pharmaceutical con-

Special effects director Koichi Kawakita, working in the film editing room at Toho, in 1988.
COURTESY OF WINTERGARDEN PRODUCTIONS

glomerate, which wants the cells too (presumably, only to foil the Saradian plan). At the same time, a subplot unfolds in which a brilliant Japanese biologist, driven to the brink of madness by his daughter's death, secretly attempts to bring her back to life by combining samples of her tissue with Godzilla cells and genetic material from a rose (her favorite flower). The results are disastrous: A gigantic gargoyle-vine monster, with the head of a rose, springs up in the middle of a nearby lake. He names the monster Biollante, taking the name from Violan, a mythological Norse nymph. Godzilla, sensing an innate attraction to and hatred for his bastard brethren, heads straight for it, and a mighty battle ensues.

What is immediately apparent in *Godzilla vs. Biollante* is the advancement in Toho's special effects technology since the dismal 1970s, and even since the so-so SFX work of *Godzilla 1985*. Godzilla has undergone a significant redesign and now resembles a more cat-like, animalistic reptile with thick, rough hide, and a stony, evil stare. Yes, Godzilla is still a man in a rubber suit — it's a matter of not only costs and technology, but also Toho tradition — but he looks better than ever, thanks not only to the improvements to the costumes but to SFX director **Koichi Kawakita**'s careful rethinking of the monster's personality. Although Godzilla reverted to villainy in the previous film, *Godzilla vs. Biollante* makes it clear that Godzilla's motivation is not to annihilate man but merely to survive in a world in which he doesn't belong. The monster is like a gigantic reptilian steamroller, flattening everything in his way and retaliating whenever man takes the offensive. His opponent, Biollante, is an inspired creation, a feminine monster with a hideous grace whose purpose seems to be to pacify Godzilla's infernal rage, but Godzilla will have none of it!

To inject new creative blood into the series, and to generate publicity for the next feature, Toho placed advertisements in Japanese newspapers in the fall of 1985, soliciting entries for a story contest. The winning entry would serve as the basis of the next film, the working title of which was *Godzilla 2*. More than 5,000 stories were submitted by the public, and to judge the entries Tanaka assembled a six-member panel consisting of himself, Toho president Isao Matsuoka, famous Japanese comics artist Dr. Osamu Tezuka, writers Chiaki Kawamata and Baku Yumemakura, and science fiction critic Mitsutoshi Ishigami. The panel initially selected 10 stories as semi-finalists, then narrowed it down to five finalists before choosing the winning entry: *Godzilla vs. Biollante*, a last-minute submission writ-

ten by **Shinichiro Kobayashi**, a dentist and occasional science-fiction writer. Kobayashi wasn't exactly a novice, for he had written scripts for Tsuburaya Productions' "Return of Ultraman" teleseries (which aired in 1971–72 on Japan's TBS network) and other shows.

THE NEW BROOD: *Godzilla vs. Biollante* is the first Godzilla movie made by the "Godzilla Generation," the men who grew up watching the original series as kids.[35] The most influential member of this group, creatively speaking, is director **Kazuki Omori**, who directed two and wrote four of the six latter-day Godzilla movies. Born on March 3, 1952, in Osaka, Omori was known as a rising young talent in the Japanese film community when producer Tanaka entrusted the new film to him in 1986, but he seemed an odd choice to direct a science-fiction film. He was known for directing Japanese "teen idol" movies, such as a trilogy starring Koji Kikkawa in the mid-1980s and *Girls in Love* (1986), starring starlet Yuki Saito. Omori began his career by making independent films while in high school, and in 1977, while attending Kyoto Medical College, he won a screenwriting award for his script *Orange Road Express*, which he made into a film the following year. Omori graduated from medical school in 1980 and passed the national medical exam in 1983, becoming a licensed practitioner, and several of his films have featured the world of medicine as a backdrop for humanist dramas. He has also directed a number of television commercials.

As the "new hope" for the Godzilla series, Omori received a lot of media attention around the time that *Godzilla vs. Biollante* was in production. His comments sometimes indicated a certain embarrassment or dislike for Godzilla, which led some fans to wonder why he'd taken the job. "I'm not such an enthusiastic fan (of Godzilla)," Omori said in an interview published in *Markalite #1*. "Although movies are, more or less, in some ways unreal or complete fabrication, Godzilla seems like the biggest fabrication of them all."

Still, at times Omori professed a fondness for the original Godzilla series and its offshoots in his youth, perhaps in an attempt to allay the fears of the devotees. "When I was in preschool, my friends' mother took us to a theater . . . to see the original *Godzilla*, and I got really scared," Omori wrote in an essay called *How I Suppressed My Fears and*

Became the Director of a Godzilla Movie. "In junior high, I lined up in front of a theater to see *Godzilla vs. The Thing* on opening day. And I eagerly awaited the release of *Ghidrah: The Three-Headed Monster.* But that's all. I don't know if the word 'graduation' is proper or not, but I started to go to theaters showing *007*, *The Great Escape*, or *The Sound of Music.*

"I wanted to make a true great entertainment film," Omori said. "The history of Japanese cinema is not only Ozu and Mizoguchi. There must have been a kingdom of entertainment films. And no one would deny that one of its kings is Godzilla."[36]

Omori apparently felt that a straight monster story, or even Kobayashi's tale of monsters spawned by out-of-control science, was not enough to create "a true great entertainment film," for he overstocked his script for *Godzilla vs. Biollante* with so many subplots that at times it's hard to decipher the story. Omori's love of the James Bond films is evident, for at times *Biollante* feels more like a spy picture than a monster movie, but his screenplay is disorganized and his direction erratic, resulting in a lack of continuity from scene to scene that is sometimes jarring. As in all Japanese monster films, there is an abundance of characters here, but so many that it's difficult to tell who the central figure is: Much time is spent at the outset with Dr. Shiragami (Koji Takahashi), but it turns out that he is really a secondary character; and the hero Kirishima (Kunihiko Mitamura) doesn't assume a commanding role in the drama until the second act. The subplot about the teen-age psychic girl, Miki Saegusa (Megumi Odaka), and her ability to read Godzilla's mind has an interesting premise but it is thrown into the story without much thought. Strangely enough, despite her marginal role here, Miki would return as a connecting character in each of the next five Godzilla pictures.

It's not that Omori's characters are uninteresting. There is Kirishima, the scientist charged with overseeing the development of a bacteria that may diffuse the nuclear arms race, but feels conflicted about participating in a project that could lead to heresy in genetic engineering; there is Shiragami, who was forced to leave Japan and its conservative scientific community in order to research new artificially-created strains of wheat that might help supply desert nations with self-sustaining food supplies;[37] Mr. Okochi, Kirishima's would-be father-in-law, who views the Godzilla Cells as a means to Japan's security; the psychic Miki, who works with ESP-gifted children and who senses the spirit of Shiragami's daughter in the elegant monster Biollante; the heroic Colonel Goro Gondo (Toru Minegishi, a standout in an otherwise bland cast), head of the defense force's one-man Godzilla office, infused with an energy and bravado that the other characters lack; and young Major Kuroki, head of an elite youth military corps, who commandeers the deployment of the Super-X2 against the mighty Godzilla. But Omori treats each of these characters in such a perfunctory way that they remain distant and impersonal. The best example of this is the death of Goro Gondo, who bravely fires the ANB capsule into Godzilla's mouth from the window of an office building, at close range, only to have the angry monster kill him. Although he was an integral part of the anti-Godzilla operation, Gondo's death is never mentioned by the other characters.

Omori also misses the boat with the Super-X2, repeating the mistake committed by screenwriter Shuichi Nagahara in *Godzilla 1985* by simply introducing the battle-craft into the story without a rationale. The Super-X2, with its fire mirror that absorbs the energy from Godzilla's ray and rebounds it at the monster with amplified force, is an interesting concept for an anti-Godzilla weapon, but it would be much more interesting if there was some drama attached to it — if it were part of a secret military program, if there were difficulties perfecting the technology, or (gasp!) if there were people inside of it. The Super-X2 is just an elaborate video game (controlled by an operator with a joystick, no less), a remote-controlled toy doomed to fail — and the buildup to its eventual destruction by Godzilla isn't very suspenseful.

More than any other entry in the series since the original *Godzilla* or perhaps *Godzilla vs. The Smog Monster*, *Biollante* is a "director's film." With Omori's then-emerging reputation as a rising film auteur in Japan, the director was given much creative leeway, resulting in a film whose style and tone are markedly different from anything seen before or since. But, after *Biollante* more or less bombed at the Japanese box office, Toho apparently tightened the reins and returned to a committee-style approach in which creative decisions are strictly supervised by the producers. Hereon, the Godzilla movies were noticeably calculated to appeal to broader audience demographics — classic Toho monsters were remade for the older fans, a baby Godzilla was created for little kids, transforming monsters and mechanical battle-crafts were introduced to grab boys' attention, feminine themes were added to draw women viewers, and so on. The formula has worked: Subsequent entries in the series continued to gain momentum at the box office. The only other director to put his personal stamp on a latter-day Godzilla movie is Kensho Yamashita in *Godzilla vs. Space Godzilla* (1994), with dismal results.

GODZILLA GETS A MAKE-OVER

Despite the story's unevenness, what works extremely well in *Godzilla vs. Biollante* is the visuals. The new Godzilla suit, the twin stages of Biollante, the miniature work, the pyrotechnics, and the opticals, all combine for a feast for the eyes. This film marks the arrival of special-effects director Koichi Kawakita (b. December 15, 1942, in Tokyo), who first joined Toho's special-effects department in 1962 in the optical compositing section and slowly worked his way up, earning his first credits as a director on several science-fiction oriented TV shows (*Ultraman Ace*, *Zone Fighter*) and debuting as a feature-film SFX director on the war drama *Samurai of the Big Sky* (1976). That film remains his favorite work, he says, because he succeeded in making a fresh picture during one of Toho's most creatively stale eras. "There have been many war movies produced by Toho, but most of them feature stock footage . . . although the producers wanted me to use stock footage, I insisted that I be allowed to use only new footage," Kawakita told *Cult Movies*. He also directed effects on *Sayonara Jupiter* (1983), the war movie *Zero* (1984), and *Gunhed* (1989) prior to *Biollante*, and he was an assistant director on the SFX staff of *Godzilla vs. The Smog Monster*, *The Last Days of Planet Earth*, and *The War in Space*.

While preserving the traditional methods invented decades before by Eiji Tsuburaya, Kawakita has put his own stamp on Toho's giant monster movies by accentuating the scope and size of Godzilla and his enemies, creating new and exciting powers and weapons for both the monsters and the military forces that combat them, and by exploring the use, albeit on a relatively limited basis due to budget constraints, of computer graphics, computer animation, and other modern techniques. Perhaps his biggest trademark is that almost all of his monsters, save for Godzilla, transform or "morph" over the course of a single film: Biollante begins as a giant, reptilian flower and later reappears as hideous creature that towers over Godzilla, seeking revenge against its brethren for attacking and killing it; King

Ghidorah is killed, only to be revamped as Mecha-Ghidorah; both Mothra and Battra undergo brilliant transformations to adult stage; MechaGodzilla combines with the Garuda warship to form Super MechaGodzilla; Space Godzilla is first seen as a crystalline creature traveling in the heavens, and then it becomes a Godzilla-like demon when it lands on Earth; and Destoroyah undergoes a variety of forms.

"I prefer to have [monsters] transform. It provides more entertainment for the members of the audience and it serves as an identifying characteristic of the current Godzilla films," Kawakita said in *Cult Movies #14*. One downside to his work, however, is that Kawakita portrays monsters as super-powered creatures who act out their aggressions not in animalistic, close combat but by waging wars at a distance, firing rays and other weapons. When he breaks from this habit — such as the titanic battle between Godzilla and Rodan in *Godzilla vs. Mecha-Godzilla*, or the fight between Godzilla Junior and Destoroyah in *Godzilla vs. Destoroyah*, the results are often outstanding. "It would almost be impossible for the monsters to wrestle with each other because of their tremendous size and weight. {And] the monsters seem too human when they wrestle with each other," he explained.

Kawakita has benefited from the many technical improvements that have occurred since the Tsuburaya days. The optical printers and digital compositors in use today have far higher resolution than the equipment used during the 1960s, enabling Kawakita to pull off a number of breathtaking composite shots in his films, such as the first view of the rose-form Biollante at Lake Ashino — a shot in which the camera pans up from the waterfront area to the lake, revealing the monster's full figure — which is beautifully executed and bears no evidence of matte lines.

The construction of the Godzilla suits, supervised on *Biollante* by veteran suit maker Noboyuki Yasumaru (a member of Tsuburaya's staff since the late 1960s, who oversaw construction of the 1970s Toho monster suits), and from *Godzilla vs. King Ghidorah* onward by Yasumaru's protégé, Tomomi Kobayashi, is more sophisticated than ever before, incorporating lighter and more durable materials and mechanisms that allow unprecedented movements, such as the tilting up and down and side to side of Godzilla's head. The structure of Toho's special effects department is also much different in the 1990s than it was in the Tsuburaya days, with most of Kawakita's staff working as freelancers rather than full-time studio employees. Thus, Kawakita has tapped some of Japan's finest designers and craftsmen from fields as divergent as animation studios and garage kit-modeling companies to help design and build his effects.

Kawakita has his shortcomings, however: As the *Heisei* Godzilla series progressed, his work tended to become more and more repetitive. In almost every film, for instance, the tide of the climactic battle turns when Godzilla, caught in a stranglehold by his opponent, uses his Nuclear Pulse, a burst of atomic energy within his body, which supercharges him and creates a concussive force that blasts the other monster away. And many of his monster designs, from his updated King Ghidorah and Mothra to the all-new Space Godzilla and Destoroyah, have been either overly derivative or completely outlandish.

Like Tsuburaya before him, Kawakita and his crew work under incredibly tight deadlines and strict restrictions on costs. "I always felt constrained by the budget and by time," he told *Cult Movies*. "We always are very rushed during both production and post-production. It's the nature of movie directors. We always want more time and more money. Most people who work in the American film industry are very surprised when they find out what the Japanese film industry is like."

KILLER WEED: *Godzilla vs. Biollante* is Koichi Kawakita's Godzilla masterpiece; while his subsequent efforts are also impressive, they don't match the spectacle of this film. The highlights are the monsters, particularly the newly designed Godzilla. Called the *Bio-Goji* design, it was created via two costumes and one robotic prosthetic of the monster's upper body and head — an updated version of the Cybot built for *Godzilla 1985*, this time constructed in the same scale as the costume, making it easier to film and ensuring that it more closely matches the details of the suit. The robot was used for close-up shots of the monster tilting its head back and roaring, revealing double rows of teeth lining its reptilian jaws (the first time ever that Godzilla had more than one set of choppers). Biollante, on the other hand, is unlike any monster in Toho's prior history, and both the "flower" version that fights Godzilla at Lake Ashino, capped by a huge rosebud and bearing a tumor-like heart that explodes when Godzilla unleashes his ray at it, and the "reptile" stage that wages the final battle with Godzilla at Wakasa, bearing

countless long, razor-sharp teeth from inside its alligator-like jaws, are something to behold. Both were costumes with an actor inside, although in both cases the stuntman didn't have much to do, standing on a platform and moving certain upper body parts with wires. The final-stage Biollante costume was built on rollers, and members of the SFX crew actually pushed the monster across the miniature set when Biollante made its charge at Godzilla, with the camera shaken violently to create the illusion of the Earth quaking as the immense creature moves across the ground. Godzilla's battle with the navy in the Uraga Strait and his attack on Osaka by night are showcases for the forced perspective and miniature photography work of Kawakita's director of special effects photography, Kenichi Eguchi.

A good amount of special effects footage shot for *Godzilla vs. Biollante* ended up on the cutting-room floor, some of which is included in the "making-of" disc in Toho's special-edition Laser Disc. A stop-motion animation sequence was filmed for the Godzilla-vs.-Biollante fight at Lake Ashino, with Biollante's animated tendrils swirling around Godzilla, but Kawakita opted not to use the footage because he felt it wouldn't match the live-action footage. After Godzilla kills Biollante at the lake and the flower dematerializes into a glowing mist, there was a scene wherein the hills around the lake are instantly covered with a blanket of colorful flowers. Although beautiful and poignant, the flowers were out-of-scale and appeared to be gigantic, and thus the footage was omitted.

Godzilla vs. Biollante is also hampered by a very lackluster and unappealing music score. Composer **Koichi Sugiyama** (b. 1931), known for writing the theme song to "The Return of Ultraman" TV series, various commercial jingles, pop songs, and the theme music to a film and video game called *Dragon Quest*, is simply not up to the task presented by the visual scope of this film. At times overly derivative of John Williams (Sugiyama's theme for the battle at Lake Ashino between Godzilla and Biollante sounds like the theme from *Jaws*, while his end-title theme is a rip-off of Williams' *Superman* main title), Sugiyama fails to come up with strong motifs for the monsters or for the Super-X2, leaving the film sputtering, without the musical energy it needs to pick up the already drawn-out pace. Apparently Tomoyuki Tanaka shared this assessment, for he utilized a rendition of Akira Ifukube's Godzilla theme from the LP *Ostinato* (a suite of newly re-corded Ifukube monster-music cuts released in the mid-1980s) for the main-title music.

GODZILLA vs. MIRAMAX

Only four-plus years lapsed between the release of *Godzilla 1985* in North America and Toho's solicitation of *Godzilla vs. Biollante* to foreign distributors, but the nature of the U.S. film business had changed. Low-budget monster movies (like the *Howling* series) were now relegated to the burgeoning straight-to-video market, where distributors avoided the mammoth costs associated with a theatrical release and made surefire profits. Meanwhile, the moviegoing public's threshold for suspending disbelief had been raised markedly by movies like *Terminator 2: Judgment Day* and *Aliens*. Could Toho's latest Godzilla movie play at the multiplexes? Fat chance.

In early 1990, Toho entered discussions with Miramax Film Corp., a distributor of foreign and art-house films (and, more recently, the studio that released Quentin Tarantino's *Pulp Fiction*), to distribute *Godzilla vs. Biollante*. The talks soon broke off, and Toho filed a lawsuit in Los Angeles federal court on August 29, 1990. In the suit, Toho accused Miramax of entering an oral agreement in June to pay Toho $500,000 for the North American, British, and Irish distribution rights to the picture, and then backing out of the deal.

The lawsuit delayed the picture's release for two years. An out-of-court settlement was eventually reached and Miramax bought the rights for an unreported figure. It is not known whether Miramax ever entertained thoughts (either before or after Toho's suit) of releasing *Biollante* in cinemas, but in the end, it gave the film minimal attention. With no publicity other than a one-page press release announcing Godzilla's "triumphant return," *Godzilla vs. Biollante* was licensed to HBO Video and released on VHS tape on October 9, 1992; it was subsequently released on Laser Disc, and shown on HBO's Cinemax cable TV channel. Thankfully, Miramax utilized Toho's uncut English-language international version of the film, and it was the first Godzilla video in widescreen format.

The Giant Rat and the Killer Plant

The Original Story of Godzilla vs. Biollante

In *Godzilla vs. Biollante*, writer Shinichiro Kobayashi opted not to use the threat of nuclear technology (a subject already covered numerous times) as the story's backdrop and instead introduced the modern themes of biotechnology and psychic powers. And, rather than challenging Godzilla with a traditional, super-powerful enemy monster, Kobayashi created a mysterious, beautiful but frightening creature. Kobayashi's story dealt with the moral dilemmas of biotechnology — this appealed to producer Tanaka, who wanted Godzilla movies to be socially relevant as well as entertaining.

Unlike the finished film that emerged later, Kobayashi's original draft of *Biollante* did not incorporate Godzilla into the central theme of bioscience-gone-wrong. In his story, a scientist named Dr. Shiranui (with financial backing from the Republic of Adelia), driven to the brink of madness by the death of his daughter, Erica, conducts a series of bizarre genetic experiments. His early research results in a genetic mutation, Deutalios, a giant monster over 50 meters long with a long tail, claws and four legs like a huge rat, created by merging fish and animal DNA. Deutalios destroys ships and eventually lands in Tokyo Bay; Godzilla, instinctively drawn to the beast, shows up and the two creatures battle in Yokohama. Deutalios, having been out of the water for too long, weakens and is easily defeated, and Godzilla eats its flesh.

Meanwhile, a young female reporter is investigating Shiranui and his top-secret experiment, called Biollante. The reporter begins to have psychic visions, in which she is surrounded by small flowers with humanoid faces, and hears a female voice calling to her. Convinced the visions are tied to her visits to Shiranui's lab, she confronts the scientist, who confesses the true nature of his research: In an attempt to preserve Erica's soul, Shiranui has combined cells from her corpse with those of a long-lived tropical plant, causing another genetic mutation. In the finale, Godzilla heads for Shiranui's lab — the forest shakes, the Earth splits and Biollante, a gigantic mutant plant with a feminine face, shoots skyward. Biollante uses the forest to extinguish fires caused by Godzilla's breath, and emits pollen that sears Godzilla's flesh. Godzilla, badly burned, retreats to the sea; Biollante, its mutation out-of-control, is consumed in a cloud of white energy.

Tanaka wanted Godzilla to be better incorporated into the story's biotechnology theme, so he hired young writer-director Kazuki Omori to develop the story. But the process took much longer than anticipated. "Before beginning, I studied for a long time," Omori said in *Japanese Giants* #8. Reading adventure novels, biotechnology and botany textbooks, etc. Finally, in the summer of 1986, I wrote the first version. Shortly after I began to write this, Toho asked me to work on another film. Thinking it would be good experience to do a movie with Toho before Godzilla, I accepted. But one and a half years passed and I did a full three films with Toho, while at the same time writing and revising my screenplay."

Over time, Omori polished the story, highlighting the psychic elements (he dropped the female reporter and substituted Miki Saegusa, the young psychic girl), eliminating the third monster Deutalios (at Tanaka's insistence), and most importantly, linking Godzilla to biotechnology. Not only did Omori have the scientist use Godzilla's radiation-based regenerative cells to give his daughter eternal life (thereby incorporating Godzilla's long-standing anti-nuclear message), he also invented a genetically engineered weapon (Anti-Nuclear Energy Bacteria) to fight Godzilla. Omori linked the story to *Godzilla* (1984) by creating the Super-x2, which cleverly uses Godzilla's atomic breath against him.

— *Jay Ghee*

MODERN-DAY MONSTER

Kenpachiro Satsuma: The Heart of Godzilla

Judging from his dedication to the role, it seems it was Kenpachiro Satsuma's destiny to play Godzilla. Even when he's not inside the bulky, 200-pound-plus latter-day Godzilla suits, Satsuma walks, talks, and thinks Godzilla. Simply put, he *is* Godzilla — at least in spirit.

A former steel worker, Satsuma (b. May 27, 1947, in Kawashima), began acting in the 1960s with bit parts in samurai films. Never much of a monster-movie fan, he was a bit taken aback when, in 1971, effects director Teruyoshi Nakano offered him the role of Hedorah, Godzilla's gooey opponent in *Godzilla vs. The Smog Monster*.

"When they told me I would be playing a monster, I became dejected, because I knew I would be completely covered by the costume," Satsuma said in a 1996 interview with *Cinefantastique* magazine. "No one would see my face. But I loved doing action scenes, and I thought it would be a unique experience.

"I really had no idea what I was doing, but I had the greatest teacher of monster-suit acting, Mr. Nakajima. He had so much experience that he knew exactly what to do. We rehearsed the scenes first without the costumes on, and even during filming he would shout out commands to me, from inside the Godzilla suit. It was a very rewarding experience, but it was also terribly difficult because the [Hedorah] costume was so heavy (nearly 300 pounds) and I could hardly move the way I was supposed to."

Satsuma (known back then by his real name, Kengo Nakayama) also played Gigan in *Godzilla on Monster Island* and *Godzilla vs. Megalon*. Eleven years later, when the actor originally hired to portray Godzilla in the monster's comeback film *Godzilla* (1984) backed out of the project, Nakano called on Satsuma again. It was a daunting assignment —

Kenpachiro Satsuma.
DAILY HERALD/ARLINGTON HEIGHTS, IL.
USED BY PERMISSION

Nakajima was closely identified with the role for decades, leaving a legacy that seemed impossible to live up to. Instead of trying to imitate Nakajima's Godzilla, Satsuma distanced himself from it and, over time, redefined the King of the Monsters' character, eschewing the humanism and humor of the 1960s and '70s and returning the beast to a more predatory, animalistic fury reminiscent of the 1954 original. When he assumed the coveted role of the monster, he viewed it as a sort of personal rebirth, and adopted his current stage name because "I wanted to start anew upon playing Godzilla," he said *in Markalite* #1.

Kenpachiro Satsuma clowns around with one of the
Bio-Goji **costumes on the set of** *Godzilla vs. Biollante.*
PHOTO BY MICHAEL BROWNING © 1989 THE MIAMI HERALD
USED BY PERMISSION

"Since Godzilla has appeared for such a long time, most people already have an image of what Godzilla should be," Satsuma said in an interview published in *Japanese Giants* #8. "He does not act like a human — he is a reptile. Haruo Nakajima defined a style for Godzilla, so I can't stray too far from that concept or people would not accept my Godzilla. In 1984 I had my first chance to play Godzilla, but I was so overwhelmed by the physical demands of the job that I could only think of the Nakajima Godzilla. However, by the time I finally felt I could succeed, the film was over! So this time, I am determined to continue from the point I left in 1984 and make a Satsuma-Godzilla. I want people to think of this Godzilla as a real animal."

Thus, like Nakajima before him, Satsuma became a fixture inside the monster — in the seven Godzilla movies made between 1984 and 1995, only once did another actor share the Godzilla role (in *Godzilla vs. Biollante*), and even then it was only due to hectic shooting schedules. He also has influenced improvements to the suit-making process, resulting in costumes that are lighter and easier to maneuver, leading to more effective monster performances. "The Godzilla costume used in *Godzilla 1985* was made to fit a man who was larger than I am, but he quit at the last minute. So, I took over the role," Satsuma said in *Cult Movies* #11. "This, along with the fact that the costume weighed 245 pounds, limited what I could do in it. The Godzilla costume used in *Godzilla vs. Biollante*, on the other hand, was made to fit me. In addition, it weighed only 180 pounds. I felt that the Godzilla costume used in *Godzilla 1985* controlled me, but that I controlled the one used in *Godzilla vs. Biollante*."

To the lay observer, acting inside the Godzilla suit might seem like child's play, a dream job. It's not. It requires incredible physical endurance and mental perseverance to withstand the weight of the suit, the grueling heat, the asphyxiation, and the lonely, dark isolation within it (Satsuma can only see the outside world through a handful of cheesecloth-like holes in Godzilla's neck). Satsuma has taken a few spills in his career — for example, during Godzilla's attack on Sapporo in *Godzilla vs. King Ghidorah*, Godzilla's foot breaks through the pavement and the monster careens to the ground. Satsuma slammed the side of his head against the miniature set platform as he fell but, fortunately, he wasn't seriously hurt. To keep himself in mental and physical shape for the role, Satsuma, who is adept at martial arts, created "Godzilla Kenpo," a combination of karate and Godzilla's movements.

"Obviously, it's very demanding physically," Satsuma told *Japanese Giants*. "The suit itself is 210 centimeters tall and weighs almost 80 kilograms. So it is big and heavy, and I need two or three people to help me in and out of the suit every time. Because of the danger from fires and explosions, I decided to wear goggles to protect my eyes. And because I cannot get any air once I am inside the costume I can barely last for 2 or 3 minutes before my head feels as if it will explode!"

Especially dangerous are the scenes filmed in the big outdoor pool on the Toho lot. The pool was constructed in 1960 for filming the naval battles in *I Bombed Pearl Harbor*, and was used subsequently over the next 30 years for many monster movies, including Godzilla's battle with the Japanese navy in *Godzilla vs. Biollante* and the battle with Mothra and Battra at sea in *Godzilla vs. Mothra*. In the 1990s, the pool was decreased in size, and later infilled and converted to a parking lot. The bottom of the pool was slick with algae and littered with debris from previous films, and a slip-and-fall accident could prove extremely hazardous.

"[The water scenes] are the most dangerous part of my job," Satsuma told *Cult Movies*. "If I fell over, I could drown. I would never be able to get back up with the Godzilla costume on." When filming a scene in the pool, or in a rainstorm (like the final battle in *Godzilla vs. Biollante*), the Godzilla suit tends to soak up large amounts of water, weighing it down and making it even more difficult to maneuver.

Even before it was announced that Godzilla would die and go on hiatus after *Godzilla vs. Destoroyah*, Kenpachiro Satsuma was approaching 50, and he had already decided to retire from the role. He has chronicled his career in several books, including the popular *Inside Godzilla* (published 1993), and another about his experience traveling to communist North Korea in the 1980s, when he played the titular character in a state-sponsored giant-monster film called *Pulgasary*, about a giant minotaur who defends feudal Korean rice farmers from marauding warlords.

"I have now done seven films as Godzilla, and I believe I have achieved most everything I have wanted to do inside the costume," he said in a 1996 interview. "Most importantly, I have always felt Godzilla should express its emotions, which is very difficult given the range of movements and expressions the suit can make. So, whatever Godzilla does — roaring, spewing his radiation breath, communicating with Godzilla Junior — I always try to add little movements that will show his emotional state, like moving his fingers, or a short glance. The *Heisei* Godzilla have a very different personality than the old Godzilla. He is very animalistic, always in motion. But I believe Godzilla is a very emotional creature."

Satsuma has become an international cult hero as the post-1985 series has gained the monster new legions of fans. But Satsuma keeps a clear perspective on the history of *kaiju eiga*, and the place that the 1990s Godzilla movies occupy in it.

"Of course, the newer films have superior special effects, because today they can build much better monster suits and miniature buildings, and computer graphics have been incorporated for some scenes. But the *Heisei* Godzilla series does not have the emotional spirit, that deep spirit that the works of Mr. Honda and Mr. Tsuburaya did. I think this was because Mr. Honda, and many members of the staff, had served during the war, and when the films depicted scenes of destruction it was a reflection somehow of their experiences in the war. There was a profoundness to those films that I do not think can be recreated."

Eighteen

THE TIME TRAVELERS

"Take that, you dinosaur!"

— Major Spielberg

GODZILLA vs. KING GHIDORAH

RATING (OUT OF FIVE STARS): ★ ★ ★

JAPANESE VERSION: GOJIRA VS. KINGUGIDORA. Released on December 14, 1991, by the Toho Motion Picture Company. Widescreen, in color. Running Time: 102 minutes. Screened at the Cannes Film Festival on May 9 and 14, 1992.

U.S. VERSION: Released directly to home video by Columbia TriStar Home Video in May 1998. Running Time: 102 minutes.

STORY: Futurians from the 23rd century travel back in time and erase Godzilla's birth from history, by preventing a dinosaur living on a South Pacific island during the 1940s from being exposed to U.S. nuclear tests; the time-travelers say their aim is to help Japan escape massive destruction by Godzilla, but their true motive — to prevent Japan's rise to economic supremacy — is revealed when they unleash King Ghidorah and demand a now Godzilla-less Japan's surrender. It doesn't work: The dinosaur becomes Godzilla anyway, kills Ghidorah and goes on a rampage; the heroes use 23rd-century technology to turn Ghidorah's corpse into Mecha-Ghidorah, a futuristic bio-mechanical robot, to defend Japan from Godzilla.

KAIJU CONUNDRUMS

Godzilla vs. Biollante was the most expensive Godzilla movie ever made, boasting a reported budget of about $10.7 million. Yet, after drawing standing-room-only crowds in its first few days of release, the film did only moderate business at the Japanese box office, and Toho wound up losing about $3 million on the picture (as reported in *Fortune* on October 7, 1991). To really put the Godzilla series back on the map, Executive Producer Tomoyuki Tanaka reneged on his vow to pit Godzilla only against all-new monsters and opted to further revitalize the series, commercially speaking, by bringing back Godzilla's greatest nemesis, the three-headed demon King Ghidorah. *Godzilla vs. King Ghidorah*, the first Godzilla movie made in the 1990s, is a wild and woolly, nostalgic throwback that recaptures the spirit of some of the best entries

265

The Godzillasaurus costume from *Godzilla vs. King Ghidora*, on display at a Godzilla exhibition in the suburban Fukuoka area, April 1992.

COURTESY OF WINTERGARDEN PRODUCTIONS

of the 1960s, most notably *Ghidrah: The Three-Headed Monster* and *Monster Zero*.

In a radical departure from classic *kaiju eiga* storytelling style, returning director-screenwriter Kazuki Omori revises Toho monster history with a mechanistic, deterministic spin in *Godzilla vs. King Ghidorah*. He re-writes the origins of Godzilla and King Ghidorah, supplying pseudo-plausible explanations for the existence of gigantic monsters that, up until now, were vaguely mythic creatures not completely understood by man. Omori makes a valiant effort to re-establish Godzilla's underlying nuclear metaphor — in this updated version of his genesis, the monster is a lonely holdover from the Age of Dinosaurs living on a South Seas island in 1944, later transformed into Godzilla by the mortal effects of nuclear testing. Omori also shows the dinosaur (called a "Godzillasaurus") defending Japanese troops during a World War II skirmish;

A close-up view of the Godzillasaurus costume.

COURTESY OF WINTERGARDEN PRODUCTIONS

The King Ghidorah costume from Godzilla vs. King Ghidorah, on
display at a Godzilla exhibition in the suburban Fukuoka area, April 1992.
COURTESY OF WINTERGARDEN PRODUCTIONS.

this event, and the kinship for the monster felt
by Shindo (a soldier saved by the dinosaur) is an
unprecedented expression of Godzilla's spiritual
relationship with Japan.

But, while Godzilla's new back-story meshes
well with the old mythology, Omori's flagrant tampering with continuity and tradition is disturbing.
When the time-travelers teleport the Godzillasaurus off Lagos Island in 1944, they erase Godzilla
from history and another Godzilla is created to
replace it — thus, the King of the Monsters in this
and all future movies through Godzilla vs. Destoroyah is a "new" beast. Even less appealing is the
birth of the new King Ghidorah, the result of three
cute, fuzzy, genetically engineered little futuristic
pets called "Drats" (sometimes spelled "Dorats")
being exposed to an H-bomb test and fusing
together into a giant monster. This cause-and-
effect rationale is silly compared to the simple-yet-
mysterious way the monster was introduced in

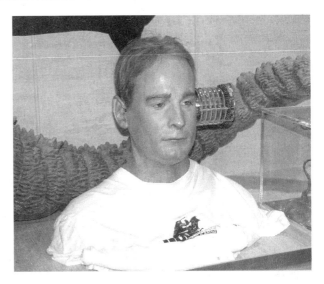

A close-up of the prosthetic M11 head, with the door
to its "disk drive" open, as seen on display at the
now-defunct "Godzilla Shop" in Kobe, circa 1993.
COURTESY OF WINTERGARDEN PRODUCTIONS

Various pieces of armature that were added to the King Ghidorah costume to create the cyborg-monster Mecha-Ghidorah in *Godzilla vs. King Ghidorah*. The props were on display at a Godzilla exhibition in the suburban Fukuoka area, April 1992.
COURTESY OF WINTERGARDEN PRODUCTIONS.

Ghidrah: The Three-Headed Monster, as a marauding space dragon roaming from planet to planet, wreaking havoc. Omori's screenplay also contains conundrums common to time-travel stories. After Godzilla is erased from history, logic dictates that present-day folk would be ignorant of him, yet everyone talks matter-of-factly about the monster. And, if the Drats were irradiated by nuclear tests in the 1950s, why does King Ghidorah wait until 1992 to appear (remember, Godzilla first showed up just months after the Operation Bravo blast)?

Released just as Japan's "bubble economy" period of the late 1980s — in which the country sailed to the forefront of world economic powers — was ebbing, the film is bogged down by crass moralizations about Japan's role in the world community and its tenuous relations with other nations. The implication seems to be that Japan is smarter and richer than everybody else, and political tensions over trade issues are borne out of America's fears of being left behind in the coming century.

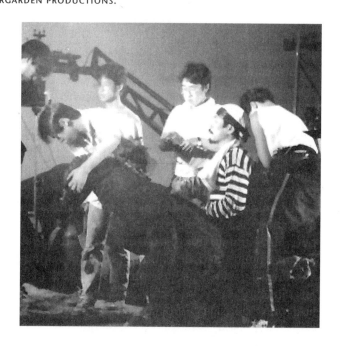

Kenpachiro Satsuma climbs into the Godzilla suit on the SFX set of *Godzilla vs. King Ghidorah*.
COURTESY OF ROBERT SCOTT FIELD

268

Robert Scott Field in burned M11 makeup. The android's emergence from a fiery car crash with its internal mechanism exposed was patterned after a scene in James Cameron's *Terminator* in which the futuristic cyborg assassin (Arnold Schwarzenegger) crawls out of a wrecked tanker-truck without its human exoskeleton.

COURTESY OF ROBERT SCOTT FIELD

At the same time, Omori expresses a certain introspective unease about Japan's immense economic power and the dangers it might bring, including the possibility that Japan might one day even arm itself with nuclear weapons. Yasuaki Shindo (Yoshio Tsuchiya), a former general-turned-developer who helped rebuild Japan's economy in the postwar era, is both a symbol of Japanese resolve and a harbinger of such danger, for he secretly procures an armed nuclear submarine to defend Japan from attack. Godzilla has the final say on the matter, however, when the submarine sent to recreate the monster (by irradiating a dinosaur deposited under the sea 46 years before, that somehow avoided drowning) is destroyed by a raging eternal force. Godzilla, according to this film, is as much a god as

a monster, an unavoidable consequence of man's nuclear folly that cannot be wiped from the slate with mere time tomfoolery.

Interestingly, in the early story-writing stages, Omori originally planned to have the Japanese government possess a nuclear weapon. "They were hiding it in order to use it to revive Godzilla in the event of a national emergency," Omori said in *Toho SF Special Effects Movie Series Vol. 6.* "But we figured the Japanese army would not cooperate with us, although I thought the story would work because it was fictitious. But we then decided the people of Japan should not have anything like a nuclear weapon, it was kind of like a policy . . . *Godzilla* movies are basically antinuclear movies, so we should not use that type of story, especially in an entertainment movie like *Godzilla.*"

Much of the fun in *Godzilla vs. King Ghidorah* stems from the villains, the time travelers who have come to cut off Japan's economic miracle at the pass. Like the *X-Seijin* from *Monster Zero*, these baddies fly around in an impressive spaceship (actually, a time machine called Mother), they have the ability to control the will of giant monsters, and of course they have an evil scheme up their seemingly benevolent sleeve. Like many Toho films of the '60s, the cast is augmented by Caucasian actors, even more than in the past, because of the large number of American characters in the film. And, as in the old days, they are non-professional actors. Most of them are quite competent, especially Chuck Wilson, an international judo champion who runs several martial-arts schools in Japan, as the leader of the Earth Union, Wilson. The futurians'

(Left to right) Director Kazuki Omori, Robert Scott Field (M11), Yoshio Tsuchiya (Shindo), Anna Nakagawa (Emi), and Megumi Odaka (Miki Saegusa) attend the premiere of *Godzilla vs. King Ghidorah* in Tokyo.

COURTESY OF ROBERT SCOTT FIELD

(Left to right) Director Kazuki Omori, Yoshio Tsuchiya, and Robert Scott Field relax in kimonos during a break in the shooting of *Godzilla vs. King Ghidorah*.
COURTESY OF ROBERT SCOTT FIELD

Richard Berger (Gurenchiko) and Robert Scott Field clown around with their scaly friend.
COURTESY OF ROBERT SCOTT FIELD

leaders also include Gurenchiko (Richard Berger), a balding, red-haired Russian and Emi Kano (Anna Nakagawa), a Japanese woman with a guilty conscience who becomes a turncoat and saves her ancestors from the doomsday scheme.

As in *Biollante*, Omori crams the script with too many characters, but because the action revolves around the time travelers and the monsters rather than innumerable intersecting plots, the players and their roles in furthering the drama are more well defined. Isao Toyohara is particularly good as Terasawa, the freelance journalist investigating the birth of Godzilla who, much to his surprise, is given a tattered copy of his own book by the futurians, years before he's written it. The minor players include Katsuhiko Sasaki (of *Megalon* and *Terror of Mecha-Godzilla*) as Dr. Masaaki, a scientist who helps the reporter decipher Godzilla's past; comic actor Koichi Ueda as a delirious ex-Japanese soldier who first reveals the story of the dinosaur who saved Japanese troops on Lagos Island in 1944; and Megumi Odaka, returning again as the psychic Miki Saegusa, now working as a Godzilla-tracker for the government.

THREE HEADS ARE BETTER

In writing his second Godzilla movie, Omori said he tried to take a somewhat more restrained approach. "I learned a lesson in filming *Biollante*: It has to be a monster drama, not just monsters in a human drama," Omori said in the *Toho SF* interview. "The main lesson I learned in these two movies is how to deal with special effects. I couldn't listen to everything director Kawakita said, because he sometimes ignores the screenplay. If I went along with him every time, I would have got tangled up in his pace and I would have lost my pace. So, I had to be grounded very solidly." Nevertheless, there is a lot going on in this movie, and inevitably some key points get lost in the shuffle. Emi reveals that in the future, Japan has become an immensely powerful nation that uses its wealth, not military might, to reign as the world's supreme power by buying up entire continents. The futurians plan to enslave the Japanese (once they have surrendered due to Ghidorah's attacks) and sabotage their future domination of world markets by forcing them to rely on technologically inferior computer technology! This idea, while vaguely interesting, is quickly tossed away, leaving the viewer to wonder why it was included in the first place, for it adds nothing to the story. Another subplot meant to have an emotional impact, yet simply dashed off, is the subtle attraction that develops between Emi and Terasawa. At the film's end, when Emi returns to her home century in the KIDS time-traveling craft, she casually reveals that she and Terasawa are distant relatives across the generations. Out of nowhere, Terasawa's girlfriend, who's been missing for the entire second half of the film, shows up beside him, and all is back to normal in his love life.

This is also Omori's first Godzilla film in which he overtly and often manifests his admiration for big-budget American blockbuster movies, with "homages" that come off as rather half-assed — something he only vaguely hinted at with the espionage elements in *Biollante*. There are references to *Back to the Future* (time travel), *Close Encounters* (the UFO appearing over Tokyo), *Gremlins* (the drats), *Star Wars* (the laser gun battle, reminiscent of the Storm Troopers), *Terminator* (the balding, Caucasian android M-11, who runs at hyperspeed by changing the camera's shutter speed), and *Aliens* (the Mecha-Ghidorah cockpit is reminiscent of the forklift-like vehicle Ripley uses to fight the creature).

Perhaps the most embarrassing (but, admittedly, very funny — although perhaps not in the way intended) scenes in the film involve the two American naval officers, who seem to be all alone on a huge destroyer ship in the middle of the Pacific in World War II. In one scene, the KIDS time machine whizzes over the navy men's heads at night, and the commander tells his subordinate not to worry about reporting it as a UFO. "You can tell your son

M11 (Robert Scott Field) on the set inside the cockpit of the KIDS time machine, preparing for the Godzilla-erasing mission to Lagos Island in 1944.
COURTESY OF ROBERT SCOTT FIELD

about it when he's born, *Major Spielberg*." The line is delivered in a hilariously effeminate voice by the commander, played by Kent Gilbert, a lawyer and former Mormon missionary well known in Japan for his family-values talks on the lecture circuit. Gilbert has been raked by readers of *G-Fan* as one of the worst actors in the modern-day Godzilla series (perhaps unfairly, since he's not an actor after all), a fact that he apologized for in a 1995 interview. "I was excited to do the film, because hey, not everybody gets to be in a Godzilla movie! I used to watch them on television when I was a kid. We did all my scenes on a real ship, a Japan Naval Self Defense Force ship that was docked in Yokosuka. Everything was shot in one day. I didn't even have a full script — we didn't know what the story was or anything."

The picture moves quickly, and is diverting enough to overcome its weaknesses. The special effects are great, particularly the final battle set amid the gigantic skyscrapers, towering over the monsters, in Tokyo's Shinjuku section. The "new" Godzilla introduced in this story stands 100 meters (about 330 feet) tall, compared to 50 meters for the 1954 original and 80 meters for the 1985–89 monster. Also impressive is an incredible battle between Godzilla and the souped-up Japanese military, complete with an updated version of the ray-shooting tanks of the classic Toho films, in the city of Sapporo. The new Ghidorah, though, is a bit of a letdown. Its design hardly departs at all from Eiji Tsuburaya's original Ghidorah, and in some ways it is inferior, moving stiffly both on the ground and in flight. The most ill-advised change is Ghidorah's

The *Ghido-Goji* Godzilla costume is readied for filming.
COURTESY OF ROBERT SCOTT FIELD

Anna Nakagawa, Robert Scott Field, and Megumi Odaka
COURTESY OF ROBERT SCOTT FIELD

Robert Scott Field with the M11 prosthetic head.
COURTESY OF NORMAN ENGLAND

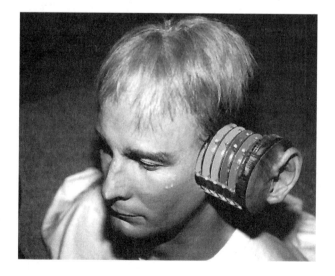

Close up of the M11 head prop.
COURTESY OF NORMAN ENGLAND

roar: In the old days, each of Ghidorah's heads had a separate, tittering cry that sounded quite eerie, but the new version emits a stock monster screech, a sort of low-rent version of Rodan's roar.

"We decided to rethink the whole image and design of King Ghidorah," SFX director Koichi Kawakita said in *Toho SF Special Effects Movie Series Vol. 6.* "I thought we should use the image and design of a Western-type dragon, from like a fantasy tale or something, instead of an Eastern or Chinese type of dragon." But the new Ghidorah design does not deviate sufficiently enough from Eiji Tsuburaya's 1964 version to establish its own identity. The main differences relate to the monster's three heads, which have no hair, and have long, straight horns around the perimeter of the face, rather than the original Ghidorah's crescent-shaped spikes.

Like the original Ghidorah, the new one is created with a man in an outsized monster suit with the aid of wire-works technicians manipulating the three heads and wings from above; but, except for an impressive shot of Ghidorah landing on top of a building during its attack on Fukuoka, the creature moves with less grace and manic energy than its predecessor — and the puppet utilized for flying scenes (including Ghidorah's battle with the fighter jets) is stiff and unconvincing. And unlike the glorious fireball birth of the monster in *Ghidrah: The Three-Headed Monster*, not much thought was given to the new Ghidorah's entrance. When the Lagos Island expedition returns to the present, Wilson simply announces that the new monster has appeared, and soon Ghidorah, preceded by an ominous shadow, is seen flying over Japan. Toho Video's special edition Laser Disc of *Godzilla vs. King Ghidorah* contains unused footage that Koichi Kawakita shot for Ghidorah's entrance, utilizing optical animation. Although the effect is somewhat fake-looking, it is more imaginative than what occurs in the finished film.

Emi returns to the 23rd century and excavates the still-living monster from the ocean floor (even more unbelievable than the dinosaur who spent less than 50 years there) and turns its body into the hull of a cyborg, Mecha-Ghidorah, to rid 1992 Japan of Godzilla. Mecha-Ghidorah features a robotic middle head that spurts a luminescent ribbon ray, and twin titanium wings replacing the dead limbs of the monster. Equipped with the Godzilla Grip (an assembly of clamps fixed to electrical cables that attach to Godzilla's hide and give him a mighty jolt) and the Machine Hand (a gigantic vice grip capable of carrying Godzilla away) the overhauled monster (which was an empty costume controlled entirely by wires, with no actor inside) impresses where King Ghidorah himself does not.

Koichi Kawakita re-deploys the two Godzilla costumes built for *Godzilla vs. Biollante* again, and due to the settling of the rubber and to several refurbishments, Godzilla actually looks better in this film than the last, with beefed-up chest musculature and arms. But the real curiosity of the picture is Godzilla's ancestor, the Godzillasaurus. According to Kazuki Omori's original story outline for *Godzilla vs. King Ghidorah*, the dinosaur that mutated into Godzilla was a tyrannosaurus. The Godzillasaurus, a hybrid of a tyrannosaur and Godzilla, was introduced by creature designer Shinji Nishikawa, who "couldn't accept that a tyrannosaur could become Godzilla."[38] The Godzillasaurus suit, which had dinosaurian claws on the backs of its feet and could tilt its head slightly upward (unlike the Godzilla suits) was worn by stuntman Wataru Fukuda. Because the dinosaur's arms are shorter than Godzilla's, the costume had no arm-holes; instead, Fukuda kept his arms inside the suit and controlled the movement of the Godzillasaurus's tiny forearms with handles. The Godzillasaurus scenes were shot outdoors, in natural sunlight, on the Toho Studios' lot, and real octopus blood was utilized for the creature's wounds, to heighten the realism. However, the Godzillasaurus' attack on the American troops hardly comes off as realistic, due to the stiff movements of the suit and the embarrassing effects of the monster's feet stepping on soldiers, and especially its tail swatting them down, which apparently was just a hand-operated prop swung around by one or more men standing off-camera. Strangest of all, when the U.S. warship opens fire on the Godzillasaurus, the monster's painful wails echo a familiar cry — it's the roar of Gamera, the giant flying turtle!

Thankfully, the Maestro Akira Ifukube was persuaded to return to the Godzilla series for the first time in 16 years. With so many new talents at work in the new Godzilla films, Ifukube's presence lends a sense of authenticity and continuity; unfortunately, his work on *Godzilla vs. King Ghidorah* is overly derivative of his older film compositions. Except for the theme heard during the Godzillasaurus's battle with the American troops, Ifukube's score features hardly any new music, and relies on his standard Godzilla theme and the Ghidorah motif introduced in *Monster Zero*, plus a piece of music culled from *Rodan* (from Rodan's battle with the jets, here used during Ghidorah's battle with jets)

and music culled from *King Kong vs. Godzilla* for the opening UFO sequence. Still, it is delightful to hear new, updated recordings of Ifukube's music, which remains forceful and passionate.

GODZILLA vs. THE YANKEES

The scene in which the young Godzillasaurus defends a Japanese regiment from American attackers generated a lot of free publicity for *Godzilla vs. King Ghidorah*. With the Japanese-U.S. trade deficit a perennial news item during George Bush's presidential term, the American media zeroed in on the film in the weeks after its Japanese premiere, taking director Kazuki Omori to task for alleged "anti-Americanism." Most of these reports weren't really thought-provoking or insightful, and all of them were worth a laugh.

The best one was aired by the syndicated TV show *Entertainment Tonight*, which showed a clip of the scene in question (surreptitiously filmed with a camcorder inside a Tokyo cinema, because Toho would not loan them the footage) and featuring interviews with Omori and Gerald Glaubitz, a crusty veteran and spokesman for the Pearl Harbor Survivors Association.

"I think it's very poor taste," said Glaubitz, who clearly was interviewed in the U.S., and who was (revealingly) not asked whether or not he had seen the movie. "People have been trying to better the relations between the two countries, and I think this just divides them more."

Entertainment Tonight also trotted out James Bailey, a scholar on Japanese films, who said, "The last three [Godzilla] films have had a very pronounced anti-American bias about them." Meanwhile, Hidekichi Yamane, a Toho spokesman, got into the act by telling the Associated Press, "Of course, I realize it may be unpleasant for Americans to watch. . . . But I think it's not as bad as those Hollywood war movies that portray Japanese soldiers with buckteeth."

For his part, Omori denied any anti-U.S. intent, but he intimated that the film was intended as a commentary on bubble-economy-era Japan's relationships with other countries. "Japan has been bashed by the rest of the world because it achieved such economic miracles. So I took this background into consideration in portraying Godzilla," Omori said. "The American actors . . . in the film were very happy about being crushed and squished by God-zilla and they went home happy. So, taking all this into consideration, I don't see any anti-Americanism in the film."

Other social critics saw *King Ghidorah* as a treatise not on Japanese-U.S. relations, but on the Japanese people's own uneasiness with their country's great wealth and opulence. Critics took note that during the final battle with Mecha-Ghidorah, as Godzilla sprays the sky with his radiation breath, he knocks down the top half of the then-new, 48-story Tokyo City Hall building in Shinjuku, a building known to the Japanese unaffectionately as the "tax tower." The 160-billion-Yen structure, built of marble and steel, "for many Tokyoites symbolized the excesses of Japan in the late '80s," said an article in the *Wall Street Journal*.

"I feel relieved when he [Godzilla] destroys build-ings," Omori said in the article. "It's as if Godzilla is destroying the city full of gaudiness."

NIKE
GODZILLA
TELEVISION COMMERCIAL

PLEAS
DO NOT
TOUCH

GODZILLA'S GREATEST BATTLE? Not really, but this Godzilla suit (seen here on display at the 1993 Marin County Fair) was made in the U.S.A. by Industrial Light and Magic and appeared in the infamous "Godzilla Vs. Barkley" commercial for Nike shoes. The spot debuted on Japanese television in 1992 and was originally set to air in Japan only, but was so successful that Nike decided to bring it to America. A snippet of the 30-second spot premiered during the Major League Baseball All-Star Game in June, 1992 and the full commercial was first shown during the MTV Music Awards broadcast on September 9, 1992. The commercial, created for Nike by Portland's Wieden & Kennedy ad agency, begins with Godzilla trashing Tokyo with his radiation breath; a giant-sized Sir Charles challenges the Big G to a game of one-on-one, and Godzilla topples into a building as Barkley scores a dunk. ILM's effects are faithful to the Toho methods: Godzilla's breath was painstakingly created with hand-drawn cel animation and the Godzilla suit is based upon the latter-day Toho G-costumes, although it emphasizes the monster's campiness with a big grin. A short documentary on the making of the commercial's special effects was broadcast on the *Scientific American* teleseries.

PHOTOS BY ALICE COOPER AND LUNA NYX

The G-Archives

S.O.L. ON THE
SATELLITE OF LOVE

Godzilla vs. Mystery Science Theater 3000

Unless you've been living under a rock (or in a place with crappy cable television service) for the past decade, you undoubtedly know about *Mystery Science Theater 3000*, the program largely responsible for the cult of "bad movie" fandom that emerged in the late 1980s and '90s. The show has the silliest, and most inventive premise to come along in a great while: a lowly janitor (Joel Robinson) at a futuristic super-corporation ("Gizmonic Institute") is banished into space by his insane, sadistic boss (Dr. Frederick Forrester). Aboard the "Satellite of Love," the janitor is subjected to brain experiments wherein he is forced to watch dozens of pathetic movies. To keep from going insane (or getting bored), the janitor and his two robot friends, Tom Servo and Crow T. Robot, supply each film with a running commentary of jokes, pop culture references, improvised dialogue, etc.

MST3K premiered on a local TV station in the Minneapolis area in 1988–89, where it ran for two seasons before being acquired by Comedy Central. In the very early going, Godzilla and his *kaiju eiga* ilk became victims to the show's comic dissection. In the show's first season, five of Daiei's Gamera movies were featured: *Gamera, Gamera vs. Barugon, Gamera vs. Gyaos, Gamera vs. Guiron*, and *Gamera vs. Zigra*. These episodes, filled with Gamera-inspired musical numbers — "Tibby, Oh Tibby," "Gamera is really neat/Gamera is full of meat," a Wagnerian "Gamera Dammerung," a bit where "Michael Feinstein" sings about Gamera à la Cole Porter, and another where Joel and the robots perform the Gamera theme in jazz, rap, reggae, rock, and other styles — remain among MST3K's all-time best.

Two Godzilla movies were beamed up to the S.O.L., both during the show's second season (1989–90). First came *Godzilla vs. Megalon*, highlighted by Joel and the robots' creative translation of the Jet Jaguar song at the end of the movie. "His head looks like Jack Nicholson," they sing, and "He'd like to bash that kid against a rock." Little Rokuro takes quite a few comedic swats throughout the film, most of them ridiculing the boy's high-pitched, badly enunciated, English-dubbed voice. Lots of potshots are taken at the shabby SFX work, such as when Megalon rises from the deep and Crow quips, "He awakens with the worst special effects of the morning," or during the military mobilization scenes, where the crew joyously points out the obvious miniatures by screaming, "Fakey!" Another highlight of the show is a running gag wherein several scenes featuring Jinkawa, the race car driver, are edited together into a "promo reel" for a mock TV detective drama called *Rex Dark, Eskimo Spy!* And when Goro calls out "Rokku-chan" to his little brother (sounding something akin to "Roxanne"), the crew launches into the famous Police song: "You don't have to put on the red light . . ."

The MST3K really show their love of Godzilla and the genre in their treatment of *Godzilla versus The Sea Monster*, which aired at the end of the second season. Although the film commentary isn't especially good, this episode is memorable for the "Godzilla Genealogy Bop," a cute, *Sesame Street*-style musical number that begins with Godzilla's origins from an atomic blast and traces his family tree, which also includes the Incredible Hulk, Kermit the Frog, and Swamp Thing. The show also featured a skit in which Crow and Tom Servo dress

CHEAP SHOTS 'R' US: The original Satellite of Love crew (silhouetted L to R): Tom Servo, Joel Hodgson, and Crow, gleefully dissect a Gamera movie.

PHOTO © BEST BRAINS INC.

up like the Infant Island fairy girls, and are visited by "Mothra" (played by then-writer and future show host Mike Nelson), who admonishes the robots for making fun of his faithful priestesses.

A weird bit of trivia: The print of *Godzilla versus The Sea Monster* used for this episode was distributed by Film Ventures International, a company not known to have ever held the U.S. rights to the film. It features an opening credits sequence comprised of footage from *Son of Godzilla* (showing Akira Kubo running away from the Gimantises), accompanied by cheapish synthesizer-type music. Several of the credits are blatantly incorrect or misspelled, including "Akira Akarada" and "Jun Fakuda," and the musical score is attributed not to Masaru Sato, but to Karl M. Demer, who apparently wrote the tacked-on opening title theme.

Nineteen

EARTH'S FINAL FURY

"My company has destroyed forests. I feel very guilty."

— Mr. Ando

GODZILLA vs. MOTHRA
a.k.a GODZILLA AND MOTHRA: THE BATTLE FOR EARTH

RATING (OUT OF FIVE STARS): ★ ★ 1/2

JAPANESE VERSION: GOJIRA VS. MOSURA. Released on December 12, 1992, by the Toho Motion Picture Company. Widescreen, in color. Running Time: 102 minutes.

U.S. VERSION: Released directly to home video by Columbia TriStar Home Video in May 1998. Running Time: 102 minutes.

STORY: A huge meteorite's impact in the Pacific Ocean sets off a chain of environmental disturbances and unearths Mothra's gigantic egg on Infant Island; a greedy developer kidnaps Mothra's tiny twin fairies, and when Mothra plunders Tokyo trying to rescue them, the military opens fire on the gigantic insect and she cocoons herself atop the Diet building, emerging as an adult moth. Meanwhile, Battra, Mothra's legendary nemesis, reawakens in the Arctic, attacks Nagoya, and battles Godzilla undersea; eventually, Mothra and Battra settle their differences and unite against their common *kaiju* enemy.

SAVE THE EARTH (AGAIN)

By reviving an old favorite like King Ghidorah, Toho regained momentum with the Godzilla series, so it was only logical to bring back another classic God-zilla nemesis. The result was *Godzilla vs. Mothra*, released the following year. Although the directorial chores were given to series newcomer **Takao Okawara** this time out, Kazuki Omori once again handled the screenwriting chores, weaving a loose remake of both *Mothra* (1961) and *Godzilla vs. The Thing* (1964) with ecological themes thrown in to update the story for modern audiences.

Godzilla vs. Mothra is the biggest money-maker of the new Godzilla films, selling 4.2 million tickets during its Japanese theatrical run, making it Japan's most successful domestic film in 1993 and second only to *Jurassic Park* in overall box office. Its great success is somewhat curious, since really it is an uneven effort, full of impressive special effects but hindered by an unfocused screenplay that bounces back and forth between heavy-handed environmentalism and a half-baked monster story. Godzilla seems to be included only for marquee value — his presence is not integral to the story until the final reel when he becomes the common enemy against which the yin and yang of Mothra and a new monster, a "black Mothra" called Battra, unite. At its heart, this is a "women's film," albeit a weak one, dominated by the feminine monster Mothra, a new pair of singing tiny twin girls, and a subplot about the failed marriage of a female government official and an Indiana Jones-like character and their young daughter. Perhaps this, more than anything else is the key to *Godzilla vs. Mothra*'s popularity, for in the early 1990s about 70 percent of Japan's movie audience was comprised of women, mostly unmarried.

Compared to the wild and woolly fun of *King Ghidorah* or the attempted intrigue of *Biollante*, this is a rather dull movie with a wafer-thin story and cookie-cutter characters. Worst of all, for the first time since *Megalon*, a child is featured prominently in the cast, a red flag signaling that Toho was backing off from the more mature tone of the first few *Heisei* Godzillas and pandering to all age groups. Much time is wasted during the first half of the film establishing the characters, their relationships, and the origins of Mothra. Takuya the treasure thief is busted for desecrating an ancient temple in Thailand while stealing an artifact (in one of Omori's Spielberg tributes); the Japanese government (including Takuya's ex-wife Masako) bails him out of jail on condition that he investigate strange phenomena on Infant Island, where some type of important development is planned. The trip to the island burns up running time without adding much to the story, padded by "funny" sequences like the collapse of a rickety suspension bridge (another Indiana Jones gag) and Masako and Ando (an executive with the development firm, who wears his suit even in the jungle) pouring water out of their soaked shoes.

Finally, they stumble across Mothra's egg and receive, from Mothra's two tiny channeler women, a long-winded history lesson about the Cosmos, a race of aliens who occupied Earth 12,000 years ago and were gifted with advanced technology. In the most contrived, childish, and preachy speech ever made in a Toho monster film, the fairies explain that the current spate of typhoons, earthquakes, volcanic eruptions, and global warming is Mother Earth's payback for mankind's unbridled environmental desecration; the same thing happened to the Cosmos ages ago — when their scientists tried to control the weather, the Earth unleashed Battra and a titanic battle was waged between Mothra (the Cosmos' protector) and the new beast. In the end, the Cosmos were wiped out and the two monsters disappeared; now that the balance of nature is upset again, the monsters this way come. Given this prophetic information, the heroes do the only logical thing: They take Mothra's egg to Japan for safekeeping, but en route Godzilla and Battra show up, and Mothra hatches and swims back to Infant Island. Then the men show their true colors: Ando, who only wanted the egg for its exploitation value, now fears losing face at his company so he kidnaps the Cosmos and brings them home; Takuya steals them back, but only to sell them to an American promoter for $1 million. In short order, both men realize the errors of their ways.

The final third of the movie is all about monsters and nothing about people, leaving the audience to ponder the point of all this mumbo-jumbo about nature's revenge and the world coming to an end, treasure-hunting adventurers, environment-plundering developers, family values, and so on — once Godzilla has been defeated, the doomsday scenarios are forgotten. While the monster action is unfolding, most of the characters watch from a great distance or on large video monitors in a government office (some of the video graphics, however, are impressive, including the heat-sensitive readout of Godzilla, after his emergence from the erupting volcano on Mount Fuji). In the end, after Battra is killed, the Cosmos reveal that the monster's true mission was to intercept a meteor on a collision course with Earth. Mothra, the most benevolent and selfless of giant insects, agrees to save the Earth from this terrible fate, and the movie ends with the monster flying into outer space.

It is necessary to recount all these plot details only because *Godzilla vs. Mothra* really has no plot, only story fragments sewn together into a loose-knit scenario that is neither interesting nor compelling. Director Takao Okawara (b. 1949) joined Toho in 1972 and was an assistant director on Shiro Moritani's *Tidal Wave* (1973), Akira Kurosawa's

Kagemusha, the Shadow Warrior (1980), and several Kihachi Okamaoto films, and he won a Kido Award for the screenplay for his directorial debut *Super Girl Reiko* (1991) starring Arisa Mizuki. But despite his impressive credits, Okawara's debut as the seventh director in the Godzilla series is rather bland — he lacks the talent to reign in and streamline Kazuki Omori's meandering screenplay and the power to overcome the Toho front office's penchant for throwing incongruous and unnecessary elements into the story to please the widest possible audience. His treatment of the drama as a light-hearted comedy, even with all its didactic environmentalism, is particularly curious. "I think that the tone of many Japanese films is too serious," Okawara said in *Cult Movies* #11. "I regard Godzilla films purely as entertainment. That's why I like to put shots offering comic relief into scenes in which people are seen panicking." Okawara is clearly a better director than Omori — this is a much smoother, more evenly paced film than the last two Godzillas, and in future efforts Okawara would prove to be the best monster-movie craftsman among Toho's latter-day talent.

A MONSTER CRIME: On March 17, 1992, as pre-production work was under way on *Godzilla vs. Mothra*, someone sneaked into Toho's special effects department and stole one of the two *Bio-Goji* Godzilla suits that was used in both *Biollante* and *King Ghidorah*, and which was slated to be used in the new film as well. A "Godzilla hunt" was launched for the stolen costume, valued at about $37,000, and it ended when an elderly woman found it in a bamboo patch in the suburbs about a week later (reported in *The Hollywood Reporter*, March 26, 1992). While the costume was AWOL, Koichi Kawakita's staff began work on a new one, cast from the same molds as the *Bio-Goji* suits. The new costume, called *Batto-Goji*, is less muscular than the last one but does not deviate much from the standard Kawakita-era Godzilla designs: small head, large body, double rows of teeth, and pronounced dorsal fins cast in heavy plastic (a separate set of dorsal plates, with electric lights installed inside, is used to enhance the glowing of the fins when Godzilla emits his atomic breath). The new suit also has more pronounced fangs jutting from the front corners of its mouth, and as for technological advancements, it was the first suit ever to have the ability to tilt its head backward and forward.

Special Effects Director Koichi Kawakita in April, 1992, showing off the Japanese academy award he won for his special effects work on *Godzilla vs. King Ghidorah*.
COURTESY OF WINTERGARDEN PRODUCTIONS

However, drastic changes were made to Godzilla's sound effects. When Toho resurrected the monster in 1984, it abandoned the high-pitched roar of the 1960s and '70s for the deep, bellowing growl of the 1954 original, but here Godzilla reverts to an elephantine screech. This change apparently did not please fans — in 1993, director Okawara told the Associated Press, "We tried a slight alteration in Godzilla's voice . . . but we got a lot of letters from angry Godzilla fans." Apparently, they didn't get quite enough letters to convince them it was a mistake, for Godzilla's roar would remain unchanged through the rest of the 1990s films. Worse is the new sound effect accompanying Godzilla's radioactive breath, a tinny noise that sounds like it was culled from a cheap video game.

Godzilla gets most of the SFX highlights in this movie, particularly his emergence from the Mt. Fuji volcano, which is far superior to a similar scene in *Biollante* (apparently, Kawakita knew he didn't get it quite right the first time and wanted another shot), flames, fireworks, and lava erupting all around the monster, lending an element of danger to the shoot for now-veteran Godzilla actor Kenpachiro Satsuma, who said it was the most difficult scene to film in his monster career. "The scene was shot at night," Satsuma said in *Cult Movies* #21. "We didn't shoot it during the day and use a filter to make it seem as if the scene were taking place at night. Many bright lights, gasoline, gun powder, and napalm were used. I had to climb up the inside of the volcano, which was very steep. Pyrotechnics were going off everywhere. There were cables and ropes everywhere. A moment after each explosion that took place in front of me, the staff members would have to pull the shell out of the way so I wouldn't step on it." Also impressive, although rather brief, is Godzilla's confrontation with the Japanese military, which deploys updated Maser cannons (first introduced in the Wakasa battle in *Biollante*, and based on the tanks from *War of the Gargantuas*) and fighter jets equipped with Maser rays, reminiscent of the X-Wing fighters from *Star Wars*.

Godzilla really plays second fiddle to Mothra and Battra, and unfortunately these two monsters are not quite as awe-inspiring. Kawakita bases his Mothra designs almost to the letter on Tsuburaya's prototypes, but he omits minor details that made the original Mothras more fun to watch, if not exactly realistic. The Mothra caterpillar prop, for instance, does not undulate up and down as it crawls across the Tokyo cityscape, but rather obviously rolls along on a set of wheels. The adult Mothra is colored more brightly than both the 1961 and '64 Mothras, making it look more like a plush children's toy than a monster; its wings are made of heavy cloth and do not flap as freely or gracefully as the old ones, and its feet — which now look more chicken-like than insectoid — are perfectly immobile, whereas the old moth had nervously moving appendages, adding to the illusion of life. Mothra's most impressive scene is her caterpillar-to-moth transformation atop the Diet Building, an homage to Honda and Tsuburaya's 1961 film, which is done entirely with traditional puppetry effects. Kawakita's crew shot an alternate version of this sequence using computer graphics to depict Mothra's wings unfolding as it emerged from the cocoon, but the shot was unused. "We used computer graphics, but we couldn't show the sensitivity of Mothra transforming into a mature moth," Kawakita said in *Toho* SF *Special Effects Movie Series Vol. 7*. "We couldn't bring that sensitivity out with computer graphics. The effect was better when I used 'hand-made' effects." The adult

Mothra is equipped with rays that fire from its antennae, and the pollen dust she emits from her giant wings now carries a glittering sparkle and is even more disabling to Godzilla than before.

Battra is a so-so creation — in its caterpillar form, it looks a lot like a cross between Mothra and the forgettable monster Megalon, and it shoots squiggly violet rays from its eyes; it also has the ability to burrow underground. The monster was created via suitmation with a live actor performing the monster's Nagoya rampage. In its adult form, Battra looks like a cross between Mothra and a giant fly.

The final three-way monster battle begins with all three creatures at odds — Battra and Mothra are engaged in an aerial dogfight, strafing each other (and a nearby bridge) with their rays, until Godzilla confronts them at an amusement park at the Yokohama waterfront. In the heat of battle, Battra atones for its misguided destruction of Nagoya and its scaring the hell out of Japan (after all, this creature really isn't a bad guy — it's a messenger of Earth's pain and suffering) by burying the hatchet with Mothra and helping to dispose of Godzilla, who's supposedly the real menace, but who only seems to be so pissed off because he's spent most of the movie trapped in the Earth's molten magma. As Mothra and Battra dump Godzilla in the drink, Godzilla pit-bull clamps onto Battra's neck, killing it; Mothra seals Godzilla at the sea bottom in an energy field shaped like the symbol of the Cosmos, a pseudo-religious imprint.

One truly great thing about *Godzilla vs. Mothra* is the music score, for which Akira Ifukube won a Japanese academy award. Although, as in the last film, Ifukube's music is highly derivative of his old works (and of Yuji Koseki's original *Mothra* score), Ifukube really charges up the final battle with a thundering theme marked by three distinct monster motifs. His new Mothra music is particularly effective, especially the piece for the monster's cocoon transformation. On the downside, Mothra's new twin fairies, played by **Keiko Imamura** and **Sayaka Osawa** (who are certainly *not* identical twins à la the Peanuts), have paper-thin voices and should have been overdubbed by more talented singers. Set against Ifukube's lush orchestration, the Cosmos' rendition of "Song of Mothra" is rather flat, to be kind.

While the main cast members are modern-day popular Japanese film and TV actors, *Godzilla vs. Mothra* also features the return, after 26 years, of Akira Takarada to the Godzilla series as Joji Minamino, head of the government's environmental agency. It's not really much of a role for Takarada — all he does is stand around and frown at the handbasket in which the world is going to hell, but he looks fit, trim, and great. In one particularly (yet unintentionally) funny moment, Takarada and his cohorts wheel around slowly on a lazy-Susan-like platform in order to get a better look at a video monitor that's only a few feet away. Also returning to the cast is Shoji Kobayashi of *Ultraman* fame, reprising his role from *King Ghidorah* as the government man Dobashi. While Toho's granting of cameos to various old-guard *kaiju eiga* faces like Takarada is a nice nod to the original series, these actors are almost always cast in meaningless or marginal roles, which undercuts the thrill of seeing them again. The lone exception was Yoshio Tsuchiya's role as Shindo in *King Ghidorah*.

According to an interview with Kenpachiro Satsuma in *Cult Movies*, the original scenario for *Godzilla vs. Mothra* had Mothra killed off at the end, and Koichi Kawakita envisioned bringing the monster back as a cyborg resembling a dragonfly, called Mecha-Mothra, in a subsequent film. While that did not happen, Kawakita got his wish, although it was not Mothra but another classic Toho foe that would fulfill his robo-ambitions. . . .

DEVELOPMENT HELL, TOHO-STYLE

Mothra vs. Bagan and Godzilla vs. Gigamoth (1990-92)

Even while *Godzilla vs. Biollante* was in production, special-effects director Kawakita and his staff were already preparing a new monster film to follow on its heels, *Mothra vs. Bagan*. In a real departure from the standard Toho line of restricting the major action to Japanese locales, a majority of this film was to take place in other countries. Mock storyboards for various scenes were prepared showing Mothra cocooning herself on a Malaysian skyscraper, battles in Indonesia, etc. A myriad of designs for Bagan, the new "bad" monster, were contemplated (one of which eventually saw the light as *Ultraman Great* monster Shilagee), but before any were selected, the project hit the skids. *Biollante* did not deliver as anticipated at the box office and Toho suddenly got cold feet over producing a film with another all-new enemy monster. Instead, the Mothra project was dumped in favor of Godzilla's rematch with King Ghidorah.

While *Godzilla vs. King Ghidorah* was in post-production, the decision was made to use Mothra as Godzilla's next foe. One of the original concepts for this matchup was submitted under the title *Godzilla vs. Gigamoth* (see *Toho SF Special Effects Movie Series Vol. 7*). Written by SFX director Koichi Kawakita, SFX designer Minoru Yoshida, and Marie Teranuma, and containing a heavy dose of far-out fantasy, psychic powers, and the introduction of an evil Mothra, this story contained a few ideas which survived into Omori's screenplay for *Godzilla vs. Mothra*.

Much like the film which was to succeed it, the story concentrates on Mothra and her "enemy," with Godzilla playing second fiddle, mostly serving as the focal point for the two adversaries to join forces at the conclusion. The impetus for the story comes from two of Tomoyuki Tanaka's favorite themes, radiation and pollution, as radioactive waste contaminates the jungle on a South Sea island, causing various mutations to occur. With the jungle stripped away by profiteers, a typhoon causes serious erosion that uncovers a gigantic egg which tumbles into the sea. While investigating this disaster, a scientist encounters a tiny woman named Mana, merely 20 centimeters tall, who warns him of the disasters that may occur if Mothra hatches from the egg near civilization. When Mothra hatches, not only does the benign caterpillar emerge, but also a hideous mutation — Gigamoth, spawned by radioactive exposure.

Kawakita's story gives Godzilla short shrift as far as an entrance scene — the Big G merely senses Gigamoth and shows up spoiling for a fight. Pushing the audience's suspension of disbelief to the brink, the story has Mana's psychic and teleportation powers allowing her to teleport inside the insect monsters and direct their actions to a degree. She helps Gigamoth defeat Godzilla, preventing him from attacking a nuclear power plant, but Gigamoth instead absorbs the radiation from the facility, helping fuel its metamorphosis into its grotesque adult form. Borrowing *Biollante*'s plot device of anti-radiation genetic material, the story has the scientist develop radiation-separation bacteria in hopes of eliminating the mutation foisted upon Gigamoth's genes by nuclear energy (and, curiously unemphasized, to take away Godzilla's powers as well). The weapon is fired at Godzilla and Gigamoth during their rematch, and while Godzilla is not affected, Gigamoth falters badly. Mana directs Mothra into the conflict, but Mothra is dealt a fatal blow by Godzilla's atomic breath. Falling atop Gigamoth's body, Mothra and Gigamoth merge to form the true Mothra, free of radioactive mutation.

The battle between Mothra and Godzilla ends with the typical uncreative resolution — monsters fall into the sea and disappear without a trace. But as if this unsatisfactory conclusion were not enough, the human drama takes a ridiculous turn: The scientist reveals he has fallen in love with Mana. She turns down his advance, telling him that his destiny lies elsewhere. Sure enough, months later the depressed scientist meets a woman who looks like Mana . . . they fall in love, and Mana's prophecy is fulfilled. *Godzilla vs. Gigamoth* provides ample evidence that SFX technicians are much better at visualizing the written word rather than writing themselves.

— Jay Ghee

Twenty

CYBORG

"The time has come, finally, to put our technology to the final test."

— The redundant Dr. Asimov

GODZILLA vs. MECHAGODZILLA
a.k.a GODZILLA vs. MECHAGODZILLA II

RATING (OUT OF FIVE STARS): ★ ★ ★ 1/2

JAPANESE VERSION: GOJIRA VS. MEKAGOJIRA. Released on December 11, 1993 by the Toho Motion Picture Company. Widescreen, in color. Running Time: 107 minutes. Alternate title (as filed with the U.S. Library of Congress, Copyright Office): *Godzilla vs. Super-MechaGodzilla*.

U.S. VERSION: Distributed directly to pay-per-view satellite television in December 1998.

STORY: Scientists at the United Nations Godzilla Countermeasures Center excavate Mecha-Ghidorah from the sea and utilize its advanced technology in the ultimate anti-Godzilla weapon, the cyborg MechGodzilla; meanwhile, a prehistoric egg discovered on Adonoa Island is brought to Kyoto, where a Godzillasaurus hatches. The military uses the little creature (called Baby) to lure Godzilla to a secluded island where MechaGodzilla can kill the Big G, but Rodan (believing it is the Baby's rightful guardian) foils the plan and the monsters instead face off in Chiba City; Godzilla is defeated by MechaGodzilla's powerful weapons and appears dead, but Rodan transfers its cosmic life-force to Godzilla, super-charging the King and enabling him to defeat his robotic replica.

TERMINATOR

If *Godzilla vs. Mothra* was a Godzilla film for girls, its immediate sequel is definitely one for the boys. Complete with all-out monster action, blood and guts, and imaginary military weaponry that rivals the best video games, *Godzilla vs. MechaGodzilla* brings back three classic Toho monsters and up-dates them for the modern era: Godzilla's robotic doppelgänger introduced in 1974's *Godzilla vs. The Cosmic Monster* (although it is the same cyborg only in name, for this time it is created by the United Nations, not by aliens), Rodan, and Baby Godzilla.

The difference between *Godzilla vs. MechaGodzilla* and the three previous films is the elimination of all the convoluted subplots that distract from the main attraction, the monsters. The film's theme is Nature

COPYRIGHT 1982 BILL GRIFFITH. USED BY PERMISSION.

vs. Technology, expressed literally and clumsily in the script as "Real Life Against Artificial Life" (which is nonsensical, since the crew that pilots the Mecha-Godzilla is alive and hardly artificial). By constructing the elaborate MechaGodzilla, the UN and Japanese forces draw a line in the sand, fully expecting Godzilla to go on the offensive. If only they realized that Godzilla would just leave them alone if they'd return the favor. Sure enough, well-meaning but foolhardy scientists steal a prehistoric egg from Adonoa Island and there's hell to pay when Godzilla comes searching for his baby. The final battle, in which Godzilla cheats death with Rodan's assistance, is a Toho fable, a simple yet poignant metaphor for man's ultimate inability to alter the course of Nature despite all his technological achievements.

Godzilla (portrayed with a new costume, the *Rado-Goji* design) looks much the same as in the three previous films, although a bit stockier — according to some sources, the costume was beefed up to give Godzilla a "maternal" look. Kenpachiro Satsuma turns in his best performance as Godzilla to date — somehow, even though he's hidden inside layers of thick rubber hide, Satsuma actually makes Godzilla a feeling, emotional creature in this film by contrasting the monster's rage with quiet moments and subtle movements. The new MechaGodzilla is more sleek and smooth than the original version, which fits better with its revisionist role as a military defense weapon rather than an alien invader. Its incredible arsenal of weapons

— including the Mega Buster (a ray fired from its mouth), its "artificial diamond" exterior coating (which absorbs energy from Godzilla's radiation breath), the Plasma Grenade (a chest-mounted ray cannon that fires that energy back at him, with amplified force), the Shock Anchor (electrical cables that pierce Godzilla's hide and give him a powerful jolt), and the G-Crusher (the ultimate weapon, which digitally locates Godzilla's secondary brain, at the base of the monster's spinal cord, then destroys it) — is imaginative and awesome. Rodan is no longer a man-in-suit monster as in *Rodan*, *Monster Zero*, and other films, but now a wire-manipulated marionette. The effect lacks some of the inherent charm and human articulation of the costume-made monsters, as this Rodan moves rather stiffly, but the monster still proves to be a formidable foe for Godzilla. Finally, there is new Baby Godzilla, a bluish junior dinosaur that is cute and friendly but still a definite improvement over the old-school Minya.

MechaGodzilla might, at first glance, seem the most ludicrous creation ever in the weird world of Japanese monster movies. But, somehow, this film has such a freewheeling, comic-book quality and is so jammed with special effects, props, and action that the impossibility of a gigantic, Godzilla-like robot (not to mention Godzilla himself) seems irrelevant. The finale, in which radioactive electric bolts crackle in the sky as Godzilla unleashes a fiery red, souped-up rendition of his radiation breath that finally trashes MechaGodzilla, is a ballet of Japanese monster destruction. The script, effectively balancing a near-continuous series of monster highlights with a lightweight yet engaging human story, was crafted by series newcomer Wataru Mimura, a film and TV writer with a style that is much more coherent than that of Kazuki Omori, who penned the three previous entries. Mimura's influences are apparent: He is an avid fan of science-fiction films, including many of Toho's early classics, and he says his writing style is most inspired by the great Shin-ichi Sekizawa. Prior to *Godzilla vs. MechaGodzilla*, Mimura's previous films included titles like *Green Boy* (1989) and *Little Sinbad* (1991), and he submitted a proposed synopsis for *Godzilla vs. Mothra* when Toho was soliciting ideas from screenwriters for that film. Writing a Godzilla movie was one of his lifelong dreams, and he gave it his all. "I feel like

I should be asking, 'Did I really write a Godzilla movie?'" Mimura said in an interview published in *Toho SF Special Effects Movie Series Vol. 8*. "The production staff has such guts. It makes me feel like, wow, I can write anything."

In an interview in *Cult Movies* #16, Mimura revealed many of the changes that *Godzilla vs. MechaGodzilla* underwent between the completion of his first draft script and the finished film. In the first draft, two pteranodons were discovered on Adonoa Island, and in a battle with MechaGodzilla, one of them was killed and the other fell into the ocean, where it was exposed to radiation and mutated into Rodan. MechaGodzilla originally had the ability to separate into two robo-vehicles (an idea later incorporated into the Mogera robot in *Godzilla vs. Space Godzilla*), and there was a brief

Kenji Sahara, veteran actor of Toho monster movies, and director Takao Okawara pose with the MechaGodzilla costume from Godzilla vs. MechaGodzilla at the Godzilla Exhibition at the Ariake Coliseum in Tokyo in January 1996.

COURTESY OF WINTERGARDEN PRODUCTIONS

scene set in prehistoric times in which a Godzilla-saurus (Godzilla's progenitor, as seen in *Godzilla vs. King Ghidorah*) battled a pteranodon. The conclusion of the film, as originally scripted, had Godzilla picking up Baby Godzilla with his teeth and heading out to sea, an idea that sounds visually interesting, but "it was thought that the scene would not be very convincing because Godzilla was so much larger than Baby Godzilla," Mimura said.

By far the most interesting revision, however, affected the film's climax and Godzilla's controversial death. In the first draft script, Godzilla was resurrected not by Fire Rodan's life force, but when radiation from the fallout of an explosion in the Garuda's nuclear reactor was absorbed by Godzilla's corpse. Although this scenario seems much better suited to Godzilla's long-standing nuclear-based mythology, Toho felt that Rodan's self-sacrifice "was more in keeping with the theme of 'Real Life Against Artificial Life,' " Mimura said.

The two subplots — Aoki's (Masahiro Takashima) disgraced demotion from G-Force and his atonement for his mistakes, and the scientists' discovery of the baby's egg and Azusa Gojo's mother-son relationship with Baby — intersect very naturally and there are no moralistic side stories about biotechnology, aliens, commercialism, and the threat of nuclear war. Any weaknesses to *Godzilla vs. MechaGodzilla*'s script stem from the absence of a clear-cut villain, leaving the audience to wonder exactly who it should be rooting for in the final battle. Godzilla is not portrayed here as a wanton destructive force but as an animal trying to protect his (or perhaps her, in this case) young. The King of the Monsters only lashes out when provoked — by Rodan, by the egg-thieving scientists, by Mecha-Godzilla, by the military men who are only interested in studying the baby to learn how to kill Godzilla, and so on. The crew of the MechaGodzilla can hardly be considered the "bad guys" either, for their anti-Godzilla mission is based on years of high-casualty tolls racked up by the monster. The real evil here is man's arrogance, symbolized by the cyborg MechaGodzilla, an attempt to re-create Godzilla in man's image and use his own size and powers (tweaked and tricked, of course) to destroy him.

"It's not really a fight between the bad guys and good guys — both sides are fighting for good," Mimura said in the *Toho SF* interview. "They're both trying to defend their own lives. . . . The theme was written so that the viewer will empathize with the creatures, so I think it's OK for MechaGodzilla to play the villain." In the end, Nature exacts her revenge when Rodan not only resurrects Godzilla with his cosmic aura, but melts the protective sheen off the robot, allowing Godzilla to decimate this icon of man's supposed supremacy in the big scheme of things. The MG crew's lives are spared — a chance to learn a lesson in respect for the natural order of things from the mighty Godzilla. However, Rodan's self-sacrifice hardly makes much sense — Godzilla and the titanic pteranodon are mortal enemies, as demonstrated by their incredible fight earlier in the picture. And Rodan, its chest blasted open by MechaGodzilla, is bleeding profusely, barely able to fly and clearly just a shade away from death itself when it drapes its body on Godzilla's, so it's hard to believe the pteranodon had much "life force" left to spare.

SON OF GODZILLA: Because of all the special-effects work on this picture, the chores of designing and creating the new Baby Godzilla were overseen not by Koichi Kawakita but by the dramatic director, Takao Okawara. While not exactly as convincing as the *Jurassic Park* dinosaurs, "Baby," as he is referred to, is a credible kid monster and a hundred times more acceptable than that lovable yet somehow detestable pug Minya. Baby is not a baby Godzilla, but a junior Godzillasaurus. Bluish, with a hint of dorsal plates just beginning to rise along his spine, the creature is cute yet believable as a sort of domesticated Godzilla pup.

"Toho wanted to bring Minya back, but I didn't. So, I redesigned him," Okawara said in *Cult Movies* #13. "Mothra is a very feminine monster, but MechaGodzilla is hard and solid. Because of this, I did intend to have *Godzilla vs. MechaGodzilla* turn out to be more serious than *Godzilla vs. Mothra*. However, I used the Baby Godzilla to provide some relief."

Baby was created via a full-body costume worn by stuntman Hurricane Ryu and an upper-half robotic prosthetic with animated eyes and mouth, which appears in the scenes where Baby munches on flowers fed by his motherly caretaker, Azusa Gojo (Ryoko Sano). The robotic prop actually emotes quite well, looking doe-eyed at the girl, but the suit is somewhat obvious when shown in its entirety, especially in the long-distance shot of Baby wading tentatively out to sea the film's end, or when he's moping around in his cage at the science institute. The most interesting scene involving Baby is his hatching, which is nicely staged and edited. As Aoki

The Godzilla and MechaGodzilla costumes from *Godzilla vs. MechaGodzilla*, on display at the Godzilla Exhibition at the Ariake Coliseum in Tokyo in January 1996. MechaGodzilla is seen here in Super-MechaGodzilla mode, with the Garuda flying warship mounted on its back.

COURTESY OF WINTERGARDEN PRODUCTIONS

(Masahiro Takashima) plays a recording of a song encrypted in a fossilized leaf, the egg begins to glow and shake. Pieces of eggshell blast out in all directions, and Azusa, trapped alone in the lab, is terrified by what she sees. Finally, the creature — seen only from behind — raises his head. Baby, covered in wet amniotic solution, peers into the camera and bellows his mini-Godzilla roar.

Kawakita's special-effects work is uneven in this film. There are some poorly designed miniatures, particularly the military hardware, and the Rodan marionette, while designed nicely, moves stiffly in flight, as do most of Kawakita's winged monsters. But overall he creates an awesome spectacle here, particularly in the two monster battles that book-end the film. This is the most graphically (although, it should be noted, not offensively) violent movie in the series since Gigan sawed open Godzilla's shoulder in 1972. In the first fight on Adonoa Island, Godzilla strangles Rodan, causing the pteranodon

to froth at the mouth, and he so batters the monster-bird that Rodan appears dead when the battle is over, only to re-emerge in the final reel as Fire Rodan, mutated and glowing red from the radiation it absorbs from Godzilla's ray. The final battle, which begins with Rodan spectacularly swiping the cargo box containing Baby from a helicopter, and ends with the mighty MechaGodzilla turned to a pile of burning titanium, is more compelling than any other monster showdown in the *Heisei* Godzillas because Baby's life hangs in the balance — if Godzilla is killed, the creature will likely be raised in captivity, and if Godzilla lives, the child will lead a normal *kaiju* life. The latter scenario unfolds and, as the movie ends, Godzilla and son swim peacefully home, with the moonlight shimmering on the ocean's surface.

This being Godzilla's 20th film appearance, there are a number of special-effects shots that pay homage to previous entries in the series, particularly

This three-story-tall replica of MechaGodzilla was erected in the
lobby of an elementary school in the Fukuoka area in 1993.

COURTESY OF BILL GUDMUNDSON

Godzilla advancing on the Yokkaichi oil refinery, an updated rendition of his attack on the same facility in *Godzilla vs. The Thing*, and a moment in the climactic battle in which Godzilla and Mecha-Godzilla's rays collide in midair, creating an explosion that blasts both monsters backward, a nice homage to *Godzilla vs. The Cosmic Monster*.

Godzilla vs. MechaGodzilla also benefits from good casting. Popular actor Masahiro Takashima isn't a leading man of Akira Takarada's caliber, but he has a screen presence and star quality lacking in most of Toho's new Godzilla movies. Takashima's father, Tadao Takashima of *King Kong vs. Godzilla* renown, makes a cameo as the head of a psychic research institute, and the stern, right-wing military men include good performances by Kenji Sahara as G-Force Chief Takayuki Segawa and Akira Nakao as Commander Aso. Megumi Odaka returns as Miki Saegusa, and although she plays a marginal role throughout most of the story, Godzilla's fate is thrust into her hands at the very end, when the military convinces her to use her psychic powers to aid in the operation to destroy Godzilla's brain and kill him. Keiko Imamura and Sayaka Osawa, the Cosmos from *Godzilla vs. Mothra*, appear as staffers at the ESP institute, speaking in unison in an obvious in-joke.

Akira Ifukube's score for this film is, in a word, awesome. The Maestro may have sounded overly self-imitating in the previous two outings, but here he delivers a tour de force proving that even in his late seventies he hasn't lost his magic touch. The highlight is his MechaGodzilla theme, a stunning, slow battle march with thundering percussion and heavy pentatonic phrasing that paints the robot as a gigantic, unstoppable force. The vocal piece sung by a group of psychic children, with lyrics written in Ainu language, is particularly haunting, and the Baby Godzilla themes and the requiem that accompanies Godzilla and son's exit at the finale are touching.

Considering how well this film turned out, it's curious to note that Toho originally had planned a remake of *King Kong vs. Godzilla* but, as revealed by Tomoyuki Tanaka in *Toho SF Special Effects Movie Series Vol. 8*, Toho was unable to obtain the rights to use the Kong character and chose to use Mecha-Godzilla instead. Koichi Kawakita, in an interview in *Cult Movies #14*, said that Toho also considered pitting Godzilla against Mechani-Kong, the cyborg built in Kong's image in *King Kong Escapes* — a scenario that sounds both unlikely and unappealing. "Toho wanted to pit Godzilla against King Kong because *King Kong vs. Godzilla* was very successful," Kawakita said. "However, the studio thought that obtaining permission to use King Kong would be very difficult. So, it instead decided to use Mechani-Kong. Soon afterward, it was discovered that obtaining permission even to use the likeness of King Kong would be difficult. So, the project was canceled. . . .

"Mechani-Kong was going to have injectors," Kawakita continued. "A number of people were going to be injected into Godzilla while the robot was wrestling with him. They then were going to do battle with Godzilla from within while Mechani-Kong continued to do battle with him from without. There were going to be many different strange worlds inside Godzilla. The concept was very much like [*Fantastic Voyage*]." Other story ideas that were submitted during the early planning stages included one in which a revenge-crazed American scientist creates MechaGodzilla (elements of this were worked into the final film — MechaGodzilla is designed by Dr. Asimov, played by the wooden amateur actor Leo Mangetti), and SFX designer Shinji Nishikawa submitted a treatment in which a female scientist attempted to turn King Kong into a cyborg.

It's also interesting to note that director Takao Okawara lobbied to kill Godzilla in *Godzilla vs. MechaGodzilla*. Okawara said in *Cult Movies #11*, "I feel that what makes *Godzilla* (1954) so powerful is the fact that Godzilla is killed at the end of the film. Because of this, I wanted to kill Godzilla. . . . However, Toho would not permit it."

Twenty-One

ENEMIES: A LOVE STORY

"Life would be sad without love."

— Shinjo

GODZILLA vs. SPACE GODZILLA

RATING (OUT OF FIVE STARS): ★

JAPANESE VERSION: GOJIRA VS. SPACEGOJIRA. Released on December 10, 1994, by the Toho Motion Picture Company. Widescreen, in color. Running Time: 111 minutes.

U.S. VERSION: Released directly to home video by Columbia TriStar Home Video in January 1999.

STORY: Godzilla cells carried into space (either by Biollante or Mothra, although no one knows for sure) are sucked into a black hole and mutated, creating a malevolent, crystal-laden monster that hurtles toward Earth. G-Force dispatches its new anti-Godzilla robot, Mogera, to intercept Space Godzilla, but the monster easily defeats the machine; after terrorizing Little Godzilla and disrupting the peace on Birth Island, Space Godzilla builds a cosmic crystal fortress in downtown Fukuoka, and it's up to Godzilla and the Mogera crew to deplete their foe's New Age powers and save the world.

GODZILLA, PHONE HOME

For every positive thing that can be said about *Godzilla vs. MechaGodzilla*, something equally negative can be said about its successor, the 21st film in the Godzilla series, *Godzilla vs. Space Godzilla*. Released just after Godzilla's 40th birthday in November 1994, *Space Godzilla* takes a series that had resurrected itself to new heights and plunges it down to the depths of films like *Godzilla vs. Megalon*. It's not that the film is any cheaper than

the recent Godzilla movies; the production values are fine. It's just that everything in the creative department — the script, the acting, the monster designs, the effects work, the musical score — appears to have been phoned in.

This is a bad movie, difficult to endure for even entrenched Godzilla fans. New director **Kensho Yamashita**, a veteran of Japanese teen-idol movies, and screenwriter Hiroshi Kashiwabara are clearly fish out of water in the giant-monster genre. The script is written as a romance between Miki Saegusa (played, as always, by actress **Megumi Odaka**, finally taking center stage) and G-Force soldier

295

A billboard announcing the release of *Godzilla vs. Space Godzilla* outside
Shinjuku Station, a major Tokyo public transportation hub, in December 1994.

PHOTO BY THE AUTHOR

Shinjo (Jun Hashizume), but their chemistry is virtually nonexistent and they spend the entire movie at arm's length. The subplot about an "industrial mafia" that hijacks G-Force's Godzilla controller, called the "T-Project," is poorly thought out, inserted into the story in midstream and then discarded just as suddenly. There is also some philosophical hogwash about a rift in the ranks of G-Force, as Commander Aso (Akira Nakao), a right-wing anti-Godzilla hawk in *Godzilla vs. MechaGodzilla*, has softened his stance and now doubts that the M-Project (a new anti-G robot called Mogera) will work — but this, too, goes nowhere. The only interesting element in the human drama is Yuuki (Akira Emoto), a soldier determined to seek revenge on Godzilla for killing his best friend (Colonel Goro Gondo, who got a little too close to the lizard in

Biollante) and who has developed his own weapon, a blood-freezing chemical, to do it. But even this story is lost in the mess as Yuuki inexplicably decides at the last minute to help Godzilla defeat Space Godzilla.

As for the monsters, things are equally bad. Little Godzilla is embarrassing. Mogera is a major comedown from the powerful MechaGodzilla. Finally, Space Godzilla, while admittedly evil-looking, is an ill-advised throwback to the anything-goes days when Toho unleashed monsters like Hedorah and Gigan. Fitted with giant crystal humps on its shoulders through which it channels new-age monster energy, Space Godzilla is blue with a reddish belly. It fires menacing rays as usual, but its most outlandish power is the Gravity Tornado, with which it levitates Godzilla (or, an empty Godzilla suit hung from wires) above the cityscape and sends him crashing into a building.

MIKI MOUSE: In her fifth consecutive outing as Miki Saegusa, Megumi Odaka is thrust from the background into the spotlight, but unfortunately all the possibilities inherent in this character, the girl with a psychic link to the King of the Monsters, remain unfulfilled. Odaka (b. 1973 in Kanagawa), began acting in television and a few film roles in the late 1980s and was also groomed as a pop idol, releasing an obligatory music album, but her real claim to fame is the Godzilla movies. And in *Space Godzilla* the truth is finally and fully revealed: She is not much of an actress. But what is most disappointing is the way her character has been portrayed: As a spineless, easily led tawn who professes an affinity for the great Godzilla, yet when the going gets tough, she always goes along with some ill-conceived plan in which her ESP powers wind up harming the monster rather than helping him. The first such incident took place in *Godzilla vs. MechaGodzilla*, when Miki was given the loathsome assignment to home in on Godzilla's nerve center and destroy it with the G-Crusher weapon. In *Space Godzilla*, Miki adamantly opposes the T-Project, a telepathic amplifier that controls and guides the monster's actions, saying it is a violation of Godzilla's rights. But when the Cosmos (Mothra's fairies from *Godzilla vs. Mothra*) appear in a vision, riding piggyback on a cheap plush toy called "Fairy Mothra" and warning of a space monster en route to destroy Earth, Miki quickly recants and supplies the psychic power to an operation co-opted by organized crime, and this leads to lots of unnecessary destruction. The following year, in *Godzilla vs. Destoroyah*, she would reluctantly use Godzilla Junior as bait to trap Godzilla, putting the kid in harm's way and ultimately leading to his death; when Miki cries for the fallen boy-monster, she ought to be ashamed of herself. With friends like Miki, Godzilla needs no enemies!

Director Yamashita joined Toho in the late 1960s and began his career as an assistant director on a comedy called *Who Am I* (1969), starring Tani Kei of the Crazy Cats. He was chief assistant director to Ishiro Honda on *Terror of MechaGodzilla* (1975), but he doesn't show much aptitude for Godzilla, despite his lofty claims of trying to expand the genre with this film. "There are two other monsters in the film and there is the conflict in G-Force, as well as the dramatic story with Emoto's character," Yamashita said in *Fangoria* #145. "I think these dramatic elements are very important to make our movie stand out from the rest. We all know that these monsters don't exist, but it is my job to approach them realistically. I just tried to express my own spirit as best I could."

This "spirit" apparently involves the conviction that Godzilla movies need an injection of sappy romance to liven up the scenery. Yamashita treats the audience to a puppy-love affair between Odaka and Hashizume, who begin their relationship at odds — she believes Godzilla should be left alone, he fights for the military agency dedicated to eradicating the monster — and evolves, via a beautiful sunset on the beach and some battle heroics by the soldier, into a tame teen-style affair, cemented when Miki uses her newfound telekinetic powers to levitate a piece of furniture during a shoot-out, enabling Shinjo to score a bullet on one of the bad guys' legs. The rest of the characters, including Shinjo's bumbling sidekick Kiyoshi Sato, the rational Dr. Chinatsu Gondo (the dead Goro Gondo's sister), and especially the mafia infiltrator Dr. Okubo (Yosuke Saito), are all trite and uninteresting.

LOST IN SPACE: Adding insult to injury are the special effects sequences, some of which are unbelievable in their ineptness. Mogera's battle with Space Godzilla in an asteroid belt, utilizing small-scale models of both monsters and staged among a constellation of foam boulders suspended by wires from the ceiling of a Toho soundstage, is laughable. The crystal formations that Space Godzilla plants at Birth Island and later in Fukuoka City look like they may have been inspired by the Fortress of Solitude from Richard Donner's *Superman* (1978), but they are wobbly and made of obvious plastic, with lights inside to illuminate them.

The monsters also invoke cringes, especially Little Godzilla, supposedly a teenage version of Baby, but which bears no resemblance to its younger self. Sporting cartoonish bug eyes, bright green skin, and a huge, dopey head, this creature is even less appealing than Minya, and he negates the positive impressions that Godzilla's offspring made in the previous film. Suddenly, the kid no longer resembles his father in any remote way, and no explanation is offered as to how the creature so utterly

Godzilla's handlers prepare the *Moge-Goji* Godzilla costume for the final showdown in Fukuoka with Space Godzilla, on the set of *Godzilla vs. Space Godzilla*. The 1990s Godzilla suits are are more advanced than the suits of the 1950s-1970s in several key ways. They are equipped with two sets of dorsal fins — one cast from latex like the suit itself, the other cast from FRP (fiber-reinforced plastic) and equipped with electric lights, used for scenes of the fins glowing (enhanced with optical animation) when Godzilla emits his atomic breath. A radio-controlled servo motor uses compressed air to power the movement of Godzilla's jaw and his head which, from *Godzilla vs. Space Godzilla* onward, is capable of tilting up and down and turning from side to side. Kenpachiro Satsuma's input has also led to several small innovations — like holes in the fingernails that allow the actor's perspiration to drain, and special boots that keep his feet in place despite the pools of perspiration that accumulate — that make the suit actor's grueling job somewhat more tolerable.

AP/WIDE WORLD PHOTOS

changed in appearance. And while the Mecha-Godzilla design was brilliantly outlandish, Mogera (an acronym — if you can believe it — for Mobile Operations Godzilla Expert Robot Aero-Type, and an updated rendition of the Mogera robots from *The Mysterians*, although there is no thematic connection) is a much more standard robot, with an angular design and vaguely humanoid shape. It sports a drill bit on the end of its snout called the Screw Crusher that enables the robot to burrow underneath the Earth, but Mogera looks like an oversized food processor.

The only monster who looks relatively normal is Godzilla. For this film, the Godzilla suit was equipped for the first time ever with a mechanism allowing the head to move not only up and down, but also from side to side — an effect repeated over and over throughout the movie. The suit also has an air duct to allow Kenpachiro Satsuma to breathe more freely, enabling him to stay inside the costume for longer periods of time, which probably came in handy during the scene where Godzilla, drawn to Birth Island when his son trips some poison gas bombs on the beach and cries pathetically for help, takes what seems like forever to wade ashore. A few shots of Godzilla use innovative

Kenpachiro Satsuma climbs into the claustrophobic Godzilla suit. A team of assistants is required to support the costume while Satsuma dons it, and to help him get out of it at the end of each take. Satsuma enters the suit through an opening along the spine, and the costume is closed with a zipper and the dorsal fins are attached with velcro. Satsuma is afforded very limited vision through several holes concealed in the folds and ribbing of Godzilla's neck, and he wears safety goggles to protect his eyes from smoke, fireworks, and other hazards.

AP/WIDE WORLD PHOTOS

A trip to the dentist? A member of Koichi Kawakita's SFX crew does some last-minute touch-up painting to Godzilla's teeth on the set of *Godzilla vs. Space Godzilla*. Unfortunately, Godzilla doesn't floss, so his breath just keeps getting worse!

PHOTO BY KOJI SASAHARA, AP /WIDE WORLD PHOTOS

camera angles, including a great long shot in which the Godzilla costume and the real-life beach landscape are perfectly integrated and composited, but the scene is drawn-out and tedious.

Further contributing to this malaise is the music score by **Takayuki Hattori**, grandson of Tadashi Hattori, who scored Akira Kurosawa's *No Regrets for Our Youth* (1946) and other pictures. Hattori composes a so-so main title theme and Mogera motif, but his themes for Godzilla and Space Godzilla are mostly nondescript; much of the time they are played so low in the mix that they just get drowned out. As in *Biollante*, the subpar score is fattened up with some of Akira Ifukube's Godzilla music (Ifukube, incidentally, declined to work on this film during the script stages), but even the Maestro's

mighty notes can't save this picture from oblivion.

Shamefully, *Godzilla vs. Space Godzilla* mimics scenes, almost note-for-note, from both *Biollante* (Godzilla's battle with the naval fleet) and the opening of *Godzilla vs. Mothra* (Big G awakening undersea when Space Godzilla's crystal meteor strikes Birth Island). On top of that, several scenes are carbon copies of *Godzilla vs. MechaGodzilla*: The opening credits sequence, in which the G-Force brass admire Mogera as it undergoes a maintenance check in its hangar, Godzilla's triumphant expulsion of fiery-red nuclear breath to deliver the coup de grace to his foe, and the denouement where Godzilla returns to the sea and swims off into the sunset (this time, without his young tyke in tow). And there is one scene that was filmed but

Godzilla and Space Godzilla prepare to face off in downtown Fukuoka, in the climactic showdown of *Godzilla vs. Space Godzilla*. Since 1991, when Toho increased Godzilla's height to 100 meters, the miniature cityscapes in the *Heisei* Godzilla have been built in 1/50 scale (compared to 1/25 scale in the older films, and 1/40 scale from 1984–89). As a result, Godzilla looks larger than ever, but the miniatures are less detailed than before.

PHOTO BY KOJI SASAHARA, AP/WIDE WORLD PHOTOS

strangely deleted — in the monster fight on Birth Island, Space Godzilla traps Little Godzilla in a crystal prism. A shot of Godzilla trying unsuccessfully to free his son from the crystal cage — which would have better explained why Godzilla heads for Japan to confront Space Godzilla — was omitted.

Despite its lackluster entertainment value, *Godzilla vs. Space Godzilla* generated a lot of publicity for Toho — dozens of reporters from around the world attended a "media day" on the special-effects set in July 1994, and there were many stories in November of that year focusing on the monster's 40th birthday. With the inking of a deal with TriStar Pictures in 1992 to produce an American-made Godzilla movie, Toho had thought it would cease production of the series — first after *MechaGodzilla* and then, after delays with the TriStar film, after *Space Godzilla* — but by late 1994 the American film had hit several roadblocks in development hell and its future was in doubt. So, Toho's men put their heads together for the ultimate publicity stunt. . . . The death of Godzilla!

Showdown: Gamera vs. Godzilla

"Gamera has formidable destructive power, but there is a weak point, and that is his unusual and overpowering kindness to children. Perhaps this can be used against him."

— *Captain of "Spaceship No. 2," from* Destroy All Planets

While Toho was enjoying increased success with its new-look 1990s Godzilla movies, its longtime rival Daiei Co. Ltd., which reformed in the late 1970s (after its infamous years-long bankruptcy shutdown) and was once again producing a limited number of new features, was quietly working on a plan to reenter the Japanese giant-monster business. Daiei explored the possibility of reviving its stone idol god, the giant Majin, but soon found that the

At a press conference commemorating Godzilla's 40th birthday in November, 1994, Toho trotted out the cast and props from *Godzilla vs. Space Godzilla*, including the ghastly Little Godzilla (Chibi Gojira) suit. At center is Toho Special Effects Director Koichi Kawakita. Looming in the background is the 10-year-old "Cybot" from *Godzilla* (1984), still making the occasional public appearance.

PHOTO BY TSUGUFUMI MATSUMOTO, AP /WIDE WORLD PHOTOS

public was more eager to see the return of the tusked wonder-turtle, Gamera.

The result, several years in the making, was *Gamera: Guardian of the Universe*, released in March 1995 to wide critical praise. Rather than imitate Toho's latest Godzillas, Daiei went off in its own direction and produced a film that, ironically enough, harks back to the spirit of the classic Honda-Tsuburaya films produced by Toho in the 1960s. Showing their creativity and confidence, Daiei's new generation of filmmakers wiped the slate clean, much as Toho did with *Godzilla 1985*, ignoring the previous cycle of Gamera films and rewriting the monster's origins. The giant turtle is the guardian

of the lost continent of Atlantis and has reawakened to battle Gyaos, the legendary enemy of his people, which comes to life in the modern world. The film borrows the concept of a psychic link between the monster and a human character, an idea that Toho only scratched the surface of with Miki Saegusa. Unlike Miki, who is useful for little more than detecting Godzilla's whereabouts, the child Asagi (Ayako Fujitani, daughter of actor Steven Seagal) becomes an extension of Gamera, sharing the pain the monster suffers when he is unjustly attacked by the defense forces.

Skillfully directed by **Shusuke Kaneko** (*Necronomicon, Summer Vacation 1999*) from a tight script by Kazunori Ito, the revitalized Gamera featured special effects by 20-something director **Shinji Higuchi**, who breathes new life into the genre. Instead of just flashy beams and rays that dazzle the eyes, Higuchi employs all the traditional Tsuburayaesque techniques (suitmation, miniatures, pyrotechnics, wire works) and adds a dose of new technology (computer animation) to heighten the suspense of the drama. The film is a highlight reel of "climax scenes," such as the military's attempt to capture the Gyaos monsters in the Fukuoka baseball stadium, Gamera's first appearance on dry land, Gyaos swooping down and snatching a dog, and the military's attacks on Gamera. The best is saved for last, when Gyaos takes downtown Tokyo hostage and lays its eggs on the Tokyo Tower. Gamera and Gyaos wage a classic battle, at one point during which the two monsters soar spectacularly toward the stratosphere. Both Gamera and Gyaos (the bat-bird first seen in *Return of the Giant*

The Little Godzilla and Space Godzilla costumes from *Godzilla vs. Space Godzilla*, on display at the Godzilla Exhibition at the Ariake Coliseum in Tokyo in January 1996.
COURTESY OF WINTERGARDEN PRODUCTIONS

The Mogera costume from *Godzilla vs. Space Godzilla*, on display at the
Godzilla Exhibition at the Ariake Coliseum in Tokyo in January 1996.

COURTESY OF WINTERGARDEN PRODUCTIONS

Monsters, 1967) are well updated for the 1990s, with Gamera shooting "plasma fireballs" instead of the flamethrower effect of the old days, and flying through the air at hyperspace speed.

Unlike the latter-day Toho Godzilla movies, Daiei's new Gamera wasted little time in making an impact in the U.S. The film was distributed theatrically, albeit on a limited basis, in 1995 and then released to home video in late 1997. It was widely praised by American critics, from Roger Ebert to Janet Maslin of the *New York Times*. Daiei followed up with an equally impressive sequel, the somewhat *X-Files*-inspired *Gamera 2: Advent of Legion*, released in July 1996, in which a swarm of alien monsters descends upon Earth and Gamera must stop it from gobbling up the planet's natural resources.

For political and legal reasons, the likelihood of an actual on-screen confrontation between Godzilla and Gamera, the two most famous Japanese movie monsters of all time (or even a team-up of the two against another monster), seems very slim. However, Daiei's new Gamera movies, in a very real sense, initiated strong competition between the two monsters in the public eye. Both *Gamera: Guardian of the Universe* and *Gamera 2: Advent of Legion* were praised by reviewers in Japan, while *Godzilla vs. Space Godzilla* and *Godzilla vs. Destoroyah*, released at roughly the same time, were mostly panned. Conversely, the two Godzilla films performed much better at the Japanese box office, owing to the superior popularity of Godzilla. Where the bottom line is concerned, Godzilla won the fight, but he suffered a hefty blow to the ego.

Twenty-Two

REQUIEM FOR A HEAVYWEIGHT

"Apparently something is happening there.
In the reactor. In Godzilla's heart.

— Professor Marvin

GODZILLA vs. DESTOROYAH
a.k.a. GODZILLA vs. DESTROYER

RATING (OUT OF FIVE STARS): ★ ★ ★

JAPANESE VERSION: Released on December 9, 1995 by the Toho Motion Picture Company. Running time: 103 minutes.

U.S. VERSION: Released directly to home video by Columbia TriStar Home Video in January 1999.

STORY: Reanimated by the after-effects of the Oxygen Destroyer in Tokyo Bay, a species of tiny, prehistoric crustaceans grows into a herd of man-sized, havoc-wreaking, crab-like creatures and eventually fuses into one gigantic monster, Destoroyah; meanwhile, uranium deposits beneath Birth Island mutate Little Godzilla into Godzilla Junior, and Godzilla glows bright red as he attacks Hong Kong, leading authorities to fear he will explode in a nuclear blast. The Super-X3's freezing lasers briefly stabilize Godzilla but the radiation in his heart escalates, threatening a China Syndrome effect; Godzilla is lured into a fight with Destoroyah in hopes he will be killed before melting down, but when Destoroyah murders Junior, Godzilla becomes enraged and defeats Destoroyah with Super-X3's help, then vaporizes into an atomic mist — but instead of wiping out Tokyo, Godzilla's radiation is absorbed by Junior's corpse, which is resurrected as the new Godzilla.

THE FINAL CHAPTER

On July 15, 1995, Toho producer **Shogo Tomiyama** announced to the world that Godzilla's movie career, at long last, was coming to an end. In *Godzilla vs. Destoroyah*, his 22nd and final film, the King of the Monsters was going to die. The purported reason for this history-making event was that, after 21 Godzilla movies, Toho simply had no more new ideas left. "That's why we've decided to put an end to the series," Tomiyama told the Reuters news service.

"We wanted to finish with Godzilla while he is still a star."

Watching *Destoroyah*, it is clear that Tomiyama's statement wasn't entirely truthful for the film is full of compelling story ideas, but many of these simply are not executed well. The real reasons for Godzilla's demise undoubtedly stemmed from economics. The *Heisei* Godzilla series had peaked with 1992's *Godzilla vs. Mothra*, which sold about 4.2 million tickets, but attendance subsequently declined for both *MechaGodzilla* and *Space Godzilla*. The 1990s Godzillas, each budgeted at about 1 billion Yen (roughly $8 million to $12 million U.S., depending on fluctuations in the exchange rate), were the most expensive movies produced in Japan, and with the series lulling toward a creative and financial slide, Toho could have scaled back the budgets and watched its monster fall into a 1970s-style abyss. Instead, the studio shrewdly re-hired the team that made *Godzilla vs. Mothra* (director Takao Okawara, screenwriter Kazuki Omori, composer

LAST AUGUST, IT WAS THE EVENT OF THE YEAR...
THIS AUGUST, IT WILL BE THE EVENT OF A LIFETIME!

G-CON '96

AUGUST 16 - 18, 1996
RADISSON HOTEL ARLINGTON HEIGHTS
CHICAGO, ILLINOIS

CLUB DAIKAIJU AND DIGITAL DAIKAIJU PRESENT IN ASSOCIATION WITH DAIKAIJU ENTERPRISES
A HISTORIC EVENT OF EPIC PROPORTIONS

HARUO NAKAJIMA · KENPACHIRO SATSUMA

IN PERSON: THE MEN WHO PLAYED GODZILLA

GUEST APPEARANCES • QUESTION & ANSWER SESSIONS • AUTOGRAPHS

IF THESE TWO LEGENDS CAN COME ALL THE WAY FROM JAPAN, WHAT'S YOUR EXCUSE FOR NOT ATTENDING?

AT G-CON '95, 600 FANS RAVAGED OUR HUGE MERCHANDISE DISPLAY. THIS YEAR...

CLUB DAIKAIJU STRIKES BACK

WITH AN EVEN LARGER SELECTION OF JAPANESE MONSTER MERCHANDISE

SO BIG... SO VAST... YOU *CAN'T* BUY IT ALL!

TOYS • MODEL KITS • COMPACT DISCS POSTERS • BOOKS • T-SHIRTS & MORE!
VISIT OUR DISPLAY IN THE G-CON '96 DEALERS ROOM
(NOT FOR THE FAINT OF HEART OR WEAK OF WALLET!)

Godzilla suit actors Kenpachiro Satsuma and Haruo Nakajima speak to hundreds of their American fans at G-Con '96 in Arlington Heights, IL., the third in an ongoing series of "unofficial" Godzilla and Japanese monster movie conventions that began with a small gathering of fans in Chicago in summer, 1994. G-Con '96 was the first time ever that the "men who played Godzilla" were invited to speak in the U.S. They returned again in 1997 and 1998.
PHOTO BY THE AUTHOR

Akira Ifukube), stacked the new movie with female characters to woo back the women's audience and, most importantly, made a media event out of Godzilla's swan song — in Tokyo, for instance, pre-release publicity efforts included signs with 20-foot-tall *kanji* characters shouting GODZILLA DIES. The strategy worked. News of the monster's death was reported around the world, and in Japan, ticket sales rebounded by about 600,000.

Considering the debacle that *Space Godzilla* was, *Destoroyah* is a major improvement, aspiring to a level of thematic importance comparable to Honda's original *Godzilla*, and it is loaded with enjoyable visual effects and action sequences. For the first time in decades Godzilla is portrayed as a sheer atomic monster, glowing fiery red and threatening

to take half of Asia with him in a doomsday explosion, and he is ultimately consumed in a nuclear funeral pyre. The new monster, Destoroyah, is a by-product of the metaphoric Oxygen Destroyer that Dr. Serizawa detonated 40 years earlier, thus raising questions about the long-term effects of man's mass-destruction weapons. The monster fest is highlighted by Godzilla Junior, a brave-fighting kid *kaiju* and the most endearing character in the film, whose untimely death and radioactive resurrection indicate Godzilla's symbolic immortality. In short, *Godzilla vs. Destoroyah* has the ingredients for what should have been by far the best film in the new series, and one of the best in the monster's entire history but, unfortunately, it comes up short — its chills are compromised by heavy-handedness and self-importance, and its thrills are often deflated by inconsistent special effects.

In July 1992, while the filming of *Godzilla vs. Mothra* was under way, a reporter for the *Daily Yomiuri* newspaper visited Toho Studios and described the activities on the special-effects set:

> "There is no high-tech equipment in the studio. The atmosphere is like that at a construction site. Young assistants, wearing helmets with tools hanging from their waists, rush around the studio. Some pull wires suspending a monster. A sheet of colored cellophane covers a lighting stand . . . Each [special-effects] cut is made painstakingly and the scenes are constructed by arranging these cuts like a jigsaw puzzle. For example, the cut in which Godzilla and (Battra) are sinking into the sea, clinging to each other, lasts only 0.5 seconds in the film. However it took more than half a day and about 100 workers to shoot that scene. Minute tests are repeated until a scene which exactly fits the plot can be produced. Koichi Kawakita, special effects director . . . said, 'Japanese special effects make the most of low-tech methods.' . . . The young staff apparently agrees with this opinion. No one complains about the simple jobs at the studio. 'Handmade taste' seems to be the key to Japanese special effects."

Despite his preference for traditional Japanese handmade techniques, Koichi Kawakita was well aware of how CGI was expanding the possibilities of special effects in U.S. films and television. Although he had dabbled with CGI before (e.g., the computer-animated meteor at the beginning of *Godzilla vs. Mothra*), Toho's strict production budgets and schedules, and the lack of access to the most sophisticated CGI software limited Kawakita's use of computers. While *Godzilla vs. Destoroyah* relies mainly on monster suits and miniature work, it contains more CGI than any previous Godzilla movie, striking a nice balance between the old-school *tokusatsu* use of piano wires, pulleys and pyrotechnics, and the newer digital methods.

Kawakita twice uses computer animation to create images that would be almost impossible with the traditional techniques. When the Super-X3 blasts Godzilla with freezing lasers, the monster becomes encrusted in ice and, in an eerie close-up, Godzilla's face is frozen solid. CGI is artfully used in the scene of Godzilla's death as the flesh melts off his bones, eventually leaving nothing but a bare skeleton (evoking the image of Godzilla's remains

on the sea bottom in Honda's original movie), which vaporizes beautifully. The computer-animated simulation of Godzilla exploding like an H-bomb in Tokyo, and another depicting a huge hole burned into the Earth's crust by the monster's meltdown, are both chilling. There are CGI-rendered helicopters and other images, but these are more run-of-the-mill.

DESTOROYAH ALL MONSTERS: Miki and Meru use their psychic powers to lead Godzilla Junior to Tokyo, where Destoroyah is casting huge, bat-shaped shadows over the city. Destoroyah slams into Junior and blasts the young monster with deadly rays. Destoroyah is poised to destroy Miki and Meru's helicopter, but at the last instant Junior knocks Destoroyah out of the sky with his atomic breath. Destoroyah transforms into its crab-form and the two giant creatures struggle, until Destoroyah uses its ray beam to topple a skyscraper onto Junior. Destoroyah pounces on the reptile, pinning Junior to the ground; although Junior fires his atomic breath and severs some of the insect's limbs, Destoroyah pierces Junior's flesh and injects him with deadly micro-oxygen. Poisoned and foaming at the mouth, Junior appears vanquished, but he unleashes a deadly atomic blast that careens Destoroyah backward into a building, seemingly killed. Godzilla and Junior are reunited, but their celebration is cut short when Destoroyah reappears in a glorious burst of energy, transformed into its "adult" form, an upright, winged creature that dwarfs Godzilla. Taking flight, Destoroyah snatches Junior and cruelly drops the young monster from high in the air, and Junior is mortally wounded by the fall. Destoroyah clamps its tail-claw around Godzilla's throat and drags the King across the tarmac of Haneda Airport. The two monsters struggle fiercely until Destoroyah morphs into a flock of small crabs that crawl all over Godzilla's body, but when Godzilla topples to the ground, the crabs vanish. Godzilla finds Junior's body and, filled with rage, he fights with all his strength, suffering oozing wounds from Destoroyah's arcing rays. Godzilla's body temperature approaches 1200 degrees Celsius and his meltdown begins, his dorsal fins liquefying and his body engulfed by hellish radioactive flame. Destoroyah tries to escape, but is killed by the Super-X3's freezing lasers and Godzilla's tragic demise unfolds.

For his last Godzilla movie, it is clear that SFX director Kawakita wanted to go out with a bang, for *Destoroyah* is packed with special-effects sequences and there are few lulls in the action. In the mode of late-1990s U.S. action/sci-fi films like *Batman and Robin* or *Lost In Space*, the movie begins with an elaborate action sequence, Godzilla's attack on Hong Kong. The radically altered appearance of Godzilla (his body burning red and steaming, his eyes burning, his breath crackling), combined with the well-conceived opening credits (the black-and-white title card from the 1954 *Godzilla* shatters, an animated Oxygen Destroyer detonates and reveals the title *Godzilla vs. Destoroyah* amid flames) and Akira Ifukube's main title theme (a re-worked, staccato rendition of Godzilla's attack music from the 1954 film) signifies from the outset that the Godzilla series has come full circle. Some of Kawakita's effects are inspired, like the composite shots of Godzilla trolling in the bay with the Hong Kong skyline behind him, the army of crab Destoroyahs invading Tokyo, Destoroyah dragging Godzilla by the neck, the swarm of crabs attacking Godzilla, and of course Godzilla's death.

However, more effects does not mean better effects, and there are lot of gaffes. The most glaring of these involves composite photography. As discussed earlier, when Godzilla's height was boosted to 100 meters in *Godzilla vs. King Ghidorah*, Kawakita had to downsize the miniatures to 1/50 scale to make the monster appear larger. The smaller miniatures were less detailed and less convincing, so in subsequent movies Kawakita used more and more composite shots, placing Godzilla into real-life backgrounds. Not a bad idea, but he should have paid more attention to the exterior footage used. In Hong Kong, pedestrians and motorists stroll and drive along casually and nonchalantly while a huge, radioactive Godzilla strolls toward them! When Godzilla enters Tokyo, motorists seem nonplused as they drive in medium traffic on the highway (this is a serious error, as the military ordered Tokyo be evacuated for fear that Godzilla will explode). At Haneda Airport, a pilot begins to taxi his airliner toward the runway, where a gigantic monster battle is under way. (In all fairness, it should be noted that it is virtually unheard of for the Japanese authorities to shut down a city street, airport, or other facility for filming.)

Like Warner Bros.' *Batman* movies and Fox's *Star Wars* pictures, Toho's Godzilla films are showcases for toys and other merchandise. Five creatures from *Godzilla vs. Destoroyah* were made available as playthings: Godzilla, Junior and the crab, flying-form and final-stage Destoroyahs. Unfortunately, Kawakita and crew missed the mark with Destoroyah, which is hardly worthy of the role of Godzilla's final opponent. The crab Destoroyahs look interesting at long range, but close-up shots reveal a plastic-looking, day-glo orange-red creature resembling a mutated arachnid-crustacean, shooting steam from its gills; brought to "life" with suitmation and prop work, the creatures seem to float slightly above ground, and it's obvious their legs are non-functional. The battle in Tokyo between the military and an army of "aggregate-form" crab Destoroyahs contains one of the biggest SFX embarrassments in the entire Godzilla series, a shot in which small Destoroyah action figures manufactured by Bandai (a Japanese toy company) were utilized instead of more highly detailed models. Worst of all is the adult Destoroyah that battles Godzilla at the film's end. Instead of a new kind of monster, as its ties to the Oxygen Destroyer would imply, Kawakita and his designers produced just another rubber suit with an array of optical beams, a nearly immobile Predator-meets-Space Godzilla clone (it even has knees similar to SG's) with big, stiff wings and clumsy, oversized feet. This creature is more laughable than menacing, and should be placed alongside Megalon and Gigan in the back rooms of the Toho monster gallery (the only impressive Destoroyah is the flying monster that battles with Junior, which looks like a truly evil, red devil-bat but is under-used, appearing only briefly). Another disappointment is the Super-X3, which may be fascinating to model kit fanatics but does not look credible on film (and, as in *Godzilla 1985* and *Biollante*, the battle-craft is thrown into the story with no dramatic buildup). It is hilarious that such a high-tech weapon cannot lock onto its target — some of the missiles fired by Super-X3, which look like kids' firecrackers, miss Godzilla by a mile.

On the bright side, there are Junior and Godzilla, both of which look great and are well portrayed by the man-in-suit stuntmen (Hurricane Ryu and Kenpachiro Satsuma, respectively). Junior Godzilla is the same creature that appeared as a pup in *Godzilla vs. MechaGodzilla* and then as a giant children's toy in *Space Godzilla* but now, having been exposed to the radiation that causes Birth Island to burn up and sink into the sea, the beast has been mutated into a small Godzilla. Junior's skin is a dark shade of green with a yellowish belly, he walks with a more hunched-forward, dinosaurian stance than Godzilla, his radioactive breath is white-hot, with a sort of bubbly sparkling shimmer, and his roar is like Godzilla's but less deep and hoarse. And, unlike the timid weakling that he was before (as Baby and Little Godzilla), Junior is a badass little dude, unafraid to fight Destoroyah even when he is over-matched. Unfortunately, because the Junior and Godzilla costumes were almost the same size, Kawakita was forced to use a smaller prop of God-zilla Junior (to show that papa Godzilla is bigger) in the scene when the two monsters are reunited; the prop is terribly unconvincing and looks as if it is propelled on rollers.

Godzilla is dreadful in this film, spewing steam from his radiation-scarred hide, causing the sea to boil and steam when he swims, and suffering terrible, intense pain (evidenced by his reddened irises and wounded roars) — perhaps his escalating temper-ature and radiation might have been better illus-trated if his appearance deteriorated during the movie, but the effect is still powerful. While com-puter animation was used to enhance Godzilla's glowing body, the basic effects involved in creating the burning Godzilla were typically low-tech. "The original idea was to have Godzilla be luminescent," Koichi Kawakita said in an interview with David Milner in Cult Movies #20. "He was going to be white and red. We tried using both luminescent paint and light reflecting tape, but they didn't look sufficiently natural. So, we ended up using the most orthodox method. We took the Godzilla costume that had been made for Godzilla vs. Space Godzilla, and put about 200 tiny orange light bulbs in it. We then put semi-transparent vinyl plates over the lights. There was a very thick power cable coming out of the end of the tail."

The added burden to the costume made work more difficult for stuntman Kenpachiro Satsuma, whose job was already cumbersome. Not only that, but Satsuma had to deal with new hazards stem-ming from Godzilla's steaming effects. "Sometimes you see Godzilla coming out of the ocean and you see him fighting, and there's gas coming out from here and there," Satsuma said later in an interview with Newsweek (June 1, 1998). "It's carbonic-acid gas. The Godzilla suit only had 12 very small holes to allow me to inhale air. When they used the gas, I'd inhale that and faint. Godzilla nearly died six times." Satsuma also commented on the relation-ship between Godzilla and Baby/Little Godzilla/ Junior, noting that Godzilla's role as a parent in the last three films made the King's gender somewhat ambiguous. "When Godzilla shows up, sometimes it's a male, sometimes a female," Satsuma said.

Monster Box Office

The approximate number of theater tickets sold in Japan for each of the 22 Godzilla features

1. *Godzilla* (1954) — 9,610,000
2. *Godzilla Raids Again* (1955) — 8,340,000
3. *King Kong vs. Godzilla* (1962) — 11,200,000
   Re-released March 21, 1970 (870,000), March 19, 1977 (480,000)
4. *Godzilla vs. The Thing* (1964) — 3,510,000
   Re-released December 19, 1970 (730,000), March 15, 1980 (2,980,000)
5. *Ghidrah: The Three-Headed Monster* (1964) — 4,320,000
   Re-released Dec. 12, 1971 (1,090,000)
6. *Monster Zero* (1965) — 3,780,000
   Re-released March 17, 1971 (1,350,000)
7. *Godzilla versus The Sea Monster* (1966) — 3,450,000
   Re-released July 22, 1972 (760,000)
8. *Son of Godzilla* (1967) — 2,480,000
   Re-released August 1, 1973 (610,000)
9. *Destroy All Monsters* (1968) — 2,580,000
10. *Godzilla's Revenge* (1969) — 1,480,000
11. *Godzilla vs. The Smog Monster* (1971) — 1,740,000
12. *Godzilla on Monster Island* (1972) — 1,780,000
13. *Godzilla vs. Megalon* (1973) — 980,000
14. *Godzilla vs. The Cosmic Monster* (1974) — 1,330,000
15. *Terror of MechaGodzilla* (1975) — 970,000
16. *Godzilla* (1984) — 3,200,000
17. *Godzilla vs. Biollante* (1989) — 2,000,000
18. *Godzilla vs. King Ghidorah* (1991) — 2,700,000
19. *Godzilla vs. Mothra* (1992) — 4,200,000
20. *Godzilla vs. MechaGodzilla* (1993) — 3,800,000
21. *Godzilla vs. Space Godzilla* (1994) — 3,400,000
22. *Godzilla vs. Destoroyah* (1995) — 4,000,000

展示物には
お手を
ふれないで下さい

A "crab-form" Destoroyah costume from *Godzilla vs. Destoroyah*, on display
at the Godzilla Exhibition at the Ariake Coliseum in Tokyo in January 1996.
COURTESY OF WINTERGARDEN PRODUCTIONS

"If you want to know about the family tree, I can't tell you. It's very complicated. But this baby was supposed to be the baby of a cousin."

ARMAGEDDON

Story-wise, one of the big problems with *Godzilla vs. Destoroyah* is that everyone already knows Godzilla is going to die. It may have been a great publicity stunt for the studio, but this steals a lot of the film's dramatic thunder. First-time viewers, knowing full well what is going to happen, are left wondering only where, when and how the monster will meet his fate. Screenwriter Kazuki Omori offsets the foregone conclusion, however, by inserting a jolting, unexpected plot twist. The death of Godzilla Junior, the young and innocent monster, is a shocking, emotional moment, and it makes the battle between Godzilla and Destoroyah (a mostly routine Toho ray-shooting exchange and slugfest) somewhat more interesting.

Like the special effects, Omori's screenplay is a mixed bag. Act One (roughly the first one-third) of the movie is probably the best *kaiju eiga* screenwriting Omori has ever done, highlighted by Godzilla's aforementioned Hong Kong attack, the introduction of the central characters, and the first appearances of the Destoroyah — a tiny organism that destroys oxygen within the tissues of other creatures, melting the flesh off its victims' bones — a living embodiment of Serizawa's Oxygen Destroyer that potentially could threaten Japan and the entire world by wiping out the air supply or turning oceans into huge graveyards. In *Godzilla vs. Biollante*, *King Ghidorah*, and *Mothra*, Omori supplemented the monster stuff with interesting characters and moral conflicts, but he also hampered those movies with his tendency to include too many characters, each with too little role in the story, and here he does the same thing. *Destoroyah* is cleverly tied to Honda's 1954 original via the central characters: Yukari, the newscaster and Kenkichi, the boy Godzilla-scholar, are descendants of the late scientist Dr. Kyohei Yamane, who discovered Godzilla years ago, while Dr. Ijuin, a scientist achieving notoriety for his work with an element called micro-oxygen, is compelled to pursue scientific advancements but knows he is walking in Serizawa's doomed shadow. There is also a wonderful cameo by Momoko Kochi (now in her sixties) as Emiko Yamane, who apparently never married Ogata after Serizawa's tragic death. Kochi warns the others not to unlock Serizawa's dark

scientific secrets, but her admonitions are mostly dismissed and her (all-too-brief) appearance is somewhat wasted. In a news report broadcast by CNN (December 1, 1995), Kochi commented on returning to the Godzilla series: "After the first Godzilla movie people pointed at me, saying, 'Godzilla, Godzilla.' As a young woman I hated Godzilla, so I thought, 'no more Godzilla for me.' But 41 years later I watched the film again and realized how great it was for its anti-nuclear theme."

In Act Two and Act Three, Omori reverts to his old ways, as the main characters fade into the woodwork or are reduced to mere commentators on the monster action. After being attacked and nearly killed by one of the crab Destoroyahs, newscaster Yukari (presumably, the female lead) takes a back seat to psychics Miki and Meru, who are tracking Godzilla Junior. Kenkichi, though he becomes the brain trust of the entire anti-Godzilla operation, remains just a know-it-all brat who watches everything on a monitor and never faces any peril (an unwitting metaphor for kids who spend much of their lives glued to computer monitors, disconnected from society). The philosophical questions raised by Dr. Ijuin's research are never elaborated upon. During the first half of the film, the dark specter of the Oxygen Destroyer casts a dark shadow (everyone knows the device is perhaps the only way to kill Godzilla before he blows up, yet the weapon is so feared that no one dares utter its name), but after Kenkichi suggests re-creating the device to save Japan, the idea goes nowhere.

As in the past two films, psychic Miki Saegusa (Megumi Odaka) makes a brief stand for "Godzilla's Rights," only to abandon her principles. Miki (portrayed here as more girlish than in her "breakthrough" role in the last picture) objects adamantly when the military opts to use Godzilla Junior as Destoroyah-bait; the military officers say they can't be sentimental about monsters, and the beret-wearing Meru threatens to complete the psychic mission herself and, as before, Miki ends up hurting rather than helping the monsters. At the climax, Miki and Meru, marginal characters throughout much of the film, are stranded amid the monster melee and must be rescued, rather undramatically. Omori also includes homages to his favorite American blockbusters again. The flame-thrower fight with the crab Destoroyahs (combined with the monsters' secondary teeth) is borrowed from *Aliens*, while the scene in which one of the crabs traps Yukari inside a car is shamelessly borrowed from *Jurassic Park*.

Before Toho pushed *Godzilla vs. Destoroyah* into production, the studio considered several interesting story ideas that ultimately went by the wayside:

- According to director Okawara, in an interview published in *Cult Movies* #18, screenwriter Omori initially submitted a story treatment called *Godzilla vs. Godzilla*, in which the ghost of the original Godzilla killed in 1954 by the Oxygen Destroyer re-materialized in Japan 40 years later and battled the *Heisei* Godzilla.

- In the original draft of the *Destoroyah* script, Godzilla and Junior did not meet at Haneda, and Junior was killed off much earlier.

- An alternate ending to *Destoroyah* was considered in which Godzilla dies, the ending credits roll, and Godzilla Junior's resurrection was shown after the credits. "We tried that, but it left too much of a gap between Godzilla's death and Godzilla Junior's resurrection," Okawara explained. "One person said that most of the members of the audience would leave during the credits, so they would never even see Godzilla Junior."

Another change to the *Destoroyah* script was made necessary due to political maneuverings in the Tokyo metropolitan government. The final monster battle and Godzilla's death were supposed to take place at World City, a $2.35-billion urban design and technology development project. However, in May 1995, right before filming was set to begin, new Tokyo Governor Yukio Aoshima axed World City because of the project's unpopularity with taxpayers. Thus, SFX director Kawakita instead staged the final battle at the Tokyo waterfront city subcenter (where World City was to have been built), and at nearby Haneda Airport. The Tokyo metropolitan government tried to use Godzilla's death as a publicity tool for the area, by staging a Godzilla exhibition at nearby Ariake Coliseum. "The waterfront area may turn out to have a special meaning for Godzilla fans, since the monster meets his fate there," a Toho spokesman told the media.

MOURNING THE MONSTER: On December 5, 1995, just a few days before the movie opened, a one-meter-tall bronze memorial statue of Godzilla was erected in a public square in the Hibiya cinema district, just a few blocks from Toho's corporate offices. The statue, hard-mounted on a stone pedestal to prevent theft, was unveiled in a dedication ceremony attended by actors Akira Takarada and Yasuko Sawaguchi (of *Godzilla 1985* fame). A Toho spokesman told the *Mainichi Daily News* that Godzilla's death was not definitely permanent, but it was unknown when the monster would return. "Even if we call him back to life, it won't be before the turn of the century."

Despite all the advance publicity of Godzilla's death, many fans were truly shocked and, according to reports in the *London Daily Telegraph* and other media, Toho was besieged with more than 10,000 protest letters in the first three days after the film's release, from fans demanding Godzilla's resurrection. Toho officials went on the defensive. Hiroshi Ono, a studio spokesman, told the *Telegraph*, "We had to kill him. We're planning to come up with a monster better suited to the 21st century . . . But his death does seem to have upset a lot of people." Distraught fans flocked to the bronze statue, many leaving 10- or 100-Yen coins under Godzilla's claws or in his mouth, as offerings for the afterlife. "One Godzilla-worshipper reverently placed an unlit cigarette between the icon's jaws. Japanese usually leave tobacco and beer at the graves of relatives who enjoyed such vice during their lives. Godzilla was not know to be a smoker, but he frequently emitted big bursts of flame from his mouth," a *Telegraph* reporter wrote. A Japanese travel agency commemorated Godzilla's death by hosting tours of the Tokyo landmarks the monster destroyed over his 40-year career.

Director Takao Okawara characterized the end of Godzilla's career as profound, telling CNN, "I want people to look at the death of Godzilla knowing that he was created by nuclear power and the most selfish existence in the world: mankind." He summed up the feelings of many Japanese, saying, "I am looking forward to seeing Godzilla in the U.S."

After the monster was symbolically buried in his homeland, attention shifted to Hollywood, where the first-ever American *Godzilla*, already in the works for three years, was about to shift from the back burner to the production fast-track at TriStar Pictures. Meanwhile, Toho remained in the giant-monster business by producing a new series of Mothra movies that featured little kids as the main characters and were geared strictly for the small-fry audiences. In *Mothra* (released December 1996), the big insect battles a creature called Death Ghidorah; in *Mothra 2* (December 1997), Mothra transforms into Aqua-Mothra to battle an undersea creature; and in *Mothra 3* (December 1998), Mothra battles King Ghidorah.

The Godzilla memorial statue in Hibiya, Tokyo.
PHOTO BY THOMAS FITCH

Interview

SWAN SONG

Maestro Akira Ifukube concludes his monster-music career with Godzilla vs. Destoroyah

In the final reel of *Godzilla vs. Destoroyah*, the King of the Monsters finally meets his match. Fittingly, it is not King Ghidorah or Mothra that sends the great beast to its demise but the stuff that spawned him in the first place, nuclear radiation. It is also fitting — poignant, even — that Godzilla's death is accompanied by a melancholy theme that is unmistakably the work of Akira Ifukube, whose signatory monster music and nationalistic military marches are trademarks of Toho's science-fiction classics. Ifukube's work has been integral to the success of the 1990s Godzilla movies, providing a bridge to the monster's past and lending a vitality that, to date, no other music composer has been able to equal. For *Godzilla vs. Destoroyah*, Ifukube wrote what is undoubtedly his last Godzilla score.

I have heard that before Godzilla vs. King Ghidorah, *you were reluctant to begin scoring Godzilla movies again.*

I did not accept the assignment for *Godzilla vs. Biollante*, but after the film was released, my daughter pointed out that they had used some of my music in the film. Also, they had made some of my music into a rock theme [the Godzilla theme is incorporated into the Andrew Lloyd Webber-style number that plays during the chase between the Japanese soldiers and Bio-Major terrorists in the beginning of the film], and I did not like that! So, my daughter encouraged me to accept the next Godzilla movie so I would have some control over how my music was used.

Has the business of scoring films changed much in Japan since back when the original Godzilla *was made?*

I still have to face the same problems: not enough time, not enough money. I always have to make last-minute changes because of editing, and often it is frustrating. In *Godzilla vs. King Ghidorah*, the Japanese air force allowed Toho to use actual footage of F-15s for the sequence when Ghidorah fights the jets, but the decision was not made until the day before the score was going to be recorded. I didn't have time to write new music for that scene, so I ended up using a theme from *Rodan*, from a very similar scene in which the Rodan monster battles with jets. It was just a matter of finding a piece of music that fit. Those kind of constraints are aggravating because I am never satisfied with the music. It doesn't sound fresh.

How do you compare working with the directors of the new Godzilla movies to working with Ishiro Honda?

Mr. Honda was very knowledgeable about the score and he had very sophisticated knowledge about music and how it should be applied in film. He would tell me, "Mr. Ifukube, you make all the decisions regarding the score." That was very flattering and it also made my work much easier. Mr. Honda paid careful attention to the music, whereas most other directors I have worked with did not. During the recording sessions, Mr. Honda would stand next to me when I was conducting sometimes. He wanted to see how things worked. No other director has done that.

You previously said that Godzilla vs. MechaGodzilla *was your last Godzilla score. How did you decide to work on* Destoroyah?

I declined to work on *Godzilla vs. Space Godzilla* because when I looked at the script, I felt it was . . . how can I say it? It wasn't right. But when I read the *Godzilla vs. Destoroyah* script I saw that it was connected thematically to the original *Godzilla*.

Maestro Akira Ifukube at his home in Tokyo.
PHOTO BY THE AUTHOR

I was also intrigued that this film was about the death of Godzilla. I was involved in the birth of Godzilla 40 years before, so I felt I should be there when he dies, too.

How did the fact that Godzilla dies in the movie affect your writing?

It didn't. I approached the film the same way as I did the other films [in the *Heisei* Godzilla series]. However, Destoroyah was a very different type of monster; he is unbelievably powerful and huge. I thought about using the original motif for the Oxygen Destroyer, but that piece was really meant to express the tragedy of Dr. Serizawa's death. I tried using it, but it didn't feel right, so I ended up writing a new theme for the Destoroyah monster.

As the end credits roll in Godzilla vs. Destoroyah, *clips of the original* Godzilla *and all the films from the* Heisei *series are shown on the screen. However, you used a piece of music from* King Kong vs. Godzilla, *which is not part of the "revised Godzilla timeline," to score this section of the film. Why?*

You are right, they do not show all the generations of Godzilla during the credits. However, I felt it was impossible to include all the Godzilla motifs during the credits, as they are relatively short, lasting only

about two and a half minutes. So, I chose the Faro Island theme from *King Kong vs. Godzilla* and the Adonoa Island theme from *Godzilla vs. Mecha-Godzilla*. I just thought these pieces fit.

I noticed that you used some themes from the original Godzilla *in this movie.*

I used the same motif of the Oxygen Destroyer as it is revealed in *Godzilla*, during the scene where Emiko has a nightmare of the Destoroyah monster. When Godzilla melts down at the end of the movie, I thought of using the same motif as when Godzilla is dissolved by the Oxygen Destroyer in Tokyo Bay in the original film. But I thought about the meaning of the two scenes, and I realized that a totally different type of atmosphere was needed. In the original film, Godzilla's death is the resolution of a tragedy, and it somehow represents hope. But in *Godzilla vs. Destoroyah*, I believe it is more pessimistic.

The theme for Godzilla's death was one of the most difficult pieces I have ever had to compose. In a way, it was as if I was composing the theme for my own death. When Godzilla was born, a phase of my life began. Now Godzilla is gone, and that phase is over. It was very emotional.

GODZILLA INVADES L.A.

Godzilla has made a habit of trashing famous Japanese landmarks, but in summer 1996 he strayed westward and stomped through downtown Los Angeles on a historic visit.

A team of handlers helps the stuntman climb into the Godzilla suit at Los Angeles City Hall, just prior to Godzilla's meeting with the Los Angeles City Council. Despite the fact that this was a "promo" costume, much lighter than the costumes actually used in the films, the stuntman was able to remain inside the suit for only short periods at a time.

PHOTO BY THE AUTHOR

Godzilla — or a somewhat flimsy looking "promo" Godzilla suit — shakes hands with Los Angeles Mayor Richard Riordan at City Hall.

PHOTO BY THE AUTHOR

The occasion was the 56th annual Nisei Week, a celebration of Japanese-American culture in the Little Tokyo section of Los Angeles. At the invitation of a community affairs group, Toho Co. Ltd. loaned out one of its "promo" Godzilla suits and shipped it in a wooden crate from Tokyo to California. Toho

Godzilla shakes hands with the kiddies in Little Tokyo.
PHOTO BY MARIO ARTAVIA

also loaned 35mm prints of three films — the "international" English-dubbed versions of *Destroy All Monsters* and *Godzilla vs. Hedora*, plus an English-subtitled print of *Terror of MechaGodzilla* — for an all-day Godzilla film festival at the Japan America Theatre in the city's Japanese American Cultural Center. The 860-seat theater was packed.

The visit began on July 29, when the suit arrived from Japan. Dan Schultz, a 39-year-old Los Angeles reserve police officer, was recruited to wear the 77-pound costume at a series of publicity appearances.

Organizers erroneously believed Toho was sending them a real "filming costume." But unlike 1985, when Toho aided New World Pictures' promotion of *Godzilla 1985* by sending one of the actual suits to America, this was instead a green, rubbery, cheapish-looking thing. One L.A. city council member was overheard wondering aloud, "Is that *really* what it looks like in person?"

Despite weighing half as much as a "real" Godzilla suit, this promo costume was still a steam-room inside, especially with the summer sun bearing down on it. Schultz, the stuntman, had to take frequent breaks, and when his handlers (several kids dressed in all-black ninja outfits) unzipped the back and pulled him out, he was soaked in sweat and had to be given 32-ounce soft drinks and blasted with electric fans. Schultz was supposed to be inside the costume when Godzilla served as Grand Marshal of the Nisei Week parade, but because of the heat, an empty Godzilla suit rode in the car instead.

Part 6

GODZILLA VS. HOLLYWOOD
The Future

"There is talk of expensive, state-of-the-art special-effects wizardry that would seem to run counter to everything Godzilla stands for. . . . Will he be scarier? Will he breathe more fire? Will he finally look real? Probably. But when he does, will he still be kind?"

— *Janet Maslin*, New York Times

"It will be the most awesome Godzilla ever. It has to be a step above. Roland and I have said this Godzilla must be to its predecessor what Tim Burton's *Batman* was to Adam West."

— *Producer-Screenwriter Dean Devlin in* Sci-Fi Universe *magazine, June 1996*

Twenty-Three

REMADE IN AMERICA

This testing done by my country left a terrible mess. We are here to clean it up.

— Agent Philippe Roache

GODZILLA

RATING (OUT OF FIVE STARS): ★ 1/2

Released on May 20, 1998. Widescreen, in color. Running time: 139 minutes. MPAA Rating: PG-13. A Sony release of a TriStar Pictures presentation of a Centropolis Entertainment production, in association with Fried Films and Independent Pictures.

STORY: Lizards exposed to French nuclear tests in the South Pacific are mutated into a new, gigantic species of reptile that can reproduce quickly and asexually, threatening to replace man as Earth's dominant creature. Dubbed "Gojira" by a superstitious Japanese sailor (the name is bastardized into Godzilla by a TV anchorman), the beast swims to New York City, burrows into the subway system, and lays hundreds of eggs in Madison Square Garden. As the military tries vainly to catch the evasive, fleet-footed Godzilla, a U.S. biologist and a team of French secret agents looking to fix their country's nuclear boo-boo kill Godzilla's hatchlings; papa (or mama?) Godzilla discovers its dead brood and, now intensely pissed off, chases the murderous humans (fleeing in a taxicab) across Manhattan and onto the Brooklyn Bridge, where the monster becomes ensnared in the suspension cables and is killed by F-18 fighter planes.

BEAST MEETS WEST

In September 1996, director **Roland Emmerich** and creature-effects designer **Patrick Tatopoulos** sat in a Tokyo conference room with members of the Toho Motion Picture Co.'s top brass, including Shogo Tomiyama and Koichi Kawakita, the producer and special-effects director, respectively, of the last six Godzilla movies. The subject of this now-historic meeting was the future of TriStar Pictures' *Godzilla*, a proposed film that had languished in Hollywood's "development hell" for four years. Emmerich, emboldened by the success of his breakthrough sci-fi blockbuster *Independence Day*, spelled out in no uncertain terms that he was willing to take on the faltering project, but only if Toho and TriStar would give him and **Dean Devlin**, his producer and writing partner (who was hospitalized in Germany and did not attend the meeting), absolute creative control. As part of the deal, the Japanese would also have to accept a new-look Godzilla designed by Tatopoulos.

The Toho men were there, ostensibly, to protect Godzilla's image and to ensure that their monster, a folk hero in its homeland, was respectfully treated by the American studio. As a matter of course, Toho had set down in writing a series of commandments establishing the parameters of the King of the Monsters' onscreen visage and persona: Godzilla's birth must be the result of a nuclear explosion; Godzilla must have four claws on its hands and feet; Godzilla must have three rows of dorsal fins along its spine; Godzilla does not eat people; Godzilla cannot die. According to reports in *Time* magazine and elsewhere, these edicts were compiled in a 75-page bible, written in legalese by Toho's lawyers. If followed to the letter, this bible ensured that any American Godzilla would largely resemble its Japanese namesake, but Emmerich's agenda was to convince the monster's corporate guardians to relax the reins. At a pivotal point in the meeting, Emmerich unveiled a sculpted maquette of Tatopoulos' new Godzilla design; the Toho men reacted with stunned silence — the creature was an upright-walking, mutoid reptile, but whereas the old Godzilla was a stocky, plodding city-flattener, this one was sleek. "I told the Japanese guys the biggest difference would be that the creature is very lean because he's very fast," Emmerich later recalled in *Time* (May 25, 1998). "I also told them, 'Guys, we either do it like this, or we don't do it at all. It's your trademark, but if you don't do it this way . . . you'll have to find someone else." The meeting was disbanded, and Emmerich was told he'd receive Toho's yay or nay tomorrow.

Much to the surprise of many — including, according to some sources, Emmerich and Tatopoulos — Toho's chief executive Isao Matsuoka greenlighted the project at 10 a.m. the next day. Why? If you believe the filmmakers and the studio, it was because the new Godzilla blew Toho away. Dean Devlin later told *SFX* magazine, "They [Toho] took a long time in deciding . . . And then they said, 'We love this look, we love your idea and we back you 100 percent. Go do it.' Because it was so different, it was like a whole rebirth of Godzilla." Patrick Tatopoulos said in *Time*, "The Japanese told me that the new Godzilla is miles away from the old creature but that I kept its spirit," while Chris Lee, the TriStar production executive who orchestrated the Toho-Emmerich summit, said Toho felt comfortable that the "TriStar Godzilla" was so different it would not be confused with the original. But the Toho chieftans likely had other, financially motivated reasons for their actions. Toho, as the Japanese distributor of *Independence Day*, was certainly impressed by Emmerich's recent box-office performance; more importantly, the deal for an American *Godzilla* was at a crossroads — no other big-name directors were vying to make the film, and the project could be derailed indefinitely if TriStar were forced to find another man. To Toho, a *gaijin* Godzilla was an opportunity to exploit the icon internationally on an unprecedented scale, reaping worldwide film and merchandising profits with little or no investment. It was too good to pass up.

Over the next year and half, Roland Emmerich made his *Godzilla*, full of loopholes that barely mask the fact he violated key points in the Toho bible. Emmerich's souped-up lizard eats people (off-camera, several Godzilla babies devour soldiers, and the full-grown beast tries to swallow a taxicab full of people) and the creature definitely dies (however, a hatchling survives at the film's end, ensuring the species' survival). Perhaps worst of all, Emmerich did away with Godzilla's atomic breath, substituting a hurricane-force gaseous snort that ignites when it comes in contact with fire. Despite a huge hype machine that led the masses to expect an incredible re-working of Japan's favorite monster, Emmerich's film was really a remake of *The Beast from 20,000 Fathoms*, with riffs carbon-copied from *Jurassic Park* (but none of that film's terror and pathos) and an ending stolen from *King Kong* (big creature gets trapped atop famous New York architectural landmark and is shot by fighter planes). Most significantly, the movie failed to supplant memories of the old Godzilla films — on the contrary, the American public became openly nostalgic for the real thing. Although it grossed upward of $300 million in theaters worldwide, the film was largely viewed a failure.

But, long before Roland Emmerich and Dean Devlin got their hands on Godzilla, TriStar Pictures had developed another screenplay, hired another director, and had a very different approach in mind.

IN THE BEGINNING

The deal between TriStar and Toho for an American *Godzilla* was announced way back in October, 1992

— more than five and a half years before Emmerich's film appeared. The *Los Angeles Times*, in a story headlined "Godzilla, Call Your Agent," was among the first media organs to report that TriStar had agreed to pay Toho an up-front fee of $400,000 plus other, undisclosed terms for rights to make a big-budget Godzilla featuring "A-list stars, screenwriter and director." The impetus for the deal reportedly came from Godzilla's longtime representative, Henry G. Saperstein. Saperstein had not co-produced a Godzilla movie since *Terror of Mecha-Godzilla*, but the monster was still making money for him — in the early 1990s, his United Productions of America was the official licensing agent for Godzilla merchandise in the U.S., and it controlled the TV and home video rights to several Toho/UPA titles including *Monster Zero*, *War of the Gargantuas*, and *Frankenstein Conquers the World*. Saperstein, who often referred to Godzilla as "the golden goose," was determined to see that the monster, at long last, laid a gigantic golden egg. "For ten years I pressured Toho to make one in America," Saperstein told *Filmfax* magazine in 1994. "Finally they agreed." Saperstein died in July 1998, two months after *Godzilla* was released.

TriStar placed a small ad in *Variety* showing the giant silhouette of Godzilla towering over the TriStar Pictures headquarters in Culver City, California, and announcing an anticipated 1994 release — a date allowing *Godzilla* to capitalize on the dinosaur mania that Steven Spielberg's *Jurassic Park* would generate the year before. Summer 1993 came and went, and *Jurassic Park* fulfilled expectations in terms of its realistic-looking dinosaurs and its gargantuan box-office success. But when 1994 arrived and it was time for Godzilla to ride the big T-Rex's coat tails (or, more appropriately, its tail), the monster was still appearing in Japanese films like *Godzilla vs. MechaGodzilla* and *Godzilla vs. Space Godzilla*, and seemed to be having trouble getting a U.S. work visa.

REVISING THE LEGEND

In May 1993, it was announced that screenwriters **Terry Rossio** and **Ted Elliott**, who had done major rewriting on the animated Disney feature *Aladdin* (1992), were hired to write an original *Godzilla* script. Rossio and Elliott seemed an odd choice for such a big assignment, especially in comparison

to other, higher-profile writers who were also considered. They included horror kingpin Clive Barker, who reportedly came up with story ideas that the studio considered "too dark," and *Predator* screenwriters Jim Thomas and John Thomas. Throughout 1993, no mention was made about a director, although both Tim Burton and Joe Dante were widely rumored to be the studio's top candidates, probably because both had previously paid homage to the King of the Monsters: Burton gave Godzilla and King Ghidorah camp cameos in *Pee Wee's Big Adventure*, and actual footage from *Godzilla vs. Biollante* was later inserted into his *Mars Attacks!*; Dante parodied Godzilla in his low-budget comedy *Hollywood Boulevard* in 1976. Dante, in fact, expressed skepticism about the viability of the project, telling *Starlog* magazine in 1993, "They (TriStar) have quite a job ahead of them trying to turn Godzilla into what they're talking about, which is a movie that will attract major stars. I don't know what you do with that time-worn plot that can be new enough to make it something special."

When Rossio and Elliott turned in their first draft script on November 11, 1993, there was still no word as to who would helm the picture. By Spring 1994 there were rumors that the project had been turned down by everyone on TriStar's short list of directors, including Ridley Scott, James Cameron, Robert Zemeckis, and — prophetically, as it later turned out — Roland Emmerich, who had recently made *Stargate*. The studio had also talked to several second-string (but nonetheless respectable) candidates, including Sam Raimi (*Evil Dead*), Barry Sonnenfeld (*Addams Family*), and Joe Johnston (*The Rocketeer*).

OHAIYO, JAN DeBONT

In May 1994, TriStar Pictures announced publicly that it was seeking a director for *Godzilla*; two months later, in July, the studio found its man, **Jan DeBont**, who had just scored a major summer hit with his first film, *Speed*. As Hollywood's newest blockbuster-maker, DeBont had his pick of big projects at several studios, and TriStar Pictures agreed to pay the director more than $4 million to woo him into the *Godzilla* camp.

DeBont gave fans reason to believe Godzilla was in good hands, telling *Fangoria* magazine that he had seen the original 1954 *Godzilla* as a child in

Jan DeBont on the set of *Speed*.
COPYRIGHT 20TH CENTURY-FOX

Holland and was wowed by it, and he even "really loved" some of the sequels. "The early ones are the best; the later ones where the big monsters start boxing now look really silly, but it used to be really funny," he said, adding that he had wanted to direct the American *Godzilla* for several years but the studio rebuffed his inquiries until he became director-du-jour. DeBont pledged to deliver a Godzilla with all the realism of modern special effects, but to retain the personable spirit that had made the Big G lovable over the years. "I'm not going to make it less funny — there's going to be a lot of humor in this movie — but it must be amazing to see a monster that big, 250 feet tall, and looks real." DeBont assembled a team and set to work on pre-production in mid-summer, 1994. He began by revising the script to suit his liking and searching for a special-effects company that could handle the ambitious film.

As details slowly began to leak out about the top-secret *Godzilla* script, it became clear that TriStar was going to take major creative liberties with cer-tain aspects of Godzilla mythology. The monster would have all-new origins, eschewing his atom-bomb beginnings. Though fearsome, Godzilla would play the role of Earth's defender against an alien creature called the Gryphon. The main char-acter of the story was a female scientist determined to slay Godzilla to avenge the death of her husband, who was killed during Godzilla's first appearance.

Synopsis: GODZILLA by Terry Rossio and Ted Elliott (1993)

In a remote location somewhere on the frozen coast of Alaska, a salvage ship excavates nuclear reactor cores that were illegally dumped at sea long ago by the Soviet Union. Suddenly, something goes awry and a huge explosion destroys the ship. On the shoreline, giant snowbanks mysteriously catch fire and a huge crevice opens in the ground, streaming an eerie red-black fluid.

In the middle of the night, Dr. Keith Llewellyn, a government scientist, is flown to the site of the accident, where the military has launched a top-secret investigation into the giant fissure in the ground (there's a scene where he regretfully leaves behind his wife, Jill, and young daughter Tina, both of whom figure in the story later). Soldiers cart away drums full of the mysterious red-black liquid which, tests show, resembles an amniotic fluid (the substance fetuses gestate upon in the womb). In the underground cavern, Keith sees what at first appears to be a huge stalactite formation but, upon inspection, is actually the claws of a huge creature imbedded in the sediment. Keith finds the head of the perfectly preserved creature — a huge dinosaur — and climbs atop its muzzle to look down the length of its 247-foot-long body. Suddenly, the beast opens one of its eyes — it's alive! — and breaks free from the ice. Everyone in the cavern is crushed, and the beast destroys the entire military camp, then heads south into the sea. Soon thereafter, the dinosaur appears at the Kuril Islands off Japan and destroys a village. It is seen by a fisherman who believes it is Godzilla, a legendary monster.

Fast-forward 12 years later. Aaron Vaught, a pseudo-scientist whose theories about dragons and dinosaurs have made him a best-selling author, and Marty Kenoshita, his assistant, sneak into a Japanese mental hospital to visit the fisherman who saw Godzilla. The fisherman shows Vaught his drawings of Godzilla, images that come to him in his dreams. In one picture, Godzilla is locked in battle with a Gryphon, leading Aaron and Marty to theorize that if Godzilla exists (as they think he does), he must have an adversary. Just then, military police arrive to escort Vaught and Marty out of the country. The men think they're being busted for sneaking into the hospital, but actually the government has a mission for them.

Meanwhile, in rural Kentucky, a huge fireball plunges into Lake Apopka, eerily raining fish and frogs on a nearby town.

Jill Llewellyn, Keith Llewellyn's widow, is now director of the top-secret St. George Project in Massachusetts, a military effort to find the beast that caused the Alaska disaster. The monster was last seen six years ago, when it destroyed an oil tanker. Jill is not pleased to learn that Vaught, the dragon enthusiast, whom she dismisses as a "folklorist,"

will be co-director of the project with her — Jill's superiors hope Vaught's popularity will help the project get funding from Congress. In the midst of this conflict, Jill gets a call from the base police: Tina, now 16, is being detained for trying to steal a car. The relationship between the workaholic mom and rebellious teen is loving, but strained.

Back at the "Godzilla womb" site in Alaska, where a military installation has been established, two military guards see streams of peculiar light coming from a yet-undiscovered ice cave and illuminating the sky.

At the same time, a mysterious alien probe — metallic, yet alive — is stirring at the bottom of Lake Apopka in Kentucky. Flowing like liquid chrome, the probe enters a cave, grabs dozens of bats, and absorbs them into its own matter. The creature then forms dozens of "probe-bats," evil creatures with 12-foot wingspans that sail out of the cave and into the night sky. Vaught, Marty, and Jill fly to Alaska and discover that red-black amniotic fluid has been flowing from the Godzilla womb, and Aaron deduces that this day is — or was supposed to be, anyway — Godzilla's birthday, had the monster not been released prematurely. The trio enter a newly opened ice cave, which is lined with intricate organic formations, a strange remnant of an ancient civilization with advanced biotechnology. No one notices when a microscopic alien organism swoops down and burrows into Marty's neck, not even Marty.

Another chain of events: In Kentucky a stable of milk cows is slaughtered overnight, their carcasses removed of limbs and organs; in the Pacific Ocean, three fishing boats are capsized when Godzilla, pursuing a giant school of fish, passes beneath at 40 knots. Another sighting is reported when Godzilla passes beneath an oil tanker, and the military figures he is headed for San Francisco.

Jill and Vaught go to the Presidio, where a command post is set up, but Marty has become ill and is taken away for medical care. Two missile carriers, a battleship, and a submarine are sent to intercept Godzilla, but the monster easily destroys two planes, then submerges and throws one of the missile carriers out of the sea, cracking it in half. Godzilla finishes off the ships by emitting a fiery breath that turns the hulls to molten metal. The military considers using a small nuclear bomb to stop Godzilla, but Vaught believes it won't work: Godzilla is a living, breathing nuclear reactor — evidenced by the fact he breathes not flame, but something so hot it actually ionizes oxygen. Jill concludes that the red-black fluid that encased Godzilla was not food, but actually a tranquilizer that kept the monster in hibernation. Barrels of the fluid are brought to San Francisco and a plan is concocted to stop Godzilla using the red-black stuff. Fire trucks spray the surface of the water entering the bay with the fluid, and as Godzilla arrives, he swims right into the trap. He bolts upright and slowly comes ashore, then, roaring weakly, collapses on the south side of the Golden Gate bridge. Using six super-helicopters, the military transports Godzilla, suspended from cables, to Massachusetts, where it is stored in a huge hangar, the tail sticking out one end. One night, young Tina sneaks into the hangar and suddenly realizes that mom's job for the past 12 years has been hunting the beast that killed her Dad. Tina, wise beyond her years, says Godzilla is a force of nature and should be respected. Her mother sends Tina to Manhattan to stay with an aunt for a while.

At a military hospital, Marty's infection is consuming his internal organs, and has turned his face into a flat, eyeless surface. Whatever has invaded his body is taking over, and begins speaking through him. Before he dies, Marty tells Jill about an alien race colonizing the universe by sending out probes that create a "doomsday beast" out of the local genetic material — by the time the alien colonists arrive, the beast has already conquered the planet. An ancient, biotech Earth civilization guarded itself against these invaders by creating Godzilla out of dinosaur genes, placing him in suspended animation to awaken when the alien probe arrives and kill it before it can reproduce. Meanwhile in Kentucky, the alien probe-bats keep absorbing critters and bringing them back to the cave, where a mysterious creature is slowly taking shape.

Vaught deduces that Godzilla was headed for the spot where the huge fireball landed, and immediately goes to Kentucky. There, Vaught is driven to Lake Apopka by Nelson Fleer, a local storekeeper (who keeps using the phrase, "weird shit," for comic effect). The men don diving gear and explore the lake bottom, and discover a tunnel that leads to a series of caves. Vaught finds what first appears to be a giant paw and, upon further inspection, proves to be attached to the Gryphon, a giant monster with the body of a cougar, wings of a bat, and a tongue of snakes, created by the alien probes out of the smaller creatures. The dormant monster is awakened when Fleer clangs one of his diving tanks against a rock. The men submerge and swim for safety, and the huge monster's roar is heard behind them; when they reach the lake's surface,

all seems normal for a moment until the monster rises with a roar and takes to the air. Flying north, the monster terrorizes Clarksburg, Virginia, where it derails a train, kills people, and fires energy bolts that destroy a gasoline storage tank. Back in Massachusetts, Godzilla senses his rival's appearance and awakens, despite a constant stream of amniotic fluid being force-fed to him. The great beast destroys the hangar and walks to the shoreline, where he drops down on all fours before going into the water.

The arch-enemies are heading straight for each other and if they hold course, they're set for a showdown in New York City. As Manhattan is evacuated, Jill tries desperately to drive into the city, hoping to save Tina. When Godzilla steps on the Queens Midtown tunnel, Jill is briefly trapped under water, but she swims to safety and, just as she reaches dry land, Godzilla's foot comes down, narrowly missing her. As the battle of the monsters begins, Jill finds Tina and they try to figure out how to get off the island safely.

The Gryphon takes flight and crashes into Godzilla, knocking him back to the shore. Godzilla wraps his tail around the frame of an under-construction building, then pulls the Gryphon near and bites its leg. The Gryphon's wounds heal instantly, miraculously, and the beast then retaliates with energy bolts that knock Godzilla back into the rows of buildings. The Gryphon keeps charging, scratching Godzilla with its talons. Helicopters circle the city, while the Gryphon flies overhead, hunting Godzilla. The two beasts again slam into one another and begin to wrestle, tumbling into a skyscraper. The Gryphon double-kicks Godzilla in the belly, sending him flying into another building, which falls on both monsters. Vaught says Godzilla can't beat the Gryphon because of a restraining device implanted in the monster's neck by the military, which gives him a constant dose of the fluid and prevents him from breathing fire. Using gunship helicopters, the military diverts the Gryphon while Vaught and Fleer remove the device from Godzilla, who lays stunned next to a building. From a helicopter, then men are lowered on wires onto Godzilla, but the Gryphon blasts the chopper and the men are stranded atop the monster. As Fleer and Vaught rig explosives to destroy the restraining device, Jill and Tina stall the Gryphon briefly by crashing a gasoline tanker into the monster. The restrainer is removed from Godzilla just before the Gryphon arrives; now Godzilla fires his breath at his opponent, wounding him, and pursues the fleeing Gryphon more vigorously.

The battle royal takes place in the East River. Godzilla breathes fire across the water's surface, creating a steam cloud that blinds the Gryphon and causes it to crash into the Brooklyn Bridge and get tangled in the cables. Godzilla bites one of the Gryphon's wings off but the monster's healing properties instantly reattach the limb. Then the Gryphon climbs skyward, turns around, and power-dives. Godzilla waits for his foe, then suddenly bends forward at the last moment and the Gryphon is sliced open on Godzilla's dorsal plates. Godzilla pulls his adversary into the river, rips its head off and sets fire to the body. Godzilla, though badly wounded, roars victoriously and sets out for the sea. Jets move in to kill the wounded beast, but Jill convinces the military commander to call off the strike. She has finally forgiven the monster. From the shore, Jill, Tina, Aaron, and Fleer watch Godzilla go home.

GODZILLA GOES PARANORMAL: There were three different versions of the unmade "Godzilla vs. Gryphon" screenplay: the first draft, summarized above, was completed Nov. 11, 1993; a second draft, in which several special-effects scenes were omitted (like Godzilla's attack on the Kuril islands) and some of the drama was rewritten (for instance, Jill Llewellyn travels to the Arctic with Keith, and is there when he dies), was completed Dec. 9, 1994; and a third draft was written by British screenwriter Donald MacPherson (1998's *The Avengers*) in May 1995. MacPherson said he was instructed to "eliminate a lot of the clichéd elements," cut special-effects sequences, pad the drama with character development, and darken the dramatic tone. MacPherson's script, which was shown to several directors in Summer 1995 — and was almost filmed by David Fincher (*Alien 3, Seven*) — included the following changes:

- The story takes place in 1999, on the eve of the millennium. The dialogue was rewritten to give the film a noirish, "X-Files" feel. At one point, a date clock on the United Nations building is damaged, and the inverted numbers read "666."
- Several characters are consolidated or eliminated. Marty Kenoshita is nixed, and Junji is a 20-something Eskimo fisherman in Alaska, rather than an old Japanese man. Instead of Marty's neck, the alien parasite implants itself in Junji's eye.
- The reactor-core excavation scene is deleted. The story opens with a shot of the alien probe, far out

in space, zooming toward Earth. On the Alaskan coast, Junji and his young son, Hiro, are ice fishing. Spots of red "blood" appear everywhere on the ice, and a huge crevasse opens in the snow, flowing with red liquid.

- Godzilla is not prematurely freed from the ice; he reawakens just as the alien probe lands on Earth. The probe lands in the state of Utah, not Kentucky.
- When Godzilla breaks free from the ice cave, only glimpses of the monster are shown, rather than his entire body as in the previous version. Jill and Junji are the only survivors as the monster wipes out the Arctic outpost; the military covers up the monster's appearance, bulldozing snow over its footprints and labeling the incident an earthquake. Junji is held prisoner in a hospital ward to prevent him from telling anyone what he saw, a monster he recognized as "Gojira."
- Fleer is a white-trash recluse who says, "I hate people." His "weird shit" slogan is changed to "weird stuff."
- The nature of Aaron Vaught and Jill's relationship is changed. Vaught, a former student of Jill's dead husband, offers to help Jill find out what really happened to Keith. Vaught suspects a massive cover-up, and that the earthquake was caused by a huge dragon. He says, "It's Hangar 18 all over again," and "exactly like Roswell back in '47." In this version, the military thinks Aaron is a "crackpot" but Jill persuades the brass to bring Aaron on the Godzilla team.
- While Fleer is getting married in a Utah church, a swarm of probe-bats invades the ceremony. Fleer's wife is killed by the Gryphon, and he joins the group in hopes that Godzilla will kill the Gryphon and avenge her death.
- During the final battle, a weak and wounded Godzilla swims to Ellis Island. There, he steps on a fireworks depot, creating a barrage of colorful explosions that continue as he kills the Gryphon, rips its head off and spikes it on the Liberty torch.
- The military moves in to kill Godzilla, but Jill and the others, aboard a helicopter, intercept a missile. As the damaged helicopter falls from the air, Godzilla catches it and places the wreck on the Statue of Liberty's crown, saving the heroes.

In retrospect, Rossio and Elliott's screenplay shows how difficult it is to create a credible Godzilla scenario for modern-day Western audiences. There are many possible directions to go in, but which is most appropriate? Exploiting the "cheese factor" in a parody like the proposed *It Ate Cleveland* seems a bad idea today, in light of the box-office failure of Tim Burton's *Mars Attacks!* In the post-*Jurassic Park* world, it's clear that audiences like their dinosaurs as realistic as possible, but Godzilla has an established reputation abroad as a campy icon, so how are these conflicting notions resolved? Should the writer ignore the past and create an entirely new Godzilla, as Steve Miner and Fred Dekker tried with their *Godzilla, King of the Monsters in 3-D* a decade before? Would audiences accept a U.S.-made Godzilla movie that is thematically linked to the Japanese series? Is Godzilla the villain or the hero?

Rossio and Elliott's *Godzilla* is hardly innovative; the characters, situations, and structure are borrowed straight out of 1950s sci-fi movies, 1990s big-budget action movies and, of course, Toho's Godzilla series — it has the familiar feel of a sequel, even while starting anew. It is obvious the authors studied their subject matter, for this Godzilla behaves similarly to Toho's *Heisei* Godzilla, as a powerful force of nature that does not attack mankind but reacts when provoked and defends his turf (in this case, not Japan but all Earth) from a hostile enemy. As written, this Godzilla, like his Japanese counterpart, is neither friend nor foe but an unstoppable, fearsome creature that causes untold damage and casualties, yet one that must be respected and reckoned with if mankind is to survive.

The writers' most serious offense, and the screenplay's greatest shortcoming, is the re-scripting of Godzilla's origins; although a low-level nuclear explosion triggers the monster's premature awakening, Godzilla is not really an atomic aberration in this story. This erases Godzilla's inherent antinuclear subtext and metaphorical value, but it is probably more a reflection of the times than anything else. A blockbuster-style *Godzilla* must appeal to the broadest common denominator, not merely the conservative sensibilities of the hard-core fan, therefore the scenarists replaced the somber message of Ishiro Honda's original *Godzilla* with a standard, 1990's-style action drama with sci-fi and monster elements. A Godzilla created by an ancient, high-tech civilization (coincidentally, a theme subsequently used in 1995's *Gamera: Guardian of the Universe*) might have been hard for purists to swallow, but it has interesting possibilities. The subplot about the scientist Vaught's search for dragons in the modern world further suggests that Godzilla is a mythological creature, a symbol of the unknown, like a legendary sea serpent.

The writers devised pseudo-scientific explanations for various phenomena (i.e., Godzilla's breath is "ionized oxygen") and filled the story with fantastic flourishes. No one knows how the Gryphon would have panned out on film, but the monster, on paper at least, had the potential to be one hell of a doomsday beast, with its Gorgon tongue and the ability to instantly heal mortal wounds. And, the writers understood one of Toho's principal themes very well: Godzilla always gets his ass kicked for a while, and teeters on the brink of defeat before finally summoning his inner strength, rising from the mat and beating the crap out of his foe. The final monster-vs.-monster battle is complicated by Godzilla's Achilles Heel, his susceptibility to the red-black amniotic fluid that acts like "Godzilla Kryptonite," rendering the great monster powerless. It's not just New York City, but the entire Earth that hangs in the balance when the two monsters meet.

The human drama is less imaginative, with stock characters like the goofy pseudo-scientist, the teenage rebel and the stiff military men. The most interesting character is Jill, who, as the writers admit, is a carbon copy of Ripley in *Aliens*. Rather than having the entire military operation focused on killing Godzilla, and one scientist trying futilely to save the monster, a more interesting conflict is established between Jill, determined to avenge her husband's death, and Vaught, who wants to capture Godzilla and figure out what it is. Through their efforts to stop Godzilla, and then to aid the monster in his battle with the enemy, the characters' relationship evolves from hostility to respect and friendship.

Of all the American *Godzilla* scripts written to date — including that which was eventually filmed — this story was the most faithful to the original character and the tone of Toho's classic Godzilla films, particularly the "giant-monsters-meet-space-aliens" films of the 1960s like *Monster Zero* and *Destroy All Monsters*. By attempting to transform Godzilla from an all-powerful villain into an Earth-defending hero within the span of one film (something that took Toho's Godzilla more than a decade), Terry Rossio and Ted Elliott probably tried to do too much. Another flaw is that Godzilla shares considerable screen time with the Gryphon, and isn't always the star of the show. Inevitably, the writers' over-zealousness likely contributed to a skyrocketing budget and the imminent derailment of Jan DeBont's tenure as director of *Godzilla*.

According to Rossio and Elliott, TriStar Pictures studio officials estimated that it would cost about $180 million to shoot the *Godzilla* script as written.

More than 500 computer-generated effects shots were planned; by comparison, James Cameron's *True Lies* (1993) had only about 150 such shots, the most ever until then. One of DeBont's first tasks was to develop a second draft with fewer effects.

The first choice for a special-effects house was Industrial Light and Magic, makers of the computer-animated dinosaurs of *Jurassic Park*. But ILM reportedly turned down the job because officials there felt the amount of computer effects required to make an all-digital *Godzilla*, plus computer-generated explosions, fire and water effects, and the Gryphon's morphing transformation, was just too much for one company to handle. In October 1994, it was announced that the effects would be done by Digital Domain, the super-special effects house founded a year earlier by director James Cameron, creature creator Stan Winston, and IBM. Stan Winston Studio in Van Nuys, California, was contracted to design the new Godzilla and Gryphon, and to create life-like robotic versions of both monsters as it had done with the *Jurassic Park* dinosaurs. The projected effects budget for *Godzilla* was reportedly $38 million to $50 million, and the cost of the entire film was pegged between $100 million and $120 million, making it one of the most expensive films to date. This was before *Waterworld* broke records with a $200 million budget; it was also just about the time TriStar's first crack at making *Godzilla* fell apart.

In Fall 1994, DeBont sent crews to a town on the Oregon coast to construct the set of a Japanese fishing village. He planned to shoot Godzilla's attack on the Kuril Islands; Godzilla and storm effects would be added to the exterior footage later using computers. It was a test of sorts. This early shoot, well before the start of principal photography (a cast hadn't even been selected yet) would help eliminate bugs in special effects technology. It also was to be used in a teaser trailer shown in theaters across the country in the summer or fall of 1995. If all went well, DeBont would begin shooting in March 1995, and the picture would hit theaters in summer 1996.

The Oregon sets were built, but no footage was shot.

Interview

NEW WAVE GODZILLA

Screenwriters Terry Rossio and Ted Elliott

Terry Rossio and Ted Elliott were 33 and 32, respectively, when they wrote *Godzilla*. They met in high school and became screenwriting partners after college, working odd jobs to pay the bills and writing four or five nights a week. Their first big break was *Little Monsters*, which was made by Hollywood Pictures, a division of Disney, in 1989; more recently, they wrote *The Mask of Zorro* and *Small Soldiers* (both 1998).

Although the duo studied Toho's Godzilla epics for reference, they opted to create a new storyline rather than follow the Japanese continuity. When this interview was conducted, in summer 1994, the writers were excited about the future as *Godzilla* was slated to begin shooting within months. Unfortunately for them, their script would be completely abandoned before the cameras began rolling (however, they did receive story credit in Roland Emmerich's film because of several minor similarities to their version).

How did you approach writing the Godzilla script?

ELLIOTT: I had been fortunate enough to see a non-reconstructed print of the original *Godzilla*, without Raymond Burr, and that's really a good movie. I think that's one of the best of those '50s atomic monster movies. It's as good as *Them!* or any of those. But when you see some of those sequels — what's the one where Godzilla and Angilas are actually talking to each other? It does get a little bizarre. And the little smoke-ring-blowing baby Godzilla, let's face it: some of that stuff, it was a little wimpy.

So we thought, what can you do with Godzilla? There's been a lot of stuff done in comics where they're kind of reconstructing the super heroes to some extent, just cleaning up some of the continuity . . . There's a comic book writer named Alan Moore who basically restructured Swamp Thing,

did a great job. The original Swamp Thing is a great character, and Moore just kicked it up to another level as far as I'm concerned. And our idea was to do basically the Alan Moore version of Godzilla. That doesn't mean Godzilla becomes some sort of tortured character, it's to embrace the really wonderful stuff about Godzilla.

There are many choices to make, and one of the choices that we made was not to do another step in the long line of Godzilla, which was an option, to have an awareness of everything that's come before and play off of it. But our choice, and the studio was happy with this, was to say: This is the first Godzilla movie. It's more of a remake of Godzilla than a sequel.

What, in your opinion, is the meaning of Godzilla?

ELLIOTT: I have a friend who is a big Godzilla fan. He really likes Godzilla, he knows all the other monsters in the series, all that stuff. And he made the observation that became for me, the key to what the story should be. What he said was, Godzilla's really not a good guy. He is incredibly territorial, he just doesn't like other monsters. And since most of the time those other monsters threaten humanity, Godzilla seems to be the defender of the Earth. But no, in fact, he's just pissing in his own territory, getting rid of anybody who interferes. And that, to me, meant you could actually present Godzilla on the side of the angels but he could still be a monster.

ROSSIO: The other thing I felt was that you would not be happy going to a Godzilla film if you weren't scared by Godzilla. There's no getting around the fact that if Godzilla's in a fight, people are probably going to root for Godzilla, but we felt it was really important that you be scared, that he be intimidating, that he be this force of nature.

ELLIOTT: Basically our approach was, let's do a

Roland Emmerich
COPYRIGHT 20TH CENTURY-FOX

Moby Dick story, where this scientist's husband is killed by Godzilla in his first appearance, and now this person wants to hunt Godzilla down and kill it. And by the time we finished the movie, a couple of months after we finished writing it, it occurred to us that it was a very similar story to *Aliens*, in which Ridley is obsessed — she is Ahab. And so I always wondered if Cameron started with an Ahab story, the same as we did. So it's a story about obsession and redemption, and inappropriate grief response.

But a lot of what we wanted to do was give Godzilla to Godzilla fans. And kind of what the movie does is, in one movie it does what about the first three Toho films did — taking him from being this horrendous threat to being defender of the Earth.

Did the agreements between Toho and TriStar restrict how you could write the script?

ROSSIO: Well, for instance, we originally wanted to have Godzilla fight King Ghidorah.

ELLIOTT: But it turned out that our contract specifically stated that we could use any monsters from the Godzilla family of monsters, with the exception of Rodan, Mothra, or King Ghidorah. I'm sure Toho believes they can license those individually, so they didn't include them in the Godzilla license, so we were left coming up with our own guy. We'll see how he works. I think thematically he actually works a little bit better than Ghidorah would have.

What were some of the other tenets of the Toho–TriStar arrangement?

ROSSIO: One of the directives that we were given by Toho, one of the 10 Commandments, was that

Godzilla's origins must be the result of a catastrophic nuclear accident. Now, having said that, it doesn't mean that we followed that precisely. That was something that we had to deal with.

ELLIOTT: As for Godzilla's appearance: he must have three rows of dorsal fins, a long tail. And they're very specific about the number of fingers, although I'm not sure why. Also, they said you must not make light of Godzilla.

There is an anti-nuclear theme, but I think it's on a larger scale. It's more encompassing, it's more about nature, and the nature of life and death. I know that sounds incredibly pretentious.

ROSSIO: Thematically, what we're doing is, Godzilla could be a metaphor for death. Death is something you can't stop. It's destructive, it's powerful.

Will your Godzilla display any anthropomorphic characteristics?

ROSSIO: I think it would be a mistake to get totally away from some humanistic things. As an example, if a submarine happened to shoot something at him, and he got hit from behind and he turned around, that's right on the edge, giving a look like he's pissed. But I think it would be a mistake to completely humanize him. He doesn't dance a jig or anything, but on the other hand he's not completely without character.

ELLIOTT: Again, we've been pushing that he is a reptilian dragon. One of the things that we've suggested is that he actually have a secondary eyelid for when he's underwater, like a crocodile does. Just little things like that can make him seem more realistic. That's such a weird word to use with Godzilla, but that's the intent.

Are you concerned that fans will reject your version of Godzilla?

ROSSIO: That's always something that we as writers are more concerned about than the studio. I think it's a fascinating question, and I think it should come up, about how a U.S. company treats this franchise versus how it was originally treated. In terms of people rejecting it, there will always be the true fan who will be upset at something that isn't the way it could have been, or maybe even should have been. But in terms of being disrespectful to the creature, I don't think we have been and I don't think we could have been, based on the restrictions Toho had put in place, and so far they've been approving of everything. Anytime you mess with a character you're on potentially shaky ground. You can only hope that what you've done is respectful, and is at least as legitimate as what was done before.

SAYONARA, DeBONT: With more than $2 billion in losses in fiscal 1994, Sony Corp. was looking for ways to trim costs across the board. So, when executives with TriStar Pictures' parent company learned that *Godzilla*'s budget was reaching historical proportions, they panicked. From October to December, 1994, a series of meetings was held between DeBont and TriStar production executives. At first, the question was how to lower the budget; then it became how to cut effects costs by replacing CGI with other, less expensive methods. Finally, it became whether or not DeBont would make the film at all. "Sources said (DeBont) was waylaid by a studio that had promised absolute freedom," reported *Variety*. According to various sources, DeBont required at least $120 million to shoot the film his way, but the studio wanted to retool the project to keep it under $100 million. In the final week of 1994, DeBont and TriStar announced that the director had jumped from the *Godzilla* ship and would be replaced.

"They were talking about five times as many digital effects shots as had been done previously, and that was crazy," said a Digital Domain effects man who worked on the aborted project. "DeBont didn't understand what was involved in all of that. He wanted a completely computer-generated Godzilla, which is certainly possible, it's just expensive, so that what was where negotiations broke down."

In press interviews, DeBont defended his big-budget approach. "It was unfortunately a little too expensive," he told *Cinefantastique*. "Though I hope they're still going to make the movie because I really think it's a great script, and it will be a great movie ultimately, as long as they do not cut out Godzilla! That's what I'm always afraid of at studios: 'It's too expensive — let's cut out more of Godzilla, let's cut out more effects shots!' And I say, 'Well, that's the leading star of the movie, and you're going to cut him out? . . . You either make it in a totally new way, where you absolutely believe this monster exists, or you make him like the Japanese do it, with a man in a costume, and then you can make it for $10 million or less. But somewhere in between would be a big, giant mistake, and that is what I hope they're not going to do. I hope they're not just going to use all miniatures, because then let's just look at the Japanese movies again. That's what they've been doing for 30 years or more, and they're fun. Listen, I have every single Godzilla movie on tape. I know my monster! I was

in Tokyo [in 1995] and I just missed the new one (*Godzilla vs. Space Godzilla*). They showed me the trailer, and I had seen the sets just before that, and they looked pretty cool. If you do it half right, that would be a mistake, in my opinion."

DeBont immediately began work on Universal Pictures' *Twister*, which starred Helen Hunt and Bill Paxton, who were reportedly DeBont's choices to play Jill Lewellyn and Nelson Fleer, *Godzilla*'s principal characters.

LOST LIZARD: One of the biggest casualties of Jan DeBont's debacle was the new Godzilla design, which was top-secret during the production and was never publicly displayed. DeBont and his production designer, Joseph C. Nemec III (*Terminator 2: Judgement Day, The Shadow, Twister, Speed 2*) hired Dark Horse Comics artist Ricardo Delgado ("Age of Reptiles") to re-design the creature. Delgado envisioned a sleeker, more agile version of the Japanese giant, incorporating elements of the *Jurassic Park* velociraptors but still strongly resembling Toho's original design, thanks to its dorsal fins and facial features. Delgado said, "I wanted to create something that was immediately recognizable as Godzilla, but that was more realistic and life-like than what had been done before. I was a huge Godzilla fan when I was young, and later on I had been able to see the original *Godzilla*, the version without Raymond Burr, and that's a very meaningful film. I based my design on the original Godzilla, but added more musculature to the lower body, with 'chicken' dinosaur legs and feet. The head, the face, the upper body, and the tail were very much like the original Godzilla.

"It was a dream come true for me to work on this film. I gave my paintings to Jan DeBont, and I also made a model. But they decided to go in a different direction, and all my design work was handed over to Stan Winston Studio, and they ended up changing the design somewhat, although it was still based on what I had done."

At Stan Winston Studio, artist Mark "Crash" McCreery, famous for his *Jurassic Park* dino designs, refined Delgado's Godzilla into a final version of the monster that was to appear in the film. Reportedly, Toho pressured DeBont to make his monster more closely resemble its Japanese progenitor. Insiders who have seen maquettes and drawings of the Stan Winston Godzilla describe it as "homogenized"

Godzilla incorporating features from the best Japanese designs with more life-like dinosaur traits. The monster was very dark brownish-gray in color, with spots and highlights all over its body and a patch of green skin on the belly. Its skin was scaly, but smoother and more dinosaur-like than the Toho versions, and its legs and feet were slender and supported the more crouched posture of a dinosaur. "It was similar to the Japanese Godzilla," said a special-effects man who worked on the aborted project. "It was still vaguely humanoid, but it was obvious it couldn't be a man in a suit because the proportions were different." Stan Winston Studio also designed the Gryphon, but this monster was not publicly revealed either.

WUNDERKINDS

By late 1995, TriStar's *Godzilla* seemed long forgotten. But a new, big-budget special-effects film was creating a huge buzz. The anticipation surrounding *Independence Day* was so great that, months before its release, TriStar Pictures began courting Emmerich and Devlin for *Godzilla*. On November 9, 1995, a source inside the studio said that studio heads had met with Emmerich, but were hesitant to make him an offer. "The Emmerich approach would be to use models, with very limited CGI effects. And the budget would be quite low, compared to where they were at last year, $65 million," the source said at that time.

On May 2, 1996, more than six months later, TriStar announced that Emmerich and Devlin would make a new version of *Godzilla*, departing entirely from the Rossio-Elliott screenplay. The deal still hinged upon Toho's approval of Emmerich's new Godzilla design (which Tatopoulos had not yet developed at that point) and storyline, which would come later at the aforementioned Tokyo meeting. At this early stage, all Emmerich knew was he wanted to do something very different than the old Zilla. "I didn't want to make the original *Godzilla*, I wanted nothing to do with it, I wanted to make my own," he later recalled in an interview with CNN. In an interview with the *TNT Rough Cut* website in 1998, he said he also knew he didn't want to do the Rossio-Elliott screenplay. "It was a very well-written script. It had some really cool things in it, but it was something I never would have done, which is starting off where . . . the sequels to *Godzilla* left off," he said. "The human involvement was kind of limited . . . the last half

[was] like watching two creatures go at it . . . I simply don't like that." He said he and Devlin agreed to take on Godzilla only after TriStar was willing to chuck the old script. "All of a sudden it was like something we originated, and we had fun doing it," he said.

Over time, Emmerich and Devlin's reasons for demanding creative freedom became clear. They never professed to being huge fans of Toho's Godzilla series; in fact, they showed a certain disdain for it, as evidenced by comments that they, and members of their crew, made to the press. Some examples:

- "We wanted to . . . reinvent it, so that when you think of Godzilla, this is the Godzilla you'll think of for the next generation." (Devlin, in an interview posted on the Sony Pictures Entertainment Web site in 1997)

- "Godzilla has always been this slow-motion man in a suit, and always standing around, looking around, smashing through buildings, looking kind of stupid. This one is an animal, a lizard, it behaves like an animal and its movements are more in the *Jurassic Park* range." (SFX supervisor Volker Engel, in an interview posted on the Sony Pictures Entertainment Web site)

- "It'll look like Godzilla but be more realistic, more to the lizard genesis than just a big fat guy in a rubber suit." (Dean Devlin, in the Honolulu *Star-Ledger* newspaper)

- "To fully background himself in the character, [Emmerich] watched 14 or 15 of the Toho Godzilla movies on laser disc. 'Then I gave up. It's just the same movie over and over again. They always had another monster in it, and I never get anything out of two monsters fighting . . . For reasons I can't explain myself, kids all over the world kept watching these movies . . .'" (*Los Angeles Times*, January 18, 1998)

As they had done with Twentieth Century Fox on *Independence Day*, Emmerich and Devlin negotiated a deal wherein their company, Centropolis Entertainment, took over virtually all aspects of film production, while the studio financed the movie and handled the merchandising, distribution, and video release. And, after *Independence Day* made them major big-budget players, there was no talk of limiting the picture to $65 million and using model effects. "It was a very, very expensive move," Devlin told the *TNT Rough Cut* Web site shortly after the picture's release. "I'm not allowed to give you the exact (budget), but I'll tell you this, quite honestly it's much more expensive than *Independence*

Day, and much less expensive than *Titanic*." Most press reports pegged *Godzilla*'s budget at $120 million, while rumors from internal sources said it was closer to $150 million.

In the era of *Waterworld*, *Batman And Robin*, *Titanic*, and other pictures costing $200 million and more, Roland Emmerich and Dean Devlin became heroes to the Hollywood industry crowd by delivering big-budget "event movies" at a discounted price. Their early films typically cost less than other summer blockbusters, and they made lots of money despite being almost unanimously panned for their brain-dead appeal. *Universal Soldier*, Emmerich's first movie, cost about $30 million and grossed $100 million; *Stargate* cost $70 million and made $200 million; and *Independence Day* cost about $90 million and reaped $800 million worldwide. Key to *Independence Day*'s success was the duo's marketing savvy, generating tremendous hype before the picture's release — much of it stemming from a pre-release trailer showing aliens blowing up the White House. With *Godzilla*, Emmerich and Devlin entered the arena of $100-million budgets and orchestrated an epic-scale marketing campaign, the centerpiece of which was the concealment of the new Godzilla's image until opening day.

Emmerich, born in 1955 in Stuttgart, Germany, is a huge fan of American movies, particularly 1970s-style American disaster movies, "Because they're unpredictable, you never know who's going to die." His idol is Irwin Allen, and his favorite films are Allen's *Towering Inferno* and *Poseidon Adventure*. He says *Independence Day* was his and Devlin's attempt to fuse the disaster-movie with the classic 1950s sci-fi genre, although he admits that he was much more influenced by *Star Wars* than *War Of The Worlds*. "To tell you the truth, I'm not a big fan of old movies, I only take an interest in them for their historical importance," he told *Tabu* on-line magazine in 1996. Emmerich is known in his native country as "Das Spielbergle" ("The Spielbergy,") or the "Swabian Spielberg" (Swabia is the region where Stuttgart is located).

Devlin (b. 1962 in Los Angeles), unlike the German director, had a Hollywood upbringing. The son of film producer Don Devlin (*The Witches Of Eastwick*, *My Bodyguard*) and Filipino-American television actress Pilar Devlin, he had boyhood aspirations of becoming a filmmaker but was unable to attend film school because of poor grades. Instead, he moved to New York and became a chauffeur for Al Pacino, who encouraged him to act, and in 1987 he landed a role on the TV drama "Hard Copy"

(not related to the news tabloid show). He gave up acting in 1992 and co-wrote the screenplay for *Universal Soldier*. After that, Devlin became a partner in Emmerich's company, Centropolis Entertainment, and the two men merged their talents.

FRAIDY LIZARD

"We were creating an animal. We weren't creating a monster."
— *Patrick Tatopoulos, in* Time *magazine, May 25, 1998*

Centropolis and Sony's principal marketing strategy for *Godzilla* was to keep the creature's new, revamped design utterly secret, while coyly piquing the public's curiosity by revealing a foot here, an eye there. The "hide-the-monster" campaign was kicked off with a short "teaser" shown in theaters with Columbia's *Men In Black*, released July 2, 1997. Filmed strictly as an advance trailer (it did not include any actual footage from the movie), the segment poked fun at the *Jurassic Park* films by showing Godzilla's foot stepping on a Tyranno-saurus Rex skeleton. As a group of school children is touring the dinosaur section of the American Museum of Natural History, the building fixtures start to shake and a big, repeating THUD! grows louder. Suddenly, the skylight above the T-Rex shatters and Godzilla's foot (created with all-CGI effects) smashes the dinosaur bones to bits, then Godzilla's tail whips past the opening in the ceiling. The trailer introduced TriStar's new *Godzilla* logo, which forms from a ball of green light (and which, despite appearing on all promotional materials, was not used in the film itself), and the monster's new roar, a digitally modified version of the classic Godzilla roar. It featured the tag line, "Guess Who's Coming To Town." A second, less amusing (and slightly longer) trailer was released in conjunction with *Starship Troopers* in November 1997, and featured a scene that appeared in the finished movie in which a wino goes fishing on the East River and hooks Godzilla on his line; this trailer introduced the slogan that would soon become synonymous with the film: SIZE DOES MATTER, an old dirty joke that Sony's marketing gurus hoped would tell audiences that: a) this is *Jurassic Park* on a bigger scale, and b) this film is tongue-in-cheek. The trailers didn't show much of Godzilla, just enough to hint that the monster was undergoing drastic changes.

Patrick Tatopoulos's prior credits as a creature designer, make-up artist, conceptual illustrator, and designer included *Independence Day* and *Stargate*, plus *The Phantom*, *Wolf*, *Demolition Man*, *Last Action Hero*, *Bram Stoker's Dracula*, *The Addams Family*, *The Doors*, *Star Trek V*, *Gremlins 2*, and other films. In his book *The Art of Godzilla* (published in Japan in 1998), Tatopoulos said, "the original *Godzilla* was one of the first movies I ever saw as a kid. It may well be the reason I got into this business. Godzilla is the monster all creature effects designers dream of designing."

As in the pre-release trailers, Tatopoulos's monster remains half-hidden throughout the first third of *Godzilla*, and is not fully revealed until it is baited into the middle of Flatiron Square with a huge pile of fish. Although it adheres to Toho's basic design criteria (an upright-walking reptile with three rows of dorsal fins) the creature is so strikingly different from anything called "Godzilla" before that comparisons are almost moot. The film's opening frames show iguanas sunning in French Polynesia before being bathed in the radiation of a nuclear test, therefore Godzilla somewhat resembles a gigantic iguana-cum-alligator. Eschewing the upright attack-stance, maple-leaf back fins and familiar face of the original, Tatopoulos-Zilla hunches low to the ground, and has jagged dorsal spikes (with two prominent growths sticking out of its shoulders), a long snout, pronounced chin (inspired by the tiger Sher Khan from Disney's *The Jungle Book*), a lizard-like sac of fleshy skin at its throat, a dog-like nose, small and expressionless yellow-brown eyes, and jagged, in-grown teeth that jut irregularly out of the lips. The creature has athletic, muscular arms, legs and chest, its fingers are long and thin with razor-sharp talons, and its feet resemble those of a bird. Its skin is alternately covered with bumps, like an alligator's, and leathery lines and creases, like a desert lizard's, and vaguely resembles the ribbed exoskeletons of H.R. Giger's aliens. Depending on the lighting, the creature changes color from scene to scene; in daylight it is a shiny black-gray; at other times its skin reveals highlights of brown, blue, and green (in the first draft of Devlin and Emmerich's screenplay, Godzilla had chameleon-like powers, reminiscent of *Predator*, that enabled him to blend into the skyscrapers and elude helicopters, but this idea was dropped). The man-sized Baby Godzillas look more or less the same as the parent creature, but with less developed musculature, thinner limbs, and stubby dorsal spikes barely sprouting from their spines.

BAD BREATH: Tatopoulos's *The Art of Godzilla* book includes some of the artist's early sketches, showing how his monster took shape and evolved into the final design. Tatopoulos started with a "lizardized" rendition of Toho's Godzilla that, from the start, showed several traits that were retained throughout his design process — the long snout, the jagged teeth, the pronounced jawline, the throat sac. His earliest sketches were somewhat Toho-like, although the monster was always lean and muscular, with long arms; one early design, which Tatopoulos never showed to Emmerich "for clearly good reason," looked somewhat like a cross between a velociraptor and a kangaroo. The book also shows the "runner-up" design that Emmerich passed over, a Tyrannosaur-esque creature with long, spindly arms and claws, tall spikes vaguely representing the Toho Godzilla's dorsal fins, and leathery skin.

The book's biggest revelation, however, is that Emmerich considered, at least briefly, giving Godzilla his classic atomic breath. Several illustrations (apparently done in mid-1996, months before the *Godzilla* script was written) show Godzilla emitting what Tatopoulos calls "the atomic beam," a concentrated stream of energy flowing alternately from his nostrils and a tongue-like membrane in his mouth; one of the sketches that was presented to Toho officials when Emmerich asked for their blessing depicted Godzilla blasting a helicopter out of the sky. Neither Emmerich nor Devlin has ever explained exactly why they decided to nix Godzilla's atomic breath, although it has been rumored that the filmmakers simply felt it was too unrealistic. In the first draft of Emmerich and Devlin's screenplay, Godzilla exhaled something called Power Breath, a gale-force wind that blew away everything that wasn't nailed down. In the script, Godzilla first used this power after being lured to the surface by the military at Flatiron Square; as the monster is chomping down the huge pile of fish, the military lobs tear-gas canisters to subdue him, but Godzilla uses his Power Breath to clear the fumes (and cars, and trucks, and people) from the air. Nick (Matthew Broderick) is swept high into the air by Godzilla's gust, but lands safely on a banner hanging from a building; meanwhile cars and trucks are blown everywhere, slamming into the military vehicles and disabling the attack forces.

When rumors circulated in 1997 that Godzilla would have Power Breath rather than his customary radioactive halitosis, many fans became irate and besieged Centropolis with phone calls, letters, and emails. It is probably no coincidence, then, that in the finished film, the aforementioned scene plays out much differently. The trigger-happy Major Hicks simply orders his troops to fire at Godzilla without provocation, the monster ducks out of the missiles' way and then flees north on Broadway; when rocket-launchers pursue Godzilla, he turns around and breathes a wall of fire (resembling a natural gas explosion) that incinerates the vehicles. This revision, replacing the Power Breath with something the producers called "incendiary breath," was obviously made after all the movie's dramatic scenes were shot, for no one mentions Godzilla's breath-weapon in the movie — not even once! — supporting the impression that the change was a capitulation to the fan community. But the effect is still unsatisfying to the Godzilla purist. Not only does Godzilla only use this ability twice in the film, he crouches low to the ground and opens his trap like a giant flame-thrower rather than rearing back and spewing forth, like a mighty dragon. Not only that, but the dreaded Power Breath *does* appear in the film — during the first face-to-face meeting between Nick and Godzilla, Godzilla yawns a mini-roar, blowing his stinky wind in the scientist's face; later, as Godzilla chases the heroes through the streets during the finale, the monster unleashes a full-power blast of his wind, sending cars and garbage cans flying.

In his interview with the *TNT Rough Cut* website, Emmerich said the incendiary breath was "a little bit of an homage" to Godzilla's traditional breath-beam. "We kind of thought of it like gas, all fishy, swallowed then thrown up again," he said. "It kind of like creates a gas and glows with an incredible force . . . The original one is more this ray than fire breath. It's a green ray coming out of the mouth. It's almost an undefined color, and all kinds of other wonderful colors later turned up in later films." SFX supervisor Volker Engel, in an article published in *Cinefex* #74, elaborated further. "Dean and Roland wanted this monster to retain a certain menace and credibility," Engel said. "But Godzilla's breath is something everyone expects to see at some point. So they came up with instances in which you would see something like the old breath, but with a kind of logic applied to it. We make the assumption that something in his breath, when it comes in contact with flame, causes combustive ignition. So you get this flame-thrower effect, which causes everything to ignite."

However, the biggest difference between Emmerich and Devlin's Godzilla and its Japanese progenitor is not the creature's look or its breath. It is not the fact that the creature moves quickly and gracefully, and *runs* at more than 200 mph. It is not the fact that Godzilla snaps tanker trucks and helicopters in its jaws (admittedly, this isn't unheard of, as Godzilla chomped a train in his 1954 debut). It isn't that the new Godzilla, at about 200 feet tall, is shorter than the 1990s Toho version (about 330 feet). And it isn't that Newzilla is not totally impervious to standard military hardware, while the Japanese monster is basically indestructible. It is Godzilla's *raison d'être,* his reason to be.

Like the original, the TriStar Godzilla is an aberration of Nature spawned by a nuclear blast, but the similarities end there. Emmerich and Devlin, in their quest to reshape the creature to something more logical and, therefore, believable and credible, reduce Godzilla to an animal merely trying to survive in a hostile world, an atomic freak of evolution that wants only to propagate its own mutated species. Although it is a huge deviation from Godzilla lore, the idea that a race of rapidly multiplying reptiles could quickly supplant man as the planet's ruling creature — presumably, feasting on human beings as their oceanic food supply runs out — is the only intelligent idea the film has to offer, raising philosophical questions about the Bomb and all the other ways man quickens the onset of his own extinction. The idea is underdeveloped, however; the military men seem not to care about Godzilla's implications, they simply attack him because, well, this is a monster movie, and that's what you're supposed to do. Only the scientist Nick seems to sense the gravity of Godzilla's appearance, and presumably he is torn between his own survival instinct (which leads him to exterminate Godzilla's eggs) and his scientific calling (to preserve the creature for study), however Nick never outwardly expresses any reservations or moral conflicts, he simply thrusts forward with the nest-busting mission because he's the hero. In any case, Godzilla only wants a safe place to lay his/her eggs; its purpose is not to deliberately destroy or kill anything, therefore the creature really isn't scary. *Au contraire*, the monster is pitiable as it shrieks in pain when struck by military weapons, gallops out of harm's way, and is finally struck down by submarine torpedoes. Godzilla only becomes angry after its young are murdered in the Madison Square Garden bombing; the monster surveys the decimated nest, sees four human beings nearby and immediately holds them responsible, and chases them across Manhattan seeking revenge. This is the movie's stupidest, most un-Godzilla-like mistake. If this were really Godzilla, he would respond by laying waste to Manhattan and taking on the military in a fierce battle. Fred Dekker, who authored the aborted *Godzilla: King of the Monsters in 3-D* more than a decade earlier, understood this aspect of the creature well; in Dekker's screenplay, Godzilla discovers its young's carcass and, furious and grieving, goes berserk in San Francisco.

DIGITIZING
GODZILLA

Independence Day contained more than 500 effects shots, combining computer-generated imaging, digital compositing, digital matte paintings, and traditional miniature model effects, among other techniques. It was one of the biggest effects films to date, and *Godzilla* was even bigger. As they had done in the past, Emmerich and his producers assembled their own model photography and CGI units to tackle the ambitious workload, rather than rely on a single effects company like ILM or Digital Domain.

As in all other aspects of Emmerich's films, there was a lot of German input into *Godzilla*'s special effects, most notably that of visual effects supervisor Volker Engel, who also worked under Emmerich on his early film *Moon 44*, plus *Stargate* and *Independence Day*. The interaction between the special effects and principal photography teams was much greater than that at Toho; in addition to the effects (involving model and CGI versions of Godzilla, miniatures, water tank effects, and large sets) that were filmed at and around the Sony/Columbia-TriStar studios in Culver City, Engel participated in nearly all the location shooting in New York, downtown Los Angeles (subbing for NYC), and Hawaii (subbing for Panama and Jamaica), helping to coordinate the background plates into which Godzilla would later be digitally composited.

At first, Emmerich did not want an all-computer-generated Godzilla, and planned to use different effects based on the type of shot involved. "Originally, there were three techniques we were going to use to create the creature," Dean Devlin told the TNT *Rough Cut* Web site. "Animatronics, digital animation and motion capture [a process whereby an actor wearing an electrode-covered suit "steers" the actions of a digitally-animated character] . . . Partially this was the decision because usually CG

doesn't hold up good when you get close to it; there's a lot of stuff you can't do with CG. So we were hoping the animatronics would do that, and when that wouldn't work, the motion capture worked . . . But something happened along the way where our CG improved to a level way beyond anything that we thought was possible . . . So very late in the process, we dumped the other two techniques. I think there's only four or five animatronic shots left in the movie, and there's only two motion capture shots. So all the rest is CG . . ."

The following is a rundown of the major special-effects techniques utilized in *Godzilla* (details gleaned from interviews with Volker Engel and SFX set designer Gary Krakoff, posted on the Sony Pictures Entertainment Web site in 1997, a behind-the-scenes on-line production report written by Will Plyler and published by godzilla.com in 1997–98, The Art of Godzilla by Patrick Tatopoulos, and other sources):

CREATURE EFFECTS: Patrick Tatopoulos Designs Inc. hired more than 170 of Hollywood's freelance SFX craftsmen — sculptors, mold makers, foam and electrical technicians, mechanical designers, and suit makers — to build several different mechanical versions of Godzilla. With so much emphasis on CGI technology, it is interesting that a more high-tech version of the so-called "suitmation" technique utilized by Toho was employed for some scenes. Tatopoulos' crew built four Godzilla suits, all in 1/24 scale and standing about seven feet tall. Two highly detailed "hero suits" were used in the scene when Godzilla first climbs out of the subway system near Flatiron Square, and again when Godzilla bursts out of Madison Square Garden, photographed at high speed à la Toho to create an illusion of size and bulk; two less-detailed "stunt suits" were used for glimpses of the monster crashing through buildings, such as the vague view of Godzilla's dorsal spikes as he tears through a skyscraper during his initial New York rampage. The suits were worn by two stunt actors who trained for three months to perfect Godzilla's movement. Like Toho's Godzilla suits, the stuntman's head was located inside Godzilla's neck, and there were only small holes through which the monster-actor could see; the suit's head was equipped with electronics that moved the eyes, mouth and nostrils by remote-control. To facilitate Godzilla's hunched-forward posture and elevated arch, the suits were fitted

A view of the Brooklyn Bridge set contructed on vacant land near the
Torrance Airport in Torrance, California, just south of Los Angeles.
PHOTO BY RICK MCCARTHY

with heavy-duty metal leg extenders enabling the actor to stand about six inches above the ground, his feet bent forward. In addition, seven Baby Godzilla costumes were built, each standing about seven feet tall and weighing about 100 pounds, and CGI was used to "multiply" these into hundreds of little Godzillas on the loose.

Tatopoulos and his crew also built a 1/6-scale animatronic Godzilla that was sculpted from foam and stood about 30 feet high, larger than the animatronic T-Rex built by Stan Winston Studio for *Jurassic Park*. Because of its unwieldy size, the robot was built from the torso up, and except for servo-controlled eyes, eyelids and nostrils, its movements were operated by pre-programmed, computer-controlled hydraulic motors. The initial plans called for the big robot Godzilla to be used in several different scenes but, in the end, it was only used when Godzilla grabs a tractor-trailer truck in his jaws, for Godzilla's face-to-face meeting with Matthew Broderick (the only time that the monster's

facial features and skin texture are truly shown up-close) and again briefly when Godzilla takes the taxicab into his mouth. Among the other props built by Tatopoulos' shop were a 30-foot section of Godzilla's tail, which is seen striking the Japanese fishing ship; a 1/1 scale set of three talons, seen tearing through the hull of the Japanese ship; a full-size set of Godzilla toes, with an 11-foot spread in between them, briefly used in when the cameraman "Animal" narrowly missed getting squished; and a 1/1 scale set of Godzilla jaws, used to illustrate the point-of-view of the people trapped in the taxicab inside his mouth.

COMPUTER ANIMATION: In contrast to the few appearances that Tatopoulos's Godzilla suits and robot made in the film, there were 185 shots of Godzilla rendered via CGI. Not only that, but various other elements of the film were also created with computers — the wrecked cargo ship that washes ashore in Jamaica was a digital rendering, as was part of the Brooklyn Bridge during Godzilla's death scene, plus several of Godzilla's footprints on the roadside, various helicopters, submarines, and other images. Even many of the buildings seen in the choppers-vs.-Godzilla chase through the New York steel canyons were constructed with CGI.

Emmerich's CGI team, called Centropolis Effects, operated as the main digital effects house, employing more than 60 animators on the film, and coordinated with several outside animation companies to get the work done. The animators began by scanning a small Godzilla maquette sculpted by Tatopoulos into the computer and constructing a wire-frame digital 3-D model of the monster, then scanning one of Tatopoulos's 1/24-scale Godzilla suits for added skin details and colors. The digital Godzilla model, called "Fred" by the technicians, was said to be capable of about 500 different expressions. The animation team boasted that the digital compositing of the live-action and CGI elements in *Godzilla* was the most complicated work of its type ever attempted, since most of the Godzilla scenes involve rain, smoke and debris, which require detailed attention to ensure that the creature becomes part of the three-dimensional action, rather than sit "on top" of it; however, these weather elements undoubtedly aided the animators in their efforts, since the creature is often obscured, making finely detailed animation less necessary.

MINIATURES, MODELS, SETS etc.: Roland Emmerich is no stranger to miniatures and the pyrotechnics involved in on-camera destruction. *Independence Day* was full of gloriously exploding models of the Empire State Building, the White House and the Citicorp Building in Los Angeles — a fact that should have bode well for Godzilla. Unfortunately, while there are lots of miniatures in this film, Godzilla really doesn't trash any of them. "I did my last movie, it was mainly like the kind of movie which blew up buildings, so I didn't want to make much destruction anymore. You don't want to repeat yourself," Emmerich told the *TNT Rough Cut* website.

Nevertheless, there are many miniatures in the film, even if Godzilla doesn't get to whack them. The most impressive destruction befalls the Flatiron Building, a triangle-shaped architectural landmark located at Fifth Avenue and Broadway, which is hit with bombs intended for Godzilla. The Flatiron was a 1/24 scale, 300-pound miniature that was said to

be so impressive, it was actually composited into the live-action background plate in several pre-destruction shots. Modelers also built a 1/24 scale section of the Chrysler building, which gets its dome blown off by Apache helicopters, and a section of the Metropolitan Life Building with a Godzilla-burrowed hole in the middle was composited with footage of the actual building.

As with the computer animation, the miniature work was farmed out simultaneously to a number of model-building shops. For the scene near the beginning of the movie where Godzilla destroys a Japanese "floating fish factory," modelers constructed a 35-foot replica of the ship. The prop was originally built as an oil supertanker, but when construction of it was almost done, Emmerich and Devlin revised the script, believing Godzilla would have more incentive to attack a fish-loaded vessel than a tanker. The ship attack scene and other water-tank effects were filmed at an artificial lake called "Lake Falls," located on the Universal Studios lot, and at a water tank originally constructed for the movie *Virus*, located on the outskirts of Los Angeles. At the climax of the film, footage of the actual Brooklyn Bridge was combined with a "stand-in" bridge shot in downtown Los Angeles and a model of a 400-foot section of the bridge, erected and filmed on vacant land at an airport in Torrance, California. There was also an "underground" set, replicating the damage wrought upon Pennsylvania Station and subway tunnels by Godzilla's burrowing. This set was one of several erected in the 40,000-square-foot Stage 15 on the Sony lot (touted as the world's largest sound stage); it took 12 weeks to build and utilized tons of lumber and Styrofoam to re-create the twisted rock and concrete. Another huge set, the interior of Madison Square Garden after it's turned into Godzilla's nest, stood a reported 80 feet from floor to ceiling.

HE'LL TAKE
MANHATTAN
On location

The making of *Godzilla* involved several lengthy and massive location shoots spanning the entire summer of 1997, and even though the Big G wasn't on the set, the filming attracted lots of media attention because of its severe impact on local traffic,

On location in the Wall Street section of New York, the *Godzilla* crew takes a break between takes. Overhead, in the middle of the street are the rainmaker machines that kept the scenes soaking wet throughout most of the picture.

PHOTO BY JIM WALSH

business and other aspects of life, especially in Manhattan.

The huge Godzilla crew shot in the New York area from May 3 to May 26. The huge influx of film trucks and other vehicles, camera cranes, rain machines, huge light standards and hundreds of extras wasn't exactly welcomed by the locals, who resented being inconvenienced by constant traffic jams. For three days, Fifth Avenue was shut down all night between 20th and 28th streets, as well as portions of Madison Avenue and Broadway, while the Flatiron Square sequence was shot, complete with a battalion of faux military vehicles (the "tanks" were actually fiberglass shells over automobiles) and a big pile of fake fish. Other locations used during the four-week shoot included the South Street Seaport and the Fulton Fish Market, where Godzilla first comes ashore, strewing fish everywhere. Large, moveable "camps," complete with trailers for the actors and crews, catering tents, wardrobe, vehicles and equipment, were set up at Madison Square Park and later at Sheep Meadow, a popular concert spot in Central Park.

While shooting in the Wall Street area, Emmerich invited the press to visit the set one day for a glimpse of a scene in which a huge crowd of people flees as Godzilla makes his way through the streets. The event, which was covered in the New York Times, on TV's "Entertainment Tonight" and elsewhere, featured several hundred extras clad in raincoats and carrying umbrellas, lots of taxicabs and other cars that bounced off the ground whenever Godzilla's foot hit the ground with a thunderous step (a mechanical effect achieved via pneumatic air pumps), and an armada of "rain machines" mounted on five-story-high cranes that constantly drenched the entire set, unleashing a storm even more powerful than the average New York downpour. Among the throng of extras was a die-hard Godzilla fan, Jim Walsh, a 33-year-old computer network consultant from New Jersey. Walsh described his experience:

> . . .We spent the morning filming on the corner of Nassau and Wall. We had come out to listen to a speech from "Mayor Ebert," and during this speech in the pouring rain, Godzilla makes his first appearance in NYC (or so we were told). At certain cues, we would turn and look down the street, and then run for it, in predetermined directions. The shots were rehearsed several times "dry" and then they added smoke and then turned on the rain! . . . After lunch, things got really intense! About a dozen of us were chosen to go down Nassau St. about 2 blocks, to the point where Godzilla was supposed to make his appearance. The camera was set up on a boom about 6 stories up, and during the shoot, it slowly came down to street level . . . We had to run up the street for about 3 blocks as the camera came down, dodging cars, a bicyclist, and a few stuntpeople who I assume fell in the panic . . . They had rigged all of the cars parked along the sides of the streets with hydraulics, and on cue they would all launch simultaneously into the air about 2 feet, as if being violently shaken by Godzilla's footsteps . . . (When) the cars start THUMPING on the street, you start to run and look back over your shoulder and up, and suddenly you are in your best dream and worst nightmare combined! Godzilla is RIGHT BEHIND YOU.

At the end of May, the production headed west for Los Angeles. Most of the shooting there took place at Sony studios, but a number of key outdoor sequences were also shot, with locales in the Skid

Row sections of town disguised to look like New York. In August, the operation moved to Oahu, Hawaii for about two weeks, then finally returned to Los Angeles for about two weeks late that month. Principal photography wrapped up in early September.

THE LIZARD QUEEN
Going Critical on Emmerich's Godzilla

In late October 1996, Emmerich and Devlin flew to a favorite isolated spot at Puerto Vallarta, Mexico and holed themselves up to write *Godzilla*. In interviews, the filmmakers said they took a number of videos with them for reference, including *The Beast from 20,000 Fathoms*, *King Kong* and "a bunch of Godzilla movies." They returned about five weeks later with a first draft screenplay, dated December 19, 1996.

Essentially, *Godzilla* the finished film is the same as that first draft. Only a few revisions were made, most notably Godzilla's death scene was moved from the George Washington Bridge to the Brooklyn Bridge, and the scene in which Godzilla traps the heroes in the Park Avenue tunnel and Nick brilliantly decides to lure the creature out into the open, was added (in the original draft, the taxicab flees Godzilla haphazardly until it winds up on the bridge where, luck would have it, the monster can be killed).

And, considering all the time and effort that went into this film, all the money spent on it, not to mention Godzilla's preceding legacy, one question looms:

What were they thinking?

At the beginning of *Godzilla*, a U.S. government agent interrupts a biologist's (Matthew Broderick) study of mutated earthworms near Chernobyl. "Dr. Niko Tapa-popolis?" the agent asks. "It's Tatopoulos," the biologist corrects him.

In Emmerich and Devlin's screenwriting textbook, the repeated mispronunciation of a Greek surname elicits guffaws from the audience. So does the gruff army general who summons Broderick all the way to Panama to help figure out what's causing a series

Matthew Broderick stars as Niko "Nick" Tatopoulos, the "clever hero" of Roland Emmerich's *Godzilla*, and whose last name no one can pronounce correctly.

of disasters, then inexplicably treats the biologist rudely and calls him "the worm guy." Also funny are stuttering military officers, a Brooklynite cameraman and his wife who say "axe" instead of "ask," a lame Siskel-and-Ebert parody and a mysterious French agent who complains about American coffee (seems he can assemble a warehouse full of black-market assault weapons, but can't locate a Starbucks) and says "thank you very much" like Elvis.

In promotional materials distributed to merchandisers, Sony pointed out that the "primary target" audience for *Godzilla* was boys 4 to 11. But Emmerich's reworking of the King of the Monsters is hardly the ass-kicking creature little boys surely expected, and there are no kids in the cast to identify with. So, whose sensibilities does this film cater to? Monster fans? Godzilla isn't a monster, but an animal acting on instinct. *Simpsons* fans? The film has three of that show's voice actors (Hank Azaria, Harry Shearer, Nancy Cartwright) but none of its wit. The French? Perhaps, for only actor Jean Reno, who portrays the intrepid Frenchman Phillippe Roache, escapes with his dignity intact.

Throughout *Godzilla*, it feels as though Emmerich is embarrassed of his subject matter; the dumb jokes and one-liners ("We need bigger guns," "That's a lot of fish," and so on) are like cynical, condescending winks to the audience. It's also obvious he wants to avoid reminders of the old Japanese films — not only is the creature itself almost totally different, but scenes that the audience expects to see in a picture called *Godzilla* are missing. Where is Godzilla smashing buildings and incinerating entire city blocks? The fierce battles between Godzilla and the army? The monster rearing back and bellowing his high-pitched roar? There are few Godzilla-like moments in the affair — for instance, when Godzilla hugs a skyscraper and wails into the night; why doesn't he push the edifice to the ground? Wasn't the point of making a mega-budget *Godzilla* the chance to relive these classic thrills with super-realistic special effects? Sure, a gigantic reptile jogging down Fifth Avenue is impressive, but the new *Godzilla* was just a way for Sony to make its own upsized, dumbed-down *Jurassic Park*

without getting sued by Steven Spielberg. The experience leaves one wondering why they bothered, for the awe of seeing CGI dinosaurs for the first time is gone, and there's little else that's new.

Emmerich tries vainly to create an atmosphere of dread by dowsing the movie with rain, but gloomy skies alone do not equal subtext. The original Godzilla was a harbinger of doom, but this one is a gutless wonder whose only desire is to eat fish and give New York the ultimate pest problem: a clutch of Baby Godzilla eggs. But once it leaves the concrete jungle, this Godzilla is quickly disposed of — far from his ominous, indestructible namesake, he's just a temporary nuisance in a "Don't Worry, Be Happy" world.

The first five minutes or so of *Godzilla* are actually enjoyable, with stock footage of nuclear tests montaged with lizards in their island habitat; the inference is that one little reptile will grow up to be the Big G. This is followed by Godzilla's exciting attack on a Japanese ship, his claws ripping the hull. Hereon, the story ranges from despicable (shirking

SIZE DOES MATTER: In the weeks preceding the release of TriStar's *Godzilla*, huge advertisements for the film began appearing in major U.S. cities, including this block-long billboard on 42nd Street in New York.
PHOTO BY THE AUTHOR

342

Left to right: Director Roland Emmerich, star Matthew Broderick, and writer-producer Dean Devlin discuss their then-upcoming Godzilla at the International Toy Fair, February 1998, in New York.

COPYRIGHT ED SUMMER/DINOSAUR INTERPANETARY GAZETTE

America's responsibility for the arms race that spawned the original Godzilla, blaming France instead) to dull (the rekindled romance between Matthew Broderick's Nick, a one-dimensional nerd scientist, and Audrey Timmonds, a whiny, lip-biting, 30-something reporter wannabe played by TV actress Maria Pitillo) to ludicrously illogical (a 200-foot lizard hiding undetectably in the Manhattan subway system). It's also unbelievably bloodless; not even the expendable characters like "Mayor Ebert" (Michael Lerner) and the pompous anchorman Charles Caiman (Harry Shearer, in role that wastes his considerable talents) get squished.

As with *Independence Day*, Emmerich apes his favorite blockbusters of the past, but this time he adds nothing to the formula. *Godzilla* mimics *Jaws*, *Aliens* and, most regrettably, it tries to one-up the "kitchen scene" from *Jurassic Park* with dozens of Baby Godzillas chasing the heroes through Madison Square Garden. This long, drawn-out and uncom-

pelling sequence glaringly shows how inferior Emmerich's talents are to those of Spielberg, who charges even his lesser films with real thrills.

Godzilla contains gaping plot holes. Why didn't all the bugs, birds and fish exposed to the French nuclear tests also turn into gigantic animals? If Godzilla is a cold-blooded animal, how can he move as swiftly as a warm-blooded creature, and why did he leave his tropical home and swim all the way to rainy New York? Doesn't anyone notice Godzilla's fire breath? How come Godzilla can fit into the subway system, but a taxi can elude him in the Park Avenue tunnel? If Godzilla runs at 200-plus mph, why can't he catch the taxi? If he can crush a helicopter in his jaws, why not the taxi? An old Japanese fisherman, the lone survivor of the shipwreck, says he saw "Gojira" (a scene replayed twice on video) but the monster's name remains mostly unexplained. And why doesn't anyone, especially Broderick's character, object to the creature's slaying?

Strangely, the special effects don't pack much wallop either. The sight of the new Godzilla, long kept secret, was a letdown when finally revealed, looking as if it's lost its dentures and bearing sleek, buffed-out arms and legs that are vaguely humanoid and, despite all the "size does matter" hype, the monster doesn't seem all that big because it's usually crouched low to the ground. The camera pulls back to provide a full-size view of the creature only a few times; usually only its feet are shown, which gets pretty annoying. Often, SFX supervisor Volker Engel masks the flaws in his work by obscuring Godzilla with heavy rain, closed window blinds or the darkness of deserted New York streets. Worst of all, this computerized Godzilla is devoid of personality, making it impossible to either love or hate him. He's not evil, for he never really attacks, but he's not that likable either; when the humans kill Godzilla's brood, no sympathy is elicited from the audience. Even Godzilla's death brings little emotional response.

The filmmakers, probably wary of comparisons to the *King Kong* movies, steer Godzilla clear of the Empire State Building and the World Trade Center, opting for less ambitious digs like the Flatiron and Chrysler buildings (both of which are destroyed by the military, not the monster). Most disappointing is that Godzilla never swims past the Statue of Liberty or walks through Times Square — stunts Emmerich had neither the guts nor inventiveness to pull off (in a scene included in the screenplay but later deleted, Godzilla was to enter a Tokyo-esque Times Square, lit up with neon, and the famous Jumbo Tron display was to be destroyed). There are nonetheless some spectacular visual effects, like Godzilla passing a group of soldiers perched on a rooftop, and the grand finale wherein the Brooklyn Bridge shudders and nearly collapses as Godzilla chases the taxicab across the East River.

Lastly, this film is marred by the thinly drawn characters, which are more like caricatures, and bad performances from otherwise good actors. Admittedly, Matthew Broderick's role gives the actor, normally a likable comic-dramatic assayer, nothing to grip onto, but Broderick makes things worse with a perpetual "yeah I know this sucks" smirk. Lerner, who was great in *Barton Fink* and other pictures, is just awful as the fat, idiotic mayor, and Maria Pitillo is simply unbearable. *Independence Day* had cardboard characters and a shallow story too, but the cast was appealing and the film had a naïve sense of wonder and fun.

Emmerich and Devlin underestimated the power of Godzilla's 40-year history and felt they could wipe it from the slate, but the monster's identity is deeply ingrained in the minds and hearts of fans around the world. Their *Godzilla* was all hype and no bite, and a blown opportunity to make a truly good monster movie, for within Godzilla's roots lies a prophetic, frightening story still waiting to be retold for modern audiences.

BACKLASH

Godzilla opened May 20, 1998 on 7,363 movie screens across the U.S., a new record. A few days later, Godzilla suitmation actors Haruo Nakajima and Kenpachiro Satsuma were in Chicago attending G-Con '98, an unofficial Godzilla convention. Midway through a screening of the American remake, Satsuma got up and walked out. "It's not Godzilla. It doesn't have his spirit," Satsuma told fans at the convention.

Satsuma's reaction is understandable, given his stake in Godzilla lore. But almost everyone, it seemed, rated the film a monster let-down. Roger Ebert, writing in the *Chicago Sun-Times*, summed up the critics' prevailing opinion, calling *Godzilla* "a cold-hearted, mechanistic vision, so starved for emotion or wit." But the film's most vociferous attackers by far were the unabashed, self-proclaimed Godzillaphiles who take the mutoid reptile to heart. After waiting years to see their hulking hell-beast stomp cities and exhale radiation breath via modern special-effects, the devotees instead got an outsize iguana that burrows underground, eats fish instead of nuclear reactors, runs away from the military, blows wind instead of flame, makes goo-goo eyes with Ferris Bueller and is easily killed with a few missiles.

In a sense, the fans' vehemence was ironic. After all, 34 years earlier, Toho re-made America's most famous giant monster in *King Kong vs. Godzilla*, a film many Kong aficionados won't even acknowledge. Dennis Bent, a G-Con participant, summed up the fans' disgust: "Godzilla's identity is well established — everybody knows he doesn't lay eggs or flee from tanks. You can't screw with Godzilla in a major way and expect the public to accept it."

And the public didn't accept it, at least not to the degree that the studio had hoped. *Godzilla* grossed about $74 million during its six-day opening spate, impressive if not for Sony's pre-release "Size Does Matter" hype, which led many to believe the film could break the $90-million Memorial Day weekend record set by *The Lost World*. But in weeks 2 and 3, the lizard's box office take plummeted to $23 million, then $10 million. By July, *Godzilla* was out of the top 10; by September, its cumulative domestic gross fizzled at about $137 million. The film had the sixth-biggest gross of Summer 1998, trailing the Bruce Willis asteroid flick *Armageddon*, Steven Spielberg's *Saving Private Ryan*, the comedy *There's Something About Mary*, Eddie Murphy's *Dr. Dolittle* remake and another asteroid picture, *Deep Impact*.

Sony maintained that *Godzilla* was profitable, and studio officials downplayed extensive media coverage portraying the film as a huge flop. However, *Godzilla*'s failure to deliver *Independence Day*-style numbers impacted more than just Sony's coffers. Theater owners, who surrender most of their opening-weekend receipts to the studio, were short-changed when the film dive-bombed quickly. Undoubtedly the biggest losers were the roughly 250

Trendmasters Toys revealed their Godzilla 1998 toy line to merchandisers at the annual Toyfair in New York City in February, 1998. To help promote *Godzilla* at the event, TriStar Pictures erected this banner outside New York's famous Flatiron Building. In the film, Godzilla first confronts the military at Flatiron Square.

© ED SUMMER/DINOSAUR INTERPLANETARY GAZETTE

merchandise licensees, who laid out hundreds of millions of dollars for rights to sell movie tie-in products. According to a *Los Angeles Times* article, Sony's major *Godzilla* promotional partners, including Taco Bell, Hershey, Duracell, Electronic Arts and Trendmasters, invested a combined $150 million into the marketing campaign in hopes of reaping a monster windfall.

With heavily merchandised movies, the goods are usually shipped to stores in advance but Sony's marketing team made retailers sign contracts forbidding them for putting *Godzilla* stuff (except items not revealing the monster's design) on the shelves before 12 a.m. on May 20, 1998. In the end, the makers of Godzilla T-shirts, toys and other paraphernalia got burned twice — first, by the "hide the monster" ploy and again when the movie failed to generate post-release sales. "A lot of plastic lizards that scream are going to end up in the sale bin," a *Newsweek* reporter wrote.

With all the bad press and negative word-of-mouth dogging their monster epic, the filmmakers proved somewhat thin-skinned. When fans sniped at the film on the G-board, a discussion forum on the official *Godzilla* Internet website (www.godzilla. com), Devlin responded with curt counter-salvos. "Our movie did what it was supposed to do. We're all happy about it. If you don't like that, to hell with you," he told one critical fan. About a week after the film's release, the G-board was closed — ostensibly, not due to the endless critical postings, but because "this board is starting to be used by others against us," a Centropolis official said.

In the weeks after the movie's release, an embarrassing fact emerged. Due to the enormous amount of special-effects work on the picture, Emmerich finished his final cut of *Godzilla* at the 11th hour and essentially shipped it straight from the editing room to the printer in order to make the May 20 release date. After test screenings of *Independence Day*, Emmerich had re-shot that film's ending (in the original cut, Randy Quaid destroyed the alien spaceship with his crop-duster plane; this was redone so that Quaid was flying a fighter jet). But with *Godzilla*, there were no test screenings and, therefore, no (much-needed) revisions.

While it was rumored that Emmerich deliberately avoided test screenings to prevent the top-secret Godzilla design from being leaked, Devlin offered a different explanation, telling Associated Press columnist Michael Fleeman in September 1998, "We were so determined to make this date [May 20] that we built a schedule where we couldn't screen test, and we should have. I think we really could have improved the film . . . Every film we've ever done [previously] we improved tremendously over the test screening." Devlin also admitted culpability for the lack of a clear-cut villain in *Godzilla*, and for the film's overzealous marketing campaign, but did not address the fans' rejection of his "take" on Godzilla as a fast-moving, wimpy creature.

For their part, Sony executives apparently had trusted Emmerich to deliver a blockbuster. According to a June 15, 1998 *Newsweek* article, no one at the studio actually saw the movie until just three weeks before it opened, when it was screened for theater owners. Realizing they had a bomb on their hands, and knowing the picture would likely not have much box-office stamina, Sony increased its marketing and advertising efforts prior to the release, luring more moviegoers into theaters early.

BEHEMOTH BETRAYED: In 1994, Toho SFX director Koichi Kawakita said he felt reassured that TriStar's *Godzilla* would stay true to its Japanese roots. "[TriStar] won't alter Godzilla's personality too much from what it has been in his recent films," Kawakita told *Asiaweek*.

Four years later, America dropped another bomb on Japan. *Godzilla* was released in Tokyo in July 1998, to generally bad reviews and the dismay of fans who, having even closer ties to the beast than their American counterparts, felt especially betrayed. Yoshiyuki Kasuya, 38, a fan who stood in line at dawn to attend a 7:20 a.m. showing on opening day, told the *Los Angeles Times* that Godzilla had been transformed into something unrecognizable. "That's not Godzilla . . . He got killed with four missiles, but the Japanese Godzilla is almost bullet-proof. And the Japanese Godzilla is handsome, but the American Godzilla is not," Kasuya said. Another fan, Masato Mukohata, 16, said simply, "My dreams were crushed."

Kawakita and Godzilla's creators at Toho remained silent during the public outcry. However, Masahiko Suzuki, a Toho spokesman, defended the movie and said it was unfair that some Japanese were suddenly claiming Godzilla as their own, after having dismissed the monster as childish for years. "Hollywood realized the sophisticated computer graphics and other technically impossible things here in Japan," Suzuki told *Agence France Presse*. "The film is enjoyable even for long-time Godzilla fans," he said. Perhaps the most insightful comment came from Shusuke Kaneko, director of Daiei's *Gamera: Guardian of the Universe* and *Gamera 2:*

Advent of Legion, who told Japan's SPA magazine, "it is interesting the U.S. version runs about trying to escape missiles . . . [Americans] seem unable to accept a creature that cannot be put down by their arms."

Nevertheless, *Godzilla* opened on a record 385 screens in Tokyo and set a new all-time high for opening-day ticket sales in Japan, with roughly 500,000 moviegoers paying about $13 for tickets, surpassing the previous record of about 350,000 set by in 1997 *The Lost World*. As in the U.S., the film's box-office returns tapered off quickly in subsequent weeks, and by the end of summer it has earned about $33.1 million in Japanese theaters. That's better than the 1990s Godzilla movies, but not significantly: *Variety* noted that 1995's *Godzilla vs. Destoroyah* grossed 3.5 billion Yen, or $24.8 million (using 1998 exchange rates). *Godzilla* was runner-up to *Deep Impact*, which scored $45 million at the Japanese box office in summer 1998, and it earned far less than *Jurassic Park* grossed during its Japanese run in 1993. "[A Columbia TriStar International official] says the Japanese results are disappointing for both dubbed version and the subtitled prints, suggesting the problem lies with the film, not in how it's translated," a *Variety* reporter wrote. In the United Kingdom, Godzilla made about $25 million and overall it had grossed about $140 million in overseas markets by summer's end, for a combined (with the U.S.) total of about $275 million. Industry analysts estimated it would pull in about $350 million by the end of its worldwide theatrical run.

GODZILLA'S REVENGE? The ending of *Godzilla* leaves open, rather uninventively, the possibility of a sequel as one of Godzilla's eggs, unscathed in the destruction of Madison Square Garden, hatches a baby. In interviews published while *Godzilla* was being filmed, Dean Devlin repeatedly said the deal between Centropolis, TriStar Pictures and Toho laid the foundation for two sequels. Devlin said the first film was Part 1 of a projected trilogy, although the second and third installments of the story arc had not been written yet. "There is an aspect to (Godzilla's) mythology which we do not explore in the first film that can take us into a new direction for the second and third," Devlin said.

Although there was no official announcement, by the end of Summer 1998 reports in the *Los Angeles Times* and elsewhere had quoted unnamed Sony officials as saying they still believed Godzilla could become a franchise and a second film would indeed be made, probably for release in the year 2000. Several early, unconfirmed rumors circulated as to who would write and direct the picture, and what the story would be about; sources close to Sony indicated that Devlin and Emmerich would not be asked to make the sequel, and if they were involved at all it would likely be as executive producers — a turnaround from earlier reports that suggested the duo would maintain creative supervision over any future American Godzillas. As to plot, it was widely rumored that in *Godzilla 2*, the lone surviving baby would grow up and face off against an old nemesis, probably King Ghidorah, on the west coast of the U.S. In an interview with the *Philadelphia Inquirer*, Emmerich said another possibility was a story about "Godzillas (as in lots of 'em)." As to what this meant, a theory was offered in September 1998 by anonymous (and supposedly well-connected) sources on the Godzilla News website (www.monsterzero. org): "[Film 3] stars off a few years down the road, and the world has reverted back to the age of dinosaurs . . . people are hiding in terror as Godzillas roam and run the planet." Other rumors said Tatopoulos's design would be scrapped in any sequels, and the King of the Monsters would look more like his old self.

On September 12, 1998, *Godzilla: The Series* premiered on the Fox TV network. This Saturday morning weekly cartoon, obviously produced with the assumption that Emmerich's *Godzilla* would be a huge hit, picked up exactly where the film ended (Episode 1 begins with an animated replay of Godzilla chasing the taxicab onto the Brooklyn Bridge and subsequently being killed). Nick Tatopoulos, portrayed as a determined young hero rather than the nerdy geek of the movie, immediately guides the military team (led by Major Hicks, voiced by Kevin Dunn, who played the same character in the film) back into the sewers to search for any remaining G-eggs. Nick witnesses the hatching of a baby Godzilla, and the young lizard develops a mother-like attachment to Nick who, along with returning scientist-characters Elsie Chapman and (constantly sneezing) Mendel Craven, dedicates himself to studying the creature. The young Godzilla is more well-behaved than its parent, and as it quickly grows to full-size Nick must help it avoid being killed by the military. In subsequent episodes, Godzilla is portrayed as a feared, misunderstood creature though not an outright villain, and he battles various monsters from around the world, using his cunning and a green atomic breath to defeat the baddies.

EPILOGUE

Godzilla: King of the Monsters! arrived at a time when cinemas were besieged by giant insects, dinosaurs and other bomb-spawned behemoths, but this beast from the east left a swath of horror and destruction across Tokyo that was unparalleled. Although born in Japan, the only nation ever to suffer a nuclear attack, Godzilla became an international superstar and for four and a half decades, while global politics evolved, wars were fought, economies soared and plummeted and science discovered new and more dangerous threats to the planet, Godzilla stood his ground, reminding us of the consequences of our destructive tendencies.

Admittedly, the original symbol of nuclear militarism de-evolved into a comic-book hero, for better or worse. His territorial instincts led him to align, perhaps reluctantly, with the interests of man, his former enemy. In his greatest outings Godzilla was the King of the Monsters. In his worst, the King of Camp. Somewhere in between, there were elements of kitsch — the boulder-tossing with King Kong, the victory dance on Planet X, the fancy footwork while battling Ghidorah — that made the once-horrible creature more human and endearing. Godzilla left a dual legacy: On the one hand, he is the disastrous by-product of contemporary civilization; on the other hand, he represents the larger-than-life possibilities of imagination and fantasy in film. And, for some people, Godzilla is worth a good laugh — that's OK too.

Godzilla is more than just a monster. Thus, it is sad that indeed that he was remade by two filmmakers whose prior claim to fame was *Independence Day*, a movie which, despite its entertainment value, has no subtext whatsoever. The American-made Godzilla was faster, leaner and more realistic than anything seen before, but it had nothing relevant to say and contributed little to the legend and lore.

The jury is still out as to whether Sony can develop the American Godzilla into a successful film franchise — and even if that happens, it seems unlikely that it would produce anything but a series of typical, easily-forgotten, big-budget summer blockbusters. Meanwhile, Toho Co. Ltd., citing Japanese fans' lack of enthusiasm for the Gaijin Godzilla, will revive the classic man-in-suit prototype in December 1999, in a film appropriately titled *Godzilla Millennium*. Thus, at the dawn of an epoch, Godzilla stands at a crossroads, poised to unleash his mighty wrath in his motherland and abroad. But, whatever incarnation of Godzilla prevails into the next century — Toho's, Sony's, another not yet dreamed of, or perhaps none — classics like *Godzilla: King of the Monsters!*, *King Kong vs. Godzilla* and *Godzilla vs. The Thing* will endure for future generations to enjoy, snapshots from an era when giant monsters ruled the screen, and Godzilla was the biggest and baddest of them all.

At the dawn of a new century, the King of the Monsters is just as relevant as the day he was born in the fire of a mushroom cloud. And, as history unfolds in the new era, Godzilla will be there, standing guard over his lord Japan — and all the world — like a faithful, fearless Samurai, yet ready to punish like a vengeful god if ever we inch toward Armageddon. Hopefully we'll hear his mighty battle-cry and heed his warning, before it's too late.

PART 7

APPENDIXES

Appendix I

CAST AND CREDITS

GODZILLA (1954)
a.k.a. GODZILLA: KING OF
THE MONSTERS! (1956)

CAST

Takashi Shimura (Dr. Kyohei Yamane), Momoko Kochi (Emiko Yamane), Akira Takarada (Hideto Ogata), Akihiko Hirata (Dr. Daisuke Serizawa), Sachio Sakai (reporter Hagiwara), Fuyuki Murakami (Dr. Tanabe), Toranosuke Ogawa (CEO of Nankai Shipping Co.), Ren Yamamoto (Masaji), Ken Hayashi (Chairman of the Diet), Keiji Sakakida (Odo Island mayor Inada), Seijiro Onda (Senator Ooyama), Kin Sugai (Senator Ozawa, the female politician), Takeo Oikawa (Defense Chief), Toshiaki Suzuki (Shinkichi), Tsuruki Mano (Shinkichi's mother), Kokuten Kodo (old fisherman), Tadashi Okabe (Dr. Tanabe's assistant), Shizuko Higashi (partygoer), Kiyoshi Kamota (partygoer's escort), Haruo Nakajima (Godzilla), Katsumi Tezuka (newspaper deskman and Godzilla), Tamae Sengo (mother). With: Ren Imaizumi, Masaki Hashi, Ichiro Tai, Yasuhisa Tsutumi, Jiro Sozukawa, Saburo Iketani.

CREDITS

Producer: Tomoyuki Tanaka. Director: Ishiro Honda. Original Story: Shigeru Kayama. Screenplay: Takeo Murata, Ishiro Honda. Music: Akira Ifukube. Director of Photography: Masao Tamai. Lighting Supervisor: Choshiro Ishii. Supervising Art Director: Takeo Kita. Art Director: Satoshi Chuko. Film Editor: Yasunobu Taira. Sound Recording: Hisashi Shimonaga. Sound and Musical Effects: Ichiro Mitsunawa. Production Manager: Teruo Maki. Assistant Director: Koji Kajita. Film Processing: Toho Laboratories.

SPECIAL EFFECTS

Director: Eiji Tsuburaya. Art Director: Akira Watanabe. Lighting Supervisor: Kuichiro Kishida. Optical Printing: Hiroshi Mukaiyama. Assistant Directors: Teisho Arikawa, Mototaka Tomioka, Yoichi Manoda, Yukio Kabayama, Hajime Tsuburaya, Masakatsu Asai. Assistant

Lighting Technician: Shinji Akiichi, Hideo Hata. Assistant Art Directors: Yasuyuki Inoue, Yoshio Irie. Prop Master: Kintaro Makino, Yoshikazu Tanaka. Grip: Mitsukazu Toshibukuro, Hajime Takayama. Props: Sadao Yamamoto. Backdrop Artist: Fukutaro Suzuki. Models: Teizo Toshimitsu, Koei Yagi, Kanji Yagi, Eizo Kaimai, Yoshio Suzuki. Plasters: Yukio Odagiri, Mitsuo Tomigashi, Sakai Terui. Mechanical Effects: Fumio Nakadai, Shoji Ogawa. Matte Painting: Takao Yuki, Tadao Izuka. Production Assistant: Yasuaki Sakamoto.

U.S. VERSION CREDITS

Cast: Raymond Burr (United World News reporter Steve Martin), Frank Iwanaga (security officer Tomo Iwanaga). Director: Terry Morse. Assistant Director: Ira Webb. Sound: Art Smith. Sets: George Rohrs. Cinematography: Guy Roe. Executive Producers: Joseph E. Levine, Terry Turner, Ed Barison. Producers: Harold Ross, Richard Kay. Presented by Jewell Enterprises Inc.

GODZILLA RAIDS AGAIN (1955)
a.k.a.
GIGANTIS: THE FIRE MONSTER (1959)

CAST

Hiroshi Koizumi (Shoichi Tsukioka), Setsuko Wakayama (Hidemi Yamaji), Yukio Kazama (Kohei Yamaji, Hidemi's father), Minoru Chiaki (Hiroshi Kobayashi), Mayuri Mokoshi (radio operator Yasuko), Sonosuke Sawamura (Mr. Shibeki), Takashi Shimura (Dr. Yamane), Masao Shimizu (Dr. Tadokoro), Takeo Oikawa (Osaka police chief), Tomonosuke Yamada (Japanese Self Defense Force chief), Seijiro Ondo (JSDF commander Terazawa), Yoshio Tsuchiya (Tajima), Ren Yamamoto (captain of landing ship), Hirotoshi Tsuchiya (fishing department chief), Nobu Ootormo, Senkichi Omura, Sokichi Maki, Shoichi Hirose, Junpei Natsuki, and Shin Yoshida (prisoners), Teruko Mita (woman innkeeper), Miyoko Hoshino (cabaret singer).

CREDITS

Producer: Tomoyuki Tanaka. Director: Motoyoshi Oda. Original Story: Shigeru Kayama. Screenplay: Takeo Murata, Shigeaki Hidaka. Music: Masaru Sato. Director of Photography: Seiichi Endo. Lighting: Masayoshi Onuma. Production Designer: Takeo Kita. Art Director: Teruaki Abe. Editor: Kazuji Taira. Sound Recording: Masanobu Miyazawa. Sound Effects: Ichiro Mitsunawa. Assistant Director: Eiji Iwashiro. Production Coordinator: Kazuo Baba. Still Photographer: Tadao Fukuda. Film Developing: Toho Laboratories.

SPECIAL EFFECTS

Director: Eiji Tsuburaya. Technicians: Akira Watanabe, Hiroshi Mukaiyama, Masao Shirota.

U.S. VERSION CREDITS

Producer: Paul Schreibman. Associate Producer: Edmund Goldman. Director and Film Editor: Hugo Grimaldi. Music Editor: Rex Lipton. Sound Effects Editor: Al Sarno. Sound: Ryder Sound Services Inc.

KING KONG vs. GODZILLA (1962)

CAST

Tadao Takashima (Osamu Sakurai), Kenji Sahara (Kazuo Fujita), Ichiro Arishima (Mr. Tako), Mie Hama (Fumiko Sakurai), Yu Fujiki (Kinzaburo Furue), Tatsuo Matsumura (Dr. Makino), Akihiko Hirata (Defense Minister Shigezawa), Jun Tazaki (Japanese Self Defence Force general), Eiko (a.k.a. Akiko) Wakabayashi (Tamiye), Senkichi Omura (Konno), Yoshio Kosuge (tribal chief), Ikio Sawamura (tribal priest), Akemi Negishi (native woman, Chikiro's mother), Somekichi Matsumoto (Dr. Ohnuki), Sachio Sakai (Obashi), Ichiro Chiba and Haruya Kato (Pacific Pharmaceutical employees), Douglas Fayne (Seahawk submarine captain), Harold S. Conway and Osman Yusef (members of Seahawk research team), Ko Mishima (JSDF naval officer), Nadao Kirino (JSDF second commander), Yoshifumi Tajima (ship captain), Yutaka Nakayama (ship crewman), Kenzo Tadake (TV show host), Ren Yamamoto (military officer in charge of explosions), Haruo Nakajima (Godzilla), Shoichi Hirose (King Kong).

CREDITS

Producer: Tomoyuki Tanaka. Director: Ishiro Honda. Screenplay: Shinichi Sekizawa. Music: Akira Ifukube. Director of Photography: Hajime Koizumi. Lighting: Toshio Takashima. Art Directors: Takeo Kita, Teruaki Abe. Editor: Reiko Kaneko. Sound Recording: Masao Fujiyoshi. Special Sound Effects: Sadatada Nishimoto. Audio Technician: Hishashi Shimonaga. Choreographer: Kenji Aoki. Production Coordinator: Shigeru Nakamura. Assistant Director: Koji Kajita. Film Developing: Tokyo Laboratories.

SPECIAL EFFECTS

Director: Eiji Tsuburaya. Directors of Photography: Teisho Arikawa, Mototaka Tomioka. Optical Photography: Takao Yuki, Yukio Manoda. Art Director: Akira Watanabe. Lighting: Kuichiro Kishida. Optical Processing: Hiroshi Mukaiyama. Production Coordinator: Kan Narita.

U.S. VERSION CREDITS

Cast: Michael Keith (reporter Eric Carter), Harry Holcombe (Dr. Arnold Johnson), James Yagi (Yataka Omura). Producer: John Beck. Director: Thomas Montgomery. Screenplay: Paul Mason, Bruce Howard. Editorial Supervision: Peter Zinner. Sound Effects: William Stevenson. Character and name of "King Kong" by permission of RKO General, Inc.@

GODZILLA vs. THE THING
a.k.a. GODZILLA vs. MOTHRA (1964)

CAST

Akira Takarada (reporter Ichiro Sakai), Yuriko Hoshi (photographer Junko Nakanishi [U.S. version: "Yoka"]), Hiroshi Koizumi (Professor Miura), Yu Fujiki (egg-loving reporter Jiro Nakamura), Kenji Sahara (Jiro Torahata), The Peanuts — Emi Ito and Yumi Ito (twin fairies), Yoshifumi Tajima (Mr. Kumayama), Jun Tazaki (newspaper city editor), Ikio Sawamura (priest), Kenzo Tadake (politician), Susumu Fujita (military commander), Yutaka Sada (school principal), Miki Yashiro (female teacher), Yoshio Kosuge (Infant Island tribal chief), Nobu Otomo (police chief), Yasuhisa Tsutumi (policeman at the dock), Ren Yamamoto (sailor), Yutaka Nakayama, Hiroshi Iwamoto, Koji Uno, Senkichi Omura, Jiro Kumagaya, Shiro Tsuchiya, and Hiroshi Aegetsu (fishermen), Haruo Nakajima (Godzilla).

CREDITS

Executive Producers: Sanezumi (a.k.a. Masumi) Fujimoto, Tomoyuki Tanaka. Director: Ishiro Honda. Screenplay: Shinichi Sekizawa. Music: Akira Ifukube. Photography: Hajime Koizumi. Lighting: Shoshichi Kojima. Art Director: Takeo Kita. Film Editor: Ryohei Fujii. Sound Recording: Fumio Yanoguchi. Sound Effects: Teisho Nishimoto. Audio Technician: Hisashi Shimonaga. Production Coordinator: Boku Norimoto. Assistant Director: Koji Kajita. Associate Producer: Tadashi Koike. Film Developing: Tokyo Laboratories.

SPECIAL EFFECTS

Director: Eiji Tsuburaya. Directors of Photography: Teisho Arikawa, Mototaka Tomioka. Optical Photography: Yukio Manoda, Yoshiyuki Tokumasa. Art Director: Akira Watanabe. Lighting: Kuichiro Kishida. Optical Processing: Hiroshi Mukaiyama. Assistant Director: Teruyoshi Nakano.

U.S. VERSION CREDITS

Re-recording (English dubbing): Titra Sound Studios. Color prints by Pathe.

GHIDRAH: THE THREE-HEADED MONSTER (1964)

CAST

Yosuke Natsuki (Shindo), Yuriko Hoshi (reporter Naoko Shindo), Hiroshi Koizumi (Professor Murai), Takashi Shimura (Dr. Tsukamoto), The Peanuts — Emi Ito and Yumi Ito (twin fairies), Eiko (a.k.a. Akiko) Wakabayashi (Mas Dorina Salno [U.S. version: Princess Selina Salno]), Hisaya Ito (Malness the assasin), Akihiko Hirata (Security Chief Okita), Kenji Sahara (Kanamaki, Naoko's editor), Yuriko Hide (mother), Kohei Nakajima and Takiyoshi Kanatsuge (boys on TV show), Senya Aozoro and Ichiya Aozora (hosts of TV show), Minoru Takada (Minister of Home Affairs), Somekichi Matsumoto (president of UFO club), Henry Okawa (man at UFO meeting), Yutaka Oka (electric company worker), Susumu Kurobe (thug 1, with pencil mustache), Toru Ibuki (thug 2), Kazuo Suzuki (thug 3), Haruya Kato (reporter Komaki), Yoshio Katsube (reporter), Eisei (a.k.a. Hideyo) Amamoto (Princess Salno's servant), Nobu Otomo (mastermind of assassination plot), Yoshibumi Tajima (ship captain), Kamayuki Tsubono (ship crewman), Ikio Sawamura (fisherman), Yutaka Nakayama (man who loses hat), Tamame Urayama (his wife), Senkichi Omura (man who picks up hat), Shoichi Hirose (villager 1), Hideo Shibuya (villager 2), Keiichiro Mastumoto (villager 3), Koji Uhno (hotel desk clerk), Kozo Nomura, Toshio Miura, Toshihiko Furuta, Kazuo Imai, and Jun Kuroki (members of research team), Haruo Nakajima (Godzilla), Masanori Shinohara (Rodan), Shoichi Hirose (King Ghidorah).

CREDITS

Producer: Tomoyuki Tanaka. Director: Ishiro Honda. Screenplay: Shinichi Sekizawa. Music: Akira Ifukube. The song *"Shiawase Wo Yobou"* ("Let's Call For Happiness," U.S. version: "Call Happiness"), words by Tokiko Iwatani, composed by Yasushi Miyagawa. Director of Photography: Hajime Koizumi. Lighting Supervisor: Shoshichi Kojima. Art Director: Takeo Kita. Film Editor: Ryohei Fujii. Sound Recordist: Fumio Yanoguchi. Sound Effects: Osamu Tomohisa. Audio Technician: Hisashi Shimonaga. Production Manager: Shigeru Nakamura. Assistant Director: Ken Sano. Associate Producer: Tadashi Koike. Film Developing: Tokyo Laboratory.

SPECIAL EFFECTS

Director: Eiji Tsuburaya. Directors of Photography: Sadamasa Arikawa, Mototaka Tomioka. Optical Photography: Yukio Manoda, Yoshiyuki Tokumasa. Optical Processing: Hiroshi Mukaiyama. Art Director: Akira Watanabe. Lighting: Kuichiro Kishida. Assistant Special Effects Director: Teruyoshi Nakano.

U.S. VERSION CREDITS

Additional Music and Sound Effects: Filmscores Inc. English Dialogue: Joe Bellucci. Post-production Consultant: Ray Angus. Prints: Movielab Inc. Additional Optical Photography (opening titles and credits): Film Cinematics Inc.

MONSTER ZERO a.k.a. GODZILLA vs. MONSTER ZERO (1965)

CAST

Nick Adams (F. Glenn), Akira Takarada (Kazuo Fuji), Kumi Mizuno (Miss Namikawa), Keiko Sawai (Haruno [Harumi] Fuji), Jun Tazaki (Dr. Sakurai), Yoshio Tsuchiya (Controller of Planet X), Akira Kubo (Tetsuo [Tatsui]); Kenzo Tadake (President of Planet X), Yoshifumi Tajima (transport officer), Noriko Sengoku (woman at Tetsuo's boarding house), Minoru Ito (reporter), Toru Ibuki and Koji Uno (World Education Corp. alien employees); Yasuhisa Tsutsumi (Captain of first research team), Hiroo Kirino (Captain of second research team), Gen Shimizu (JSDF representative), Fuyuki Murakami (medical academy representative), Toki Shiozawa (feminist group representative), Somekichi Matsumoto (priest), Haruo Nakajima (Godzilla), Masanori Shinohara (Rodan), Shoichi Hirose (King Ghidorah). With: Takamaru Sasaki, Kazuo Suzuki, Masaaki Tachibana, Kamayuki Tsubono, Rinsaku Ogata, Tadashi Okabe, Yoshizo Tatake, Mitzuo Tsuda, Hideki Furukawa, Rioji Shimizu, Goro Naya, Yutaka Oka, Takuzo Kumagaya.

CREDITS

Producer: Tomoyuki Tanaka. Director: Ishiro Honda. Screenplay: Shinichi Sekizawa. Music: Akira Ifukube. Director of Photography: Hajime Koizumi. Lighting: Shohichi Kojima. Art Director: Takeo Kita. Editing: Ryohei Fujii. Sound Recording: Wataru Konuma. Sound Effects: Teisho Nishimoto. Audio Technician: Hisashi Shimonaga. Production Managers: Masao Suzuki, Tadashi Koike. Assistant Director: Koji Kajita. Film Developing: Tokyo Developing Lab.

SPECIAL EFFECTS

Director: Eiji Tsuburaya. Directors of Photography: Teisho Arikawa, Mototaka Tomioka. Optical Photography: Yukio Manoda, Sadao Iizuka. Optical Processing: Hiroshi Mukaiyama. Assistant Director: Teruyoshi Nakano. Art Director: Akira Watanabe. Lighting: Kuichiro Kishida. Mechanical Effects: Fumio Nakadai.

U.S. VERSION CREDITS

Executive Producers: Henry G. Saperstein, Reuben Bercovitch. Sound Recording (English dubbing): Glenn Glenn Sound. Production Supervisor: Richard Krown.

GODZILLA VERSUS THE SEA MONSTER (1966)

CAST

Akira Takarada (Yoshimura, the bank robber), Kumi Mizuno (Daiyo), Akihiko Hirata (Red Bamboo captain), Jun Tazaki (Red Bamboo general), Toru Watanabe (Ryota), Toru Ibuki (Yata), Hideo Sunazuka (Ninda), Chotaro Togin (Ichino), Eisei (a.k.a. Hideyo) Amamoto (ship captain), Ikio Sawamura (old native man), Hisaya Ito and Tadashi Okabe (nuclear reactor workers), Fumiko Ohma (Kane, Ryota's mother), Chieko Nakakita (spiritual medium), Izuko Ikeda and Yutaka Sada (old fishermen), Hideo Shibuya (policeman), Kenichiro Murayama and Tsune Omae (reporters), Haruo Nakajima (Godzilla), Hiroshi Sekita (Ebirah), Shoichi Hirose and Tazuo Suzuki (natives who flee in canoe), The Bambi Pair (twin fairies of Infant Island), Studio No. 1 Dancers (Infant Island natives).

CREDITS

Producer: Tomoyuki Tanaka. Director: Jun Fukuda. Screenplay: Shinichi Sekizawa. Music: Masaru Sato. Director of Photography: Kazuo Yamada. Lighting: Kiichi Onda. Art Director: Takeo Kita. Sound Recordist: Shoichi Yoshizawa. Sound Effects: Toshiaki Kane. Audio Technician: Hisashi Shimonaga. Assistant Director: Takeshi Sano. Associate Producer: Yasuaki Sakamoto.

SPECIAL EFFECTS

Director: Eiji Tsuburaya. Assistant Director: Teisho Arikawa. Directors of Photography: Mototaka Tomioka, Yoichi Manoda. Optical Photography: Yoshiyuki Norimasa. Art Director: Yasuyuki Inoue. Lightng: Kuichiro Kishida. Mechanical Effects: Fumio Nakadai. Optical Prodessing: Hiroshi Mukaiyama. Assistant Director: Teruyoshi Nakano.

SON OF GODZILLA (1967)

CAST

Tadao Takashima (Dr. Kusumi), Bibari (a.k.a. Beverly) Maeda (Saeko Matsumiya, "Reiko" in U.S. version), Akira Kubo (reporter Goro Maki), Akihiko Hirata (radio operator Fujisaki), Kenji Sahara (Morio), Yoshio Tsuchiya (Furukawa), Yasuhiko Saijo (Suzuki), Kenichiro

Murayama (Ozawa), Seishiro Kuno (Tashiro), Susumu Kurobe (captain of weather plane team), Kazuo Suzuki (pilot), Tsune Omae (radio man), Chotaro Togin (weather plane navigator), Hiroshi Sekita, Seiji Onaka, and Haruo Nakajima (Godzilla), Marchan the Dwarf (Son of Godzilla).

CREDITS

Producer: Tomoyuki Tanaka. Director: Jun Fukuda. Screenplay: Shinichi Sekizawa, Kazue Shiba. Music: Masaru Sato. Director of Photography: Kazuo Yamada. Lighting: Eiji Yamaguchi, Shoshichi Kojima. Art Director: Takeo Kita. Film Editor: Ryohei Fuji. Sound Recordists: Nobu Watari, Toshiya Ban. Sound Effects: Minoru Kanayama. Audio Technician: Hisashi Shimonaga. Production Manager: Yasuaki Sakamoto. Assistant Director: Takashi Nagano. Film Developing: Tokyo Laboratory. Special thanks to Pan American Airlines.

SPECIAL EFFECTS

Supervisor: Eiji Tsuburaya. Director: Teisho Arikawa. Director of Photography: Totoyasu Inoue. Lighting: Fumiyoshi Hara. Optical Processing: Hiroshi Mukalyama. Mechanical Effects: Fumio Nakadai. Assistant Director: Teruyoshi Nakano.

DESTROY ALL MONSTERS (1968)

CAST

Akira Kubo (SY-3 Capt. Katsuo Yamabe), Yukiko Kobayashi (Kyoko Manabe), Kyoko Ai (Queen of Kilaak), Jun Tazaki (Dr. Yoshida), Yoshio Tsuchiya (Dr. Otani), Kenji Sahara (SY-3 navigator Nishikawa), Andrew Hughes (Dr. Stevenson), Chotaro Togin (Okada), Hisaya Ito (Ota, military Chief of Staff), Yoshifumi Tajima (Military Cmdr. Sugiyama), Ikio Sawamura (old farmer), Yutaka Sada (policeman), Susumu Kurobe, Kazuo Suzuki, Minoru Ito, Toru Ibuki, Rinsaku Ogata and Haruya Sakamoto (Monsterland staff members), Nadao Kirino, Naoya Kusagawa, Kamayuki Tsubono, Yasuhiko Saijo, Seishiro Hisano and Wataru Omae (Interpol detectives), Keiko Miyauchi, Atsuko Takahashi, Ari Sagawa, Yoshiko Miyata, Kyoko Mori, Midori Uchiyama, Wakako Tanabe and Michiko Ishii (Kilaak women), Yoshio Katsube (young scientist), Henry Okawa (engineer 1), Kenichiro Maruyama (engineer 2), Hiroshi Okada (doctor), Hideo Shibuya (reporter 1), Yutaka Oka (reporter 2), Ken Echigo (SY-3 engineer), Haruo Nakajima (Godzilla), Teruoshi Nigaki (Rodan), Marchan the Dwarf (Son of Godzilla), Susumu Utsumi (King Ghidorah), Hiroshi Sekita (Angilas).

CREDITS

Executive Producer: Tomoyuki Tanaka. Director: Ishiro Honda. Screenplay: Kaoru Mabuchi, Ishiro Honda. Music: Akira Ifukube. Director of Photography: Taichi Kankura. Lighting: Kiyohisa Hirano. Art Director: Takeo Kita. Film Editor: Ryohei Fujii. Sound Recording: Shoichi Yoshizawa. Sound Effects: Sadamasa Kishimoto. Audio Technician: Hisashi Shimonaga. Production Manager: Yasuaki Sakamoto. Assistant Director: Seiji Tani. Film Processing: Tokyo Laboratory Ltd.

SPECIAL EFFECTS

Supervisor: Eiji Tsuburaya. Director: Teisho Arikawa. Directors of Photography: Mototaka Tomioka, Yoichi Manoda. Art Director: Yasuyuki Inoue. Optical Photography: Yoshiyuki

Tokumasa. Lighting: Fumiyoshi Hara. Optical Processing: Hiroshi Mukaiyama. Mechanical Effects: Fumio Nakadai. Assistant Director: Teruyoshi Nakano.

U.S. VERSION CREDITS

Producer: Sal Billitteri. Re-recording: Titra Studios. Postproduction Director: Peter Fernandez.

GODZILLA'S REVENGE (1969)

CAST

Tomonori Yazaki (Ichiro Mitsuki), Kenji Sahara (Kenichi, Ichiro's dad), Machiko Naka (Tamiko, Ichiro's mom), Eisei (a.k.a. Hideyo) Amamoto (toy inventor Shinpei Minami), Shigeki Ishida (apartment building manager), Ikio Sawamura (noodle shop owner), Sachio Sakai (Sembayashi, the smart robber), Kazuo Suzuki (Okuda, the dumb robber), Junichi Ito (Gabara the boy), Hidemi Ito (Sachiko, Ichiro's friend), Yukiko Mori (Sachiko's mom), Yoshifumi Tajima and Chotaro Togin (police detectives), Yutaka Sada (Kenichi's co-worker), Yutaka Nakayama (sign painter), Haruo Nakajima (Godzilla), Marchan the Dwarf (Minya), Yasuhiko Kakuyuki (Gabara the monster), Midori Uchiyama (Minya's voice in Japanese version).

CREDITS

Producer: Tomoyuki Tanaka. Director: Screenplay: Shinichi Sekizawa. Music: Kunio Miyauchi. Theme song, *"Kaiju March"* (a.k.a. "March of the Monsters"), lyrics by Shinichi Sekizawa, music by Genta Kanou, arranged by Jinzou Kosugi, sung by Rie Sasaki, released by Crown Records. Director of Photography: Mototaka Tomioka. Lighting: Fumiyoshi Hara. Art Director: Takeo Kita. Film Editor: Masahisa Shoumi. Sound Recordist: Norio Tone. Audio Technician: Hisashi Shimonaga. Assistant Directors: Masaaki Hisamatsu, Teruyoshi Nakano. Associate Producer: Yasushi Sakai. Film Developing: Tokyo Laboratory.

SPECIAL EFFECTS

Supervisor: Eiji Tsuburaya. Optical Processing: Hiroshi Mukaiyama. Operations: Fumio Nakadai.

U.S. VERSION CREDITS

Sound Recording: Ryder Sound Services, Inc. Titles: Consolidated Film Industries. Postproduction: Riley Jackson.

GODZILLA vs. THE SMOG MONSTER a.k.a. GODZILLA vs. HEDORAH (1971)

CAST

Akira Yamaguchi (Dr. Toru Yano), Toshie Kimura (Mrs. Toshie Yano), Hiroyuki Kawase (Ken Yano), Toshio Shibaki (Yukio Mori), Keiko Mari (a.k.a. Rikako Asa) (Miki Fujimiya), Yoshio Yoshida (Grandpa Gohei), Haruo Suzuki (Japanese Self Defense Force cadet), Yoshio

Katsube (JSDF engineer), Tadashi Okabe and Kentaro Watanabe (news anchors), Wataru Omae (policeman), Tadashi Okabe (scholar), Shigeo Kato (fireman), Takuya Yuki (communications officer), Yukihiko Gondo (helicopter pilot), Haruo Nakazawa (young guy), Haruo Nakajima (Godzilla), Kengo Nakayama (Hedorah).

CREDITS

Executive Producer: Tomoyuki Tanaka. Director: Yoshimitsu Banno. Screenplay: Kaoru Mabuchi, Yoshimitsu Banno. Music: Riichiro Manabe. Director of Photography: Yoichi Manoda. Lighting: Fumiyoshi Hara. Art Director: Yasuyuki Inoue. Film Editor: Yoshitami Kuroiwa. Sound Recording: Masao Fujiyoshi. Audio: Toho Recording Center. Assistant Director: Heikichi Tsushima. Film Developing: Tokyo Laboratory Ltd.

SPECIAL EFFECTS

Special Effects Technician: Teruyoshi Nakano. Operations: Shoji Ogawa. Optical Photography: Yoshiyuki Tokumasa. Optical Processing: Saburo Doi.

U.S. VERSION CREDITS

Producer: Salvatore Billiteri. Postproduction: Titan Productions, Inc. Director: Lee Kressel. Editor: Eli Haviv. Song "Save the Earth," lyrics by Guy Hemric and Adryan Russ, sung by Adryan Russ.

GODZILLA ON MONSTER ISLAND
a.k.a. GODZILLA vs. GIGAN (1972)

CAST

Hiroshi Ishikawa (Gengo Kotaka), Tomoko Umeda (Machiko Shima), Yuriko Hishimi (Tomoko Tomoe), Minoru Takashima (Shosako Kosugi), Zan Fujita (Fumio/the Chairman), Toshiaki Nishizawa (Kubota/the Secretary), Kunio Murai (Takashi Shima), Gen Shimizu (Japanese Self Defense Force station commander), Yukie Omiya (JSDF central chief), Kuniko Ashihara (old woman), Zeko Nakamura (priest), Akio Muto (comic book editor), Naoya Kusakawa (police officer), Wataru Omae, Hirofumi Kimura, Nobutake Saito, and Sadao Watanabe (alien subordinates), Haruo Nakajima (Godzilla), Yukihiro Omiya (Angilas), Kanta Ina (King Ghidorah), Kengo Nakayama (Gigan).

CREDITS

Producer: Tomoyuki Tanaka. Director: Jun Fukuda. Screenplay: Shinichi Sekizawa. Music: Akira Ifukube. "Godzilla March," lyrics by Shinichi Sekizawa and Jun Fukuda, music by Tetsuaki Hagiwara, sung by Susumu Ishikawa, released by Toho Records. Director of Photography: Kiyoshi Hasegawa. Lighting: Kojiro Sato. Art Director: Yoshifumi Honda. Film Editor: Yoshio Tamura. Sound Recording: Fumio Yanoguchi. Foley: Toho Foley Group. Audio: Toho Recording Center. Production Manager: Takahide Morichi. Assistant Director: Fumisuke Okada. Developing: Tokyo Laboratory.

Director: Teruyoshi Nakano. Director of Photography: Mototaka Tomioka. Operations: Fumio Nakadai. Optical Photography: Yoshiyuki Tokumasa. Art Director: Toshiro Aoki. Optical Processing: Saburo Doi.

GODZILLA vs. MEGALON (1973)

CAST

Katsuhiko Sasaki (Goro Ibuki), Hiroyuki Kawase (Rokuro, Goro's little brother), Yutaka Hayashi (Hiroshi Jingawa, Goro's buddy), Kotaro Tomita (Seatopian agent in black), Wolf Ohtsuke (Seatopian agent in gray), Robert Dunham (Antonio, King of Seatopia), Gen Nakajima (truck driver), Sakyo Mikami (truck driver's assistant), Kanta Mori (Japanese Self Defense Force commander), Rolf Jessup (Seatopian communications officer), Eisuke Nakanishi (nuclear testing staff), Shinji Takagi (Godzilla), Hideto Date (Megalon), Kengo Nakayama (Gigan), Tsugutoshi Komada (Jet Jaguar).

CREDITS

Producer: Tomoyuki Tanaka. Director: Jun Fukuda. Original Story: Shinichi Sekizawa. Screenplay: Jun Fukuda. Music: Riichiro Manabe. Theme song, *"Gojira to Jagger de Punch Punch Punch"* ("Godzilla and Jaguar Punch-Punch-Punch"), lyrics by Shinichi Sekizawa, music by Riichiro Manabe, sung by Masato Shimon, released by Toho Records. Director of Photography: Yuzuru Aizawa. Lighting: Masakuni Morimoto. Art Director: Yoshifumi Honda. Film Editor: Michiko Ikeda. Sound Recording: Teishiro Haysahi. Foley: Toho Foley Group. Unit Production Manager: Keisuke Shinoda. Assistant Director: Tsunesaburo Nishikawa. Film Processing: Tokyo Laboratory.

SPECIAL EFFECTS

Director: Teruyoshi Nakano. Director of Photography: Mototaka Tomioka. Art Director: Toshio Aoki. Optical Photography: Takeshi Miyanishi. Operations: Shoji Ogawa. Optical Processing: Kazunobu Sanbin.

GODZILLA vs. THE COSMIC MONSTER
a.k.a. GODZILLA vs. MECHAGODZILLA (1974)

CAST

Masaaki Daimon (Keisuke Shimizu), Kazuya Aoyama (Masahiko Shimizu), Reiko Tajima (Saeko Kanashiro), Berbera Lynn (Naomi Kokto), Masao Imafuku (Izumi priest Tengan Kokto), Hiromi Matsushita (Iko Miyajima), Akihiko Hirata (Dr. Hideto Miyajima), Hiroshi Koizumi (Professor Wagura), Goro Mutsu (Kuronuma, captain of alien forces), Shin Kishida (Interpol Agent Nanbara), Daigoku Sano (Yanagawa), Hiroyasu Tori (Interpol Agent Kamura), Kenji Sahara (ship captain), Yasuzo Ogawa (field inspector), Takmitsu Watanabe (alien), Isao Zushi (Godzilla), Kazunari Mori (MechaGodzilla), Satoru Kuzumi (Angilas and King Seesar).

CREDITS

Producer: Tomoyuki Tanaka. Director: Jun Fukuda. Original Story: Shinichi Sekizawa, Masami Fukushima. Screenplay: Jun Fukuda, Hiroyasu Yamaura. Music: Masaru Sato. "Miyarabi's Prayer" ("*Miyarabi no Inori*"), lyrics by Jun Fukuda, music by Masaru Sato, sung by Berbera Lynn. Director of Photography: Yuzuru Aizawa. Lighting: Masakuni Morimoto. Art Director: Kazuo Satsuya. Film Editor: Michiko Ikeda. Sound Recordist: Fumio Yanoguchi. Foley: Toho Foley Group. Audio Technician: Toho Recording Center. Associate Producer: Keisuke Shinoda. Assistant Director: Tsunesaburo Nishikawa. Film Processing: Tokyo Laboratory. Special thanks to Nippon Highspeed Ferry, All Nippon Airways, Okinawa Prefecture, Gyokusen Cave, Shokkoku Yusen Ship Lines.

SPECIAL EFFECTS

Director: Teruyoshi Nakano. Directors of Photography: Mototaka Tomioka, Takeshi Yamamoto. Art Directors: Toshio Aoki, Kan Komura. Optical Processing: Kazunobu Sanbin. Optical Photography: Takeshi Miyanishi. Matte Paintings: Tadashi Kawana. Operations: Shoji Ogawa.

TERROR OF MECHAGODZILLA (1975) a.k.a. THE TERROR OF GODZILLA

CAST

Katsuhiko Sasaki (Akira Ichinose), Tomoko Ai (Katsura Mafune), Akihiko Hirata (Dr. Shinzo Mafune), Tadao Nakamaru (Interpol Chief Tagawa), Goro Mutsu (Captain Mugar [English-language version: "Mugan"], leader of alien invasion), Katsumasa Uchida (Jiro Murakoshi), Tomoe Mari (Yuri Yamamoto), Toru Ibuki (Tsuda, Mugan's right-hand man), Mokoto Roppongi (Yuichi Wakayama), Kotaro Tomita (Mr. Ota), Ikio Sawamura (Mafune's elderly servant), Kenji Sahara (Japanese Self Defense Force commander), Masaaki Daimon (Interpol Agent Kusugari), Akinori Umezu (boy in city), Kazuo Suzuki, Yoshio Kirishima, Masata Kakiguchi, Takuya Yuki and Jun Nishihara (aliens), Toru Kawai (Godzilla), Kazunari Mori (MechaGodzilla 2); Tatsumi Fuyamoto (Titanosaurus).

CREDITS

Producer: Tomoyuki Tanaka. Director: Ishiro Honda. Screenplay: Yukiko Takayama. Music: Akira Ifukube. Director of Photography: Mototaka Tomioka. Lighting: Toshio Takashima. Art Director: Yoshibumi Honda. Film Editor: Yoshitami Kuroiwa. Sound Recording: Fumio Yanoguchi. Foley: Toho Foley Group. Audio: Toho Recording Center. Assistant Director: Kensho Yamashita. Associate Producer: Keisuke Shinoda. Assistant Producer: Kenji Tokoro. Film Processing: Tokyo Laboratory.

SPECIAL EFFECTS

Director: Teruyoshi Nakano. Art Directors: Toshiro Aoki, Kan Komura. Optical Processing: Kazunobu Sanbin. Assistant Director: Yoshio Tabuchi. Optical Photography: Yoshikazu

Manoda. Matte Paintings: Yoshio Ishii. Operations: Koji Matsumoto. Technician: Tadaaki Watanabe.

U.S. VERSION CREDITS:

Released by The MechaGodzilla Company. Special Material: UPA Productions of America. Production Supervisor: S. Richard Krown. Opening Montage: Richard Bansbach, Michael McCann. Sound: Quality Sound Company. Titles: Freeze Frame.

GODZILLA (1984) a.k.a. GODZILLA 1985 (1985)

CAST

Keiju Kobayashi (Prime Minister Mitamura), Ken Tanaka (Goro Maki), Yasuko Sawaguchi (Naoko Okumura), Shin Takuma (Hiroshi [U.S. version: "Ken"] Okumura), Tetsuya Takeda (bum), Yosuke Natsuke (Professor Hayashida), Hiroshi Koizumi (Dr. Minami), Taketoshi Naito (cabinet secretary Takegami), Itaro Ozawa (finance minister), Mizuho Suzuki (foreign minister), Junkichi Orimoto (Defense Agency Chief Mohri), Shinsuke Mikimoto (chief of staff Kakurai), Mikita Mori (National Land Agency Chief Ohkochi), Nobuo Kaneko (Home Affairs Minister Isomura), Kiyoshi Yamamoto (Director of Science and Technology Kajita), Takeshi Kato (Internal Trade and Industry Minister Kasaoka), Yoshibumi Tajima (Director General of the Environment Hidaka), Yasuhiko Kohno (Maritime Forces Chief of Staff Kishimoto), Eiji Kanai (Ground Forces Chief of Staff Imafuji), Isao Hirano (Air Force Chief of Staff Kiyohara), Kenichi Urata (Ishimaru), Kei Sato (Gondo), Kunio Murai (Henmi), Takenori Emoto (Kitagawa), Takeo Morimoto (newscaster), Takashi Ebata (Yahata Maru captain), Shigeo Katoh and Sennosuke Tahara (Yahata Maru crewmen), Shinpei Hayashiya (cameraman), Hiroshi Kamayatsu (bullet train passenger), Kohji Ishizaka (power plant employee), Alexander Kailis (Soviet Ambassador Chevsky), Walter Nicholas (U.S. Ambassador Rosenberg), Luke Johnson (Captain Kathren), Kenpachiro Satsuma (Godzilla).

CREDITS

Executive Producer: Tomoyuki Tanaka. Assistant Producer: Fumio Tanaka. Director: Koji Hashimoto. Original story: Tomoyuki Tanaka. Screenplay: Shuichi Nagahara. Music: Reijiro Koroku, performed by the Tokyo Symphony Orchestra, conducted by Katsuaki Nakaya, published by Toho Music Publishing Co., Ltd. "Godzilla," lyrics by Linda Henrick, composed by Reijiro Koroku, sung by the Star Sisters. Director of Photography: Kazutami Hara. Lighting: Shinji Kojima. Production Designer: Akira Sakuragi. Film Editor: Yoshitami Kuroiwa. Sound Recording Mixer: Noboyuki Tanaka. Assistant Director: Takao Okawara. Production Manager: Takahide Morichi. Special advisors: Hitoshi Takeuchi (Professor Emeritus, Tokyo University), Hideo Aoki (military consultant), Yorihiko Ohsaki (doctor of engineering), Klein Uberstein (science-fiction writer), Sohichiro Tahara (journalist).

SPECIAL EFFECTS

Director: Teruyoshi Nakano. Directors of Photography: Toshimitsu Oneda, Takeshi Yamamoto. Lighting: Kohei Mikami. Production Design: Yasuyuki Inoue. Miniature Pyrotechnics: Tadaaki Watanabe, Mamoru Kume. Godzilla Suits: Noboyuki Yasumaru. Wire Works: Kohji Matsumoto, Mitsuo Miyakawa. Matte Photography: Takeaki Tsukuda, Yoshio Ishii. Optical

Photography: Takeshi Miyanishi, Yoshizaku Manoda. Assistant Director: Eichi Asada. Production Manager: Masayuki Ikeda.

U.S. VERSION CREDITS:

Cast: Raymond Burr (Steven Martin), Warren Kemmerling (General Goodhue), Jame Hess (Colonel Raschen), Travis Swords (Major McDonough), Crawford Binion (Lieutenant), Justin Gocke (Kyle), Bobby Brown, Patrick Feren, Mark Sino, Shepard Stern, and Alan D. Waserman (extras). Producer: Anthony Randel. Director: R.J. Kizer. Screenplay: Lisa Tomei. Film Editor: Michael Spence. Photography: Steven Dubin. Assistant Director: Lee S. Berger. Postproduction Coordinator: James Melkonian. Postproduction Sound Services: Ryder Sound, Inc. Sound Director: Leo Chaloukian. Re-recording Mixers: John "Doc" Wilkinson, Charles "Bud" Grenzbach, Joseph Citarella. Additional Music: Chris Young, copyright 1985 New World Pictures. Additional Optical Effects: Ray Mercer & Co. Special thanks to the Dr. Pepper Bottling Co., Inc. Prints by Technicolor.

GODZILLA vs. BIOLLANTE (1989)

CAST

Kuniko Mitamura (Kazuhito Kirishima), Yoshiko Tanaka (Asuka Okochi), Masanobu Takashima (Major Sho Kuroki), Megumi Odaka (Miki Saegusa), Toru Minegishi (Lieutenant Goro Gondo), Ryunosuke Kaneda (Mr. Seido Okochi), Koji Takahashi (Dr. Genichiro Shiragami), Yasuko Sawaguchi (Erica Shiragami), Toshiyuki Nagashima (Director of Technical Division Seiichi Yamamoto), Yoshiko Kuga (Chief Cabinet Secretary Keiko Owada), Manjhat Beti (Saradian Agent SSS9), Koichi Ueda (Japanese Self Defense Force Chairman Yamaji), Isao Toyohara and Kyoka Suzuki (Super-X2 operators), Kenji Hunt (John Lee), Derrick Holmes (Michael Low), Hirohisa Nakata (Director General of Defense Agency Koyama), Katsuhiko Sasaki (Director of Science Technology Takeda), Kenzo Hagiwara (Ground Forces staff officer), Kazuyuki Senba (Maritime officer), Koji Yamanaka (air force officer), Iden Yamanrahl (Abdul Saulman), Hiroshi Inoue, Kazuma Matsubara, Ryota Yoshimitsu, Tetsu Kawai, and Yasunori Yumiya (JSDF officials), Shin Tatsuma (Director of Giant Plant Observation Akiyama), Shu Minagawa, Kazuma Matsuoka, and Shoichiro Sakata (operations room staff members), Mehedijadi Soleiman (Sirhan), Abudula Herahl (researcher), Curtis Kramer, Brian Wool, and Robert Conner (commandos), Beth Blatt (CCN newscaster Susan Horn), Demon Kogure (himself), Isao Takeno (Super-X2 repair crew chief), Kenpachiro Satsuma, Shigreu Shibazaki, and Yoshitaka Kimura (Godzilla), Masao Takegami (Biollante).

CREDITS

Executive Producer: Tomoyuki Tanaka. Associate Producer: Shogo Tomiyama. Director and Screenplay: Kazuki Omori. Original Story: Shinichiro Kobayashi. Director of Photography: Yudai Kato. Production Designer: Shigekazu Ikuno. Lighting: Takeshi Awakibara. Film Editor: Michiko Ikeda. Recording Mixer: Kazuo Miyauchi. Music: Koichi Sugiyama. Music Arrangement: David Howell. Godzilla Theme Music: Akira Ifukube.

SPECIAL EFFECTS

Director: Koichi Kawakita. Director of Photography: Kenichi Eguchi. Art Directors: Tetsuzo Osawa, Takashi Naganoma. Lighting: Kaoru Saito. Monster Suits: Noboyuki Yasumaru, Fuyuki Shinada. Wire Works: Koji Matsumoto. Pyrotechnics: Tadaaki Watanabe, Mamoru Kumi.

GODZILLA vs. KING GHIDORAH (1991)

CAST

Anna Nakagawa (Emi Kano), Isao Toyohara (Kenichiro Terasawa), Megumi Odaka (Miki Saegusa), Kiwako Harada (Chiaki Morimura), Katsuhiko Sasaki (Dr. Hironori Masaaki), Yoshio Tsuchiya (Yasuaki Shindo), Shoji Kobayashi (Yuzo Dobashi), Kenji Sahara (Prime Minister), Chuck Wilson (Wilson), Tokuma Nishioka (Takehiko Fujio), Richard Berger (Gurenchiko), Robert Scottfield (Android M-11), Kent Gilbert (U.S. Navy commander), Daniel Kahl (Major Spielberg), Koichi Ueda (Ikehata), Wataru Fukuda (Godzillasaurus), Hurricane Ryu (King Ghidorah), Kenpachiro Satsuma (Godzilla).

CREDITS

Executive Producer: Tomoyuki Tanaka. Producer: Shogo Tomiyama. Director and Screenplay: Kazuki Omori. Music: Akira Ifukube, conducted by Satoshi Imai. Director of Photography: Yoshinoru Sakiguchi. Lighting: Tsuyoshi Awakihara. Art Director: Ken Sakai. Film Editor: Michiko Ideda. Sound Recording: Katsuo Miyahara. Sound: Toho Recording Center. Dolby Stereo Consultant: Mikio Mori.

SPECIAL EFFECTS

Director: Koichi Kawakita. Directors of Photography: Kenichi Eguchi, Toshimitsu Oneda. Art Director: Tetsuzo Osawa. Lighting: Kaoru Saito. Pyrotechnics: Tadaaki Watanabe. Wire Works: Koji Matsumoto. Sculpting: Tomoki Kobayashi. Assistant Director: Kenji Suzuki.

GODZILLA vs. MOTHRA
a.k.a. GODZILLA AND MOTHRA: THE BATTLE FOR EARTH (1992)

CAST

Tetsuya Bessho (Takuya Fujita), Satomi Kobayashi (Masako Tezuka), Takehiro Murata (Kenji Ando), Megumi Odaka (Miki Saegusa), Shiori Yonezawa (Midori Tezuka), Makoto Otake (Takeshi Tomokane), Shoji Kobayashi (Ryuzo Dobashi), Koichi Ueda (Minoru Omae), Shinya Owada (ship captain), Keiko Imamura and Sayaka Osawa (the Cosmos), Saburo Shinoda (Shigeki Fukazawa), Akira Takarada (Environmental Planning Board head Jyoji Minamino), Hurricane Ryu (Battra), Kenpachiro Satsuma (Godzilla).

CREDITS

Executive Producer: Tomoyuki Tanaka. Producer: Shogo Tomiyama. Director: Takao Okawara. Screenplay: Kazuki Omori. Music: Akira Ifukube. Director of Photography: Masahiro Kishimoto. Lighting: Hidechi Mochizuki. Art Director: Ken Sakai. Film Editor: Miho Yoneda. Sound Recording: Teiichi Saito. Assistant Director: Kunio Miyoshi. Production Heads: Yoshihide Moritomo, Koji Maeda.

SPECIAL EFFECTS

Director: Koichi Kawakita. Director of Photography: Kenichi Eguchi. Art Director: Tetsuzo Ozawa. Lighting: Kaoru Saito. Wire Works: Koji Matsumoto. Pyrotechnics: Tadaaki Watanabe. Assistant Director: Kenji Suzuki. Production Head: Taro Kojima.

GODZILLA vs. MECHAGODZILLA
a.k.a.
GODZILLA vs. MECHAGODZILLA II (1993)

CAST

Masahiro Takashima (Kazuma Aoki), Ryoko Sano (Azusa Gojo), Megumi Odaka (Miki Saegusa), Daijiro Harada (Takuya Sasaki), Ichirota Miyagawa (Jun Sonezaki), Kenji Sahara (G-Force Chief Takayuki Segawa), Lasalle Ishii (Kunio Katsuragi), Tadao Takashima (Mind Institute Head Mr. Hosono), Akira Nakao (Commander Aso), Yusuke Kawazu (Professor Omae), Leo Mangetti (Dr. Asimov), Keiko Imamura and Sayaka Osawa (psychic school-teachers), Wataru Fukuda (MechaGodzilla), Hurricane Ryu (Baby Godzilla), Kenpachiro Satsuma (Godzilla).

CREDITS

Executive Producer: Tomoyuki Tanaka. Producer: Shogo Tomiyama. Director: Takao Okawara. Screenplay: Wataru Mimura. Music: Akira Ifukube. Director of Photography: Yoshinori Sekiguchi. Lighting: Hideki Mochizuki. Art Director: Ken Sakai. Film Editor: Miho Yoneda. Sound Recording: Kazuo Miyauchi. Assistant Director: Kunio Miyoshi. Production Head: Koji Maeda.

SPECIAL EFFECTS

Director: Koichi Kawakita. Director of Photography: Kenichi Eguchi. Lighting: Kaoru Saito. Art Director: Tetsuzo Ozawa. Puppetry: Yutaku Suzuki. Special Effects: Tadaaki Watanabe. Assistant Director: Kenji Suzuki. Production Head: Taro Kojima.

GODZILLA vs. SPACE GODZILLA (1994)

CAST

Jun Hashizume (Koji Shinjo), Megumi Odaka (Miki Saegusa), Zenkichi Yoneyama (Kiyoshi Sato), Towako Yoshikawa (Chinatsu Gondo), Akira Emoto (Akira Yuuki), Yosuke Saito (Susumu Okubo), Keiko Imamura and Sayaka Osawa (the Cosmos), Kenji Sahara (G-Force Director Takayuki Segawa), Akira Nakao (Commander Takaki Aso), Koichi Ueda (Deputy Commander Iwao Hyodo), Ed Sardi (Eric Gould), Ronald Hea (Professor Alexander Mammilov), Tom Duran (McKay, the mafia boss), Little Frankie (Little Godzilla), Wataru Fukuda (MOGERA), Ryo Hariya (Space Godzilla), Kenpachiro Satsuma (Godzilla).

Executive Producer: Tomoyuki Tanaka. Producer: Shogo Tomiyama. Director: Kensho Yamashita. Screenplay: Hiroshi Kashiwabara. Director of Photography: Masahiro Kishimoto. Music: Takayuki Hattori. "Echoes of Love," performed by Date of Birth. Special Effects Director: Koichi Kawakita. SFX Photography: Kenichi Eguchi.

GODZILLA vs. DESTOROYAH (1995)
a.k.a. GODZILLA vs. DESTROYER

CAST

Tatsumi Takuro (Dr. Ijuin), Yoko Ishino (Yukari Yamane), Yasufumi Hayashi (Kenkichi Yamane), Megumi Odaka (Miki Saegusa), Momoko Kochi (Emiko Yamane), Akira Nakao (General Takaki Aso), Masahiro Takashima (Sho Kuroki), Sayaka Osawa (Meru Ozawa), Koichi Ueda (night watchman at aquarium), Ronald Hea (Professor Marvin), Takehiro Murata (Yukari's editor), Hariken Ryu (Godzilla Junior), Ryo Hariya (Destroyer), Kenpachiro Satsuma (Godzilla).

CREDITS

Executive Producer: Tomoyuki Tanaka. Producer: Shogo Tomiyama. Director: Takao Okawara. Screenplay: Kazuki Omori. Music: Akira Ifukube. Special Effects Director: Koichi Kawakita. SFX Photography: Kenichi Eguchi.

GODZILLA (1998)

CAST

Matthew Broderick (Dr. Niko Tatopoulos), Jean Reno (Philippe Roache), Maria Pitillo (Audrey Timmonds), Hank Azaria (Victor "Animal" Palotti), Kevin Dunn (Col. Hicks), Michael Lerner (Mayor Ebert), Harry Shearer (Charles Caiman), Arabella Field (Lucy), Vicki Lewis (Dr. Elsie Chapman), Doug Savant (Sgt. O'Neal), Malcolm Danare (Dr. Mendel Craven), Lorry Goldman (Gene), Christian Aubert (Jean-Luc), Philippe Bergeron (Jean-Claude), Frank Bruynbroek (Jean-Pierre), Francois Giroday (Jean-Philippe).

CREDITS

Producer: Dean Devlin. Executive Producers: Roland Emmerich, Ute Emmerich, William Fay. Co-Executive Producers: Robert N. Fried, Cary Woods. Co-Producers: Peter Winther, Kelly Van Horn. Director: Roland Emmerich. Screenplay: Roland Emmerich And Dean Devlin. Story: Terry Rossio And Ted Elliott, Dean Devlin And Roland Emmerich. Director Of Photography: Ueli Steiger. Editors: Peter Amundson, David J. Siegel. Music: David Arnold. Production Designer: Oliver Scholl. Supervising Art Director: William Ladd Skinner. Art Director: Robert Woodruff. Set Decorator: Victor Zolfo. Costume Designer: Joseph Porro. Sound: Jose Antonio Garcia. Creature Designer And Supervisor: Patrick Tatopoulos. Visual-Effects Supervisor: Volker Engel. Assistant Director: Kim Winther. Second Unit Director: Josef Rusnak. Second Unit Camera: Peter Joachim Krause. Stunt Coordinator: R.A. Rondell. Casting: April Webster, David Bloch.

Appendix II

GODZILLA ON VIDEO

The following list covers all Godzilla movies available on home video in the U.S. as of 1998, plus information on selected out-of-print videos. All videos are in pan-and-scan (full-frame) format unless noted otherwise.

Godzilla: King of The Monsters!
Simitar Entertainment (DVD, ep or sp VHS tape). Previously available from Paramount Gateway Home Video (LD, ep VHS tape), Vestron Video (LD, sp VHS tape) and Goodtimes Home Video (ep VHS tape).

Gigantis: The Fire Monster
a.k.a. Godzilla Raids Again
Not currently available. Previously available from Video Treasures (ep or lp VHS tape).

King Kong vs. Godzilla
Goodtimes Home Video (DVD, ep VHS tape).

Godzilla vs. The Thing
a.k.a. Godzilla vs. Mothra
Simitar Entertainment (pan-and-scan/widescreen DVD, pan-and-scan ep or sp VHS tape, widescreen sp VHS tape). Previously available from Paramount Gateway Home Video (LD, ep VHS tape) and Paramount Home Video (sp VHS tape).

Ghidrah: The Three-Headed Monster
Anchor Bay Entertainment (ep VHS tape; sp edition available by special-order). Previously available from Video Treasures (lp VHS tape). Unlicensed, inferior quality videotapes of this film have been issued by several distributors.

Monster Zero
a.k.a. Godzilla vs. Monster Zero
Simitar Entertainment (pan-and-scan/widescreen DVD, pan-and-scan ep or sp VHS tape, widescreen sp VHS tape). Previously available from Paramount Gateway Home Video (LD, ep VHS tape) and Paramount Home Video (sp VHS tape).

Godzilla versus The Sea Monster
Goodtimes Home Video (ep VHS tape). Previously available from Video Treasures (lp VHS tape). Unlicensed, inferior quality videotapes of this film have been issued by several distributors.

Son of Godzilla
Anchor Bay Entertainment (ep VHS tape; sp edition available by special-order). Previously available from Video Treasures (lp VHS tape). Unlicensed, inferior quality videotapes of this film have been issued by several distributors.

Destroy All Monsters

ADV Films (widescreen sp VHS tape). Note: This is the "international" English-dubbed version, which is different from the original U.S. version distributed by American International Pictures. The AIP version has never been officially released on home video, although "bootleg" tapes abound.

Godzilla's Revenge

Simitar Entertainment (pan-and-scan/widescreen DVD, pan-and-scan ep or sp VHS tape, widescreen sp VHS tape). Previously available from Paramount Gateway Home Video (LD, ep VHS tape).

Godzilla vs. The Smog Monster
a.k.a. Godzilla vs. Hedorah

Not currently available. Previously available from Orion Home Video (double LD with *Monster from a Prehistoric Planet*, sp VHS tape) and Simitar Entertainment (ep VHS tape).

Godzilla On Monster Island
a.k.a. Godzilla vs. Gigan

Anchor Bay Entertainment as *Godzilla vs. Gigan* (ep VHS tape; sp edition available by special-order). Previously available from New World Video (double LD with *Godzilla vs. MechaGodzilla*, sp VHS tape). Note: This is the "international" English-dubbed version. Unlicensed videotapes of *Godzilla on Monster Island* have been issued by several distributors.

Godzilla vs. Megalon

Anchor Bay Entertainment (ep VHS tape; sp edition available by special-order). Unlicensed videotapes of this film have been issued by numerous distributors; most U.S. video releases, licensed or unlicensed, are of poor image quality.

Godzilla vs. The Cosmic Monster
a.k.a. Godzilla vs. MechaGodzilla

Anchor Bay Entertainment as *Godzilla vs. Mecha-Godzilla* (ep VHS tape; sp edition available by special-order). Previously available from New World Video (double LD with *Godzilla vs. Gigan*, sp VHS tape). Note: This is the "international" English-dubbed version. Unlicensed videotapes of *Godzilla vs. The Cosmic Monster* have been issued by several distributors.

Terror of MechaGodzilla

Simitar Entertainment (DVD, ep or sp VHS tape). Previously available from Paramount Gateway Home Video (LD, ep VHS tape) and Paramount Home Video (sp VHS tape). Note: All videos utilize the edited version released to theaters in 1978, originally titled *The Terror of Godzilla*. A more complete version was syndicated to television through the mid-1980's (see Chapter 15) but has never been issued on home video.

Godzilla 1985

Anchor Bay Entertainment (ep VHS tape; sp edition available by special-order). Previously available from New World Video (LD, sp VHS tape).

Godzilla vs. Biollante

HBO Video (widescreen LD and sp VHS tape).

Godzilla vs. King Ghidorah

Columbia TriStar Home Video (double DVD with *Godzilla and Mothra: The Battle for Earth*, ep VHS tape).

Godzilla and Mothra
a.k.a. Godzilla vs. Mothra: The Battle for Earth

Columbia TriStar Home Video (double DVD with *Godzilla vs. King Ghidorah*, ep VHS tape).

Godzilla vs. Space Godzilla (1999)

Columbia TriStar Home Video (ep VHS tape)

Godzilla vs. Destoroyah
a.k.a. Godzilla vs. Destroyer (1999)

Columbia TriStar Home Video (ep VHS tape)

Godzilla (1998)

Columbia TriStar Home Video (widescreen or pan-and-scan DVD, LD and sp VHS tape).

BOXED SETS

Several video distributors have packaged different Godzilla videotapes together and sold them as boxed sets. In 1998, Simitar Entertainment released a set containing *Godzilla: King of the Monsters!*, *Godzilla vs. Mothra*, *Godzilla vs. Monster Zero*, *Godzilla's Revenge* and *Terror of MechaGodzilla* (all in pan-and-scan format, in ep or sp mode); another containing *Godzilla vs. Mothra*, *Godzilla vs. Monster Zero* and *Godzilla's Revenge* (all in widescreen format, sp mode) and another containing *Godzilla: King of The Monsters!* and *Terror of MechaGodzilla* plus a third tape featuring movie clips and stills.

Other boxed sets and twin-packs containing different Godzilla movies, in various combinations, have been released by Anchor Bay Entertainment, Starmaker Video, and Goodtimes Home Video.

JAPANESE VERSIONS

The original, uncut Japanese versions of all 22 Godzilla movies, from *Godzilla* (1954) to *Godzilla vs.*

Destoroyah (1995) are available on VHS videotape and LD from Toho Video in Japan. In addition, all films from *Godzilla vs. Biollante* to *Destoroyah* were issued in collector's edition LD boxed sets in CAV format, each with a bonus disc featuring behind-the-scenes footage. LD boxed sets featuring both the Japanese and U.S. versions of *Godzilla* (1954) and *Godzilla vs. The Thing*, and an eight-disc boxed set featuring the edited-down "Champion Festival" versions of seven Godzilla films and *Mothra* (1961) have also been issued. The U.S. versions of *Godzilla: King of The Monsters!* And *Godzilla 1985* have been released on VHS tape in Japan as well. Toho Video products are available outside Japan by import only and can be special-ordered from some video and LD retailers.

Appendix III

Cyberspace Godzilla

*Selected resources for Godzilla
information and news on the Internet*

Barry's Temple of Godzilla
http://www.stomptokyo.com/godzillatemple

Godzilla.Com — official web site for *Godzilla* (1998)
http://www.godzilla.com

Godzilla News
http://www.monsterzero.org

Goji-World
http://www.inteleco.com/gojiworld/index/html

Kaiju-Direct — an exhaustive list with URL's for hundreds of web sites, with links
http://www2.arkansas.net/~gsraptor/godzilla.html

Conster's Museum of Godzilla
http://members.xoom.com/Conster74/welcome.html

Godzilla FAQ by Chia-Ning Kao
http://www.stomptokyo.com/godzillatemple/godfaq.htm

Sentai/Kaiju/Tokusatsu (Steve's Link Universe)
http://www.otaking.com/otaking/links/LnkSentai.html

The World of Godzilla: Online Encyclopedia of the King of the Monsters
http://ultdownload.digiweb.com/Godzilla/The_World_of_Godzilla.html

Godzilla 98 Websites (Extinctions Fossil Company)
http://www.extinctions.com/sites/movies/godzilla/godzilla.htm

Appendix IV

ENDNOTES

1 Tomoyuki Tanaka's quote is taken from an article in the January 14, 1985 issue of *People* magazine. The entire account of the making of *Godzilla* in Chapter 1 is synthesized from many sources, principally *Testimony: Birth of Godzilla, The Complete History of Toho Special Effects Movies, Eiji Tsuburaya's World of Images, Toho SF Special Effects Movie Series Vol. 3,* and *The Visual Guide Book of First Godzilla.*

2 Information on Japanese movies about the Bomb is taken from "Japan: An Ambivalent Nation, An Ambivalent Cinema" by David Desser, *Currents in Japanese Cinema* by Tadao Sato, and other sources.

3 This account of the Lucky Dragon accident is based upon information in *The Fifties* by David Halberstam and other sources.

4 Takeo Murata's quotation is taken from an interview published in *Toho SF Special Effects Movie Series Vol. 3.*

5 This account of the birth of Toho Studios is based upon information in *Mr. Smith Goes to Tokyo* by Kyoko Hirano and *The Japanese Film* by Anderson and Richie, and other sources.

6 This information is from *The Illustrated Encyclopedia of Godzilla* by Godziszewski.

7 Akira Takarada's quotation is taken from an interview published in *Toho SF Special Effects Movie Series Vol. 7: Godzilla vs. Mothra.*

8 Biographical information on Tomoyuki Tanaka is derived from his bio in *The Complete History of Toho Special Effects Movies* and other sources.

9 Biographical information on Ishiro Honda is derived from his bio in *The Complete History of Toho Special Effects Movies* and other sources.

10 Eiji Tsuburaya's quotation is taken from a February 2, 1961 *Associated Press* article by syndicated columnist Bob Thomas.

11 Information on Eiji Tsuburaya's early special effects career is taken from "A Walk Through the Monster Films of the Past" by Hiroshi Takeuchi, published in *Markalite #1, Eiji Tsuburaya's World of Images,* and other sources.

12 Teisho Arikawa's quotation is taken from his essay in the book *Godzilla Days.*

13 Quotations from the dialogue of *Gigantis* and the spelling "Anguillasaurus" are taken from a copy of the English-language dubbing script for *Gigantis: The Fire Monster,* on file at the Warner Bros. Archive in Los Angeles, CA.

14 This information is according to documents on file at the Warner Bros. Archive in Los Angeles, CA. Acknowledgments to Stuart Galbraith IV.

15 These figures are from the Japanese version; the figures for the egg's price in the U.S. version are different.

16 Godzilla's trembling lip in *Godzilla Vs. The Thing* is the result of an accident. Mid-way through filming, the problem was fixed and the lip no longer quivered. This discrepancy has led to rumors that two *Mosu-Goji* costumes were constructed, one with a moving lip and one without.

17 In the Japanese version of the film, when Mothra leaves to fight Ghidorah alone, it appears that Godzilla and Rodan are "talking" to Mothra, with human voices super-imposed over their monster roars. Upon careful review, it becomes clear that the monsters are *not* talking; the voices heard are those of the human cast, calling from a hillside for Rodan and Godzilla to join the fight.

18 This information is taken from an interview with Henry Saperstein by Stuart Galbraith IV, published in *Filmfax #45*.

19 In the Japanese version of *Monster Zero*, the story is set in the future. A title card at the beginning of the film says the action takes place in the year "198X." Thus, it can be assumed that all the Godzilla movies 1966–75 occurred before *Monster Zero*, except for *Destroy All Monsters* (set in 1999) and *Godzilla's Revenge* (a boy's dream). Whew!

20 Teisho Arikawa's quote is taken from the book *Godzilla Days*.

21 Saperstein announced the film in the trade papers in 1966 as *Invasion Of The Astros* (not *Invasion Of The Astro-Monsters*, which is the title of Toho's "international" version). Evidence suggests Saperstein originally planned to release the picture with this title (35-millimeter theatrical film prints were made, and posters were printed — both of which have made their way into the hands of latter-day collectors).

22 For an exhaustive comparison of the editing changes to *Monster Zero* and *Invasion Of The Astro-Monsters*, see "Godzilla in America" in *G-Fan #13*.

23 This information on the dubbing of *The Killing Bottle* is taken from on interview with Peter Fernandez, conducted by the author.

24 Biographical information on Jun Fukuda's career is taken from his bio in *The Complete History of Toho Special Effects Movies*, and other sources.

25 Teisho Arikawa's quotation is taken from his essay in *The Complete History of Toho Special Effects Movies*. Biographical information about Arikawa in this chapter is taken from this essay, plus his biography in the same book, his essay in *Godzilla Days*, and other sources.

26 Although Toho's theatrical trailer and publicity materials for *Son of Godzilla* give "Minira" as the name of Godzilla's son, the creature is referred to simply as "baby Godzilla" in the film.

27 What these numbers do not show is that the types of films being made in Japan during the 1970s had changed drastically. Sex and violence were accentuated as the studios attempted to lure back viewers who had defected to TV.

28 This information from *The Japanese: Portrait of a Nation*, by Peter Tasker.

29 This information is according to *The Illustrated Encyclopedia of Godzilla* by Godziszewski.

30 Information the origins of Jet Jaguar's design is taken from *The Complete History of Toho Special Effects Movies*.

31 Acknowledgments to articles published in *Markalite*, *Sentai* and *Oriental Cinema* for translations of *Zone Fighter* episode titles.

32 This information is according to an interview with Yukiko Takayama by David Milner in *Cult Movies #12*.

33 In an interview published in *Toho SF Special Effects Movie Series Vol. 1: Godzilla (1984)*, Hashimoto said he has worked on several kaiju movies, but did not name the films.

34 This information on the special-effects shoot is taken from the press kit for *Godzilla 1985*.

35 Most of the information on the making of *Godzilla vs. Biollante* in Chapter 17 is taken from articles in *Japanese Giants #8*, *Markalite #1*, and various issues of *Cult Movies*, as well as the making-of disc included in Toho Video's *Godzilla vs. Biollante* Laser Disc boxed set.

36 Kazuki Omori's quotation is taken from an interview published in *Markalite #1*.

37 Dr. Shiragami's disgust with restrictions on scientific research in Japan is a timely topic. As of the late 1980s, Japan had only won three Nobel Prizes for science; the most recent was awarded in 1987 to a scientist who was forced to leave Japan and conduct his research in immunology in the U.S.

Appendix V

SELECTED
BIBLIOGRAPHY

Books

Anderson, Joseph L., and Donald Richie. *The Japanese Film*. New York: Grove Press, 1960.

Barrell, Tony, and Rick Tanaka. *Higher Than Heaven: Japan, War and Everything*. Australia: Private Guy International, 1995.

Baxter, John. *Science Fiction in the Cinema*. New York: Paperback Library, 1970.

Bock, Audie. *Japanese Film Directors*. New York: Kodansha International, 1978.

Brosnan, John. *Movie Magic: The Story of Special Effects in the Movies*. New York: New American Library, 1974.

Clarens, Carlos. *An Illustrated History of the Horror Film*. New York: Capricorn Books, 1967.

Galbraith, Stuart, IV. *Japanese Science Fiction, Fantasy and Horror Films*. North Carolina: McFarland, 1993.

Galbraith, Stuart, IV. *The Japanese Filmography*. North Carolina: McFarland, 1995.

Godziszewski, Ed. *The Illustrated Encyclopedia of Godzilla*. Daikaiju Enterprises, 1996.

Halberstam, David. *The Fifties*. New York: Fawcett Columbine, 1993.

Hirano, Kyoko. *Mr. Smith Goes to Tokyo*. Washington: Smithsonian Institute Press, 1992.

Huss, Roy, and T.J. Ross, eds. *Focus on the Horror Film*. New Jersey: Prentice-Hall, 1972.

Lent, John, ed. *The Asian Film Industry*. Austin: University of Texas Press, 1990.

Peary, Danny. *Cult Movies 2*. New York: Dell, 1983.

Richie, Donald. *The Japanese Movie*. New York: Kodansha International, 1966/1982.

Rovin, Jeff. *The Encyclopedia of Monsters*. New York: Facts on File, 1989.

Sato, Tadao. *Currents in Japanese Cinema*. New York: Kodansha International, 1982.

Svensson, Arne. *Screen Series: Japan*. New York: Barnes, 1971.

Tasker, Peter. *The Japanese: Portrait of a Nation*. New York: Meridian, 1987.

Willis, Donald, ed. *Variety's Complete Science Fiction Reviews*. New York: Garland Publishing, 1985.

Japanese-Language Books

The Complete History of Toho Special Effects Movies (Toho Tokusha Eiga Zenshi). Tokyo: Toho Co. Ltd. Publishing Division, 1983.

Eiji Tsuburaya's World of Images (Tsuburaya Eiji no Eizo Sekai). Tokyo: Jitsugyo no Nihonsha, 1983.

Godzilla Days: 40 Years of Godzilla Movies (Godzilla Days: Gojira Eiga Yonjunen Shi). Tokyo: Shueisha Kabushiki Gaisha, 1993.

Higuchi, Naofunai. *Good Morning, Godzilla: The Period of Director Ishiro Honda and the Studio.* Tokyo: Chikuma Shobo, 1992.

Satsuma, Kenpachiro. *Inside Godzilla (Gojira no Nakami).* Tokyo: Chikuma Shobo, 1993.

The Making of Godzilla 1985. Tokyo: Shogakukan, 1985.

Yamada, Masami. *The Pictorial History of Godzilla.* Vols. 1 and 2. Tokyo: Hobby Japan Co. Ltd., 1995.

Inoue, Hideyuki. *Testimony: Birth of Godzilla (Kensho: Gojira Tanjo).* Tokyo: Kabushiki Gaisha Asahi Sonorama, 1994.

Toho SF Special Effects Movie Series, vol. 1: *Godzilla* (1984). Tokyo: Toho Publishing Products Division.

Toho SF Special Effects Movie Series, vol. 2: *Mothra/Mothra vs. Godzilla.* Tokyo: Toho Publishing Products Division.

Toho SF Special Effects Movie Series, vol. 3: *Godzilla/Godzilla Raids Again/Varan the Unbelievable.* Tokyo: Toho Publishing Products Division.

Toho SF Special Effects Movie Series, vol. 5: *King Kong vs. Godzilla/The Mysterians.* Tokyo: Toho Publishing Products Division.

Toho SF Special Effects Movie Series, vol. 6: *Godzilla vs. King Ghidorah.* Tokyo: Toho Publishing Products Division.

Toho SF Special Effects Movie Series, vol. 7: *Godzilla vs. Mothra.* Tokyo: Toho Publishing Products Division.

Toho SF Special Effects Movie Series, vol. 8: *Godzilla vs. MechaGodzilla.* Tokyo: Toho Publishing Products Division.

Toho SF Special Effects Movie Series, vol. 9: *Godzilla vs. Space Godzilla.* Tokyo: Toho Publishing Products Division.

Toho SF Special Effects Movie Series, vol. 10: *Godzilla vs. Destoroyah.* Tokyo: Toho Publishing Products Division.

The Visual Guide Book of First Godzilla. Tokyo: Tokuma Shoten, 1983.

Periodicals

G-FAN. Published by the Godzilla Society of North America, a.k.a. Daikaiju Enterprises, Manitoba, Canada. Various issues, 1993–present.

Japanese Fantasy Film Journal. Fanzine, Toledo, OH. Various issues.

Japanese Giants. Fanzine, Chicago. Various issues.

Markalite, The Magazine of Japanese Fantasy. Published by Pacific Rim Publishing Co., Oakland, CA, issues 1–3, 1990–91.

Oriental Cinema. Draculina Publishing, Centralia, IL. Various issues.

Cult Movies. Hollywood, CA. Various issues.

Articles

"Hiroshima in Film. Japan: An Ambivalent Nation, an Ambivalent Cinema" by David M. Desser. *Swords and Ploughshares, the Bulletin of the Program in Arms Control, Disarmament and International Security*, Vol. IX No. 3–4, Spring–Summer, 1995. Published by University of Illinois at Urbana-Champaign.

"Godzilla and the Japanese Nightmare: When *Them!* Is Us" by Chon Noriega. *Cinema Journal* 27, No. 1, Fall 1987.

Steve Ryfle visiting the bronze statue of Godzilla in Tokyo, January 1996.